The Battle against Anarchist Terrorism

G000155957

This is the first global history of the secret diplomatic and police campaign that was waged against anarchist terrorism from 1878 to the 1920s. Anarchist terrorism was at that time the dominant form of terrorism and for many continued to be synonymous with terrorism as late as the 1930s. Ranging from Europe and the Americas to the Middle East and Asia, Richard Bach Jensen explores how anarchist terrorism emerged as a global phenomenon during the first great era of economic and social globalization at the end of the nineteenth and beginning of the twentieth centuries and reveals why some nations were so much more successful in combating this new threat than others. He shows how the challenge of dealing with this new form of terrorism led to the fundamental modernization of policing in many countries and also discusses its impact on criminology and international law.

RICHARD BACH JENSEN is Professor of History at the Louisiana Scholars' College at Northwestern State University. He is a recognized authority on the repression of anarchist terrorism and has published widely in the field. His previous publications include *Liberty and Order: The Theory and Practice of Italian Public Security Policy, 1848 to the Crisis of the 1890s* (1991).

The Battle against Anarchist Terrorism

An International History, 1878–1934

Richard Bach Jensen

CAMBRIDGE
UNIVERSITY PRESS

CAMBRIDGE
UNIVERSITY PRESS

University Printing House, Cambridge CB2 8BS, United Kingdom

Cambridge University Press is part of the University of Cambridge.

It furthers the University's mission by disseminating knowledge in the pursuit of education, learning and research at the highest international levels of excellence.

www.cambridge.org
Information on this title: www.cambridge.org/9781107595538

First published 2014
First paperback edition 2015

A catalogue record for this publication is available from the British Library

Library of Congress Cataloguing in Publication data
Jensen, Richard Bach.
The battle against anarchist terrorism : an international history, 1878–1934 / Richard Bach Jensen.
    pages   cm
Includes bibliographical references and index.
ISBN 978-1-107-03405-1 (hardback)
1. Anarchism–History.   2. Terrorism–History.   3. Political violence–History.   I. Title.
HX828.J46 2014
363.32509′041–dc23
2013028562

ISBN 978-1-107-03405-1 Hardback
ISBN 978-1-107-59553-8 Paperback

Dedicated to my father, James Helge Jensen, and to the memory of my mother, Ruth Bach Jensen

Contents

Illustrations

Abbreviations

ACS	Archivo centrale dello Stato, Rome
Adm.Reg.	Administrative Registratur (Haus- Hof- and Staatarchiv, Vienna)
b.	Busta (document file)
bd.	Band (volume)
BDIL	British Digest of International Law, ed. Clive Parry. Part 6: The Individual in International Law (London, 1965)
BDFA	British Documents on Foreign Affairs
BPA	Bundespolizeiarchiv, Vienna, Austria
c.	carton
CIR	Conférence internationale de Rome pour la défense sociale contre les anarchistes: 24 Novembre-21 Décembre 1898. Confidential. Rome. Imprimerie du ministère des affaires étrangères, 1899 (the secret official record of the 1898 Rome Anti-Anarchist Conference).
CPC	casellario politico centrale (central political file or registry)
DDF	Documents diplomatiques français, 1871–1914
DDI	I documenti diplomatici italiani
DDS	Documents diplomatiques suisse
DGPS	General Directorate of Public Security, interior ministry of Italy
Eur. Gen.	Europa Generalia
f.	fascicolo (folder)
FO	Foreign Office or Foreign Office papers, Public Record Office [the National Archives], London
GCSAP	German Central State Archive, Potsdam, Germany
GCSAM	Deutsches Zentrales Staatsarchiv, formerly in Merseburg, now in Berlin-Dahlem, Germany

GFO	German Foreign Office (records filmed at Whaddon Hall, Bucks, December 1958)
HHStA	Haus- Hof- and Staatarchiv, Vienna
HO	Home Office or Home Office papers, Public Record Office [the National Archives], London
IB	Informationsbüro (Haus- Hof- and Staatarchiv, Vienna)
IFM	Italian foreign ministry archive, Rome
JDIP	Journal du droit international privé
k.	Karton (document carton)
l.	legajo (file)
LC	Library of Congress
M.plen	Ministro plenipotentiario
NA	National Archives, College Park, Maryland, United States
nr.	Number
OP	Orden Público (public order)
PI	Polizia internazionale record group at the Italian foreign ministry archive
PRO	Public Record Office, London; since 2003, combined with the National Archives (United Kingdom).
PS	Pubblica sicurezza. Public security
Rap.dip.USA	I fondi archivistici…delle Rappresentanze Diplomatiche Italiane negli USA
SFM	Spanish foreign ministry, Archivo Histórico, Madrid
SP	Staarsarchive Potsdam: Brandenburgischen Landeshauptarchive, Orangerie, Potsdam
UR	ufficio riservato (private office)

Foreword

I first became intrigued with Richard Bach Jensen's work when *Terrorism and Political Violence* published a fascinating article by him in the spring of 2001. In that article he discussed Theodore Roosevelt's efforts to launch an international crusade to eliminate anarchist terrorism after President McKinley's assassination in September 1901. Six months after the article appeared, and a century after Roosevelt's crusade began, a second one was launched when President George W. Bush in response to 9/11 declared a "war (that) would not end until every terrorist group of global reach has been found, stopped and defeated."

The similarities and differences between these two dramatic events were so striking that I thought that many would be deeply interested in exploring the history of terrorism, to see what could be learned to help us understand the contemporary situation and future possibilities better. However, although 9/11 did stimulate an extraordinary number of popular and academic accounts of contemporary terrorism, very little work on the history of the phenomena appeared. This negligence reflected a common view deeply embedded in our culture and was expressed conspicuously a number of times. When the Soviet Union collapsed, most existing terrorist groups that were part of a terrorism wave that had emerged in the 1960s disappeared; the US stopped funding terrorism research and reduced security and counterterrorism efforts, assuming that without the Soviet Union, terrorism could no longer be significant.[1]

A large portion of the academic world seems to understand terrorism in the same way. In 1933, for example, when anarchist terrorism had virtually disappeared, an article on the subject in the first edition of the *Encyclopedia of the Social Sciences* concluded that soon only antiquarians would find the subject interesting, because modern technology made it impossible for small groups to be serious elements in our political world where only classes and masses mattered! Were the editors of the second

---

[1] Aiding Islamic forces against the Soviets in Afghanistan also helped the US believe it would not be the target of Islamic terror as it had been in the 1980s.

edition of the *Encyclopedia* (1968) impressed by their predecessors' "wisdom"? Whatever their reason, they did not explain their decision to exclude the subject, even though in the period between the two editions a number of states were established partly by terrorist campaigns, for example, Israel, Cyprus, and Algeria. Perhaps the editors thought that since events occurred in Western colonial empires that no longer existed, terrorism would vanish too! The editors also missed the fact that a few years before they published the new edition a number of New Left terrorist groups began to emerge. They were not alone in ignoring these facts. The *Encyclopaedia Britannica* in 1968 omitted terrorism too, although earlier editions published important classic articles on the subject.

It is not easy to understand why we keep making the same mistake when terrorist activity seems to diminish greatly, but our misconceptions may be linked to the fact that we know so little about the history of modern terrorism, a history characterized by a series of waves that emerge suddenly and then recede after reaching a certain high point. Since we tend to focus on one period only, it seems "obvious" that the activity is linked solely to a particular political context and will disappear when that context is altered.

Tracing the origin and process of modern non-state terror should help us understand our contemporary scene better.[2] A number of uprisings broke out in the capital cities of many European states throughout the first seventy-one years of the nineteenth century, aiming to achieve one or more of the French Revolution's various promises. The major mechanism for insurrection was the "mob" and, as the century developed, mobs became more internationalized, attracting recruits from other European states. But mob efforts failed and produced increasingly bloody aftermaths. Revolutionaries in the 1880s were stimulated to produce a new form of violence, one that would be less bloody! Small underground groups began employing the bomb, a new weapon the invention of dynamite made easy to use effectively and which has remained the terrorist's principal weapon ever since. Terrorism spread throughout Europe quickly and became a global phenomenon reaching every continent except Antarctica – the unpopulated one. Most groups had strong anarchist inclinations but some had important nationalist ingredients, and the wave persisted for a generation.

---

[2] See my "Before the Bombs There were the Mobs: American Experiences with Terror," *Terrorism and Political Violence* 20:2 (2008) and "The Four Waves of Modern Terrorism," in *Attacking Terrorism: Elements of a Grand Strategy*, ed. Audrey Kurth Cronin and James M. Ludes. Washington, DC: Georgetown University Press, 2004, 43–76.

Critical changes in communication pattern provided the publicity those small groups needed for their violent acts, which they described as "propaganda of the deed." The transatlantic cable telegraph enabled the new daily newspapers with mass circulations to report events throughout the world in a day. Mass rail transportation networks were available enabling extensive emigrations from poor countries to others, creating diaspora communities very interested in the politics in both their old and new homes. The technological circumstances essential for small groups to become so important grew more favorable over time, encouraging similar sized groups with their own political objectives to become terrorists in different eras.

As the title of Professor Jensen's book indicates, his principal concern is the analysis of the various international and domestic counterterror campaigns organized to cope with the first modern, or anarchist, wave. He has been working on the subject since 1981, and this volume provides the most complete and authoritative study of government campaigns available, partly attributable to the author's ability to read five languages, which gave him access to many government documents. Many documents had been kept secret; others were unknown because they were unpublished and/or not previously consulted.

The global character of anarchism made it essential for states to develop policies of cooperation. But the differences between states over other political issues created difficulties that were only partially overcome. Bilateral efforts were more effective that multilateral ones. Police cooperation was easier to sustain: sometimes police officials went abroad to train foreign forces. Still, not all states had appropriate police forces, and the frequent presence of foreign forces in many states could create problems.

Terrorism transformed the police. To deal with mobs, uniformed police forces were first established and worked well. Now police had to take their uniforms off to become invisible and infiltrate groups at home and abroad to get information before terrorist acts were committed. The ability of terrorists to move easily meant that centralization was mandatory, a process some states opposed.

The importance of gaining information before acts of terror occurred created difficult new political problems. Torture, which had been banished in European states, became common again and martial courts often replaced civilian ones. Infiltrators employed as *agents provocateurs* made the police responsible for many important terrorist deeds, which might not have occurred otherwise, embarrassing governments and creating rage among some elements of the public.

Media coverage provoked crucial issues. It frequently mischaracterized the threat by describing virtually every act of violence as anarchist even when other motives and political agendas were involved. It continually exaggerated the threat, a process that both contributed to the spectacular growth of newspapers and made the public tolerate government overreactions and misdeeds. Governments often tried to link particular opposition parties falsely to anarchist activity.

Jensen compares the different responses of seven states in Europe and the Americas including their labor and immigration reforms to explain state successes and failures. Hopefully this illuminating study of counterterrorism will inspire comparative efforts in subsequent terrorism waves to see what governments learned or failed to learn. It is worth pointing out that second or anti-colonial wave terrorists abandoned the assassination of prominent persons – previously the principal target – and restrained their global activities; decisions that helped contribute to the first terrorist successes.

Remember why Clausewitz, the founder of the science of war, was so obsessed with history! "Examples from history," he said, "make everything clear, and furnish the best description of proof in the empirical sciences. This applies with more force to the Art of War than to any other." I would add that what is true for war is true for terrorism also.

David C. Rapoport,
Professor Emeritus, Founding Editor
Terrorism and Political Violence

Preface

Reading Barbara Tuchman's *The Proud Tower* in the 1970s, I was intrigued by her brief mention of the International Anti-Anarchist Conference of Rome. Little was known about this highly secret diplomatic conference whose minutes had allegedly been burned in December 1898 to preserve its secrecy. It became my obsession to find these minutes as well as more about an event that had been omitted from historical accounts. In 1981, I published the first scholarly article on the conference and subsequently began the research that led to the present work. Regretfully, due to space limitations, I have had to cut one entire chapter from this book devoted to national, bilateral, and regional anti-anarchist policing, 1900–1914. I hope to publish material from this chapter at a later date.

It is customary to thank all the people who have assisted the author in one way or another in the research and writing of this book. I particularly wish to thank Ann Larabee, Michigan State University, and Mary Gibson, John Jay College, CUNY, who read the entire manuscript and offered many excellent suggestions. David Rapoport, Professor Emeritus at UCLA and Founding Editor of the journal *Terrorism and Political Violence*, has continuously supported my work on the history of anarchist terrorism, for which I am profoundly grateful. The same could be said of John Thayer, my former adviser at the University of Minnesota, who has supported me in all of my historical work over the years, insisted I learn German, and encouraged me to apply for my first Fulbright Fellowship (to Italy), which I would never have done otherwise. Much of my research was conducted with the support of the Council for International Exchange of Scholars, which administers the Fulbright program. Besides the CIES, I would like to thank the American people, whose taxpayer dollars support it, for the extraordinary opportunities that two Fulbright Fellowships afforded me. This book is an attempt to repay that debt. I also received grants from IREX, the American Philosophical Society, the University of Minnesota, Skidmore College, and Northwestern State University that at various points allowed me to continue my research. I must also thank Jacqueline Hawkins and her predecessors at Northwestern State's interlibrary loan office and many librarians at the other institutions where I have taught. Sonny Carter assisted me in scanning images for the book's illustrations. The personnel at the Archivio Centrale dello Stato were unfailingly helpful, as was Stefania Ruggeri and other archivists at the Italian foreign ministry archive in Rome. I also owe a debt of gratitude to the staffs of the Haus-, Hof- und Staatsarchiv in Vienna, the Bundespolizeiarchiv in Vienna, various archives in Germany, the Public Record Office in London, the foreign ministry and national archives in Madrid, the Archive of Antonio Maura in Madrid, the Archivo General de la Nación in Buenos Aires, the Library of Congress, and the National Archives, College Park, Maryland. Ambassador Allende Salazar was extraordinarily kind in making his ancestor's papers available to me before they were deposited at the foreign ministry archive in Madrid. Prof. Ingo Materna, Humbolt University, was very helpful and kind when I did research in East Germany in 1988. Eric Rauchway generously shared some of his unpublished research with me, as did John C. G. Röhl. Sadeem El Nahhas provided editorial assistance. Barbara Akin, Frank Schicketanz, Ken Berri, Christine Ferrell, Viviane Winteroy, Lisa Wolff, Francesco Tamburini, and Nathalie Kasselis all helped me with language questions and, in some cases, translations from German, French, Spanish, Dutch, and Italian. I assume responsibility for any errors. For their excellent critical comments and suggestions, I am extremely grateful to the editors and their assistants, both in-house and out of house, at Cambridge University Press. No one could ask for a better press with which to work. Finally I wish to express my appreciation for Janina Darling's support and friendship over the years since we first met in Rome in 1974. There are probably many others I should be thanking as well; I apologize for any unintentional oversights. This book is dedicated to my father, James H. Jensen, and to the memory of my mother, Ruth Bach Jensen. Expressing my full gratitude to them would require an additional preface unto itself.

Introduction

In one of his brilliant aphorisms, Nietzsche astutely observes that "only that which has no history is definable."[1] Since terrorism definitely has a long history, this may be the best response to the inconclusive scholarly debate over its precise definition. For the purposes of this book it will include bombings, assassinations, and attempted bombings and assassinations (*attentats*) carried out by anarchists, or those widely alleged to be anarchists, during the last decades of the nineteenth century and the first decades of the twentieth. It is very little exaggeration to claim that anarchism *was* the terrorism of the era between the years 1878 and 1934. In the public mind, however erroneously, anarchism and anarchist became synonymous with terrorism and terrorist. The press identified "Anarchists with bombs."[2] An editorial that appeared in 1909 in the English language *Buenos Aires Herald* and was devoted to the shocking anarchist assassination of the police chief of Buenos Aires and his secretary provides an example. The editorial, "Rampant Anarchism," demonstrates this equivalency by the repeated usage of the same adjective in its title and in its content, referring to the fact that "rampant anarchy has established itself here" and that "rampant terrorism is in our midst."[3]

The equivalency was also emphasized by developments in international law that defined anarchist acts of violence as "social crimes" outside the protection provided political crimes in extradition treaties, as the Institute of International Law did in 1892. In 1898, the Rome Anti-Anarchist Conference of European diplomats and policemen defined the "anarchist act" as aimed at the violent destruction of "all social organization," suggesting a level of violence with breathtaking dimensions. At least in theory, this definition fundamentally

---

[1] *On the Genealogy of Morals*, trans. Walter Kaufmann and R. J. Hollingdale (New York: Random House, [1887] 1967), II: 13.
[2] L. S. Bevington, "Anarchism and Violence" (Chiswick: James Tochatti, 1896), 3.
[3] *Buenos Aires Herald*, 15 November 1909.

1

differentiated anarchist terrorism from other forms of political violence perpetrated by nationalists and Russian revolutionaries (although the "nihilists" were often confused with the anarchists) who aimed at narrower political goals. The equivalence between anarchist acts, or social crimes, and terrorism was definitively made explicit in 1934 by the International Conference for the Unification of Penal Law (ironically just at the moment that anarchist terrorism was about to be superseded by other forms of terror).[4]

I have three specific aims in writing this book: First, and foremost, I want to narrate and analyze the history of the *international* and especially the *multilateral* diplomatic and police responses to anarchist terrorism, 1878–1914, with an epilogue covering the period 1914–1934. Beginning in the 1890s growing bilateral anti-anarchist police cooperation was followed by major efforts at multilateral cooperation in 1898 at the Rome Conference and in 1904 with the St. Petersburg Protocol. Regional anti-anarchist agreements were signed in the Americas. Paralleling these efforts was the creation by individual states of extensive international police networks to monitor the anarchists.

I argue that in the pre-war era careful police intelligence work and international police cooperation, together with a more rigorously professional system of protection for monarchs and heads of state, aided in curbing anarchist terrorism, while heavy-handed repression only worsened it. Britain provided the best example of anti-anarchist policing and Spain the worst. After 1900, Italy followed in Britain's footsteps: it revamped and professionalized its police force and the king's corps of bodyguards, and expanded and improved its intelligence-gathering service abroad.

The book's second major aim is to provide greater understanding of the phenomenon of anarchist terrorism, particularly as it was depicted by the print media. Anarchist terrorism was a worldwide phenomenon and my book places it in the context of the first great era of economic and social globalization at the end of the nineteenth and beginning of the twentieth centuries. The book includes information on the problem of anarchist violence and its repression in such regions and countries as the Middle East, Morocco, India, China, and Japan. My major focus, however, will be on Europe and the Americas, especially the United States and Argentina, which were the sites of the most important acts of anarchist terrorism in the Western Hemisphere.

Of some significance is that anarchist suicide bombings and assassinations took place during this period, a phenomenon that was not to

---

[4] See Chapter 10.

reoccur until the present era of terrorism.[5] Although I have reservations about the claim, it should be mentioned that several authors have pointed out many similarities, or even the equivalency, between nineteenth century anarchism and al-Qaeda.[6] While most general texts on terrorism end their discussion of anarchist "propaganda by the deed" in 1914, if not earlier, this book carries it through to the mid-1930s. Anarchist violence had been on the decline since the mid-1920s, but it was only in the next decade that the phenomenon was clearly replaced by a new form of terrorism.

During its heyday, sensationalistic newspapers, together with their fearful readers and the anarchists (and would-be anarchists) themselves, took the violent deeds of anarchists and others and created the myth of anarchist terrorism as a powerful conspiratorial force moving throughout the world. This myth was as important in the history of the development of anarchist terrorism – and its containment – as were the heterogeneous acts of violence themselves. In a sense, my book aims to "shatter" the fearsome myth of anarchist terrorism by showing the wide gap that existed between what the media, the public, and governments perceived and what actually took place. The anarchists organized very few conspiracies and many acts of "anarchist" terrorism were not committed by the anarchists at all, but by nationalists, radicals, socialists, police spies, and the mentally unbalanced.

Third, I want to explore the reasons why certain nations were more successful than others in dealing with anarchist terrorism. By comparing and contrasting the experience of countries – Spain par excellence – that experienced severe problems with anarchist terrorism during the key period 1878–1914 with those nations (Britain, Germany, and Austria) in which anarchist violence was not a significant domestic issue after the 1880s, or after 1900 (France and Italy), the book will seek to identify which factors caused some societies to evolve in ways inimical to terrorist bomb-throwing and assassination attempts.

---

[5] I owe this information to David C. Rapoport, whose four wave theory of the evolution of terrorism is the most persuasive historical analysis of this phenomenon currently available. David C. Rapoport, "The Four Waves of Modern Terrorism," 46–73.

[6] James Gelvin, "Al-Qaeda and Anarchism: A Historian's Reply to Terrorology," *Terrorism and Political Violence*, 20:4 (2008), 563–581. Gelvin cites eight other commentators, ranging from *The Economist* to the historian Niall Ferguson, who briefly allude to these alleged similarities. For a critique of Gelvin's views, see Richard Bach Jensen, "Nineteenth Century Anarchist Terrorism: How Comparable to the Terrorism of al-Qaeda?", *Terrorism and Political Violence*, 20:4 (2008): 589–596; George Esenwein, "Comments on James L. Gelvin's 'Al-Qaeda and Anarchism: A Historian's Repy to Terrorology'," 597–600, and the other contributions in this issue.

A fundamental nineteenth-century debate in Italy and other European countries was over whether law and order should be maintained through "prevention" or "repression," and these terms can also serve to frame a discussion of how governments dealt with anarchist terrorism. Preventative methods called for actions to forestall illegalities and outbreaks of violence, but at the risk of violating people's legal and constitutional rights. They might involve prohibiting meetings and carrying out arrests, even mass arrests, of people suspected of involvement in crime or social upheavals although they had not carried out any illegal activities. Censorship and violating the freedom of the mails would also fall under the category of "prevention." "Prevention, not repression" smacked of the despotic policies of the Old Regime. Tsarist Russia was infamous for such prevention and it often involved the use of *agents provocateurs*. Liberals and progressives therefore championed "repression, not prevention" since it left individuals unmolested by the police until they had actually committed crimes. In practice, such clear-cut distinctions between conservative and liberal approaches to maintaining order were rarely if ever uniformly applied. Moreover, they became particularly problematical when applied to terrorism. No political entity, no matter how progressive, could or can complacently allow its leaders to be assassinated, or crowded cafés and opera houses to be bombed, or symbolically important buildings to be blown up on the simple assurance that after the deed the perpetrators would soon be brought to justice. These murders and bombings were usually too shocking and potentially destabilizing to society to allow such laissez-faire responses.

When examining anti-anarchist policies during the late nineteenth and early twentieth centuries, it is possible to trace an evolution and refinement of both policies of "prevention" and of "repression." Initially in the 1890s acts of anarchist terrorism were not prevented because governments had relatively little knowledge about who the bomb-throwers and assassins were or what groups they belonged to. France, Italy, Portugal, Spain, Russia, Argentina (after 1900), and other countries responded with brutal and widespread repression, including in some cases torture, as well as attempts to legislate prevention through the prohibition of anarchist meetings, associations, and publications. On the whole, the attempt to prevent terrorism through legislation produced meager results and, together with brutal police repression, produced a backlash against these assaults on civil liberties and on the persons of the anarchists themselves.

More successful were preventative measures that involved careful and secret intelligence work to monitor (rather than smash) the anarchists to find out what they were doing and possibly stop the odd terrorist plot. Such precisely focused prevention required a good deal of money, skillful organization, careful selection of personnel, and international cooperation. It included the creation or improvement of security forces to protect the head of state and other government officials. In the new century, Italy and France combined this refined and restricted prevention with what might be described as wider, "socially preventive" policies. Social and political reforms could drain off or diminish the discontent that formed the source of so many anarchist *attentats*. These "micro" and "macro" preventative approaches made it possible to avoid the iron-fisted policies of repression and prevention during the 1890s that had embittered the atmosphere in so many countries and that often provoked violent anarchist acts of revenge.

Two final points are worth making about the significance of the subject of international cooperation against anarchist terrorism. Because of its secrecy, it has been omitted from history books on politics and foreign relations. The battle against anarchist terrorism deserves a much more prominent place in such works. In part this is because it shows how nations were secretly bound together in previously unknown ways and how, in the end, anti-terrorism proved insufficiently strong to counter the centrifugal pull of national rivalries and divergent political goals. National perspectives colored views of who should be considered a terrorist: a dangerous "anarchist" terrorist in Russia might simply be a political dissident in Britain, Switzerland, or Italy.

Second, my book argues – providing a new, or at least little known, chapter in police history – that the challenge of anarchist terrorism led to a fundamental modernization of the police in many countries. This modernization included the institution of new or better identification systems, better police education, and more centralized policing. For example, the Rome Conference called for the universal adoption of Bertillon's *portrait parlé*, at the time the most advanced system of criminal identification, leading to its adoption by many European states. The professionalization of protective measures for heads of state during this era was also important, and even critical, for preventing further assassinations.

Crucial to understanding anarchist violence and how governments and societies reacted to it is understanding its complex origins. This is the subject of the next two chapters.

1   The origins of anarchist terrorism

Alfred Nobel's invention of dynamite in 1866 transformed the world.[1] Not only did it make possible spectacular construction projects such as blasting railroad tunnels through the Alps and digging the Panama Canal, but it also put into the hands of terrorists a source of power almost unimaginable in its dimensions. A popular Spanish periodical of 1908 captured this image when it described the attributes and allegorized the power of dynamite:

> Its irresistible force, its formidable power. It seems that the spirit of Shiva, the god of destruction, eternal destroyer of life, resides in the depths of its strange composition. All the great phenomena of Nature resemble it in their effects... it creates and it destroys, it annihilates and it gives life; it is chained Prometheus and angry Jupiter; it illuminates and darkens. From civilization's necessity, it becomes its chastiser... it has changed into a social anathema, into the dissident sects' weapon of terrorism.[2]

Nobel's Promethean invention that so troubled his times produced a "super-explosion" twenty times more violent than black powder, which for more than 800 years had been virtually the world's only known explosive. In a fraction of the time and with a much smaller amount of explosive than was needed in the case of black powder, dynamite could shatter granite and other rocks of adamantine hardness into tiny bits. Earlier, in 1846, the powerful explosives nitroglycerin and guncotton had been invented. Because of their highly unstable composition, however, they were liable to explode at any time, or not at all in the case of nitroglycerin, which, after being ignited by a fuse, might simply burn but not explode. For most practical purposes these high explosives were unusable until Nobel devised the blasting cap and employed

---

[1] Much of this chapter originally appeared as "Daggers, Rifles and Dynamite: Anarchist Terrorism in Nineteenth Century Europe," *Terrorism and Political Violence*, 16:1 (2004): 116–153.

[2] Jose Pérez Guerrero, "Prologo," *Regicidios y crimenes politicos* (Madrid: Los sucessos, c. 1908–1909): 2.

the stabilizing element kieselguhr, a spongy, absorbent clay abundant in northern Germany.[3]

The wave of terrorism brought forth by this immense new physical power,[4] as well as by economic, social, and political discontent, began in the late 1870s, reached a climax in the 1890s, and, after a few years' pause, resurfaced in the early twentieth century. The Russian Revolution of 1905 and World War I unleashed new, if less well-known, waves of terrorism. These were usually identified with the anarchist movement. Because of anarchism's potentially fearsome physical power and explosive ideas, one Italian author described it as "the most important ethical deviation that may ever have disturbed the world." In 1893, an American historian judged it "the most dangerous theory which civilization has ever had to encounter." After the assassinations of the Empress Elisabeth and President McKinley, German newspapers noted that "society...dances on a volcano" and that "a very small number of unscrupulous fanatics terrorize the entire human race...The danger for all countries is very great and urgent."[5] While in popular imagination the terrorist bomber and the anarchist became the same thing, in retrospect we know this was not true. Few anarchists became bomb-throwers or carried out violent acts. Moreover, not all the alleged "anarchist" terrorists were anarchists, the label "anarchist" simply becoming the easiest means for many journalists and some politicians and police to identify the myriad, often obscure malcontents who carried out violent deeds during the late nineteenth and early twentieth centuries.

But if there was never a perfect fit between "anarchist" and "terrorist," there was a history of theoretical and practical involvement by anarchists in carrying out violent deeds to achieve their aims. In this chapter and the following we will look at the growth of the anarchist movement, the development of political and social terrorism, and the persistent gap between historical reality and public perception.

---

[3] The technical term for the violent force of dynamite is its "brisance," which is the shattering or crushing effect of an explosive (*Webster's New Collegiate Dictionary*). William S. Dutton, *One Thousand Years of Explosives: From Wildfire to the H-Bomb* (Philadelphia: John C. Winston, 1960): 5–6, 109–110, 128, 134, 136.

[4] On September 27, 1893, *The New York Times*, 4, declared: "It is plain that the strength of the modern Anarchical movements is in the faith that high explosives have been invented which are useless for every innocent purpose to which gunpowder is applied, but are of great efficacy in the work of demolition. In other words, dynamite is the main support of Anarchism."

[5] Ettore Zoccoli, *L'anarchia* (Rome: Fratelli Bocca 1907): vii, cited by Saverio Cilibrizzi, *Storia parlamentare politica e diplomatica d'Italia da Novara a Vittorio Veneto* (Milan: Società editrice Dante Alighieri, 1925–1943): 3: 131. Richard T. Ely, "Anarchy," *Harper's Weekly*, 37 (1893), 1226; *Staatsburger Zeitung*, 13 September 1898; *Die Post* (Berlin), September 16, 1901.

The development of the anarchist movement in nineteenth-century Europe

Ever since anarchism was born in the nineteenth century as an ideology and a political and social movement, it has meant many different things, both to its supporters and to its opponents. In general it has signified chaos and destruction to its enemies, while to its exponents it has promised hope of a better life built on juster foundations than those to be found in the status quo. A good way to begin to understand it, at least from the anarchists' point of view, is to turn to the definition developed by one of its most famous practitioners, the Russian anarchist and former prince, Peter Kropotkin. Invited by the *Encyclopaedia Britannica* to define anarchism for its eleventh edition (1910), he wrote at the beginning of his lengthy entry on the subject that anarchism was:

The name given to a principle or theory of life and conduct under which society is conceived without government (from Gr[eek] αν- and αρχη, without authority) – harmony in such a society being obtained, not by submission to law, or by obedience to any authority, but by free agreements concluded between the various groups, territorial and professional, freely constituted for the sake of production and consumption, as also for the satisfaction of the infinite variety of needs and aspirations of a civilized being.[6]

Although it had precursors in such thinkers as William Godwin, for the most part the European anarchist movement grew out of an amalgam of the ideas and practices of the Frenchman Pierre-Joseph Proudhon and the Russian Mikhail Bakunin. Proudhon was a thinker and writer, Bakunin was a man of action, a theorist, and Proudhon's self-declared disciple (although he did not agree with all of Proudhon's ideas) – both men advocated a non-authoritarian form of socialism.[7] They sought to bring about a revolution of workers and peasants against the established order of property-owners, the church, and the government. Proudhon, the first person to proudly proclaim himself an anarchist, wrote in his 1840 work *What is Property?* that "property is theft" and called for "scientific socialism," "equality," and "justice." He praised: "Anarchy, that is the absence of a ruler or sovereign. This is the form of government we are moving closer to every day."[8] The two pillars of Proudhon's thought, his vehicles for achieving "Anarchy, or the government of each man by himself," were

[6] *Encyclopaedia Britannica*, "Anarchism."
[7] Bakunin rejected Proudhon's utopian scheme for a mutual bank and his ideas on property and possession. George Woodcock, *Anarchism: A History of Libertarian Ideas and Movements* (New York: World Publishing 1962): 152, 164.
[8] *Selected Writings of Pierre-Joseph Proudhon*, ed. Steward Edwards, trans. Elizabeth Fraser (Garden City, New York: Doubleday, 1969): 88–89; Woodcock, *Anarchism*, 11–12.

federalism and mutualism.[9] Federalism aimed to replace centralized governments by federations of local communities or communes. Mutualism sought to base society on small, mutually supporting economic groups and, by eliminating the capitalist middleman through the creation of new forms of contract and a People's Bank, to secure for the worker the full value of the goods he had produced.[10] By the mid-1860s followers of Proudhon dominated the French working-class movement.

Bakunin, the son of a prominent Russian landowner, became a heavily-bearded, wildman revolutionary during the European revolts of 1848–1849. Arrested, he spent a decade in prison. After his escape in 1860, he increasingly embraced Proudhon's vision as the necessary framework for the coming social revolution. Bakunin's charm and eloquence helped bring Proudhonist ideas, together with Bakunin's own beliefs in collective action, to the watchmakers of the Jura in western Switzerland, to the people of Italy, and – most momentously of all, in 1868 through an intermediary named Giuseppe Fanelli – to the peasants and workers of Spain.

In the 1860s few clear-cut distinctions existed between the various socialist groups that were sprouting up all over Europe. In 1869 Bakunin and his followers affiliated with the International Workingmen's Association (the First International), which Karl Marx and others had founded in London in 1864. Marx exercised considerable influence over the anarchists' economic thinking, but Bakunin completely rejected his authoritarianism and his desire that the party of the workers should participate in bourgeois politics. Even after the First International expelled Bakunin in 1872 and moved its headquarters to New York City (and later Philadelphia) in order to elude the grasp of the charismatic Russian, socialists of the Marxist and anarchist persuasions continued to mix at the local and national levels.

To evaluate the threat that anarchism and its terrorist offshoot posed for established society during the nineteenth-century, it would be helpful to know the size of the movement. This is a question open to much dispute, particularly since the police, journalists, various authors, and the anarchists themselves often greatly exaggerated anarchist numbers. One authoritative source calculated that in Spain alone – where, ostensibly as part of the First International, anarchism had taken root and come to dominate the working-class movement – the International had attracted 300,000 supporters.[11] This is clearly wrong, and although an exact count is impossible, a more plausible estimate for the size of Spanish anarchism

---

[9] *The Federal Principal* (1863), in *Selected Writings of Pierre-Joseph Proudhon*, 91.
[10] *Selected Writings of Pierre-Joseph Proudhon*, 56–63, 75–79.
[11] The *Encyclopedia universada illustrada europeo-Americana*, 'Anarquismo', 357, cites the figure of 300,000.

at a highpoint in the early 1880s is almost 60,000 adherents.[12] Bakuninism also found many followers in Italy, where in 1874 a report confiscated by the Italian police estimated membership to be 32,000.[13] In 1882 an interior ministry report claimed that the number of anarchists had shrunk to 5,617, but this oddly precise figure may well be unreliable.[14] In 1894, the Italian anarchist Pietro Gori, who should have been in a position to know, claimed that the police greatly underestimated the number of anarchists and that no less than 5,000–6,000 anarchists lived in Milan alone.[15] For France, the historian Jean Maitron estimates that in 1894 anarchism attracted 1,000 militant followers, 4,500 sympathizers who purchased anarchist journals and 100,000 others who were faintly supportive.[16] Anarchist groups also sprang up in Switzerland, Germany, Austria-Hungary, Russia, and in the Americas, especially in the United States and Argentina, where growing immigrant populations brought anarchist ideas with them. Here too the estimates vary greatly. In 1889, a contemporary historian thought that not more than 10,000 anarchists resided in the United States.[17] Of these, at least according to the Haymarket grand jury, not more than 100 and probably not more than 40 or 50 could be considered dangerous.[18] Paul Avrich, one of the foremost historians of anarchism, thinks these figures are underestimates, and that there were tens of thousands at the peak of the movement between 1880 and 1920, "with 3,000 in Chicago alone during the last decades of the nineteenth century and comparable numbers in Paterson and New York."[19] For Argentina, several sources give an estimate of 10,000 anarchists residing in Buenos Aires in the early twentieth century.[20]

[12] George Richard Esenwein, *Anarchist Ideology and the Working-Class Movement in Spain, 1868–1898* (Berkeley: University of California Press, 1989): 83 and 229n9.
[13] Report of the Italian Federation of the anti-authoritarian, or Bakuninist, International to the International Commission, Brussels. Nunzio Pernicone, *Italian Anarchism, 1864–1892* (Princeton University Press, 1993): 75–76. Pernicone believes the report's figures were exaggerated and estimates that, at the movement's height, some 25,000 Bakuninists and many more sympathizers resided in Italy (4).
[14] Pernicone, *Italian Anarchism*, 238.
[15] "Le idee dell'anarchico avv. Gori," *La Sera* (Milan), March 12–13, 1894.
[16] The police compiled a list giving a total of 4,489 anarchists living in France and North Africa. Jean Maitron, *Histoire du Mouvement Anarchiste en France (1880–1914)*, 2nd editon (Paris: Société universitaire d'éditions de libraire, 1955): 124.
[17] Herbert Osgood, "Scientific Anarchism," *Political Science Quarterly* 4 (1889) 30, cited by Sidney Fine, "Anarchism and the Assassination of McKinley," *American Historical Review* 60 (1955): 777.
[18] Fine, "Anarchism and the Assassination of McKinley," 777.
[19] Paul Avrich, *An American Anarchist: The Life of Voltairine de Cleyre* (Princeton University Press, 1978), xvii–xviii.
[20] Macchi di Cellere, Italian Legation, Buenos Aires to Foreign Minister Giulio Prinetti, Rome, August 9, 1901. PI, file 28, Italian foreign ministry archive (hereafter cited as IFM); *The Times* (London), November 17, 1909, 5.

The anarchists came from all classes of the population: from the nobility and the proletariat, from the illiterate peasantry and middle-class intellectuals. The ideas of Bakunin and Proudhon often appealed to those who were harmed or angered by the exploitation of the working people during the harsh, early days of the industrial revolution. It also appealed to those angered by the middle classes' and the liberals' abuses of their economic, social, and political power, and by the failure of aristocratic rulers to adjust their regimes to the demands for freedom and equality that had issued forth during and after the French Revolution. In most countries anarchism remained the ideology of a small minority, but in Spain it became a mass movement involving the laboring classes, and long dominated that country's organizations for industrial workers. In Argentina as well, at least for some years at the beginning of the twentieth century, anarchism held sway over the labor movement. Anarchism enjoyed a strong presence in the labor unions of Italy, France, Portugal, and other countries.[21] Contrary to the stereotype, anarchism's strongest appeal was to those who were *not* destitute and whose literacy rate was higher than the local or regional average.[22] Artisans were the most characteristic adherents to the movement. Mechanics, bricklayers, carpenters, bakers, butchers, carters, skilled vine tenders, tailors, watchmakers in western Switzerland, and craftsmen who made casks for the sherry of Andalusia all flocked to the black banner of anarchism. Shoemakers and barbers were particularly important components of the anarchist movement. In southern Spain, Italy, and elsewhere, barbers were crucial because besides clipping hair, they often served as distributors for anarchist newspapers and journals, collected money for subscriptions and held political discussions in their shops.[23] In general, artisans looked to the anarchist movement as the best means of opposing encroachment and exploitation by sherry merchants or large industrialists or other members

---

[21] Peter Merten, *Anarchismus und Arbeiterkampf in Portugal* (Hamburg: Libertäre Association, 1981).

[22] This has been best documented for Spain: Temma Kaplan, *Anarchists of Andalusia, 1868–1903* (Princeton University Press): Chapter 3, and Kaplan, "The Social Base of Nineteenth-Century Andalusian Anarchism in Jerez de la Frontera," *Journal of Interdisciplinary History* 6 (1975): 47–70. Francis H. Nichols, a journalist, denied that Italian anarchists in the United States had a "hard lot" or lived on "starvation wages." Instead "almost without exception the Italian Anarchists are regularly employed in some trade at fair pay. Some have comfortable savings-bank accounts." "The Anarchists in America," *The Outlook in America*, 68 (1901): 859.

[23] Kaplan, *Anarchists*, 171. Pierre Milza, *Française et italiens à la fin du XIXe siècle* (Rome: École française de Rome, 1981): 866–867, notes that *coiffeur* was the profession indicated for 15 of the 882 Italian anarchists expelled from France between 1894 and 1903. The largest single professional group of Italian anarchist expellees was made up of shoemakers (85), followed by bricklayers (*maçons*) (65), and day laborers (55). The profession of 142 of the expellees remained unidentified. In 1906 an Italian barber named Gabbianelli

of the upper classes. Anarchism offered the artisans "a chance of establishing social justice while retaining their treasured independence."[24]

In Spain, although rarely in other countries, anarchism attracted the support of many peasants and rural people. These included not only seasonal workers, landless day laborers, and the unemployed, but also peasant landowners, tenants, sharecroppers, small vineyard proprietors, shepherds, and rural schoolteachers, all of whom found the ideas and social organizations of the anarchists attractive.[25] It remains a mystery why anarchism never found a mass following among the peasants and landless day laborers of southern Italy, where Bakunin had lived for over a year, exercising great influence over the rising generation, including the young Errico Malatesta, and where social conditions and sufferings resembled so closely those of southern Spain.[26]

Despite Russia's contribution of many of the greatest anarchist leaders and thinkers, its huge peasant population also proved largely immune to

was supposedly at the center of a plot to blow up King Victor Emmanuel III's train near Ancona (*Corriere della Sera*, June 6, 1906). In West Hoboken, where many Italian emigrants lived, Nicola Quintavalle, an alleged accomplice of Bresci, ran a barbershop that was a rendezvous for anarchists (*New York Times*, August 2, 1900).

[24] Woodcock, *Anarchism*, 194; see also James Joll, *The Anarchists*, 2nd edition (Cambridge, MA: Harvard University Press, 1980): 79–80, and Kaplan, *Anarchists*, 80–82.

[25] Only a few works have been devoted to the social history of European and American anarchism. Among the best is Kaplan's work on Andalusian anarchism. See also Esenwein, *Anarchist Ideology*, 61, 68, 83, 110, and Carl Levy, "Italian Anarchism, 1870–1926," in David Goodway (ed.), *For Anarchism: History, Theory, and Practice* (London: Routledge, 1989): 26–29. For an analysis of Andalusian anarchism from the perspective of an anthropologist and ethnographer see John R. Corbin, *The Anarchist Passion: Class Conflict in Southern Spain, 1810–1965* (Aldershot: Avebury, 1993).

[26] Pernicone, *Italian Anarchism*, 23–27. Eva Civolani, *L'anarchismo dopo la comune: I casi italiano e spagnolo* (Milan: Franco Angeli, 1981): 47–59, believes that the greater influence of the International among Spanish peasants was due to a number of reasons, including the discontent caused by the disintegration of small peasant property holdings and the liquidation of church lands in 1836. Church property usually fell into the hands of large landowners. While such phenomena occurred in Italy as well, they came at a later date, after the unification of the country, and at a time when the International was no longer so influential. Civolani also claims that the Spanish peasants were more open to class-based organizations and the Spanish section of the International more active in working with peasants, but does not clarify why this was truer of Spain than Italy. Finally, Civolani suggests that anarchism developed in those areas with latifundia, i.e., vast, low-yield estates often owned by absentee landlords, that were close to areas of dynamic agricultural and industrial capitalism. This allowed the rural areas to benefit from the experiences of the urban-based anarchists, and vice versa. In southern Italy, however, the regions of relatively advanced, export-oriented agriculture in parts of Sicily and Apulia were too distant from the industrialized areas in the north to benefit from such an interchange. Civolani does not prove the existence of this beneficial rural-urban interchange. Certainly industrial and commercial Barcelona, Spain's greatest center of urban anarchism, was no closer to poverty-stricken and rural Andalusia than industrial Milan and the other Italian anarchist centers in Romagna and Naples were to rural and peasant Sicily and Apulia.

anarchism. The early development and continuing influence of Russian populism and of populism's successor, the Socialist Revolutionary movement (neither of which rejected rule by a central state, as anarchism did), help to explain this, as well as the ferocious repression of the tsarist police. In order to flourish, anarchism needed at least a modicum of official tolerance or the breakdown of central authority.

The emergence of anarchist terrorism

At first the anarchists did not espouse terrorism as a weapon to foment revolution. What brought that about, and what brought about the popular identification of anarchism with terrorism, was a complex web of factors configured somewhat differently for each country. Italian, French, and Russian propagandists and theorists, events in Paris and St. Petersburg, economic difficulties, government repression, and historical chance: all of these were important as catalysts in producing the theory of "propaganda by the deed" and the actions of the terrorists.

Neither Proudhon nor Bakunin called for assassination attempts and terrorist bombings. Proudhon stressed the necessity for each individual to begin his personal moral reform and that this would ultimately lead to the reformation of society. As he indicated in a May 1846 letter to Marx, Proudhon was equivocal about or even opposed to immediate revolutionary action.[27] In the populist newspaper that he had founded during the Revolution of 1848, Proudhon declared that: "Killing people is the worst method for combating principles. It's only through ideas that we triumph over ideas."[28]

Bakunin, physically gigantic and possessed of enormous appetites of all kinds (except the sexual), was attracted to violence and revolution, and wrote, famously and even before he became an anarchist, that "the urge to destroy is also a creative urge."[29] Bakunin predicted that in the future, masses of peasants and workers would rise in terrible and bloody revolts: "Of course it is a pity that humanity has not yet invented a more peaceful means of progress, but until now every forward step in history has been achieved only after it has been baptized in blood."[30] Although

[27] Joll, *The Anarchists*, 52–53; Woodcock, *Anarchism*, 132–133.
[28] *Représentant du Peuple*, April 20, 1848, cited in John Ehrenberg, *Proudhon and his Age*. (Atlantic Highlands, NJ: Humanities Press, 1996): 92.
[29] This statement appears in his Hegelian-influenced essay, *Reaction in Germany*. Woodcock, *Anarchism*, 150–151.
[30] This appears in a Bakunin pamphlet published in 1870 that denounced the Swiss authorities' collaboration with the Russian government, *Les Ours de Berne et l'Ours de Saint-Pétersbourg* [1870] (Lausanne: La Cité-éditeur, 1972): 23; English translation in Mikhail

fascinated by the young Russian terrorists of the 1860s and later, he still rejected regicide and premeditated terrorism. In *The Program of the International Brotherhood* (1869) Bakunin noted that

kings, the oppressors, exploiters of all kinds…are evildoers who are not guilty, since they, too, are involuntary products of the present social order. It will not be surprising if the rebellious people kill a great many of them at first. This will be a misfortune, as unavoidable as the ravages caused by a sudden tempest, and as quickly over; but this natural act will be neither moral nor even useful.[31]

Rather than conspiring to murder tsars, government ministers and other individuals, Bakunin advocated the destruction of property and the institutions of government and society, views that his key writings, such as the *National Catechism* (1866) and *The Program of the International Brotherhood*, make clear.

At the outset (when the people, for just reasons, spontaneously turn against their tormentors) the Revolution will very likely be bloody and vindictive. But this phase will not last long and will never [degenerate into] cold, systematic terrorism…It will be war, not against particular men, but primarily against the anti-social institutions upon which their power and privileges depend.[32]

In 1869–70 Bakunin briefly collaborated with Sergei Nechaev, a ruthless Russian terrorist whose proletarian background and, even more, his "colossal" and "savage energy" attracted Bakunin and seemed to bring great advantage to the revolutionary cause. After Nechaev murdered a fellow revolutionary, however, Bakunin became disillusioned with his brutal compatriot and rejected Nechaev's "catechism" (which advocated robbery and assassination) and his whole "Jesuitical system."[33]

Bakunin, *The Political Philosophy of Bakunin: Scientific Anarchism*, ed. G. P. Maximoff (Glencoe, IL: The Free Press, 1953): 372.
[31] Mikhail Bakunin, *Bakunin on Anarchism*, ed. Sam Dolgoff (New York: Knopf, 1972): 150. For Bakunin's opposition to regicide, see his letter to Alexander Herzen, a fellow revolutionary, cited by Richard Saltman, *The Social and Political Thought of Michael Bakunin* (Westport, CT: Greenwood Press, 1983): 134. For similar views see also Bakunin's "A Circular Letter to My Friends in Italy" (1871) in *The Political Philosophy of Bakunin*, 413.
[32] Bakunin, "The National Catechism," 99, and "The Program of the International Brotherhood" in *Bakunin on Anarchism*, 149, 151.
[33] Saltman, *Social and Political Thought*, 135, demonstrates that Bakunin was primarily attracted to Nechaev's energy. Once thought to have authored *Catechism of a Revolutionary*, in 1966 the discovery of a letter dated June 2, 1870, from Bakunin to Nechaev demonstrates that the latter was the author, although "Bakunin may have helped with the writing or editing." See Chapter 3 of Paul Avrich, *Anarchist Portraits* (Princeton University Press, 1988): especially 40. Aileen Kelly, *Mikhail Bakunin: A Study in the Psychology and Politics of Utopianism* (Oxford University Press, 1982): 210–213; 269–272, is determined to expose the Russian as an advocate of terrorism, but is countered by Saltman, *Social and Political Thought*, 131, and Dolgoff ("Introduction," *Bakunin on Anarchism*, 1) who see a "flagrant contradiction between the *Catechism*'s

Instead Bakunin sought through endless conspiracies and anarchist-led insurrections to bring down the old social order. Bakunin also saw possibilities in organizing workers and farm laborers into a revolutionary force. Because of his propensity for political solutions through mass efforts, whether they were insurrectionary or labor-oriented, Bakunin's brand of anarchism came to be referred to as "collectivist."

While the majority of anarchists certainly believed that violence would accompany a future social revolution, it should be pointed out that an important pacifist, or at least non-violent, strain existed in the movement. This was exemplified in the late eighteenth century works of the English writer William Godwin, in the later writings of the novelist (turned prophet) Leo Tolstoy, and in the thinking of the Dutch anarchist Ferdinand Domela Nieuwenhuis (although Nieuwenhuis's fervent rejection of war did not exclude his approval of tyrannicide).[34]

The brief success of the Paris Commune in the spring of 1871, when radicals (some influenced by Proudhon's ideas) took over the capital for three months before the French government summoned sufficient troops from the provinces to crush the rebellion, thrilled Internationalists everywhere. The Commune acquired a tremendous notoriety and terrified the middle classes because of its bloody excesses, which included shooting the Archbishop of Paris and other hostages, and destroying such landmarks as the city hall and the Place Vendome's Napoleonic column. The emergence of the Paris Commune convinced much of the bourgeoisie and many governments that the International was an organization of immense power, despite the fact that genuine adherents of the International had played only a small part in the uprising. The Paris Commune also convinced Internationalists throughout the world that it might indeed be possible to launch a successful insurrection against the established order.

How illusory was the power of the International became apparent during the 1870s, when the insurrectionist strategy proved a complete failure. A spontaneous peasant revolt in southern Spain failed in 1873, an uprising in the Romagna led by Bakunin fizzled in 1874, and an expedition led by the anarchists Malatesta and Carlo Cafiero to revolutionize the peasants of southern Italy failed in 1877. Overreacting to the

---

negativist violence and any other manuscript, speech or action attributed to Bakunin." While this may be an overstatement, it is clear that Bakunin's most well-known and widely circulated writings not only failed to advocate a policy of terrorism, but also disparaged its value.

[34] For Nieuwenhuis's support of the assassination of Spanish leaders, Juan Avilés Farré, "Contra Alfonso XIII: Atentados frustrados y conspiración revolucionaria," in Juan Avilés Farré (ed.), *El nacimiento del terrorismo en occidente* (Madrid: Siglo XXI de España, 2008): 144.

actual threat posed by these events, governments in Italy, France, Spain, and Germany cracked down hard, not only on the Internationalists, but also on the entire labor movement. The International was suppressed in France in 1872, in Spain in 1874, and in Italy at various dates throughout the 1870s; Germany outlawed the Social Democratic Party in October 1878.

It was in the context of the apparent failure of Bakunin's collectivism together with the increasing repressiveness of the police and the authorities that the theory of "propaganda by deed" developed and became widely known. In December 1876 at the Berne Congress of the Bakuninist wing of the International, Malatesta and Cafiero announced as the policy of the Italian Internationalists, that the "insurrectionary deed, designed to promote the principles of socialism by acts, is the most effective means of propaganda and the one which ... penetrates to the deepest social stratum and attracts the living forces of humanity in the struggle that upholds the International."[35] While Malatesta and Cafiero emphasized popular revolt (and carried their idea into practice during their 1877 guerrilla expedition into the Matese mountains northeast of Naples), Paul Brousse, a French anarchist who had emigrated to Barcelona and then Berne after the suppression of the Commune, developed the concept further. Brousse, apparently the first person to use the phrase "propaganda by the deed" (in an article published two weeks after the Italian statement), suggested that the tactic could be employed not only by small bands of conspirators, but also by individuals.[36] In December 1880, Cafiero, in a famous article published in *Le Révolté*, the Geneva-based newspaper founded a year before by Peter Kropotkin, called for:

Action and still more action ... Our action must be permanent revolt by the spoken and written word, by the dagger, the rifle, dynamite ... We will use any weapon when it comes to striking as rebels. Everything is good for us that is not legal.[37]

Kropotkin, the brilliant, exiled young Russian of noble descent who in the last decades of the nineteenth century became anarchism's foremost spokesman and theoretician, echoed many of Cafiero's ideas. Never as

[35] Cited by Esenwein, *Anarchist Ideology*, 60–61, and Ze'ev Ivianski, "Individual Terror: Concept and Typology," *Journal of Contemporary History* 12 (1977), 45.

[36] Caroline Cahm, *Kropotkin and the Rise of Revolutionary Anarchism, 1872–1886* (Cambridge University Press, 1989): 80, 302n1; Esenwein, *Anarchist Ideology*, 62.

[37] "*L'Action*," *Le Révolté*, December 25, 1880, quoted by Pernicone, *Italian Anarchism*, 186–187. This article is often erroneously attributed to Kropotkin, rather than Cafiero, e.g., Walter Laqueur, *The Age of Terrorism* (Boston: Little, Brown, 1987), 48; Joll, *The Anarchists*, 109. Cahm, *Kropotkin*, 140, points out Kropotkin's reservations about Cafiero's approach. For a recent analysis of Cafiero's ideas, see Chapter 2 of Richard Drake, *Italy's Marxist Revolutionary Tradition* (Cambridge, MA, and London: Harvard University Press, 2003).

radical as the fiery Italian, in May 1881 in a widely distributed newspaper article and pamphlet, Kropotkin exalted "acts of illegal protest, of revolt, of vengeance" carried out by "lonely sentinels." "By actions which compel general attention," Kropotkin claimed, "the new idea [of revolution] seeps into people's minds and wins converts." Each act of these so-called "madmen" could "in a few days, make more propaganda than thousands of pamphlets."[38]

A month and a half after the appearance of Kropotkin's article, in July 1881, an international congress of anarchists, including Kropotkin and Malatesta, met in London and officially adopted the policy of "propaganda by the deed," a policy of illegal *acts*. These acts aimed against institutions and toward revolt and revolution were necessary since verbal and written propaganda had proved ineffectual. Excited by the recent assassination of the tsar and urged on by two shady characters, Edward Nathan-Ganz (alias Rodanow) and "Serraux" (alias for Égide Spilleux, secret agent of the Parisian prefect of police), the congress passed a resolution calling for the study of the technical sciences, such as chemistry, in order to make bombs that could be used for offensive and defensive purposes.[39] Nathan-Ganz, who resided in Boston but at the congress represented Mexican workers, also urged the creation of a military school to train anarchists in the military sciences and "chemistry" (a euphemism for dynamite). Kropotkin, who in the debates voiced his preference for nonviolent propaganda, and others opposed this.[40]

It must be emphasized again that Kropotkin and many other anarchists assumed bombs and propaganda by the deed would be used in the service of mass revolution, rather than of random acts of terror. Subsequently, however, Johann Most (1846–1906) and several lesser-known figures explicitly recommended terrorism. Most, a violent German publicist

---

[38] "The Spirit of Revolt," *Le Révolté* (Geneva), May 14, 28; June 26; July 9, 1881. The combined newspaper articles were published as a pamphlet in October 1881 and reissued in 1882. An English translation appeared in the English *Commonweal* in 1892. Cahm, *Kropotkin*, 166, 323n26; Peter Kropotkin, *The Essential Kropotkin*, ed. Emile Capouya and Keitha Tompkins (New York: Liveright, 1975): 293. The quotations are from *The Essential Kropotkin*, 6–7; also Cahm, *Kropotkin*, 161–162.

[39] Cahm, *Kropotkin*, 152–177. The resolutions of the London congress were published in *Le Révolté* (July 23, 1881), 1–2, and are reproduced, in English translation, in Cahm, *Kropotkin*, 157–158, and Andrew Carlson, *Anarchism in Germany. Vol. 1: The Early Movement* (Metuchen, NJ: Scarecrow Press, 1972): 62–63. For Serraux, see Pernicone, *Italian Anarchism*, 193–194, and *Sans patrie ni frontiers Dictionnaire international des militants anarchists*, http://militants-anarchistes.info/spip.php?article5694, accessed January 19, 2013.

[40] Given his enthusiasm for terrorism, Nathan-Ganz was suspected of being an *agent provocateur*, but this was never proved. The anarchist Benjamin Tucker later described him as being a "fascinating crook." Avrich, *The Haymarket Tragedy* (Princeton University Press, 1984): 57–58; Pernicone, *Italian Anarchism*, 194.

and orator nicknamed "the Wild Beast," published detailed directions for manufacturing and using explosives and advocated using bombs, burglary, poison, and arson against the bourgeoisie whenever possible.[41] This equivocation over the exact meaning of "propaganda by the deed," and whether it justified individual terrorism or not, was never to be decisively resolved or clarified by the anarchists.[42]

While anarchist leaders were debating theoretical issues involving the use of violence, a dramatic series of assassinations took place. During 1878, revolutionaries and assassins attacked officials throughout Europe: the chief of the St. Petersburg police was shot, the German kaiser was first fired at and then, less than a month later, peppered with shotgun pellets, and finally, on separate occasions, the kings of Spain and Italy were assaulted. The culminating *attentat* took place in March 1881, when a secret organization of Russian populists or "nihilists," to use the term first coined by the novelist Turgenev and later taken up by the popular press, tossed a lethal bomb at Tsar Alexander II. These assassination attempts had little direct connection with anarchist ideology (nor were they part of any grand conspiracy), yet because the anarchists generally applauded them, they came to be seen as anarchist and furthermore influenced subsequent anarchist views on the use of violence. The assassination of Alexander II, Europe's most despotic and reactionary ruler (at least in the eyes of the left), electrified the anarchists, who believed this deed demonstrated that revolutionary changes might indeed be possible and imminent. As Kropotkin wrote in *La Révolte*: "When the Russian revolutionaries had killed the Czar... the European anarchists imagined that, from then on, a handful of fervent revolutionaries, armed with a few bombs, would be enough to bring about the social revolution."[43] Ironically, therefore, the desires of the anarchists and the misperceptions and sensationalism of the popular media once again collaborated to reinforce the picture of a mighty international conspiracy undermining the entire established order.[44]

Driven by fears of this mostly phantom International, governments throughout the continent ordered massive police repression, rounded up thousands of people, and harassed or dissolved scores of labor organizations. This repression only convinced many anarchists that legal activity

---

[41] Max Nomad, *Apostles of Revolution* (Boston: Little, Brown, 1939): 281; Carlson, *Anarchism in Germany*, 253–254.

[42] Esenwein, *Anarchist Ideology*, 63.

[43] *La Révolte*, March 18–24, 1891, cited by Maitron, *Histoire*, 246, and translated by Janet Langmaid, in Walter Laqueur (ed.), *The Terrorism Reader: A Historical Anthology* (New York: New American Library, 1978): 99. For the enthusiasm that the assassination of the tsar aroused among Italian anarchists, see Pernicone, *Italian Anarchism*, 188–189.

[44] Esenwein, *Anarchist Ideology*, 62.

was pointless or impossible, and that terrorism was the revolutionaries' only effective arm. Anarchists abandoned "collectivism" for the anarchist-communist ideas of Kropotkin, who wanted a more egalitarian division of the products of labor than Bakunin and feared that too much involvement in labor union activity would dull the revolutionary impulse of the workers.

Historians have disputed whether this turn toward Kropotkin's "communism" promoted a strategy of violence, or whether indeed there is any direct link between anarchist ideology and the acts of violence that occurred during the 1880s and 1890s and were labeled "anarchist."[45] The Spanish historian Joaquín Romero Maura has written that in Spain the small groupings of anarchists encouraged by Kropotkin's communism provided fertile soil for the growth of violent plots.[46] On the other hand, it can be argued that the deepening influence of Kropotkin's ideas on the anarchist movement worked as much against terrorism as in favor of it. For example, in Italy during the 1880s and early 1890s, anarchists increasingly embraced fatalistic views – derived mainly from Kropotkin – about the inevitability of the coming revolution, rather than becoming violent activists.[47] On the whole, however, by discouraging anarchist involvement in the labor movement, anarchist communism helped create a mindset more congenial to terrorist activities than had been true earlier when Bakunin's collectivism had predominated.

Despite contemporary allegations to the contrary, little or no evidence exists that the spokesmen and leaders of anarchism conspired with the assassins and bomb-throwers. While a few anarchist thinkers such as Élisée Reclus sympathized with the dynamiters,[48] in the early 1890s Kropotkin, Most, and Malatesta explicitly denounced terrorism (although their position on assassination was much more equivocal). Kropotkin declared that: "A structure [i.e., authoritarian European society] built on centuries of history can not be destroyed with a few kilos of explosives."[49] Malatesta described those anarchists who supported

---

[45] Marie Fleming, "Propaganda by the Deed: Terrorism and Anarchist Theory in Late Nineteenth-Century Europe," *Terrorism* 4 (1980): 1–23, argues that violent acts of propaganda by the deed "became central to the elaboration of anarchist theory and that a philosophical justification of individual, as well as collective, violence developed logically out of it." Woodcock, *Anarchism*; Murray Bookchin, *The Spanish Anarchists: The Heroic Years, 1868–1936* (New York: Free Life Editions, 1977), and others dispute any intrinsic connection between terrorism and anarchism.

[46] Joaquín Romero Maura, "Terrorism in Barcelona and its Impact on Spanish Politics 1904–1909," *Past and Present* 41 (1968), 151–154; Esenwein, *Anarchist Ideology*, 131–133, 170.

[47] Pernicone, *Italian Anarchism*, 242–243.   [48] Maitron, *Histoire*, 212.

[49] Kropotkin, *La Révolte*, March 18–24, 1891 and *La Révolte*, January 16–22, 1892. Maitron, *Histoire*, 246, 209.

Ravachol's violent deeds as having missed the point about the anarchist struggle. "It's no longer love for the human race that guides them, but the feeling of vendetta joined to the cult of an abstract idea, of a theoretical phantasm."[50] While Malatesta justified tyrannicide,[51] he also told a reporter that he "would rather kill chickens than kill kings. Chickens are good to eat. But a king, of what use is he?"[52] Given anarchism's emphasis on individual freedom and initiative, of course, what the leaders thought about terrorism was much less influential than it would have been in other political ideologies and movements.

During the 1880s and 1890s various acts of social revolt and violence took place in Italy, France, Spain, Germany, Russia, and the United States, but these acts were almost always closely connected to local conditions and traditions in which violent response to social problems had long been the norm, rather than being solely or mostly due to anarchist instigation. In southern Spain violence against the rich had been a common popular tactic much before the Spanish section of the International called for such attacks. Especially during times of high unemployment or in periods of government repression, Spaniards often stole food, cut down vines, and set wheat fields or olive groves on fire; they resorted to frequent daylight robberies and even murders.[53] In Italy there was a long tradition, preceding the emergence of anarchism and reinforced by the *Risorgimento* or struggle for national unification, of taking revenge for injustice by killing tyrants.[54] Giuseppe Garibaldi was a supporter of tyrannicide and Felice Orsini, a former follower of Mazzini, became a national hero after trying to assassinate Napoleon III for his failure to assist the Italian cause.[55] The example provided by Italian nationalists for assassination, as well as for violent insurrection,

---

[50] Malatesta to Luisa Minguzzi Pezzi, April 29, 1892, in Malatesta, *Rivoluzione e lotta quotidiana*, ed. Gino Cerrito (Milan: Edizioni Antistato, 1982). Writing in the French anarchist journal *L'En Dehors*, August 21, 1892, Malatesta publicly opposed *attentats* (Maitron, *Histoire*, 227).

[51] Malatesta's article "The Duties of the Present Hour," *Liberty* (August 1894), cited by Carl Levy, "Malatesta in London: The Era of Dynamite," *The Italianist*, **13** (1993): 33.

[52] August 17, 1900 interview with Malatesta published by *The Daily Graphic* (London), cited by Levy, "Malatesta in London," 39.

[53] Kaplan, *Anarchists*, 28, 117–119, 143, 163.

[54] Nunzio Pernicone, "Luigi Galleani and Italian Anarchist Terrorism in the United States," *Studi emigrazione/Etudes Migrations* 30:11 (1993): 470–472, and Pernicone, *Italian Anarchism*, 13.

[55] Denis Mack Smith, *Mazzini* (New Haven and London: Yale University Press, 1994): 122, 166. Giuseppe Mazzini opposed terrorism, but "would not deter ... individuals if they sincerely and in good conscience resisted his contrary arguments." In 1833 he provided money and a knife for an assassination attempt on Piedmontese King Charles Albert. Smith, *Mazzini*, 9–10.

proved influential inside and outside of Italy. Italian anarchists soon became famous as the great regicides of Europe, although they used the traditional dagger and the pistol, rather than the new weapon of mass terror: dynamite.[56]

Anarchist terrorism also developed within the context of painful social and economic changes taking place throughout Europe and the Americas at the end of the nineteenth century. Some historians view propaganda by the deed violence as coinciding with the "transition period of a pre-capitalist economy to the establishment of organized capitalism" just as the earlier "insurrectional phase" of anarchism had coincided with "agrarian anarchism."[57] In southern Spain the collapse of the sherry market in the 1860s drove small peasant proprietors and vine tenders to the verge of bankruptcy and into the anarchist movement. Throughout Europe the coming of the Great Depression in the late 1870s brought a steady decline in agricultural prices and sharpening international competition between industrial manufacturers. Such developments particularly hurt artisans and Europeans living in the countryside, while in contrast urban factory workers experienced a rising standard of living.

These structural causes for violence, found in hunger, unemployment, and other degrading living and working conditions, while important, should not be overemphasized or focused on too narrowly. Nor, in the case of Spain, should the blame for terrorism be put on the shoulders of the wretched agrarian masses of Andalusia infected by anarcho-communism.[58] While the deeds of some of the assassins and bomb-throwers may be considered the desperate protests of those "crushed beneath the wheels of industrialization and modernization," other anarchists acted for coolly plotted political reasons and came from the middle classes and intelligentsia.[59] As for Spain, men from outside the south carried out most of the famous assassinations and bombings.

In a broad sense, however, the "Social Question" was fundamental to the genesis of anarchist terrorism and helps to distinguish it from some later forms of terrorism. The Social Question can be defined as the ethical, social, and political issues raised and the injustices and sufferings caused by nineteenth century industrialism, or "the consciousness

---

[56] Pernicone, "Luigi Galleani," 470–472, and Pernicone, *Italian Anarchism*, 13.
[57] Ulrich Linse, "'Propaganda by Deed' and 'Direct Action': Two Concepts of Anarchist Violence," in Wolfgang Mommsen and Gerhard Hirschfeld (eds.), *Social Protest, Violence and Terror in Nineteenth- and Twentieth-century Europe* (New York: St. Martin's Press, 1982): 207.
[58] Cf. Walther Bernecker, "The Strategies of 'Direct Action' and Violence in Spanish Anarchism," in Mommsen and Hirschfeld, *Social Protest*, 88–111, especially 102–104.
[59] Iviansky, "Individual Terror," 51.

of a contradiction between economic development and the social ideal of liberty and equality."[60] The problem posed by the Social Question was not only one of frustrated and downtrodden artisans and proletarians deciding to violently strike out in desperation (or in careful calculation). It also encompassed a fearful and unimaginative (and sometimes cynical) governing class wishing to avoid social upheaval (or even defeat at the next election) by turning the solution of the Social Question into an issue of repressing terrorism. This helps explain the unusual numbers of *agents provocateurs* and corrupt police during this period who contributed to fomenting the very terrorism they were supposed to be eliminating. The importance of the Social Question to an understanding of anarchist terrorism would seem to differentiate it fundamentally from the twenty-first century's religiously inflected terrorism, despite the efforts of recent commentators to depict al-Qaeda as a form of anarchism.[61]

A proper understanding of the origins of anarchist terrorism at the end of the nineteenth century must take into account not only a variety of causes, some of them contradictory, but also a baffling gap between rhetoric and reality. Malatesta and Kropotkin had called for propaganda by the deed, meaning actions aimed at insurrection and revolution, but soon got random acts of murder about which they harbored deep misgivings. Loath to abandon the lowly instigators of these deeds, the anarchist leaders apologized for them, and thus enabled, or at least assisted, the popular press and numerous politicians in finding someone to blame, or to scapegoat, for miscellaneous anti-social acts. Equal in its irony, many governments, seeking to end the violent insurrectionism that they blamed on a largely phantom International, sought to crush the organized labor movement, only to sow the seeds for a crop of revenge-seekers who trumpeted the cause of defiant anarchism. Police brutality ignited chain reactions of violence in which the anarchists met acts of police brutality with bloody responses. Massive government crackdowns followed, but only provoked even more spectacular assassinations and terrorist bombings. Traditional means of maintaining social order no longer seemed effective against an enemy who picked such nontraditional targets as religious processions, opera performances, and outdoor cafés. Or who came out of nowhere, made up of obscure individuals arriving from abroad (since anarchism, driven by police expulsions and mass migration, had metastasized to the four corners of the earth). Adding to the confusion and contributing to the violence were regional and national traditions of social warfare and justified regicide. These had long preceded the writings of Proudhon and the actions and words of Bakunin,

---

[60] Ira W. Howerth cites this oft-quoted passage by the German economist Adolph Wagner in "The Social Question of Today," *The American Journal of Sociology* 12:2 (1906): 259.
[61] See Gelvin and others in *Terrorism and Political Violence* 20:4 (2008).

yet after the 1860s they were all labeled "anarchist." Just as confusing and even more contradictory, is the little documented clandestine role of police agents and politicians in provoking or assisting terrorist violence in the hopes of achieving a variety of political goals.

Therefore, it can be argued that the wave of anarchist terror that swept through Europe during the 1880s and 1890s drew its growing strength from a curious combination of the acts of ideologically committed anarchists and of the violent deeds of a miscellany of perpetrators who shared dubious or no connections with anarchism. The assassination of Tsar Alexander, attempts on the German kaiser and Italian king in 1878, the abortive bombing of the Greenwich Observatory (at the instigation of the tsarist police?), scores of mysterious bombings in Barcelona between 1904 and 1909, attacks on British civilians and officials in India, the Italian soldier Masetti's assault on his commanding officer in 1911, and other acts of violence were all co-opted into the terrorist "black wave," not only by the prejudices (and sometimes the instigation) of the media, police, and politicians, but also by the fervent desires of many anarchists, who saw in them dazzling images of proletarian power.

Anarchist terrorism after 1878

In retrospect, widely publicized assassination attempts in 1878 began a miscellany of violent incidents in Europe and the United States that can be viewed as the beginning of the era of anarchist terrorism. Several historians see the Russian populist Vera Zasulich's assault on General Trepov, the brutal tsarist governor of St. Petersburg, on January 24, 1878, as the spark that ignited a series of assassination attempts inside and outside Russia.[62] Assaults followed in May and June against the German kaiser, Wilhelm I, in October against the Spanish King Alfonso XII, and in November against the Italian monarch, Umberto I. Bombs were hurled at monarchist crowds in Florence (February 9 and November 18; the latter assault killed four people and injured many others) and in Pisa (November 20). Who threw these bombs has never been indisputably established. At the time some blamed the anarchists, but one scholar has argued that police agents may have been involved.[63] While

---

[62] Anna Geifman, *Thou Shalt Kill. Revolutionary Terrorism in Russia, 1894–1917* (Princeton University Press, 1995): 85; Alex Butterworth, *The World That Never Was: A True Story of Dreamers, Schemers, Anarchists and Secret Agents* (New York: Pantheon, 2010): 128; Pernicone, *Italian Anarchism*, 147–48. Ernest Alfred Vizetelly, *The Anarchists* (London: John Land, 1911): 41, emphasizes the German assassination attempts.

[63] Paola Feri, as cited in Pernicone, *Italian Anarchism*, 148–152, especially 149n.

perhaps only Max Hödel, the attempted assassin of the kaiser, and Juan Oliva y Moncasi, the alleged assailant against the Spanish king, could definitely be considered anarchists (or Bakuninist members of the First International), newspapers and worried governments attributed this entire hodgepodge of incidents to the sinister designs of the Black International. Moreover the anarchists themselves were quick to celebrate Max Hödel and Karl Nobiling – the man responsible for the June assassination attempt on the kaiser – as anarchist heroes, whatever their real political affiliation.[64] Indicative of future developments was not only the fear of widespread conspiracy and the facile use of the anarchist label for these events, but also the possible involvement of *agents provocateurs* and the connection between a desire for publicity and violent anarchist deeds. Before his *attentat* on Wilhelm I, Hödel had his photograph taken because he was sure he would soon become famous and his picture would be much in demand.[65] Hödel's belief that he would not survive his attack (and Nobiling's suicide after he had fired on the German emperor) foreshadowed the tendency of latter anarchist terrorists to look upon their deeds as calls to martyrdom.

As already mentioned, the most spectacular assassination of this period took place in March 1881 when the People's Will succeeded in mortally wounding the Russian emperor, Alexander II. The People's Will was not an anarchist organization, since it was authoritarian and hierarchical and intended to create a popular dictatorship after toppling the tsar. Most anarchists rejected authoritarian political structures, even if

---

[64] Historians are divided on the motivations and political backgrounds of the two German assassins. Carlson argues that the assassination attempts were part of a single conspiracy orchestrated by the anarchist-identified German section of the Jura Federation in Switzerland; Carlson, *Anarchism*, 122–123, 147–149, and "Anarchism and Individual Terror in the German Empire, 1879–90," in Mommsen and Hirschfeld (eds.), *Social Protest, Violence and Terror*: 178. Carlson states that "the police demonstrated beyond the shadow of a doubt that Hödel was an anarchist" ("Anarchism and Individual Terror," 150). On the other hand Otto Pflanze, the foremost contemporary historian of Bismarck, states that "there was no evidence that the two men [Hödel and Nobiling] knew each other or that either had co-conspirators." Pflanze points out the political vacillations of the two men and suggests that the key to understanding their deeds was not anarchist, let alone socialist, ideology, but that both "were psychopaths eager for attention and notoriety." Pflanze, *Bismarck and the Development of Germany* 3 vols. (Princeton University Press, 1990): 2:393. Contemporaries were prone to identify Hödel and Nobiling as anarchists (e.g., the magisterial article by the international law expert, William Loubat, "De la legislation contre les anarchistes au point de vue internation," *Journal du Droit international privé*, 23 (1896): 306; the Jesuit newspaper *Civiltà cattolica*, January 27, 1903). The anarchist press praised and identified with their actions. The Geneva section of the Jura Federation even passed a resolution declaring Hödel to be a "martyr for the rights of mankind." (Carlson, *Anarchism*, 149).

[65] Carlson, *Anarchism*, 122.

devised by themselves, and after the revolution favored turning power over to autonomous local groups and organizations. But the People's Will did share with the anarchists the famous practice of employing dynamite for terrorism; indeed the Russians pioneered its use and provided the anarchists with a model.

In 1875 Nobel's invention of an even more powerful explosive, variously called blasting gelatin, gelatin dynamite, or gelignite, excited the Russian revolutionaries. Nobel found a way to dispense with kieselguhr, the spongy clay he had used to stabilize nitroglycerine but which diminished its force, by mixing nitroglycerine with collodion, a low nitrated, soluble form of guncotton (which is cotton treated with a mixture of acids and very explosive). According to an illustrative, if probably apocryphal, account, Nobel made his discovery in curious fashion, realizing the possibilities of the odd combination of ingredients after painting a cut on his finger with collodion, which was used at the time as a quick-drying bandage for wounds.[66] The mixture of collodion and nitroglycerin produced a pale yellow substance that looked like jelly and was for many decades "the most powerful nonmilitary explosive in existence."[67]

The People's Will used gelatin dynamite for all its attempted assassinations, even though the conventional pistol was more easily available, cheaper, and probably stood a greater chance of success. The stated reason for this was that the revolutionaries believed that an assassination caused by a dynamite explosion would have a much greater psychological impact: it would express "a new stage in the revolutionary movement" rather than being "interpreted as an ordinary murder."[68] Of course, in most cases, setting off a dynamite bomb allowed the perpetrator a better chance of escaping than if he had used a dagger or a revolver and this may have been an unstated reason behind its use.

During the 1880s, attempted assassinations and murders of leading police and political figures occurred, but more characteristic of the period were violent acts involving labor disputes and pure acts of criminality, such as robbery and the murder of ordinary citizens. A strand developed (and long continued) in anarchism – described by one historian as a mutant offshoot – that advocated expropriation of the bourgeoisie as a legitimate tool in the promotion of revolution.[69] The first act of propaganda by the deed during the 1880s (unless one counts the police-assisted bombing of a statue of Adolphe Thiers) occurred in October 1881, when

---

[66] Dutton, *One Thousand Years of Explosives*, 147–152. Norman Gardiner Johnson refers to the story of Nobel's cut finger and collodion as a "legend," *Encyclopaedia Britannica*, 1970 "Explosives."

[67] Dutton, *One Thousand Years of Explosives*, 152; *Encyclopaedia Britannica*, "Explosives."

[68] Iviansky, "Individual Terror," 47.   [69] Pernicone, *Italian Anarchism*, 239.

the young French anarchist Émile Florion attempted to assassinate a bourgeois gentleman he met by chance. Florion, an unemployed weaver, had initially intended to shoot the famous republican leader Leon Gambetta, but after failing to locate his intended victim, shot twice at, but missed, the little-known Dr. Meymar. Florion then tried, but failed, to kill himself.[70]

A much more significant assassination attempt took place against the German kaiser in September 1883. If a badly sprained ankle had not led the chief conspirator, August Reinsdorf, to turn the plot over to his incompetent followers, German anarchism might have succeeded in carrying out the most spectacular piece of propaganda by the deed of the nineteenth century, blowing up not only the kaiser and the crown prince, but also many top generals, aristocrats and government officials. All of these prominent people were scheduled to attend the dedication of a great monument symbolizing Germania on a high ridge of the Niederwald overlooking the Rhine River. But the anarchists' attempt was foiled by a wet fuse that failed to ignite sixteen pounds of dynamite placed in a drainage pipe. In a subsequent effort they blew up an almost empty concert hall in nearby Rüdesheim on the mistaken assumption that the German emperor intended this place for a visit.[71] While the anarchists failed to kill the kaiser, their attempts succeeded in terrorizing some members of the imperial family. According to one source, the Crown Princess Victoria was "terrified of attempts on her life" and "discussed with somebody in great detail the further security measures which might be taken. She demanded a considerable increase in the police estimates and the formulation of a large and efficient secret police."[72]

The failure of the Niederwald attempt illustrated some of the practical problems of utilizing dynamite. Although for fifty years dynamite preserved its reputation among anarchists, revolutionaries, and the public as the miracle weapon of destruction, a gap existed between the potent symbol and the mundane reality. Dynamite was much more powerful than previous explosives, but in practice it often proved less lethal and more cumbersome than expected. Most's and later anarchist manuals on explosives were inaccurate and attempts by amateurs to concoct dynamite bombs often ended in premature explosions. Even when the terrorists stole or purchased commercially produced dynamite (which Most

---

[70] Maitron, *Histoire*, 198.
[71] Carlson, *Anarchism*, 289–299.
[72] Diary entry of Friedrich von Holstein, a German Foreign Office official, August 27, 1884, cited in Carlson, *Anarchism*, 274.

recommended over homemade varieties), huge quantities were often necessary to guarantee success.

Some commentators feared that the anarchists would move on from dynamite to other means of mass destruction, including bio-terrorism. Since the early 1880s, Most and Nathan-Ganz had been advocating various diabolical schemes to poison or blow up the bourgeoisie.[73] In 1894 the British weekly magazine *Tit-Bits*, claimed the discovery of evidence, provided by a highly placed detective, of a plot to release disease into the air or the country's water supply.[74] Italian police agent Ettore Sernicoli, whose job was to keep an eye on anarchists in the French capital, wrote that he knew of anarchist projects to put barrels of nitroglycerine into the water pipes of Paris, which would create explosions in every home, or else the anarchists might set off blasts by breaking gas pipes near houses and other buildings.[75] But these claims and reports, as well as so much else about the anarchist threat, proved to be sheer fantasies, daydreams never followed up by attempts at implementation.

Soon after the failure of the Niederwald attempt and the explosion in Rüdesheim, the police arrested Reinsdorf and another anarchist; both were tried and executed for their part in the assassination attempt. Perhaps in revenge for this sentence, in January 1885 an unknown assailant stabbed to death the police chief of Frankfurt, a man who had played an important role in convicting Reinsdorf. Circumstantial evidence was used to convict the anarchist Julius Lieske of the deed.[76] After his sentencing, Lieske called for revenge, as did Most's New York-based German-language newspaper, *Freiheit* (*Freedom*).

But the murder of Police Chief Rumpf and the execution of Lieske proved to be the end of propaganda by the deed in Germany except for a few sporadic incidents later on. Rather than leading to a new chain reaction of revenge and repression, these events were accompanied by a rapid decline in the German anarchist movement, which in any case was rather small, consisting in the 1880s of no more than perhaps a couple of dozen groups and around 200 members.[77] While the police rounded up

---

[73] Ann Larabee, "A Brief History of Terrorism in the United States," in David Clarke (ed.), *Technology and Terrorism* (New Brunswick, NJ: Transaction Publishers, 2003): 19–40.

[74] Bernard Porter, *The Origins of the Vigilant State: The London Metropolitan Police Special Branch Before the First World War* (London: Weidenfeld and Nicolson 1987): 103, 132.

[75] Ettore Sernicoli, *L'anarchia e gli anarchici. Studio storico e politico*, 2 vols., 2nd edition (Milan: Treves, 1894): 1:195. To his credit, Sernicoli labels these projects "daydreams" (*fantasticherie*).

[76] Carlson, *Anarchism*, 302–310.

[77] Dieter Fricke, *Bismarck's Praetorianer* (Berlin: Rutten and Loening, 1962): 153; E. V. Zenker, *Anarchism: A Criticism and History of the Anarchist Theory* (London: Methuen, 1898): 239.

or exiled anarchist leaders and dissolved their organizations, the German anarchists had a major falling out among themselves and used up their energies squabbling. Although the anti-socialist law harmed both the Social Democrats and the anarchists, the socialists were better able to survive since many of their leaders, as deputies elected to the Reichstag, remained safe from prosecution. In the late 1880s, German anarchism, which had always been much smaller than the movements in France, Italy, and Spain, went into a rapid decline. Since the majority of the German anarchists had been handicraft workers, the powerful development of German industry and the growth of socialist-dominated labor unions greatly undermined the movement's social base.[78]

Besides the events in Russia and Germany, the only other significant act of "symbolic" terrorism in Europe during the 1880s took place in France. In 1886 the anarchist Charles Gallo threw a bottle of prussic acid into the Paris stock exchange, fired his revolver at random, and shouted "*Vive l'Anarchie!*" The sole harm done was to the stockbrokers' noses, assaulted by the abominable stench of the acid.

Acts of propaganda by the deed connected with labor disputes were more characteristic of the 1880s. In 1882 a mysterious "Black Band" was accused of terrorist acts against local mine operators and religious and political authorities in Bois du Verne and Montceau-les-Mines, seventy miles north of Lyon, and of bombings in Lyons itself, where Kropotkin and other anarchist leaders were later tried for instigating these crimes. If anarchists were indeed involved in the 1882 bombings, which is debatable, it would have been the first instance of anarchists using dynamite to commit terrorist acts.[79] The historian Maitron believes that the authors of these first dynamite attempts were miners and other workers angered by economic exploitation and religious repression who might have been exposed to some anarchist ideas and literature, but were not part of any self-consciously anarchist movement.[80] This distinction was lost on the authorities and the public, however, due to the anarchist press's glorification of the "admirable anarchist movement" at Montceau and attempts by the anarchists of Lyons to make contact with the Montceau miners.[81]

[78] Carlson, *Anarchism*, 395.
[79] Woodcock, *Anarchism*, 250; Maitron *Histoire*, leaves open the question as to whether or not an anarchist journalist named Antoine Cyvoct was guilty of bombing the restaurant of the Bellecour Theater, Lyon, an explosion that killed one young employee (Maitron, *Histoire*, 161–162, 169–170).
[80] The manager of the mines at Montceau, a certain Chagot, ruled the miners like a dictator, arbitrarily reducing wages and, for example, decreeing a church burial for one newly deceased young man, although the latter had expressed the desire to be buried in a civil ceremony. Maitron, *Histoire*, 160, 163–164.
[81] Maitron, *Histoire*, 162.

From the very beginning, then, a pattern emerged that was to character-
ize the entire era of anarchist terrorism. The anarchists' desire for signs
of a rising proletarian revolt combined with the authorities' and the public's fears of a vast anarchist conspiracy to create the mirage of a powerful
movement of anarchist terrorism. But the anarchists' involvement in violence was not entirely a mirage, since evidence exists that they instigated a
wave of dynamite explosions in 1883–1884.[82]

During the same years that the "Black Band" was operating in France,
the equally mysterious "Black Hand" was accused of perpetrating violent
deeds in southern Spain. Since murders and other acts of violence had
long characterized the bitter class struggle in Andalusia, it is not at all
certain that the Black Hand existed outside the minds of the police and
the newspapers.[83] Nonetheless the trials and executions of the alleged
members of the *Mano Negra*, all anarchists, served as an effective means
of crushing the Andalusian labor movement.

The most famous of all the labor disputes connected with propaganda
by the deed involved the campaign for the eight-hour day in the United
States, which culminated in the Haymarket Bombing of May 4, 1886.
This took place in the context of increasingly embittered labor relations
in Chicago and the ascendancy of Johann Most over the revolutionary
left in the United States.[84] Most, who had immigrated to New York City
in 1882, after being imprisoned first in Germany and then in England,
was a brilliant editor of New York's *Freiheit*, an influential pamphleteer,
and an orator who "electrified, all but bewitched every listener."[85] While
Most spoke and wrote in German, at this time millions in the United
States could understand him. The second half of the nineteenth century witnessed the high tide of German immigration; in 1880, eighty
German-language dailies were being published in the country.[86] Before
Haymarket, the Chicago anarchist press serialized parts of Most's *Science
of Revolutionary War*. It was also sold for ten cents a copy at picnics and
meetings and at the offices of anarchist newspapers.[87] The anarchist press
incessantly extolled the virtues of dynamite in articles, editorials, and
poetry: "Hurrah for science! Hurrah for dynamite! – the power which
in our hands shall make an end of tyranny."[88] When in the spring of
1886 a campaign began in Chicago for the eight-hour workday, it was

---

[82] Maitron, *Histoire*, 156–157.
[83] See Kaplan's and Esenwein's discussions of the arguments for and against the existence
of the *Mano Negra* in, respectively, *Anarchists*, 126–134, and *Anarchist Ideology*, 88–92.
[84] Avrich, *Haymarket*, 67.
[85] According to an anarchist who had heard Most speak. Avrich, *Haymarket*, 65.
[86] Frederic Trautmann, *The Voice of Terror: A Biography of Johann Most* (Westport, CT:
Greenwood Press, 1980): 113–114.
[87] Avrich, *Haymarket*, 165.   [88] Avrich, *Haymarket*, 167.

in an atmosphere influenced by Most's propaganda and full of "apocalyptic fervour... that social revolution was imminent and physical force unavoidable."[89]

On May 3, Chicago police fired into a crowd of unarmed, but rock-throwing, strikers, killing two men. When a peaceful protest meeting was held the next day near Haymarket Square, the police abruptly marched in and ordered it terminated. At this point, an unknown assailant threw a bomb at the police and the latter began firing wildly. Subsequent investigations showed that the bomb indubitably killed only a single policeman. Three other police died due to a combination of bomb fragments and police bullets. Panicky police firing caused the eventual death of 11–14 law officers and 7–8 civilians, and the injury of 80–90 civilians and police. This was not the impression that the public received, however, since the press attributed most of the dead and wounded to the anarchist bomb. The bomb-thrower, who may have been an anarchist from New York, was never conclusively identified, but, in a travesty of justice, eight Chicago anarchists were rounded up, tried, and convicted; four were hanged for the deed.[90] This misguided act of judicial murder propelled the fallen men into the front ranks of anarchist martyrs, inspiring generations of anarchists and, eventually, anarchist terrorists.

During the 1880s many of the most notorious anarchist deeds were hardly more than common crimes. Between 1882 and 1884 Austrian radicals and anarchists robbed and murdered a shoe manufacturer, a policeman, and, most shockingly of all, a moneychanger and his nine- and eleven-year-old sons.[91] In France a former employee killed the mother superior of the convent where he had been working; in Germany anarchists robbed and killed a pharmacist and a banker, using the expropriated funds to finance propaganda.[92] In the late 1880s, exiled Italian anarchists in Paris led by Vittorio Pini and Luigi Parmeggiani robbed and used part of their proceeds to finance a few issues of an anarchist publication. Élisée Reclus, a well-known geographer and anarchist publicist, and Sébastien Faure, a journalist and libertarian philosopher, applauded these robberies as revolutionary acts against the immorality of property ownership and in support of friends. Other French anarchists agreed, although there were some who did not.[93] In February 1889 Pini

[89] Avrich, *Haymarket*, 455.

[90] Avrich, *Haymarket*, 206–210; 437–445. James Green, *Death in the Haymarket: A Story of Chicago, the First Labor Movement, and the Bombing that Divided Gilded Age America* (New York: Anchor Books, 2006), provides no new light on the identity of the bomb-thrower.

[91] Carlson, *Anarchism*, 256–269. See also Anna Staudacher's *Sozialrevolutionäre und Anarchisten: Die Andere Arbeiterbewegung vor Hainfeld: die Radikale Arbeiter-Partei Österreichs (1880–1884)* (Vienna: Verlag für Gesellschafts Kritik, 1988).

[92] Carlson, *Anarchism*, 260.   [93] Maitron, *Histoire*, 182–183.

and Parmeggiani traveled to Emilia in north-central Italy and stabbed a former Internationalist in revenge for his criticism of their tactics.[94]

These dreadful deeds, as well as the other acts of anarchist violence during the 1880s, exercised limited impact. They were isolated events and produced little or no panic among the public at large, although they preoccupied the authorities. Chain reactions of violence, repression, and revenge had either failed to ignite or proved to be short-lived. Calls for revenge against the execution of Lieske in Germany and of the robber-murderers in Austria met no response. In Germany and Austria, at least, severe police repression combined with a lack of sympathy for the anarchist murderers (and the smallness of the local anarchist population) not only ended terrorism, but also effectively marginalized anarchism as a social and political movement. In France the terrorist events of the 1880s had been even more isolated, with fewer immediate repercussions than in the German-speaking countries. Throughout Europe, with the exception of the death of Alexander II in 1881, the various assassination attempts against crowned heads and ruling politicians had been unsuccessful.

Anarchist terrorism in the 1890s

All of this was to change in the 1890s. Then, to quote a popular British journal, anarchist terrorism became a deadly "epidemic … almost as mysterious and universal as the influenza" against which "police precautions appear to be as useless as prophylactics against the fatal sneeze."[95] The years 1892 to 1901 became the decade of regicide, during which more monarchs, presidents, and prime ministers of major world powers were assassinated than at any other time in history (President Marie François Sadi Carnot of France in 1894, Prime Minister Antonio Cánovas del Castillo of Spain in 1897, the Empress Elisabeth of Austria in 1898, King Umberto I of Italy in 1900, and President William McKinley of the United States in 1901).[96] Carnot's murder was the first assassination of a

---

[94] Pernicone, *Italian Anarchism*, 239–241.
[95] *Review of Reviews*, 5 (1892): 435, quoted in Porter, *Vigilant State*, 102.
[96] The extensive listing in Murray Clark Havens, Carl Leiden, and Karl Schmitt, *The Politics of Assassination* (Englewood Cliffs, NJ: Prentice-Hall, 1970): 161–167, would seem to undermine the anarchists' reputation as history's supreme regicides. During two eight-year periods (1918–1925 and 1961–1968) assassins killed more heads of government and state (eight during the post-war era – plus one additional leader killed by the anarchists – and 12 during the 1960s). In each period, however, only one of the leaders was from a major power, i.e., Premier Takashi Hara of Japan in 1921 and President Kennedy in 1963. During both sets of years, the rash of assassinations took place primarily in newly independent or highly unstable countries, often in the midst of

French head of state since 1610 and Umberto's the first of a member of the house of Savoy in 700 years.

The 1890s also became the era of the anarchist terrorist bloodbath, as anarchists hurled explosive devices into crowded cafés, religious processions, and operatic performances where they killed men, women and children. In November 1893 an anarchist, Santiago Salvador, threw a bomb onto the heads of the elegantly dressed audience attending a performance at Barcelona's grand Liceo (or Liceu) Theater of Rossini's *William Tell* (an opera, appropriately enough from the anarchists' viewpoint, extolling freedom and tyrannicide). The bomb killed more than thirty people – more than twice the number who perished as a result of anarchist actions in France during the whole of the 1890s and as many as all the incidents of the 1880s combined.[97] Ironically, this act of terrorism, one of the anarchists' deadliest, was carried out, not by a dynamite explosion, but with an "Orsini bomb," whose technology had been invented back in 1858 by Orsini, the attempted assassin of Emperor Napoleon III. Orsini was no anarchist, but rather an Italian nationalist. The ingenious bombs that he and his accomplices threw at the carriage of Napoleon III, who, curiously, was also on his way to hear that dangerous opera *William Tell*, were oblong, ranging in size from that of an orange to a small melon. The average bomb weighed about three pounds. They were filled with mercury fulminate and black powder and detonated when protruding "nipples" were violently pushed back into the core of the bomb by collision with a solid object, such as a paving stone or the side of a carriage.[98]

On June 7, 1896, a bomb was dropped on a Corpus Christi procession on Calle de los Cambios Nuevos in Barcelona. This ultimately led to the death of twelve people, most of whom were women and children, as well

revolutions (e.g., President Carranza of Mexico in 1920). On the other hand, the figures assassinated between 1894 and 1901 were all leaders of relatively stable and long-lasting (i.e., at least several decades old) regimes.

[97] The Barcelona Liceo bombing initially killed fifteen and injured fifty (Esenwein, *Anarchist Ideology*, 186), but at least another fifteen died of their injuries. See *The Times* (London), November 9, 1893, 3, and the *New York Times*, December 20, 1893, 8. T. L. Jouffray, writing years later ("Warnings and Teachings of the Church on Anarchism," *The Catholic World* 74 (1901): 207) speaks of the bombs "killing fifteen … on the spot and mortally injuring two score more," which would mean fifty-five deaths, although no other source gives such a high figure. An accurate count is difficult since the government prohibited Spanish press coverage of these events and provided no official tally. The court case summary cites twenty killed and twenty-seven injured. A. Herrerin, "España: La Propaganda por la Represión, 1892–1900," in Farré, *El nacimiento* (Madrid: Siglo XXI de España, 2008): 111.

[98] Michael St. John Packe, *Orsini, the Story of a Conspirator* (Boston: Little Brown): 234–236, 288–290.

as to injury to scores of people.[99] In an age unaccustomed to terrorist attacks on women and children, the shocking spectacle of their murder at the hands of anarchists drove many observers into a frenzy. William Tallack, president of the Howard Association, wrote the London *Times* in June 1897 that

these deeds are not only wicked, but also contemptible to the last degree. For unspeakably cowardly it is to hurl fatal explosives among women and children! These dastardly outrages are, in the nostrils of mankind, as the fetid repulsiveness of the most nauseous of animals.[100]

While during the 1880s, the most prominent acts of anarchist terrorism took place in Germany, Austria, and the United States, in the next decade the geography of terrorism shifted. During the 1890s a few bombs shook Greenwich, Constantinople, and Zurich, but terrorism centered in western and southern continental Europe – in France, Belgium, Spain, and Italy and, to a lesser degree, in Portugal. While the number of victims was relatively small, the political and social prominence of many of them greatly increased the impact and notoriety of these violent deeds. Adding to their force was the fact that they took place in such great urban centers as Paris, Barcelona, and Rome; in the 1880s, except for the incidents in Vienna and Chicago, the sites of most anarchist deeds had been in the countryside or small towns. Compounding the terror of the anarchist bombings, especially between 1892 and 1894, was the fact that the blasts seemed linked together in chain reactions of violence that were impervious to police efforts at prevention. Moreover, the dynamiting and assassinations often took place in several countries simultaneously, which magnified their psychological impact and made them seem part of one vast terrorist conspiracy. Italian anarchists journeyed to France in 1894 and Spain in 1897 to avenge their martyred French and Spanish comrades by killing the French president and the Spanish prime minister. The Italian parliament rushed through draconian anti-anarchist legislation not only because of violence in Rome, but also because of its horror at events taking place in France and Spain.

[99] Romero Maura, "Terrorism," 130, provides the figure of 12 killed and 44 wounded. At first the *New York Times* published reports of 6 killed, but these were soon revised to 11 killed and 40 wounded. It noted on June 10 that several of the latter "have since died and others are moribund" (*New York Times*, June 9 and 10, 1896). Rafael Núñez Florencio, *El Terrorismo Anarquista (1888–1909)* (Madrid: Siglo veintiuno, 1983): 57, relying on the contemporary anarchist account of Ramón Sempau, gives a figure of 6 killed and 42 injured, "some" of whom later died.
[100] *The Times*, June 7, 1897.

The mass of the population reacted to these violent incidents with growing concern and even panic. In France the panic began when the arrest in March 1892 of Ravachol, the most famous of all the anarchist terrorists, did not bring an end to the bombings in Paris.[101] Since Ravachol, besides robbing graves and murdering old misers, had given money to the wives and children of imprisoned anarchists, spoken eloquently at his trial, and behaved bravely at his execution, in the eyes of many he became a folk hero and martyr. Celebrated in novels and in such popular songs as *"La Ravachole,"* he came to symbolize the retribution of the poor against the rich.[102] At his trial, Ravachol had called for revenge, and his words proved prophetic, since nine bombing attacks followed his death on the guillotine.[103] Reviewing the case of Ravachol, it is difficult not to grant a share of the responsibility for the outbreak of sustained terrorism in France to chance. Who could have predicted that the actions of Ravachol, the author of so many unsavory deeds, would have exercised such a fascination over the minds of men that they would give up their lives to vindicate his anarchist ideals and to avenge his death?

In Belgium an attempt was made to blow up the Spanish Legation in February 1892 and later threats, taken very seriously by the police, to do the same to the French Legation.[104] On May 1, 1892, a series of dynamite explosions in Liège, instigated by anarchist painters, closely followed Ravachol's bombings in Paris. A number of aristocratic homes were targets, including that of the former president of the Belgian senate, and a church was heavily damaged. In 1894, explosions again troubled Liège and in 1897 a bomb in Brussels planted by an anarchist counterfeiter gravely wounded a policeman.[105]

Less than two weeks after the beheading of Ravachol, Alexander Berkman, a young Russian emigrant to the United States, repeatedly shot and stabbed Henry Clay Frick, the operating manager of Carnegie Steel, in his office in Pittsburgh. This proved to be the only anarchist *attentat*

---

[101] Henri Varennes [Henri Vonoven], *De Ravachol à Caserio (notes d'audience)* (Paris: Garnier Frères, 1895): 8.

[102] Besides *"La Ravachole,"* at least two other contemporary songs were written to celebrate the exploits of Ravachol (Maitron, *Histoire*, 211). During the 1890s, at least twenty songs were composed praising the anarchist *attentats* as acts of vengeance for the oppression of the working class. Richard Sonn, *Anarchism and Cultural Politics in Fin de Siècle France* (Lincoln, NE, and London: University of Nebraska Press, 1989): 123.

[103] Maitron, *Histoire*, 242–243.

[104] Copy of Martin Gosselin, Brussels, to Salisbury, London, April 30, 1892, in HO/144/587B2840C, PRO.

[105] "Les Explosions de Liège," *Le Petit Parisien*, May 6, 1892, 2; Luc Keunigs, "Ordre Public et peur du rouge au XIXème siecle. La police, les socialistes et les anarchistes à Bruxelles 1886–1914," *Revue belge d'histoire contemporaine* 25:3–4 (1994–1995): 361.

on American soil during the 1890s. Indignant over Frick's ruthless use of Pinkerton detectives to crush a strike (in one melee a little boy had been killed), the twenty-one-year old Berkman, together with the devoted Emma Goldman, plotted to avenge the wrongs done to the Carnegie Steel workers.[106] Berkman, who worshiped "the Cause" and "the grand, mysterious, yet so near and real, People," asserted in his memoirs published in 1912 that "the removal of a tyrant is not merely justifiable; it is the highest duty of every true revolutionist."[107] Frick seemed to be such a tyrant and Berkman's attempted murder (after a few months Frick recovered from his multiple wounds) akin to the deeds of both the Russian nihilists and the Italian tyrannicides.

In Spain, the era of terrorism began in September 1893 when Paulino Pallás threw two bombs at Martínez Campos, the captain general of Catalonia, slightly wounding the general, but killing two other people. Pallás had acted to avenge a sentence of garroting – strangulation by means of a continually tightened iron collar – ordered by a military court to be carried out against several anarchists for participation in a revolt. At Pallás's trial he declared that, for his own execution, "Vengeance will be terrible!" Like Ravachol, Pallás's words proved prophetic since bombings and assassinations continued in Spain for the next four years.

In Italy, too, a cycle of social protest, government repression, and anarchist revenge unfolded in the winter of 1893–1894 and the following spring and summer. The Italian government responded to violent popular confrontations in Sicily and a rising of the anarchist marble workers of Tuscany with massive military repression. Subsequently, in March 1894, a mysterious bomb exploded just outside the Italian parliament, not only damaging the building but also killing two people and injuring six more, and, in June, an anarchist shot at and slightly wounded the prime minister. In May 1894 blasts went off near the Justice and War Ministries, allegedly in revenge for the harsh sentencing of one of the leaders of the Sicilian popular movement (the *fasci siciliani*). In July, an anarchist stabbed to death a Tuscan journalist who had strongly condemned the anarchists for their involvement in the assassination of Carnot.

On February 4, 1896, in Lisbon, Portugal, a huge explosion severely damaged the building where one of the doctors lived who had certified an anarchist as insane, subsequently sending him to a lunatic asylum. The police had recently arrested the anarchist because he had thrown a

---

[106] Emma Goldman, *Living My Life* (New York: AMS Press, 1970): 85, 91.
[107] Alexander Berkman, *Prison Memoirs of an Anarchist* (New York: Schocken, [1912] 1970): 5, 7.

rock at the Portuguese king. This incident led to the passage of some of the most ferocious anti-anarchist legislation ever written.[108]

One act of propaganda by the deed, emblematic of its increasingly global impact, occurred in Australia. On July 27, 1893, the anarchist Laurence (Larry) Petrie (or De Petrie) set off a bomb on the non-union ship SS *Aramac* as it sailed near Brisbane. Two women were slightly injured. Earlier Petrie had been foiled in his plan to blow up Sydney's Circular Quay together with nearby shipping.[109]

While the symbolic power of and fear caused by all these anarchist bombings and assassinations were enormous, the number of casualties they produced was, by present day standards, modest in size. During the 1890s real or alleged anarchists in Europe, the United, States, and Australia killed more than sixty and injured over 200 people with bombs, pistols, and daggers. For the period 1878–1914 (excluding Russia) more than 220 people died and over 750 were injured as a result of real or alleged anarchist attacks throughout the globe. This includes a number of anarchists who accidentally blew themselves up with their own bombs.[110] If we include estimates for Russia, which must remain highly speculative given the chaotic conditions of the country after the 1905 Revolution and the tendency to label all violence "anarchist," the death toll may be over 1,000 and the injured may number into the thousands.[111] The true size of anarchist terrorism may long remain an unknown, "dark figure," because of this tendency to false attribution and because many obscure acts of anarchist violence are unknown to historians, as a casual browse through the newspapers of the period reveals. Nonetheless, these forgotten incidents would have left their imprint on contemporaries.

---

[108] *The Times* (London), February 6, 10, 13, 1896; Loubat, "De la législation contre les anarchistes," 19; Angel Ruota, Spanish Minister, Lisbon, to Minister of State, Madrid, reports 33, 36, and 38, of February 5, 9, and 13, 1896, Spanish foreign ministry archive (hereafter abbreviated SFM), Legajo (hereafter abbreviated 'L') 2750, *Orden Público*. 1892–1898. The Portuguese anti-anarchist law of February 13, 1896, punished *both* private and public provocation to, or apology for, subversive acts and acts menacing the safety of persons and property. It also forbade the press to report on anarchist acts of violence and on the trials of anarchists. The accused were tried without juries. Perhaps most astonishingly, art. 5 of the law made it retroactive in order to cover proceedings against recently arrested anarchists.

[109] Bob James, "Larry Petrie (1859–1901) – Australian Revolutionist?" *Red & Black* Summer 1978/1979, www.takver.com/history/petrie.htm (accessed July 7, 2013); Bob James, "Introduction," in *A Reader of Australian Anarchism, 1886–1896* (Canberra: Canberra Publishing, 1979).

[110] My calculations are based on Maitron, Esenwein, Vizetelly, Carlson, Núñez Florencio, newspaper accounts, and other sources.

[111] Anna Geifman claims that the majority of the "estimated seventeen thousand casualties of terrorist acts [in Russia] between 1901 and 1916 were the victims of anarchist attacks." *Thou Shalt Kill*, 124–125.

2 Conspiracies, panics, *agents provocateurs,* mass journalism, and globalization

Anarchist conspiracies?

Were the various acts of violence chronicled in the previous chapter and later on the product of widespread conspiracies? Contemporary opinion believed so. Ambassador Benomar, Spain's representative in Rome, wrote to Madrid on February 15, 1892, that

the demonstrations that have taken place in some cities in Italy upon receiving notice of the execution of the assassins of Jerez [i.e., the alleged anarchist fomenters of the January 1892 rising] demonstrate that the crimes committed there and the agitation in Barcelona have their origin in, if indeed they don't obey, an international anarchist impulse.[1]

In 1897 the Italian Queen Margherita wrote that the "infamous sect" had chosen Pietro Acciarito by lot to assassinate her husband.[2] "Chosen by lot" became, quite erroneously, the standard explanation for how anarchist assassins were selected; in fact no evidence has been produced that this method was ever used. The *Corriere della Sera,* a prominent Milan daily, declared shortly after the assassination of Umberto I in 1900 that

There is general agreement here that one is dealing with a plot...aimed not only at the King of Italy, but at all European sovereigns...the vastness of the plan of the anarchists and of the aims they propose to reach, allows one to hope that we will be able to discover the truth more easily.[3]

Both the police and governments in private and the media in public subscribed to the theory of a vast anarchist conspiracy to assassinate and terrorize.[4] Much evidence contradicts the contention sometimes made

[1] Benomar, Rome, to foreign ministry, Madrid, February 15, 1892, OP, l. 2750, SFM.
[2] Margherita to General Osio, Rome, June 27, 1897, cited in Giovanni Artieri, *Cronaca del Regno D'Italia. 1: Da Porta Pia all'Intervento* (Milan: Arnoldo Mondadori, 1977): 608.
[3] *Corriere della Sera,* August 5–6, 1900.
[4] After the murder of the Empress Elisabeth in 1898, the Russian and France authorities informed Italy of evidence that this was but the beginning of a wider anarchist plot to assassinate heads of state. Italian consulate, Zurich, to foreign ministry, Rome, September 13, 1898, and tel. Morra, St. Petersburg, to foreign ministry, Rome, September 9, 1898.

that the police knew these vast anarchist conspiracies were all shibboleths.[5] Yet exhaustive government investigations and searches for accomplices found little evidence of conspiracies, particularly of conspiracies with international ties. In France and Italy, at least, the anarchist assassin or bomb-thrower was usually a lone individual.[6] A small number of accomplices, as in the cases of Ravachol and Berkman, might assist the anarchist bomber or assassin, but he often received little more than emotional support and meager financial assistance from a few friends and sympathizers.

More of a case can be made for international or wide-ranging conspiracies in regard to Spain (and for attempted assassinations of Spanish leaders traveling outside of the peninsula). The leaders of the Cuban exiles in Paris, eager to undermine the Spanish government and hasten their island's independence, probably gave Michele Angiolillo, the Italian anarchist, the idea of assassinating Prime Minister Cánovas (rather than the queen regent or her son, as had earlier been his intention) and may have provided funds for his trip to Madrid in 1897. Sympathizers in Spain provided him both with money and a deadly revolver.[7] Several Spanish historians have constructed elaborate arguments to show that the 1905 and 1906 assassination attempts against the life of King Alfonso XIII of Spain, both of which missed the king but killed and injured many bystanders, were the fruit of complex plots. The "mastermind" behind all these was Francisco Ferrer y Guardia, the well-known anarchist educator, assisted by Alejandro Lerroux and his radical republicans. Lerroux hoped to benefit from the political chaos that would likely follow the extermination

---

Pos. P, busta (hereafter cited as b.) 606, pos. 550, IFM. On November 8, 1893 the hugely popular New York *Evening World* printed an Associated Press story alleging that the Spanish "police had discovered documentary evidence that the conspiracy [of the anarchists associated with Paulino Pallas] was widespread." No such evidence, however, was ever published. Giulio Diena, a distinguished professor of international law, wrote of a "great worldwide [anarchist] conspiracy" that menaces every state, and that "anarchist delinquents['] … crimes are connected for the most part to vast plots." "I provvedimenti contro gli anarchici e la prossima conferenza internazionale," *Rivista di diritto internazionale e di legislazione comparata* 1:6 (1898), 247, 250, 257. A distinguished French international law journal made the same point ("Espagne—Anarchistes—Entente internationale," *Revue général de droit publique* 1 [1894]: 59). Police Inspector Sernicoli, head of the Italian anarchist surveillance service in Paris, concluded that "in Italy at least, anarchist crimes are more often the work of gangs [*combriccole*] than of isolated individuals." *I delinquenti dell'anarchia: Nuovo studio storico e politica* (Rome: E. Voghera, 1899): 77.

[5] For example, Scotland Yard's Robert Anderson reported in January 1899 that the police had recently broken up a conspiracy to assassinate the king of Italy. January 14, 1899. Home Office (hereafter cited as HO) 45/10254/x36450. PRO.

[6] Woodcock, *Anarchism*, 301, asserts that "all terrorist acts by French anarchists [were] acts of individuals or at most of minute circles of three or four people, prompted by personal and not by group decisions," but provides no source for this information.

[7] Francesco Tamburini, "Michele Angiolillo e l'assassinio di Cánovas del Castillo," *Spagna contemporanea* 4:9 (1996): 110–118.

of the king and the possible collapse of the monarchy (since the young Alfonso had not yet produced an heir).[8] Probably Ferrer knew ahead of time about the 1905 and 1906 attempts, but the evidence for a deeper involvement in the plots, while compelling, still remains inconclusive.[9]

Kropotkin's communism, which animated Spanish anarchism in the 1890s, encouraged association in small groups, and it was in these "*grupitos*" or *grupos de afinidad* that the origin of many acts of violence was to be found. Precise information about these groups is difficult to unearth. Five to ten dedicated anarchists would meet at a working class café to debate politics and plan propaganda efforts. This might take the form of maintaining a small library to help educate workers to read and write. Some *grupitos* also put out a small newspaper. Inside the *grupito* might be an even smaller group of intimate friends who met secretly and planned reprisals against the bourgeoisie. *Grupitos* gave themselves names such as *Salut, Fortuna, Avant, Benvenuto*, and later *Mártires de Ravachol*. While one may attribute to the *grupitos* a series of mostly harmless bombings – harmless since many of the bombs were concocted from such objects as tin pans, coffee-grinders, metal boxes, and banister knobs – that continuously rattled Barcelona and other Spanish cities during the early twentieth century, little evidence exists of meaningful links between them and the deeds of the famous assassins and bomb-throwers such as Pallás and Salvador.[10]

Anarchist terrorism and moral panics

In Spain the inability of the police to prevent individuals or small groups from carrying out their violent exploits, as well as the unpredictability of the anarchists' targets, created an atmosphere of panic. In January 1894, José Echegaray wrote in the periodical *La Lectura*:

Explosives are on the order of the day in the Chambers [of parliament], in the disorder of the night in the theaters; they hang as a menace over the entire bourgeoisie, without respecting the poor worker if they encounter him in passing, and

[8] Romero Maura, "Terrorism," 130–183, especially 137–146. Juan Avilés Farré, *Francisco Ferrer y Guardia: pedagogo, anarquista y mártir* (Madrid: Marcial Pons Ediciones de Historia, 2006).

[9] Núñez Florencio, *Terrorismo*, 73, and Pere Solá, "Morral y Ferrer vistos por Alban Rosell," *Tiempo de Historia* 43 (1978): 38–45, who cites new evidence. For further discussion of this controversy, see Chapter 9.

[10] Gerald Brenan, *The Spanish Labyrinth* (Cambridge University Press, 1971): 163n; Esenwein, *Anarchist Ideology*, 131–133, 170; Núñez Florencio, *Terrorismo*, 16. Romero Maura, "Terrorism," 151–154, describes in detail the anarchist group *Juventud Libertaria*, which the author blames for some of the bombings that plagued Barcelona between 1904 and 1909. Esenwein, *Anarchist Ideology*, 86, 89–92, discusses a secret revolutionary anarchist group called the Disinherited Ones that advocated propaganda by the deed in Andalusia during the 1880s.

there is no person who does not worry about dynamite, nitroglycerine, panclastites [another class of explosives], and detonators. ...

Modern explosives have come to upset everything: ideas and property and social relations.

The lowliest wretch in the worst social rubbish heap [*pudridero social*] holds a threat over the entire society, like a horde of barbarians showing their monstrous heads over the frontier. The result is that the least becomes the first, if not by power, by terror ... Satan has made himself a dynamiter and tries to be equal with God, and threatens his shadow [on earth].[11]

The nervous mood described by Echegaray led to fearful responses. After the Liceo bombing in Barcelona, Martínez Campos reported that public opinion was "overexcited" and "horrified."[12] The theaters remained deserted.[13] On December 26, 1893, in Madrid, the governor of the city received two letters threatening to blow up the Opera House where the queen regent and the infanta planned to attend a performance. The governor warned Maria Christina not to attend, and when news of this warning reached the audience, it caused a panic. The people made a rush for the doors and, although they exited without serious injury, this abrupt departure spread, in the words of the Associated Press, "alarm and excitement throughout Madrid, and all through the night the wildest rumors were in circulation."[14]

During the first half of 1894, the Spanish press constantly reported news of anarchist deeds of terrorism, particularly those occurring in France, where events mirrored events in Spain. The execution of Émile Henry, the instigator of so many Parisian bombings, took place on May 21, 1894, the same day as the execution of six Spanish anarchists accused of the bombing of the Liceo Theater. Although in this case it might seem implausible, such strange coincidences helped perpetuate the idea frequently voiced in the Spanish press of linkages between the anarchists of various nations who were alleged to be involved in an international conspiracy against society.[15] In actual fact, the linkage between the violent deeds in Spain and France was created less by any conspiracy than by reports in the media. According to an anarchist who knew the

---

[11] José Echegaray, "Los Explosivos," *La Lectura* **61** (1894): 54, 56. God's "shadow" presumably refers to God's duly ordained governments and His people on earth. Cf. Psalms 91:1–2: "He who dwells in the shelter of the Most High, who abides in the shadow of the Almighty, will say to the Lord, 'My refuge and my fortress; my God, in whom I trust.'"

[12] Telegraphic conference between Martínez Campos and ministers of interior and war, November 8, 1893, cited by Eduardo González Calleja, *La razón de la fuerza: orden público, subversión y violencia política en la España de la Restauración (1875–1917)* (Madrid: Consejo superior de investigaciones científicas, 1998): 273.

[13] González Calleja, *La razón de la fuerza*, 273.

[14] *The Evening World* (New York), December 27, 1893.

[15] Núñez Florencio, *Terrorismo*, 54, 56.

terrorist Henry, "the bombs of Barcelona hypnotized him; the only thing he thought of was to strike a blow and die."[16]

A fear of terrorism amounting to panic also affected Italy. In March 1894, after the bombing of the Italian parliament, a Rome newspaper wrote that the "impression produced on the citizenry" was "most painful"; people were "seriously and justly terrified about an explosion that massacred men and ruined property."[17] Even two days after the bombing, it formed "the topic of every conversation at every gathering" in the city.[18] When explosions shook government buildings again in May, the newspaper *La Tribuna* referred to the "extraordinary gravity" of these occurrences and the astonishing inability of the police and government to protect the "quiet and tranquility of the populace" after months of searching for the perpetrators of the earlier bombing.[19] Despite its admonitions to the government, *La Tribuna* seemed less interested in preserving the "quiet and tranquility of the populace" than in selling newspapers, and began a column entitled "Chronicle of the Bombs" that ran sporadically for a month.[20] In early July 1894 Prime Minister Francesco Crispi spoke to Domenico Farini, the head of the Italian senate, about "the anarchists, about the danger that menaces everything and everybody." A few days later the king told Senator Farini that "many are fearful; many people no longer leave their homes. I have anonymous threatening letters from every part [of Italy] ... Crispi is continually menaced."[21]

Paris provides the best-documented case of mass hysteria. Prior to 1892, Parisians had been indifferent to the various isolated incidents of anarchist violence. What changed that and led to a moral panic were the initial, rapid succession of bombings at different locales and the inability of the police to discover the perpetrators or prevent new explosions. Compounding the fear was that the public knew that Ravachol and his friends had stolen an enormous quantity of dynamite (according to one contemporary source, 360 kilograms or almost 800 pounds, although in reality the amount may have been much smaller) from a quarry southeast of Paris and that much of this had

---

[16] Charles Malato, "Some Anarchist Portraits," *The Fortnightly Review*, September 1, 1894, 315–333.

[17] "Cronaca di Roma," *La Tribuna* (Rome), March 10, 1894. For details of the bombing, the injured and the dead, see *Tribuna*, March 9, 10, 11, and 16, 1894.

[18] "Cronaca di Roma," *Tribuna*, March 11, 1894.

[19] *Tribuna*, June 1, 1894.

[20] *Tribuna*, May 14 and 15 and June 2, 1894; other articles on bombings were published May 10, 11, 12, and 13 and June 1 and 3, 1894.

[21] Diary entries for July 1 and 6, 1894 in Domenico Farini, *Diario di fine secolo*, ed. Emilia Morelli, 2 vols. (Rome: Bardi 1961–62): 1:536, 542.

been hidden, ready for new bomb attacks.[22] Moreover, the terrorists seemed to be progressing technologically having advanced from using dynamite to the potentially more powerful melinite or panclastite explosives.[23]

Consequently the public flooded the offices of the Paris police with reports of suspected bombs and bombings. The Parisian correspondent of the Italian periodical *Illustrazione Italiana* writes of an "unspeakable panic" seizing the Parisians.[24] The slogan "Long Live Anarchy!" appeared everywhere in the French capital, spoken in private discussions and shouted at public meetings, printed in the newspapers and scrawled on innumerable walls. The police imagined they heard it whenever encountering resistance, although the culprit might be a tipsy railway clerk rather than a dangerous anarchist.[25] In one case police and the investigating magistrate browbeat a seventeen-year-old youth, after he had stabbed a man, into a false confession that he was an anarchist.[26] In other cases robbers willingly cloaked their deeds with the mantle of the anarchist cause, even though this meant a death sentence rather than imprisonment.[27] The police found themselves carefully extracting suspicious objects from the garbage, taking them to the municipal laboratories and opening them with a thousand precautions, only to discover that the deadly device was no more than a sardine can.[28] Once again police and non-anarchists alike unwittingly collaborated in magnifying the anarchist menace out of all proportion to its true size.

Among the general public, even small incidents led to panic. In separate events in Paris, faulty electrical wiring on a streetcar and the collapse of some scenery at a theater sent people rushing about, screaming hysterically because they were fearful of impending explosions.[29] The police of Paris were themselves terrorized, with policemen under the authority of Commissioner Raynaud requesting transfers and resigning in order

---

[22] Italian police inspector Sernicoli, who provides the figure of 360 kilograms (*L'anarchia e gli anarchici*, 315) was in very close relations with the Parisian police and should have been well informed. John Merriman, *The Dynamite Club: How a Bombing in Fin-de-Siécle Paris Ignited the Age of Modern Terror* (Boston and NewYork: Houghton Mifflin Harcourt, 2009): 79, gives a figure of only 30 kilograms (around 65 pounds). Even if the larger number is incorrect, it is significant since it shows how contemporaries tended to magnify the deeds of the anarchists.

[23] *L'Illustrazione italiana*, April 3, 1892, 210.

[24] R. Alt, "Ravachol in Corte d'Assise. Il trionfo dell'anarchismo," *Illustrazione Italiana*, May 1, 1892, 282.

[25] Ernest Raynaud, *Souvenirs de Police au temps de Ravachol* (Paris: Payot 1923): 106, 113. Raynaud was a police official in the Chapelle quarter on the outskirts of Paris.

[26] Vizetelly, *The Anarchists*, 166.   [27] Varennes, *De Ravachol à Caserio*, 95–96.

[28] Varennes, *De Ravachol à Caserio*, 7.   [29] Vizetelly, *The Anarchists*, 163–164.

to avoid the bombings in which several of their fellow officers had been killed.[30] Spreading the panic were thousands of anonymous letters, the product of private grudges, containing threats to blow up landlords, concierges, and neighbors. One letter threatened to blow up a bakery unless the owner promised in eight days to reduce the price of bread.[31] The newspapers added to the overexcitement with daily columns devoted to "dynamitings."[32] In the words of a contemporary, the anarchists who carried out ferocious deeds "were no longer two, three, but a swarm [*une nuée*]."[33]

While police and newspaper reports and memoirs provide enough evidence to demonstrate that many among the Parisian middle and upper classes were indignant, upset, and horrified, the extent of the panic was certainly limited by class and in duration.[34] The French bourgeoisie and foreign tourists might be fearful of attending the opera and theaters, or going to restaurants and fine shops, or even riding in the Bois de Boulogne,[35] but little evidence exists that the large numbers of poor and working-class people living in Paris were terrorized. The less-privileged classes might not approve of Ravachol's deeds, but they had little to fear from them. Moreover, according to Sernicoli, the Italian police inspector and long-time Paris resident, by late 1893 after an initial period in which "the city was terrorized," the bourgeoisie had gotten over its anxiety:

The most recent attentats instead produced a much different effect; the fashion [*moda*] had passed and Paris does not feel the same impression twice. Dynamite, like cholera [which had appeared on the outskirts of the city], had become customary [*è entrata nei costumi*]. The anarchist attentats didn't arouse more than a feeling of curiosity mixed with a little indignation.

[30] Raynaud, *Souvenirs de Police*, 310.
[31] Hsi-Huey Liang, *The Rise of Modern Police and the European State System from Metternich to the First World War* (Cambridge University Press, 1992): 156.
[32] Maitron, *Histoire*, 215–216.
[33] Pierre Morel, *La police á Paris* (Paris: Sociéte d'édition et de publications, 1907): 157. Morel was a *conseiller municipal* in Paris. For examples of the "veritable psychosis that took hold of Paris," see Merriman, *The Dynamite Club*, 85–86, 111, 163.
[34] *Le Petit Parisien* referred to the Boulevard Saint-Germain explosion as "absolutely terrifying" (March 13, 1892) and claimed that both that bombing and the Lobau barracks explosion were "more than what is necessary to highly upset [*émotionner*] the Parisians. But let's hope that they don't publish in foreign newspapers that the great city was seized by a riotous panic" (March 17, 1892). On March 29, 1892, after the Rue Clichy bombing, *Le Petit Parisien* wrote that anarchist *attentats* had excited "general indignation" and produced "a movement of horror…in Paris…that will have an echo throughout the entire world."
[35] Writing almost forty years after visiting Paris in 1892, the English author and critic Ford Madox Ford remembered a city terrorized and paralyzed by rumors of anarchist bombings, robberies and murders. He also cited to the same effect the words of Fernand Evrard, a contemporary journalist. *Return to Yesterday* (New York: Horace Liveright, 1932): 107–108.

In support of his view, Sernicoli cites two articles in the Paris *Journal*. On December 12, 1893, "Madame Séverine" (the pseudonym of Caroline Remy) noted the absolute calm of the Parisians after Vaillant's bombing of the French parliament. Since Madame Séverine also praised their great courage, she clearly implied that there was much to be frightened of. Following Henry's bombing of the Café Terminus in February 1894, a writer in the same journal claimed that up to that point the anarchists had never "succeeded in inspiring terror." This, however, seems to have been a minority opinion.[36]

Informers and *agents provocateurs*

The authorities themselves contributed to the creation of the phenomenon of anarchist terrorism through their misuse of informers, particularly of *agents provocateurs*. The latter were police spies who encouraged anarchists, either directly or through subsidizing anarchist newspapers, to commit or plan to commit crimes so that they might be apprehended and punished and their organizations destroyed. Provocateurs caused simmering discontent to boil over into violence. A central argument about the counterproductive effect of using informers is that, both for them and for their police handlers, the temptation was ever present to instigate terrorist acts in order to justify their existence and keep their jobs.[37] The nineteenth century has been termed the "classical age of the police informer" and the police were involved at some level in a surprising number of acts of propaganda by the deed, although a comprehensive history of *agents provocateurs* before World War I still awaits its historian.[38] A reasonable conclusion might be that to a limited extent police funding contributed to spreading anarchist propaganda and, in a relatively small number of cases, provocation helped to generate terrorist acts that might otherwise never have occurred.

The use of *agents provocateurs* was often thought to be characteristic of absolutist and authoritarian regimes, like those of Napoleon III,

---

[36] A writer named Coppée denied any terror. Sernicoli, *L'anarchia e gli anarchici*, 192–195, contradicts himself, since on the one hand he agrees with Coppée and on the other he claims that Paris was "surprised" and "terrorized" when the *attentats* began in 1892.

[37] Jean-Marc Berlière, *Le Monde des polices en France XIXe-XXe siècle* (Paris: Le Monde, 1996): 155–162.

[38] Laqueur, *Age of Terrorism*, 134. Two older works need to be updated and expanded. The best is Alexander Bekzadian, *Der Agent-Provocateur (Lockspitzel) mit besonderer Berücksichtigung der politischen Provokation in Russland. Ein Beitrag zum Strafrecht und zur Kriminalpolitik* (Zurich: Leemann, 1913). Ernst Deubert, *Der Agent Provocateur und seine Beurteilung nach dem Reichsstrafgesetzbuche* (NeunKirchen: C. A. Ohle, 1910), focuses on issues of criminal law.

Bismarck, and tsarist Russia.[39] One historian estimates that the Russian police employed 10,000 informants from 1880 to 1917 (although most of these individuals only worked for a few years).[40] It also turned out that many liberal countries such as Britain, Republican France, and post-1900 Italy employed them. The role of *agents provocateurs* was especially important during the 1880s, perhaps somewhat less during the 1890s, but acquired new significance after 1900, particularly because of their astounding activities in Russia and Spain.

We have already seen how *agents provocateurs* urged the adoption of violent tactics at the 1881 London congress, although the congress would probably have approved a resolution favoring terrorism even without their urging, such was the excitement over the recent murder of the Russian tsar.[41] The first so-called "anarchist" act of terrorism during the 1880s (and in French history) occurred *before* the London anarchist congress when, in June 1881, at Saint-Germain, a bomb blew up under a statue of Adolphe Thiers, the French leader who had crushed the Paris Commune. This deed, which caused almost no damage, merely leaving a dark stain on the statue's base, was probably instigated by *agents provocateurs* placed among the anarchists by Louis Andrieux, the prefect, or head, of the Paris police. In his memoirs Andrieux implies that his agents, by directing the anarchists toward attacking the statue, had diverted them from bombing the parliament building or some other prominent structure. But his memoirs also make clear that the anarchists were hesitant to turn their violent words into deeds (and made no immediate effort to follow up on this comic first act of terrorism).[42] At this time it seems likely that no bombing of any sort would have occurred if it had not been for the provocation of the police spy.[43]

Andrieux also reveals that in September 1880 he secretly financed the creation of *La Révolution Sociale*, the first anarchist periodical published in France.[44] According to Kropotkin, this journal "was of an unheard-of-violence; burning, assassination, dynamite bombs – there was nothing

[39] Bekzadian, *Der Agent-Provocateur*, 16; Louis Andrieux, *Souvenirs d'un Prefect de Police* (Paris: Memoire Du Livre, [1885] 2002): 147.
[40] Jonathan Daly, "Security Services in Imperial and Soviet Russia," *Kritika* 4:4 (2003): 955–973.
[41] Pernicone, *Italian Anarchism*, 194; Avrich, *Haymarket*, 58.
[42] Andrieux, *Souvenirs*, 261–266.
[43] During the 1880s, other French policemen besides Andrieux were also provoking terrorist incidents. In 1882, just prior to the bombing of the Bellecour Theater, a police agent apparently wrote an article for a Lyon anarchist paper that advocated the destruction of the "dens" of the bourgeois. The anarchist Cyvoct was falsely blamed for writing this article, which was used as evidence to convict him of the bombing itself. Maitron, *Histoire*, 159–161, 164.
[44] Maitron, *Histoire*, 134.

but that in it."[45] It even printed detailed (one hopes faulty) instructions for fabricating dynamite. Andrieux argues that the creation of this fire-breathing periodical allowed him to "place a telephone [line] between the conspiracy room and the office of the prefect of police."[46] As the episode of the Thiers statue bombing should indicate, it is doubtful whether this connection prevented any genuine terrorist acts.

Given that no acts of anarchist terrorism had occurred in France up until this point (and that as of yet few were likely, at least in Paris), why did Andrieux found *La Révolution Sociale*? In his memoirs Andrieux says he wished to spread mistrust about the revolutionaries and thereby render them impotent.[47] More specifically, circumstantial evidence suggests that it was because of government concern over the impact of the recent amnesty extended to victims of the repression of the Commune and the repatriation of former communards to France from their places of imprisonment in New Caledonia and other locales. Andrieux, who had opposed the wide amnesty ultimately conceded, was obviously very concerned about the impact of these returning social revolutionaries (and Louise Michel, the famous, recently released communard, was deeply involved in *La Révolution Sociale*).[48] The newspaper had other uses as well: in it Andrieux inserted articles intended to besmirch his political enemies and influence the electorate (if only by encouraging anarchist sympathizers to boycott elections).[49] Such a tactic benefited Andrieux personally because he had remained a deputy in parliament even while serving as police prefect. This episode demonstrates how intimately anarchism was involved in politics, as much as its enemies wanted to label it non-political and simply criminal.

La Révolution Sociale was only one among the many newspapers of the anarchists (who, more than most other political movements, were perpetually short of cash) that the police secretly funded or contributed articles to. One historian even asserts that "a considerable proportion of the terrorist journals of the 1880s and 1890s [both anarchist and non-anarchist] were in fact founded or maintained by secret-police money."[50] An example would be several anarchist newspapers in southern Italy founded by the anarchist Giovanni Domanico, who was a police agent between 1894 and 1899.[51]

[45] Kropotkin, *Memoirs of a Revolutionist,* ed. and intro. by Nicolas Walter (New York: Dover, 1988): 479–480.

[46] Andrieux, *Souvenirs,* 257.   [47] Andrieux, *Souvenirs,* 256–57.

[48] Jean-Paul Morel, "Préface: Louis Andrieux alias M. Mystère," in Andrieux, *Souvenirs,* 15. Unfortunately Gérald Dittmar, *Louise Michel (1830–1905)* (Paris: Ditmar, 2004): 183, says little about his subject's role in *La Révolution Sociale.*

[49] Andrieux, *Souvenirs,* 258–261.   [50] Laqueur, *Age of Terrorism,* 135.

[51] Pietro Di Paola, "The Spies who Came in from the Heat: The International Surveillance of the Anarchists in London," *European History Quarterly,* 37:2 (2007): 193.

During the 1880s Germany and Austria were the places where *agents provocateurs* figured most prominently among the anarchists and socialists and where they contributed the most to terrorism. These episodes have left a lasting impression on historical memory. Chancellor Otto von Bismarck was determined to destroy the Social Democratic Party in Germany by blaming it for assassinations and bombings. He also wanted to use the issue of opposition to terrorism to pressure the National Liberal Party into becoming a more compliant supporter of his policies. Bismarck's first reaction after learning of Nobiling's assault on Wilhelm I was not concern for the aged kaiser's health but how to exploit the event for political advantage.[52] While there is no evidence that police spies participated in 1878's two assassination attempts, a spy was at least marginally involved in the 1883 conspiracy to assassinate the emperor and top German officials at the Niederwald monument. The police agent Rudolf Palm lent money to one of the conspirators in order to enable him to travel to the site of the planned assassination and was also somehow involved in the bombing of a restaurant in 1883.[53] Bismarck carefully stage-managed the release of the news of the failed Niederwald attempt to facilitate the renewal of the anti-socialist law.[54] Various other German police spies helped run or contributed incendiary articles to Johann Most's newspaper *Freiheit*, which championed violent propaganda by the deed. The government subsequently cited the inflammatory articles that it had itself planted as further reasons to renew the anti-socialist law.[55] The Berlin police may even have helped fund *Freiheit* although the evidence for this is inconclusive.[56] Another agent of the Berlin police named Ferdinand Ihring, alias Mahlow, tried to infiltrate a group of Social Democrats in order to teach them how to use dynamite.[57] Two German police agents attended an August 1883 meeting in St. Gallen, Switzerland, where violent deeds were planned that subsequently led to several murders in Strasburg, Stuttgart, and Vienna.[58] While the agents did not carry out the murders, they did nothing to stop them. In the 1880s, 1890s, and as late as 1904 German *agents provocateurs* who had infiltrated the German-speaking radical community of Chicago preached the assassination of American officials, but without result.[59]

---

[52] Pflanze, *Bismarck*, 2:397–399.   [53] Carlson, *Anarchism*, 288–89, 293.
[54] Carlson, "Anarchism and Individual Terror," 190.
[55] Carlson, "Anarchism and Individual Terror," 185.
[56] Carlson, *Anarchism*, 233–235.
[57] Vernon Lidtke, *The Outlawed Party. Social Democracy in Germany, 1878–1890* (Princeton University Press, 1966): 242.
[58] Carlson, *Anarchism*, 258–267.
[59] Dirk Hoerder, *Plutocrats and Socialists: Reports by German Diplomats and Agents on the American Labor Movement, 1878–1917* (Munich: K. G. Saur, 1981): 371, 382–383.

Evidence from police memoirs and works by a French historian writing in the 1930s and a popular historian suggest that *agents provocateurs* were involved in Ravachol's robbery of dynamite, Henry's bombing of the Café Terminus, Félix Fénéon's attack on the Café Véry, Pauwels's bombing of Parisian churches, Vaillant's bombing of the French Chamber of Deputies, and even the assassination of Carnot.[60] They argue, for example, that the police deliberately supplied Vailliant with a bomb, which was very weak and only caused minor injuries, in order to provide an excuse for passing draconian anti-anarchist laws. Since this view is based on the testimony of a single source, who was perhaps an anarchist that the police pressured to become an informer, it must remain conjecture.[61]

In a dramatic and widely publicized speech in November 1898, the Social Democratic leader August Bebel took incidents such as these together with a number of others that involved not only *agents provocateurs* employed by the German, but also by the French, Belgian,[62] Italian, Russian, and even the British police as evidence that propaganda by the deed was little more than police-instigated terrorism designed to discredit law-abiding socialists.[63] In his speech, the only example he cites of an anarchist acting *without* being persuaded by or involved with police spies is Santo Caserio's assassination of the French president.

While Bebel's allegations about the nefarious doings of police spies were often correct, his overall conclusion equating terrorism with the deeds of *agents provocateurs* is greatly exaggerated. Bebel's claims should be seen as essentially a defensive tactic designed to distance the Marxian socialists from the anarchists, to protect the SDP against charges of being an accomplice to terrorism, and to prevent the enactment of new anti-socialist

---

[60] Butterworth, *World That Never Was*, 333–334; 343–344.

[61] Testimony of Charles Jacot to Police Commissioner Ernest Raynaud, *La vie intime des commissariats* (Paris: Payot 1926) : 42–44 and especially 43n1; Henri Rollin, *L'Apocalypse de notre temps. Les dessous de la propaganda allemande d'apreès des documents inédits* (Paris: Allia, [1939] 1991): 537–538.

[62] In 1887–1888 Lèonard Pourbaix, working for the Belgian police and intending to discredit the socialists, infiltrated the Belgian Republican Socialist Party. There he advocated a *"Grand Complot"* to overturn society, utilizing a general strike and dynamite. www. goens-pourbaix.be/multima-pourbaix/leonart/POURBAIX%20Leonard.htm (accessed July 7, 2013). Belgian socialists wanted to deduce from this that "anarchism amounts to police provocation," but the historian Jan Moulaert denies any "serious indication" of a "police infiltration into the bosom of the anarchist movement." *Le mouvement anarchiste en Belgique*, trans. Sophie Haupert (Ottignies: Quorum, 1996): 343. Butterworth, *World That Never Was*, 294.

[63] August Bebel, *Assassinations and Socialism*, trans. Boris Reinstein (New York: New York Labor News Company, *c.* 1898); original German in Iring Fetscher, *Terrorismus und Reaktion mit einem Anhang, August Bebel, Attentate und Sozialdemokratie* (Cologne: Europäische Verlagsanstalt, 1978).

laws.[64] Among his false allegations is the claim that Luigi Lucheni had been persuaded by Italian police agents to murder the Empress Elisabeth. No evidence of this emerged at Lucheni's trial or subsequently. Bebel also criticized the involvement of a police spy with Ravachol; indeed one of Ravachol's accomplices, Chaumentin (called Chaumartin) gave evidence against him at his trial.[65] But later research has shown that Chaumentin was not an *agent provocateur* and only decided to cooperate with the police five days *after* Ravachol's first bombing once he had been betrayed by a spy who had befriended him and his wife.[66] As for Britain, the major historian of the Special Branch, the British secret police, who has examined confidential Home Office records, finds that "there is no conclusive proof of the participation of *agents provocateurs* in any Fenian or anarchist incident of the 1880s and 1890s, but there is a great deal of circumstantial evidence which seems to point that way."[67] While the acts of British secret agents *may* have led to the imprisonment of a few innocent people and to encouragement "to commit indictable crimes," at least as regards the anarchists, they did not result in any actual violence.[68] If there was a direct correlation between political policing, informers, and terrorist incidents, as Bebel suggests, then propaganda by the deed should have increased exponentially after the great expansion of the French police in 1894 and of the Italian police after 1901, since both enlargements, particularly the French, were due, at least in part, to the anarchist threat. Instead, terrorism in both countries went into steep decline.

After 1900 Russia became the country par excellence of the *agent provocateur* as double agent, although more in regard to the Socialist Revolutionaries (SRs) than to the anarchists who possessed no central group for planning terrorism that could be infiltrated. Evno Filipovich Azef, who rose to a leadership position in the SR party and took command of its terrorist Combat Organization, was a secret agent who worked both to help the police and the revolutionaries.[69] He "apparently masterminded" the 1904–1905 assassinations of Interior Minister Plehve and Grand Duke Sergei, the tsar's uncle.[70] In 1912 the anarchist turncoat and

[64] Elun Gabriel, *Anarchism, Social Democracy and the Political Culture of Imperial Germany* (DeKalb: Northern Illinois Press, 2014).
[65] Bebel, *Assassinations and Socialism*, 30.
[66] Maitron, *Histoire*, 215n, 459–461. [67] Porter, *Vigilant State*, 190–191.
[68] Butterworth, *World That Never Was*, 298–299, emphasizes the connection between the actions of a police spy that led to the arrest of the Walsall anarchists and the Special Branch's need to justify its existence and prevent funding cutbacks.
[69] Geifman, *Thou Shalt Kill*, 232–237, and *Entangled in Terror: The Azef Affair and the Russian Revolution* (Wilmington, DE: Scholarly Resources, 2000).
[70] Jonathan Daly, *The Watchful State: Security Police and Opposition in Russia 1906–1917* (DeKalb: Northern Illinois University Press, 2004): 90. Geifman, *Entangled*, disputes the view that Azef was a double agent.

police spy Dmitrii Bogrov, who had been given a ticket to the theater by the police, assassinated Prime Minister Stolypin at the opera in Kiev. This was an example of the police's inept handling of its agents, since the Okhrana had failed to notice evident signs of Bogrov's shifting allegiance.[71]

After 1900, problematic cases of *agents provocateurs* also crop up in western Europe. The press charged that the attempted assassination of the shah of Persia in August 1900, while he was visiting Paris, may have been faked by a police spy.[72] Another example regarding France is that of Marius Jacob who, according to Maitron, might never have begun his long career (1900–1903) of illegalism, robberies carried out partially on behalf of the anarchist cause, if earlier an agent had not betrayed him and made a normal working life impossible.[73] In 1902 the Italian anarchist and *agent provocateur* Gennaro Rubino (or Rubini) tried to assassinate the king of Belgium.[74]

In Spain we find examples of the police fomenting false plots, carrying out bombing attacks, and paying anarchist informers to discover bombs that the informers themselves had planted.[75] On the other hand, historians have suggested that one case that at the time seemed the likely product of an *agent provocateur*, i.e., the Corpus Christi bombing of 1896 – which missed the dignitaries at the beginning of the procession and killed mostly ordinary people at the tail end – was in actuality the work of an anarchist.[76] As for secret agents gone wrong, the most famous Spanish case is that of Juan (or Joan) Rull, a Catalonian anarchist who in 1906–1907 worked as a paid informant for several governors of Barcelona. The governors hired him to prevent explosions in the city but, when payments were suspended, Rull and his family set off numerous bombs in order to get reinstated on the payroll. As many as three people were killed and eighteen injured during the period of Rull's activities, although it is unclear whether all these casualties were due to the efforts of Rull and his gang. Their arrest and Rull's execution did not end the explosions.[77] In regard to the Barcelona bombings, the careful conclusion of the foremost historian of Spanish anarchist terrorism during this period could be applied in large part to the entire phenomenon of police-facilitated terrorism before World War I:

[71] Daly, *Watchful State, 125–126.*   [72] See Chapter 6.
[73] Maitron, *Histoire*, 393.   [74] See Chapter 9.
[75] For the (false) Coronation Plot of 1902, the deeds of Captain Morales in 1903, and other examples, see Romero Maura, "Terrorism," 140n172.
[76] Romero Maura, "Terrorism," 131n, and Esenwein, *Anarchist Ideology*, 191–192, provide evidence that the perpetrator was an anarchist named Jean Girault who fled to Argentina.
[77] González Calleja, *La razón de la fuerza*, 398–400; Romero Maura, "Terrorism", 156–157; Núñez Florencio, *Terrorismo*, 81–82, 164–168.

The fact that one had some plots hatched [*tramados*] by informers, does not justify [*autoriza*] thinking that they were responsible for *all* the explosions that these years produced in Barcelona; their participation in some of the cases is indisputable, and in others one can reckon as very probable. But many other explosions remain mysterious.[78]

And I would add that, whatever the mystery in Barcelona, many explosions and assassinations throughout Europe were in fact carried out by anarchists. Of twenty-four known Italian anarchist *attentateurs*, 1880–1914, only one (Rubino) can be firmly identified as a police agent, while two others were suspected of being, but never definitely proved to be, police agents. The later two cases remain highly speculative. One piece of evidence comes from the British police:

It is believed that Agiolillo [sic] who murdered Senor Canovas was denounced in Paris by his Anarchist confréres as a Police spy, came over to London where this reputation followed him and made his life so unendurable that he was impelled by similar considerations to the crime he committed. And the history of the Anarchist Lega convicted of attempting the life of the ex Premier Caprivi [Crispi] is much the same.[79]

The presence of two errors, one in spelling (Angiolillo) and the other in fact (the Italian not the German prime minister) do not inspire confidence in this report. Nor does the most recent study of anarchist terrorism in Italy accept the *agent provocateur* thesis for these two anarchists, although it is true that police harassment and multiple arrests made it difficult for Lega to find work and therefore contributed to the desperation he felt before his *attentat*.[80]

As Andrieux had foreseen, the actions of *agents provocateurs* spread mistrust and infighting among the anarchists and other revolutionaries, but it also spread mistrust between citizens and the authorities. The enormous scandal over Azef's dual role greatly discredited the SR's terrorist strategy, but it also blackened the Russian government's reputation.[81] In France, the "black legend" of the "crimes" of the political police helped to undermine the Third Republic.[82] This was an ominous development, since one of government's most valuable weapons in fighting terrorism was the belief that it upholds justice while terrorists perpetrate criminality.

[78] Núñez Florencio, *Terrorismo*, 80.
[79] E. R. Henry, Chief Commissioner, Metropolitan Police, memo, to Kenelm Digby, Home Office, March 16, 1903. HO144/545, PRO.
[80] Erika Diemoz, *A morte il tiranno. Anarchia e violenza da Crispi a Mussolini* (Turin: Giulio Einaudi, 2011): 83–85.
[81] The revelations about Azef "devastated" the SR Party and "caused a massive exodus." Daly, *Watchful State*, 94, 109.
[82] Although perhaps more after World War I than before; Berlière, *Le Monde*, 160–162.

Moreover, by spreading mistrust, *agents provocateurs* unleashed a wave of suspicion and accusations among the anarchists that sometimes backfired. An amazing number of anarchists including, absurdly, Malatesta and Most were falsely accused of being police spies.[83] This undermined the authority of Malatesta, who opposed terrorism,[84] and, it could be argued, left the way open for irresponsible lone wolves to strike out on their own. All of this fueled the legend of anarchist terrorism as no more than police provocation.

In conclusion, as far as we know – outside of Russia – during 1880–1914 all or nearly all of the most famous and bloody assassinations and bombings, and a large majority of the lesser known *attentats*, were *not* carried out at the instigation of police agents but rather by real or self-proclaimed anarchists in protest against socio-economic, political, and other abuses or by nationalists and radicals mislabeled as anarchists. The public scandals caused by the cynical machinations of Bismarck and his cronies and by Andrieux and the inept tactics of the tsarist police in their use of *agents provocateurs*, together with such notorious cases as those of Pourbaix, Chaumentin, Rubino, Rull, etc., have obscured this truth. Perhaps it is worth noting the obvious, that people who are not inclined toward participating in violent deeds can rarely be provoked into committing acts of terrorism.[85] Nonetheless, to a certain, relatively limited extent, the phenomenon of anarchist terrorism was due directly or indirectly to actions by the police and government authorities.

Anarchist terrorism and the age of mass journalism

The age of anarchist terrorism coincided with the beginning of the age of mass journalism, which played a crucial role in whipping up hysteria over anarchist acts of violence. Since the mass media was and is crucial to the generation of terrorism, nineteenth-century anarchist terrorism has a fair claim to be considered the first completely modern form of terrorism. The print media's relentless tendency to oversimplify and to exploit dominant stereotypes about anarchist violence provided the essential glue that bound together and transformed disparate incidents into a formidable edifice of terrorism. In Britain, the United States, and

---

[83] William Liebknecht allegedly, and incorrectly, claimed that Most was in the pay of the German police. Hoerder, *Plutocrats and Socialists*, 370. Even Lenin, no anarchist, was accused of being a police spy. Porter, *Vigilant State*, 66.

[84] Di Paola, "Spies," 204.

[85] Gary T. Marx, "Thoughts on a Neglected Category of Social Movement Participant: The Agent Provocateur and the Informant," *American Journal of Sociology* 80:2 (1974): 402–442.

throughout the Western world, the 1880s witnessed the emergence of a "new journalism." Pioneered by such editors as Joseph Pulitzer with his *St. Louis Post-Dispatch*, and later his *New York World*, and W. T. Stead in his *Pall Mall Gazette*, the "new journalism," with its sensational headlines in heavy black lettering, was less interested in hewing to a single political line or providing in-depth and long-range analysis than churning out exciting news for mass consumption and entertainment.[86] The circulation of the new mass newspapers surged. After 1880, newspaper after newspaper, their prices often slashed – in England many were cut to a halfpenny an issue – surpassed 100,000 circulations. In 1896, *Lloyd's Weekly Newspaper* of London reached a million, and around 1900, the French daily paper *Le Petit Parisien* reached a similar figure.[87] Between 1880 and 1910 the circulation of newspapers in Paris rose from 1,947,000 to 4,937,000 copies; between 1871 and 1910 the real cost of Parisian newspapers for laborers in the provinces dropped over 50 percent as national press circulation expanded more than eight times.[88] Reflecting the European media's fascination with anarchist terrorism, week after week *Le Petit Parisien* published illustrated supplements with self-described "superb engravings" depicting the explosions on the Rue de Clichy and in the Café Véry, the arrest of Ravachol (with his portrait), and other acts of anarchist terrorism.[89]

In New York City, Pulitzer's *World* (or *Evening World*) vied with William Randolph Hearst's *Evening Journal* to provide the most sensational and popular accounts. When it came to events in Europe, both papers almost always scooped the more staid and expensive (during the early 1890s, three cents an issue as compared to the *World* and *Evening Journal*'s penny a copy) *New York Times*. This paid off at the newsstand when the *World* reported, on the day it happened in 1893, the bombing of the Liceo Theater. In an "extra" edition and in its last edition, the *World* gave the leading place to the large, bold front-page headline:

BOMBS IN A THEATRE
Anarchist Casts Two Deadly Missiles into an Audience
Eighteen People Die

[86] Anthony Smith, *The Newspaper: An International History* (London: Thames & Hudson 1979): 152–160. In 1893 the circulation of *Le Petit Journal* was 400,000 and by 1903, 1,300,000 copies. Micheline Dupuy, *Le Petit Parisien* (Paris: Plon, 1989): 60, 71.

[87] E. J. Hobsbawm, *The Age of Empire, 1875–1914* (New York: Random House, 1989): 53; Smith, *The Newspaper*, 155–156.

[88] Between 1875 and 1914 France's total daily press circulation rose from 1.5 million to 12.5 million copies. Roger Price, *A Social History of Nineteenth-century France* (New York: Homes and Meier, 1987): 354.

[89] Examples of advertisements for these illustrated supplements can be found in *Le Petit Parisien*, April 1 and 9 and May 5, 1892.

Mad Panic Follows a Terrible Explosion in Liceo Theatre, Barcelona
Many Trampled under Foot
Nearly Four Thousand People Engaged in the Wild Rush

Two days later, the *World* boasted that the November 8 issue that printed this news, together with the dramatic results of the New York elections, had sold more copies (629,176) than any other single issue in the history of American journalism. Hearst's *Evening Journal* was even more sensationalistic in its format than the *World*. Although devoted in its daily coverage to American stories of sports, fashion, and murder, the *Evening Journal* still gave top billing to the assassination of the Empress Elisabeth on September 10, 1898. A giant headline stretched across the entire top of the front page, "**AUSTRIA'S EMPRESS FOULLY ASSASSINATED BY AN ITALIAN ANARCHIST**," accompanied by a large sketch of a youthful and attractive crowned head in a low-cut evening gown (apparently based on a photo of Elisabeth in her younger days). Ample coverage of the assassination filled the columns of the first and second pages.

The new journalism was slower to arrive in Italy and Spain where illiteracy remained high (in 1900, 56 percent of Spaniards over ten years of age and 49 percent of Italians over six could not read or write) and readership was therefore more limited than in wealthier countries. Nonetheless, one can still see its impact in the coverage afforded terrorist deeds. For example, the *Corriere della Sera* of Milan, one of Italy's most important newspapers, issued two extraordinary editions in a single day with news of the assassination of King Umberto I. The headline of July 30–31, 1900, trumpeting this event was unprecedented in its size and format (two black bands framing a huge banner headline). By comparison the headline of March 5–6, 1896, announced Italy's disastrous and decisive defeat by the Ethiopians at the battle of Adowa (with the loss of 5,000 Italian dead – more than had died in all the wars for Italian unification) and the resignation of Francesco Crispi, the quasi-dictatorial prime minister. These events were of equal or greater importance than the death of the mediocre Umberto, but they received a less spectacular treatment. Examples such as this could be multiplied for both Europe and America. They demonstrate that the gripping details of anarchist assassinations and bombings provided perfect fodder for the new "mass media," a term that first became applicable only at the end of the nineteenth century.[90]

A vigorous crop of anarchist publications sprang up in the shadow of the new mass media and played a significant role in glorifying those

---

[90] Hobsbawm, *Age of Empire*, 53.

"martyrs" for the anarchist cause who, after committing violent acts, gave up their freedom and their lives. These publications were often short-lived and could never compete with the bourgeois press in terms of circulation. By the late 1880s *La Révolte*, at the time the most important anarchist paper in Paris, printed about 8,000 copies every two weeks. *Les Temp Nouveaux* debuted in 1895 with 18,000 copies but by 1901 had stabilized at 7,000. Before the First World War, the French anarchists never managed to achieve their dream of a daily paper except on a few occasions and for brief periods (the longest being ten months).[91] In 1923, in response to the sensational trial of Germaine Berton, an anarchist who had assassinated a right-wing journalist, a daily French anarchist newspaper once again became a reality for fifteen months.[92] The Argentinean *La Protesta*, the greatest of the pre-war anarchist newspapers and, beginning in 1904, one of the world's very few anarchist dailies, reached a peak circulation of 16,000 in early 1910. By comparison, in 1900 the largest bourgeois dailies of Buenos Aires had been publishing well over 100,000 copies. Reflecting the influence of the new journalism, *La Protesta* (admittedly an exception) incorporated news cabled from abroad, maintained contacts with major anarchist publications throughout the world, and issued illustrated supplements.[93] Worldwide, the total number of anarchist publications was impressive: in 1906 a Parisian newspaper estimated their number at 250.[94]

These anarchist periodicals often distributed their copies globally and sometimes were financed from abroad. Almost a third of the initial financing that launched *Les Temps Nouveaux* came from the gift of a "comrade" in Buenos Aires.[95] As for the global reach of the anarchist press, *La Révolte* had subscribers, although often only one or two, in twenty-five countries including Australia, Egypt, the Cape of southern Africa, Guatemala, and Turkey.[96] In Buenos Aires, anarchist newspapers from Spain were "circulated so widely that when six Spanish anarchists in this city formed the group *Los Desheredados* (The Disinherited) in 1889, they called for new affiliates by placing an advertisement in Barcelona's *El Productor*."[97] The Italian-language *La Questione Sociale*, based in Paterson, New Jersey, sent two-thirds of its 3,000 weekly issues to readers throughout the United

[91] Maitron, *Histoire*, 132–143, 434–440.
[92] Richard Sonn, *Sex, Violence and the Avant-Garde: Anarchism in Interwar France* (University Park: Pennsylvania State University Press, 2010): 9, 39, 42.
[93] Juan Suriano, *Anarquistas: Cultura y política libertaria en Buenos Aires, 1890–1910* (Buenos Aires: Manantial, 2001): 188, 211n7.
[94] "Bloc-Notes Parisien: La presse anarchiste," *Le Gaulois,* 6 June 1906, 1.
[95] Maitron, *Histoire*, 434.   [96] Maitron, *Histoire*, 137–38.
[97] Moya, *Cousins and Strangers: Spanish Immigrants in Buenos Aires, 1850–1930* (Berkeley: University of California Press, 1998): 308.

States and the world.[98] After police searched the room of the French terrorist Émile Henry, they found an Italian newspaper with bomb-making
instructions.[99]

Anarchist periodicals normally exalted the memories of anarchist
assassins and dynamiters who had martyred themselves for the cause and
exaggerated the importance of propaganda by the deed. According to an
Italian police agent, for example, in 1883 Most's newspaper *Freiheit* took
the news of a harmless, small explosion in Lyon and made it into a major
incident of class warfare in which the palace of a rich merchant had
suffered enormous damage, although "unfortunately" no one had been
injured.[100] Most's and other anarchists' journals also published recipes
for concocting bombs. After 1900, however, only a few anarchist periodicals openly championed terrorism as a tactic (and if they did, issues and
authors were usually liable to be confiscated and prosecuted).[101]

Sir Howard Vincent, who helped found Scotland Yard's Criminal
Investigation Department and later represented Britain at the 1898
Rome Anti-Anarchist Conference, was not alone in believing that all
the publicity that both bourgeois and anarchist print media generated
about anarchist deeds exercised a powerful effect on the minds of many
potential terrorists. Writing confidentially in 1906 after a bloody bombing attack in Madrid, Vincent opined that

> the rapidly increasing means of location, the spread of information, and the incen-
> diary influence of publicity and notoriety [make police cooperation] more and
> more essential...The "advertisement" of anarchism, as of many other crimes,
> infallibly leads to imitation.[102]

While this seems exaggerated, several notable examples support Vincent's
conclusion. Luigi Lucheni, who murdered the Empress Elisabeth, longed

---

[98] George W. Carrey, "*La Questione Sociale*, an Anarchist Newspaper in Paterson, NJ,
(1895–1908)," in Lydio F. Tomasi (ed.), *Italian Americans. New Perspectives in Italian
Immigration and Ethnicity* (New York: Center for Migration Studies, 1985): 291. Pier
Carlo Masini, *Storia degli anarchici italiani da Bakunin a Malatesta (1862–1892)* (Milan:
Rizzoli, 1969): 131.

[99] Merriman, *The Dynamite Club*, 91–92

[100] Ettore Sernicoli, *L'anarchia e gli anarchici*, 189.

[101] E.g., Laurent Tailhade writing in *Le Libertaire* in September 1901. Maitron, *Histoire*,
438–439; Suriano, *Anarquistas*, 198. Even during the 1890s, Maitron, *Histoire*, notes the
lack of any wholehearted support for terrorism in the French anarchist press.

[102] Vincent to Herbert Gladstone, Home Secretary, *Précis of the Proceedings at the
Anti-Anarchist Conference Convened at Rome, in November 1898*, July 6, 1906.
HO144/757/118516/sub. 15. PRO. In 1894, the Spanish interior ministry undersecretary expressed similar views, claiming that it was impossible "to deny the influence,
at times decisive, that the daily exposition of anarchist doctrines in the press [both
bourgeois and anarchist], as well as news of the [anarchist] crimes," including their trial
testimony, "exercises on some exalted spirits." Undersecretary, Public Order, interior
ministry, to secretary of state, [Madrid], September 21, 1894. SFM, OP, L. 2750.

to get into the newspapers as a famous anarchist assassin. Leon Czolgosz, who shot President McKinley, regarded a newspaper that he had purchased recounting the assassination of Umberto I as a precious object. He took it to bed with him every night. In her memoirs, May Picqueray, one of the few anarchist women who tried to carry out an assassination attempt, asserts that in 1921 she sent a bomb to the American ambassador to France in order to get the large newspapers to pay more attention to the Sacco and Vanzetti case. She succeeded.[103]

As we shall see in the following chapters, the authorities responded to the challenge posed by media-driven terrorism in a number of ways. These ranged from passing laws restraining publication and completely censoring terrorist news (as with Spain, on occasion, and Russia) to complete freedom (as with the US before 1901). A liberal approach, punctuated by occasional crackdowns, characterized the British, the Swiss (after 1894), and the Italian (after 1901) approaches. Attempts to downplay anarchist terrorism by refusing to give it special attention or keeping news of thwarted anarchist *attentats* secret, and thus out of the press, also characterized the approaches of certain British and Italian governments.

Any simple correlation between publicity in the print media and acts of propaganda by the deed, however, is disproved by the experience of Argentina. In the 1890s, many anarchist journals vehemently applauded personal acts of violence and terror, but no assassinations or bombings took place. As a prominent Argentine historian concludes, what was characteristic of Argentine anarchism in the 1890s was terrorist rhetoric (*palabrerío terrorista*) rather than terrorist deeds.[104] This was not the first time, nor the last, that violent words from the left substituted for concrete actions. What was needed to turn words into terrorist deeds was the changed political and social conditions of the early twentieth century, when the Argentine authorities reacted to the militancy of a burgeoning labor movement with ill-considered brutality and repression.

It should also be pointed out that the media helped curb anarchist terrorism as well as promote it. "The arrest of Ravachol was due in great part to the press," which had widely publicized his description, enabling a waiter at the Café Véry to identify him.[105]

---

[103] May Picqueray, *May La Refractaire* (Paris: Marcel Jullian, 1979): 60–61. Ferdinando Sacco and Bartolomeo Vanzetti were convicted of murdering two men during an armed robbery in 1920. After a trial characterized by many irregularities, the two men were executed in August 1927, although one or both may have been innocent.

[104] Literally, "verbiage" or "hot air." Oved, *El anarquismo y el movimiento obrero en argentina* (Mexico City" Siglo XXI, 1978): 54–61.

[105] R. Alt, "Lettere da Parigi," *L'Illustrazione Italiana*, April 24, 1892.

Globalization and anarchist terrorism

The birth of a worldwide mass media was but one aspect of the globalized economy and culture that developed at the end of the nineteenth century. It could be argued that another was the spread of anarchism and anarchist terrorism throughout the world. Otherwise they might have remained mostly European phenomena, with the exception of a few intellectuals living overseas. While the world economy had been globalizing since at least 1492, a pronounced phase of that development took place during the decades before World War I. During this mighty era of globalization the size of the world economy doubled (1890–1914) and the "greatest international migration of people in history" took place.[106] Globalization stoked the discontent that led some people into the anarchist fold by favoring the "great acceleration," the rapid urbanization and industrialization of the world, developments that increasingly disrupted traditional society.[107]

In many respects, this globalization suited the anarchists very well. They saw themselves as part of a universal movement that rejected the constraints of the nation-state (although in reality language barriers and different national cultures undermined this cosmopolitanism, not so much among the anarchist elites but at the grassroots level).[108] Many of the leading anarchists were extraordinarily peripatetic, their movements often compelled by police persecution and expulsion, probably more mobile than the leaders of any other political movement of the time. For example, the Italian anarchist Errico Malatesta led an amazing career founding or editing anarchist journals in Italy, France, England, Switzerland, Argentina, and the United States, founding the first militant labor union in Argentina (which subsequently exercised a great influence) and in 1882 journeying to Egypt to help the Arabs in their revolt against European imperialists. He went on lecture tours of Cuba, Spain, the United States, and visited Romania, Belgium (during major strikes), and Holland (where he attended an international anarchist congress in

---

[106] Hobsbawm notes that the world merchant marine almost doubled during this period (1890–1914) and views this as a rough indicator of the expansion of the international economy. Hobsbawm, *Age of Empire*, 50, 153. The economists Kevin H. O'Rourke and Jeffrey G. Williamson, *Globalization and History: The Evolution of a Nineteenth-Century Atlantic Economy* (Cambridge, MA: MIT Press, 1999): 4, label the end of the nineteenth–beginning of the twentieth century as "the first great globalization boom."

[107] Christopher Alan Bayly, *The Birth of the Modern World 1780–1914* (Malden, MA: Blackwell, 2004): 472.

[108] Carl Levy, "Anarchism, Internationalism and Nationalism in Europe, 1860–1939," *Australian Journal of Politics and History* 50:3 (2004): 330–342; Constance Bantman, "Internationalism without an International? Cross-channel Anarchist Networks, 1880–1914," *Revue belge de philologie et d'histoire* 84 (2006): 961–981.

1907).[109] Other Italian anarchists, besides bringing anarchism to Spain and labor militancy to Argentina, played crucial global roles in launching the Brazilian and Peruvian labor movements.[110] As this list of countries suggests, anarchist internationalism was easiest among peoples speaking similar Romance languages.

As with the spread of print media, the relation between globalization and the spread of anarchist terrorism is a complicated one. In a general sense, anarchist terrorism was spread (because anarchists were spread) and connected by migration, and by worldwide webs of shipping lines, communication networks, and cheap publications. Most of the relevant migration was from Europe to the rest of the world, but occasionally it went the other way. Chinese, particularly Chinese students, living in Paris and Tokyo began the transfer of anarchist ideas back to China, where the first anarchist association was founded in 1912. Chinese radicals attracted to anarchism soon began promoting assassination as a necessary tool to promote revolution.[111]

World fairs, which became regular features of international life after London's famous Great Exhibition of 1851 at the Crystal Palace, also facilitated terrorism. In 1894 French President Carnot was stabbed to death in Lyon not long after touring its Universal, International and Colonial Exposition. To cross the Atlantic from his immigrant home in New Jersey, Gaetano Bresci, the assassin of Umberto I of Italy, took advantage of the discounted fares made available to those traveling to the Paris Exhibition of 1900, which he visited before carrying out his deadly deed. The Pan-American Exposition held in Buffalo in 1901 attracted President McKinley as well as his assassin, whose deadly plan was facilitated and masked by the surging crowd of fairgoers. The Milan Exposition of 1906 might have witnessed a royal assassination had the police not successfully intervened.[112]

More fundamental than international expositions in promoting anarchist migration and, in some cases, terrorism, was the vast increase in shipping, especially shipping at increasingly low cost.[113] This made it

---

[109] For Malatesta, see Carl Levy's articles "Malatesta in Exile," *Annali della Fondazione Luigi Einaudi* **15** (1981): 245–280, and "Malatesta in London." The most recent scholarly biography of Malatesta is Giampietro Berti, *Errico Malatesta e il movimento anarchico italiano e internazionale, 1872–1932* (Milan: FrancoAngeli, 2003). Carl Levy's biography is forthcoming.

[110] Levy, "Malatesta in Exile," 246.

[111] Arif Dirlik, *Anarchism in the Chinese Revolution* (Berkeley: University of California Press, 1991): 10, 13, 25–26, 71–72.

[112] See Chapter 10.

[113] O'Rourke and Williamson, *Globalization and History*, 33–36. The authors view falling transport costs, which declined 45 percent between 1870 and 1913, as the fundamental factor promoting globalization.

possible for Italian workers to travel 14,000 miles to Argentina and back for a single season of harvesting the fields. Rail fares dropped as well. The era's fundamental belief in liberalism proclaimed that labor, as well as goods and capital, should be as free as possible to flow around the world with minimal restrictions and regulations.[114] Money also flowed across the ocean as the more affluent immigrants in the Americas responded to appeals for funds from their anarchist cousins in Europe.[115] Sometimes this money went into the hands of radical individuals and groups supporting propaganda by the deed although it is hard to identify convincingly cases in which it was crucial in facilitating *attentats*. The most conspicuous funder of the anarchist cause, and perhaps terrorism, was not some American or Argentine millionaire but Francisco Ferrer, the Spanish anarchist revolutionary and educational reformer, who had inherited from a French woman a small fortune that he invested wisely.[116]

Conclusion

The myth of anarchist terrorism and of the power of dynamite as created by sensationalistic newspapers, a fearful populace and discontented anarchists was as important in the development, and containment, of anarchist terrorism as were the heterogeneous acts of violence themselves. Although some terrorist deeds were due to *agents provocateurs* and secret agents gone wrong, real acts of anarchist violence did take place, the product of harsh socio-economic conditions in Europe and America, regional and national traditions of social warfare and justified regicide, government repression of more peaceful and organized forms of protest and labor activity, the spellbinding examples of the Paris Commune and the assassination of Tsar Alexander II, the invention of dynamite, incitement to propaganda by the deed, and historical chance. The globalization of the world economy spread anarchism and propaganda by the deed throughout the world helping it to become the first truly international form of terrorism. Indeed the era of anarchist terrorism roughly coincided with the first great period of globalization and one of the factors that can be cited for its eventual decline was the restrictions on free migration enacted in the 1920s. While the number of heads of state, government chiefs, and monarchs who were assassinated is noteworthy, and the unprecedented blowing up of innocent bystanders marked a terrible milestone in the history of terrorism, one is struck by how relatively few,

---

[114] Moya, *Cousins and Strangers*, 18–25.   [115] Moya, *Cousins and Strangers*, 308–309.
[116] Avilés Farré, *Francisco Ferrer y Guardia*.

outside of Spain (and, after 1905, Russia), were the victims of anarchist violence. Nonetheless, the anarchists' thirst for dramatic signs of a coming proletarian revolt and of vindication against their enemies now combined with the authorities' and the public's fears of a vast anarchist conspiracy to create the mirage of a powerful terrorist movement. In the context of these fears, governments and police tended to overreact, which in turn added more fuel to the anarchist desires for revenge. Chain reactions of repression and revenge swept through nations and across the world, with anarchist violence seemingly beyond the capacity of any police force to prevent or control. It was in this dreary quandary that much of Europe remained until the turn of the century.

3 International action against subversives: 1815–1889

In the decade between 1894 and 1904 Europe constructed an elaborate system of international police cooperation designed to monitor anarchist movements and prevent anarchist violence. The creation of this extensive anti-anarchist police system, the unacknowledged, but earliest and most notable forerunner of Interpol, raises a number of questions.[1] In an age of intense nationalism, what induced the European states to overcome their mutual suspicions and rivalries, as well as their innate inertia, and reach out to cooperate with one another? Who led this movement toward police cooperation and what was the pattern or shape of the system that evolved? Was the anti-anarchist campaign a façade for more sinister official designs, such as an attack on the socialists and others singled out as "subversives"? And finally, did the anti-anarchist campaign at the end of the nineteenth century have parallels or even roots in and direct connections to earlier efforts to stem subversion and disorder in society?

Certainly the elaborate system of spies, censorship, and general repression chiefly inspired and masterminded by the Austrian Prince Metternich between 1815 and 1848 bore striking resemblances to the anti-anarchist system created decades later on. So great indeed was the similarity, that critics on the left labeled the attempts to thwart anarchist terrorism a new "Holy Alliance," recalling the alliance based on Christian principles proposed by the Emperor Alexander I of Russia in 1815.[2] The Holy Alliance, whatever Alexander's original intention and however inaccurately, came to symbolize the campaign conducted against liberalism and revolution

---

[1] For the links between the anti-anarchist system and Interpol, see Richard Bach Jensen, "The International Anti-Anarchist Conference of 1898 and the Origins of Interpol," *Journal of Contemporary History* 16 (1981): 334, 338–339.

[2] Many on the left applied this label to the International Anti-Anarchist Conference held in Rome, November–December 1898. The official German socialist newspaper, *Vorwärts*, wrote that the organizers of the Rome Anti-Anarchist Conference, "Have a fixed idea regarding it: to raise the Metternichean Holy Police-Alliance [sic] from the dead" (*Vorwärts*, November 30, 1898). See also the statements of the Deputies Dejeante and Zévaès in the French parliament, *Ann. Cham. Dep*, sess.ext., November 24, 1898, 202, 211–212.

by Europe's reactionary monarchies between the fall of Napoleon and the Revolutions of 1848.

The true orchestrator of the anti-liberal and anti-revolutionary campaign in Europe was not Alexander, but Klemens von Metternich, the wily Austrian foreign minister and later chancellor, nicknamed "Old Plaster Face" because of his inscrutability during diplomatic negotiations. In collaboration with most of the governments of the European continent, he utilized and resorted to international treaties and conferences, bilateral diplomacy, and the secret police to uproot and destroy all revolutionary menace to the conservative order that had been created in Europe at the Congress of Vienna in 1814–1815.

International congresses held between 1818 and 1825 at Aix-la-Chapelle, Troppau, Laibach, and Verona brought all the Great Powers together to discuss issues of international concern, chiefly threats to the established order. While at Aix-la-Chapelle Britain blocked Russia's proposal that Europe's sovereigns unite against the forces of revolution, at Troppau in 1820 Austria, Prussia, and Russia agreed not to recognize revolutionary governments and even approved the principle of intervening against rebellion. This alliance of the three Eastern monarchies succeeded in enacting its conservative agenda once again at the 1821 Congress of Laibach, entrusting Austria, over the protests of Britain, to put down rebellions in Italy. In 1822, further revolutionary disturbances led to the calling of the Congress of Verona, which authorized France to quash a revolution in Spain. After Verona, Britain refused to attend any further congresses and this method of sanctioning international repression came to an end. Even earlier, in 1817, Metternich's proposal that a central bureau should be created for collecting information on conspiratorial activity throughout Europe had met with heavy opposition from British Foreign Secretary Castlereagh and been left abandoned.[3]

While British opposition made pan-European cooperation against revolution difficult, Metternich succeeded in spinning out an elaborate anti-conspiracy web on the continent, especially amongst the states of the German confederation and the Italian peninsula. In 1816, in the Austrian-controlled city of Milan, Metternich set up a Central Observation Agency to collect information on Italian subversives. Austria also helped establish a common postal system for the Italian states that allowed Metternich's intelligence service to pry open letters and read them. Secret police agents and paid informers scoured the Italian countryside for news of nationalist conspiracies.

[3] Alan Palmer, *Metternich* (New York: Harper and Row), 1972.

In 1819 Metternich maneuvered the states of the German Confederation into agreeing to the Carlsbad Decrees, a set of laws designed to exterminate liberalism, nationalism, and all other threats to the established order. These decrees gave each state the right to veto publications of more than twenty pages printed anywhere within the German Confederation, placed the universities under strict surveillance, prohibited secret societies, and set up a central commission in Mainz to receive reports on and investigate revolutionary activity. The authorities ordered librarians to compile lists of the books that professors read. Those considered too radical or nationalist were dismissed from their positions. The Carlsbad Decrees remained in effect for almost twenty years. The secret Austrian cipher chancellery functioned a decade longer, busily opening up German mail, as well as the post of any other nation it could get its hands on, to snoop for plots and conspiracies.

Whenever possible, Metternich promoted international police cooperation against subversives. For some years even France agreed to a regular exchange of police information.[4] On occasion Prussia and Bavaria asked for Austrian police agents to watch out for intrigues and secret societies and to spy on other nations.[5] The Austrian police also cooperated with the Russian authorities, although political jealousies prevented the close collaboration characteristic of its relations with the German states.

As was to be true later in the century, Britain and Switzerland were the two thorns in the conservatives' side, since these two countries traditionally gave refuge to political refugees and allowed greater freedom of the press. Metternich's attempts to curb the radical press in Britain were unavailing, but proved more successful with Switzerland. In 1823 Austria, assisted by diplomats from other European powers, forced the Swiss Diet to impose severe limitations on foreigners and to censor Swiss newspapers' publication of foreign news.[6] In the years to come – and notably during the anarchist scare at the turn of the century – its stronger neighbors would once again force Switzerland to modify its liberal policies.

Despite Metternich's ceaseless efforts, the Austrian foreign minister failed to prevent the outbreak of revolutions in 1820, 1821, 1830, and 1848. Nor did all those opened letters and the information acquired by a myriad of secret agents and informers provide Metternich with an accurate understanding of the enemy he faced. In 1817 Metternich believed that hundreds of thousands of adherents to the "sects" infested Italy, but this number was

---

[4] Donald Emerson, *Metternich and the Political Police: Security and Subversion in the Hapsburg Monarchy (1815–1830)* (The Hague: Martinus Nijhoff, 1968): 52.
[5] Emerson, *Metternich*, 53.   [6] Emerson, *Metternich*, 54.

a wild exaggeration.[7] Deluded as well was Metternich's conviction that an international conspiracy menaced Europe. By the mid-1820s foreign diplomats had taken to dubbing Metternich "the Grand Inquisitor of Europe." Seeking details of the alleged Europe-wide conspiracy, the Austrian foreign minister even stooped to entering the cell of Count Federico Confalonieri, a liberal revolutionary from Milan, after Confalonieri was brought to Vienna on his way to a dungeon in Moravia. But Old Plaster Face's famous personal interrogation of Confalonieri failed to unearth evidence of a conspiracy; nor did it reveal – as it should have – that the foreign minister's idea was a delusional fixation, not a concrete reality.[8]

The Revolutions of 1848 sent Metternich fleeing to London and destroyed his system of police repression, spying, and censorship that, outside of Russia, had been severer than anything enacted later on against the anarchists. It was only partially restored in 1851 at the instigation of K. L. F. von Hinckeldey, the head of the Berlin police. He convinced police authorities from Austria, Prussia, Saxony, Hannover, Bavaria, Würtemberg, and Baden to set up a seven-member "Police Union of the more important German States." This organization, which operated without any formal legal or official sanction, aimed to suppress revolutionary activities by monitoring the activities of subversives, opening their mail, and confiscating their publications. Each police department exchanged information directly with the police of other union members, without having to go through diplomatic channels. The Berlin police sent a police officer to carry out surveillance in London, and the Police Union placed secret agents in New York, Paris, London, and Brussels. Attempts to foster closer collaboration with the British and French police, however, failed.[9] Nonetheless, the German Police Union demonstrated that secret anti-subversive police cooperation could flourish even without explicit government authorization, foreshadowing developments in anti-anarchist policing at the end of the century.

The re-establishment across Europe of a fuller version of the Metternichean system was obstructed and delayed by the emergence of a less conservative France, first under the Republic in 1848 and then three years later, under Napoleon III, and by the protracted struggles for Italian and German unification. The German Police Union, already on the decline, collapsed in 1866 when Prussia and Austria went to war. The completion of German and Italian unification in 1870–1871 promoted a new equilibrium in Europe and peace for almost forty-five years. But Bismarck's defeat of Napoleon III and proclamation of the German

---

[7] Emerson, *Metternich*, 99.   [8] Palmer, *Metternich*, 225–226.
[9] Mathieu Deflem. "International Policing in 19th-Century Europe: The Police Union of German States, 1851–1866," *International Criminal Justice Review* 6 (1996): 36–57.

Empire also led to the rising of the Paris Commune and to growing fears of a new menace, the Red International.

Fears of subversion and the re-emergence of international police cooperation after 1870

After 1870 new, and often overblown, fears of subversion combined with real and mounting acts of violence to propel Europe toward international police cooperation. The centralization and development of policing within the individual European nations and an increasing level of bilateral communications between the police departments of the different states prepared the way for later collaboration.

Germany was the first nation to urge international action against subversives, despite the paradoxical fact that after unification it was the continental power least in danger of a bloody social upheaval. In 1871, in response to the violent eruption of the Paris Commune, Chancellor Bismarck called for a great European alliance to fight the International (despite the fact that, as already mentioned, genuine Internationalists had played only a small part in the uprising). Bismarck proposed that all the European powers exchange information on subversives and, in order to allow their easier extradition into the clutches of the police, exclude revolutionary activities from the normal protection allowed political offenses.[10]

Britain rejected the latter measure, helping to sabotage Bismarck's project. Britain's refusal before 1898 to participate in Europe-wide anti-anarchist or anti-revolutionary projects was to be characteristic of its policy and a major obstacle to reaching agreement on such issues. Britain also rejected Spain's call months later, in February 1872, for European police cooperation against the International. This Spanish failure was also characteristic. Spain, unstable and beset by throngs of domestic enemies, often looked for external assistance to cope with internal difficulties. Too weak to count much in the international diplomatic game, Madrid saw the failure of almost all its initiatives and pleas for help. Even Bismarck refused to embrace the Spanish proposal, finding the excuse that he was too involved in Germany's domestic problems.[11]

Equally futile was the invitation, issued in the spring of 1872 by the much more powerful government of Russia, for all the European states to take collective steps against the Socialist International.[12] But fear of the anarchist and socialist menace did serve as one of the principle

---

[10] Even before the Commune, in September 1870, Bismarck had put out feelers toward the Austrian and Russian governments for a common front against subversive movements. Pflanze, *Bismarck*, 2:294.

[11] Pflanze, *Bismarck*, 2:294–295.   [12] Liang, *Modern Police*, 88.

underpinnings of the Three Emperors' League, made up of Germany, Austria, and Russia, that came into being in the autumn of 1873.[13] Harking back to the conservative entente established by Metternich in 1820, the league survived five years, to 1878. A second, and more formal, Three Emperors' Alliance followed in 1881 and lasted until 1884. Even after these agreements ended, the three conservative empires led the fight against "subversion" in general and anarchist terrorism in particular until the outbreak of the First World War.

The opposition of Britain, political divisions between the continental states, and the absence of a sustained threat to the established order prevented the development of any kind of Europe-wide cooperation against the International after the Commune was crushed in 1871. Similar reasons account for the failure of the appeal made a decade later for international action after the assassination of Tsar Alexander II. In its desire to destroy the entire Russian revolutionary movement, both at home and abroad, St. Petersburg, joined by Berlin and Vienna, called for an international conference to exclude assassination or attempted assassination from the list of crimes exempted from extradition due to their political nature, and to promote international police cooperation against assassins.[14] While the governments and middle and upper classes of Europe were shocked, and the anarchists and other extreme leftists elated, by the murder of the Russian emperor, the nihilist threat was insufficient to provide the stimulus for an international conference since it was confined to a single country. Moreover, Britain disliked the idea of political policing and "successfully nipped [the 'Nihilist Conference'] in the bud" by persuading France not to participate.[15]

In its absence, during the late 1870s and the 1880s, several nations took unilateral or bilateral action to counter what was perceived to be a continuing and growing "subversive" menace. In September 1883, Russia and Germany agreed to direct communications between their border authorities regarding suspected persons; later, comparable agreements were signed between Russia and Austria (1886), and Russia and Romania.[16] Reacting to, first, the nihilists', then, the Irish Fenians', and finally, the anarchists' practice of using dynamite to attack their enemies,

[13] Pflanze, *Bismarck*, 2:258–260; Fricke, *Bismarck's Praetorianer*, 165; Francis R. Bridge, *The Habsburg Monarchy Among the Great Powers, 1815–1918* (New York, Oxford, and Munich: Berg, 1990): 109–110. The text of the agreements aligning the three empires is at 381–382.

[14] Fricke, *Bismarck's Praetorianer*, 166; Porter, *Vigilant State*, 40.

[15] Ambassador Ampthill to Foreign Secretary Granville, May 7, 1881, cited in Bernard Porter, "The *Freiheit* Prosecutions, 1881–1882", *The Historical Journal* 23:4 (1980): 848n.

[16] Zuckerman, *The Tsarist Secret Police Abroad: Policing Europe in a Modernising World* (Hampshire: Palgrave Macmillan, 2003): 58.

four countries in northern and central Europe passed laws against the criminal use of explosives: Britain on April 10, 1883; Germany on June 9, 1884; Austria on May 27, 1885; and Belgium on May 22, 1886.[17]

In addition to legislative enactments, several countries began creating an embryonic international policing apparatus. The latter development was particularly significant since, during the 1890s, this apparatus expanded considerably and took over the duties of the antianarchist campaign. Germany, wealthy, powerful, but uneasy about its internal security given the recent date of German unification, was once again the first to act. After the assassination attempts of May and June 1878 against the German kaiser, Bismarck put the blame on the Social Democratic Party and forced anti-socialist laws through parliament. By November 1878 the Prussian police had begun posting spies to Paris, Geneva, London, and Budapest to watch anarchists, socialists, and others on the extreme left. By 1881 Berlin had posted agents as well to Zurich and Brussels.[18] In 1882 the Germans even sent an agent to New York City, where he remained until the anti-socialist laws lapsed in 1890; a new agent came over in 1900 to remain until 1917.[19] After the September 1883 attempt to blow up the kaiser, Germany and Russia agreed to direct communications between their border authorities regarding the activities of subversives. In January 1885 they signed an extradition agreement denying asylum to those accused of murderous attempts against a monarch or his family.[20] (An April 1888 treaty between Russia and Spain went even further, making all political crimes extraditable.[21])

In the early 1880s, Italy decided to set up an anti-subversive police surveillance and spy agency in Paris. As was often to be the case, the initiative for this momentous step came from local officials rather than from the central government.[22] On March 19, 1880, Baron Marochetti, the chargé d'affaires at the Italian embassy in Paris, asked Rome for permission to hire an Italian-speaking Corsican employed by the Parisian police who might provide "exact notices on various Internationalists, who

---

[17] Eugenio Florian, *Trattato di Diritto Penale. 2: Introduzione ai delitti in ispecie delitti contro la sicurezza della Stato*, 2nd edition (Milan: Vallardi, 1915): 138–161; Loubat, "De la legislation contre les anarchistes."

[18] Hoerder, *Plutocrats and Socialists*, xxxi; Fricke, *Bismarck's Praetorianer*, 286.

[19] Hoerder, *Plutocrats and Socialists*, xxxiii.

[20] Fricke, *Bismarck's Praetorianer*, 167–168.

[21] Lassa Oppenheim. *International Law: A Treatise*, 2 vols (London: Longmans, Green, 1921), 1:522–523.

[22] Stefania Ruggeri, "Il fondo 'Polizia Internazionale'," in F. Grassi and G. C. Donno (eds.), *Il movimento socialista e popolare in Puglia dalle origini alla Costituzione (1874–1946)* (Bari: Laterza, 1986): 155, leaves the impression that the initiative came from Interior Minister Depretis on April 3, 1880, although, in fact, Marochetti's note preceded Depretis's.

previously took part in the Paris Commune" since the "diplomatic route is not always the best for [obtaining] these, considering the reluctance of the [French] Republic to give news about individuals who took part in the Commune, even if they are now suspected as Internationalists." Marochetti believed that one reason for this reluctance might be because some of the former members of the Commune, e.g., Camille Barrère, now held official positions or were honored in other ways.[23] The Ministry of the Interior in Rome readily agreed to Marochetti's request for a special agent "to watch out for the plots of the Italians belonging to subversive parties."[24]

After the assassination of Tsar Alexander, the Italian government feared the growing "boldness of the lawless [*facinorosi*] of every country [which] has made it necessary that the surveillance of Italian anarchists who have fled abroad should be stricter and more vigilant than ever." Therefore the royal government wished to "to organize there [in Paris] on its own account and at its expense a special surveillance service [*un servizio particolare di sorveglianza*]."[25] To meet this end, the Italian ambassador suggested hiring an Italian policeman, and in May 1882 the interior ministry sent Public Security Inspector Ettore Sernicoli, who had served in Paris during the Universal Exposition of 1878.[26] Previously police officers had been sent on missions to foreign cities, but their stays had been temporary. In 1882 a Vice-Inspector Amede had served in London before he was abruptly recalled after his identity had become public.[27] Before 1882, the permanent monitoring of subversives had almost always been in the hands, not of full-time policemen, but of the Italian consuls or vice-consuls who hired informants to gather information. Once Sernicoli arrived in the French capital, he took over these duties. Sernicoli would remain in Paris, well known to the French authorities and in semi-official relations with them, until 1895.[28]

---

[23] Marochetti, Paris, to foreign ministry, Rome, March 19, 1880. Polizia internazionale (hereafter cited as PI), b. 26, IFM.

[24] Malvano, foreign ministry, Rome, conveying the view of the interior ministry, to Barone Marochetti, Paris, April 7, 1880. PI, b. 26, IFM

[25] Malvano, foreign ministry, Rome to General Cialdini, duke of Gaeta, Paris, March 25, 1881. IFM., PI, b. 26.

[26] Cialdini, Paris, to Malvano, Rome, March 25, 1881; Malvano to Marochetti, May 1, 1882. PI, b. 26, IFM.

[27] Di Paola, "Spies," 192. An Italian policeman may also have been temporarily posted to Geneva. See Mauro Canali, *Le spie del regime* (Bologna: Mulino, 2004): 16.

[28] See Ambassador Tornielli's fascinating report on the Italian system of political policing in France, Tornielli, Paris, to Foreign Minister Canevaro, July 20, 1898, IFM, PI, b. 36. For Sernicoli's career, see Giovanna Tosatti, "La repressione del dissenso politico tra l'età liberale e il fascismo. L'organizzazione della polizia," *Studi storici* 38 (1997): 219n.

Soon after his arrival, in late May 1882, he began to exchange information with the Russian Foreign Agency in Paris. At the time, the Italian chargé d'affaires noted that

the Russian embassy in Paris is also here organizing, on a vast scale, a political police administration, aimed at keeping an eye on the movements of members of the nihilist sect. On several occasions [my] previous communications have demonstrated that frequent and continual connections exist between the Russian nihilists and the Italian socialists.

On May 30, 1882, the Italian government "fully approved" this "advantageous" reciprocal exchange of information.[29]

Denied their international conference after the death of the tsar, in June 1883 the Russians set up a secret political police center in the basement of their embassy in Paris, the so-called "Foreign Agency" (the *Zagranichnaia Agentura*; literally, the "Foreign Secret Service").[30] The Foreign Agency was to develop into the greatest foreign political police apparatus in the world. At its height in 1914, it had three Russian policemen (as case officers), forty police detectives (all foreigners), and about twenty-five Russian informers operating in, at one time or another, Paris (all the police and about half the detectives), London (a handful of detectives), Berlin (two to three detectives), Italy (after 1912, six detectives), Bulgaria, and Romania.[31] Many of these detectives had formerly worked for the police of their own countries.[32] The Russian police abroad also had paid informers among the Berlin and Geneva police and carried out surveillance in Switzerland, Belgium, and the Baltic countries with the assistance of the local police or of detectives sent out from the main center in Paris.[33] Russian agents operated as well in New York and Chicago.[34] The focus of the Foreign Agency was on monitoring the activities of the People's Will and the Socialist Revolutionary party among the Russian emigrant communities, but it was easy enough for the Foreign Agency to include

---

[29] Marochetti, chargé d'affaires, Paris, to Mancini, minister of foreign affairs, Rome, May 23, 1882; foreign ministry, Rome, to Marochetti, Paris, May 30, 1882. IFM, PI, b. 26.

[30] Jonathan Daly, *Autocracy under Siege: Security Police and Opposition in Russia, 1866–1905* (DeKalb: Northern Illinois University Press, 1998): 45.

[31] Richard J. Johnson, "*Zagranichnaia Agentura*: The Tsarist Political Police in Europe," in George Mosse (ed.), *Police Forces in History* (London: Sage Publications, 1975): 22–25; Johnson, *The Okhrana Abroad, 1885–1917: A Study in International Police Cooperation* (PhD Dissertation, Columbia University, 1971): 22, 25. Independent of control from Paris, the St. Petersburg government also occasionally sent out confidential agents to monitor revolutionaries abroad. Johnson, *Okhrana Abroad*, 26.

[32] Frederic Scott Zuckerman, 'The Russian Political Police at Home and Abroad (1880–1917): Its Structure, Functions, and Methods, and its Struggle with the Organized Opposition' (PhD Dissertation, New York University, 1973): 524.

[33] Johnson, "*Zagranichnaia Agentura*," 25–26.

[34] Hoerder, *Plutocrats and Socialists*, 371.

anarchists on its enemies' list since the Russian government usually por-
trayed *all* revolutionaries as anarchists and terrorists (although it certainly
knew better).[35] Peter Rachkovsky, the skillful, media savvy, smiling *bon
vivant* who headed the Foreign Agency between 1885 and 1902, published pamphlets in which he argued that members of the People's Will,
the group that had assassinated the tsar, were "the intellectual brethren
of the anarchists."[36] Incidentally, according to a contemporary account,
Rachkovsky was so esteemed by the French that President Émile Loubet,
after being warned of a possible *attentat* during a visit to Lyon, asked
the Russians, rather than the *Sûreté*, to handle his security.[37] Less to his
credit, Rachkovsky may have been at the center of a web of *agent provocateur* bombings in Liège, London, and Paris designed to scare Western
governments and make them more amenable to tsarist efforts to harass
Russian revolutionaries. Butterworth even suggests that in December
1890 Rachkovsky instigated the murder of General Seliverstov, the former
head of the St. Petersburg police because he was a possible rival.[38]

Arguably, after the Russians, the British created the most formidable international anti-terrorist network of police and agents during the
1880s, although this was not in response to subversives on the far left
but to the Fenians. The Fenians were Irish-American terrorists seeking
Ireland's independence from Britain. Because they were to have such
a direct impact on its later endeavors to contain anarchism, Britain's
actions merit some careful analysis. The Fenian campaign grew out of
the efforts of two Irish-American organizations based in the United
States, Clan na Gael and Jeremiah O'Donovan Rossa's Skirmishers.
Targeting London and two other British cities between January 1881
and January 1885 (and in June 1887 threatening to blow up Westminster
Abbey during Queen Victoria's jubilee celebration),[39] it began the first
modern terrorist campaign. It differed from previous campaigns because
it largely eschewed attempts at assassinating political leaders (in contrast
to the People's Will), and emphasized, in order to cause general terror,

[35] In January 1894 Rachkovsky tried to arrange a secret anti-anarchist agreement with the
French *Sûreté* but was informed by police headquarters in St. Petersburg that "even if
such a pact were concluded, it would not deal with revolutionaries, who comprised most
of the émigré problem." Johnson, *Okhrana Abroad*, 70.

[36] Zuckerman, *Russian Political Police*, 531. For Rachkovsky's character see Christopher
Andrew and Oleg Gordievsky, *KGB: The Inside Story of Its Foreign Operations from Lenin
to Gorbachev* (New York: HarperCollins, 1990): 23, and Zuckerman, "Political Police and
Revolution: The Impact of the 1905 Revolution on the Tsarist Secret Police," *Journal of
Contemporary History*, 27 (1992): 283.

[37] Daly, *Autocracy under Siege*, 46.

[38] Butterworth, *World That Never Was*, 276, 343–344.

[39] A British secret agent, assisted by some unsuspecting Fenians, originated the "Jubilee
Plot." Porter, *Vigilant State*, 88–90.

blowing up sites frequented by the public.[40] While the Irish (or at least Clan na Gael; O'Donovan Rossa was more indiscriminate) tried to direct their blasts toward destroying famous buildings, rather than killing people, one bomb that was detonated in the London underground railway injured seventy.[41]

Appalled, in the words of Home Secretary Harcourt, by "the absolute want of information ... in regard to Fenian organisation in London," in March of 1883 the British government created a Special Irish Branch at Scotland Yard.[42] While the Special Branch was eventually to have a great future, at the time an even more important development was the creation of a separate intelligence network of policemen and informers in Dublin, and later, under the intrepid Edward Jenkinson, its introduction into Britain. Jenkinson took "charge of all anti-Fenian intelligence worldwide."[43] As spymaster, he was ably supported in the north of England by Nicholas Gosselin. With considerable success, this intelligence network penetrated the Fenian organizations in the British Isles and the United States, from whose safe haven the Fenians carried out much of their plotting and drew most of their money.

Historians of the Irish-American dynamiters cite five or six major factors that explain why the Fenian terrorist campaign came to an end. Political and diplomatic developments were crucial. By 1885 the parliamentary success of the Irish political leader Parnell and his party by 1885 had strengthened the Irish Republic Brotherhood in its opposition to the use of dynamite, while factional infighting in the Clan na Gael led it to a change of strategy. Diplomatically, in mid-March 1885, the French police began raiding the residences of Fenians in Paris and deporting them. Moreover, "there may have been intimations that the American sanctuary was in danger of being lost as the French sanctuary had been withdrawn."[44]

Two other reasons for the end of the dynamite campaign had to do with British police actions. First, because of the increasing sophistication of its intelligence operation, the police inflicted heavy losses on the ranks of the dynamiters; more than twenty were arrested, tried, and imprisoned. Even if the very idea caused horrified reactions amongst the top political leadership, considerable evidence suggests that this intelligence operation went as far as employing *agents provocateurs* to encourage

---

[40] "Only in the case of John Daly, arrested in 1884, was there any claim that Clan na Gael had embarked on the path of assassination." Kenneth Short, *The Dynamite War: Irish-American Bombers in Victorian Britain* (Dublin: Gill and Macmillan, 1979): 3.

[41] Although the Fenian attempt in 1867 to destroy a Clerkenwell prison wall led to the death of twelve people in nearby houses, this was unintentional.

[42] Porter, *Vigilant State*, 41.   [43] Porter, *Vigilant State*, 51.

[44] Short, *Dynamite War*, 227; Niall Whelehan, *The Dynamiters: Irish Nationalism and Political Violence in the Wider World, 1867–1900* (Cambridge University Press, 2012).

the Fenians to undertake violent actions that would make them liable to arrest and prosecution. Second, fifty-four police were sent to watch British and continental ports and they succeeded in making the importation of dynamite into Britain almost impossible. In and of themselves, the historian K. R. M. Short argues, police operations could never have stopped all the dynamiters, but these efforts to stop terrorism were greatly assisted by evolving attitudes among members of the Irish and Irish-American organizations that sapped the will for continued acts of violence.[45] In similar fashion, improved policing together with changing anarchist attitudes toward terrorism would later on be crucial in the decline of propaganda by the deed.

Deserving emphasis as well is the fact that Britain's response to Fenianism was relatively measured. While the British penal system could be gruesome, in this case it produced no martyrs and few executions. The only examples of the latter were the hanging of the rogue Fenians who in May 1882 had brutally knifed to death both the chief secretary and the permanent undersecretary for Ireland while they were walking together, unguarded, in Dublin's Phoenix Park.

Some anarchists (e.g., those who helped edit *Freiheit*, the London-based newspaper of the incarcerated Johann Most) applauded these cruel murders but no evidence exists that anarchist propaganda ever inspired the Fenians.[46] Nonetheless, the deeds of the Irish terrorists in the British Isles foreshadowed the even bloodier actions of the continental anarchists during the 1890s.

Conclusion

In Austria and Germany in particular, but also in Spain, Italy and France, the legacy of the pre-1848 (or pre-1870, or, in the case of Britain, pre-1889) subversive policing system provided a model and a mindset easily applicable to anarchist terrorism at the end of the century. In both periods the fear of conspiratorial subversion grossly exceeded its reality. Similarly, spies, police agents (including agents posted to foreign countries), letter-opening, bilateral accords, and police cooperation played a vital part in the anti-anarchist campaign as they had previously. Austria and Germany also played a leading role in both eras, although more covertly in the second. But if the end of the century repression was similar

---

[45] Short, *Dynamite War*, 213, 225–227, 234, 240–241. For the issue of *agents provocateurs*, see Porter, *Vigilant State*, 68–79, 88–90.

[46] Frederic Trautmann, *Voice of Terror*, 69–70; John Newsinger, *Fenianism in Mid-Victorian Britain* (London: Pluto Press, 1994): 23–24, cites the influence of Italian nationalist revolutionaries and conspirators on the Fenians after the Revolutions of 1848.

to the old, it was not exactly the same. Censorship, at least outside of Spain and Russia, was less utilized, as was probably also the case with the firing of teachers of politically advanced views. Liberalism's increasingly influential claims about the advantages of a free marketplace of ideas had proved too potent for that to occur. Nor did a single directing mind, like Metternich's, succeed in welding together the efforts of Europeans in an anti-subversive crusade. Moreover, the definition of what was dangerously subversive and inherently violent had changed and constricted since the beginning of the century. In most countries peaceable socialists and nationalists were not considered the criminals that they had been previously. Therefore post-1890 anarchist repression was narrower in scope than the earlier Metternichean system, but more concrete and extensive in terms of international agreements and understandings between major European states. International law also played a larger role in suppressing the anarchists since more of a consensus existed that violent anarchists were outside the law than had been true earlier regarding the criminality of nationalists and socialists.

4   The terrorist 1890s and increasing police cooperation: 1890–1898

In the 1890s more intensive, systematic, and widespread police and diplomatic collaboration against the anarchists replaced the sporadic police and diplomatic cooperation against them (and other terrorist groups) of the previous decade. In the 1880s, the actions of the Russian nihilists and Irish Fenians had each been restricted to one or two countries, but in the 1890s anarchist terrorism spread throughout Europe with incidents in the United States and Australia. The difficulty that the European authorities, the public, and the mass media found in defining "anarchist" and "anarchism," and the authorities' frequent inability to distinguish anarchism from other forms of socialism and extreme political belief made "anarchist terrorism" a greater phenomenon than it really was and led to a central paradox. While overblown fears of anarchism provided the energy that moved governments to cooperate internationally, their vague and inaccurate understanding of the phenomenon made it difficult, perhaps impossible, to cope with this threat effectively. Good intelligence skillfully utilized was crucial for a more effective reaction.

How did the European states respond to the challenge? After 1890, the French were the first on the continent to be forced to develop an anti-terrorist/anti-anarchist policy, since the wave of anarchist bombings that made the 1890s the pre-eminent decade of nineteenth-century terrorism began in Paris in March 1892. Domestically, France pursued increasingly ruthless policies of spying on, searching, rounding up, imprisoning, and executing anarchists. In response to the seemingly unending series of violent anarchist attempts, in February 1894, the Paris prefecture of police decided to centralize all intelligence-gathering in the city in one organization under Louis Puibaraud (or Puybaraud), a former high-ranking bureaucrat of the interior ministry. As Paris's all-powerful *directeur-géneral des recherches* (1894–1903), Puibaraud ruled a curious empire of hundreds of men, some devoted to watching gamblers and lodging houses, while others monitored the anarchists.[1] The third, or anarchist, squad (*brigade*),

---

[1] Jean-Marc Berlière, "A Republican Political Police? Political Policing in France under the Third Republic, 1875–1940," 27–55, and Clive Emsley, "Introduction: Political Police

under a Commissaire Fédée, was composed of more than 100 detectives. It compiled a detailed directory of anarchists listing their names and addresses; it was also kept informed of their activities and meetings, of even their least important movements inside France, and of when they left the country.[2] Spies and *agents provocateurs* infiltrated anarchist meetings and groups, with as many as five police agents taking notes at a single anarchist gathering![3] In 1894 the anthropometric identification and photographic services, together with a central card index of suspects and criminals (*sommiers judiciaries*) were attached to Puibaraud's directorate. Housed in an airless, sunless garret, tropical in summer and frigid in winter, the labyrinthine office of *Identité judiciaire* eventually acquired an international reputation for the excellence of its research.[4] The pre-eminent historian of the French police has attributed considerable significance to this centralization of authority under Puibaraud. It created "a formidable power realizing the ideal of every political [policing] service: to group together every resource [*moyen*], all the plain-clothes men, all the brigades, all the card indexes, all the informers."[5] A police official who had worked for Puibaraud claimed in a book written many years afterwards that he had "saved" France from the "anarchist peril" with his ruthless policies and widespread use of *agents provocateurs*.[6] Contemporaries and several modern historians have disputed this view.

At this time, the French Foreign Office was also investigating the anarchists. In 1892 a Captain Eugéne Bazeries, seconded from the French army, broke some of the codes that the anarchists used in their correspondence, but whether this prevented any terrorist acts has never been proved.[7]

In the provinces, "Special Railway Commissioners," detectives with wide-ranging legal powers and attached to the *Sûreté Générale*, played an important role in monitoring the peripatetic anarchists on their rambles,[8] and as we shall see, in protecting visiting royalty. The Special Railway Commissioners performed the same function in the *Sûreté* as the

and the European Nation-State in the Nineteenth Century," in Mark Mazower (ed.), *The Policing of Politics in the Twentieth Century* (Providence and Oxford: Berghahn Books, 1997): 35, 18; Jean-Marc Berlière, *Le Préfet Lépine* (Paris: Denoël, 1993) (paris: Robert Laffont, 2005): 104–105.

[2] Claude Charlot, "Brigades," Michel Aubouin et al. (eds.) in *Histoire et Dictionnaire de la Police*, gives a figure of 104 *fonctionnaires* in the *3e brigade* in 1894; "Bloc-Notes Parisien," *Le Gaulois*, October 27, 1894.

[3] Maitron, *Histoire*, 427–432.   [4] Berlière, *Le Monde*, 47–48.

[5] Berlière, *Le Monde*, 145.   [6] Ernest Raynaud, *La vie intime*, 33.

[7] Douglas Porch, *The French Secret Services from the Dreyfus Affair to the Gulf War* (New York: Farrar, Straus and Giroux, 1995): 35.

[8] Marie-Josèphe Dhavernas, "La surveillance des anarchistes individualistes (1894–1914)," in Philippe Vigier (ed.), *Maintien de l'ordre et polices en France et en Europe au XIXe siècle* (Paris: Créaphis, 1987): 352–353.

research brigades in the Paris Prefecture. After Vaillant tossed his bomb into the French assembly, parliament authorized a "dramatic increase" in their numbers and enlarged their jurisdiction to include many cities.[9] The Third Brigade also increased in size: according to the Italian secret police in Paris, by 1908, it had 150 inspectors to monitor "subversives."[10]

On January 1, 1894, a few weeks after Vaillant's *attentat*, the police carried out about 2,000 searches of anarchists throughout France.[11] When these failed to prevent a new round of lethal bombings, most anarchist newspapers were closed down and "innumerable" arrests carried out. But according to one of our best contemporary chroniclers, the journalist Henri "Varennes," these sorts of crackdowns, by harassing many innocent people, were useless and only exasperated anarchist feelings of hatred.[12] The police historian Jean-Marc Berlière cites the memoirs of several contemporary members of the *Sûreté* (admittedly an organization in rivalry with the police of Paris) who shared Varennes's view. Berlière concludes that "by subjecting anarchists to special laws, humiliating surveillance, arrests and endless searches, subversion was nourished rather than fought." Inspector Rossignol even went so far as to declare that "I realized why political squads never find any anarchists despite the money they spend on searching for them. Most of the anarchists are informers, 'finks.' If the squads arrested them, they would have no more business and no more reason for being."[13]

It is difficult to disagree with the harsh verdict that, at least for the early and mid-1890s, the French police perpetuated the very problem of violent anarchism that it was supposed to be resolving. Only later, by the end of the 1890s, once the hastily enacted reforms and expansion of the police had had time to fully mature and bear fruit, can the modernization of the French police probably be credited with reducing the problem of terrorism.[14] But a fundamental resolution of the terrorist threat also

---

[9] Berlière, "A Republican Political Police," 33, and "Police spéciale des chemins de fer," in Aubouin, *Histoire et Dictionnaire de la Police*: 827.

[10] Beniamino Wenzel to commendatore [Scrocca], Paris November 15, 1908, DGPS, 1909, b. 2, *Archivio Centrale dello Stato*, Rome (hereafter cited as ACS). Morel, *La police*, 156, gives a figure of 125 *inspecteurs* for the anarchist brigade.

[11] Italian Ambassador Costantino Ressmann, Paris, to foreign ministry, Rome, January 2, 1894. PI, b. 27, IFM.

[12] Maitron, *Histoire*, 237–238; Varennes, *De Ravachol à Caserio*, 209. Morel, *La police*, 156–161, shares Varennes's view.

[13] Gustave Rossignol, *Mémoires de Rossignol ex-Inspecteur principal de la Sûreté* (Paris: 1900): 167, cited by Berlière "A Republican Political Police," 47. Berlière also cites the contemporary accounts by M.-F. Goron (1897) and Pierre Morel (1907).

[14] Evidence for modernization can perhaps be found in Prime Minister Georges Clemenceau's (1906–1909), very favorable impression of the *Sûreté*'s ability to break the codes of left-wing revolutionaries. Porch, *French Secret Services*, 48.

required political reforms, changes in the operation of French justice, and changes in the attitudes of the anarchists themselves.

Internationally, the French government began both working more closely with foreign police and sending agents to monitor foreign and French anarchists residing abroad. Paris asked for closer police cooperation with Britain and began forwarding names of anarchists departing for London.[15] During the 1890s French informers, and probably undercover policemen as well, were posted to the British capital and began sending back information on the anarchist movement.[16] The newspapers even spoke of a "secret anti-anarchist squad" in London maintained by the Paris Prefecture of Police but this may be an exaggeration.[17] A French police *commissaire* with his staff operated in Barcelona with the full permission of the Spanish authorities (and offered to share information on the anarchists with the consulates of Italy and other states).[18]

Unlike Spain, Switzerland opposed the French desire to set up a spy service on its territory, and was able to prevent this by offering to provide the French police with all the information it wanted.[19] As a 1898 report by Charles Lardy, Swiss Minister to France, on his conversation with Charles Blanc, Paris Police Prefect and former director of the *Sûreté*, indicates, France believed that one of the keys to effective control of anarchism and terrorists was close cooperation between frontier police so that the passage of anarchists from one country to another could be communicated quickly. The French police agent in Barcelona was essential in facilitating that communication since, in the view of the French, the Spanish police were incompetent. Although France was unable to place an agent inside Switzerland, it succeeded in establishing an information exchange between the police of Geneva and the French police across the frontier, as well as the police on both sides of the Franco–Belgian border.

---

[15] Porter, *Vigilant State*, 111; "R.A." (presumably Robert Anderson, assistant commissioner of Scotland Yard's criminal investigation department), wrote that he was glad to have the names of the four Italian anarchists on their way to join Malatesta in London, although he already knew of their arrival. Copy of D'Estournelles de Constant, French embassy, to earl of Kimberley, London, September 22, 1894, with accompanying confidential minute, September 27, 1894. Home Office 144/587/B2840c/48, Public Record Office (hereafter PRO; these records are now stored at the British National Archives).

[16] Liang, *Modern Police*, 165–166; E. Thomas Wood, Introduction, 'Wars on Terror: French and British Responses to the Anarchist Violence of the 1890s' (M. Phil, University of Cambridge, 2002).

[17] *New York Herald*, June 7, 1903, 2.

[18] Liang, *Modern Police*, 165–166; Sensales, DGPS, Rome, to foreign ministry, August 13, 1895. PI, b. 36, IFM.

[19] Liang, *Modern Police*, 160–161.

French officials also sought to strengthen police surveillance of anarchists inside France and to expel foreign anarchists across the frontier. After the Paris bombings began in 1892, the French rushed to expel hundreds of foreign anarchists, but without any concern as to whether or not individual anarchists were nationals of the countries to which they were being sent and without any prior notification being given to the authorities of those countries. The British felt particularly vulnerable to and aggrieved by this policy since, until the passage of the Aliens Act in 1905, Britain had no legal means of restricting immigration. Nor could Britain expel an undesirable person by administrative or police fiat. The only recourse the British government had was to apply diplomatic pressure, and consequently, it protested against French policy; in the future France promised not to deport any more anarchists across the channel.[20]

Beginning in May 1894, the French police began compiling lists of foreign anarchists it had expelled and, on a periodic basis, forwarding these lists to neighboring countries. Even more frequently, it sent out individual police bulletins notifying foreign authorities of transfers to the border and the destinations of dangerous anarchists.[21] In August 1894, Jules Herbette, the French ambassador to Germany, told his Austrian colleague that this spontaneous provision of information had led to mutual cooperation with the security forces of other countries and eventually favored the creation of binding agreements.[22] Spain and Italy found the French anarchist lists of "great usefulness" and "most useful." But in September 1897 Madrid complained that none had been transmitted since January 1895 (an omission that in this case Paris quickly remedied).[23] Rome complained that the French would only send information about the movements of Italian anarchists in France, not about French or other anarchists.[24]

This "unilateralism" was characteristic of French policy. The police historian Hsi-Huey Liang has characterized the French strategy for policing as "*défense du territorie*," a nationally self-centered, politically

---

[20] Home Office memo, "Expulsion from France to England of persons obnoxious to the French Government," March 22, 1897, HO144/587/B2840c, PRO.

[21] Velics, Austrian embassy, Berlin, to Austrian Foreign Minister Kálnoky, August 4, 1894. n. 30.B. Political Archive (hereafter "PA") Interna. Liasse XXVII. f. 155–158, Haus-Hof- und Staat Archiv (Vienna) (hereafter HHStA).

[22] Ibid.

[23] Ambassador Marques de Novallas, Paris, to foreign ministry, Madrid, September 9, 1897; mss. foreign ministry, Madrid to embassy, Paris, September 20, 1897; Undersecretary del Valillo to foreign secretary, September 25, 1897. OP, l. 2750, SFM. Sensales, interior ministry, Rome, to foreign minister, August 31, 1894. PI, b. 36, IFM.

[24] Telegrams between Italian foreign ministry and Paris embassy, October 1895. PI, b. 27, IFM .

opportunistic policy.[25] Moreover the French gave repeated indications that they believed multilateral (as opposed to bilateral) cooperation, whether this meant attending international anti-anarchist conferences or signing international anti-anarchist conventions, was a waste of time.[26]

The Spanish had a completely different view, which soon became evident when Spain overtook France as the leading country of anarchist terrorism beginning in September 1893. The Spanish authorities had great difficulties in finding the instigators of many anarchist assaults. Spain was poor and its police backward; it would take a much longer time than its wealthier French neighbor to reform and modernize its system. Antonio Tressols, one of the aces of the Barcelona police force charged with stopping the anarchist onslaught, could barely read or write.[27] In the early 1890s, the Spanish police still had no scientific way of identifying lawbreakers. They had not yet installed the complicated and expensive French system of Bertillonage (which involved measuring twelve body parts), and fingerprinting was virtually unknown in Europe at this time. Therefore, it was logical for Spain to turn to the international community for help.

Spain proposes an international anti-anarchist accord, 1893

Spain approached Britain first. On November 20, 1893, twelve days after the bombing of the Liceo Theater, the Spanish ambassador in London inquired if the British "would be disposed to enter into arrangements for common international action against the anarchists. If so, the Spanish government were prepared to take the initiative and to propose measures for carrying out the object in view."[28] In confidence the Spanish foreign minister, Segismundo Moret – who, incidentally, was quite the Anglophile: the grandson of an English general, he had lived in London and read the London *Times* his whole life – informed the British that he was "very anxious on this subject, as he anticipates great danger from

---

[25] Liang, *Modern Police*, 46.
[26] Report of Charles Lardy, Swiss Minister to France, regarding conversation with Paris Police Prefect Charles Blanc, November 8, 1898.
[27] Núñez Florencio, *Terrorismo*, 90.
[28] See the telegram from Moret, foreign ministry, Madrid, to Spanish ambassador, London, November 19, 1893, l. 2750, SFM, and Lord Roseberry's summation of his discussion with the ambassador on November 20. Rosebery to H. Wolff, Madrid, November 22, 1893. Foreign Office (hereafter FO) 72/1923. N. 164, PRO. The Spanish had been interested in convening international conferences against revolutionaries and subversives for a long time. Cánovas had proposed such a gathering in 1878 and Interior Minister Francisco Silvela had proposed an anti-anarchist entente in 1891. González Calleja, *La razón de la fuerza*, 270.

this source."[29] On December 11, emboldened by the widespread shock over the recent bombing of the French parliament, Spain proposed to the whole of Europe "legislation" and joint "international action" against the anarchists.[30] Two days later Britain said "no."[31] On November 22, even before the entire cabinet had decided the issue, Lord Rosebery, the prime minister, indicated to the Spanish ambassador the reasons for Britain's reluctance to participate. Rosebery explained that

it was not easy to draw a clear line between anarchism and other forms of more or less extreme opinion. In the next place legislation would be required, and all legislation of this kind was regarded with the most jealous suspicion in this country.[32]

The British felt that existing laws were quite adequate to deal with anarchist crimes and did not wish "to enter into any international engagement which might hamper or complicate [our] liberty of action."[33] The Liberal Gladstone cabinet (1893–1895) operated on the assumption that neither public opinion nor parliament could be convinced to sanction the kind of restrictive, anti-anarchist legislation that the continent seemed to want, although in private Home Secretary Asquith told the Austrians that it would be desirable if the printing for distribution abroad of publications that advocated murder and assassination could be restricted, something the current British laws on freedom of the press did not allow.[34] The Conservative party had not so many qualms, at least about *introducing* anti-anarchist legislation into parliament, and if it had been in power, the British might have proved more open to cooperation.

Common opinion during the 1890s and more recently has held that the British rejection of the Spanish proposal killed the projected anti-anarchist conference or international agreement.[35] This view fit in well

---

[29] British Ambassador Wolff, Madrid, reporting on his conversation with Moret, November 20, 1893, to Roseberry, London. FO 72/1928, PRO; Raymond Carr, *Spain 1808–1975*, 2nd edition (Oxford: Clarendon Press, 1982): 470.

[30] Foreign minister, Madrid to Spanish representatives abroad, December 11, 1893, OP, l. 2750, SFM

[31] Draft, FO to Ambassador del Mazo, London, December 13, 1893. FO72/1938, PRO.

[32] Rosebery, FO, to Wolff, Madrid, November 22, 1893. FO72/1923, PRO; *British Digest of International Law*. ed. Clive Parry. Part 6: *The Individual in International Law* (London, 1965): 70.

[33] Draft note from Rosebery to del Mazo, December 13, 1893. FO72/1973. Rosebery's reply to the Spanish proposal closely followed the recommendations of the Home Office. (Minute, initialed by Lushington, December 8, 1893. Home Office [cited hereafter as "HO"] 45/10254/x3650/8), PRO.

[34] Docket Sheet notes, November 28–December 1, 1893, FO 72/1938, PRO; Deym, London, to Kálnoky, Vienna, December 13, 1893. N. 37.E. PA. XL.Interna. Liasse XXVII, HHStA.

[35] "Espagne—Anarchistes—Entente internationale," *Revue géneral de droit publique* 1 (1894): 58; Alcide Darras, *Repertoire de droit international privè et de droit penal international*, 428; "Chronique," *Journal du droit international privè et de la jurisprudence comparée*

with the European mainland's stereotype of a selfish Britain that assured its own impunity from bomb attacks by offering anarchists an asylum that they exploited by venturing forth to assault the population and rulers of the continent.[36] A contemporary cartoon in a German magazine depicted a complacent Queen Victoria as a brooding hen sitting atop a nest swarming with little "anarchist crocodiles" about to swim across to the continent to perpetrate various misdeeds.[37] The construction of this stereotype had long preceded the deeds of the anarchists and was not without some basis in fact. Orsini's attack on Napoleon III had been plotted in England and some of the bombs he used had been manufactured by a British engineer in Birmingham.[38] In December 1893 French Premier Casimir-Périer told the Austrian ambassador that Britain was the place "where the anarchists find today their principal refuge and where the laws and customs oppose the employment of police measures suitable for purging that country of the anarchist leprosy."[39] The anarchists themselves seem to have cherished this vision of a benevolent Britain, despite the British authorities' occasional act of harsh repression. In the late fall of 1893 placards, supposedly printed in London, were posted in Paris and Orleans declaring "England alone has been spared on account of her hospitality to the anarchists."[40]

The diplomatic archives dispel the notion of a British veto single-handedly killing the proposed anti-anarchist agreement. Certainly some countries were hesitant to adhere to the Spanish proposal unless London agreed to it as well. During initial discussions, Francesco Crispi, the Italian prime minister, accepted the Spanish proposal in principle, but delayed an official response since the Spanish plan might be modified or even lapse due to rumored British opposition.[41] When London's

(1906), 770–771; Ulrich Linse, *Organisierter Anarchismus im Deutschen Kaiserreich von 1871* (Berlin: Dunker and Humbolt, 1969): 25, cites Swiss and English opposition as especially important in causing the agreement to miscarry.

[36] Liang, *Modern Police*, 173; Porter, *Vigilant State*, 111; the *Daily Graphic*, August 11, 1900, noted: "The common cry that we permit London to be the hatching ground for Anarchist plots."

[37] *Kladderadatsch*, August 26 1894, reprinted in Porter, *Vigilant State*, following 144. The Austrian ambassador to Britain shared *Kladderadatsch*'s point of view. In a report dated July 26, 1894, Graf Wydenbruck wrote Austrian Foreign Minister Kálnoky that it was an "indisputable fact" that London was the headquarters of European anarchism and the place of refuge of those who committed propaganda by the deed. PA, XL. Interna Liasse XXVI, f. 108, HHStA.

[38] Packe, *Orsini*, 288–290.

[39] Hoyos, Paris, to Kálnoky, Vienna, December 14, 1893. PA XL, Interna XXVII, HHStA.

[40] See HO docket sheet dated December 1, 1893. HO 144/545/55176/5, PRO.

[41] Report of the Austrian ambassador to Rome, Baron Bruck, December 18, 1893, to the Austrian foreign ministry. tel. n. 318; Bruck to Austrian Foreign Minister Kálnoky, Rome, December 29, 1893. HHStA. PA XL. Interna XXVII, 33; 62.

refusal was confirmed, Rome backpedaled even from this tepid support, merely assuring Madrid that it would "simply study the proposition."[42] Ironically, given Crispi's support within seven months for draconian legislation aimed at the anarchists and his wholesale repression of the left in September 1894 without distinguishing anarchist from non-anarchist, during conversations at this time with the Spanish and Austrian ambassadors he expressed concern over the difficulty in establishing the difference between political and anarchist crimes.[43] These considerations apparently outweighed Crispi's earlier desire, expressed three and a half years before to the Austrians following an apparent assassination attempt, for an international anti-anarchist agreement.[44]

Nonetheless, despite Italian reservations and the British refusal, Spain continued to push for an agreement. On December 18, when the Spanish ambassador to Italy asked Madrid if it intended to abandon the idea of an anti-anarchist understanding, the Spanish foreign minister wired: "Far from abandoning I am continuing negotiations over the international accord." Moret also expressed his frustration, noting, "I cannot tell Your Excellency whether all the continental powers will agree to an exchange of ideas on this subject. Everyone seems at the same time disposed to and indecisive."[45] On December 12, Austria became the first country to accede to the Spanish initiative, at least in principle, and it was followed by Portugal and Russia. Belgium, Italy, Sweden, and Denmark also agreed, but contingent on the positive attitude of the Great Powers.[46] Germany also agreed in principle, but with some delay

---

[42] Austrian ambassador Bruck quotes Italian Foreign Minister Blanc. Bruck to Austrian Foreign Minister Kálnoky, Rome, December 29, 1893. HHStA. PA XL. Interna XXVII, f. 62.

[43] Telegram copy, Rascon, Rome, to Spanish foreign ministry, December 12, 1893. SFM. L. 2750. Bruck to Austrian foreign ministry, December 18, 1893, tel. n. 318. HHStA. PA XL. Interna XXVII, 33.

[44] Copy, confidential report, Ambassador von Bruck, Rome, May 20, 1890. PA. Informationsbüro (hereafter cited as IB) 1890. GZ 16/1481, HHStA. On September 13, 1889, Emilo Caporali threw a rock at Crispi, injuring the prime minister. Subsequently Crispi remained consistent in his skepticism regarding an international anti-anarchist agreement. Writing for the *Daily Mail* (November 30, 1898) about the upcoming Rome Anti-Anarchist Conference, Crispi opined that "it is doubtful if the conference will have practical results... Anarchism is a grave social disease for which I can see no remedy save in assiduous and conscientious effort on the part of every Government to eliminate at home the causes of those crying social inequalities which fertilise and develop the sad and cruel germs of social destruction."

[45] Rascon, Rome, to foreign ministry, Madrid, and foreign ministry, Madrid, to ambassador, Rome, December 18, 1893. OP, l. 2750, SFM.

[46] Tel. Valera, Vienna, to foreign ministry, Madrid, December 12, 1893; foreign ministry, Madrid, to Spanish embassy, Paris, December 18, 1893. OP. l. 2750, SFM. A memorandum entitled "*Anarquistas*," setting forth the situation as of January 8, 1894, provides

and contingent on the answer of France, whose participation Berlin considered "indispensable."[47]

It was the refusal of France to adhere to the Spanish initiative that doomed Spain's proposed agreement. In an encoded telegram, the Spanish foreign ministry wired its minister in Brussels on December 20, 1893: "I hope [for] a decisive answer from France. On its decision depends whether the negotiations are formally carried out."[48] On December 21 the French prime minister told Ambassador Fernando León y Castillo that the French council of ministers had decided that an anti-anarchist accord was "impossible" and unnecessary. Like the British, the French were unwilling to propose to their Chamber of Deputies legislation resulting from an international accord. Moreover, France did not see the necessity of new agreements since a *de facto* accord already existed between Spain and France by which the police of the two countries communicated to each other all types of information regarding the repression of anarchism.[49]

Why did the Spanish initiative of 1893 fail? In the candid assessment of the Austrian representative to Berlin, it was because Spain had given no precise or concrete information on either the contents of the anti-anarchist proposal it intended to suggest or the methods of implementing it. "Even the opening pourparlers completely lacked a concrete kernel."[50] The Spanish attempt to achieve the widest possible consensus by making deliberately vague proposals, which would hopefully attract even the skittish British, had therefore boomeranged. In the harsh opinion of the Austrian foreign minister "the Spaniards... an impractical people... had, as usual, 'made a mess of it.'"[51]

Italian policy, 1892–1896

Italy, like Spain, found it difficult to forge a successful response to anarchist terrorism and flip-flopped in its commitment to international policing, whether that be in cooperation with other states or with its own agents.

an overview of the positions of the different European states. OP, l. 2750, Parte General 1892–1898, SFM.
[47] See Austrian Ambassador Szögyény's account of Germany's policy. Szögyény, Berlin, to Kálnoky, Vienna, December 23, 1893, HHStA. PA XL. Int. XXVII. 48–49. Berlin believed that the Spanish initiative would come to no practical result.
[48] OP, l.2750, SFM.
[49] Leon y Castillo, Paris, to foreign minister, Madrid, December 21, 1893. OP, l.2750, SFM.
[50] Vélics, Berlin, to Kálnoky, Vienna, no. 30.B, August 4, 1894, XL. interna XXVII. f. 158, HHStA. The Swiss, who feared opposing France, also objected to the Spanish proposal's lack of clarity. Conseil Fédéral minutes, January 9, 1894, DDS, 4:274.
[51] Edmond Monson, Vienna, to Rosebery, London, February 20, 1894. FO 7/1213, PRO.

Plagued by mounting political, economic, and financial difficulties, in the early 1890s the Italian government soured on the idea of policing subversives through Italian police officers and confidents assigned to foreign countries. In the summer of 1893, the young, dynamic new prime minister, Giovanni Giolitti, who was committed to improving relations between the laboring people, their organizations, and the government, and also determined to maintain such basic civil liberties as the right to associate, ordered a reduction of funding for policing abroad. Beginning July 1, 1893, Rome reduced the funding for Sernicoli's "public security" expenses in Paris by more than 42 percent, from 350 to 200 lire monthly. The foreign ministry explained to the Italian embassy in Paris that, according to Giolitti, this reduction was necessary:

for reasons of economy, and having regard to the very few [*pochissime*] interactions that the subversive parties and their adherents presently have with their comrades in France, and especially in Paris.[52]

Earlier in June Giolitti had told the Foreign Ministry that he also wished to suppress the secret service accounts at some consulates, such as those in Corfu, Athens, Alexandria (Egypt), Algiers, and Lyon. "This was because experience has not demonstrated that the utility of the service corresponded to the size of the expense, nor was there any necessity for establishing a permanent police service abroad."[53] Giolitti justified a reduction of secret service expenses in Geneva because the cantonal government was less friendly to subversives than it used to be and therefore many had gone elsewhere.[54] When Pietro Rosano, a close friend as well as undersecretary at the interior ministry, suggested a rather creative method of fighting anarchists, i.e., providing them money to facilitate their departure for America (in this case, of two "socialist anarchists"), Giolitti was typically practical and wryly humorous in his reply. "It seems to me a bad system to pay for the anarchists' trip since that way whoever wants to emigrate will begin to affiliate with the anarchist sect."[55]

Crispi, Giolitti's successor as prime minister (December 1893–March 1896), reversed his policies, reinstituting the secret service expenses that had been cut back.[56] In personality and life experience, Crispi was Giolitti's opposite. Born in Sicily in 1818, he was twenty-four years

---

[52] Malvano, foreign ministry, Rome, to Ambassador Ressman, Paris, June 20, 1893. PI, b. 27, IFM.

[53] Giolitti to foreign minister, June 1, 16, and 20, 1893. PI, b. 22, IFM.

[54] Giolitti, interior ministry, to foreign minister, Rome, June 1, 1893. IFM. PI, b. 22.

[55] Rosano, Rome, to Giolitti, Cavour, January 7, 1893, no. 156, and Giolitti, Cavour, to Rosano, January 1893, no. 157. *Quarant'anni di politica italiana. Dalle carte di Giovanni Giolitti.* (Milan: Feltrinelli, 1962): 1:121.

[56] DGPS to foreign minister, Rome, March 10, 1894. PI, b. 24, IFM.

older than his northern Italian predecessor. Crispi had conspired with Garibaldi in 1860 to launch the semi-clandestine expedition to liberate the south from Bourbon rule. A former plotter himself, he was highly suspicious of anarchist, socialist, and others' plots to overthrow the state that he had been so instrumental in creating. Besides spending more on secret service expenses, he also sent out more agents. For example, in March 1894, at Monaco's request, he agreed to post a confidential informant (although not a policeman) to watch over the Italian anarchists residing in the principality. Monaco paid all expenses.[57]

In January 1894, the Italian foreign ministry's reply to a Turkish request for information about Italian policing abroad shows us what it was like at the beginning of Crispi's second term in office. The memorandum forwarded to Constantinople declared that, while no special surveillance service existed for foreign anarchists, Italian anarchists who had fled abroad were watched by "special secret agents" attached to Italian embassies and consulates. These secret agents were to enter into relationships with the anarchists in order to monitor their movements and thwart their plots. They were to pass on any information they discovered to Italian diplomats who in turn would immediately inform the Italian foreign ministry. If the anarchist plots regarded foreign states, then the Italian government would inform them of these matters. If their projects involved Italy, then the foreign minister would immediately notify the interior minister so that he could take all necessary steps "that the law allows." The names, distinguishing features, and deeds of the anarchists under surveillance were to be registered in the archives of the foreign ministry and, in so far as they regarded Italian internal security, in the archives of the interior ministry.[58]

Four months later, on May 25, 1894, accessibility to information on the anarchists and others was dramatically increased with the creation inside the interior ministry's General Directorate of Public Security of a centralized service that systematically compiled personal files on "members of the subversive parties."[59] In 1896 these records were famously denominated "The Central Political File" (*Casellario politico centrale*). The head of public security described the Central Political File as a

---

[57] General directorate of public security to foreign minister, Rome, February 25, 1894 and March 31, 1894, PI, b. 24, IFM.

[58] Mss. *Promemoria for the Turkish government on the International Police Service in the Kingdom of Italy*, January 20, 1894, PI, b. 24, IFM. Printed in Ruggeri, "Polizia Internazionale," 154.

[59] Giovanna Tosatti, "Il Ministero degli interni: le origini del Casellario politico centrale." In *Le reforme crispine: Amministrazione statale* (Milan: Giuffrè, 1990): 462.

filing system having for its purpose the surveillance of the anarchists and dangerous affiliates of other parties ... on the filing cards are also transcribed all the information that this Ministry succeeds in obtaining on how the anarchists, especially, operate abroad.[60]

Although many of these records were later destroyed, one researcher estimates that for the years 1894–1896 a little over 48 percent of the files of "dangerous subversives" were classified as anarchists, a slightly smaller percentage as socialists, and the rest as "revolutionary republicans."[61] To speed up even further the often-cumbersome process of communicating information about subversives, on June 7, 1894, the foreign minister authorized Italy's diplomatic representatives abroad to correspond directly with the public security chief.[62] In November a secret code, K3, was created for use in telegrams dealing with international policing.[63]

At some point in 1894, presumably prior to the creation of the Central Political File, Crispi also instituted a "special" office within the General Directorate to receive and dispense information both at home and abroad regarding dangerous subversives. This *Ufficio riservato*, or Confidential Bureau, as it eventually came to be called, coordinated the efforts of the Italian authorities in investigating and repressing political crime, although little has been written about its exact nature and composition.[64]

In 1894 Italian Prime Minister Crispi also proposed a sweeping series of anti-anarchist laws. Parliament, frightened by continuing anarchist *attentats* in Italy, Spain, and France – particularly by the assassination of French President Carnot – passed them on July 19. The first law punished the criminal use of explosives, and while it did not specifically use the word "terrorism," included the comparable phrase "to incite public fear" (*incutere pubblico timore*).[65] Another law penalized instigating others to such crimes via the press and inciting hatred between the social classes in a manner dangerous to public peace. Crispi's most notorious anti-anarchist law was a temporary measure lasting a year and a half (but

---

[60] Leonardi, DGPS, Rome, to foreign minister, September 17, 1900, PI, b. 35, IFM.

[61] Tosatti, "Il Ministero degli interni," 466–467.

[62] Ruggeri, "Polizia Internazionale," 157.

[63] Sensales, DGPS, Rome, November 8, 1894 to foreign ministry; foreign ministry, Rome, to DGPS, confidential, November 14, 1894, PI, b. 36, IFM.

[64] The first veiled reference to this new bureau is in Giuseppe Sensales, "L'anagrafe di polizia," *Nuova Antologia* 177 (1901): 246–247. Canali, *Le spie del regime*, 9, 13. At least until 1906 correspondence regarding anarchists was sent to the "gabinetto," the office or bureau, of the DGPS, rather than the *Ufficio riservato*. For example, Consul General Testa, Rosario (Argentina) to MI, DGPS (Gabinetto), Rome, December 24, 1906. Serie P, politica, f. 47, IFM. By February 1907 the correspondence of the DGPS is on stationary with "Ufficio riservato" listed as the address (February 18, 1907, Leonardi, MI, DGPS. *Ufficio riservato*, to foreign ministry, Rome. PI, b. 47, IFM.

[65] Eugenio Floren, *Trarrato di diritto penale*, 2:158.

revived between July 17, 1898, and June 30, 1899) that made it easier for the government to forcibly detain people on islands off the coast of Italy and to dissolve associations and meetings aimed at subverting the social order through violent acts (*vie di fatto*). As a result of this law 3,021 suspected subversives were rounded up by the police and sent to remote islands such as the Tremiti in the Adriatic and the Lipari north of (and Pantelleria south of) Sicily. Some historians have viewed these laws as directed more against the socialists than the anarchists but they fail to see them in the context of international panic over anarchist *attentats* or note the testimony of contemporaries. Ultimately Crispi exploited the laws to crack down on socialists and anarchists alike, but this does not deny their original anti-anarchist nature.[66]

Germany and anti-anarchist policing

While Italy was absorbed in its own domestic troubles and therefore eschewed a leading European role, the cautious stance of the much more powerful and stable German Empire deserves explanation since it helps us understand why no international anti-terrorist agreement was reached in 1893–1894. After Bismarck's departure from office in 1890, German political leaders proved unwilling for the country to take a leading role in the fight against "subversion," as it had done, for example, when the Paris Commune emerged in 1871. At the time of the Spanish proposal in late 1893, Prime Minister Leo von Caprivi concluded that it was undesirable for Germany to assume the initiative. This was, first of all, because of the refusal or at least half-hearted attitude of various Great Powers, namely Britain, France, Italy and Russia, to take a stand on this issue. Second, it was inadvisable to direct the attention of the "subversive elements" against Germany when, thanks to Germany's "healthy institutions," the subversives were only imperiling the "Latin" states.[67] Berlin wished Paris, in particular, to take the lead and, as Foreign Minister Marschall told the British ambassador, was irritated

that the French [news]papers had recently been attributing various apocryphal utterances to the [German] emperor, to the effect that Draconian measures must

---

[66] See Giovanni Rosadi, *Del domicilio coatto e dei delinquent recidivi* (Florence: Bocca, 1900), 99; Richard Bach Jensen, *Liberty and Order: The Theory and Practice of Italian Public Security Policy, 1848 to the Crisis of the 1890s* (New York: Garland, 1991): 85–92.

[67] See the memo of Foreign Minister Bülow to Reichschancellor Hohenlohe-Schilingsfürst, Berlin, June 22, 1898, in which Bülow reviewed past German policy regarding international action toward the anarchists. German Central State Archive (Potsdam) (hereafter abbreviated as GCSAP). Alte Reichskanzlei. Justizachten: Bekämpfung der Umsturzbestrebungen. 755/4. folio 65 (microfilm n. 12155/56).

be adopted towards the anarchists, and it might be the wish of the French to shelter themselves by allowing the idea to spread that if international repressive measures were adopted the initiative had come from here [i.e., Berlin].[68]

Purely domestic considerations also disinclined and inhibited the Caprivi government from playing a leading role. Almost from the moment of his appointment as imperial chancellor in 1890, Caprivi had been forced to battle against the intrigues of ultra-conservatives and reactionaries who looked for, and often found, support in the views of the youthful kaiser, Wilhelm II. A moderate conservative of courage and integrity who was not afraid to stand up to the volatile and headstrong Wilhelm, General Caprivi refused to countenance extreme policies that threatened to overturn the German constitution and possibly lead to a public revolt, if not indeed a revolution. Therefore when in November 1893 the kaiser suggested to Caprivi the need for special legislation against anarchism, the chancellor proceeded with caution.[69]

On November 26, 1893, the kaiser and Caprivi received letters attached to explosive devices mailed from Orleans, France, perhaps the first anarchist use of letter, or parcel, bombs (although the sending of such bombs goes back at least to the eighteenth century).[70] These were detected and disarmed but their perpetrators remained unidentified. According to the Spanish ambassador, the bombs "produced momentarily an intense impression and indignation in all classes of this society." Public opinion concluded that they must be the product either "of some crazy person or an anarchist."[71] Despite this and a couple of other mysterious explosions during 1893, a reign of anarchist terror never agitated German cities during the 1890s in the way it did Paris, Barcelona, and Rome. Nonetheless after the murder of President Carnot and the kaiser's renewed demands, the chancellor felt compelled to draft legislation exacerbating penalties against activities that might promote violent revolution. But this "Anti-Revolution Bill" soon became the tool whereby such arch reactionaries as Botho Graf zu Eulenburg, minister president of Prussia, hoped not only to crack down on anarchism, but also to suppress the Social Democratic Party and prepare the

---

[68] E. Malet, Berlin, to Rosebery, London, December 16, 1893, regarding a conversation with German Foreign Ministry State Secretary Baron von Marschall. FO 64/1295, PRO.

[69] J. Alden Nichols, *Germany after Bismarck: The Caprivi Era 1890–1894* (Cambridge, MA: Harvard University Press, 1958): 333.

[70] Joachim Wagner, *Politischer Terrorismus und Strafrecht im Deutschen Kaiserreich von 1871* (Heidelberg and Hamburg: von Decker, 1981): 15; John C. G. Röhl, *Wilhelm II: The Kaiser's Personal Monarchy, 1888–1900,* trans. Sheila De Bellaigue (New York: Cambridge University Press, 2004): 501.

[71] Felipe Mendez de Vega, Berlin, to foreign minister, Madrid, November 30, 1893. OP, 1.2750, SFM.

way for the abolition of universal suffrage and perhaps for a reactionary *coup d'état*.[72]

While Caprivi seems to have understood the difference between anarchist terrorism and the peaceful expression of extreme opinion, whether that was anarchist or socialist, many German conservatives did not, including officials in the government and the kaiser himself.[73] An interior ministry memo from May 1894 quoted the views of representatives of the Prussian state government:

> To recognize a fundamental distinction between anarchists and social democrats is neither correct, nor practically feasible. The goal of both revolutionary Parties is the same, mainly the violent overthrow of the existing [order]. The difference exists only in this, that the anarchists admitted this goal openly, while the Social Democrats sought to deceive. The dividing line between socialists and anarchists is to be regarded as correspondingly fluid and social democracy as the breeding ground out of which anarchism grew again and again. From the outset, therefore, legal action limited to anarchism promised little success.[74]

The kaiser saw as little distinction between anarchism and socialism as the Prussian officials, and it was the failure to make this crucial distinction – or the even more fundamental distinction between those who practiced terrorism and those who simply held extreme opinions – that proved such an obstacle to obtaining broad international cooperation. The British and the French governments, in particular, since they were more reliant on elected parliaments than the German authorities, were more conscious of such distinctions and less willing to offend powerful constituencies on the far left or to limit civil liberties.

At the same time, Wilhelm II had genuine reasons to be concerned about his personal security and that of his family.[75] The Anti-Revolution Bill of 1894–1895 was not simply the result of cynical exploitation of chimerical fears, as Bismarck's 1878 anti-socialist law had been, but of real, or at least plausible, dangers. Bombings and assassinations were sweeping across much of Europe from the autumn of 1893 to the summer of 1894,

---

[72] Nichols, *Germany after Bismarck*, 339–340; John C. G. Röhl, *Germany without Bismarck: The Crisis of Government in the Second Reich, 1890–1900* (Berkeley: University of California, 1967): 112–113. Differences over the "Bill for the Amendment and Amplification of the Criminal Code, the Military Penal Code, and the Press Law," to give the Anti-Revolution Bill its formal title, were central to the crisis that led to Caprivi's resignation and dismissal in October 1894. Prince Hohenlohe-Schillingsfürst, who replaced Caprivi as Chancellor, revived the bill, which, although much amended, was voted down overwhelmingly by the Reichstag in May 1895.

[73] For the Caprivi government's moderate views, see Nichols, *Germany after Bismarck*, 33. For the kaiser's reactionary inclinations, Nichols, *Germany after Bismarck*, 338–343, and Röhl, *Germany without Bismarck*, 114–115.

[74] Reich ministry of the interior memo, Berlin, May 10, 1894, f. 175, GCSAP.

[75] Nichols, *Germany after Bismarck*, 338.

and the German public, as well as its kaiser, who worried about his wife and children, was very anxious.[76] In August 1894, the Italian embassy reported that the police had discovered in Berlin a "nest of anarchists," two bombs, and chemical substances for explosives. "It seems however that one is dealing with an isolated band, of little danger and without connections abroad." To Ambassador Calvi the reasons for Germany's immunity to "this dangerous [anarchist] agitation" (at least for the most part) was

not so much the high quality of the German police as to its social legislation, which on the one hand does not allow the formation of that substratum [*fondo*] of unemployed and misfits, from which the anarchists then emerge, and on the other, serves as a stimulant to emigration due to its very intricacy.[77]

To Chancellor Caprivi's credit, he sought to contain hysterical fears at home and avoid extreme policies there and abroad that would only play into the hands of his right-wing opponents. He therefore had little incentive to lead an international anti-anarchist crusade; nor, in fact, did he possess the means. During 1894 the Reich interior minister approached the foreign ministry with a project for increasing European police cooperation in the monitoring of "the anarchists and other social revolutionaries." The foreign ministry agreed, but wished to begin the project by linking together the various police forces of the constituent states of the German Empire, designating the Berlin police as the central office for coordinating this information exchange. But the south German states, such as Bavaria and Baden, refused to subjugate themselves to the Prussian capital, preventing the implementation of the plan.[78] The lack of a centralized police force together with Caprivi's determination not to stoke the fires of internal reaction therefore account for Germany's failure to follow in the footsteps of Bismarck and lead an international crusade against the anarchist menace.

Bilateral anti-anarchist police accords: 1894–1896

The failure to achieve an international accord in the winter of 1893–1894 at the invitation of Spain did not prevent a complex web of police agreements from being spun across Europe between 1894 and 1896. Indeed

---

[76] Robert Lougee, "The Anti-Revolution Bill of 1894 in Wilhelmine Germany," *Central European History* **15** (1982): 226; Nichols, *Germany after Bismarck*, 331–332, 339; Röhl, *Wilhelm II: The Kaiser's Personal Monarchy*, 606–608.

[77] G. Calvi, Berlin, to Foreign Minister Blanc, Rome, August 20, 1894. PI, b. 24, IFM.

[78] Foreign Minister Bülow to Chancellor Hohenlohe, Berlin, June 22, 1898. Reichskanzlei, f. 65, GCSAP. Bülow to kaiser, Semmering, September 13, 1898, Europa generalia 91, GFO.

the failed negotiations regarding the Spanish proposal may have laid the groundwork or at least prepared opinion for the later agreements. While the French had demurred at joining Spain and the rest of Europe in legislative action or a wide-ranging diplomatic agreement, in December 1893 they had clearly indicated that they would have no objection to increased police cooperation. According to a report by the Austrian ambassador, French Premier Casimir-Périer and the president of the Chamber of Deputies, Charles Dupuy, expressed the belief that the exchange of information about and closer surveillance of the anarchists might be very effective. The Austrians were delighted to hear this, since previously the French had provided little or no help in tracking down Austrian or Hungarian anarchists.[79]

During 1894 the wave of anarchist bombings and assassinations swept away the remaining reservations of most European governments – Britain once again being the chief exception – regarding new anti-anarchist laws and increased international police cooperation. France (April 29, 1892, December 12 and 18, 1893, and July 28, 1894), Denmark (April 1, 1894 and April 7, 1899), Switzerland (April 12, 1894), Spain (July 10, 1894 and September 2, 1896), Italy (July 19, 1894), and Portugal (April 21, 1892 and February 13, 1896) passed laws increasing the penalties for the criminal use of explosives, or in some cases punishing provocation in the press to commit murder and arson, and penalizing other actions that might conceivably favor anarchist propaganda by the deed, such as, in the case of France, the publication of trial records.[80] The Italian and Spanish legislators punished inspiring public fear (*timore*) or alarm (*alarma*). The Swiss law of April 12, 1894, appears to have been the first anti-anarchist law explicitly directed against "terrorism" since it stated that "whoever, with the intention of spreading terror [*repandre la terreur* or *schrecken zu verbreiten*] in the population or disturbing [*ébranler*] public security, incites to commit crimes against persons or property, or gives instruction for their [explosives'] preparation" would be punished.[81] The

---

[79] Count Hoyos, Paris, to Kálnoky, Vienna, December 14, 1893. PA. XL. interna XXVII. n. 96, D, HHStA. The Austrian Prime Minister, in consultation with the interior minister, arrived at views almost identical to those of the French leaders. In a memo to Foreign Minister Kálnoky, the Austrian leaders expressed their concerns about the difficulties of passing common anti-anarchist legislation, as well as the fruitful possibilities of international police cooperation. Vienna, January 22, 1894. PA. XL. interna XXVII. f. 77–78, HHStA.

[80] Florian, *Trattato di Diritto Penale*, 138–161; Loubat, "De la legislation contre les anarchistes"; Cristóbal Buñuel Zaera et al., *El asesinato de D. José Canalejas* (Madrid: Juan Perez Torres, 1912): 31–46.

[81] Florian, *Trattato di Diritto Penale*, 156; *Conférence internationale de Rome pour la défense sociale contre les anarchistes: 24 Novembre–21 Décembre 1898.* Confidential (Rome: Imprimerie du ministère des affaires étrangères, 1899) (hereafter cited as CIR): 145.

Swiss law would also seem to have been the only legislation that punished those who "furnished instructions" for the execution of crimes against persons and property. Presumably this would have included those who provided bomb-making instructions. As of December 1902, this law had yet to be applied.[82]

During 1894 Europeans reached the first of a series of formal agreements to exchange information between border police regarding anarchists. This was the result, not of bold central government initiatives, but of low-level suggestions being taken up by higher authorities and extended in scope. In mid-July a French police commissioner on the Franco–Italian border near Nice proposed to the local Italian police delegate that they exchange information on the passage and arrest of anarchists.[83] It is unclear whether this local French initiative, authorized by the prefect of Nice, had previously been decreed by Paris. The French government had disclosed in December 1893 at the time of the negotiation over the Spanish conference proposal (and reiterated in August 1894), that it was just this kind of police cooperation that it endorsed.[84]

In any case the Italian police official passed this proposal on to Rome with a recommendation for its approval. This led the director general of public security, the official ranking just below the interior minister and responsible for civilian police activity throughout Italy, to suggest to the Italian foreign minister that such cooperation be extended along the entire frontier. The Italian foreign minister therefore proposed that the Swiss and Austrians also be approached to arrange border accords.[85] The French (on July 17), the Austrians (on July 18), and, with some reluctance, the Swiss (on July 31), agreed to this information exchange between frontier police.[86] Interestingly, the French "insisted" that the Italians conclude an agreement with Berne, if necessary "forcing their [i.e., the Swiss] hand by citing the consent of France."[87] The Swiss feared that the accord would compel them to hand over expelled anarchists at the border into the custody of the *carabinieri*, the Italian military police. This would constitute a

---

[82] Florian, *Trattato di Diritto Penale*, 156; message, December 15, 1902, Swiss Federal Council to the Federal Assembly concerning a proposed law amending the Federal Penal Code of February 4, 1853.

[83] Tel. Sensales, Director General of PS, to foreign ministry, Rome, July 14, 1894. PI, b. 36, IFM.

[84] For the growing police cooperation between France and Italy, see Milza, *Français et Italiens*, 2:872.

[85] Telegrams nos. 10793 and 1699, Director General of PS Sensales and Foreign Minister Blanc, Rome, July 14, 1894, PI, b. 36, IFM.

[86] Foreign Minister Blanc, Rome, to Italian embassy Vienna and legation, Berne, July 19, 1894. PI, b. 36, IFM.

[87] Ressman, Italian embassy, Paris, to foreign ministry, Rome, July 18, 1894. PI, b. 36, IFM;

form of "disguised extradition" and would be against the law. Assured by the Italians that anarchism was no longer considered a political crime by any nation and that these measures would be "police measures conducted administratively and in private," the Swiss consented.[88]

The Austrians now wished to proceed one step further. They suggested to the Italians drawing up an agreement that would provide not only for the exchange of information at the border, but also for direct communications, bypassing time-consuming diplomatic channels, between *central* police organizations in Vienna, Trieste, and Rome. Such an agreement

would result in the double advantage that, on the one hand, the process of exchanging information could be done more promptly and that, on the other hand, this information could be transmitted immediately to the authority which exercises control over individuals professing anarchist tendencies and which, from then on, is in a position to judge the importance of each piece of news communicated to it, and to act accordingly.[89]

The Austrian minute therefore made the telling point that it was not just a question of obtaining more information quickly about potential terrorist actions (much of which would doubtless be of little importance), but that this information be rapidly *evaluated* at the highest level by authorities who had access to the broadest range of intelligence. The Italians accepted this Austrian addition and then turned to France and Switzerland with similar proposals.[90] Both acceded to the Italian suggestions, the Swiss, on September 25, 1894, with reservations. Subsequently, the Italians used the Swiss accord as their norm for all agreements on anarchist information exchange between central police authorities.[91] In the spring of 1896 Hungary, which as an equal member of the Dual Monarchy exercised sovereign control over its internal policing, joined the Italian police communications network, both at the local level (through the Hungarian-controlled port of Fiume on the Adriatic) and at the national. In the fall of that same year Belgium agreed to direct communications between the central police authorities in Brussels and Rome regarding the anarchists.[92]

---

[88] Peirolari, Italian Legation, Berne, to foreign minister, Rome, July 19 and 31, 1894. PI, b. 36, IFM.
[89] Copy of a minute from the Austro-Hungarian foreign ministry to the Italian embassy, Vienna, August 18, 1894. PI, b. 42, IFM.
[90] Italian foreign ministry to Italian ambassador, Vienna, August 30, 1894. PI, b. 42, IFM.
[91] Mss. letter, Visconti Venosta, Rome, to interior ministry, September 22, 1896. PI, b. 36, IFM.
[92] For Hungary, Sensales, DGPS, Rome to foreign ministry, March 22, 1896. n. 3044. For Belgium, mss. letter, Visconti Venosta Rome, to interior ministry, September 22, 1896;

On the other hand, Spain balked at Italy's request in August 1894 for "full" (*complete*) exchanges at "*regular*" intervals of information on each other's anarchist and subversive movements and their contacts internationally. Italy desired this "considering that in every country the adherents and centers of propaganda and of organization of the anarchist sect maintain relations with all their affiliates in other nations."[93] This passage illustrates how the pervading fear of a "Black International" was not just a figment of yellow journalism, but also was an idea deeply imbedded in official thinking. While the Spanish foreign ministry had initially accepted the Italian proposal, the Spanish interior ministry rejected providing regular reports since it claimed that in Spain anarchism had been mostly crushed and that investigations had not yet been able to uncover links between Spanish and foreign anarchists. It was willing to communicate information on the "ups and downs" (*alternativas*) of the anarchist movement as they occurred, and news and records (*noticias y antecedents*) of interest. This satisfied Rome.[94] Indeed, the Italians soon asked for and received reports on the anarchist movement in Spain and the means used to repress it (particularly as they impacted Italians in Barcelona).[95] One suspects that the true reason that the Spanish interior minister was reluctant to promise the *regular* reports that Italy so much desired was because its police was faulty and lacked reliable informers.

During this period, Germany, Austria, Switzerland, Saxony, and Bavaria also concluded agreements providing for more direct communications regarding the activities of the anarchists. In these efforts, Austria hoped to take the lead in tandem with the German Empire.

Directing Vienna's policies was Count Gustav von Kálnoky, the publicity-shy (he boasted that he had never received a newspaperman) Habsburg foreign minister who by 1894 had been in office for more than thirteen years.[96] An ultra-conservative aristocrat, he had been a keen

---

Imperiali, Brussels, to Visconti Venosta, Rome, September 15 1896, and Belgian foreign minister to the Italian Legation, Brussels, October 7, 1896. The latter document sets out the terms of the information exchange accord. PI, b. 36, IFM.

[93] Alberto de Foresta, Italian embassy, Madrid, to Moret, Madrid, August 31, 1894. OP, l. 2750, SFM.

[94] In a note dated September 25, 1894, the Italian ambassador prematurely thanked the Spanish foreign minister for his "adhesion to the [Italian] request made to procure ... regular news on the anarchist movement in this peninsula." The ambassador also informed the minister that while there were no Spanish anarchists in Italy, his government would keep Spain apprised of any "subversives plots" that might interest Madrid. Maffei [di Boglio] to foreign minister, Madrid. SFM, OP, L. 2750.

[95] Undersecretary interior ministry, to secretary of state (Madrid), September 21, 1894. The report on anarchism in Spain and the means used to repress it was forwarded on February 21, 1895. SFM, OP, L. 2750; González Calleja, *La razón de la fuerza*, 276.

[96] Joseph Redlich, *Emperor Francis Joseph of Austria* (1929; reprinted Hamden, CT: Archon Books, 1965): 429.

GRÓF KÁLNOKY GUSZTÁV.

Figure 1 Count Gustav von Kálnoky, Austro-Hungarian minister of foreign affairs, 1881–1895, and promoter of European police cooperation against the anarchists.
Source: Wikimedia Commons. http://commons.wikimedia.org/wiki/File%3AK%C3%A1lnoky_Guszt%C3%A1v_1898–8.jpg

supporter of the Three Emperors' Alliance as a bulwark against revolution. Despite his Hungarian name, Kálnoky was by birth a German Moravian. The German ambassador described him as "of medium stature, rather fat, and with a pudgy face. His outward appearance was not attractive, nor could his manner be called engaging... [His] rudeness to diplomats was notorious."[97] Dry and reserved, his stiff, military manner made his haughtiness all the more unbearable. Kálnoky usually kept a monocle fixed in his eye. He was also intelligent and hard-working, writing by hand many of his own dispatches, and his devotion to Catholicism and conservatism endeared him to Emperor Franz Joseph.[98]

The Austrian foreign minister had long been a supporter of multinational action against the anarchists. In 1891, Austria had been the only country to agree to Spain's proposal for an international entente against anarchism and in 1893 had been the first state to accede to Madrid's call for an international conference on the subject.[99] On July 28, 1894, Kálnoky presented his views on the current terrorist crisis to the minister presidents of Austria and Hungary. He noted that "the recent infamous deeds of the anarchists, especially the murder of the president of the French Republic, had recently brought into question the adoption of international measures against the subversives." Reports from the Austrian ambassador to Berlin indicated that Chancellor Caprivi believed that achieving international agreement on legal means to repress the anarchists was hopeless. An effective campaign against them would only be possible if there came about "a fundamental change in England's present unrestrained right of asylum." This still left open the possibility of each country on its own amending domestic legislation to protect itself against this social menace.

Kálnoky proposed, however, additional measures to "parallel" and complement these internal actions. He meant "police and other administrative provisions" that would serve to avoid time-consuming diplomatic action. If Germany and Austria, whose legislation was constructed on similar principles, could coordinate their administrative and legislative actions, this would not only be a big step forward in itself, but it could "exert a fundamental influence on the attitude of other governments."[100] In the meantime, Kálnoky said it would give him

great satisfaction, if from the Austro-Hungarian side effective measures would be adopted as a stimulus and as a basis for the increased protection of the State

[97] Arthur May, *The Hapsburg Monarchy, 1867–1914* (Cambridge, MA: Harvard University Press, 1951): 277.
[98] Bridge, *Habsburg Monarchy*, 150; *The Holstein Papers. 1: Memoirs*, ed. Norman Rich and M. H. Fisher (Cambridge University Press, 1955): 150–151.
[99] For 1891, see González Calleja, *La razón de la fuerza*, 270.
[100] Austria's law of May 27, 1885, *Anordnungen gegen den gemeingefährlichen Gebrauch von Sprengstoffen und die gemeingefährliche Gebarung mit denselben*, strongly resembled

and of the Social Order, and for an international understanding, as all parties call for.[101]

Responding at the end of August 1894, Austrian Premier Alfred Windischgrätz agreed to this initiative, suggesting as an immediate step agreements with neighboring states along the lines of the accord concluded with Italy in July, which had provided for regular, secret information exchange regarding the border crossing, surveillance, and arrests of anarchists. For a long time, Windischgrätz noted, the Viennese *Polizeidirektion* and Berlin's *Polizeipräsidum* had regularly exchanged information, and this relationship did not need to be changed. Comparable links between Vienna and the central police authorities of Austria's neighbors were to be recommended. The essential point was the concentration of intelligence in order to clarify the significance of any anarchist movement and proceed with the necessary rapidity. The prime minister also recommended the amendment of extradition treaties to allow the handing over of persons who, in order to alter the existing social order, had committed crimes against the security of persons or property or in order to abolish the entire political order.[102]

In a marginal note responding to the Austrian prime minister's memorandum, Kálnoky asked why the initial agreements should be limited to "neighboring states."[103] Nonetheless, he proceeded on October 19, 1894, to propose agreements on the Italian model with Switzerland, Bavaria, and Saxony. The latter two were of course member states of the German Empire, but, due to the decentralized structure of the German police (and Reich), on their own territories they retained control over border security.[104] By March 1895, Austria had reached agreement with both Bavaria and Saxony regarding the exchange, at the local and central levels, of information on the anarchists.[105] The Habsburg interior minister requested that the border

Germany's legislation of June 9, 1884. The Austrian law punished anyone who prepared, procured, held, or delivered explosive materials or devices with the intention to place in danger the property, health, or life of another. As in the German legislation, the death penalty was decreed if the penalized act was premeditated and resulted in someone's death. The public provocation to, apology for, and justification of the crimes comprised in the law were also punished, as was the failure to reveal plots utilizing explosives. Eugenio Florian, *Trattato di Diritto Penale*, 143–144; Loubat, "De la legislation contre les anarchistes," 310–311.

101 Copy of memo to both minister-presidents, Vienna, July 28, 1894. PA XL. Int. Liasse XXVII, HHStA.
102 Windischgrätz to Kálnoky, Vienna, August 22, 1894. IB. 1894. carton (hereafter, c.) 340, gz. 29, HHStA.
103 See Kálnoky's marginal comment on ibid.
104 Decree, Vienna, October 19, 1894, to Von Seiller, Bern, Prince Wrede, Munich, Count Chotek, Dresden, IB 1894. c. 340 gz. 29, HHStA.
105 K.K. minister of interior to foreign ministry, Vienna, March 22, 1895, memorandum n. 89. IB, 1894 c. 340 cz. 29, HHStA.

authorities be allowed a "free hand" to work out the details of the information exchange without this becoming part of an international treaty.

The Swiss, however, balked at cooperation between border police, but agreed to a direct exchange of intelligence between the Vienna *Polizeidirektion* and the attorney general's office in Bern. Although this only partly satisfied Austria's original request, the Habsburg minister of the interior recommended accepting the Swiss offer. This was because he realized that the number of detained and arrested anarchists in Switzerland was very numerous and past experience had shown the difficulty that the Swiss had in providing information about individual cases.[106] The problem was compounded by the fact that, unlike the Italians, Bavarians, and Saxons, the Swiss had no central police force to monitor the anarchists. This illustrates a central and often overlooked issue regarding the anti-anarchist campaign. With both Switzerland and, as we have seen, Germany, closer international cooperation in the surveillance of the anarchists required a reform, and especially a centralization, of national police forces. Many individual countries simply lacked the capacity to gather and distribute information about the anarchists without important structural changes in the organization of their police. A second major stumbling block for the Swiss, as for the British, was that they had long upheld the right of asylum for political exiles and were not eager to have their hands tied by an international agreement. Instead the Swiss preferred to judge the question of each anarchist on a case-by-case basis.[107] On March 22, 1895, Vienna informed Bern that it agreed to accept the limited police accord desired by the Swiss.[108]

While all of these agreements were a considerable accomplishment, Kálnoky's plans to make Austria-Hungary into the gray eminence of the anti-anarchist campaign failed. The German kaiser was enthusiastic for a frontal assault on the "revolutionary parties," but his government was not and gave only tepid support to Kálnoky's proposals. In October 1894, Kálnoky observed in a dispatch to the imperial and royal ambassador in Berlin that the degree of communications between the German and Austrian police had worked well for many years, but that the surveillance of the subversive elements

---

[106] Interior minister to foreign minister, Vienna, January 31, 1895. IB 1894. c, 349, gz. 29, HHStA.

[107] See the copy of the report by Busch, the German representative at Bern, to Chancellor Caprivi, July 12, 1894. Central State Archive, Merseburg (hereafter GCSAM; now in Berlin) Ministry of the Interior, Rep. 77. Tit. 2512 n. 4 bd. 1.

[108] Foreign ministry, Vienna, to Seiller, Bern, March 22, 1895. IB. 1894. c. 340 gz. 29, HHStA.

could still be improved.[109] In November, the new German chancellor, Prince Hohenlohe-Schillingsfürst, responded by agreeing that the surveillance of traffic along the Prussian-Austrian border had functioned well, and that for the moment this was sufficient and needed no further expansion.[110] The Austrian government drew up new anti-anarchist legislation, including an amendment to the 1885 act on the criminal use of explosives and a proposed definition of anarchism, and in great secrecy shared its proposals with Germany.[111] Unlike the Germans, the Austrians did not make the mistake of lumping together anarchists and socialists, but sought to make a clear distinction between the two. In 1894 Vienna issued its security forces an instruction on the surveillance of anarchists that excluded as "not belonging to anarchism...the supporters of Social Democracy or other social political doctrines."[112] Unfortunately the Austrians failed to make the even more vital distinction between violent anarchists and those who advocated extreme ideas in a peaceful fashion.[113] The legislation contemplated by Kálnoky was apparently never submitted to the Austrian parliament and it was not until 1909 that a proposed revision of the Austrian penal code sought to heap additional punishments on the anarchists, e.g., restricting their right to associate.[114]

Hungarian opposition also undermined Kálnoky's desire to make Vienna the hub or co-leader of the anti-anarchist campaign in Europe. In July 1895 the Hungarian Minister President Bánffy informed the Austrians that his country believed that those states with large numbers of anarchists should take the lead in proposing international measures, not Austria-Hungary. Moreover Hungary did not wish to change its laws in order to coordinate them with the anti-anarchist legislation of other nations. The only area in which Hungary was willing to cooperate was in the promotion of direct communications between the various European police forces.[115]

---

[109] Copy, foreign ministry, Vienna to Szögyény, Berlin, October 29, 1894. HHStA. PA XL. Int. XXVII. folio 242, HHStA.

[110] Szögyény, Berlin, to Kálnoky. No. 44E, November 10, 1894. HHStA. IB. 1894, HHStA.

[111] Windischgrätz to Kálnoky, Vienna, September 21, 1894. 927/MP; (draft) foreign ministry, Vienna, to Szögyény, Berlin, October 25, 1894; and Szögyény, Berlin, to Kálnoky, Vienna, November 10, 1894. n. 44E; for a draft of the revision of the 1885 law, folios 183–186, in PA. XL Interna Liasse, XXVII, HHStA.

[112] Liang, *Modern Police*, 163–164.

[113] For example, see the 1894 directive of the Austrian interior ministry to the country's public security offices. Liang, *Modern Police*, 163–164.

[114] Florian, *Trattato di Diritto Penale*, 2:143–144.

[115] Translation of memo, Bánffy to foreign minister Goluchowski, July 28, 1895. no. 1290. IB. 1894. K. 340, GZ. 29, HHStA.

After making a few tactless remarks on Hungarian policy regarding church–state relations that led to a political uproar, Kálnoky resigned as foreign minister in May 1895. This ended for several years Austria's efforts, to a considerable degree successful in so far as they regarded inter-police communications with its neighbors, to play a prominent role in the anti-anarchist campaign.

In August 1896, Emilio Visconti Venosta, the extraordinarily cautious and widely respected foreign minister and elder statesman of Italy, provided a trenchant analysis of the system of communications between central police authorities that Kálnoky had done so much to promote. Writing to the Italian minister in Brussels, Visconti Venosta noted that the accords for the exchange of information about the anarchists had been

in vigor for some years between Italy on the one hand and Austria, France, Spain, Switzerland on the other, and have always given good results promoting promptness and efficacy in the service concerned. The bases of the accords themselves are, generally speaking, the following:

I. The exchange of correspondence concerning the anarchists occurs between our General Directorate of Public Security and the central authority designated by the other concerned State.
II. Such an exchange is limited in absolute fashion to information about the anarchists, their sectarian plots, etc. etc.
III. It is understood that the accord is concluded in provisional fashion and under the qualification of an experiment.
IV. Any question that does not refer to information about the anarchists continues to be treated in the customary diplomatic fashion.[116]

The Austrians also attested to the efficacy of the recently constituted system of inter-police communication. Referring to a report dated November 8, 1895, emanating from the imperial and royal ministry of the interior, Austrian Premier Badeni pronounced the experience of the police treaty with Italy to be "favorable." This was important, since recent Italian government crackdowns on the numerous anarchists residing in Italy threatened to force them and their "dangerous activities" into the bordering Austrian crownlands. So far, luckily, this had not occurred, and instead the anarchists had fled to Switzerland, Belgium, France, and the United States, or, if from southern Italy, to South America. The Austrians were particularly pleased by the "excellent cooperation" of the Italian authorities in proving the falsity of a report that the anarchist Pietro Conti was planning to assassinate Emperor Franz Joseph.[117]

[116] Visconti Venosta, Rome, to Cantagalli, Brussels. (mss) protocol no. 31699/451. August 22, 1896. PI, b, 36, IFM.
[117] Badeni, Vienna, to Goluchowski, November 14, 1895. IB. 1894. K. 340. GZ. 29, HHStA.

Besides the efficacy of the police communication system, another noteworthy aspect of Visconti Venosta's confidential communication to the Belgians was the care with which the Italians sought to limit its application to the anarchists alone, rather than to a larger category of "subversives." This Italian statement, along with the regulations disseminated by the Austrian interior minister in 1894, belies in part the fears of those who saw the anti-anarchist crusade as simply a ruse for a more general crackdown on political opponents of all kinds. But their fears can only be partially discounted since police and governments often found it difficult to distinguish between anarchists and socialists and other social reformers, or even between anarchists and nationalists, and in some cases, these categories overlapped or were not clearly differentiated. Furthermore, not all Italian, not to mention European, governments were as enlightened as Caprivi between 1890 and 1894, or the Di Rudinì cabinet in 1896, whose policies were in reaction against the previous, increasingly despotic Crispi regime.[118] Nor did the relatively progressive Di Rudinì of 1896 retain his moderation after widespread rioting engulfed Italy during the spring of 1898. Instead, he came down with an iron fist on the "revolutionaries" who had supposedly instigated the riots, imprisoning "subversives" of all sorts, anarchists, socialists, and even intransigent Catholics. Russia was even less interested in making distinctions between violent terrorists and peaceful political opponents.

Argentina, Italy, and the anarchist menace, 1885–1898[119]

The inconsistencies and problems of the emerging anti-anarchist dragnet were demonstrated as well by Italy's collaboration with Argentina. Europe's economic and political difficulties at the end of the nineteenth century, the possibility of achieving prosperity in the New World, inexpensive transportation costs, and the era's liberal immigration policies led millions of people to cross the Atlantic. By 1895 Buenos Aires, soon to become the largest city in Latin America, had a population of 50 percent foreign born; the entire country was over 25 percent foreign born.[120] The largest number

---

[118] For Rudinì's remarkably enlightened attitude to the anarchists forcibly detained without trial by Crispi, see Richard Bach Jensen, "Italy's Peculiar Institution: Internal Police Exile, 1861–1914," in June K. Burton (ed.), *Essays in European History* (Lanham: University Press of America, 1989): 99–114.

[119] Much of this section is drawn from my forthcoming chapter: "Global Terrorism and Transnational Counterterrorism: Policing Anarchist Migration Across the Atlantic. Italy and Argentina, 1890s–1914," in Carola Dietze and Claudia Verhoeven (eds.), *The Oxford Handbook of the History of Terrorism* (Oxford University Press, 2014).

[120] Ronaldo Munck with Ricardo Falcón and Bernardo Galitelli, *Argentina: From Anarchism to Peronism* (London and Atlantic Highlands, NJ: Zed Books, 1987): 26, 43–44. Luis

of these immigrants came from Italy (49 percent), followed by those from Spain (19.8 percent) and France (9.4 percent).[121] By 1914, the nation's population was one-third immigrant, giving it the highest proportion of immigrant to native population of any country in the world.[122]

Some of the immigrants, fleeing political repression and harsh economic conditions in their home countries, were anarchists before they arrived in Argentina. After their arrival, the immigrants' difficulties in adjustment, economic exploitation, and political marginalization in a country dominated until 1916 by a small oligarchy provided fertile terrain for the further growth of anarchist ideas and organizations. Beginning in the 1870s, French, Spanish, and Italian speakers each formed anarchist groups. Errico Malatesta, the foremost Italian anarchist, traveled to Argentina where he lived between 1885 and 1889. In 1887 he helped the bakers of Buenos Aires organize the first militant workers' union. Other anarchist-dominated unions and organizations followed, as well as newspapers and public libraries. According to the calculations of the Argentine police, by 1900, 6,000 anarchists resided in the country, 1,500 of them in Buenos Aires. Of these the local authorities considered about 150, mostly Italians, to be "eminently dangerous."[123] Other estimates give much higher estimates of the anarchist population. Francesco Parrella, an Italian police inspector posted to Argentina, asserted that there were 7,000 anarchists in Buenos Aires alone, and most of these were Italians.[124] While Parrella may have wanted to inflate the numbers in order to keep his job, a German correspondent came up with an even bigger figure, alleging that, in 1900, 20,000 anarchists lived in Buenos Aires.[125] Whatever the exact figures, by the early twentieth century, the Argentine capital had become the greatest anarchist center in the world not only because of the large anarchist population, but also because of the amazing number of anarchist publications and social and political organizations, and because of the anarchists' pervasive influence over the labor movement.[126]

Alberto Romero, *A History of Argentina in the Twentieth Century* (University Park, Pennsylvania: State University Press, 2004): 18.

[121] Munck et al., *Argentina*, 26.

[122] Iaacov Oved, *Anarquismo*, 31. In 1914, "almost 1 million Italians and more than 800,000 Spaniards lived in Argentina." David Rock, *Argentina 1516–1982* (Berkeley: University of California Press, 1985): 166.

[123] See the copy of a report from the Italian Legation, Buenos Aires, to Saracco, premier and interior minister, Rome, confidential, August 22, 1900. IFM. PI, b. 28. This figure may well have been an underestimate.

[124] See Parrella's report to Minister Malespina, Italian Legation, Buenos Aires, January 20, 1901. IFM. PI, b.28.

[125] *Berliner Neueste Nachrichten*, September 19, 1900.

[126] For a comparison between Barcelona, the other formidable anarchist metropolis, and Buenos Aires, see Jensen, "Global Terrorism."

During the early 1890s, many of Argentina's anarchists fell under the spell of propaganda by the deed, and their periodicals exalted violence and the glory of dynamite. Interestingly, inflammatory words did not as yet translate into destructive deeds, and after 1895 more and more Argentine anarchists spoke out against individual acts of terrorism and in favor of mass action.[127] Involvement in organizing Argentine workers promised to yield greater benefits for the anarchist cause than throwing bombs.[128] In a speech given in Buenos Aires in 1898, Pietro Gori, a well-known Italian anarchist, pointed out how Argentine anarchists enjoyed greater liberty of thought and expression than their much persecuted brethren in Italy and Spain (and, by implication, less reason to resort to extreme measures of resistance and revenge).[129] Like Malatesta, Gori favored anarchist participation in the labor movement.[130]

While Argentine soil remained free of terrorism during the 1890s, it is noteworthy that two famous anarchist bomb-throwers, Auguste Vaillant (1861–1894) and Paulino Pallás (1863?-93), resided for several years in Argentina prior to returning to Europe to carry out their notorious deeds. Vaillant, already radicalized before traveling abroad, suffered from starvation wages and broken promises when he went to work in the interior of Argentina. Later he found employment with a French-language anarchist periodical in Buenos Aires that supported terrorism.[131] As for Pallás, who as a youth emigrated from Spain with his family, he apparently became an anarchist once in Argentina, where he worked as an apprentice typesetter. Pallás later moved to Brazil, where on May Day 1892 he began his terrorist career by tossing a small petard into the luxurious Alcantara Theater in Rio de Janeiro.[132] Since so little has been documented about their lives in South America, the connection that may have existed between these men's immigrant experience in the New World and their impulse to carry out vindictive acts in the Old against its more repressive authorities remains unclear. It may have simply been that Pallás and Vaillant's failure to find prosperity in "America" sent them back embittered to their European homelands, ready to take revenge for the dismal prospects of the working class.

A more instructive case may be that of Francesco Momo, an Italian emigrant who helped to found Buenos Aires's union of bakers. A

[127] Oved, *Anarquismo*, 55–59.   [128] Oved, *Anarquismo*, 64.
[129] Oved, *Anarquismo*, 109–10.   [130] Munck et al., *Argentina*, 49.
[131] Joseph C. Longoni, *Four Patients of Dr. Deibler. A Study in Anarchy* (London: Lawrence and Wishart, 1970): 85–87; Oved, *Anarquismo*, 56; Maitron, *Histoire*, 218–219; *Dictionnaire biographique du mouvement ouvrier française*, part 3, 14:265.
[132] Esenwein, *Anarchist Ideology*, 185; Giampietro Berti, *Errico Malatesta*, 190.

militant, but peaceful, labor organizer in Argentina, he became a terrorist in Spain, where in 1893 he allegedly supplied explosives for Pallás and certainly blew himself up trying to concoct an Orsini bomb.[133] Put more succinctly, Spain, not Argentina, made Momo a terrorist.

By no means did the Argentine press and government rest assured that the prospect of greater prosperity and liberty in Argentina would prevent the eruption of violent incidents like those in Europe and viewed with mounting nervousness the increasing flow of immigrants, some of whom harbored anarchist sympathies. On June 20, 1894 Argentina's chargé d'affaires proposed to the Italian foreign ministry that the two countries sign an agreement designed "to forewarn, reciprocally, against anarchists going onto the territory of the other."[134] If possible, the Argentines wanted to know the "distinguishing features" of each anarchist.[135] Presumably because of the recent attempt on Crispi's life and the assassination of President Carnot on June 25, Rome initially greeted Buenos Aires's proposal with enthusiasm. In a passage omitted from the final draft of his response, the Italian foreign minister even asserted that the Argentine proposals:

will serve me as the basis of study for those international accords that are already being aired between some European states and that perhaps, in a not distant future[,] will be translated into pacts expressed between all civilized nations.[136]

The Italian interior ministry soon threw cold water on the Argentine proposal, objecting that the proposed agreement would be "impossible" to enforce in a comprehensive fashion, given the widespread diffusion of anarchist doctrines, the "hundreds of emigrants leaving Italy for abroad at every departure of a steamship," and the emigrants' option of leaving their country clandestinely or via ports in France. Moreover, Rome had little direct interest in the expulsion of Italian anarchists from Argentina (after all, they might come back to Italy!).[137] The Italian minister in

---

[133] Pallás claimed that Momo supplied the bombs that he threw at the Captain General of Catalonia in September 1893. This may well have been a ruse to shield the real suppliers since Momo was already dead. Núnez Florencio, *Terrorismo*, 115; Osvaldo Bayer, "L'influenza dell'immigrazione italiana nel movimento anarchico argentino," in Bruno Bezza (ed.), *Gli Italiani fuori d'Italia: gli emigrati italiani nei movimenti operai dei paesi d'adozione, 1880–1940* (Milan: F. Angeli, 1983): 533.

[134] Mss. foreign minister, Rome, to A. Del Viso, chargé d'affaires, Argentina, Rome, June 25, 1894. PI, b. 28, IFM

[135] Italian Legation Buenos Ayres, to foreign ministry, Rome, July 31, 1894. PI, b. 28, IFM.

[136] Mss. foreign minister, Rome, to A. Del Viso, chargé d'affaires, Argentina, Rome, June 25, 1894. PI, b. 28, IFM.

[137] Interior ministry to foreign minister, September 15, 1894, PI, b. 28; copy, foreign minister, Rome, to Italian Legation, Buenos Ayres, September 21, 1894, PI, b. 28, IFM.

Argentina informed his superiors that, in the past, the Argentine police had failed to keep careful watch over the arrival of anarchists and had not been able to let him know when, or if, they subsequently departed.[138] In short, the Argentines might not be able to keep up their end of the bargain. This was a critical issue for Italy, since about 50 percent of Italian emigrants to Argentina later returned to their homeland, and many, whom the Argentines nicknamed the "swallows," returned to Italy after only a single season of helping to harvest the crops.[139] Instead of Argentina's comprehensive plan of surveillance, Interior Minister Crispi (who was also prime minister, since in Italy the two offices were almost invariably linked) suggested "accords ... for a reciprocal communication of all news that might come to the knowledge of the Italian and Argentine police regarding anarchists and anarchist plots."[140] These communications, if agreed to and without the necessity of a formal convention, might transpire directly between the police department in Buenos Aires and the General Directorate of Public Security in Rome.[141] In other words, an agreement similar to those already made between Italy and France, Switzerland, Austria-Hungary, Bavaria, and other countries in August and September 1894.[142]

Argentina accepted Crispi's plan but remained less than satisfied. In November 1897 Buenos Aires requested that the agreement be extended to involve directly the provincial prefects, especially those at Naples, Livorno, and Genoa, Italy's major ports. The prefects were asked to notify consular "agents of the Argentine Republic" regarding the "departure of persons affiliated with the subversive parties, whenever the occasion presented itself." Argentina would adopt analogous measures in regard to its ports, informing Italian consuls about the embarkation of subversives for Italy.[143] Surprisingly, the Italian foreign ministry ignored the objections of Giovanni Alfazio, the new director general of public security, and agreed to the Argentine proposal, which it hoped would increase the reliability and speed up the process of identifying dangerous subversives.[144] Included in the agreement, along with the anarchists, were all members of the "subversive parties." While these parties were

---

[138] Italian Legation, Buenos Ayres, to foreign ministry, Rome, July 31, 1894. PI, b. 28, IFM.
[139] Munck et al., *Argentina*, 25–26, 43.
[140] Interior ministry to foreign minister, Rome, September 15, 1894, PI, b. 28, IFM.
[141] Interior ministry to foreign minister, Rome, April 29, 1895. PI, b. 28, IFM.
[142] Foreign minister, Rome, to Italian Legation, Buenos Ayres, May 6, 1895. PI, b. 36, IFM.
[143] Mss. Visconti Venosta to interior ministry, Rome, November 30, 1897. PI, b. 28, IFM.
[144] Bonin, foreign ministry, Rome, to interior ministry, December 19, 1897. PI, b. 28, IFM.

not better identified, it is difficult to imagine them not encompassing the socialists. On December 21, 1897, the interior minister and premier, Antonio Di Rudinì, ordered the prefects to begin enforcing the agreement with Argentina.[145] While the reasons for the change in Italian policy are unclear, they were made against a background of increasing social upheaval and violence. In Rome on April 22, 1897 the anarchist Pietro Acciarito nearly succeeded in stabbing the king and in October disorders broke out in the capital ending in bloodshed. Rudinì erroneously blamed the disorder on the socialists.[146]

The concerns of the Public Security department (and earlier, of the Crispi government) proved accurate and the Italo-Argentine anti-anarchist agreement soon backfired, at least from Rome's point of view. At the end of March 1898 the Argentine authorities forbade Emilio Mei of Livorno, furnished with a regular passport, to disembark at Buenos Aires, and then arrested him, because the Italian police had identified Mei as an anarchist.[147] According to the Italians, Mei might have been an anarchist, but he was neither dangerous nor guilty of any crimes. Foreign Minister Visconti Venosta believed that the agreement with Argentina was "aimed only at facilitating surveillance but not at prohibiting the embarkation of the above mentioned Emilio Mei."[148] This violated

norms accepted universally, according to which States as a rule do not prohibit the disembarkation of citizens of another State and only expel them when they act in a manner that disturbs order or contravenes the laws of the country of which they are guests.

Ascribing to fanatical ideas or being associated with anarchist circles was not against the immigration laws currently enforced in the Argentine republic.[149] The foreign minister's defense of the rights of an anarchist Italian is more than a little ironic, given how often during the 1890s, especially, under the Crispi government, anarchists had been imprisoned or forcibly detained for their beliefs.

Subsequently the Argentinean courts ruled that the government lacked any legal authority to bar immigrants, and the police ordered that all anarchists arriving in Buenos Aires be granted free entrance.

---

[145] Rudinì, interior ministry, Rome, to the prefects of the Realm, December 21, 1897. PI, b. 28, IFM.
[146] Jensen, *Liberty and Order*, 155.
[147] Di Cariati, chargé d'affaires, Buenos Aires, to foreign ministry, Rome, April 3, 1898; mss. Visconti Venosta, foreign ministry, Rome, to Prince di Cariati, Buenos Aires, April 20, 1898. PI, b. 28, IFM.
[148] Ibid.
[149] Ibid.; copy, di Cariati to Amancio Alcorta, Buenos Aires, May 16, 1898. PI, b. 28, IFM.

Argentine Foreign Minister Alcorta noted bitterly that his government, unlike those in Europe, except for Britain, lacked the authority to expel, and once "affiliates of the subversive sects" had embarked, they "had to be considered as equals of Argentinean citizens." In Alcorta's personal opinion, therefore, the Argentine-Italian anarchist accord was of no "practical importance" and he was ready to denounce it.[150] In the end, Buenos Aires was forced to acquiesce in Rome's interpretation of the agreement.[151]

Spain, Europe, and the anarchists: 1893–1898

The efficient and effective network of bilateral agreements at the local, national, and international level served as a substitute for more comprehensive cooperation against the anarchists. But even in this restricted field Spain remained a loose wire. The difficulties it faced in confronting the challenge of anarchist terrorism were immense. Spain had more anarchists and fewer effective policemen per capita than any country in Europe, if not indeed the world with the possible exception of Argentina. After the assassination of President Carnot of France in 1894, most of Europe enjoyed a four-year respite from terrorism. But in the Iberian Peninsula the bombings and assassination attempts continued, most spectacularly with the bombing of the Corpus Christi procession in Barcelona in June 1896.

To cope with the challenge of terrorism, the Spanish lacked not only an effective domestic police force, but also consistent help from abroad. The French never developed the same kind of close cooperation with the Spanish police that they had, beginning in 1892, with the Swiss, and in 1894, with the Italian security forces. The Pyrenees, rather than an impenetrable mountain barrier, proved to be a sieve through which dynamite and assassins poured into Spain. This lack of cooperation was in all likelihood due to France's disdain for the incompetence of the Spanish police (e.g., in 1898, the Paris police prefect noted that "in Spain anarchists and simple republicans are thrown in the same pot and ... information provided by the Spanish police cannot be taken seriously").[152]

Since Spain could not usually rely on its own police for security against terrorism, Madrid not only allowed, but also pleaded for the stationing of foreign police on Spanish soil. By the mid-1890s Paris had posted a police *commissaire* in Barcelona to monitor the anarchists. In August

---

[150] Malaspina, Buenos Aires, to Canevaro, Rome, September 3, 1898, PI, b. 30, IFM.
[151] Mss. Malvano, foreign ministry, Rome, to Malaspina, Italian Legation, Buenos Ayres, October 8, 1898. PI, b. 30, IFM.
[152] Reported by Charles Lardy, the Swiss minister to France. Liang, *Modern Police*, 166.

1895, this *commissaire* offered to exchange information on anarchists with the Italian consulate. But the Francophobe Crispi government in Rome was suspicious of the French offer, instructing the Italian consul to cooperate merely on a case-by-case basis.[153]

The new coalition government in Italy that came in under the conservative Marquis Di Rudinì in March 1896 was much friendlier toward the French, and continued Crispi's cordial relations with the Spanish. In April 1896, at the suggestion of the Italian consul in Barcelona, Di Rudinì reversed Crispi's policy and agreed to "reciprocal exchange ... of information concerning the plots of the anarchists and facts relating to international policing" between the French *Commissaire* Thiellement and the Italian consulate.[154] In January 1897 Rome spontaneously forwarded information picked up by the Italian consul in Geneva on the plots of Spanish anarchists in that city. For this news, the Spanish showed themselves extremely thankful.[155] In August 1897, the Spanish foreign minister, the duke of Tetuan, asked for an Italian police functionary who could be placed on permanent assignment in Barcelona to keep a close watch on Italian anarchists in Spain.[156] The Italian consul general estimated that there were about a hundred of them living in Barcelona, more if one counted those who had been detained for years in the forbidding hill-top fortress prison of Montjuich.[157] In October 1897 the Italian interior ministry sent *Delegato di pubblica sicurezza* Francesco Petrilli to the great Catalonian port city, despite the fact that he spoke only mediocre Spanish and no Catalan, although fairly good French.[158] The latter ability helped when the consul put him in contact with *Commissaire* Thiellement so that they might "exchange on an equal basis services and assistance."[159] Nonetheless, the lack of Spanish created plenty of difficulties. Indeed, the language problem was to bedevil many European states in their hasty attempts to set up police systems abroad, given that most policemen lacked advanced education.

In February 1898 Petrilli was recalled, although not because of his linguistic deficiencies. His experience demonstrated that an effective anti-anarchist monitoring system could not be carried out easily or on

---

[153] Sensales, DGPS, to foreign ministry, Rome, August 13, 1895. PI, b. 36, memo n. 8325, IFM.
[154] Alfazio, DGPS, Rome, to foreign ministry, no. 4733, April 29, 1896. PI, b. 36, IFM.
[155] Italian ambassador to the foreign minister, duke of Tetuán, January 26, 1897. OP, l. 2750, SFM.
[156] Italian ambassador, Zaranz, August 31, 1897, to Visconti Venosta, PI, b. 36; Bonin, foreign ministry to interior ministry, September 9, 1897, PI, b. 36, IFM.
[157] Consul general, Barcelona, to foreign ministry, Rome, October 19, 1897. PI, b. 36, IFM.
[158] Ibid.   [159] Ibid.

the cheap. The Italian consul pointed out that working alone the Italian policeman would find it difficult to carry out his "quite delicate and dangerous" mission. He needed

to establish his own special office with an archive – registers – records – creating a file for every single anarchist, in a word, establishing a new secret service that might also serve as a basis and a guide for the eventual successor of Mr. Petrilli. In my view it is necessary that the [police] functionary could count on the help of some informers, at least two, one Spanish and the other Italian, chosen by the [police] delegate and who act under his complete responsibility and whom he pays according to services rendered.

This service would cost an estimated 150 lira a month. For his part, the consul was willing to put a room in the new consular residence at the policeman's disposal.[160] Due to severe financial constraints, neither the Italian interior nor foreign ministries were willing to allocate these additional funds; moreover the former now expressed doubts about the "practical utility" of the service. The government therefore decided in February 1898 to recall the police agent (after he had recuperated from three weeks of the gout), and make do with an informer working out of the consulate general.[161]

A policy that its neighbors found less attractive than Spain's hospitality toward foreign agents was its propensity to expel across its borders, without any prior notice, scores of both foreign and domestic anarchists. A shocking terrorist act, such as the bombing of the Liceo Theater or the Corpus Christi massacre, was often the occasion for wholesale expulsions. This practice particularly annoyed France. On January 8, 1894, the French embassy in Madrid and the Spanish foreign ministry exchanged notes regulating the expulsion of anarchists to each country, since the Franco–Spanish Convention of January 7, 1862, did not address this question. According to the understanding, only individuals of French nationality were to be expelled to France and France would expel only Spaniards back to Spain.[162] Despite this agreement, and Madrid's frequent attempts at enforcement, France continually complained that local Spanish authorities failed to obey it.[163]

[160] Ibid.
[161] Alfazio, DGPS, to foreign ministry, Rome, October 20, 1897, and February 5 and 18, 1898; Consul General, Barcelona, to foreign ministry, Rome, February 11, 1898. PI, b. 36, IFM.
[162] Memo, Sección de Política, foreign ministry, to interior ministry [*Gobernación*], Palacio March 10[?], 1894. OP, l. 2750/20; mss. minute, foreign minister to interior minister, Madrid, July 23, 1894, OP, l. 2750/2; French embassy to Moret, Madrid, July 19, 1894, OP, l. 2750/14, SFM.
[163] French embassy to Moret, Madrid, July 19, 1894, l. 2750/14; Subsecretaría Orden Público to foreign minister, August 10, 1894, l. 2750/4; French Ambassador Reverseaux to Foreign Minister Tetuan, Madrid, June 13, 1896, L. 2750/14, SFM.

A critical period for Franco–Spanish relations came in the aftermath of the Corpus Christi bombing. Unable to find concrete evidence identifying the murderer, the Barcelona authorities arrested 300–400 anarchists and others suspected of being sympathetic to the anarchists, including radicals, Catalan republicans, and anti-clericals.[164] Since the jails of Barcelona were filled to overflowing, many of the arrested were imprisoned in the Montjuich fortress overlooking the city. There police tried to extract confessions by resorting to horrible tortures. Prisoners were forced to go without food or sleep for more than a week. The guards beat them repeatedly with rods until their skin ruptured under the blows, or branded them with hot irons. Fingernails and toenails were ripped out and testicles crushed or tied off with guitar string until they atrophied. Due to these torments, at least one man went mad.[165] In a secret trial characterized by many illegalities, a military tribunal tried eighty-seven of the prisoners, sentencing eight to death and sixty to terms of from eight to twenty years of hard labor. Upon appeal, the highest military court reduced the number of death sentences to five and acquitted sixty-one, leaving about a score to face penal servitude and imprisonment.

The use of military tribunals to punish those accused of the homicidal bombings of the mid-1890s proved to be characteristic of Spanish policy. Even after 1900, the Spanish government continued to resort to military solutions for resolving the dilemma of anarchist terrorism. In 1894, the Spanish parliament passed new anti-anarchist measures punishing the illicit use of explosives, conspiracy, and instigation to commit such crimes either by word of mouth or by other means of publicity (and also banned associations aimed at executing such crimes). While the 1894 law left enforcement in the hands of the civilian judiciary, in 1896 the Cortes made the penalties of the earlier law severer, and handed over the more serious crimes to military tribunals. Initially temporary and only for Madrid and Barcelona, it was extended to all of Spain in 1897 and lasted until 1902.[166]

Following the Montjuich trial, Prime Minister Cánovas threatened to send those acquitted to the hellish penal colony of Río de Oro in the Western Sahara.[167] Eventually 195 people were ordered to leave Spain, some after

---

[164] Esenwein, *Anarchist Ideology*, 193; Núñez Florencio, *Terrorismo*, 58; Angel Herrerin, "España: La Propaganda por la Represión, 1892–1900," in Farré, *El nacimientote* (Madrid: Siglo XXI de España, 2008): 103–139.

[165] Esenwein, *Anarchist Ideology*,195; Núñez Florencio, *Terrorismo*, 95.

[166] Florian, *Trattato di Diritto Penale*, 2:153–55; Loubat, "De la legislation contre les anarchistes," 2:302–305; González Calleja, *La razón de la fuerza*, 274–283.

[167] Vizetelly, *The Anarchists*, 203–204. Although it is often stated that the sixty-one were in fact sent to Africa, Cánovas, under the pressure of both Spanish and foreign opinion, apparently demurred at taking this step. Instead the acquitted anarchists were expelled to France and England.

being detained in prison for almost a year.[168] Following a verbal accord between the Spanish ambassador in Paris and the French interior minister, the government of the Republic agreed to give asylum to a certain number of expelled Spaniards, as long as their records were free of any criminal convictions and their identities could be determined precisely.[169] In June 1897, the Spanish transported forty-five anarchists (the French government had expected twenty) to the border at Cerbére, on the Mediterranean coast. Instead of first ensuring that all the prisoners possessed proper credentials and then turning them over to the French police, the Spanish *Guardia Civil* (Civil Guard) "literally abandoned" the anarchists on French territory and immediately departed. The French warned that any new convoy of expellees would be barred from crossing the border.[170] At the end of July, when the governor of Barcelona wished to ship thirty-seven anarchists to Marseilles, the French government peremptorily refused his request.[171]

With the door to France closed, Spain turned toward Britain. In May 1897 a Spanish woman called on the British consul in Barcelona, inquiring whether a passport was needed for travel to England. The woman was a relative of Jaime Torrents, a prisoner detained in the fortress of Montjuich for his alleged participation in the Corpus Christi massacre. Consul Wyndham informed the woman that no passport was needed to visit Britain. He also wrote the captain general of Catalonia about her request, noting as well that he had heard that another prisoner in Montjuich had asked to be sent to England. Wyndham therefore requested "the names, [Bertillonage] measurements, and antecedents if possible of the prisoners who wish to go to England. These antecedents and facts are for the information of the Authorities in England so that they may take the measures they think needful."[172] Early in July the secretary of the civil governor of Barcelona "enquired from me [i.e., the British consul] what papers were necessary from any Anarchist proceeding to England, and was informed by me that immigration was free in England."[173] Understandably, the Spanish authorities concluded from this that they could now ship all their troublesome subversives to Britain.

[168] Royal Order, December 6, 1897, Madrid, in HO144/587/B2840c/97, PRO.
[169] Ambassador Reverseaux to Tetuan, Madrid, June 13, 1897. l. 2750/2, SFM.
[170] Ambassador Reverseaux to Tetuan, Madrid, June 30, 1897. l. 2750/2, SFM; Barclay, the British chargé d'affaires PRO, San Sebastian, to FO, July 23, 1897. FO 72/2036, PRO.
[171] Cos Gayon, interior minister, to foreign minister, Madrid, July 20, 1897; Novallas, chargé d'affaires, Spanish embassy, Paris, to foreign ministry, Madrid, July 22, 1897. OP. l. 2750/2, SFM.
[172] Translation, Wyndham to captain general of Catalonia, May 21, 1897 in dispatch no. 193, Ambassador Wolff to Salisbury, San Sebastian, July 30, 1897. FO 72/2035, PRO.
[173] Wyndham to George Barclay, San Sebastian, July 27, 1897 (included in dispatch no. 193). FO 72/2035, PRO.

On July 15, twenty-eight Spanish anarchists (and one Italian) embarked on the aging hulk *Isla de Luzon* bound for Liverpool.[174] Only after the ship's embarkation did Spain reveal the news to Britain, together with the deportees' names, ages, descriptions, and antecedents.[175] This lack of forewarning provoked consternation in the British government and questions in the House of Commons. The expellees had been required to pay for their own deportation, and the British presumed, in the words of the Home Office, that they would soon have on their doorstep a

considerable number of destitute Spaniards of Anarchist opinions. Such a proceeding necessarily throws upon the police of this country a serious addition of labour and responsibility, and probably entails also a considerable expenditure of the funds appropriated to poor relief.[176]

Since the British realized they had no statutory authority to forbid the entrance of the anarchists into England, they clearly saw the possibility, particularly in light of the French refusal, of becoming the depository for all of Spain's unwanted anarchists.[177] On July 22, the British chargé d'affaires informed the Spanish foreign minister that instructions were "now on their way directing me to protest earnestly against the action of the Spanish Government in sending to England without previously consulting HM Government a number of destitute Spaniards of anarchist opinions."[178] Fearing to antagonize the powerful British (to whom Spain frequently looked for diplomatic and other kinds of support), the duke of Tetuan immediately acceded to London's desires and avoided a "formal" protest.[179]

Unfortunately the government in Madrid often had difficulty controlling the behavior of the Spanish authorities in Barcelona, especially since that city was so often under martial law, and the military was committed to drastic and effective action against the anarchists, not to the niceties of diplomatic, led alone judicial, form. Reports surfaced that the Spanish government planned to liberate all the remaining anarchist prisoners, "giving them money with the intimation that if found in Spain after a certain date they will be deported to Fernando Po [in equatorial Africa, i.e.,

---

[174] Undersecretary of Interior Vadillo to undersecretary, foreign ministry, July 1897. L. 2750/2, SFM.

[175] The British documentation for this incident can be found in FO 72/2032, 2034–2036, 2048, PRO.

[176] Copy of Home Office letter, in dispatch no. 169 to Barclay. FO 72/2032, PRO.

[177] Home Office "Draft for Approval," July 1897, and note by C. Murdoch, July 19, 1897. HO144/587/B2840c/70 and 68, PRO.

[178] Barclay, San Sebastian, to Salisbury, London, July 23, 1897. FO72/2034, PRO.

[179] Translation. Tetuan to Barclay, San Sebastian, July 22, 1897, in Barclay to Salisbury, July 23, 1893. FO/2034, PRO.

Spain's Devil's Island]."[180] Since Britain was the only European country that could not bar their entry, especially if they entered as travelers rather than prisoners, the anarchists would of course flock there. The British ambassador fancied that this measure was "taken with the approval if not the instigation of the other [European] Embassies."[181] On August 4, the duke of Tetuan reiterated his country's promise not to send new convoys of anarchists to England, without prior consent, although by now it was clear that neither the French nor the British would give consent unless the anarchists were, respectively, of French or British nationality. At the same time, the Spanish foreign minister tried to bring to heel the author- ities in Barcelona.[182]

Meanwhile, the twenty-eight anarchists arrived in Liverpool to a warm welcome from local socialists and London anarchists who had journeyed up to the port. To help raise funds for the penniless arrivals, anarchist groups gave balls and organized benefits in the metropolis. Rather than being stereotypically wild young men from the lower depths of society, the English newspapers revealed that the anarchists were mostly mid- dle-aged and from "the well-to-do class."[183] Nonetheless, the Liverpool police closely watched the arrivals and escorted to London those who wished to stay in the capital. The Metropolitan Police, long accustomed to dealing with the large anarchist population of London, thought such precautions demonstrated an undue zeal, giving "'bold advertisement' and undue prominence to the wretched fellows."[184]

The typically low-key approach of the Metropolitan Police and its Special Branch contrasted with the widely publicized brutality of the Spanish and for many years proved more successful in dealing with the anarchists than the policy, or police, of any other country. The record of the British Foreign Office was more equivocal. Its persistent protests succeeded in stopping the flow of Spanish "anarchists" to Britain, but no thought was given to the fact that many, if not all, of these anarchists or anarchist-sympathizers were more fit to be received as political refugees who had suffered a year of unjust imprisonment and torture, than as dangerous people who would be drags upon society. Moreover the British

[180] Wolff, San Sebastian, to FO, August 5 and 6, 1897. FO72/2036, PRO.
[181] Ibid.
[182] Tetuan to Wolff, San Sebastian, August 4, 1897, included in Wolff to Salisbury, no. 199, August 4, 1897. FO72/2035, PRO; foreign minister to interior minister, San Sebastian, August 3, 1897. OP. l. 2750/2, SFM.
[183] See the unnamed English-language newspaper clippings forwarded by the Spanish embassy in London to the foreign ministry, Madrid, July 26 and 29, 1897. OP, l. 2750/2, SFM.
[184] William MacNaghten, Metropolitan Police, to Murdoch, HO, July 30, 1897. HO144/587/B2840c/83, PRO.

government failed to lodge even the most minimal protest against the horrifying human rights abuses in Spanish prisons. This was at the same time that a widely publicized protest campaign against the cruelties perpetrated in the Montjuich prison caused a stir in many European countries. Since a good number of the prisoners were well-educated writers, lawyers, and other professionals, they were able to draw up compelling accounts of their gruesome experiences and feed them to the world press. In England repeated mass rallies were held in Trafalgar Square where prisoners who had been released addressed the crowds and opened their shirts to reveal horrible scars and burned flesh.[185]

On June 4, some days after one of these mass meetings, Joseph Perry, head of the Freedom Anarchist-Communist Group and secretary of the Spanish Atrocities Committee, which included delegates not only from the anarchists, but also from the Humanitarian League, the Fabian Society, the Independent Labor Party, and the Social Democratic Federation, sent a letter to Lord Salisbury.[186] Based on a resolution passed by those gathered in Trafalgar Square on May 30, 1897, this petition called for a searching inquiry into the reported Spanish tortures and for allowing prisoners in Montjuich to go free to whatever country they wished, and not be forced – as was rumored – to go to Río de Oro. Permanent Undersecretary of State Sanderson noted on the back of Perry's letter: "The Spanish Ambassador would I think like us to answer that we understand that the Spanish government altogether deny the truth of these allegations. Would there be any objection to an answer in this sense?" A further annotation, initialed "S" in red ink, for "Salisbury," concluded: "Better simply acknowledge. It is not our affair."[187]

Simply acknowledging these petitions and inquiries, but remaining passive and indifferent to the terrible conditions inside Spain, continued to be official British policy. William Tallack, president of the Howard Association, received much the same treatment as Joseph Perry when he wrote Salisbury on June 9 asking if, "*Possibly* you might be able to invite the British Ambassador in Madrid to seek some *suitable* opportunity of using his influence to prevent, or lessen, the use of the Torture in Spain, *if* any such opportunity offers." On the same date, Tallack also

---

[185] Esenwein, *Anarchist Ideology*, 194–195; Núñez Florencio, *Terrorismo*, 94; Hermia Oliver, *The International Anarchist Movement in Late Victorian London* (London: Croom Helm, 1983): 114.

[186] For the work of the Spanish Atrocities Committee, see Oliver, *International Anarchist Movement*, 114, and Teresa Abelló i Güell, *Les relacions internacionals de l'anarquisme català (1881–1914)* (Barcelona: Edicions 62, 1987): 166–169.

[187] FO72/2048, Salisbury always initialed in red ink official documents submitted to him. A. L. Kennedy, *Salisbury, 1830–1903: Portrait of a Statesman* (London: John Murray, 1953): vii.

sent a second, private letter to Undersecretary Sanderson expressing his view that the anarchists were "fools" and that he would have nothing to do with the Spanish Atrocities Committee, but that there were too many eyewitness reports on tortures to think them totally untrue. "Where there is so much 'smoke' there must be *some* 'fire'." On July 13, the permanent undersecretary responded with a private letter mentioning another proverb:

if you throw enough mud, some of it will stick. I do not venture an opinion which [proverb] is the most applicable to the present case. Nor could I undertake to affirm that cruelties are never practised in Spanish prisons. All that can be said is that the Spanish Government and authorities utterly repudiate such malpractices and do not require – would indeed resent – exhortations to do so.

In a minute regarding Tallack's letter, Sanderson added "I have answered this[.] His uncharitable desire to convict the Spaniards of atrocities is rather amusing." Salisbury's "S" follows without comment.[188]

The failure of international opinion and the Spanish government to halt the torture of anarchists imprisoned in Montjuich and the abuses of the secret trials cast doubt on the validity of Spanish justice and displaced onto the authorities much of the public's anger against the anarchists aroused at the time of the Corpus Christi bombing. This was a grave development, since repression without justice rarely succeeds in destroying terrorism in countries that, like Spain, hold pretenses to being liberal, parliamentary, and, after 1890, democratic. While the British Foreign Office did nothing to restrain the barbarities of the Spanish police and military authorities, the Spanish government, undoubtedly influenced in part by public opinion both inside and outside Spain, eventually relented in its persecution of the anarchists. With no countries willing to accept most of the detainees under order of expulsion, the Madrid decided to liberate those still on Spanish soil. In addition, on December 6, 1897, it ordered that those who had already been expatriated, but who wished to return to Spain, might do so provided they gave notice to the authorities of the place where they wished to reside.[189]

The international question of anarchist expulsions, 1894–1898

Spain's actions in 1897 provide the most dramatic episode in the history of anarchist expulsion, but they were but part of a larger unresolved issue involving all of Europe and eventually the whole world: what to do

[188] Kennedy, *Salisbury*, vii.
[189] Translation of Royal Order, December 6, 1897. HO144/587/B2840c/97, PRO.

with unwanted anarchists? After anarchist bombs began to shake Paris in 1892, the French government responded by expelling increasingly large numbers of foreign anarchists across its borders into Belgium and Britain. Belgium responded by expelling them back into France or Luxembourg, or sending them over to Britain. Britain protested vehemently against its neighbors' policies, but incidents continued to occur.

In November 1894, after Belgium had deported a millionaire French anarchist named Henri Dupont and a destitute American lunatic to England, the British government strongly remonstrated.[190] The Belgians responded that their law gave deported persons the right of choosing to which foreign country they wished to go; while the Belgian authorities did their best "to so arrange expulsions as not to inconvenience neighboring countries,"[191] "these exportations were often the work of the local police of which the Central Government might not always be informed."[192] On another occasion Belgium's director general for public safety complained that "it is unfair to expect a little country like Belgium to be the receptacle of the overflow from others," and suggested that "all the Great Powers interested should … come to a common understanding on this subject, in virtue of which each should be responsible for the anarchists of its own nationality."[193] Belgium had reason for concern, since per capita, after Switzerland, more foreigners resided there than in any other European country on the continent.[194] In February 1897 repeated British complaints finally led Brussels to assure London that it would do its best not to send to England any persons who were not British subjects.[195]

Britain shared Belgium's, and one might add, Argentina's, worries about becoming an anarchist dumping ground, and felt even more vulnerable since, in the words of the Home Office undersecretary, "if other states possess and exercise the power of expelling anarchists from their countries and England alone does not, all the anarchists are bound to come

---

[190] Plunkett to Belgian foreign minister, Count de Merode Westerloo, November 11, 1894. HO144/594/B16627/7, PRO. See also Plunkett to British Foreign Secretary Kimberley, December 1, 1894. HO144/587/B2840c/sub. 52, PRO.

[191] Interview between Count de Mérode and Plunkett, in Plunkett to Kimberley, Brussels, December 1, 1894, HO144/587/B2840c/sub.51, PRO.

[192] Plunkett to Kimberley, Brussels, November 10,1894, HO144/594/B16627/7, PRO.

[193] Cited in Monson, Brussels, to Rosebery, March 23, 1893. HO144/587/B2840c/21c, PRO.

[194] Alfred Eric Senn, *The Russian Revolution in Switzerland 1914–1917* (Madison: University of Wisconsin Press, 1971): 4. In 1910, of every 1,000 residents of Belgium, 31 were citizens of another country; this compared to 11 in Holland, 17 in Germany, and 27 in France.

[195] Handwritten note addressed to Mr. Murdoch, March 17, 1897. HO144/587/B2840c/sub.3°, PRO.

to England."[196] The British dilemma illustrated a certain hypocrisy in the attitude of the continental states, which were happy to expel anarchists to Britain, but complained that the island kingdom was becoming a nest of assassins and bomb-throwers. As a stopgap measure, the British government had, in 1892, asked Robert Anderson, Assistant Commissioner in charge of Scotland Yard's Criminal Investigation Department (CID), to note anarchists coming into the country and post officers in continental and British ports to monitor departures and arrivals.[197] A more effective, indeed obvious, solution, barring the conclusion of an international accord, would have been for Britain to legalize the government's right to expel undesirable aliens. But Britain refused, clinging to its great liberal tradition and remembering the evils of the early nineteenth-century system of transportation to Australia and other places. In 1894 Sir Howard Vincent, a Conservative MP, asked in the House of Commons when the government proposed to limit the immigration of dangerous characters to England. Herbert Asquith, the Liberal Home Secretary, replied that "the extension of the power of expulsion on suspicion ... is apt to confound the innocent with the guilty, and to shift the burden and the danger from one country to another." Instead he asserted that

in our opinion, the direction which international efforts can most fruitfully take is to be found ... in a more constant and concerted interchange of information and combined action, both detective and punitive, between the Government and police authorities of the different nations of the world.[198]

On February 20, 1894, Count Kálnoky responded readily to Asquith's declaration, informing Ambassador Monson in Vienna that more communications regarding the anarchists were needed with the British.[199] The Austrians, and the continental states in general, were never quite satisfied with the British response to dealing with the anarchists. While on a case-by-case basis London, like Berne, responded willingly to inquiries and always tried to inform the continental governments of possible bomb plots and assassination attempts, it refused to provide systematic reports on the status and movements of anarchists living on British territory.[200]

---

[196] Godfrey Lushington, Home Office undersecretary, note on docket sheet, April 6, 1893. HO 144/587/B2840c/sub.3, PRO.

[197] Minute dated May 3, 1892, appended to Anderson to undersecretary of state, PRO, Home Office, New Scotland Yard, April 29, 1892; a memo by Anderson, September 19, 1894, refers to "officers of my Department stationed at Antwerp and Harwich." HO144/587/B2840c, PRO.

[198] House of Commons, February 19, reported in *The Times* (London), February 20, 1894.

[199] Porter, *Vigilant State*, 111.

[200] For example, see Rosebery, London, to Edward Malet, Berlin, secret and by messenger, January 13, 1893, regarding the alleged intention of the "group of International Anarchists in London" to assist the Parisian Communists in a revolutionary outbreak on January 15, 1893. FO 244/501, PRO.

While France had also resorted to expulsions, and irritated its neighbors Belgium and Britain because of them, its policy differed from Spain's since it expelled only foreign anarchists. Spain became one of the few countries in the world, along with Russia, that expelled its own nationals. This was indeed an additional confession of the weakness of the Spanish police and the government's lack of confidence in it. The Spanish authorities realized there was no guarantee that the police would be able to keep track of any anarchists who remained inside the country and thus turned in desperation to a general purging of the anarchist population, terrorist or not – and most Spanish anarchists were peaceful and harmless. The creation of a special Spanish anti-anarchist police in September 1896, the *Cuerpo especial de policia judicial*, did nothing to alter the critical situation of public security in the peninsula. A reform of the entire Spanish police system, the hiring of better, more well-educated personnel, the development of a better command structure, and improved technical and scientific methods (especially of identification) were needed to resolve the defects of the Spanish police, not another set of uniforms.

The British response to anarchism

If during the 1890s Spain was the country least successful in responding to the threat of anarchist terrorism, the most successful was Britain. Whether this was inevitable, due to luck, or, in some measure, because of the excellence of the English detective and the Metropolitan Police force with its anti-terrorist Special Branch is open to debate. Certainly British society and its political institutions seemed sounder than many of those on the continent and therefore less obvious targets for terrorist attack. Economic and labor conditions, while far from perfect (in 1893 unemployment reached 7.5 percent and, during strike riots at the mining village of Featherstone, the militia shot and killed two men), were better than across the Channel. Average wages increased slightly during the 1890s while prices declined due to cheaper imports into tariff-less Britain.[201] While by 1892–1893 financial scandals and ruthless bursts of repression had discredited the governments of France, Italy, and Spain, much of the British political leadership, pre-eminently Queen Victoria, retained respect and even popularity. The two leading political figures of the first half of the 1890s, William Gladstone and Lord Salisbury, were well known for their integrity, and Gladstone possessed far more grassroots appeal among the common people of Britain (and probably

---

[201] Brian R. Mitchell, *European Historical Statistics, 1750–1970*, abridged edition (New York: Columbia University Press, 1978): 66, 72; G. D. H. Cole and Raymond Postgate, *The British People: 1746–1946* (New York: Knopf, 1947): 370, 372, 375, 458.

Ireland) than any politician in France, Spain, Portugal, or Italy had among their own populations.

While London was full of anarchists at the end of the nineteenth century, most of these were foreign. The British police estimated that only 3 percent of the kingdom's anarchists were native born.[202] Simply because they were foreign, of course, did not make them potentially less dangerous. Italian anarchists traveled all over Europe to assassinate prime ministers and heads of state that they considered guilty of grave injustices. On the other hand, few – except, perhaps, for some Irish nationalists – felt that the British leaders or monarch deserved the ultimate punishment.

Ireland, or more specifically the legacy that Britain carried over from its successful response to the Fenian outrages of the 1880s, may help us to understand why the British coped so well with anarchism in the 1890s. The Fenian episode left the British with anti-explosives legislation on the books that could later be used against the anarchists, and more importantly, with a police organization that was more experienced in dealing with terrorism than the security forces of any other country, with the possible exception of Russia. While the British were at first caught completely off guard by the Irish-American dynamiters, they eventually mastered the tricky business of creating an intelligence-gathering operation through the use of informers. Despite a four-and-a-half-year pause between the terrorist alarms of the 1880s and the 1890s, the British police never let down its guard.[203] In fact Britain further centralized and improved its secret police operations (and the extreme fragmentation of police authority in Britain had been one of the reasons for initial police ineffectiveness in countering Fenianism).[204] After Jenkinson resigned his position in January 1887, the government replaced him with James Monro, who also headed Scotland Yard's Criminal Investigation Department (CID), which included the Irish counterterrorist unit. This marked the foundation of the modern Special Branch, although, confusingly, there were actually two Special Branches inside the CID, Section D, the successor to Jenkinson's organization, and Section B, the anti-Fenian bureau. But, according to their historian "it is highly likely that they worked closely together, as two sections of what was in practical terms one body."[205] Initially Section D was quite small, made up of only four inspectors. What happened to Jenkinson's private anti-Fenian agents remains unknown.[206] During the early 1890s the two sections had a combined strength of twenty-five, expanding through the

[202] E. R. Henry, Memorandum, January 7, 1902, Inclosure 2 in No. 2, Correspondence respecting the Measures to be taken for the Prevention of Anarchist Crimes. FO 412/68. The original is in HO45/10254/X36450, sub. 126, PRO.
[203] Porter, *Vigilant State*, 90–91.   [204] Short, *Dynamite War*, 202.
[205] Porter, *Vigilant State*, 87.   [206] Porter, *Vigilant State*, 85

years to thirty-eight in July 1909.[207] Another element of continuity with
the anti-Fenian campaign of the 1880s was Gosselin's spy organization.
In March 1892, Gosselin employed in the United States one secret agent,
seven informants, and two "sub-agents." In the British Isles, he had agents
in Dublin, Newcastle, London, and Manchester, and eleven informants,
plus some clerical and London police help. Soon afterwards, however,
the government drastically reduced Gosselin's organization, although it
continued to maintain agents and informants in Britain, Paris, and the
United States.[208]

Interestingly, at least if a later report by the head of the CID is accurate, a focus on the anarchist threat began early. "Since 1887 the observation of Anarchists has been intrusted [sic] to the special branch of the
Metropolitan Police."[209] Assistant Commissioner Henry also speaks of an
"Anarchists' Register" having been established a dozen years ago, i.e., in
1890, but does not specify exactly what information was put into the register. At a minimum it would have included the addresses of anarchists in the
London metropolitan area, where almost all foreign anarchists resided, but
the dossiers presumably contained much more information than this. If an
anarchist was expelled from the continent and headed for Britain, a foreign
government might, or might not, inform the British. The Home Office also
had informal contacts abroad that might be able to alert London. Then a
special police officer at either Calais or Dover would take note of the suspected anarchist and send on this information; at Dover an officer would
interrogate the man.[210] If the anarchist were thought to be dangerous, the
police would keep him "under more or less sustained observation."[211]

It is worth adding that if the Anarchists' Register did go into effective
operation in 1890, then Britain was ahead of Spain, Italy, and perhaps
Germany. The latter countries did not set up centralized and effective
files on the anarchists until 1894 (with Italy's *Casellario politico centrale*)
and December 1898 (with Germany's Anarchist Album; since at least
the early 1880s, however, Berlin had maintained a massive register for
"all politically suspect persons").[212] In September 1896, Spain created a

---

[207] Porter, *Vigilant State*, 154. Since the size of Section "B" was raised to twenty-five in
December 1894 (Porter, *Vigilant State*, 118), and presumably Section "D" still had its
four inspectors, the combined total for the two branches must have been 29 by 1895.

[208] Porter, *Vigilant State*, 118.

[209] E. R. Henry, Memorandum, January 7, 1902, Inclos. 2 in No. 2, Correspondence
respecting the Measures to be taken for the Prevention of Anarchist Crimes. FO
412/68, PRO.

[210] Porter, *Vigilant State*, 122–123.

[211] E. R. Henry, January 7, 1902, FO 412/68, PRO.

[212] Fricke, *Bismarck's Praetorianer*, 112; Hoerder, *Plutocrats and Socialists*, xxxiii; Linse,
Organisierter, 28.

central anthropometric identification office in the Madrid cellular prison, but for many years this functioned poorly or not at all. In December 1902 the energetic Maura government created a special file listing suspected foreigners, anarchists, vagabonds, and persons lacking documentation. In 1904 Maura reorganized the identification service once again, which suggests that it was still malfunctioning.[213]

Crucial to the success of the British "system" was the placement of judiciously selected confidential informants inside the anarchist movement and, just as important, their expert handling by the police. Prior to the 1880s, the British had "accepted disclosures from informers, but did not go out of their way to cultivate them." They did not plant full-time agents inside subversive groups, lest they become *agents provocateurs*.[214] This all changed after the Fenian dynamite campaign. Chief Inspector Donald Swanson explained the system in June 1893:

> In dealing with informers proper, it is the practice of the Met.[ropolitan] Police CID officer to disburse secretly small sums from his own pocket to enable the informer to get and supply the required information. No receipts are given for obvious reasons, and it is looked upon as an unpardonable violation of duty to disclose such an informer's name. Each officer has his own informers, and they are not generally known. The method is for the officers to compare with each other the information they may have received before action is taken. In cases where good service has been rendered, the informer is regarded in the same way as the witness [in court cases] except that for the object of secrecy he is dealt with in such a way as not to disclose his identity.[215]

This British police method of comparing secret information from different spies and carefully evaluating it in cooperative fashion before taking action was not always adopted by the continental police and probably accounts for the generally superior quality of British intelligence. We have many fewer examples of wild stories of anarchist conspiracies coming out of Britain than out of the rest of Europe.

The use of informers, possibly including *agents provocateurs*, as well as techniques of constant surveillance were some of the new and illegal methods that "crept into the Special Branch's armoury" during the 1890s, although they may also have been used against the Fenians during the 1880s.[216] CID Chief Anderson's January 1899 confidential report is very explicit:

---

[213] Martin Turrado Vidal, *Estudios sobre historia de la policía* (Madrid: Ministerio del Interior, 1986): 41. Vicente Rodríguez Ferrer, *Manual de Identificatión judicial* (Madrid: De Angel Alcoy, 1914): 4.

[214] Porter, *Vigilant State*, 59, 184.

[215] Report Chief Inspector Swanson, in R.A. [Robert Anderson] memo, June 27, 1893. Metropolitan police, CID, HO 144/249/A54906, PRO.

[216] Porter, *Vigilant State*, 184–185.

I am clear that the measure of peace & order wh.[ich] we have been able to maintain in recent years has been due to action taken by this dep[artmen]t wh.[ich] was (if I may coin a word) extra-legal: I hesitate to use the ordinary word wh.[ich] seems applicable to it...The experience of all the years during wh.[ich] I have held my present office [i.e., since August 1888] has been this: For more or less prolonged intervals these men [foreign anarchists] have been treated under the ordinary law, with the invariable result that they have assumed a menacing attitude, and taken to dangerous plots. Then some "extra-legal" action has been adopted by the Police, & they have at once grown quiet & timid.[217]

On occasion the judiciary and other official bodies colluded in these "extra-legal" practices. According to Anderson, a magistrate "winked at the action of the Police" and ordered an Italian anarchist consigned to jail after he had reacted violently to being put under dubiously legal police surveillance.[218] Anarchists' letters were also opened, people recruited to boo or even attack the anarchists at their rallies, and pressure put on landlords and employers to evict or fire anarchists.[219] Quite often during the 1890s, the police raided anarchist newspaper offices and clubs. In April 1892 and June 1894, raids on the offices of the anarchist journal *Commonweal* did so much damage that it was forced to stop publication.[220]

Especially at times when fears of anarchist terrorism were at their height, the British authorities cracked down hard on those who advocated assassination. In the spring of 1892, when Ravachol was planting his bombs throughout Paris, the police arrested, and the courts sentenced to eighteen months in prison, David Nicoll, the editor of *Commonweal*. He was convicted of publishing death threats against figures in the government, judiciary, and police. In August 1894, not long after the assassination of President Carnot, two British anarchists were imprisoned for allegedly advocating the murder of members of the royal family.[221]

It should be emphasized, however, that if the British authorities sometimes bent or broke the law, they did not abandon it altogether as the Spanish did with their widespread practice of torture and as the Italians did with their wholesale arrests on flimsy charges of thousands of "subversives." The British imprisoned fewer than a dozen anarchists and one Russian Socialist Revolutionary during the entire decade of the 1890s; on more than one occasion they refused to jail or even prosecute anarchists guilty of suspicious or illegal activities.[222] By comparison, during 1894

---

[217] Robert Anderson, January 14, 1899. HO45/10254/x36450, PRO.
[218] Robert Anderson, January 14, 1899. HO45/10254/x36450, PRO.
[219] Porter, *Vigilant State*, 130.   [220] Porter, *Vigilant State*, 125.
[221] Porter, *Vigilant State*, 117; Hermia Oliver, *International Anarchist Movement*, 109.
[222] Porter, *Vigilant State*, 117.

alone, Italian Premier Crispi used the anti-anarchist and other legislation to arrest and place under forced detention more than 3,000 anarchists and other supposed enemies of society.[223]

The extreme measures of the Italians and Spanish were in part the frustrated reactions of the government and police to difficulties in tracking down and identifying terrorists. Those who in the spring of 1894 had thrown bombs at parliament and government ministries in Rome were never found or identified. This is understandable given Crispi's bitter complaints at the time that, because of economic considerations, the registry system that he had created in 1887 to keep track of criminals and shady characters had been abolished by his successors, along with the police's detective service.[224] Prefect Guiccioli of Rome, who was ultimately responsible for public security in the capital, wrote in his diary that the parliamentary bombers would not be found since "there is not a trace of organization in our police service."[225] Crispi tried to create a detective force modeled on Britain's but his efforts were not continued by his successor.[226]

Another reason that, despite some questionable police actions and overly harsh jail sentences, the anarchists had less cause to feel abused in Britain than elsewhere was that they could publish, meet, and speak with much greater freedom than in Italy, Spain, or almost any other European country. In 1894 after his inflammatory and scurrilous anarchist newspaper, *Père Peinard*, had been suppressed in France, Émile Pouget escaped to London, where the police kept track of him but did nothing to prevent him from publishing anew.[227] The advances that the British workers had achieved through trade union and strike activity impressed Pouget as well as Malatesta, who lived in London for most of the 1890s. Both anarchist leaders became spirited advocates of anarchist involvement in the labor movement. While in London, Pouget also observed that the English anarchists were uninterested in explosives and wished to avoid provoking the full wrath of society and the government.[228]

During the 1890s, excellent detective work led the Special Branch to forestall at least one bombing in Britain and possibly two, to capture two French anarchists accused of bombings in Paris, and perhaps to prevent

[223] Jensen, *Liberty and Order*, 92.
[224] Farini, *Diario*, 1:455; Francesco Crispi, *Discorsi parlamentari*. 3 vols. (Rome: Tipografia della Camera dei deputati, 1915), 3:733; Jensen, *Liberty and Order*, 93.
[225] March 9, 1894, diary entry. Alessandro Guiccioli. *Diario di un conservatore* (Milan: Borghese, 1973): 189.
[226] Sensales, "L'anagrafe di polizia," 228–229; Tosatti, "Il Ministero degli interni," 455. For Crispi's January 31, 1894 directive creating a secret police detective service, see Natale Musarra, "Le confidenze di "Francesco" G. Domanico al Conte Codronchi, *Rivista storica dell'anarchismo* 3:1 (1996): 45–92.
[227] Oliver, *International Anarchist Movement*, 110.
[228] Oliver, *International Anarchist Movement*, 110, 113. Levy, "Malatesta in London," 29–30.

the assassination of foreign royalty. In his memoirs, Special Branch Constable Melville MacNaghten, who arrested many anarchists during the 1890s, asserted that "in anarchist circles our information was always so good that, had a plot been in the hatching, I think the Yard would have got wind of it within twenty-four hours."[229] In January 1892, with the help of an informer, the police discovered a bomb-making factory in Walsall, north of Birmingham.[230] On the basis of the Explosives Act of 1883, two British, an Italian, and a French anarchist were convicted and imprisoned, although the bombs they built may have been intended for Russian targets. A tsarist target may also have been the real destination for the bomb that in February 1894 blew up prematurely near Greenwich observatory, killing the French-born anarchist Martial Bourdin and providing the factual kernel for Joseph Conrad's famous novel, *The Secret Agent.*

More serious, at least for Britain, was the plot hatched by Francesco Polti, the eighteen-year-old friend of Bourdin, and Giuseppe Farnara, an older man, to blow up the Royal Exchange, which might have led to the death of dozens.[231] (Or it might have led to the death of no one, since most of the time the Royal Exchange was nearly empty! At the end of the nineteenth century its former role had long since been taken over by the larger Stock Exchange and it no longer remained a den of capitalists, as Farnara mistakenly claimed after his arrest. *Perhaps* he meant to target the Stock Exchange). Farnara was amazed that the police were able to locate him at a house in Stratford, in a room occupied by six other men: "I should like to know how you learned I was here. How is it you came straight to my bed? You are well informed."[232] The Special Branch achieved this feat after convincing an anarchist informer, who they discovered was in the employ of the Italians, to help them.[233] One British newspaper claimed that Farnara was "chosen to direct operations in England at a conference of anarchist delegates from all parts of the world held at The Hague two years ago ... [Farnara, alias "Carnot",] described himself as the 'Financial organiser of International Anarchy'."[234] But no solid evidence supports either of these claims, and both Farnara and Polti appear in fact to have been the most inept of terrorists.

---

[229] He admitted, however, that police were helpless against a crank or lunatic who may "be willing to throw his own life away" in order to assassinate an enemy. MacNaghten fails to mention that few of the anarchist assassins during the 1890s were involved in plots involving numerous accomplices or wider anarchist circles. *Days of My Years* (London: Edward Arnold, 1915): 83.

[230] Auguste Coulon, the informer, may also have been an *agent provocateur.* Porter, *Vigilant State*, 138–142, carefully examines the evidence and concludes that although it may have been true "there is no saying for sure."

[231] Oliver, *International Anarchist Movement*, 111–112; Porter, *Vigilant State*, 127.

[232] *The Times* (London), April 24, 1894, 13.   [233] Di Paola, "Spies," 200.

[234] "Arrest of an Anarchist Leader," *Standard*, April 23 1894, HO 144/259/A55860, PRO. Despite Quail's assertions (*The Slow Burning Fuse* [London: Paladin, 1978]: 173) about

William Melville, the head of the Special Branch, achieved another apparent success in 1899. According to his testimony years later, the police "frustrated an attempt to assassinate King Alfonso and his mother by the discovery of a plot against them in London and the pursuit and capture of the plotters at Bordeaux while they were on their way to" Spain.[235]

Successes in forestalling anarchist plots during the 1890s fueled the growing prestige of the British detective. In the 1880s detective work had not been considered suited to the "genius of the English race," in the opinion of Sir Charles Warren, chief commissioner of the Metropolitan Police, and his view had been widely shared. The French were thought to be much better at it.[236] All of this changed by the 1890s. Literature proved prophetic as Sherlock Holmes, who first appeared in a story in 1887, became all the rage in the next decade. Moreover, foreign government after government expressed interest in studying the British detective "system" and occasionally borrowing the detectives themselves.[237] The British government denied the existence of any detective system, however, and usually refused to let foreigners send observers to Scotland Yard. In 1900 Prime Minister Salisbury denied Germany's request for its detectives to be allowed to see Scotland Yard at work. In a personal and private postscript to the German ambassador, however, the prime minister suggested that the German visit would have been useless, since Metropolitan Police Chief Bradford's

success does not lie in any system or rules, but in a remarkable power for choosing the best men, keeping personal knowledge of them, and employing them for the purposes for which they are fitted. I say as far as I have been able to learn because although singularly clear-headed he is very bad at explaining, and the clearer he seems, the less able he is to explain.[238]

Bomb disposal in Britain and France

While the British were loath to let foreigners study their methods, they occasionally profited from adopting continental anti-terrorist practices. After the February 1894 bomb explosion outside the Greenwich Observatory, which caused England's only terrorist fatality during the 1890s, Vivian Majendie, the Home Office's chief inspector of explosives, asked as a precaution that he be allowed to go to Paris and study methods for bomb disposal there since the French had had more recent experience

a mysterious third anarchist plotter named Carnot, *The Times* (April 24, 1894, 13) makes clear that Farnara, "Piemonte," and "Carnot" were one and the same person.
[235] *Daily Telegraph* (London) cited by the *New York Times* (June 4, 1906), 1.
[236] Porter, *Vigilant State*, 63, 84.   [237] Porter, *Vigilant State*, 97.
[238] Salisbury to Count Hatzfeldt, London, August 9, 1900. FO64/1507, PRO.

with that problem than the British. According to Majendie, only "luck" which "has favored us in a most remarkable degree," had so far saved the English from such tragedies as the 1892 *Rue des Bons Enfants* explosion in which four Parisian policemen (and an office boy) had been killed while trying to deactivate a complicated anarchist bomb fitted inside an iron cooking pot.[239] In Paris the *Sûreté* cordially received Majendie and showed him around. According to his report, which provides a fascinating window into Paris's methods, the French had a Municipal Laboratory, staffed day and night, that dealt with bombs. Should notice of a bomb be received, a police officer or assistant from this laboratory would immediately proceed to the site. In the case of a serious threat, a cart would convey the bomb to one of four bastions "fitted up for the purpose of examining and opening infernal machines." The bomb cart was

simply a one-horse phaeton, such as is used by commercial travelers; it is provided with good springs, the wheels are furnished with india-rubber tyres.

The bomb is deposited on a quantity of wood shavings or similar elastic material in the body of the phaeton...At one time the idea was entertained of constructing a bomb proof cart for this purpose – or at any rate a cart which by means of iron shields would prevent the lateral dispersion of fragments should the bomb unfortunately explode in transit. But the idea was abandoned in view of the fact that the infernal machines in some cases contained very large charges of explosives (e.g. the machine [planted by Ravachol in 1892] which exploded at the Rue de Clichy contained between 50 and 60 lbs), and of the considerations, 1st. that a cart which would resist the explosion of such a charge would have to be of so cumbrous a character as to require 3 horses to draw it, and would be proportionally inconvenient to bring into action, besides attracting much attention...and that in the event of a bomb containing a charge in excess of what the cart was calculated to resist exploding therein, the iron and stout structure of the cart itself would probably seriously aggravate the effect.

The bomb sheds at the Parisian bastions (de Bercy, Pont de Jour, Porte de Versailles, and the furthest out – three miles – from the center of Paris, Aubervilliers) were surrounded by stout earth parapets and equipped with a hydraulic press for crushing the bombs. Normally crushing left all parts of the bomb undisturbed, but even if an explosion occurred, the cracking of the outer shell greatly diminished the bomb's explosive power. Small dynamite charges might also be used to open bombs, as well as

an apparatus with 3 moveable arms or holders, into which machines of different sizes can be fixed and lowered into a bath of mercury, to a sufficient depth to bring the mercury into contact with a portion of the solder, and it is the practice

[239] Majendie to Secretary of State, Home Office, London, March 1, 1894. HO.45/9741/ A55680, PRO.

in such cases to allow the machine to remain in the mercury bath for about 24 hours, by which time the solder is sufficiently acted upon to enable the box to be opened without risk.

If removal involved "appreciable risk," however, the French preferred to blow up the bomb on the spot, despite the damage caused. Majendie disagreed with this approach and recommended accepting some risk so as to avoid, in effect, seconding and supplementing the anarchist's efforts.

It is impossible to regard with complacency the deliberate explosion of a powerful infernal machine, in some valuable building, as the House of Commons, the Home Office !! [exclamation points appended, presumably, by the Home Secretary], the National Gallery or St. Paul's Cathedral.

Majendie recommended "prompt adoption" of a modified version of the French bomb disposal system. To improve communications, Majendie recommended that his home and that of his chief assistant be connected by telephone with Scotland Yard. "We should then have a complete telephonic system with the Home Office and through Scotland yard." He also recommended the construction of a light, covered handcart for bomb removal.

The enormous, thickly populated area of London as compared to smaller-sized Paris posed a problem in finding a suitable site for disposing the bombs. Majendie assumed that the "two main centers of possible anarchical activity" would be "the district of which the Home Office and Scotland yard may be regarded as the centre" and the "City district, which comprises St. Pauls Cathedral, the Bank, the Mint, the Guildhall and Mansion House, the Tower and other places of importance." It was therefore necessary to find locations close to these areas. Majendie recommended three: Duck Island in St. James's Park, the Tower Ditch, and Hyde Park (e.g., the "enclosed space known as the 'Gravel Pit'"). For bombs that could be safely transferred out of the metropolis, he recommended conveyance to the grounds of the great Royal Arsenal at Woolwich, southeast of London, perhaps to the "Thunderer Cell", "i.e. a cell which was constructed to burst one of the [battleship] Thunderer's Guns").[240]

The government soon authorized the creation of bomb disposal sites at Duck Island (practically complete by November 1894) and Hyde

---

[240] Majendie to Secretary of State, HO, London, April 12, 1894. HO.45/9741/A55680, PRO. A *Reclams Universum* article republished in *Scientific American* 105:5 (1911): 100–101, provides a somewhat veiled description of the Paris bomb laboratory. The Thunderer reference is to the 1880 recreation of the accidental bursting of one of the guns of the battleship HMS *Thunderer*. Thomas Brassey, *The British Navy: Its Strength, Resources, and Administration* (London: Longmans, Green, 1882): 85.

Park. Because of the extreme dampness of the first location, a man who lived on Duck Island and acted as bird-keeper was hired to keep the machinery and implements for opening bombs oiled, cleaned, and in good order. On the remonstrance of CID chief Anderson that the officers needed more protection (and Majendie does seem to have been less concerned with their safety than with that of public monuments), the War Office designed a special "truck" for disposing of bombs that was finished in November 1895. All of these arrangements, of course, were kept completely secret.[241]

Neither Duck Island nor Hyde Park seem to have been put to much use as bomb disposal sites and were not crucial to the British anti-anarchist strategy. Essential for its success was effective police surveillance of the anarchists on British territory, the placement of confidential agents inside the movement, the careful handling of these agents, and the judicious evaluation of the information they provided. The early creation of an Anarchist Register suggests that the British had learned their lesson from combating Fenianism about the importance of information-gathering and intelligence. While the British approach was usually low key, occasional, but severe, police and judicial reactions against extreme words and deeds left no doubt in many anarchists' minds that the police were vigilantly observing their activities. Even if the police crossed the line into "extralegal" territory, this was done judiciously and infrequently enough to avoid a revenge-seeking backlash as occurred in France, Italy, and Spain.

Conclusion

Several generalizations can be made about the international war against terrorism and anarchism waged between 1871 and 1898. First of all, at the highest level, political divisions between the different European states made it impossible to conclude a comprehensive international agreement regarding the proper defenses against terrorism. Britain, France, Switzerland, and even Italy, despite the fact that at this time it was going through a particularly reactionary period of its history, were unsure about the practicality of distinguishing between anarchism and other kinds of extreme political opinion, opinion that might be perfectly legal. At this time and also in later years, where agreement could be reached beyond the glare of publicity and without risking parliamentary debate, that is, at the level of secret police and administrative arrangements, a great deal

---

[241] Majendie report, to Secretary of State, HO, November 23, 1894, and letters of June 15 and November 29, 1895. HO.45/9741/A55680, PRO.

of European cooperation became possible. This grew up not as some gigantic scheme of repression, not as some new "Holy Alliance" against subversives, but piecemeal and in response to the onslaught of anarchist bombings and assassinations in the winter of 1893 and through the first half of 1894, when a "critical mass" of governmental and public concern provided the energy to overcome long-standing inertia and suspicions of foreign police and governments. Another point worth stressing is that the suggestions of low-ranking police and diplomatic agents in the field, rather than of high officials in national capitals, provided the catalyst for many – although certainly not every – agreement.

The French, Italian, and Argentinian police improved their intelligence-gathering services during the 1890s. Spain tried to enact similar reforms but these remained superficial and ineffective. Some may view this as marking the first, sometimes stumbling, steps toward an all-seeing, "panopticon" society, after the mid-century hiatus caused by the collapse of the Metternichean system.

While anti-anarchist agreements were knitting together much of the continent, Britain stayed largely apart. Protected by the relative stability and popularity of its institutions, leaders, and laws, and by the excellence of the anti-terrorist procedures and police it had developed at the time of the Fenian crisis, Britain saw no pressing need for closer cooperation with European security forces. Britain was never tempted to conflate anarchist terrorism with other potential enemies of the status quo, be they trade unionists or socialists.[242] Just the opposite was true of Russia, and at times Germany, Spain, Portugal, and Italy, which tried to jump on the anti-anarchist bandwagon in order to more effectively combat their enemies on the far left. This effort was usually not successful or only temporarily successful. Policies of repression without justice backfired by discrediting the governments that adopted them and making their victims into martyrs, most prominently in the case of Spain. Given the increasingly important part that socialist parties played in the political life of many European states, a clear focus on anarchism, and the exclusion of socialism, was the *sine qua non* for the achievement of most forms of international cooperation. While bilateral anti-anarchist agreements spread like a web across the face of central and western Europe in 1894–1895, with extensions as far as Argentina (and with secret agents dispatched to the United States), it still required a peculiar conjunction of place and circumstances to make possible a higher level of cooperation and the calling of the first international conference against terrorism.

---

[242] Porter, *Vigilant State*, 92–93.

5 The first international conference on terrorism: Rome 1898

On the afternoon of September 10, 1898, a young, robust Italian rushed up to the aging, slender Elisabeth, Empress of Austria and Queen of Hungary (b. 1837), as she was walking toward a ferry-steamer docked at Geneva, Switzerland. The Italian anarchist Luigi Lucheni plunged a three-edged file, its tip honed needle-sharp, into her chest, and with his blow knocked the empress to the ground.[1] Lucheni fled but was quickly apprehended by passersby and the police. The Empress Elisabeth managed to regain her feet and board the steamer, but Lucheni's crude, stiletto-like weapon had made a tiny perforation into her chest three and a third inches deep, piercing the heart and lung. Soon after boarding, Elisabeth collapsed, fell into unconsciousness, revived briefly, but, shortly after being carried back to her hotel in Geneva, died.[2]

This quixotic anarchist assassination had immediate repercussions throughout Europe and ultimately led the Italian government to convene a conference with representatives from the whole of Europe. This "International Conference for the Defense of Society against the Anarchists" met in Rome between November 24 and December 21, 1898.

The agreements reached there played a key role in the quarter-century-long international campaign against anarchism. Despite the significance of the conference, the only Europe-wide anti-anarchist congress ever held and the first international gathering convened to combat terrorism,

This chapter is an extensively revised and expanded version of my article, "The International Anti-Anarchist Conference of 1898 and the Origins of Interpol," *Journal of Contemporary History*, 16 (1981), 323-47.

[1] Many authors mistakenly spell Lucheni's name with two "c"s, i.e., Luccheni. The historian Egon Corti prints a photograph of a letter by Lucheni in which the Italian spells his name with one "c" (*Elizabeth, Empress of Austria*, trans. Catherine Alison Phillips [New Haven: Yale University Press, 1936]: following 476). In his preface to Lucheni's recently discovered memoirs, Santo Cappon provides a definitive explanation of the origin of the spelling confusion. "L'histoire de l'assassin d'Élisabeth, dite Sissi, impératrice d'Autriche et reine de Hongrie," in Luigi Lucheni, *Mémoires de l'assassin de Sissi* (Paris: Le cherche midi, 1998): 43.

[2] Letter, A. Didier, Head of Department of Justice and Police of Geneva, Geneva, to E. Brenner, Head of Swiss Department of Justice and Police, September 10, 1898. *DDS*, 4:596.

it has long remained wrapped in mystery and denied much importance. Because the sessions were carefully kept secret and its records rumored to have been burned, until recently historians have written little on the conference and, in what they have, often fallen grossly into error. Due to the lack of information even the existence of the 1898 conference has been denied.[3] Otherwise, the general opinion has been that the conference must have been abortive with few, if any, practical results.[4] French Ambassador Camille Barrère, who headed his country's delegation at the conference, wrote in a letter that its propositions possessed no more value than "the paper they were written on."[5] Barrère, a former communard who, like many of the anarchists, had been forced to find asylum in London, may not have been the most objective of witnesses.[6] As the following chapter will show, a more balanced assessment would conclude that some of the conference's propositions proved to be dead letters, but others were not and in fact proved quite influential.

Why did the assassination of the Empress Elisabeth lead to an international conference when so many earlier (and much bloodier) terrorist deeds had not? This was due in part to the particular qualities of the victim, as we shall see. Even more important, however, was the fact that

[3] *Dizionario biografico degli italiani*, "Canevaro," by M. Gabriele, 69.
[4] Saverio Cilibrizzi, *Storia parlamentare, politica e diplomatica d'Italia* (Naples: Tosi, 1939–1952): 3:133; Pietro Vigo, *Annali d'Italia. Storia degli ultimi trent' anni del secolo XIX*, 7 vols. (Milan: Treves, 1915): 7:348; Ferruccio Quintavalle, *Storia della unità italiana (1814–1924)* (Milan: Hoepli, 1926): 409; Christopher Seton-Watson, *Italy from Liberalism to Fascism* (London 1967): 189; *Enciclopedia universal ilustrada*, "Anarquismo," 364; Vizetelly, *The Anarchists*, 238; Gian Franco Vené, "Il braccio della legge contro gli anarchici," *Storia illustrata* October 1973: 147–154. Francesco Tamburini, "La conferenza internazionale di Roma per la difesa sociale contro gli anarchici (24 November–21 Dicembre 1898)," *Clio* 33:2 (1997): 227–265, stresses the "limits and incurable contradictions" of the conference (262). González Calleja, *La razón de la fuerza*, 259, claims "the Conference ended without having adopted any substantial accord." Liang, *Modern Police*, 157–166, gives a more balanced account of the Rome meeting. Liang concludes that the calling of the conference was of considerable significance, since it raised the question whether the European States "had become so closely linked to one another that their defense was now a collective necessity" even if this meant domination by "autocratic regimes" pushing for strict anti-anarchist measures. While in the end this did not prove to be the case, and "as an instrument for the suppression of anarchism it was inadequate," the conference did lead to increased exchange of police information between European capitals. The best discussions of the Rome Conference, based on archival research, are Tamburini, "La conferenza internazionale di Roma," and Jensen, "International Anti-Anarchist Conference," 323–347.
[5] Barrère, Rome, to Foreign Minister Delcassé, Paris, December 30, 1898, cited by Maitron, *Historie*, 433n8.
[6] During the Paris Commune of 1871, Barrère may have commanded a detachment of artillery and certainly acted as a revolutionary journalist. Léon Noël, *Camille Barrère, Ambassadeur de France* (Paris: Tardy, 1948): 18, 32; Milza, *Français et Italiens*, 2:928–929.

Figure 2 The assassination of the Empress Elisabeth of Austria as reported by the old journalism. *The New York Times*, September 11, 1898.

since the murder was committed by an Italian against an Austrian on Swiss soil, it was a bona fide international crime seeming to demand an international response. Second, several states held a grudge against Switzerland for providing asylum to so many subversives for so long. Moreover, in the fall of 1898, Italy was especially well positioned to host an international conference since its membership in the Triple Alliance tied it closely to Austria and Germany, while at the same time it had preserved its friendship with England and had begun improving its relations with France. The issue of troublesome anarchist refugees concerned both of the latter countries.

As regards the victim, even in an era of frequent anarchist assassinations and bombings, the murder of the Empress Elisabeth appeared horrifying, capturing the imagination of the world, in the words of one contemporary writer, as "the most vile and most wicked among all the

Figure 3 The assassination of the Empress Elisabeth of Austria as reported by the new journalism. *New York Journal*, September 10, 1898.

anarchist crimes."[7] In large part, this reaction was due to the victim's gender. "Even in the disordered minds of anarchists and assassins," the

---

[7] Giulio Diena, "I provvedimenti contro gli anarchici e la prossima conferenza internazionale." *Rivista di diritto internazionale e di legislazione comparata* 1:6 (1898): 252.

Figure 4 The assassination of the Empress Elisabeth of Austria as reported by the new journalism. *New York Journal*, September 11, 1898.

New York Times editorialized, "the universal sentiment that prompts male humanity to exempt woman from the consequences of ferocious passion has commonly held sway." Lucheni's violation of this accepted restraint made his crime "almost unexampled in its heartlessness."[8] Contributing to the horror felt at his crime was Elisabeth's reputation for goodness (according to the London *Times* she was "an incarnation of charity and beneficence") and her many personal tragedies, such as the suicide of her only son Rudolf.[9] Also compounding the poignancy of her demise was the fact that many people considered Elisabeth to be the most

[8] *New York Times*, September 11, 1898, 16. Many other newspapers echoed these sentiments. See *The Times* (London), September 12, 1898, 3, with excerpts from continental newspapers.
[9] "Worldwide Sorrow," September 12, 1898.

beautiful woman in Europe, if not indeed the entire world, an image she succeeded in preserving to the end by avoiding being photographed in her later years.[10] In reality, in 1898 Elisabeth was over sixty, in failing health, and anorexic, half-starved by her obsessive dieting and exercise.[11] Nevertheless, at the time of her death many commentators still alluded to her great beauty.[12]

Lucheni's motivation

What was Lucheni's motive in assassinating Elisabeth? Many of his public statements point to the Social Question. Interrogated after the crime as to who had urged him to strike at the empress, he replied "wretchedness [*miseria*]."[13] In a letter mailed from prison to *Don Marzio*, a Neapolitan newspaper, Lucheni attacked "the greed with which [the ruling class] sucks the blood of its fellow men." Unless this was curbed, "the just blows of the undersigned must fall upon all royalties, presidents and ministers, and everyone who attempts to bring his fellow-men into subjection for his own profit." He added, curiously echoing St. Paul (2 Thess. 3:10), that "he who does not work shall not eat" and signed his letter "Luigi Lucheni, the most convinced of anarchists."[14] By way of justifying his murderous action, at his trial he repeated the phrase: "He who does not work shall not eat."[15]

Perhaps the motives for his actions should be linked more concretely to his personal circumstances and character.[16] Abandoned soon after birth at a foundling hospital in Paris, and shortly thereafter transferred to a children's home in Parma, he spent most of his existence as a rootless wanderer. Although after the assassination of Elisabeth he claimed to have been an anarchist since the age of thirteen, it is by no means

---

[10] Brigitte Hamann, *The Reluctant Empress* (New York: Knopf, 1986): 360. The Viennese correspondent of London's *Pall Mall Gazette* (September 17, 1898) asserts that the last photograph of Elisabeth was taken "more than fifteen years ago," i.e., before 1883.

[11] Walter Vandereycken and Ron VanDeth, "The Anorectic Empress: Elisabeth of Austria," *History Today* 46: 4 (1996): 12–19.

[12] "The Murdered Empress," *New York Times*, September 11, 1898, 1; *Pall Mall Gazette* (London), September 17, 1898. Joseph Pulitzer's *The World*, which was the *Evening Journal*'s main rival for the mass reading public of New York City, published on its front page a large drawing of Elisabeth "at the height of her beauty" (September 11, 1898).

[13] Alfred Gautier, "Le process Lucheni," *Revue Pènale Suisse* (1898): 344.

[14] Letter dated September 11, 1898. Brigitte Hamann, "Der Mord an Kaiserin Elisabeth," in Leopold Spira (ed.), *Attentate, die Österreich eschütterten* (Vienna: Löcker, 1981): 28; Corti, *Elizabeth*, 387.

[15] Corti, *Elizabeth*, 387, 391.

[16] Franklin L. Ford, *Political Murder: From Tyrannicide to Terrorism* (Cambridge University Press, 1985): 209, overemphasizes Lucheni's ideological motivation.

clear that he adopted such views before he left for Switzerland. Some historians believe he was never a "true" anarchist.[17] In Italy Lucheni had expressed monarchist sentiments and in 1896 had proven an excellent soldier during the Italian campaign in Abyssinia. The next year, after his release from the military, Lucheni's life had become one of continual frustration and disappointment at the hands of officialdom and his employer. The Prince d'Aragona, his commander in Africa, had hired Lucheni as a servant, but after Lucheni stalked off having been denied a raise in wages, refused to accept him back once Lucheni repented of his impetuous action. Several times he applied to the government for a post in the public service, but was ignored; on two occasions, his requests for help from Italian consulates in Switzerland landed him in jail.[18] Ignored by officialdom and by his previous aristocratic patron, and with few other prospects, the twenty-five-year-old Lucheni found in the anarchist ideas circulating among the expatriate Italians working in Switzerland a way of explaining the grievous misfortunes of his young life and a vehicle for expressing his thwarted ambitions.[19] In this he was typical of many, although not the majority of, anarchist assassins, who were often footloose young men who had left their native countries to find fortune abroad, only to meet with disappointment and suffering. Alienated from the culture and often the language of their new habitations, these men easily fell in with and adopted the ideas of co-nationals holding radical opinions on social and political issues.

Impulsive and theatrical by nature, Lucheni desired to do some deed that would give significance to his life and ensure the immortality of his

---

[17] Masini, *Storia ... attentati*, 117; Tamburini, "La conferenza internazionale di Roma," 229.

[18] Gautier, "Le pròces Lucheni," 345–346.

[19] Some accounts, including that of the public prosecutor at Lucheni's trial, assert that the assassin became an anarchist in Italy *before* immigrating to Switzerland (Gautier, "Le pròces Lucheni," 338). The newspapers reported that Lucheni had allegedly told the examining magistrate after the assassination that, at the time he was a valet in the service of the Prince d'Aragona in Naples, "anarchist ideas began to possess his mind, and – to use his own words – 'prevented me from remaining in servitude.'" ("The Assassin Tells All," *New York Times*, September 13, 1898). This may well have been nothing more than justification after the fact, an attempt to provide ideological window dressing for Lucheni's impulsive resignation from the Prince's service. Professor Gautier of Geneva, who has written one of the most convincing contemporary accounts of the case, believed that Lucheni did not become an anarchist until he mixed with Italian workers in Lausanne, among whom anarchism was actively preached (Gautier, "Le pròces Lucheni," 346). This is also the view of Elisabeth's recent biographer, Brigitte Hamann (*Reluctant Empress*, 369). Even if Lucheni was exposed to some anarchist ideas in Italy, it was only after his emigration to Lausanne that evidence exists of him becoming active in the movement, interacting with other anarchists, and helping to distribute *L'Agitatore*, an anarchist newspaper (see Lucheni's file, no. 2866, *Casellario politico centrale*, ACS). *Before* the assassination, Lucheni's name did not appear on the Italian interior ministry's list of anarchists, but that proves little since the list was frequently faulty.

name. The foremost anarchist child of the age of mass media, Lucheni told an acquaintance: "Ah! How I should like to kill somebody; but it must be some person of great importance, so that it might get into the papers."[20] At his judicial hearing, he informed the judge "I wanted to kill a big personage, 'a Mont-Blanc [i.e., the highest mountain in the Alps],' one of those who after nineteen centuries oppress the worker and exploit the people."[21] The assassin clearly had no particular animus against Elisabeth, other than her role as a representative of the aristocracy and the ruling class. Indeed, at first Lucheni had intended to murder Henri of Orléans, pretender to the French throne, but Henry had left Geneva before Lucheni's arrival. This choice of aristocratic targets may appear odd since at this time neither Elisabeth nor Henri exercised any political power. It is not so surprising, however, if one remembers that a number of deadly anarchist acts were aimed at purely symbolic subjects, and that, by adopting this tactic, Lucheni could express his anger at the treatment he had received from another aristocrat, his erstwhile benefactor the Prince d'Aragona.

While Lucheni attacked a symbol, he also embraced a myth: that of the powerful anarchist able to exercise a terrifying sway over people and societies. His self-identification as "one of the most dangerous of [anarchists]," as he wrote to the president of the Swiss Confederation,[22] is surely of more interest and historical consequence than whether or not he had mastered the classics of anarchist literature. In almost every country anarchists were pursued and harassed by the police. Anarchism possessed no state sponsor, no country of secure refuge for its adherents, no powerful organization, and little or no money. Yet Lucheni, and many others, still gloried in its name as the most potent human symbol of resistance to oppression and of the vindication of injustice.

Reactions to the assassination of the Empress Elisabeth

For European governments an even more compelling concern than the death of Elisabeth was signs that this was just the beginning of a much larger anarchist conspiracy. The Russian government informed Rome the day following the murder that it had discovered information on a plot hatched by anarchists in Zurich to kill other European heads of state, beginning with the king of Italy, and the Parisian police corroborated this information.[23] In October, Egyptian authorities exposed an alleged

---

[20] Corti, *Elizabeth*, 373.   [21] Gautier, "Le procès Lucheni," 344.
[22] Corti, *Elizabeth*, 387.
[23] Italian Ambassador Morra, St. Petersburg, to foreign ministry, Rome, September 11, 1898, and Italian Consulate, Zurich, to foreign ministry, Rome, September 13, 1898, series "P" (1891–1916), b. 606, IFM. "A message has arrived at the Ministry [of the

conspiracy by some Italian anarchists living in Alexandria to assassinate Kaiser Wilhelm II, who was then making a tour of the Ottoman Empire.[24] The immediate reaction to this looming anarchist menace was arrests and increased surveillance of anarchists throughout Europe. Even in New York City, Emma Goldman found herself "shadowed by police and pilloried by the press" after the Geneva murder.[25] Bowing to international pressure, Switzerland initiated a series of measures to crack down on foreign anarchists.

After Switzerland, the country most directly affected by the assassination was the Austro-Hungarian Empire. The Empress Elisabeth was popular throughout the Dual Monarchy. When the news of her murder reached Budapest, men and women could be seen weeping openly in the streets and black mourning banners were displayed everywhere.[26] At her funeral in Vienna hundreds of thousands of people filed past her coffin.[27] Her death also sparked anti-Italian demonstrations and rioting in Trieste, Ljubljana, Fiume, and Budapest, as well as in several villages. Mobs sacked the homes and schools of immigrant Italian workers and other Italian-speakers residing in the Austrian Empire. In Trieste, they wrecked Italian cafés and a gymnastic center; in Linz and Budapest, employers summarily fired Italian workers. Hundreds of Italians fled back to Italy.[28]

In its reaction to Elisabeth's murder, the Austrian government acted with restraint, although the death of his wife deeply hurt Emperor Franz Joseph, who on receiving news of the murder broke down weeping. Nonetheless, demonstrating his famous devotion to duty, he refused to allow Foreign Minister Goluchowski to initiate any diplomatic action that might damage relations with either Switzerland or Italy.[29] Franz Joseph felt especially well disposed toward Switzerland, where large numbers of citizens had paraded through the streets of Geneva, voicing their indignation against the anarchists and sympathy for the dead empress.[30]

Interior] from the Paris Prefect of Police, that in a meeting held there by Italian anarchists there taken refuge, it may have been decided to take the next opportunity to attempt the life of His Majesty, the King." Chief of Police to inspectors, September 15, 1898, no. 3631, *Archivio di Stato*, Milan, Questura, cartella 84.

[24] Ferruccio Quintavalle, *Storia*, 409; Silvio Furlani, "La conferenza internazionale di Roma del 1898 contro l'anarchismo," in Aldo Mola (ed.), *La svolta di Giolitti. Dalla reazione di fine Ottocento al culmine dell'età liberale* (Foggia: Bastogi, 2000): 24–25.

[25] Emma Goldman, *Living My Life*, 1:231.

[26] *New York Times*, September 11, 1898, 1.   [27] Corti, *Elizabeth*, 390.

[28] *La Stampa* (Turin), September 11, 16, and 17, 1898.

[29] Rudolf Dannecker, *Die Schweiz und Österreich-Ungarn: Diplomatische und militärische Beziehungen von 1866 bis zum ersten Weltkrieg* (Basel and Stuttgart: von Helbing and Lichtenhahn, 1966): 143; 159; Bernard von Bülow, *Memoirs* (Boston: Little, Brown, 1931–1932): 1:277.

[30] Dannecker, *Schweiz und Österreich-Ungarn*, 143.

The murder of the empress also horrified public opinion in the German Reich. A Cologne newspaper noted that "a cry of universal indignation rises from the whole civilized world. It would be impossible to find words to describe this villainous act."[31] On the outskirts of Berlin a mob burned down a slum-dwelling housing fifty itinerant Italian workers (although the Italian ambassador thought this violence due to a dispute over scab labor rather than to anger over the Geneva crime).[32] Throughout Germany flags were set at half-mast in sign of mourning. In his youth Wilhelm II had worshiped the gorgeous Elisabeth[33] and in 1898 became even more vehemently in favor of taking strong measures against the anarchists than Elisabeth's husband. In a telegram of condolence to the Austrian emperor, sent without consulting his government, Wilhelm described anarchism as arising from "liberalism, humanitarian slop, demagogy, and above all, from the cowardice of parliaments." He encouraged the Austrians to suggest common anti-anarchist measures and ended his message with the exclamation, "Something must be done!"[34]

Wilhelm and his ministers had an opportunity to coordinate joint measures with the Austrian government when they journeyed to Vienna on Saturday, September 17, to attend the empress's funeral. The German kaiser was accompanied by Prince Chlodwig zu Hohenlohe-Schillingsfürst, his aged and ineffectual chancellor, and Bernard von Bülow, his young and charming foreign minister. Although the kings of Saxony, Romania, and Serbia, as well as a host of European nobility, attended the funeral, Wilhelm received special treatment. Franz Joseph went to the train station to meet Wilhelm and they rode together in the same carriage to the funeral ceremonies. The older (sixty-eight), courtly Franz Joseph never found the impulsive, manic Wilhelm II, who was only thirty-nine, a pleasant companion, but evidence points to some kind of accord being reached by the two about the necessity for general European action against the anarchists.[35] Count Goluchowski, the Austrian foreign minister, also spoke with Wilhelm.[36]

The Italians needed little prodding from Berlin or Vienna to realize how difficult their international situation had become. Two days after

---

[31] Quoted by the Berlin correspondent of the *Times* (London), September 12, 1898.

[32] *La Stampa* (Turin), September 11, 1898; Lanza (Berlin) to Italian foreign ministry, no. 2633, September 15, 1898, *Telegrammi in arrivo*, vol. 236, IFM.

[33] Röhl, *Wilhelm II: The Kaiser's Personal Monarchy*, 945.

[34] Bülow, *Memoirs*, 1:278.   [35] Linse, *Organisierter*, 25.

[36] Mss. [Nigra] to Italian foreign ministry, Vienna, September 27, 1898, 3049/727. *Ambasciata d'Italia a Vienna*, b. 168, IFM. Nigra wrote to correct the false impression conveyed in his dispatch of September 19, 1898 (IFM, *Telegrammi in arrivo*, no. 2686, vol. 236.) that it was *only* the two monarchs who had originated the idea of an international conference.

the assassination of Elisabeth, the editorialist of a major Turin newspaper lamented that, according to world opinion, the name "Italy" and
"assassin" had become nearly synonymous.[37] Confiding in his diary, the
president of the Italian senate expressed the fear that the Italians were
in danger of "being lynched by Europe."[38] The violent reprisals against
Italians living abroad gave substance to these fears and strained Rome's
relations with Vienna. Only with difficulty did the government prevent anti-Austrian demonstrations from erupting within Italy. Foreign
Minister Napoleone Canevaro later expressed the suspicion that behind
the operations of the "sect," which he believed was obeying orders and
perhaps being financed from "across the mountains," i.e., from France,
was a plan to undermine the monarchical principle and the Triple
Alliance.[39]

Rome was especially anxious for the life of King Umberto I, since it
took seriously the persistent rumors that the king's name stood next after
Elisabeth's on the anarchist "hit list." General Luigi Pelloux, the Italian
prime minister, was devoted to Umberto, a bond reinforced by the general's attachment to the region of Savoy, which was both his own birthplace and the ancestral home of the ruling dynasty. Soon after the death
of Elisabeth, Pelloux ordered an increased surveillance of anarchists in
Italy and a crackdown on their publications and activities.[40] The newspapers reported scores of arrests.[41]

Within days of Lucheni's blow, Pelloux addressed an excited memorandum marked "most reserved; personal" to Italy's minister of justice.
Deploring the "execrable crime of Geneva," and mentioning reports from
foreign "powers" and "our confidants abroad" about "a vast conspiracy
against the life of every head of state, and especially against the King of
Italy," the prime minister demanded immediate measures. Subversive
newspapers and associations must be curbed. "At the same time I have
already given instructions to the Foreign Minister about the line of action
to adopt with friendly and allied powers for those eventual international
accords that the situation demands."[42]

---

[37] Literally, the term he used was *accoltellatore*, "stabber" or "cutthroat"; *La Stampa* (Turin)
September 12, 1898.

[38] Domenico Farini, *Diario*, 2:1350.

[39] Canevaro to Nigra, Vienna, September 29, 1898, DDI (3), 3:51; Canevaro to Lanza,
Berlin, February 21, 1899, DDI (3), 3:102.

[40] Prefect, Rome, to Commander *Carabinieri* and secretary general of police, September
10 and 11, 1898. *Archivio di Stato* of Rome. Questura. fascicolo (hereafter "f.") 229, sot-
tofascicolo (hereafter s.f.) 404A.

[41] *Avanti!*, September 14, 1898.

[42] Mss. letter, prime minister to the minister of justice, originally dated September 12, then
revised and redated September 14, 1898. ACS, *Presidenza del Consiglio* (hereafter cited as

Especially irritating to the Italian prime minister were the actions of Switzerland. Among other lapses, the Swiss had allowed the imprisoned Lucheni to carry on a published correspondence regarding the assassination with a Neapolitan newspaper. This was but one example, according to Pelloux, of the excessive permissiveness that the Swiss allowed the anarchists in their country.[43] (The Swiss, on the other hand, thought these complaints were a case of the Italians "looking for the straw in our eye instead of the beam which is in theirs."[44]) The Italian government was convinced that Lucheni had only become actively involved in anarchism once he had left his homeland and crossed the border into Switzerland, that den of subversives from all over Europe.[45]

The government in Rome cherished other grievances against its northern neighbor as well. During May 1898 Italy had feared an "invasion" from Switzerland of several hundred expatriate Italian anarchists and other militants.[46] At the frontier the Swiss and Italian authorities easily thwarted this rag tag column, but Rome nonetheless found the attack most alarming, because of its intention to assist protestors in Milan who, the authorities erroneously believed, were engaged in a plot to provoke a general revolution throughout the country.[47] Foreign Minister Canevaro even thought that the Milanese disturbances were the direct result of machinations, "anarchist plots," by Italian subversives residing in Switzerland.[48] Since the latter continued to agitate and publish incendiary propaganda from across the border, particularly in the Italian-speaking canton of Ticino, Rome felt doubly justified in calling the Swiss to account.[49]

Presidenza), *Gabinetto* Pelloux, 1898, f. 210. Printed in Umberto Levra, *Il colpo di Stato della borghesia* (Milan: Feltrinelli, 1975): 263–264.

[43] Pelloux to foreign minister, Rome, September 16, 1898, ACS, *Presidenza*, *Gabinetto* Pelloux, 1898, f. 210.

[44] Ruffy, Berne, to chargé d'affaires, Dumartheray, Vienna, September 21, 1898. DDS, 4:602.

[45] Canevaro, sixth plenary session, December 20, 1898, CIR, 2.

[46] Marc Vuilleumier, "L'emigrazione italiana in Svizzera e gli avvenimenti del 1898," in *Anna Kuliscioff e l'età del riformismo* (Milan: Mondo Operaio, 1978): 85–103.

[47] For the seriousness with which the government took the anarchist "invasion" from Switzerland (despite its comic opera results) see Fernando Manzotti, "I rapporti italosvizzeri e la crisi italiana del 1898," *Accademia di scienza, lettere e arti in Modena. Atti e memorie* 6 (1962): 181; Mario Belardinelli, *Un esperimento liberal-conservatore: i governi di Rudinì (1896–1898)* (Rome: Elia, 1976): 353–354.

[48] Choffat, Swiss Legation, Rome, to Ruffy, October 3, 1898. DDS 4:609; Sir George Bonham, British chargé d'affaires in Rome, to FO, September 17, 1898, FO. 43/176, PRO.

[49] Canevaro, Rome, to diplomatic representatives, September 15, 1898. no. 62, DDI. (3) 3:38–39.

Negotiations for joint actions against Switzerland and the anarchists

On September 15, Canevaro issued a circular dispatch to all diplomatic representatives residing in Rome.[50] The foreign minister noted that Switzerland's laws and, even more, its lax administration allowed "the worst evil-doers" of every country to gather there, spreading their propaganda and inciting others to commit abominable crimes. After the tragic events of Geneva, the Italian government felt that it should remind the Swiss authorities of their responsibilities and the necessity for finding remedies. First, however, Italy desired to consult with the other European Powers, in case they should wish to join Italy in making recommendations to Switzerland in the interests of preserving the safety of the whole of European society.[51] The European powers generally indicated their support for the Italian position, although England expressed some reservations.

With international pressure looming, on September 23 the Swiss government expelled thirty-six anarchists, mostly Italians (in future years this federal decree of September 23 provided a precedent for additional expulsions).[52] In October and November Switzerland expelled over forty more anarchists. The authorities closed down several subversive journals.[53] The Federal Council, the central executive authority of Switzerland, invited the cantonal governments to note any foreigners entering their territory and to communicate this information to Berne. The cantons were also asked to exercise strict surveillance over anarchist conspiracies, disclosing their findings, especially regarding any infraction of the Swiss anti-anarchist law of 1894, to the Confederation's attorney general (*procureur général*).[54] The Swiss government also charged the attorney general with reporting on and formulating proposals to deal with "dangerous anarchists" and with foreigners who facilitated anarchist propaganda. Furthermore the authorities in Berne studied the possibility of enacting new legislation to control the activity of foreign anarchists.[55] These measures satisfied at least some of the demands of Switzerland's

---

[50] Ibid.   [51] Ibid.

[52] "Faits et informations," *Journal du droit international privé* 33 (1906): 954–955; Giovanni Casagrande, "Mises en fiche du début du siecle: le cas Luigi Bertoni," in *Cent ans de police politique en Suisse (1889–1989)* (Lausanne: Editions d'enbas, 1992): 74.

[53] Johann Langhard, *Die anarchistische Bewegung in der Schweiz von ihren Anfängen bis zur Gegenwart und die internationalen Führer* (Berlin: O. Häring, 1903): 414–416.

[54] No. 83, DDI (3), 3:50; Naum Reichesberg, "Anarchisme," in *Dictionnaire Historique et Biographique de la Suisse*, 1:316; "Contre les anarchistes," *L'Italie*, September 25, 1898.

[55] "Contre les anarchistes," *L'Italie* (Rome), September 25, 1898; Reichesberg, "Anarchisme," 316.

Figure 5 Count Agenor Maria Goluchowski, Austro-Hungarian minister of foreign affairs, 1895–1906, and covert father of the Rome Anti-Anarchist Conference of 1898.

foreign critics and made combined diplomatic action against Berne no longer so urgent or opportune.[56]

Italy now changed its course from pressuring Switzerland to broaching the idea of convoking an international conference of diplomats and police representatives.[57] Behind Rome's historic step lay the inspiration and

[56] Canevaro to Italian ambassadors Paris, Berlin, and Vienna, and chargé d'affaires, London, September 28, 1898, DDI (3), 3:50.
[57] Currie to Salisbury, October 18, 1898, FO 45, PRO.

prodding, above all, of Austria, but also of Germany. Count Goluchowski, the Austro-Hungarian foreign minister, has quite rightly been declared the "primary father" of the Rome Anti-Anarchist Conference.[58] Following in the footsteps of Kálnoky, Austria resumed its role as the gray eminence of anti-anarchist diplomacy. As early as September 14 Goluchowski suggested to the Italians that they not limit their diplomatic initiative to Switzerland but give it a more universal character, involving all European states in the struggle against anarchism.[59] On September 18, the Swiss minister in Vienna reported that Goluchowski mentioned the need for an "international police league" and an "international league against anarchism."[60] On September 19, Costantino Nigra, the veteran Italian ambassador in Vienna, informed Rome that, in Goluchowski's view, pressure on Switzerland "might not be sufficient."

The two Emperors of Austria-Hungary and of Germany, he [Goluchowski] added, think that in order to obtain an effective result all the powers should come to an agreement about measures to take in common. They believe, therefore, that the Royal [Italian] Government should assume the initiative of urgently proposing the meeting, for such a purpose, of an international conference, which the representatives of the Justice and Interior or Foreign Affairs Ministries would attend.[61]

The next day, responding to Nigra's telegram, Foreign Minister Canevaro explicitly confirmed the Austro-German parentage of the conference:

Please tell [Count] Goluchowski that the Royal [Italian] Government shares the view of the two emperors about the opportunity of an understanding among the powers directed to fix measures to take in common against the anarchists. The Government of the king would not be opposed to being the initiator of such an international conference… [I]n the eventuality of a meeting of the conference, I would like to know which, according to the thinking of the Count, should be the states to whom it [Italy] should send an invitation.[62]

Rome subsequently piggy-backed the Austro-German proposal onto Italy's suggestion for anti-Swiss action by asking Italian diplomats to mention it orally to foreign governments.[63]

---

[58] Dannecker, *Schweiz und Österreich-Ungarn*, 156.
[59] Copy telegram, Goluchowski, Vienna, to Ambassador Müller, Rome, September 14, 1898. PA XXVII/64. HHStA.
[60] Dannecker, *Schweiz und Österreich-Ungarn*, 145–146; A. de Claparède, Vienna, to E. Ruffy, President of the Swiss Confederation, Vienna September 18, 1898. DDS, 4:598.
[61] Nigra, Vienna, to foreign ministry, Rome, September 19, 1898, *Telegrammi in arrivo*, no. 2686, vol. 236, IFM.
[62] Canevaro to Nigra, Rome, September 20, 1898, DDI (3), 3:44, no. 72.
[63] Dannecker, *Schweiz und Österreich-Ungarn*, 154.

German policy and the anti-anarchist conference

The references to the "two emperors" in the telegrams exchanged between Vienna and Rome indicate how the inspiration for the conference came not only from Austria's Franz Joseph (or, more importantly, Count Goluchowski), but also from Germany's Wilhelm II. The German kaiser's outrage over the death of Elisabeth has already been cited. While Austria wanted Italy to step forward and take the initiative in order to avoid the appearance of acting out of a desire for revenge, the German government wished to remain in the background in order to spare Wilhelm the wrath of the anarchists as well as avoid domestic complications.

Three days after the assassination, Foreign Secretary Bülow wired Wilhelm, agreeing with him that the government must take advantage of the opportunity provided by the widespread anger against the abominable criminal act in Geneva. Outrage against Elisabeth's murder should be used both to implement long-standing plans to centralize the German police and to conclude administrative agreements with Germany's neighbors to improve surveillance of "anarchists and other social revolutionaries." Germany, of course, would listen willingly to any Austrian or other suggestions for international action.[64] In the end, at least in regards to international measures, Germany decided to let Austria and Italy take the lead. On October 8, 1898, Velics, the Austrian chargé d'affaires in Berlin, explained to Foreign Minister Goluchowski why Germany, despite its enthusiasm for taking strong measures, resisted presenting its own anti-anarchist proposals.[65] Kaiser Wilhelm and Foreign Secretary Bülow were scheduled to leave on a trip to the Middle East on October 12, and would therefore be unable to supervise diplomatic negotiations. Moreover, the French would "probably refuse to accept special German proposals" simply because they were German.

Even before the Italians had taken the initiative, a German government official had told Velics confidentially that, although the kaiser was "personally inclined to take energetic steps," the government was cautious because of the failure of earlier anti-subversive conferences (presumably a reference to the 1893 Spanish proposal or perhaps to Bismarck's proposals after the Paris Commune) and because of domestic considerations. In particular, how could Berlin lead a campaign against the anarchists, when the Prussian and imperial German legal codes had so

---

[64] Tel., Bülow, Semmering, to Kaiser Wilhelm, September 13, 1898. Eur. Gen. 91. reel 108. GFO.
[65] Velics, Berlin, to Goluchowski, Vienna, *Streng vertraulich*, n. 40 E, October 8, 1898. PAXXVII/64. HHStA.

many gaps that needed to be filled in? In 1894–1895 the government had proposed anti-subversive legislation, but this had never been approved, which meant that, for example, the glorification of anarchist deeds still went unpunished in Germany.

Another consideration was that, in its overwhelming majority, the German press was adverse to all measures that might affect, not only individualist anarchists, but also other opposition groups. The imperial government had to be cautious, otherwise it might provide the Social Democrats with a new weapon for agitation in the upcoming Prussian general elections. Finally, if Germany took a leading role in the anti-anarchist campaign, this step might pose a serious threat for Wilhelm II by exposing him to an anarchist assassination attempt, especially since the kaiser was about to embark on an extended trip to the Middle East and his custom was to move everywhere with the freedom of an ordinary tourist.

Italy, the Vatican, and the proposed conference site

On September 29, strongly encouraged by Germany and Austria, Italy sent out a dispatch to every Italian embassy and legation in Europe with a formal proposal for an anti-anarchist conference.[66] The diplomatic note called for

the meeting of an international conference whose object would be to establish among the European powers, in the interest of defending society [*défense social*], a practical agreement [*entente*] aimed at successfully combating anarchist associations and their followers.[67]

At the suggestion of the Austrian foreign minister and in order to convoke the conference quickly, the Italian government decided to limit the invitations to European states.[68] Critics later took Canevaro to task for not inviting the United States, home to so many anarchists who had emigrated from Europe.[69] Canevaro answered this objection by declaring that such a course was impractical. If America had been asked, then it would have been necessary to extend invitations to the whole world and this would have caused too much delay in opening the conference and,

[66] Canevaro to Italian ambassadors in Paris, St. Petersburg, Berlin, Vienna, and the chargé d'affaires in London, Rome, September 28, 1898. DDI (3), 3:50, no. 83.
[67] Canevaro to Royal embassies and legations in Europe, Rome, September 29, 1898, DGPS, (1879–1903), *Ufficio riservato*, b. 1, fasc. 14/71. ACS.
[68] Nigra, Vienna, to foreign ministry, Rome, September 21, 1898, *Telegrammi in arrivo*, no. 2714, vol. 236, IFM.
[69] Senator Pierantoni, *Atti parlamentari, Senato, Discussioni*, February 2, 1901, 1119.

in fact, "more than one country from overseas" had asked him why it had not been invited.[70] Among those countries that had been formally contacted, Italy's allies, first Germany and then Austria-Hungary, accepted on October 4. Russia indicated its adherence by October 14 and France on October 17.[71] Most of the other European states had accepted by October 18 and Switzerland consented to attend on October 21.[72] Only Britain remained undecided.

The Spanish foreign minister, the duke of Almodóvar del Río, had early on approved of the Italian initiative "without reserve."[73] Unfortunately, as he later wrote the Spanish ambassador to Rome, Spain's "police resources" were "too meager" (*demasiado escasos*) for it "to take a prominent part in the discussions."[74] This sounds odd since five years earlier Madrid had taken the initiative in calling for an anti-anarchist conference. But it makes sense if one remembers that since 1893 the enormous scandal over the police torturing of anarchist prisoners in the Montjuich fortress had occurred and blackened not only the reputation of Spain's security forces but of the government itself. The battle against anarchist terrorism revealed the glaring inadequacy of many countries' police while at the same time proving a powerful force for police modernization.

A difficulty arose over the selection of the conference site. Russia, France, and Austria-Hungary, not wishing to strain their relations with the Vatican, which had never accepted Italy's annexation of Rome in 1870, preferred Florence (although apparently Austria had initially hinted that the Italian capital might be acceptable given the "exceptional importance of the gathering.")[75] Venice was also suggested. Much to the chagrin of the octogenarian Pope Leo XIII, however, the Eternal

---

[70] See Canevaro's speech to the Italian Senate, *Atti parlamentari, Senato, Discussioni*, February 2, 1901, 1121–1122. Despite the fact that there is no evidence that America was invited or even informally approached, James Beck, US Assistant Attorney General, later asserted that "the fear that the word 'anarchist' might be construed to include political offenders prevented the United States from taking any part in this conference" ("The Suppression of Anarchy," *American Law Review* 36 [1902]: 200). The authors of the official biography of Howard Vincent also maintain that America "refused to send delegates to the Conference." S. H. Jeyes and F. D. How, *The Life of Sir Howard Vincent* (London: George Allen, 1912): 307.

[71] DDI (3), 3: 52, 53, 56, nos. 88 and 95; Currie to Salisbury, no. 206, confidential, Rome, 18 October 1898, FO 45/206, PRO.

[72] Currie informed Salisbury that "Germany, Austria, Russia, Sweden, Holland, Servia had accepted officially. France, Portugal, Spain, & Bulgaria had stated that they would accept." Currie to Salisbury, Rome, October 18, 1898, FO 45, PRO.

[73] Di Cariati, Madrid, to foreign ministry, Rome, October 5, 1898. PI, b. 30, IFM.

[74] Almodòvar, Madrid, to Spanish ambassador, Rome, November 24, 1898. OP, l. 2750, IFM.

[75] Ambassador De Reverseaux to Delcassé, Vienna, November 9, 1898, DDF, 780; *L'Italie*, November 14, 1898 ; Nigra, Vienna, to Italian foreign ministry, Rome, September 21, 1898, *Ambasciata d'Italia a Vienna*, b. 168 (1899), IFM.

City was finally chosen as the conference site. For failing to prevent this action, the pope blamed Austria and Germany. Berlin repeatedly denied the papal allegation, attributing the rumor to French intrigue and to the Vatican's unreliable source in Vienna (the nuncio there was subsequently reprimanded for his chattiness).[76] In the Vatican's view, the growth of anarchism, particularly in Italy, was due to a lamentable deficiency in European religious education. Conversing with Howard Vincent, a British delegate to the conference, Cardinal Secretary of State Rampolla pointed to Lucheni as an example of this dangerous deficiency, since the assassin had supposedly declared that he had never been taught the duty of going to church.[77]

Why did Britain agree to attend the anti-anarchist conference?

The greatest potential obstacle to the convening and subsequent success of the conference was British opposition. So firmly ingrained was – and is – the image of Victorian Britain, with its liberal tradition, as contrary to all coordinated international action against subversives, that some near-contemporaries, as well as many later historians, have denied that it attended the Rome conference.[78] If the British had refused to participate, this might have led other countries, such as Switzerland, to boycott the meeting. And without Britain and Switzerland, the two major European centers for anarchist exiles and propaganda, the conference would have lost much of its value. Why then did Britain break with its mid-Victorian tradition and attend the 1898 conference?

In part it was because the assassination of the Empress Elisabeth stunned public opinion in Britain quite as much as in the rest of the world, temporarily diverting its attention from a growing confrontation with France in Africa over control of the upper Nile valley.[79] Rome's tactful diplomacy and the cordial relations between Italy and Britain also facilitated British acceptance. Sounded out by the Italian government in late September as to Britain's opinion on making a collective

[76] Foreign Minister Bülow to Chancellor zu Hohenlohe Schillingsfürst, November 15, 1898. *Acten betreffend: Die Anti-anarchist Conference in Rom vom 1898.* Europa Generalia 91 nr. 1. GFO. See also Silvio Furlani's discussion of this question based on German and other documents. "La conferenza internazionale di Roma del 1898 contro 'anarchismo,'" in *La svolta di Giolitti: dalla reazione di fine ottocento al culmine dell'età liberale* (Foggia: Bastogi, 2000): 23–41.

[77] Jeyes and How, *Howard Vincent,* 305.

[78] Quintavalle, *Storia,* 409; Vigo, *Annali d'Italia,* 7:348; Linse, *Organisierter,* 27; duke of Arcos, "International Control of Anarchists," *North American Review* 173 (1901): 764.

[79] Geoffray to Delcassé, September 12 and 28, 1898, DDF, 544 and 597.

representation to the Swiss government regarding its handling of anarchist subversion, the British replied to the Italian chargé d'affaires that Her Majesty's government was "no less concerned than those of other countries in the adoption of reasonable precautions against such atrocious crimes as that which had recently horrified all Europe." Before making further commitments, however, it desired more particulars about proposed measures.[80]

In mid-October, Foreign Minister Canevaro clarified the Italian position on the aims and methods of the conference.[81] He assured the British that the conference program would be very moderate. Its primary objects would be to define anarchism "unofficially" and endeavor to arrive at an understanding for putting anarchists on the same footing as offenders against common law. Participation in the conference would be non-binding, since all decisions reached by the delegates would have to be ratified by home governments.[82]

Despite these reassurances, when Lord Salisbury spoke with Italian Ambassador De Renzis on October 20, he continued to emphasize the difficulties involved in British adherence. English tradition, particularly the historic right of asylum for political exiles, blocked acceptance of new anti-anarchist measures. Smiling, Salisbury quipped that, "Personally, I am of the opinion of the Government of the Netherlands, that perhaps the Conference is a danger, because it gives too much importance to anarchy whose members live on vanity above all!" But the prime minister also repeatedly stressed his wish to do Italy a favor and his opinion that, for Britain, representation at the conference would be a simple act of courtesy.[83]

Indeed at this time and later, Britain owed Italy an "act of courtesy."[84] During September and October, while Rome was making diplomatic preparations for the conference, a political confrontation between France and Britain was coming to a boil over control of the headwaters of the Nile in southern Sudan. During the so-called Fashoda crisis, Italy, although officially neutral, remained benevolently pro-British. At the end

---

[80] Salisbury as reported in Sanderson to Count Costa, Italian chargé d'affaires, September 29, 1898, FO. 45/392, PRO. At the same time that the British were making this moderately favorable reply to the Italians, they led the French to think the reverse, i.e., that they would decline to participate in any joint anti-anarchist measures. Geoffray to Delcassé, September 28, 1898, *DDF*, 597.

[81] De Renzis, London, to Canevaro, October 20, 1898, *DDI* (3), 3:57–58.

[82] Currie, Rome, to FO, copy tel. no. 87, October 18, 1898, FO 43, PRO.

[83] DeRenzis to Canevaro, October 20, 1898, DDI (3), 3:57–58. In his dispatch, De Renzis annotated Salisbury's reference to the Netherlands with an "(?)".

[84] "La Grande-Bretagne laquelle n'a adhéré que par déférence pour le Gouvernement italien et afin de se le conserver bien disposé dans ses démêlés actuels avec la France." Carlin, Rome, to Ruffy, Berne, November 10, 1898. DDS 4:623.

of October 1898, Italian naval bases were put in readiness in case of a possible pre-emptive French attack.[85]

The opinion of Queen Victoria also influenced Salisbury. While parliament and the cabinet controlled foreign policy, the monarch still had the right to be consulted and to advise, and in the case of Salisbury, Queen Victoria's advice mattered a good deal. The heavy-set, six-foot-four prime minister and the tiny old queen, at seventy-nine more than ten years older than her head of government, made an odd couple, but Salisbury respected Victoria's experience, common sense, and wisdom, and this regard was mutual, creating a strong rapport between the two.[86] One biographer even asserts that although Salisbury paid little attention to women, "two women, his wife and the Queen, exercised far more influence over him than all his male acquaintances put together" and "commonly helped him make up his mind."[87]

Victoria's reaction to the death of the Empress Elisabeth and the call for an international anti-anarchist conference was therefore bound to have some effect on British policy. In her journal entry for September 10, Victoria noted that the "startling and awful news" of Elisabeth's assassination "gave us all a terrible shock."[88] In earlier years, on the occasions when she visited the country to go hunting, the Empress Elisabeth had made friends in Great Britain, including Victoria herself.[89] When Victoria wrote in her journal months after the assassination, the impact of Elisabeth's brutal death was still apparent:

The last day [i.e., 31 December 1898] of a very eventful year, full of victories, but also of sad events, one in particular, very dreadful, the assassination of the sweet, good and beautiful Empress of Austria![90]

Victoria pressed Salisbury to take some kind of action against the anarchists, and on October 19, the prime minister spoke with Sir Edward Bradford, the commissioner of the Metropolitan Police.[91] The latter strongly opposed taking international measures against the anarchists "as such" because of the impossibility of defining "anarchist." Questioned closely by Salisbury regarding the queen's safety, the police commissioner replied that "of course

---

[85] Canevaro to Saletta, *Capo di Stato Maggiore dell'esercito*, December 6, 1898, DDI (3) 3: 72; James L. Granville, "Italy's Relations with England," *Johns Hopkins University Studies in Historical and Political Science* 52 (1934): 61–63; Seton-Watson, *Italy*, 209.

[86] Paul Kennedy, *The Realities Behind Diplomacy: Background Influences on British External Policy, 1865–1980* (London: George Allen and Unwin, 1981): 66–67.

[87] Kennedy, *Salisbury*, 329.

[88] Queen Victoria, *The Letters of Queen Victoria*, vol. 3, 3rd series (New York: Longmans Green, 1932), 227.

[89] Victoria, *Letters*, 222; *The Times* (London), September 12, 1898, 7.

[90] Victoria, *Letters*, 327.   [91] Victoria, *Letters*, 294–295.

he would take any further measures that were thought expedient; but that in his conviction [Her] Majesty was as safe as any person in [her] dominions." He even averred that "no English anarchist had ever been found," and that foreign anarchists resident in Britain made no criminal attempts, because the "atmosphere of opinion" was so strongly against such actions. Nonetheless, Bradford was agreeable to an extension of the government's general power to expel aliens if parliament would permit it. But the police commissioner thought that unlikely, an opinion that Salisbury shared.[92]

In July 1894, the conservative leader had introduced into parliament a bill allowing the government to expel indigent immigrants and foreigners suspected of threatening British security; it had failed to pass. The bill's introduction was prompted in part by the presence of several French anarchists who sought safety in England after carrying out bombings in Paris. In 1898, Salisbury tried once again to secure passage of his aliens bill. The House of Lords passed the first part of the bill, regarding foreign paupers, but, since the House of Commons failed to act, the measure died.[93]

On October 27, 1898, the cabinet finally reached a decision on the proposal to attend the anti-anarchist conference. The same day in a ciphered telegram, Salisbury informed the queen that the answer agreed upon was affirmative "in accordance with the view your Majesty expressed to Lord Salisbury."[94] In its message to Rome, London qualified its acceptance by noting that parliament, in all probability, would not be disposed to sanction any legislation departing from "the principles traditionally accepted here with regard to the individual freedom of all persons, whether natives or foreigners, whatever opinions they may hold, so long as no substantial evidence of crime or criminal intentions can be produced against them."[95]

The British cabinet consented to the conference not only because Conservatives who worried about immigration issues were in power and because the government desired – or at least was willing – to extend courtesies to Queen Victoria and Italy, but also because at this juncture it would have been unwise to remain isolated from the rest of Europe. With the Fashoda crisis, in particular, still unresolved and the prodromes evident of a conflict in South Africa, this was no time to needlessly affront the Triple Alliance. Since March 1898, Chamberlain had been seeking an understanding with Germany, which as we have seen was one of the prime instigators of the conference.

[92] Victoria, *Letters*, 284 and 295.
[93] *BDIL*, 6:12, 100; Elie Halévy, *A History of the English People*, trans. E. I. Watkin and Ernst Benn, 5 vols. (London: T. Fisher Unwin, 1924–1947): 5:373; Porter, *Vigilant State*, 110–111.
[94] Victoria, *Letters*, 299.
[95] Salisbury to Ambassador Currie, Rome, no. 144, October 27, 1898, FO 45, PRO.

The French attitude

The attitude of France also influenced Britain. In late October, the Italian ambassador informed Rome that "Lord Salisbury finally, before I took my leave, asked me repeatedly if among the governments favorable to the Conference there was France."[96] Indeed, French participation was even more crucial than British, since several important states – notably Germany and Austria – were willing to support a gathering made up of *only* continental countries.[97] In 1898 a growing rapprochement with Italy after years of bitter acrimony characterized French policy. Theophile Delcassé, who began his long tenure (1898–1905) as foreign minister in June 1898, and Camille Barrère, the able new French ambassador in Rome, were determined to improve relations with Italy in order to undermine its alliance with Germany and Austria-Hungary.[98] In the fall of 1898, secret talks in Paris, begun in May 1897, continued in an effort to end a ten-year-old Franco–Italian trade war. On November 21, 1898, France and Italy successfully concluded a new Commercial Agreement.

At the same time that trade relations were improving, France and Italy were able to concur on joint action against the anarchists. France wished neither to offend Italy nor to humiliate Switzerland. Delcassé repeatedly assured the Swiss ambassador that he was a friend of Switzerland. He encouraged the Swiss both to keep him informed of their actions and to take vigorous measures against the anarchists, because this was the only way to definitively block the Italian initiative.[99] At the same time France gave lip service to the Italian *démarche*. If all the Great Powers agreed (which was by no means assured given Britain's cautious attitude), and if the communication to the Swiss government avoided a threatening tone, France was willing to go along with the Italian proposal to pressure Switzerland and participate in concerted action against the anarchists.[100] Delcassé made plain to Italian Ambassador Tornielli, however, that simply putting pressure on Switzerland promised little advantage to France since the Swiss reaction would simply be to expel foreign subversives who would ultimately end up in London. Residing there, they would pose just

---

[96] De Renzis to Canevaro, October 20, 1898, DDI (3), 3:58.
[97] Velics, Berlin, to Goluchowski, Vienna, September 24, 1898. PA XXVII/64, HHStA.
[98] Seton-Watson, *Italy*, 207–208.
[99] Chargé d'affaires Boissier, Paris, to Swiss Confederation President Ruffy, September 19, 1898. Cited by Dannecker, *Schweiz und Österreich-Ungarn*, 147–148; Adolf Lacher, *Die Schweiz und Frankreich vor dem Ersten Weltkrieg. Diplomatische und politische Beziehungen im Zeichen des deutsch-franzosischen Gegensatzes 1883–1914* (Basil: Helbing and Lichtenhahn, 1967): 115–117.
[100] Tornielli, Paris, to Canevaro, September 22, 1898, DDI (3), 3: 46; Sanderson memorandum, "Anarchists in Switzerland," summarizing discussion with French minister, September 24, 1898. FO 43, PRO.

Figure 6 Palazzo Corsini alla Lungara, Rome. Site of the Anti-Anarchist Conference of 1898.
Source: Lalupa, Wikimedia Commons http://commons.wikimedia.org/wiki/File:3ATrastevere_-_Palazzo_Corsini_alla_Lungara_1040126.JPG

as much danger to France. Action that led to a British crackdown on the "conspiracies of the worst agitators," would be much more desirable.[101] This helps explain why, having helped Switzerland avoid a slap in the face at the hands of the Triple Alliance, on October 17 Paris was ready to accept Rome's more congenial invitation to attend an international anti-anarchist conference including Britain.[102] While France thought any new anti-anarchist legislation "impractical," "police precautions to be internationally arranged" might be worth discussing.[103]

The Rome conference opens and defines anarchism

Amid, according to the newspapers, "an enormous display of police force" to guard against possible anarchist attacks, the conference opened

---

[101] Tornielli, Paris, to Canevaro, September 22, 1898, DDI (3), 3: 46
[102] Currie to Salisbury, no. 206, confidential, Rome, October 18, 1898, FO 45/206, PRO.
[103] British Ambassador Monson, Paris, October 19, 1898, FO27/3400. PRO.

Figure 7 Sir Charles Edward Howard Vincent, first director of Scotland Yard's Criminal Investigation Department, and initiator of the secret meetings between police representatives held at the 1898 Rome Anti-Anarchist Conference.

on November 24 in the Palazzo Corsini on the west bank of the Tiber. Fifty-four delegates representing twenty-one countries attended.[104] This was the whole of Europe (Montenegro sent no delegate but was represented by Russia). Besides ambassadors, diplomats of lesser rank, and

[104] The *Daily Mail* (London), November 25, 1898, 5, speaks of the preventative arrest of 2,000 anarchists in Rome, but this may be an exaggeration, since the anarchist population of the city probably numbered in the hundreds not the thousands; Prefect Serrao to *Commissario capo di pubblica sicurezza*, Rome, November 25, 1898, *Archivio di Stato di Roma, Questura*, f. 302.

miscellaneous interior and justice ministry bureaucrats, the national police heads of Russia, France and Belgium, as well as the municipal police chief of Stockholm, the head of the Berlin political police, and a high-ranking representative of the Viennese police participated.[105] The presence of some of Europe's most experienced and able diplomats, such as France's Camille Barrère, Russia's Alexander Ivanovich Nelidov, and Britain's Sir Philip Currie, together with high-ranking police and government officials, made this one of the most impressive international conferences since the Congress of Berlin in 1878. After the opening session, the Rome meeting was held in secrecy in order to avoid terrorist reprisals against those delegates who recommended harsh repressive measures. Even the gathering's secret minutes usually do not identify how countries voted.[106] It was almost as if the conference, mimicking its enemy, wished to create a vast, secret anti-terrorist conspiracy to battle the vast, secret – although phantom – international conspiracy of the anarchists. Ironically, or perhaps appropriately, the rules of the conference were based on those adopted by several international conferences on sanitation devoted to stopping infectious diseases (appropriate since anarchism was often compared to a disease or vermin).[107]

In the month-long discussions that now began and lasted until December 21, Russia and Germany took the lead and were closely followed by Austria-Hungary and Turkey. These were the four most conservative, indeed reactionary, states attending the Rome meeting. The German ambassador informed the chancellor that, in accordance with the latter's directives, "I was in continual contact with my Russian colleague throughout the entire duration of the Conference."[108] Since the sessions of the conference were confidential, Germany could now assume the prominent role it had long hesitated to take in public, and put into action plans that it had had under consideration since 1894. The three central and eastern European empires attempted with some success to enact what amounted to a common program. According to the British ambassador, Italy, Spain, and Turkey almost invariably supported the three empires, and France usually voted with them as well, although it

---

[105] S. E. Zwoliansky [Zvolianskii], Director of the Russian Police Department (1897–1902); Jean Samuel Maurice Viguié, Director of France's *Sûreté Général* (1897–1899); and François Charles de Latour, Belgium's Director General of Public Security and of Prisons since 1890.

[106] Canvaro's speech to the Italian Senate, *Atti parlamentari*, Senato, discussioni, February 2, 1901, 1116–17.

[107] CIR, 17.

[108] Saurma, Rome, to Hohenlohe-Schillingsfurst, Berlin, December 22, 1898, f. 168, interior ministry, Rep. 77, tit. 2512, no. 7, vol .1, GCSAM.

dissented on a number of key issues.[109] Despite, or because of, the fact that it was the host country, Italy acted simply as a facilitator, chairing the various sessions and committee meetings, but rarely intervening (the minutes record only one instance, i.e., when Canevaro spoke out on the necessity of the death penalty for assassins).[110] Britain participated actively in the proceedings, especially at the outset, when it proposed amendments and tried to moderate those resolutions it disliked. But these efforts attracted so little support that this tactic was soon abandoned. On December 1, Maurice de Bunsen, a secretary to the British delegation at the conference, recorded in his diary that: "It seems not improbable that the British Delegates will have to leave the Conference, or at least give up active participation in the discussions."[111] The British adopted the latter course and subsequently abstained on most ballots, continuing, however, to work behind the scenes to tone down the more extreme proposals.[112]

During the first ten days of the meeting, the delegates hotly debated the fundamental question of the definition of anarchism and finally accepted a compromise resolution. In the process definite patterns of allegiance emerged and the entire conference threatened to break apart due to disagreements between the more liberal countries, such as Britain and France, and the more conservative, spearheaded by a reactionary Russia and Germany. A legal definition of what constituted "anarchism" was crucial, since no parliament or court in Europe had clearly resolved this question. Hector de Rolland, diplomat, legislator, and prosecuting attorney before the supreme court of Monaco, proposed a definition that focused on the "anarchist act." He defined this as an action "having as its aim the destruction through violent means of all social organization [*toute organisation sociale*]." An anarchist was simply one who committed such an act. Russia and Germany desired a more detailed and comprehensive definition that explicitly included propagandists of anarchist ideas and those who acted like anarchists even if they did not call themselves that, but their resolutions lost out to the Monacan proposal.[113]

[109] Currie to Salisbury, December 22, 1898, FO 881/7179, no. 33, 100, PRO.
[110] Tamburini, "La conferenza internazionale di Roma," 263.
[111] Edgar T. S. Dugdale, *Maurice de Bunsen: Diplomat and Friend* (London: John Murray, 1934): 165.
[112] Howard Vincent to Salisbury, December 8, 1898, reprinted in Jeyes and How, *Howard Vincent*, 303.
[113] Germany and Russia proposed similar definitions, which they later amended in a vain attempt to obtain majority support. The initial German proposal, presented on November 26 by Ferdinand von Martitz, a distinguished professor of international law, stated that "under the name of anarchists, whatever designation they may give themselves, are comprised all individuals who have the goal of overthrowing the social order

While Germany and Russia disliked the narrowness of the definition of the anarchist, its ambiguity and vagueness caused problems for
other countries.[114] The French word *toute* could be translated as "any,"
although it is clear from the comments of British officials that "all" was
the intended meaning.[115] De Rolland's definition did have the advantage of precedent. In 1892 the Institute of International Law, made up
of eminent jurists from various countries and arguably the world's most
important fount of international law theory, held a meeting in Geneva
that adopted a definition for extradition cases similar to de Rolland's.
This definition was designed to exclude anarchists from the protection of
the political asylum clause found in many laws and treaties.

[Art. 4] Ne son point réputé délits politiques au point de vue de l'application des
règles qui précèdent, les faits délictueux qui sont dirigés contre les bases de toute
organisation sociale, et non pas seulement contre tel Etat déterminé ou contre
telle forme de gouvernement.

Criminal acts directed against the bases of all social organization, and not only
against a certain State or a certain form of government, are not considered political offences in the application of the preceding rules [regarding extradition].[116]

Curiously this important validation of de Rolland's definition did not figure prominently in the discussions at the Rome meeting. Whatever its
limitations, de Rolland's definition had tremendous implications, since it
declared that anarchism aimed at an apocalyptic destruction of all social
organizations: governments, churches, businesses, the family, etc. If such an
all-encompassing, limitless program of violence was implicit in the "anarchist act," what need was there to use a word like "terrorism" to describe or

in order to replace it by a new state of affairs without law and without authority and
who, in order to attain this end, do not hesitate in respect to [using] any means, whether
trying to stir up minds through their subversive theories, or committing or endorsing
or glorifying crimes." CIR, 80. On November 28, Russian police chief Zvolianskii proposed that: "Under the name of anarchists, whatever designation they may give themselves, are comprised all those whose acts have as a goal the destruction of all social
organization [*toute organization sociale*], whatever may be its form, by having recourse
to violent means, or provoking them [i.e., violent means] through the propagation of
their theories." Second meeting of the commission, CIR, 84. See also the fourth plenary
session, December 3, 1898, CIR, 35–37.

[114] In his final report to the Spanish foreign ministry, Aramburu wrote of the "excessive
generality of the phrase" used to define anarchism, *Memoria*, page 12 of unnumbered
text. OP, l. 2750, SFM.

[115] Salisbury to Currie, London, December 2, 1898; inclosure 1 in Currie to Salisbury,
Rome, December 3, 1898. FO 881/7179, PRO.

[116] See the French and English versions provided in Christine Van den Wijngaert, *The
Political Offence Exception to Extradition* (Netherlands: Kluwer, 1980): 16. The English
translation is that of James Brown Scott, *Resolutions of the Institute of International Law*
(1916): 103. Ludovic Beauchet, *Traité de l'extradition* (Paris: A. Chevalier-Marescq,
1899): 232–233, quotes from Albéric Rolin's report on this proposed article, in which
Rolin explicitly links it with the deeds of such anarchists as Ravachol.

qualify it? For everyone other than the anarchists, it made anarchism virtually synonymous with terrorism and, at least potentially, with the most frightening form of terrorism that has ever existed before or since.

After defining anarchism, the conference was free to move on to other issues. The delegates decided to divide up their labors by forming two large committees, one devoted to legislative and the other to administrative matters; later they established a sub-committee made up of representatives from the regular committees and charged with handling the delicate problems of the expulsion and extradition of anarchists.

A set of Spanish propositions presented to the legislative committee were the only ones at the conference that tried to address the fundamental economic, social, political, and even spiritual causes of anarchist terrorism. Agreeing with the Vatican, Spain called for the reinforcement of religious belief, of the moral sense, and of the means for sound education. Another Spanish resolution called for the "wise and progressive amelioration of institutions, laws and customs which incubated injustices or gave a reasonable pretext for the spirit of revolt." A third proposed that each state seek to improve the "conditions of the indigent" through the work of "charitable societies and industrial enterprises."[117] Many of the delegates agreed with Spain that to overcome anarchism required basic reforms. As Baron de Rolland noted in his final report on the committee's work,

anarchism is nothing but the brutal manifestation of a profound illness, from which a set of repressive laws would not suffice to deliver society. It will not be able to triumph, all clear headed people recognize, than with the aid of reforms resolutely undertaken simultaneously in the social, moral and religious order.[118]

Despite this agreement, the Spanish program was quickly tabled and had no influence. Most delegates believed that these questions were for their home government to resolve; attempts by the conference to formulate solutions for society's malaise would lead the delegates into unauthorized discussions and decisions far exceeding their diplomatic mandates.[119] Equally unsuccessful was Spain's proposal that anarchists be shipped off to an island or distant region where they would be left free to put their theories into practice.[120]

Most of the resolutions eventually adopted by the legislative commission were the work of Baron de Rolland. In reality, de Rolland acted as a mouthpiece for France, which through this stratagem hoped to avoid an open

---

[117] Felix Aramburu, December 1, 1898, CIR, 129–130.   [118] CIR, 183.
[119] Report of the legislative committee, CIR, 183.
[120] CIR, 130.

confrontation with its ally, Russia.[121] Briefly stated, de Rolland's program called for prohibiting and punishing the possession or use of explosives for illegitimate reasons, membership in anarchist associations, provocation to or support of anarchist acts, spreading anarchist propaganda, publicizing of anarchist trials, and rendering assistance to anarchists (e.g., providing lodgings, instruments of crime, etc.). De Rolland's proposals also included measures restricting anarchists' movement once outside prison and forcing them to remain in solitary confinement when incarcerated. Despite opposition from both liberal and conservative critics, the conference accepted most of de Roland's program without amendment.[122]

In addition, the Austro-German-Russian bloc succeeded in passing legislative proposals that punished anarchist propaganda in the armed forces and complicity of any sort in anarchist deeds and that required the non-public execution of anarchists. Recognizing the crucial role that the media played in the spread of terrorism, the conference also adopted by the narrowest of margins a cautious Austro-German resolution calling on governments to limit press coverage of anarchist actions. Toward the end of the conference, on December 19, German Ambassador Saurma von Jeltsch presented a very controversial proposal demanding that the death penalty be made mandatory for all assassinations of sovereigns and heads of state. Even though Italy had abolished the death penalty, Foreign Minister Canevaro (under strong pressure from the German ambassador) spoke in favor of its adoption since he believed that, if capital punishment had been legal in both Geneva and Italy, the murder of Elisabeth would never have taken place.[123] (It is difficult to credit Canevaro's view since Lucheni had declared that he *regretted* the absence of the death penalty in Geneva and, without compulsion, would have "bound up the steps of the beloved guillotine," if his petition requesting this had been accepted by the President of the Swiss Confederation. It was not.[124]) Since the German proposal did not specifically mention anarchism, the Swedish delegate thought it out of order.[125] Nonetheless, the plenary session finally accepted the measure, although seven out of the twenty delegates abstained from voting: Portugal, Romania, the Netherlands (all three of which had abolished capital punishment), Britain, Switzerland, Sweden-Norway, and Denmark.[126]

[121] Currie to Salisbury, November 30, 1898, FO 881/7179, N. 8, 10. PRO.
[122] Report of the legislative committee, CIR, 172.
[123] Saurma, Rome, to Hohenlohe-Schillingsfurst, Berlin, December 22, 1898, f. 168, interior ministry, Rep. 77, tit. 2512, no. 7, vol .1, GCSAM; Canevaro, December 20, 1898, CIR, 50.
[124] Corti, *Elizabeth*, 387–388.
[125] Baron de Bildt, December 20, 1898, CIR, 51.
[126] Saurma, Rome, to German foreign ministry, December 21, 1898. Rep. 77, tit. 2512, no. 7 vol. 1, GCSAM.

The question of extraditing anarchists also provoked much discussion at the conference. The delegates finally agreed on Germany's proposal that anarchist crimes be considered non-political for extradition purposes and that various violent acts typically the work of anarchists, such as fabricating bombs, be made subject to extradition.[127] Despite the assurances of various countries, however, few if any seem to have subsequently altered their legislation on extradition along these lines so as to conform with Rome's wishes.

More influential was a Russian proposal presented by Ambassador Nelidov with the support of the Belgians. Nelidov's resolution asked that attempts against the life or liberty of a sovereign or chief of state, or of their families, be made grounds in every case for extradition proceedings. This was a version of the famous "Belgian" or *attentat* clause devised in 1856 after an unsuccessful attempt to blow up a train carrying Napoleon III between Lille and Calais. The perpetrators of this deed fled to Belgium but Brussels refused to extradite them since they were protected as political offenders by the "political exclusion clause" of the Franco–Belgian extradition treaty. Subsequently France pressured its small neighbor into amending its laws to provide for the extradition of those who attempted the lives of foreign heads of state or their families.[128] Since neither the original *attentat* clause nor the Russian proposal referred specifically to anarchism, the French and Swiss delegates criticized it as out of order. Nonetheless the conference adopted the resolution without a single opposing vote and with only five countries out of twenty abstaining. Although the minutes do not record how each country voted, France and Switzerland were probably joined in their abstentions by Britain, Greece, and perhaps Sweden.[129]

Equally, if not more, controversial was the question of the administrative expulsion of anarchists. The delegates approved two resolutions on the question, one supported by Germany and the second by Russia. The German-backed motion provided that all foreigners expelled as anarchists be directed back to the frontiers of their native countries, and that the police authorities involved be given sufficient forewarning of the impending expulsions. If the expellee lived in a non-bordering country, all intervening states would help effect said person's transfer back to his homeland. Then on December 7, the Russians presented a resolution calling for negotiations between governments prior to an expulsion in

[127] Report of the subcommittee on extradition and expulsion, CIR, 205–210.
[128] Jean Beaudéant, *L'Attentat contre les chefs d'Etat* (Toulouse: Divion, 1911); *Digest of International Law*, ed. Marjorie Millace Whiteman (Washington, DC: US Government Printing Office, 1963–1973): 856–857, 860–861.
[129] December 20, 1898, CIR, 54–55.

which a prospective expellee faced possible arrest after deportation to his homeland. This highly controversial resolution infuriated the French, who considered the measure license for the disguised extradition of political offenders.[130] Despite French opposition, the delegates adopted the Russian proposal, but by the barest of majorities: ten to eight with Britain and Greece abstaining.[131] The heated debate on this issue had exposed a profound divergence between Paris and St. Petersburg and the development of deep cracks in the recent Franco–Russian Alliance (1893/1894). Already in a private letter dated December 4, Ambassador Barrère had warned the French foreign minister that the Russians were proving every day more and more intransigent, and that the whole conference was in danger of "fizzling out."[132] A few days later, Sir Howard Vincent, a British delegate, noted in a letter to Lord Salisbury that "the remarkable thing is the *éloignement* [estrangement or antipathy] between the representatives of Russia and France, amounting almost to hostility."[133]

Administrative issues and secret police sessions

Ultimately more significant for the future than the conference's recommendations on expulsion and extradition was its work involving administrative and police questions. When the administrative committee began meeting on December 1, 1898, Germany once again took the initiative, proposing that each country: 1) keep a close watch over its anarchists; 2) establish a central agency to carry out this task; and 3) facilitate direct communication and information exchange between the central agencies.[134] This project was hardly a new one, since the German interior ministry had been recommending it to the Foreign Office as long ago as mid-1894, at the time of the assassination of President Carnot. The interior ministry wanted the conclusion of such an agreement with as many foreign states as possible, including the United States.[135] The conference approved the German policing measures by near-unanimous votes, with only Britain abstaining.[136]

---

[130] Viguié, December 7, 1898, CIR, 102–103; 104–105.

[131] December 13, 1898, CIR, 200.

[132] "*De tourner en eau de boudin*," DDF (1), XIV, no. 555, December 4, 1898.

[133] Vincent, Rome, to Salisbury, December 8, 1898, cited in Jeyes and How, *Howard Vincent*, 303.

[134] CIR, 89–90.

[135] Bülow, Berlin, to Hohenlohe-Schillingsfürst, June 22, 1898. Film 12155/56. fol. 65. Reichskanzlei. GCSAP; Tel., Bülow, Semmering, to Kaiser Wilhelm, September 13, 1898. Eur. Gen. 91, reel 108, GFO.

[136] December 7, 1898, CIR, 102; see also the report of the administrative commission, CIR, 115.

The efficacy of these resolutions was enhanced by the work of a highly secret committee of police chiefs and representatives. While no minutes were kept at the mysterious meetings, Sir Howard Vincent, a Conservative member of parliament and ex-director of Scotland Yard's criminal investigation unit, reported on their discussions to the Foreign Office and later mentioned them in a 1906 London *Times* interview. In the interview, Vincent claimed that it was he who instigated these informal secret meetings and this fact is corroborated by Karl Brzesowsky, a high-ranking Viennese police official who also participated in the secret gatherings.[137] In his confidential report to Ambassador Currie, Vincent states that at first he did not propose himself to attend, since at the time, he had no special police attribute. He only changed his mind "in deference to the strongly expressed general wish."[138]

It may seem odd that Britain should have taken such a leading role, given its detached policy of abstaining on most issues brought before the conference. Vincent probably went beyond what his government wanted, since in his official report to London he makes no mention of his personal initiative. In many ways, however, Vincent was the ideal person to bring European police officials together for a meeting. Blue-eyed, with an enormous drooping mustache, Vincent possessed great energy, as well as a taste for intrigue and a talent for organization. He spoke (although often with an atrocious accent) all the major European languages, including Russian.[139] He was personally acquainted with the leadership and structure of the major European police systems, and was sympathetic with continental problems in dealing with anarchists. As far back as 1878, when Vincent had helped found the Criminal Investigation Department of the London Metropolitan Police, he had fought, with only partial success, to expedite international police communications, bypassing cumbersome diplomatic procedures.[140] As a policeman in the early 1880s, Vincent had also struggled to defeat the Fenian bombing campaign in England.

According to Vincent, "some fourteen or fifteen police forces were represented at the meetings."[141] Brzesowsky mentions a gathering on

[137] *The Times* (London) June 5, 1906, p.3; Brzesowsky to Pasetti, inclosure in dispatch, Rome, December 26, 1898. Politisches Archiv. XXVII/65. HHStA.

[138] 19 FO 881/7179, p.68. PRO.

[139] Jeyes and How, *Howard Vincent*, 128, 180, 347.

[140] Copy of circular, London, June 1, 1878 and Vincent memorandum, November 6, 1878; translation of Vincent's *revised* circular of June 1, 1878 included with dispatch of chargé d'affaires, Stuttgart, April 25, 1879, to undersecretary of state, HO. HO45/9569/76261. PRO.

[141] Vincent's Confidential Report, December 17, 1898. Inclosure no. 30 in Currie to Salisbury, secret, December 20, 1898, FO 881/7179, p. 68. PRO. In the *Times* interview held almost eight years after the event, Vincent speaks of sixteen present at the meeting,

WHO CAN TELL HOW SOON IT MAY TURN ITS HEAD THIS WAY

Figure 8 The anarchist menace as it appeared in the aftermath of the assassination of Italian King Umberto I. *New York Herald*, August 1, 1900.

December 14, as well as the one on December 12, but lists only eleven participating countries: Austria-Hungary, Germany, Belgium, France, Britain, Italy, Russia, Sweden, Turkey, Switzerland, and Holland.[142] Italy's director general of public security attended, although he was not an official participant in the Rome conference.[143] Spain, which had sent a distinguished professor of penal law but no police official to the conference, was apparently unrepresented at the meetings.[144] This was an unfortunate omission since, of all countries, Spain was the most in need of help in the policing of anarchists. The sessions were strictly private, held round a small table, and limited to those persons directly concerned. No formal speeches were made, no minutes taken, and no written report drawn up. According to Vincent's and Brzesowsky's accounts, three matters were dealt with: 1) the expulsion of undesirable foreigners; 2) cooperation between the police forces of Europe; and 3) descriptive methods of identifying criminals, particularly *portrait parlé*.

Most of Vincent's confidential report was devoted to summarizing the views and information exchanged by the police officials on the subject of expulsion, a topic of great interest to the British government. Nine countries, plus Britain, reported their procedures and practice. In practice, Vincent wrote, Britain had become the great "depot for the expelled of all countries." Since foreign governments so frequently dumped anarchists and the destitute on British shores, Vincent naturally felt that "the law and practice of expulsion as now enforced are in direct opposition to international comity." In his confidential report, Vincent endorsed as "beneficial" the resolution of the administrative commission providing for the expulsion of anarchists to their native states after prior notification of the country affected.[145]

Another important item discussed by the police committee was descriptive methods of identifying criminals. The committee, and later the conference, decided that *portrait parlé*, in Vincent's words, was "by far the most complete and handy as to accuracy, information, size and material" and should be adopted by all countries for common criminals

---

but this must be a lapse in memory. *The Times* (London), June 5, 1906, 3. Nine current or former police officials were official representatives at the conference. *Conférence internationale ... Rome 1898. Liste des délégués.* Presidenza Pelloux. f. 365. ACS.

[142] Brzesowsky to Pasetti, inclosure in dispatch, Rome, December 26, 1898. Politisches Archiv. XXVII/65. HHStA; Sir Howard Vincent, confidential report, December 17, 1898. Inclosure no. 30 in Currie to Salisbury, December 20, 1898. FO 881/7179, PRO.

[143] Memoir, *riservata*, Rome, September 17, 1900. Series Z., b. 51. IFM.

[144] Felix de Aramburu y Zuloaga, rector of the University of Oviedo.

[145] Vincent's confidential report, December 17, 1898. Inclosure no. 30 in Currie to Salisbury, December 20, 1898, FO 881/7179. PRO.

and anarchists alike.[146] What was *portrait parlé*? The "speaking likeness" system was an offshoot of the famous French criminologist Alphonse Bertillon's complex method of identification termed anthropometry or Bertillonage, which was the world's first precise, and apparently "scientific," system of describing the human body. Bertillon took prisoners' measurements with specially designed calipers, gauges, and rulers. Using a scale of seven derived from a study of the work of the anatomist Adophe Quetelet, he then classified the size of various parts of the head and body. This descriptive information, together with data about a criminal's color of hair, eyes and skin, scars and tattoos, exact body measurements (e.g., the length of the foot, the forearm, etc.), and other pertinent information, could be squeezed onto a folded *portrait parlé* card and carried in a pocket.[147] If available, a photograph of the subject, carefully posed full-face and in profile might also be added. This system was of special use in the apprehension of criminals operating across borders since the dozen or so pieces of information vital to the positive identification of a suspect could be transmitted by telephone or telegraph, a process facilitated by reducing descriptions of physical traits to a few letters and numbers.[148]

While anthropometry was useful for the positive identification of criminals already under detention, *portrait parlé* was helpful in recognizing suspected individuals still at large. *Portrait parlé* aided in recognition rather than unequivocally establishing the identify of a suspect. In the words of the director general of the French *Sûrete*, Jean Viguié, it was a question of using "the eye and no longer the compass," as in Bertillonage's complicated measurements. Viguié explained to the delegates assembled at Rome that descriptions of criminals had previously been composed of "terms too vague and artificial" (*termes synthétiques fort vagues*) that were "more harmful than helpful, because [they] could almost always apply indiscriminately to many persons." On the other hand, *portrait parlé*, by focusing on the dozen or so fixed qualities of the human face (such as the shape of the ear and the forehead) and describing them in a systematic and precise fashion, would enable an observer to pick out a suspect "in any place, at any hour."

[146] Ibid., 70.
[147] Alphone Bertillon, *Identification Anthropométrique. Instructions Signalétiques*, 2 vols. (Melun: Imprimerie administrative, 1893): 2:137. This *portrait parlé* card was therefore a hybrid made up of Bertillonage measurements and *portrait parlé* proper, which was purely visual and descriptive.
[148] The most recent authoritative account of *portrait parlé* and other systems of criminal identification is Simon Cole, *Suspect Identities: A History of Fingerprinting and Criminal Identification* (Cambridge, MA: Harvard University Press, 2001): especially 47–53.

Portrait parlé presents itself as a new tool, perfected and scientific, placed in the hands of agents charged with the pursuit of fleeing lawbreakers.

If the police of every country definitively adopt it, it will be like a universal eye staring at noted criminals as they pass by and infallibly unmasking them despite the perfection of their most well executed disguises.

The acquisition of this "universal" unmasking "eye" required, according to Viguié, "only" thirty lessons of two hours each.[149] The facilitation of inter-European police cooperation was the most important result of both the police meeting and of the anti-anarchist conference as a whole. The assembled police delegates had to deal with the most basic questions. They therefore began by identifying for each other the official designation and address of each country's police authority to which news of any anticipated anarchist outrage or of its perpetrators could be most expeditiously communicated. A list containing this information was prepared for forwarding to the various police forces. Several of the European police authorities promised to communicate to each other a monthly descriptive roll of persons expelled and the reasons for their expulsion.[150] In his report, Vincent declared, "I have little doubt that the result of these confidential meetings of Heads of Police will do good, if only by forming reciprocal friendships leading to greater cooperation."[151] Brzesowsky noted that Vincent "promised the most far-reaching consideration of the eventual wishes of the continental central [police] departments."[152] This statement certainly stands in stark contrast with the official British position of abstaining from any commitment to the conference's proposals. While larger political differences might divide their countries, the international police confraternity clearly found much to agree on in the fight against anarchism.[153]

On December 19, during one of the final plenary sessions, Britain made a more public gesture of agreement with the conference's anti-anarchist agenda. Ambassador Sir Philip Currie pledged his country's support for new anti-anarchist laws. Currie acknowledged that it was Britain's "international duty" and "duty as a member of the European family" to assist in coping with anarchist violence, and that toward this

---

[149] Report of the administrative committee, CIR, 122–123.

[150] Report of the administrative committee, CIR, 122–123, and Brzesowsky to Pasetti, inclosure in dispatch, Rome, December 26, 1898. Politisches Archiv. XXVII/65. HHStA.

[151] Confidential report, December 17, 1898. Inclosure no. 30 in Currie to Salisbury, December 20, 1898, FO 881/7179. PRO.

[152] Brzesowsky to Pasetti, inclosure in despatch, Rome, December 26, 1898. Politisches Archiv. XXVII/65 HHStA.

[153] For the creation of an "international police culture" during the nineteenth century that increasingly promoted cooperation, Mathieu Deflem, *Policing World Society: Historical Foundations of International Police Cooperation* (Oxford University Press, 2002).

end the cabinet in London intended to prepare several bills for presentation to parliament. These bills envisaged an extension of the Explosives Act so that it would punish not only the case of a criminally instigated or planned explosion in Great Britain, but also such a crime when carried out or plotted for execution abroad. In addition, these crimes would be made subject to extradition. The crime of simple assassination, be it of a chief of state or of any other individual, would also be specified as liable to extradition and as not falling under the category of a political crime. Finally, the government promised to study ways in which the law could be improved in order to impede, whether in Britain or elsewhere, the distribution of documents that incited persons to crimes of violence.[154] The Currie address was extremely well received, and when the ambassador reported back to London, he noted that the Russian, German, and Austrian ambassadors had termed the British promises "the most important result obtained by the conference."[155]

At the conference's final session on December 21, Italian Foreign Minister Canevaro demonstrated his talent for papering over the conservative-liberal rift that had so recently threatened to break up the Rome gathering. Canevaro restated his conviction that it had never been the delegates' task to "dictate new laws or engage the freedom of action of our governments." The delegates' only duty had been to indicate general guidelines for the defense of society against the anarchists, guidelines which the Great Powers might follow as they saw fit.[156] Ambassador Barrére expressed his complete agreement with the Italian foreign minister's remarks, making "superfluous" any of the additional reservations that France had previously intended to make prior to signing the Final Protocol.[157] At the conclusion of the session, the head of every delegation, except for the British ambassador, signed the *Acte Final*, a document that listed the proposals adopted by the conference as well as the reservations of individual nations. Rather than following Britain's example, the liberal continental states, such as Switzerland, followed France's lead and signed the protocol.[158]

The impact of the Rome conference

Despite this felicitous conclusion to the Rome conference, its results were clearly mixed. Little, if any, new legislation went into effect as a result of the conference, but it did influence the practice of extradition

[154] Fifth plenary session, December 19, 1898, CIR, 40–41.
[155] Currie to Salisbury, December 22, 1898, FO 881/7179, no. 32, p. 91. PRO.
[156] Seventh plenary session, CIR, 58.   [157] Seventh plenary session, CIR, 58.
[158] Luxembourg did not sign since its delegate had left the conference. Liang, *Modern Police*, 166, errs when he asserts that Switzerland refused to sign. The names of all the Swiss delegates were affixed to the *Acte Finale*. CIR, 61–65.

and expulsion, promote the wider use of *portrait parlé*, and above all, increase inter-European police cooperation. According to one authority, it prevented new anarchist outrages for about a year and a half.

The countries whose representatives had met in Rome were requested to inform Italy within three months, later extended to seven, of the actions they planned to take in response to the conference's decisions. These statements would be collected in a special protocol. In the diplomatic responses they sent to Rome during 1899, a large number of countries promised to study the question of introducing new legislation or modifying their old along the lines advocated by the conference; these included Britain, Sweden and Belgium, as well as Italy, Spain, Luxembourg, Monaco, Serbia, Bulgaria and, of course, the three east and central European empires. As mentioned, not much seems to have ever been enacted, at least by the major powers. In Italy Foreign Minister Canevaro exerted great pressure to have the death penalty reinstated, even threatening to resign over the issue, but he fell from office in May of 1899, and subsequent governments did not pursue the matter.[159] The proposed Italian anti-anarchist law of February 1901 contained several recommendations of the conference, but never passed parliament.[160]

Interestingly the only major country that actually drafted new legislation especially "for giving effect to the proposals of the Conference" was Great Britain, even though it had not made any binding commitment nor signed the Final Protocol.[161] In her February 1899 speech at the opening of parliament, Queen Victoria spoke of her government's intentions to amend the extradition and explosives acts.[162] As late as February 1902, the foreign secretary informed the German government that it still intended to introduce the promised bills, but that the state of business in the House of Commons made it impossible to assure that these measures would pass "in the near future." And indeed they never seem to have been brought before parliament, although legislation on these questions was certainly drawn up and has since been located in the archives of the Home Office.[163] Precisely why the bills were never brought before parliament is unknown, although years later Howard Vincent said that it was because, soon after the conference ended, the British government's attention became completely absorbed by the confrontation with the Boers in

---

[159] Italy, *Atti parlamentari, Senato, discussioni*, February 2, 1901, 1116–1117.
[160] See Chapter 6.
[161] Sanderson (for Salisbury) to DeRenzis, London, March 30, 1899. PI, b. 32, IFM. See also DeRenzis to Canevaro, April 8, 1899, DDI (3), III, no. 220.
[162] Great Britain. Parliament. Parliamentary Debates (Lords), 4th series, 66 (1899), 3–4.
[163] Lansdowne to Lascelles, Berlin, February 4, 1902, printed in BDIL, 6:73–75. For the draft bills on extradition and explosives, see BDIL, 6:678–679.

South Africa – which in October 1899 led to war.[164] War aside, Britain's political leaders felt, rightly or wrongly, that public opinion would not countenance an erosion of Britain's traditional liberties, especially if proposed in the absence of any recent anarchist outrage on British soil.[165]

Regarding the question of new anti-anarchist legislation, whether it was in Britain or elsewhere, the secrecy of the Rome conference proved disadvantageous in several respects. While secrecy helped to promote international police cooperation, it kept public opinion in the dark, and therefore could do little to persuade the media and society that new legislation was required to confront the terrorist threat.

The Rome conference's proposals on expulsion and extradition exercised some impact. It was particularly significant that Switzerland agreed to all the administrative proposals, including procedures for expulsion, except for the measure, originally sponsored by Russia that seemed to turn expulsion into the disguised extradition of an offender. In March 1899 Berne issued instructions to the effect that all expelled anarchists were to be returned to their native lands after the police authorities of those countries had been duly forewarned. Switzerland also agreed to transport across its territory anarchists expelled by third countries and being returned to their home states.[166] At the same time Berne insisted it was taking these measures "as an autonomous act and not as a contractual obligation." It reserved the liberty "to release itself" from these obligations "if circumstances or a change in legislation" dictated.[167]

The recommendation for the inclusion of the Belgian or *attentat* clause in treaties of extradition may have been even more influential. It reinforced, for example, a change in Italian extradition policy already underway at the end of the nineteenth century. Formerly the peninsula, along with Britain and Switzerland, had shunned the *attentat* clause. Italy's reluctance to embrace the *attentat* clause reflected the nationalist feeling of the Risorgimento, which had excoriated foreign and domestic despots for oppressing Italy and had sympathized with tyrannicides such as Orsini. In a well-known case in 1870, Italy had refused France's request for the clause's insertion in a bilateral treaty of extradition, demonstrating

---

[164] Vincent memo, *Précis of the Proceedings at the Anti-Anarchist Conference*, to Home Secretary Gladstone, July 6, 1906. HO144/757/118516/sub. 15, PRO.

[165] Porter, *Vigilant State*, 112–113.

[166] The Swiss regulations were dated "3/21 March 1899." See the Declaration of the Swiss Federal Council regarding the Rome Final Act, May 16, 1899, PI, b. 32, IFM; Conseil fédéral, Procès-verbal de la séance du 3 mars 1899, DDS 4:653–654; Swiss response to the Russo-German démarche of April 1902, "Réservations du Conseil Fédéral suisses," May 29, 1902. Deutsche Gesandtshaft in Bern. Anarchistisches, f. 4. GFO.

[167] Declaration of Swiss Government, May 16, 1899, PI, b. 32, IFM; Marc Vuilleumier, "La police politique en Suisse, 1889–1914. Aperçu historique," in *Cent ans de police*

itself to be "the most obstinately opposed of all countries to extradition for political murder or assassination."[168]

But with the wave of assassinations during the 1890s, including an unsuccessful attempt on the life of Umberto I in April 1897, Italy altered its practice. Rome signed treaties containing the *attentat* clause with the French protectorate of Tunisia in September 1896 and with San Marino in June 1897.[169] When at last the king fell victim to an assassin's bullet on July 29, 1900, the clause became more compelling than ever. Responding to a parliamentary interpellation by Admiral Canevaro in February 1901, the Italian government informed the senate that it "insisted" upon using the Rome conference's formulas whenever there was "occasion to negotiate or renew or complete extradition treaties."[170] This pledge meant introducing the conference-recommended Belgian clause into such agreements, which Italy did with Mexico in 1899, with Montenegro in 1901, and with many other countries in later years.

Italy's redirection of policy was not unique. In February 1901 the Italian justice minister noted that the Belgian clause was "little by little conquering the opinion of diplomats in every country."[171] By World War I, Western nations had increasingly come to accept the Belgian clause as standard practice. A number of Latin American countries wrote it into the multinational extradition conventions that they concluded between themselves in 1902, 1907, and 1911. Norway, Russia, and Sweden made it part of their national extradition statues in 1908, 1911, and 1912 respectively.[172]

The secret police committee, and later conference, recommendation of *portrait parlé* as a means of criminal identification was also very influential. Although Germany had been utilizing Bertillonage since 1896–1897, in early 1899 the anarchists' press linked the decisions of the Rome conference to the fact that the German police had begun a campaign

---

politique en Suisse (Lausanne: Association pour l'etude de l'histoire du mouvement ouvrier and Editions d'en bas, 1992): 55.

[168] Albéric Rolin, "Quelques questions relatives à l'extradition," *Recueil des cours: Académie de Droit International* 1 (1923): 210.

[169] Much has been written about the importance for Franco–Italian relations of the series of treaties dated September 28, 1896 that regulated Italy's relations with the French protectorate of Tunisia. What has been overlooked is the considerable significance of the extradition convention.

[170] Visconti Venosta, Italy, *Atti parlamentari*, Senato, Discussioni, February 2, 1901, 1118.

[171] Gianturco, *Atti parlamentari*, Senato, Discussioni, February 2, 1901, 1124.

[172] The Latin American extradition conventions referred to are the Pan American Convention of 1902, the Central American Treaty of 1907, and the Caracas Convention of 1911. The projected Russian law on extradition apparently never went into effect. Francois Joseph Saint-Aubin, *L'extradition et le droit extraditionnal: Théorique et Appliqué.* 2 vols. (Paris: A. Pedone, 1913): 2: 984–988.

in which they required suspected anarchists to undergo anthropometric measurement.[173] This may have been a false connection, however, since the conference had only called for use of the eye, *portrait parlé*, and not the measuring compass. In mid-March 1899 the Italian interior ministry sent a senior police functionary to Paris to study *portrait parlé*. By July the government had begun putting the system into operation for common criminals and anarchists alike.[174] This was a notable development for the peninsula, since previously the Italian police had been the only security force in Europe, outside the Ottoman Empire, that had completely ignored Bertillon's techniques.[175] The complexity, difficulty, and rigorous precision required of Bertillonage, however, produced problems for Italy and other countries. One expert subsequently labeled the new criminal identification method introduced by Rome as "completely primitive," so much below the scientific standards of Bertillon that it would "serve more often to confound a gentleman with a bandit than to facilitate an arrest."[176] Italy finally began introducing a more reliable identification system derived from Bertillon's methods in 1902.[177]

While all the countries at the Rome conference, except Britain, gave blanket endorsements of the policing measures recommended by the Final Act, five other countries besides Italy specifically promised to study and possibly utilize the speaking likeness (or verbal portrait) method: Austria-Hungary, Sweden-Norway, Switzerland, Romania, and Turkey.[178] Several of these sent agents to Paris to study the system at the same time that Italy did.[179] Except for Turkey and perhaps Hungary, all of these countries eventually adopted *portrait parlé*, at least for use in major urban centers. Switzerland, Denmark, Portugal, and possibly Norway, Holland, and Romania, had begun to put the system into effect as early as 1900.[180]

[173] Edmond Locard, "Les services actuels d'identification et la fiche internationale," *Archives d'anthropologie criminelle et de criminologie* 21 (1906): 190.

[174] Memorandum, DGPS, interior ministry, December 28, 1898, and Pelloux, interior ministry to foreign ministry, July 4, 1899, DGPS–Ufficio riservato, b. 3A/5, ACS.

[175] Giuseppe Alongi, *Manuale di polizia scientifica* (Milan: Sonzogno, 1898): 178.

[176] Edmond Locard, *Traité de criminalistique, Vol. 4: Les Preuves de l'identité* (Lyon: J. Desvigne, 1932–1933): 728.

[177] Locard, *Traité de criminalistique, Vol. 4*, and *Novissimo Digesto Italiano*, "Ritratto parlato," by Ugo Sorrentino, 204.

[178] While *portrait parlé* was already in use in Vienna, Austria promised to introduce it into the rest of Austrian-controlled territory. PI, b. 32, IFM.

[179] The in-house publication of the Italian interior ministry lists Sweden, Norway, and Denmark (with Austria having preceded them) as having sent representatives to Paris in March 1899. M., "Il servizio antropometrico negli uffici di P.S.," *Manuale di publica sicurezza* (December 1899).

[180] By July 1899, the Austrians reported that Swiss officials had journeyed to Paris to study *portrait parlé*. Giskra, Bern, to Goluchowski, Vienna, July 3, 1899. PA XXVII/65. HHStA; Vuilleumier, "La police politique," 56.

Since the data from the secondary sources are incomplete and sometimes contradictory, it is difficult to chart anthropometry's advance with great precision. As a broad generalization, however, one can say that, within a decade after 1898, the use of Bertillonage had spread to all of Europe, except for most of the Balkans, although Romania adopted *portrait parlé*.[181] It had also been introduced into Tunisia, Bengal in India (1893), the United States, Canada (1887), Mexico (1895), and most of South America.[182]

The unchallenged triumph of anthropometry, a trend that the Rome conference clearly promoted, proved to be short-lived, although *portrait parlé* was to be more durable. In 1901 Scotland Yard, which had been using a watered-down version of Bertillonage since 1895, discontinued its use for identifying criminals in favor of a newly developed system of classification by fingerprints. Fingerprinting did not require the expensive measuring equipment and rigorous training of Bertillonage. Moreover, according to one expert, on an average it only took four minutes to locate a fingerprint file as opposed to twenty minutes for an anthropometric record.[183] Other police forces soon followed the British example in abandoning Bertillonage, although as late as the 1930s France, Germany, Spain, the Scandinavian states, and others continued to rely partially or completely on the Frenchman's system.[184] Moreover, even as it was being discontinued in parts of Europe, Bertillonage was being introduced into cities in the United States.[185]

Because, strictly speaking, *portrait parlé* is a precise system of describing the body and, more especially, the face for visual recognition, and is independent of Bertillonage's cumbersome requirements for measurement, it enjoyed a longer life. In 1903 Bertillon created the DKV album containing thousands of photographs of criminals and of persons expelled from France classified according to the *portrait parlé* system. Variations on the French DKV album soon appeared in Italy and, in 1910, in Spain.[186] Giovanni Gasti, an early champion of fingerprinting and head

[181] Ridolfo Livi, *Antropometria* (Milan: Hoepli, 1900): 196; Salvatore Ottolenghi, "L'estensione del Bertillonage e la lotta contro gli anarchici," *Rivista d'Italia* 6 (1901): 7; Eugene Stockis, *L'identification Judiciaire et le Signalement International* (Brussels: Larcier, 1908): 68; Edmond Locard, "Les Services," 161–188.

[182] Cole, *Suspect Identities*, 52–53.   [183] Cole, *Suspect Identities*, 162.

[184] Locard, *Traité de criminalistique*, 4:179, 771; Cole, *Suspect Identities*, 152.

[185] Raymond Fosdick, "The Passing of the Bertillon System of Identification," *Journal of Criminal Law and Criminology* 6 (1915): 363–369.

[186] Locard, *Traité de criminalistique*, 3:180–185. José Jiménez Jerez, a Spanish police secretary, emphasizes the continuing importance of *portrait parlè* despite the triumph of dactiloscopy. *Sistema dactiloscópico de Olóriz y retrato hablado de Bertillon* (Madrid: Alvarez, 1913): 107.

of Italy's identification bureau, believed, together with many others, that an important role for anthropometry, and particularly *portrait parlé*, continued to exist alongside dactyloscopy.[187] Eugene Stockis, a well-known Belgian criminologist, also wanted to abandon anthropometry, but retain *portrait parlé*.[188] Even in Britain, the birthplace of fingerprinting, Howard Vincent claimed in 1906 that the conference's recommendation that "*portrait parlé*... be used as the international descriptive form... has practically been done" and, as evidence, pointed to the twelfth edition of his *Police Code*.[189] Under the heading "Description," Vincent's practical manual for policemen recommends a *portrait parlé*-like format for recording a suspect's description and mentions that the "speaking likeness" system was "adopted at the Anti-Anarchist Conference at Rome by the representatives of the Police of the Nations."[190] Since the *Code* was widely used in England and throughout the British Empire and went through at least fifteen editions, its influence was immense. Until the 1990s, Interpol, and presumably other police organizations, continued to utilize *portrait parlé* files.[191]

Increased police cooperation and a crackdown on anarchism, 1898–1900

The Rome conference's most important result was to expedite closer international cooperation and faster communication between Europe's police forces. With the exceptions of Britain, which never signed the Final Protocol, and France, all of Europe had adhered to the resolution calling for direct communications between central police authorities and the mutual exchange of all pertinent information. France set itself apart by emphasizing its unilateral adoption of these measures. In its declaration of April 20, 1899, Paris declared that, while for some time it had already

---

[187] Giovanni Gasti, *La missione attuale dell'antropometria nelle funzioni di polizia*. Report, June 17, 1911, submitted to the 1912 annual conference of the International Chiefs of Police, Rochester, NY. DGPS, 1912. b. 6, ACS.

[188] Stockis, *L'identification*, 64. R. A. Reiss claims that his *Manuel du portrait parlé (signalment)* (Paris: G. Roustan, 1914): viii, first published in 1904 and reissued in 1914, led to a revival of Bertillon's method, which began "to be employed everywhere."

[189] Vincent, confidential memo, to Home Minister Gladstone, July 6, 1906. HO144/757/119516. sub. 15. PRO.

[190] Not that Vincent tried to replicate exactly the immensely detailed terminology of Bertillon's *portrait parlé*; nor did Bertillon use the term "Jewish" nose! *The Police Code and General Manual of the Criminal Law*, 12th edition (London: Francis Edwards and Simpkin, Marshall, Hamilton, Kent, and co., 1904): 61–63.

[191] Michael Fooner, *Interpol* (Chicago: Henry Regnery, 1973): 50; Interpol's fiftieth anniversary commemorative publication (Paris 1973): 37. Henry Rhodes, *Alphonse Bertillon: Father of Scientific Detection* (New York: Abelard-Schuman, 1956): 104; Interpol Press Office email, February 18, 2003.

been carrying out such communications, it did not think it "necessary to sanction" them "by an international accord," since such an agreement "could be interpreted by public opinion as comprising a veritable service of international police" and might cause "certain inconveniences from a political point of view."[192]

Some contemporaries believed that closer ties between European police forces were instrumental in preventing anarchist *attentats* for over a year. In an interview given in 1900, Sir Howard Vincent insisted that the secret police committee "had decided on plans which...prevented any outrage for fifteen months."[193] In 1906 he told a *Times* correspondent that after the 1898 meeting:

an international system was effectively established, and for 18 months prevented any anarchic outrages of a serious character [Vincent is presumably counting his months from the death of Elisabeth rather than the conclusion of the Rome Conference three months later]. If these precautions had been continued to be observed, it is probable that some of those events which the world recently had to deplore would have been averted. But as always happens after a period of freedom from crime or outrage, the police precautions began to be relaxed and the illustrious personages for whose safety they have to be taken themselves got worried by the attentions paid to them by the authorities, and naturally longed for the freedom enjoyed by private individuals. Unfortunately [on April 5, 1900] there was the well-known attempt of Sipido at Brussels, followed soon afterwards [on July 29] by the assassination of that gallant gentleman King Humbert [Umberto].[194]

Whether Vincent is accurate or not in his assessment,[195] it is striking to observe that, after the occurrence of at least one violent anarchist act every year beginning in 1892 (or even in 1881, if one includes the

---

[192] Diplomatic responses to the Final Act of France and other states; submitted to Rome between March and July 1899. PI, b. 32, IFM; note from French ambassador accompanying the French declaration. In 1901, the French foreign minister, while citing Rome's imprimatur, reiterated to the German ambassador Paris's basically unilateral approach: "anarchists in France are the object of a permanent and continuous surveillance; foreign administrations, in conformity with the resolutions adopted at Rome, are regularly informed of all that they have an interest in knowing on the subject of anarchists; and, especially in that which concerns expulsions, notice of expulsions is carefully given to the police of the countries to which the expellees belong." Copy, Note Verbal, forwarded by Ambassador Radolin, Paris, December 27, 1901. Auswärtiges Amt, 13688/1, GCSAP.

[193] "How to Deal with Anarchists. An Interview with Sir Howard Vincent," *Daily Graphic*, August 11, 1900.

[194] *The Times* (London), June 5, 1906, 3.

[195] Scattered, but inconclusive, evidence supports Vincent's claim that European authorities grew complacent after 1898. According to Casagrande ("Mises en fiche," 68n), Switzerland and Italy stopped sending out monthly reports on the anarchists by 1900, although this assertion, based on a 1930 note by the Swiss *procureur general*, seems to be contradicted by Liang (*Modern Police*, 168), who has also examined the Swiss archives. Romania stopped sending reports soon after the Rome Conference ended

death and injuries that accompanied the Rome May Day riot of 1891 in which anarchists were involved), no acts of anarchist terrorism took place in the whole of 1899 and the first three months of 1900. Some in the contemporary media found this long period of anarchist quiescence noteworthy.[196]

During the year or so that followed the murder of the Empress Elisabeth and the Rome conference, European anti-anarchist police activity increased significantly. The anarchists themselves observed (or at least felt) this, as is made clear in a March 1899 news item from the London anarchist newspaper *Freedom*:

The so-called secrets of the anti-anarchist conference begin to slowly leak out. An Italian comrade, a working mason, who had the audacity to speak at a meeting in Hungary, three weeks ago, has been arrested and handed over to the Italian police. In England the Italian comrades are being systematically coerced and terrorized by Scotland Yard … the "shadowed" increase in number.[197]

While these events may have reflected intensified police activity following the Rome conference, their interpretation may have simply mirrored the exaggerated fears of the anarchists, with a phantom Black International now finding its double in a phantom police international. As Vincent later remarked "nothing but good can come out of International Police Conferences. Their very mystery inspires criminal conspirators with fear, and the exchange of views and mutual confidence engendered are conducive to successful activity and cooperation."[198] Italian Prime Minister Pelloux shared Vincent's view, telling the president of the Italian senate that "the subversive elements are frightened by the [police] raids that have been carried out everywhere, above all after the assassination of the empress of Austria. Also the deliberations of the anti-anarchist conference, because secret, have scared many people."[199]

In early March 1899 the Swiss Federal Council asked the country's justice and police department to investigate whether "the control of the anarchists could be made better and more intensive," especially with the "anarchists residing in Switzerland being placed under continual

(Liang, *Modern Police*, 168). The German police inspector in Strassburg complained in 1905 that no official communications about expelled anarchists had been received from France since September 1900. Bauer, Strassburg, to Berlin Polizeipräsidum, October 28, 1905, Rep 30 tit. 94, 8672, f. 48, Brandenburgischen Landeshauptarchivs Potsdam (Staatsarchive Potsdam, hereafter cited as SP).

[196] *The Times* (London), April 6, 1900, 9; "Faits et informations: Angleterre et Belgique," *Journal du Droit international privé* 37 (1900): 435–436.

[197] "International Notes," *Freedom*, March 1899, 23.

[198] Vincent, confidential memo, to Home Minister Gladstone, July 6, 1906. HO144/757/119516. sub. 15. PRO.

[199] Farini, *Diario*, 2:1400–1401.

surveillance."[200] Already in 1898 Berne had created a filing card system to identify the anarchists and the confederation's public prosecutor began sending out circulars to inform the cantons of anarchist activities inside the country. These circulars continued at irregular intervals until 1914.[201] In the spring of 1899, an anarchist newspaper reported that in Switzerland frequent expulsions, arrests, and harassment of Italian anarchists and socialists continued as in the previous fall.[202] Thus, according to a Swiss historian, something new emerged among most of the Swiss cantons during the 1890s: a "scheme for systematic political ... surveillance."[203]

Complying with the decisions taken by the assembled police heads at the anti-anarchist conference, in 1899 many European states began regularly exchanging information about anarchists on their territories and anarchists they had expelled. Italy, France, Holland, Belgium, Switzerland, Romania, and other countries began sending out monthly, or at least fairly regular reports.[204] In April the police chief of Rotterdam sent the Berlin police two volumes of photos of anarchists; in June, Rotterdam received the photos of 150 anarchists from Berlin.[205] The British received periodic reports on the anarchist movement, occasionally including information on anarchist expulsions, from France, Belgium, Holland, Italy, Switzerland, Austria Hungary, and Greece. Some of these reports had been sent prior to 1898 (e.g., those from France and Austria-Hungary), but others were clearly a result of the Rome meeting.[206]

During the next decade and a half, Italy repeatedly demonstrated the seriousness with which it took the administrative decisions of the Rome conference.[207] A German diplomat claimed that one of the main reasons that, in 1900, Italy started posting police agents abroad to create a far-flung system of anarchist surveillance was the impact of the Rome

[200] Conseil fédéral, *Procès-verbal de la séance du 3 mars* 1899, DDS 4:654.
[201] Casagrande, ("Mises en fiche," 68.
[202] "Suisse mouvement social," *Temps nouveau*, March 11–17, 1899, 4.
[203] Vuilleumier, "La police politique," 49.
[204] For Italy and France, see Giskra, Bern, to Goluchowski, Vienna, July 3, 1899, HHStA; for Holland and Belgium, see Justice Ministry, The Hague, February 28, 1899, no. 88, confidential, Rep 30, Berlin, 8755, f. 76, SP, and copy of de Favereau, Brussels, to Count de Wallwitz, German embassy, December 19, 1901, 13688/1, f. 16, German interior ministry, GCSAP. For Switzerland, Casagrande, 68, 71; see also *Rapport mensuel no. 1* (January–February 1899), f. 100, Polizei präsidium Berlin, Pr. Br. Rep. 30 tit. 94, lit. A, no. 290, SP.
[205] Rep 30. Berlin C. tit. 94, lit. A no. 360, 8757, f. 108, SP.
[206] Porter, *Vigilant State*, 122; memorandum, E. R. Henry, head of the Criminal Investigation Department, January 7, 1902. FO 412/68, PRO; also in HO45/10254/A36450. Henry gives no dates for the appearance of these reports.
[207] E.g., Giolitti, DGPS, Rome, to foreign minister, December 19, 1901, PI, b. 48, IFM.

Conference (as well as the assassination of Umberto I).[208] While this may be an over-attribution, the conference's call for centralizing information gathering finds an echo in the Italian foreign ministry's request on April 15, 1899 that all anti-anarchist policing services in the United States be concentrated in the consulate of New York City.[209] Ironically Italy sometimes used the Rome agreement as an excuse not to adhere to more far-reaching accords. For example, in 1908, when Germany requested anew that Italy sign the St. Petersburg Protocol providing for increased anti-anarchist police cooperation, the response of the security department's director general was that Italy was already cooperating:

the Director General of P.S. in this Ministry has always followed the conclusions and the arrangements established by the various states, Italy included, at the Conference against the anarchists held in Rome in 1898.

Hitherto it has not been noticed that other states in their relations with Italy have failed to carry out the practices instituted by those accords, and one can, especially in as much as it pertains to Germany, assert that such exchanges continue and that direct correspondence regarding public security affairs is rather frequent, particularly regarding the anarchists, and is still maintained exclusively on the basis of the accords established in the aforementioned International Conference of 1898 between our General Directorate of P.S. and the Police President of Berlin.[210]

While France opposed the creation of a pan-European police system sanctioned by treaty, in practice it continued to cooperate with other European police forces. Already for some years before 1898, Paris had been communicating directly with the central police authorities of many of its neighbors.[211] France never refused a request from another country for information about an anarchist.[212] In late 1901, France claimed that

in conformity with the resolutions adopted at Rome, foreign [police] administrations are regularly informed of everything of interest for them to know on the subject of the anarchist movement; and, especially as regards expulsions, the police of the countries having jurisdiction over the expellees are carefully notified.[213]

The British, at least, complained that these expulsion reports from France and elsewhere often arrived weeks after the event and in no case had "a

208   Metternich, London, to Foreign Office, Berlin, March 18, 1903. Rep. 30, Berlin, tit. 94, lit. A no. 360, 8756, f. 40, SP.
209   Mss. Italian ambassador, Washington, DC, to Brusati, first royal aide-de-camp, February 24, 1903. Rap.dip.USA (1901–09), b. 119, IFM.
210   Leonardi, DGPS, Rome, to Italian foreign minister, July 19, 1908. Ser. P, b. 47, IFM.
211   Presumably this statement is a reference to the bilateral treaties signed in 1894.
212   Maitron, *Histoire*, 433. After the Rome Conference, Maitron (*Histoire*, 433–434) does not detect any increase in French police communications with foreign authorities regarding anarchists, which were already frequent.
213   Copy, verbal note of French foreign minister, forwarded by German Ambassador Radolin, Paris, December 27, 1901. German foreign ministry, 13688/1, fol. 21. GCSAP

foreign Government given [the British] notice of their intention to expel, or of the impending arrival in this country of '*expulsés*.'"[214]

Due to improving diplomatic relations, police cooperation between France and Italy strengthened after the Rome conference.[215] In June 1899 the French interior ministry authorized the prefects to correspond directly with the Italian consuls in order to ensure a rapid exchange of information regarding anarchist surveillance.[216] Also during 1899 the expulsion of foreign anarchists from France, and particularly of Italian anarchists, increased.[217] In early 1900, confronted by a police offensive on a grand scale made up of both French officers and Italian policemen and secret agents who had entered France, the Italian anarchist colony in Paris gave up any further attempts to hold meetings.[218]

Was the Anti-Anarchist Conference a ruse to provide cover for an attack on the socialists, as many of the latter feared and as some later historians have asserted? Little or no evidence in the archives supports this view, although concern was certainly justified. Prominent political figures, such as Farini, the president of the Italian senate and an indefatigable diarist, asserted in December 1898 that the "the socialists now have fused themselves with the anarchists."[219] While several of the more reactionary European governments would doubtless have liked to have found a way to turn the anti-anarchist conference into a general campaign against "subversives," if they had adopted such a ploy, the liberal states would have peremptorily abandoned the Rome meeting and effectively wrecked the conference. Even the conservative Prussian justice minister, Karl Heinrich von Schönstedt, saw realistic political reasons for differentiating between the two leftist movements, rather than shackling them together. In February 1899 he lamented to the interior ministry the fact that, for legal and extradition purposes, the conference had failed to adopt a definition of anarchists that more clearly distinguished it from socialism. New anti-anarchist legislation and revisions of extradition treaties would have to obtain the Reichstag's consent.

Such could only be hoped for, if it would have been guaranteed by a clear definition of anarchists, that the intended measures could only be applied against the anarchists and not also against other elements of the population opposed to the government, especially not against the social democrats.[220]

---

[214] CID Chief E. R. Henry, Memorandum, January 7, 1902. FO 412/68. PRO.
[215] Milza, *Français et Italiens*, 2:872.
[216] Genovefa Etienne and Claude Moniquet. *Histoire de l'espionnage mondial. Les services secrets, de Ramsès II à nos jours* (Paris: Luc Pire and du Fèlin, 1997): 87.
[217] In 1898, 76 anarchists were expelled, including 49 Italians; in 1899, the number rose to 87 total and 80 Italian. Milza, *Français et Italiens*, 2:865.
[218] Milza, *Français et Italiens*, 2:873.   [219] Farini, *Diario*, 2:1401.
[220] Berlin, February 18, 1899, no. 7, vol. 1, fol. 160–163. Interior ministry. Rep. 77, tit. 2512, no. 7, vol. 1, GCSAM.

On the other hand, the Russian government, which among all the European authorities made the least effort to distinguish between anarchists and other sorts of revolutionaries, continually tried to expand the scope of the Rome agreement and use it as a cover for action against non-anarchists. In 1903 the Foreign Agency in Paris supplied Russian police agents carrying out anti-revolutionary surveillance in Switzerland with a certificate affirming that:

The bearer [...] is a special agent of the Department of police of the Imperial Russian Ministry of the Interior...The police authorities having adhered to the Conference of Rome (1898) are requested to convey [porter] to the bearer of the present their aid and support within the limits of the laws of their country.[221]

Bilateral anti-anarchist accords and police reorganization, September 1898–May 1899

Besides the international conference, the assassination of the Empress Elisabeth and the Swiss expulsions of anarchists spawned a series of diplomatic agreements and police reforms that were nearly as important, one could argue, as the Rome meeting itself.

In the German Empire, the assassination of the Empress Elisabeth became the impetus for the government to push through a proposal it had wanted to enact for years: the centralization in Berlin of information exchange concerning anarchist movements and activities.[222] Previously public opinion, due to various police scandals in Berlin and to the local loyalties of the non-Prussian German states, particularly in south Germany, had opposed concentrating more authority in the police department of the Prussian capital.[223] This opposition now collapsed in the face of public horror over the murder of the Bavarian-born empress (she was a Wittelsbach). In its initial proposal made in mid-September, the government had wanted to include "social revolutionaries" as well as anarchists in a new agreement on cooperation between the police of the German states, but dropped this idea in the face of Bavaria's objections. On December 1, 1898 the implementation of a nationwide system of anarchist surveillance according to uniform rules and with the Berlin police department designated as the central exchange center for collecting and dispersing this information officially began. The agreement also provided for direct communications between the police departments of

---

[221] Vuilleumier, "La police politique," 60–61.   [222] See Chapter 4.
[223] Mss. D[erenthall], Berlin, telegram to State Secretary Bülow, Semmering, September 12, 1898; Bülow, Semmering, telegram to foreign ministry, Berlin, September 14, 1898, Eur. Gen., 91 bd. 1, GFO. Linse, *Organisierter*, 27–28.

the different states and for the expulsion of all foreign anarchists from the country.[224] In its diplomatic response to the accord reached at the Rome meeting in December 1898, the German government opined that the conference's request for Europe-wide police communication simply meant "developing and extending the administrative measures" already undertaken by the German states.[225] The German plan, secretly drawn up in 1894, for greater anti-anarchist police cooperation inside Germany and with foreign countries outside the Reich now seemed to have finally been achieved.

In the spring of 1899, as another consequence of this domestic police reform, the Berlin police department produced an "Anarchist Album" listing the names and addresses of all anarchists in Germany, together with, when possible, their photographs and handwriting samples. The album was to be periodically updated. The first album contained the pictures of 240 German and foreign anarchists who had lived in Germany or might be expected to carry out propaganda there. The different German states were also to inform Berlin, as well as each other, of any expulsion of a foreign anarchist or their changes of address, and of any notable events occurring in the anarchist movement. Available for purchase by the police departments of the empire, it initially cost a little over seventy marks, although newer editions of the constantly updated album cost less.[226] On April 4, 1899, the first edition of the German "wanted" newspaper (*Deutsches Fahndungsblatt*) appeared, published daily and with a column on the front page listing the foreign anarchists expelled from the country.[227]

Switzerland's, as well as France's, expulsion of scores of anarchists (Paris expelled fifty anarchists in early October)[228] prompted several European states to seek ways of controlling, or at least monitoring, the potential chaos and danger created by these multiplying expulsions. The French received a verbal promise from the Swiss government, under pledge of reciprocity, that the Swiss police would inform the French police ahead of time of any expulsion of an anarchist over the French

---

[224] Prussia enacted internal regulations along these lines in January 1898. Prussian interior minister, Prussian state ministries meeting, Berlin, September 6, 1900, film 1215/56, GCSAM. For the circular implementing the new accord, see the interior ministry circular, Berlin, November 28, 1898, C. 13073, copy in 13689, German interior ministry, GCSAP; Linse, *Organisierter*, 28; *Vorwärts*, December 15, 1898.

[225] German declaration, March 25, 1899, PI, b. 32, IFM.

[226] Linse, *Organisierter*, 28; Memo, Berlin, May 15, 1899. Lit. A. Nr. 360. 8757. fol. 121, SP.

[227] Rep 30. Berlin C. Tit. 94, LitA Nr. 360, 8757, f. 104 and 106, SP.

[228] Mayor, Italian Legation, Berne, to foreign ministry, Rome, October 10, 1898. PI, b. 32, IFM.

border.[229] The Germans (and later the Austrians and Italians) received a similar promise, after German Minister Rotenhahn reminded the head of the Swiss justice department "that one must at least inform one's neighbor, if one lets loose a wild beast onto his territory."[230] Although at this time, apart from Russia, passports were not generally used in Europe, Germany and Italy contemplated reinstituting their use for travelers from Switzerland so as to exercise better control over expelled anarchists (a move the Swiss objected to since it would have hindered their profitable tourist trade). In the end, both countries decided against this measure.[231] On October 8, Austria went a step further and promised to inform Berlin of any anarchist, expelled or not, who crossed the German border; Berlin (and Bavaria) agreed to act in a similar fashion with anarchists crossing the Austrian border.[232] By the end of October, Hungary had agreed with Germany to exchange information on expellees and provide their photographs.[233] Hungary also requested that Vienna ask the United States and all of Europe (except for Montenegro and Portugal) to forward information and photos on expelled anarchists.[234] The Netherlands, Luxembourg, Spain, Italy, Serbia, Bulgaria, and Austria-Hungary also entered into agreements with each other, unless prior accords existed, as between Italy and Austria-Hungary, to exchange information about expelled anarchists, including photos and descriptions.[235] Brussels and

---

[229] Copy, Rotenhahn, Berne, to Hohenlohe-Schillingsfurt, Berlin, October 6, 1898. Interior ministry, Rep 77, tit. 2512, no. 8, vol. 2, GCSAM.

[230] Ibid.; Kuefstein, Berne, to Goluchowski, Vienna, secret, October 13, 1898, IB, 1898, c. 389, HHStA; Italian Legation, Berne, to foreign minister, Rome, November 9, 1898, PI, b. 35, IFM.

[231] See the Italian minister in Berne's report of a conversation with the German minister, and the former's recommendation for similar measures. Mayor, Italian Legation, Berne, to foreign ministry, Rome, November 9, 1898; Riva, Berne, to foreign ministry, Rome, December 16, 1898, PI, b. 35, IFM.

[232] Vienna police president, October 8, 1898; German reply October 14, 1898; Prussian ambassador, Munich, to Bülow, Berlin, December 22, 1900, secret, in Berlin C, Rep. 30, 8755, SP.

[233] Mss note, October 25, 1898, interior ministry, rep. 77, tit. 2512, no. 8, vol. 2, GCSAM. Linse, *Organisierter*, 26, misdates this agreement as October 1899.

[234] Austrian foreign minister to missions abroad, Vienna, October 11, 1898, IB 1898, k. 390, HHStA.

[235] Dutch Legation to Austrian foreign ministry, Vienna, October 18, 1898, and Austrian interior ministry to foreign minister, Vienna, December 5, 1898, IB 1898, c. 389, HHStA; Italian foreign ministry to J. London, Dutch embassy, Rome, October 29, 1898, PI, b. 34, IFM; regarding Luxembourg, see Italian foreign ministry to Italian ambassador, The Hague, November 3, 1898, PI, b. 36, IFM; Austro-Hungarian ambassador to Spanish foreign minister, Madrid, October 20, 1898, Ambassador Leon y Castillo, Paris to foreign minister, Madrid, 19 October 1898, and undersecretary, foreign minister, Spanish foreign ministry to Dutch plenipotentiary, November 2, 1898, all in l. 2750, SFM; Serbian ambassador, Vienna, to Austrian foreign minister, October 2/14, 1898, Informationsbüro, 1898, c. 389, HHStA.

Rome, which since 1896 had communicated directly with each other on anarchist questions, now fine-tuned and speeded up the system by instituting a correspondence in secret code. This would of course permit telegraphic exchanges.[236]

Agreements forewarning neighboring states of an imminent expulsion hardly resolved the difficulties surrounding this question since the duly alerted receiving state might then deny admittance to the unwelcome visitor. To its displeasure, Switzerland soon found this out, as France, Germany, and Austria proceeded to reject its Italian anarchist expellees.[237] Even more grave was the possibility that these administrative expulsions would become cases of disguised extradition. Germany decided to delay the conclusion of any further agreements until after the Rome conference's decisions. Austria also looked to the conference to resolve its expulsion difficulties with the Swiss, and set clear guidelines for agreements made in principle with various other European states.[238] The two empires were not disappointed since Switzerland agreed to implement most of the proposals on expulsion approved by the Rome conference.

Conclusion

The immediate reaction to the death of the Empress Elisabeth in September 1898 was as important in promoting police modernization and criminalistics as the later Rome conference. The reforms of the German and Swiss police are the primary examples of this, with one historian ominously noting that by the end of the 1890s a scheme for systematic political surveillance had emerged in Switzerland for the first time.

Given the wide political differences between the European states, the mixed results of the Rome Anti-Anarchist Conference were probably the best that could have been achieved at the time. In order to create some kind of consensus Italian Foreign Minister Canevaro had sacrificed a legally binding program for a set of suggested options about the best way to confront violent anarchism. The same search for consensus, together with a reluctance to infringe on the sovereign prerogatives of the different nation-states, had prevented any discussion of the deeper economic and social causes of anarchist terrorism. But the image of a failed conference, so memorably captured by Barrère's damning judgment, was only

---

[236] Imperiali, Brussels, to Canevaro, Rome, October 24, 1898, PI, b. 36, IFM.
[237] Riva, Berne, to foreign minister, Rome, November 24, 1898, no. 3001, PI, b. 35, IFM.
[238] Foreign ministry to interior ministry, October 27, 1898, GCSAM, interior ministry, rep. 77, tit. 2512, no. 8, vol. 2; Kuefstein, Berne, to Goluchowski, Vienna, October 25, 1898, and Imperial interior minister to foreign minister, Vienna, November 27, 1898, HHStA, IB, 1898, c. 389.

partially true. Besides promoting the *attentat* clause and *portrait parlé*, the Rome meeting led to increased European police cooperation. While difficult to evaluate or quantify with great precision, almost all observers attested to this increase, which was the crucial legacy, the real achievement of the first conference on terrorism.

Significant as well was the leading role from behind the scenes that Austria, the most multinational of all the European states, played in initiating the conference. Once again it seemed to be following in the steps of Metternich, although this time potently seconded by a unified Germany. From behind the scenes as well, Britain played a larger part than the European public believed since Howard Vincent initiated the influential secret meeting of police officials within the secret diplomatic meeting. Despite London's liberal qualms and official standoffishness, the British police was quite willing to cooperate with the continental security forces and this proved to be a consistent theme throughout the pre-war period.

Perhaps the most arresting phrase to come out of the conference was the French police chief's description of *portrait parlé* as a "universal eye... unmasking criminals." A product of scientific policing, the widespread introduction of this new method of identification was a noteworthy benchmark on the continuum that has seen an ever-widening intrusion of government via technical means into the privacy of individuals.

If the reality of the Rome conference's achievements was modest, the illusion it temporarily created – due to its secrecy – was powerful. As Vincent remarked: "mystery inspires fear." A phantom police international now mimicked the phantom Black International, with perhaps a bit more substance, and may have helped effect the short hiatus in anarchist *attentats*.

6

1900: three assassination attempts and
the Russo-German anti-anarchist initiative

In 1900 three assassination attempts against royalty, one spectacularly successful, shattered the pause in violent anarchist acts that had followed the murder of the Empress Elisabeth and the meeting of the Rome conference. The phenomenon of anarchist terrorism entered a new phase, spreading from Europe and becoming increasingly transatlantic. European and other countries scrambled to find new strategies to cope with this expanding threat. Some chose to use the proposals of the Rome conference as a point of departure for strengthening international cooperation against anarchism. Others were uninterested in new multinational accords and opted for mostly national solutions, either working to centralize and perfect their existent police forces, which was in line with the recommendations of the Rome conference, or creating new networks of police and secret agents, often posted in foreign countries and overseas. Several countries saw the key to preventing new anarchist assassinations in building up or creating for the first time corps of professional bodyguards to protect their leaders. European attempts to pass new anti-anarchist legislation failed. The unheralded expulsions of troublesome anarchists continued to bedevil diplomatic relations, as did – at least for the more conservative European states – Britain and Switzerland's liberal polices of free expression and asylum.

Sipido's attempt on the prince of Wales

On April 4, 1900, the period of anarchist quiescence following Elisabeth's death came to an end. A 15-year-old Belgian with a round, boyish face, black eyes, and dark hair, "excited and spurred on by the taunts of his companions," jumped onto the footboard of a train carriage just as it began moving out of Brussels's Gare du Nord. He then fired one or more shots through an open window at the fifty-eight-year-old Edward, prince of Wales. According to newspaper accounts, one of the bullets passed 12 inches over the prince's head, ricocheted against a metal hand-rest and came to rest on the carriage seat.[1] The station chief then rushed at the boy, "putting his left arm around his neck and grasping his right hand in his own right hand." The two then "rolled together on the platform, during which a second shot was fired."[2] After he was subdued, the attempted assassin, who was identified as Jean-Baptiste Sipido, was found with his pockets stuffed with anarchist literature. Edward, who preferred to travel without guards since he believed his personal popularity would protect him, escaped unharmed.[3] While the prince joked about his assailant's bad marksmanship, his wife Alexandra, who was sitting next to him at the time of the attack, "suffered severely from the shock." According to *The Times*, "from all parts of the civilized world come expressions of the horror and indignation which the abominable attack" had excited.[4]

This incident was both an adolescent prank and indicative of more serious developments, specifically an increasing effort by anarchists and other extremists to subvert national armies and thwart military adventures. Sipido, a tinsmith from a poor family of nine children, apparently bet his youthful cronies five francs that he would shoot the prince of Wales. Sipido frequented the workingman's *Maison du Peuple* as well as left-wing clubs (e.g., the Socialist Advance Guard of St. Gilles) where socialists and anarchists preached anti-militarism. Some newspapers claimed that Sipido was a socialist rather than an anarchist, although other accounts pointed out that, despite its name, the Socialist Advance Guard was of an "anarchical tendency."[5] Confusion over Sipido's affiliation might be clarified if one remembered that, whatever ideological differences might be emphasized by the leaders of the two political movements, at the grassroots level people, especially young people, of socialist and anarchist ideas mixed easily with one another and formed a single radical subculture.[6] As for his personal motive, Sipido claimed that he wished to kill the prince because Edward had "caused thousands of men to be slaughtered in South Africa."[7] After the outbreak of the Boer War in October 1899, Brussels had become, according to some accounts, the foremost

[1] *The Times* (London), April 7, 1900, 13.
[2] *The Times* (London), April 7, 1900, 13; official account provided by the British minister in Brussels, reprinted *The Times* (London), April 6, 1900. Accounts disagree as to how many bullets were fired during the *attentat*.
[3] Harold Brust [Peter Cheyney], *"I Guarded Kings." The Memoirs of a Political Police Officer* (London: Stanley Paul, 1935): 37.
[4] *The Times* (London), April 6, 1900, 9.
[5] *The Times* (London), April 6, 1900.
[6] Regarding Italy, Carl Levy speaks of a popular socialism, a "second socialist culture," that read anarchist books (aside from the *Communist Manifesto*, Marx's were too voluminous and indigestible), sang anarchist songs, and resonated to anarchist symbols, and where committed anarchists were welcome. "Italian Anarchism," 44–46, 69–70.
[7] *The Times*, April 5, 1900, 6.

European center of pro-Boer and anti-British sentiment.[8] Many, especially in England, blamed the excessive virulence of the Belgian press, as well as the anti-Boer War propaganda of the Belgian socialist party, with inciting the impressionable Sipido to commit his deed.[9]

The assassination of Umberto I of Italy

While the contemporary press wrote off Sipido's attempt on the aging prince of Wales as the "imbecile" deed of a "hare-brained" youth,[10] the assassination of King Umberto I in July proved a more serious matter with important consequences for Italy and for international efforts to control terrorism. While Edward had joked that the anarchists were not very good shots and that they were more to be feared for their daggers, Gaetano Bresci practiced incessantly before shooting Umberto in the heart on July 29, 1900, with an American-made revolver.[11] Bresci's act raised the false specter of a great transatlantic anarchist conspiracy as well as the real necessity for more systematic and professional protection to be accorded heads of state and government.

Questions still remain regarding Bresci's character and his involvement with other anarchists in carrying out the assassination. Bresci was the son of a small farmer from near Prato, Tuscany, who had fallen on hard times with the agricultural depression of the 1880s. As a youth Bresci found work in a textile factory, where he worked fourteen hours a day, six days a week, and eventually became a skilled silk weaver and dyer, a relatively well-paid position.[12] Anarchist ideas attracted many in Tuscany and Bresci had become an active exponent by the time he was fifteen.[13] A man of no tolerance for what he saw as injustice, at twenty-two years of age Bresci began shouting at the police for fining a poor shop boy. For this the courts sentenced him to two weeks in jail. When in 1894–1895 Crispi carried out mass arrests of subversives, Bresci was forced to spend over a year of detention (*domicilio coatto*) on the island of Lampedusa, off the southern coast of Sicily. With plenty of time of his hands, he began an intensive reading of anarchist texts. The experience of *domicilio coatto*, in Bresci's case as well as in that of other young Italians, resulted, not in effective punishment or admonition, but in increasingly radicalized

[8] Paris correspondent, *The Times*, April 5, 1900, 6.
[9] *The Times*, April 6, 1900, 9. The socialists held a big anti-war rally in Brussels the day prior to Sipido's attempt.
[10] *The Times*, April 6 and 9, 1900, citing *Le Temps* (Paris) and *Die Information* (Vienna).
[11] Sidney Lee, *King Edward VII* 2 vols (New York: Macmillan, 1925), 1:777; Petacco, *L'anarchico che venne dall'America* (Milan: Mondadori, 1974): 34.
[12] Petacco, *L'anarchico*, 97.   [13] Petacco, *L'anarchico*, 18.

beliefs.[14] Ironically enough, *domicilio coatto* became the anarchists' "university," as anarchists from all over Italy were brought together and devoted their abundant free time to discussing their ideas. Released from detention, Bresci had difficulty finding work. In January 1897, after receiving a regular passport from the authorities who were doubtless glad to be rid of this troublesome anarchist, Bresci emigrated to the United States, where he found employment in the great textile mills of Paterson, New Jersey.

After Umberto's assassination, Paterson acquired the somewhat ill-deserved reputation of being the world's foremost center of anarchism and anarchist terrorism.[15] About 1,000 people in Paterson (among a larger Italian immigrant population of 10,000) subscribed to the anarchist *La Questione Sociale*, and this suggests the possible size of the anarchist or anarchist-sympathetic community.[16] All these Italians had been drawn to this heavily industrialized city of 100,000 people by the opportunity to work in the silk mills, since Paterson, nicknamed "the silk city," was America's largest producer of silk. Many northern Italians had experience in this industry because their own nation had long been "the silk factory of Europe."[17] The owners of the silk mills told the Italian ambassador that their workers were "from the province of Como and the young ones all came [*giungere*] more or less stained with anarchism [*tinti di anarchismo*]."[18] Because of the almost unlimited power provided by its Great Falls, a seventy-seven-foot drop in the Passaic River, Alexander Hamilton had selected Paterson as the nation's first planned industrial center.[19] By the end of nineteenth century, however, it had become a squalid industrial town of ramshackle wooden houses and dirty brick factories with chimneys continually emitting smoke and with no municipal sewage system.[20]

---

[14] Petacco, *L'anarchico*, 18. Besides Bresci, the most well-known (and similarly radicalized) survivor of *domicilio coatto* was Amedeo Boschi, *Ricordi del domicilio coatto* (Turin: Seme anarchicico, 1954): 43–44. See also Vittorio Buttis, *Memorie di vita di tempeste sociali* (Chicago: n.p., 1940): 37–38.

[15] Nichols, "Anarchists in America," 860.

[16] George W. Carrey, "*La Questione Sociale*," 292. Arrigo Petacco, an Italian journalist turned historian, cites a *New York Times* article claiming that 2,500 Italian anarchists lived in Paterson. Unfortunately, the December 18, 1898 issue of the *New York Times*, cited by Petacco (*L'anarchico*, 27) as his source, has no article on this topic, nor does the index to *The Times* for the entire 1890s provide such a citation. L. V. Ferraris, "L'assassinio di Umberto I e gli anarchici di Paterson," *Rassegna storica del Risorgimento* **60** (1968): 52, cites an article by the *New York Tribune*, July 31, 1900, giving the number of anarchists in Paterson as 1,500–2,000, but judges this to be excessive.

[17] Petacco, *L'anarchico*, 23; Seton-Watson, *Italy*, 21, 285n.

[18] Ambassador Mayor, Manchester, Massachusetts, to Prinetti, Rome, August 16, 1902. IFM, PI, b. 35.

[19] J. Palmer Murphy and Margaret Murphy, *Paterson & Passaic County: An Illustrated History* (Northridge, CA: Windsor Publications, 1987), 59–60.

[20] Petacco, *L'anarchico*, 23.

In 1894 acidic fumes from the polluted Passaic River caused the paint on houses to peel and blister.[21] Relations between the American industrialists (some of whom lived in palatial mansions, such as Lambert's Castle, furnished with fabulous art collections) and their immigrant employees were often embittered.[22] In such an atmosphere, anarchism flourished, and not only among Italians, but also among Spanish, French, German, Austrian, and eastern European, especially Jewish, immigrants. Several anarchist newspapers were founded in Paterson, including the Spanish *El Despertar* (*The Awakening*), the French *Germinal*, and most importantly, the bi-weekly Italian *La Questione Sociale*. Altogether the latter had about 3,000 readers scattered throughout the world.[23]

Many of the most prominent Italian anarchist leaders visited or lived in Paterson for a time. Saverio Merlino, who later defended Bresci at his trial, arrived in 1892, becoming the editor of an Italian-language anarchist newspaper in New York City. In 1895, he was followed by the popular lawyer-advocate, "poet," and songwriter of anarchism, Pietro Gori, who together with the Spaniard Pedro Esteve, founded *La Questione Sociale*.[24] The incendiary agitator, Giuseppe Ciancabilla, a socialist who converted to anarchism, arrived in 1898, when he took over the editorship of *La Questione Sociale* before being replaced in September 1899 by the most famous Italian anarchist of all, Errico Malatesta. Ciancabilla moved to nearby West Hoboken where he founded another anarchist periodical, *L'Aurora* (*The Dawn*). In the spring of 1900 Malatesta returned to London, which became his abode for more than a decade, and was replaced as editor by Esteve and others.

The largest anarchist group in Paterson was "The Society for the Right to Existence" (*Società per il diritto all'esistenza*), which backed *La Questione Sociale* and which Bresci joined shortly after immigrating. In fact Bresci rented a room in the very building, Bertholdi's Hotel, where the Right to Existence held its weekly meetings and where *La Questione Sociale* and *El Despertar* were published. According to a US Secret Service report drawn up after the assassination of Umberto with the aid of an informer, the group had "about forty active members."[25]

The principal group meets every Wednesday about eight o'clock on the second floor of #353 Market Street [i.e., Bertholdi's Hotel]. Their sessions usually last

[21] Murphy and Murphy, *Paterson & Passaic County*, 13, 16.

[22] Murphy and Murphy, *Paterson & Passaic County*, 69–70; 136–139.

[23] Carrey, "*La Questione Sociale*," 291. Masini, *Storia … attentati*, 131. See also the sometimes unreliable report by police Captain George McClusky of the New York City Detective Bureau, August 1900. Copy included with letter of Ambassador Fava to Acting Secretary of State, A. A. Adee, September 19, 1900. RG 60, Department of Justice, NA.

[24] Masini, *Storia … attentati*, 77; Carrey, "*La Questione Sociale*," 291.

[25] Carrey estimates the number of "active members" at 90. "*La Questione Sociale*," 292.

about an hour and a half, & there is no regular programme of exercises. The various members drop in & drop out. They have no such thing as a President or a Presiding officer, but Pedro Esteve, the editor of "La Questione Sociale" and "El Despertar", the principal organs of the Anarchists, usually directs the proceeding. Occasionally Francis Widmar, an Austrian who has long been identified with the group assumes these duties.[26]

While these meetings were mostly devoted to the discussion of political, philosophical, and social problems, occasionally the anarchists held dances and, allegedly, drank plenty of beer.[27] According to a *New York Times* reporter who visited the "dingy" premises, two big medallion busts of Angiolillo, the assassin of Prime Minister Cánovas, hung on the walls and big pictures of him were also scattered in various parts of the room.[28] (One wants to ask, why just Angiolillo? why not Caserio, assassin of Carnot? Why not Bakunin and Malatesta? Perhaps the reporter could not tell one anarchist from another.)

The Right to Existence group mostly identified with Malatesta's approach calling for organization, based on "cooperation and solidarity" rather than hierarchy, in order to prepare the way for social revolution. Malatesta rejected a narrow individualism that acted on impulse and glorified assassinations and bomb-throwings.[29]

But it was just this narrow individualism that seems to have appealed to Bresci, as well as to certain other anarchist leaders, such as Ciancabilla. Although Bresci had joined the Right to Existence, the Secret Service report states that he was also a member of another association, the Group of Thought and Action, "their creed being that it was an idle waste of money to attempt to bring about reforms through newspaper agitations, and that each individual should act for himself whether against king, or the simple factory owner or foreman."[30] The report lists seven "principal members" in this group, including Ciancabilla and, curiously enough, Malatesta, as well as Bresci.[31] Other than this, very little is known about the Group of Thought and Action and whether, indeed, it may have been at the center of a plot to kill the king of Italy. The Secret Service report

---

[26] The Secret Service was responding to requests from the Italian government. John E. Wilkie, Secret Service, to Treasury Secretary [Lyman Gage], Washington, DC, November 2, 1900. Forwarded to Department of State, November 3, 1900. File No. 11717/1900. RG 60, Department of Justice, NA.

[27] Petacco, *L'anarchico*, 27.

[28] "Searching Among Paterson Anarchists," *New York Times*, August 1, 1900, 1.

[29] Petacco *L'anarchico*, 8–10.

[30] Wilke to Secretary of Treasury, Washington, DC, November 2, 1900. File No. 11717/1900. RG 60, Department of Justice, NA.

[31] The other members listed were: V. Garbaccio, M. Tambonini, Gaspar Ferrario, and Gildo Zoppatti.

denied the existence of any conspiracy.[32] After his arrest and during his interrogation, Bresci made no mention of this radical group, although he did say that "six months before leaving [the United States] I withdrew from every political association in order to be freer."[33] Moreover, he had left the Right to Existence society after only two months because "it seemed to me that its members did not truly profess socialist anarchist ideas," i.e., presumably, because its anarchism was insufficiently revolutionary. At his interrogation and trial, Bresci repeatedly claimed to hold "revolutionary anarchist principles."[34]

While the workings of the Group of Thought and Action remain obscure, the actions and motivations of Bresci are relatively well documented. As has already been mentioned, Bresci was intolerant toward what he perceived to be injustice. His brother Lorenzo said that if Bresci saw someone whom "poverty [*la miseria*] had forced to beg, the blood rushed to his face."[35] Sophie Knieland, his Irish-American companion, said she remembered Bresci weep and curse against the "murderer king" at the thought of his role in the bloody repression of social discontent in Italy during the 1890s.[36] At his trial Bresci declared "it was after the states of siege [i.e., martial law] in Sicily [in 1894] and Milan [in 1898], established illegally by royal decree, that I decided to kill the king in order to vindicate those pale and bleeding victims." Moreover, Bresci explained, the king was at fault for awarding a medal to the general that had shot down the men, women, and children of Milan who were protesting against rising bread prices and unpopular government policies.

When in Paterson I read about the events in Milan where even cannon were used [against the protesters], I wept from anger and I prepared myself for revenge... Besides avenging the victims, I also wanted to revenge myself, forced, after a very difficult life, to emigrate.[37]

Having done little to provide for his escape after the assassination, Bresci hoped to be freed from prison by an imminent revolution, which he thought would take place within a couple of months.[38]

Was Bresci unbalanced or even insane? Many contemporaries and later commentators claimed he was. An August 2 editorial in *Avanti!*, the official Italian socialist newspaper, categorized Bresci as a "criminal madman" (but *Avanti!* also described former Italian Prime Minister Pelloux as

---

[32] Wilke to Secretary of Treasury, Washington, DC, November 2, 1900. File No. 11717/1900. RG 60, Department of Justice, NA.
[33] Petacco, *L'anarchico*, 92.   [34] Petacco, *L'anarchico*, 68.
[35] Ugoberto Alfassio Grimaldi, *Il re "buono,"* 5th ed. (Milan: Feltrinelli, 1973): 444.
[36] Petacco, *L'anarchico*, 33.   [37] Petacco, *L'anarchico*, 91.
[38] Petacco, *L'anarchico*, 103, 120. "Il complotto", *La Tribuna* (Rome), August 4, 1900.

a madman!).[39] The American Secret Service spy, presumably E. Moretti, who supposedly had been a "trusted member" of the Right to Existence group for three months, beginning in 1898 and in correspondence with leading members afterwards, reported that Bresci was "an eccentric, who was regarded by his companions as mentally unsound, and an 'individualist' of the pronounced type."[40] Moretti does not claim, however, that he ever personally met Bresci; the informer joined the Right to Existence only after Bresci had left the group. It is true that Bresci was an eccentric. For example, on trial virtually for his life (Italy had abolished the death penalty, but few survived a long sentence of solitary confinement without going mad or committing suicide), he spent thirty minutes of his two-hour interview with Filippo Turati, the socialist leader whom he had asked to defend him, complaining about petty injustices, such as the fact that the police had removed a metal stud from his shirt.[41]

But Bresci was not mentally unbalanced in any pronounced or clinical sense. His foreman at the Hamil and Booth silk mill in Paterson characterized Bresci as "a good workman and a man who had never made any trouble."[42] At his trial, a man who had worked with Bresci for six or seven years in Italy offered a similar assessment: "he was a good citizen, quiet by nature."[43] Sophie Knieland, the mother of two of his children, was astonished that he had committed the assassination since "he was always of such a timid, retiring disposition." He was also "a loving husband and father, and never drank to excess."[44] Even the famous criminologist Cesare Lombroso, who was quick to discover mental illness, degeneration, and hereditary criminality in almost every anarchist he came across, found nothing of the sort in Bresci. A handsome, muscular

---

[39] The *New York Times* ("Bressi's Deed," July 31, 1900) agreed "Bressi [sic] was not sane – we may assume that with entire certainty – and he had no effective respect of law and no restraining horror of murder."

[40] Treasury Secretary Gage described the unnamed Secret Service "operative" who reported on Bresci as "in the employ of the St. Louis and Southwestern Railway in Texas, and no longer an agent of the Secret Service. He is an Italian and a most capable man. He has already been communicated with a view to making a further investigation for this Department." Lyman Gage, Treasury Secretary, to Justice Department, Washington, DC, August 11, 1900; Wilkie to Secretary of Treasury [Gage], Washington, DC, November 2, 1900. File no. 11717/1900. RG 60, Department of Justice, NA. Charles Dawes, comptroller of the US currency and close to President McKinley, cites in his memoirs a report furnished "two years ago" (i.e., 1898) to the US Government by an "Italian-American resident of New York City, named E. Moretti...relative to a Grotto of Socialists located in Patterson [sic] N.J." and speaking of a vast conspiracy by "Anarchists or Socialists." *A Journal of the McKinley Years* (Chicago: Lakeside Press; R. R. Donnelley, 1950): 240.

[41] Undated letter [composed August 18, 1900] from Alfredo Bertesi to Camillo Prampolini, reprinted in Petacco *L'anarchico*, 81.

[42] *New York Times*, July 3, 1900.   [43] Petacco, *L'anarchico*, 96.

[44] *New York Times*, August 1, 1900.

man of medium stature, Bresci possessed none of those atavistic traits found in "born criminals." According to Lombroso, Bresci was, "even psychologically," as well as physically, an "average man" who in his formative adolescent years had become obsessed with anarchist ideas. A fanatic, Bresci carried out his violent deed after residence in a "free and economically happy" country, the US, had underscored for him the "terribly grave political conditions" in Italy.[45] Not that life in America was unalloyed pleasure: at his trial, Bresci said that "in America they even call us [Italians] swine."[46] Testimony at his trial also failed to establish Bresci's insanity. The Italian procurator general was forced to declare: "I would have liked to find [in Bresci] a lunatic [*demente*], in the hope of seeing, in this way, the gravity of the crime committed diminished in front of our Country. But I have found nothing of this in him."[47]

Was Bresci involved in a widespread anarchist plot to kill Umberto, as so many contemporary newspapers and some later historians wrote?[48] Just as had been true in the case of Sipido, the newspapers tried to link Bresci with the assassin of the Empress Elisabeth, associating together violent men who actually had little to do with one another.[49] *Le Matin* claimed that Bresci might have met Lucheni in Geneva and Swiss authorities interviewed the latter in his prison cell to learn if he knew anything.[50] Lucheni was delighted at the news of Umberto's death, but knew nothing of a conspiracy (testimony that failed to prevent an American newspaper from asserting that the incarcerated assassin's interrogation had "assured [the police] that the crimes of recent years have been the successive phases of a plot").[51] Even if Bresci was unconnected to Lucheni, was the former an "agent" of an anarchist group in Paterson or even of the great Malatesta, who pulled poor Bresci's strings from distant

[45] Lombroso's analysis of Bresci first appeared in the Venetian newspaper, *L'Adriatico* (September 23, 1900), 1–2, and was then republished in a slightly modified and updated form as a chapter in *Delitti vecchi e delitti nuovi* (Turin: Bocca, 1902): 245–252.

[46] Petacco, *L'anarchico*, 120.

[47] Petacco, *L'anarchico*, 101.

[48] *Corriere della Sera*, August 5–6, 1900; "Il complotto anarchico," *Perseveranza* (Milan), April 20, 1900; Robert Pinkerton, "Detective Surveillance of Anarchists," *The North American Review* 173 (1901): 612; "Il complotto," *La Tribuna* (Rome), August 4, 1900; "Other Assassins and their Victims," *New York Times*, October 15, 1912, 3. Alfredo Comandini and Antonio Monti, *L'Italia nei cento anni del secolo xix (1801–1900)* (Milan: Vallardi, 1930–1942): 5:1552. Gaetano Natale, *Giolitti e gli italiani* (Milan: Garzanti, 1949): 412; Martin Miller, "The Intellectual Origins of Modern Terrorism in Europe," in Martha Crenshaw (ed.), *Terrorism in Context*, (University Park, Pennsylvania: State University Press, 1995): 47.

[49] See the report from Vienna, April 5. *The Times*, April 6, 1900.

[50] *L'Italie* (Rome), August 2, 1900, cited *Le Matin*'s claim.

[51] "I documenti segreti nel processo Luccheni," *Corriere della Sera*, August 9–10, 1900; *New York Herald*, August 1, 1900, 4.

London?[52] During late August and September 1900, by which time the truth should have been apparent, several Roman newspapers continued to assert Malatesta's complicity, including the semi-official French language *L'Italie*.[53] *Il popolo romano* claimed that, "It is he [Malatesta] that prepared the assassination of King Umberto and who designated the assassin."[54] *Outlook*, a prominent American journal, declared that, "silent, cold, and plotting, [Malatesta] is, rather, the living, working genius of Anarchy itself...Enrico [sic] Malatesta was the head and moving spirit of all the conspiracies which have recently startled the world by the awful success which attended their execution." The *New York Herald* expressed similar views.[55] While the prosecution at Bresci's trial was no more specific than claiming that the Tuscan anarchist's deed was the fruit of a conspiracy originating in Paterson, the Milanese police assumed, at least for a time, that Malatesta was behind it all.[56] That Malatesta should have been identified as the ringleader of the assassination plot against Umberto and others suggests how little the media and many government figures understood him or the anarchists. As mentioned earlier, ever since 1892 Malatesta had spoken out against anarchist involvement in terrorism (although he undercut the force of his position by almost invariably finding, after the deed, much to justify the actions of anarchist assassins, including Bresci).[57] Malatesta favored organized action, especially inside the labor movement, to promote revolution, not individual acts of violence.

On the other hand, a peculiar assassination that took place in Paterson on July 20 seemed to offer evidence of a conspiracy against Umberto.

---

[52] "Bresci seems to have been the chosen agent of an anarchist group in Paterson, New Jersey." Woodcock, *Anarchism*, 146. Walter Laqueur, *Age of Terrorism*, 51, and Joll, *The Anarchists*, 122, repeat Woodcock's unfounded assertion. Giovanni Artieri, an Italian journalist and former senator, writes in his massive *Cronaca del Regno d'italia* (Milan: Mondadori, 1977): 740, that "The true and greater instigator [of the assassination of Umberto] was, as we know, Malatesta." Artieri alleges, without providing documentation, that Malatesta prepared the regicide while he was in the United States in 1899. *Cronaca*, 727, 737, 741, 744, 765, 773.

[53] *L'Italie*, August 25, 1900, asserted that despite the denials of certain American and English journals, Malatesta "is, more than ever, indicated as the principle organizer of the plot against Umberto."

[54] *Il popolo romano*, September 6, 1900, cited in *Gli anarchici*, ed. Aldo De Jaco (Rome: Riuniti, 1971): 658. *La Tribuna* ("Il complotto," August 4, 1900), however, noted that in the US, Malatesta headed those who opposed attentats.

[55] Francis Nichols, "Anarchists in America," 860–861. *New York Herald*, August 3, 1900, 3.

[56] See statement by Procurator General Francesco Ricciuti, in Petacco, *L'anachico*, 101; report, questura of Milan, July 30, 1900, in Giuliano Turone, "Il proceso per il regicidio di Umberto I," *Risorgimento* 34 (1982): 44–45.

[57] Malatesta, "Causa ed effetti. 1898–1900." Reprinted as "La tragedia di Monza" in Errico Malatesta, *Rivoluzione e lotta quotidiana*.

Sperandio Carbone, an unemployed textile worker and sometime pian-
ist, shot to death a much hated, and somewhat shady, plant manager
named Giulio Pessina. After his arrest Carbone committed suicide, but
left a strange note pinned to his shirt saying that "the good and honored
society" to which he belonged had chosen him by lot to kill the king of
Italy. Instead, Carbone had decided to kill Pessina. Various versions of
this note exist since the original was destroyed by the police prior to the
assassination of the Italian monarch, and it later had to be reconstructed
from memory. One version, at the time much publicized in Italy, said
that Carbone ceded to Bresci the honor of killing Umberto.

Although this fable has found its way into the history books, further
investigation demolished its credibility.[58] After official inquiries, both the
Italian and American governments dismissed the story. Italian Consul
General Branchi wrote the Italian foreign ministry that "I obtained the
original [?] of the now famous letter of Cariboni [sic], and with this
and with the declarations of informers, I believe to have proved beyond
a shadow of a doubt that the same has nothing to do with the supposed Paterson conspiracy."[59] Paterson Prosecutor Eugene Emley, in a
report eventually forwarded by the governor of New Jersey to Secretary
of State Hay, reached a similar conclusion. Emley had been unable to
discover that

any such purpose [as a plot] was shared by any other Italians here, or that there
was any combination or confederacy...looking to that end...I do not believe
that any combination or conspiracy has existed there which has as its object the
murder of King Humbert [Umberto], and what the culprit [i.e., Bresci] did was
done by him...acting upon his own responsibility.[60]

While American investigators were notoriously ill-informed about foreign anarchists, in this case it seems that Emley's conclusions were correct. Carbone may not even have written the letter attributed to him,
since later investigation suggested not only that he was not an anarchist,
but also that he was almost illiterate. Even if he did somehow compose it,
both local Italian anarchists and Consul General Branchi dismissed the
message as the ravings of a nutcase.[61]

The informer-based Secret Service report of November 2, 1900, also
denied any conspiracy involving Carbone or any of the Italians from

---

[58] Artieri, Cronaca, 744.
[59] G. Branchi, New York City, to G. Malvano, Rome, September 5, 1900. Affari politici, ser.
    P, b. 47. IFM.
[60] Quoted by Lowell Blaisdell, "The Assassination of Humbert I," Quarterly of the National
    Archives 27:3 (1995): 244.
[61] Branchi, New York, to foreign ministry, Rome, August 11, 1900, IFM, Affari politici, ser.
    P, b. 49; Petacco, L'anarchico, 65.

Paterson who happened to journey to Italy about the same time as Bresci. Despite the allegations of the media and ill-informed New York City Detective McClusky,

no cable was received by the members of the [Right to Existence] group announcing the assassination, and there was none of that suppressed excitement which would surely have manifested itself had they been waiting comsummation [sic] of a plot in which they were directly interested.[62]

Since confidential agents tend to exaggerate and invent conspiracies, rather than deny them, this skepticism adds a certain credibility to the report. Indeed the ten or so co-conspirators arrested and held by the Italian government for more than a year eventually had to be released for lack of evidence.

Nonetheless, Bresci probably had one accomplice from Paterson, Luigi Granotti. A murky figure, his name does not appear on the Secret Service list of principal members of the Right to Existence society and his role has only been substantially clarified since the complete records of Bresci's trial and the investigations of his alleged accomplices, moldering in the Milan archives, came to light in the late 1970s.[63] Giuliano Turone's article proves beyond a doubt that Granotti, Bresci's melancholic friend who followed him around like a faithful dog, was with the assassin in Monza between July 27 and 30, just at the time of Umberto's murder. While Granotti's activities during that period are largely unknown, it strains credulity to think that he had come to Monza simply to pay Bresci a friendly visit (although this was what Bresci repeatedly claimed).[64] Was Granotti, as the newspapers theorized, at the gymnastic field in Monza at the time of the assassination, assisting Bresci by watching one of the two exits?[65] Granotti subsequently went to stay with his cousin, Giacomo Bussetti, in Piedmont north of Biella, before crossing the Swiss border on August 2 with the help of a guide and, apparently, escaping to America where he went into hiding.[66] Interrogated by the police, Bussetti said that he had deduced from conversations with his cousin that, if Bresci had missed, Granotti would have had to fire on the king.[67] Through a

---

[62] Wilke to Secretary of Treasury, Washington, DC, November 2, 1900. File no. 11717/1900. RG 60, Department of Justice, NA.

[63] Turone, "Umberto I," 37.

[64] Giuseppe Galzerano, *Gaetano Bresci* (Casalvelino Scalo: Galzerano, 2001): 351–353; 357.

[65] See unidentified (but presumably the *Osservatore romano*) newspaper account dated Monza, night of July 31 to August 1, 1900, reprinted in Petacco, *L'anarchico*, 212–216.

[66] An anarchist newspaper reported that Granotti died in New York in 1949. Galzerano, *Gaetano Bresci*, 389.

[67] Turone, "Umberto I," 41.

lawyer, Granotti's family later denied that he had any responsibility for the murder.[68] Bussetti fled to South America and, according to one of his acquaintances, repudiated his testimony since it had been extorted by police brutality.[69] Nonetheless, in November 1901 the Italian courts condemned Granotti *in absentia* to life imprisonment. Confidentially, Interior Minister Giolitti admitted to the Italian foreign minister that all the evidence gathered so far amounted to

rumors and circumstantial evidence [*voci e indizi*], that point to the existence of an accord among the anarchists of Paterson and to monetary help loaned by them to the regicide Bresci; but from the aforementioned records clear and evident facts affirming the existence of a plot could not be inferred.

Moreover, Giolitti continued, since all the evidence had been acquired confidentially, it would not stand up in court.[70] Giolitti, to his credit, does not hint at even the most minimal involvement of Malatesta. Without providing convincing evidence, however, some historians continue to speculate about the latter's responsibility, as well as, with somewhat more justification, that of Carlo Colombo and others.[71] Giuseppe Galzerano's massive and well-documented *Gaetano Bresci* and another recent study deny that there was a plot.[72]

Defects in Umberto's security guard and its reform

The Italian government drew two major conclusions from the assassination of King Umberto. The first was that it needed to be better informed about the activities of Italian anarchists residing abroad. The second was that the personal security provided the head of state needed to be much

---

[68] Turone, "Umberto I," 42; Galzerano, *Gaetano Bresci*, 369–371.

[69] Galzerano, *Gaetano Bresci*, 370; Blaisdell, "Humbert I," 245. The *New York Times*, "Bresci's Friend Accused" (October 22, 1900), 2, cites one "Joseph" Mercandino, a resident of Paterson who said he had met Granotti and Bussetti in their village in Italy. Mercandino alleged that Bussetti told him that "he had signed a confession to escape torture in a dungeon." Petacco, citing an old Italian American from Pittsburgh, alleges that Granotti made his way to Paterson in 1902 where he spent the rest of his life.

[70] Giolitti, Rome, to minister of Foreign Affairs, March 7, 1901. IFM, PI, b. 30.

[71] E.g., Artieri, *Cronaca*, 744, whose account is based in part on diaries and letters of members of the royal court. Berti, *Errico Malatesta*, 315–316, speculates, without offering proof, that Malatesta must have known about Bresci's plans.

[72] Galzerano, *Gaetano Bresci*, 329–426; Carl Levy, "The Anarchist Assassin and Italian History, 1870s to 1930s," in Stephen Gundle and Lucia Rinaldi (eds.), *Assassinations and Murder in Modern Italy. Transformations in Society and Culture* (New York: Palgrave Macmillan, 2007): 214, 211. The only real evidence of Colombo's involvement was a vague statement by Galleani ten years later that Colombo had been at Monza. Maurizio Antonioli, "Colombo, Carlo" and Antonioli and Giampietro Berti, "Bresci, Gaetano" in *Dizionario biografico degli anarchici italiani*. Carl Levy's forthcoming biography of Malatesta may well clarify many of these questions.

improved. Romanin-Jacur, the assistant minister of the interior, headed up an official inquest into the causes of Umberto's assassination, but his findings have never been published or located by historians.[73] The inquest carried out by the *carabinieri* command has also remained secret, although Prime Minister Saracco shared with parliament some of the findings from both inquests.[74]

While it would be very instructive to be able to examine the inquests, the major gaps in the security net provided for the king can be readily inferred from contemporary accounts. Improvident, ill-coordinated, and undermanned, the forces assigned to protect the head of the Italian state were of two sorts: the *carabinieri*, in their striking uniforms and beautiful plumed hats, and the more mundanely dressed public security police. Inspector Galeazzi, the head of Umberto's police security squad, drew up a report that was leaked to the press.[75] Galeazzi declared that the sub-prefect of Monza charged the local *carabiniere* lieutenant with providing security arrangements for the king's visit to a gymnastics tournament the night of July 29. This was doubtless a normal arrangement since the *carabinieri*, a militarized police forming part of the Italian army, were generally assigned duties in small towns, such as Monza, and the countryside. The *carabinieri*, who normally performed routine police duties rather than the complex tasks and detective work involved in urban policing, were not the best force for the complex job of protecting the king. For example, Galeazzi asserts that the *carabiniere* lieutenant, in collaboration with the royal household's master of the horse, chose a long and vulnerable route for the royal carriage to pass the short distance (450 meters or less, i.e., less than a third of a mile) between the king's villa and the outdoor sports complex where the monarch was to attend a gymnastics competition. According to Galeazzi, he insisted that the route be shifted to one that was half as long and less dangerous. Three or four *carabinieri* stood in and around the sports field, two near the royal box and the rest along the short street leading back to the villa.[76] It is clear, however, that the major responsibility for safeguarding the king fell on the civilian police, traditional rivals of the military force. There were only ten of these

[73] *Corriere della Sera* (Milan), September 1–2, 1900.
[74] Italy, Chamber of Deputies, November 26, 1900, 561–562, 570.
[75] Initially published by "Provincia di Cremona;" republished by *Corriere della Sera*, August 11–12, 1900.
[76] Ugo Pesci, *Il re martire: la vita e il regno di Umberto I: date, aneddoti, ricordi, 1844–1900* (Bologna: Ditta Nicola Zanichelli, 1901): 408. Pesci claims that his account of the assassination was based on "an eye witness who due to his office was in a position to be exactly and minutely informed" (*Il re martire*, 406). Pesci writes that when the king arrived at the stadium "much confusion in the maintenance of order seemed to be everywhere; because everyone was commanding and no one was obeying" (*Il re martire*, 408).

civilian *Guardie di pubblica sicurezza*, six of whom were strung along the approach route to the event, and only four available to guard the king inside the sports complex.

Critics were unanimous in criticizing this disposition of forces.[77] The newspapers contended that the king had been led into a virtual "trap" where it was easy to commit the crime.[78] Galeazzi himself admitted that there were too few civilian and military police to handle the large crowds – 2,000 people attended the gymnastics competition.[79] Galeazzi lamented as well the decision to schedule the royal visit for such a late hour (the king arrived at 9:30 p.m. and departed at 10:30 p.m.). Part of the reason for the lateness was the suffocating heat: 36 degrees centigrade or almost 97 Fahrenheit.[80] The electric arc lights illuminating the sports field were so high up that they gave off only an uncertain light,[81] making it difficult for the police to spot potential troublemakers in the shadows. Dangerous as well was the narrowness of the avenue for the royal vehicle to approach and exit from the viewing stand. This made it difficult to keep the public at a safe distance, and as the king's carriage tried to leave, it was obstructed and much slowed by the crowd. It was just at this moment that Bresci stood up on his chair in the public seating three rows back, less than twelve feet from the carriage, and fired his revolver three times.[82] Allegedly, he had scored the tips of his bullets to make them more deadly, believing the grooves would introduce dirt and germs into the wound, but this is unproven. Since the king was said to wear armor or a mailed vest in public (although one historian dismisses this as a "clerical legend"),[83] Bresci hoped that even a small penetration would prove mortal.[84] As it turned out, the king had worn no armor that night and the autopsy revealed that two of the three shots had been lethal.

Giuseppe Sensales, who had headed the General Directorate of Public Security in the Crispi government of 1893–1896, provides us with an interesting, and rarely cited, analysis of the failure of the police to protect Umberto. In a 1901 article, Sensales noted, first, that no preventative steps had been taken. For example, no effort had been made to learn the names of the gymnasts from Italy and abroad who were participating in

---

[77] "In a really stupefying manner, the most elementary measures of public security seem to have been neglected." "*Come e dove fu consumato l'assassinio,*" *La Tribuna* (Rome), August 2, 1900.

[78] *Corriere della Sera* (Milan), August 3–4, 1900, quoting the Roman newspaper *Esercito.*

[79] De Jaco, *Gli anarchici*, 642.   [80] Grimaldi, *Il re "buono,"* 445.

[81] Pesci, *Il re martire,* 405–406.

[82] Petacco, *L'anarchico,* 50. Pelloux's notes composed in 1900 say that, according to the official inquest, Bresci was a meter from the king, while the latter's bodyguards were at least five or six meters away. Scatolla 28, f. 33. Pelloux Archive, ACS.

[83] Artieri, *Cronaca,* 747.   [84] Petacco, *L'anarchico,* 86–87.

the event. Second, the placement of police inside and outside the sports arena was ineffective. It was useless to position only a few guards along the king's route; those in charge should have posted sufficient forces to form a chain of security men that could prevent mischief-makers from approaching the royal carriage. Given the late hour and darkness of the street, the surveillance along the avenue should have been entrusted to *carabinieri* on horseback. Inside the sports stadium, the placement of the few police guards was also defective:

They would have been overwhelmed by the crowd at the first sign of confusion.

In similar circumstances, in order to deal with events not difficult to foresee, skilled officials have never failed to post the greatest possible number of guards in civilian attire around the royal vehicle; especially during the arrival at the meeting place and at the departure, the moments of greater crowding caused by [people's] natural and normal curiosity.[85]

The newspapers agreed with Sensales. Given the few police agents available, they should have been posted close around Umberto in order to cover the person of the king, rather than standing at the foot of the sports stand and where the chairs of the audience were located.[86] All of this just proved, as Sensales declared, "the absolute deficiency of our system of public security."[87]

Sensales suggested, and the Saracco government as well as other observers concurred, that crucial to Bresci's success was the lack of a rigorous system of royal protection directed by an able and foresighted head. This was partially due to the opposition of the monarch, who, understandably enough, hated a heavy-handed surveillance of his activities and demanded as much as possible that his protectors remain out of sight.[88] In Rome, if the king decided to take a drive, he did not give notice to anyone, and his bodyguard had to follow as best it could, if necessary renting public carriages at the last moment (and these carriages could never keep up with the king's horses).[89] This royal attitude, combined with the maneuvering of the police administration and royal household, led, only ten days before the assassination, to the removal of an extremely capable official in charge of the king's safety. In his *Memoirs*, Prime Minister Pelloux (1898–1900) revealed that after the 1897 anarchist assassination attempt on the king, Prime Minister Di Rudinì had wanted to reinforce

---

[85] Sensales, "L'anagrafe di polizia," 248.   [86] *La Tribuna* (Rome), August 2, 1900.
[87] Sensales, "L'anagrafe di polizia," 248. The *Corriere della Sera*, August 23–24, 1900, contended that Italy had "one of the most incapable and unfit police mechanisms."
[88] Fiorenza Fiorentino, *Ordine pubblico nell'Italia giolittiana* (Rome: Carecas, 1978): 24.
[89] Inspector Galeazzi to Questore, Rome, May 19, 1897, f. 285, Questura. Archivio di Stato di Roma.

the royal security service, as well as get rid of the good-hearted, but semi-incompetent, Inspector Leopoldo Galeazzi. Umberto, however, "with his well known fanaticism, did not wish to speak of any change in his entourage, and the Marquis de Rudinì did not insist."[90]

At first the king also refused when Pelloux demanded greater security measures in the summer of 1898. After the Empress Elisabeth's assassination in September, however, the prime minister succeeded in forcing him to accept the assignment of a second man to head up the royal protection squad alongside Galeazzi, whom the king found congenial. For this new position Pelloux chose a "truly exceptional" police inspector from Turin named Federico Piano.[91] Pelloux also sought to increase the number of the king's bodyguards, aiming at doubling its size, although it is unclear if he succeeded in this endeavor.[92] Piano's assiduous and severe manner of protecting the royal couple, however, caused complaints. Nonetheless, according to the prime minister's secretary, the king liked Piano and praised his work; after the assassination, the widowed Queen Margherita specifically requested that Piano accompany her from Monza to Rome.[93] Galeazzi and the minister in charge of the royal household, however, were jealous of his authority and good standing with Umberto. The prefect of Rome, who for administrative reasons, was slated to become Piano's nominal superior, found him arrogant and proposed that he be replaced – a change to which the minister of the royal household readily assented. Pelloux thought that, if Piano had remained at his post, Umberto's assassination could have been prevented, either because Piano would have been right next to him at all times (Galleazzi was faulted for leaving the monarch's side, just prior to Bresci's assault, in order to deal with the carriage horses),[94] or else because Piano would have vetoed altogether the hazardous night journey to the gymnastics event.

In the face of a torrent of public and parliamentary criticism of Italy's policing apparatus, the government of the aged Prime Minister Giuseppe

[90] Fiorentino, *Ordine pubblico*, 24; Giacomo Morando, Italy, Chamber of Deputies, *Discussioni*, November 26, 1900, 570; Luigi Pelloux, *Quelques souvenirs de ma vie Rome*, ed. Gastone Manacorda (Rome: Istituto per la storia del risorgimento italiano, 1967): 187.

[91] Pelloux, *Quelques souvenirs*, 187–188.

[92] In his memoirs (*Quelques souvenirs*, 187) and notes, Pelloux makes it clear that "a better choice of personnel" was more important than more guards. "Assassinio del Re Umberto e appunti per una interpellanza," scatola 28, Pelloux Archive, ACS.

[93] Pelloux, *Quelques souvenirs*, 213, 215; Raffaele Cafiero, who had been in the Prime Minister's secretariat under both Pelloux and Saracco, wrote to Pelloux, December 2, 1900, that "as you know [the king] approved of Piano and willingly praised his work." Scatola 28, Pelloux Archive, ACS.

[94] Saracco told Parliament that Galeazzi had failed in his duty and acted irrationally. Italy, *Atti parlamentari* Chamber of Deputies, Discussioni, November 26, 1900, 561.

Saracco (1900–1901) decided to do two things for which he has rarely been given sufficient credit: field an international police force to monitor Italy's far-flung emigrant communities, especially their anarchist offshoots, and, second, create a special security force to protect the head of state. Galeazzi was fired and, on November 6, 1900, a decree officially instituted the Royal Commissariat (or General Inspectorate) of Public Security for the Royal Household.[95] Relatively little is known about this organization. The prime minister told parliament that the new police force guarding the royal family was "constituted by a sufficient number of select and experienced officers and many agents" and was "governed by an appropriate set of regulations, whose rules were the product of the most careful study by the interior ministry in cooperation with the Royal Household."[96] At some point the able Piano was brought back to protect the sovereign.[97] Senator Astengo, one of the government's severest critics on the question of past deficiencies in royal protection, lauded Saracco's efforts, claiming to find the new security service, about which Astengo said he had become thoroughly acquainted, "excellent" (ottimo).[98] During the king's trips, the Royal Commissariat now received a mountain of reports from all over Italy about persons held to be "politically dangerous" and whom the police had temporarily lost sight of. No doubt this was an improvement over the previous situation with its lack of intelligence, although in 1910 Inspector General Paoli Sessi complained that much of the information was worthless and, after ten years on the job, he no longer had any place to store it all.[99] As to the size of the royal security force, evidence from 1912 shows that it was made up of an inspector general and five other policemen of various ranks; this could be compared, presumably, with the one or two officials who had been permanently assigned to guard Umberto.[100] In November 1900, the newspapers reported that "another forty cuirassiers" had been added to the king's guard, although Victor Emmanuel III still enjoyed driving his wife about Rome in his carriage without any sort of guard or entourage.[101] Such actions, since unannounced, were relatively safe; Umberto's fatal

---

[95] Saracco's statement to parliament suggested that it had come into being even before this; he said the Commissariat had been in existence "da qualche mese," "for some months." Saracco, Italy, Atti parlamentari, Senate, Discussioni, November 27, 1900, 242.

[96] Saracco, Italy, Atti parlamentari, Senate, Discussioni, February 2, 1901, 1126.

[97] For evidence of Piano's continued presence, see: "Il Re a Livorno," Corriere della Sera, October 30–31, 1902.

[98] Astengo, Italy, Atti parlamentari, Senate, Discussioni, February 2, 1901, 1127.

[99] Sessi, Racconigi, to DGPS, Rome, on July 21, 1910. ACS, Dir.AA.GG.RR. massime, b.3.

[100] ACS, DGPS, ufficio riservato, 1912, b. 13.

[101] Corriere della Sera, November 6–7, 1900.

trip to the gymnastics tournament, on the other hand, had been widely publicized. In January 1901, Italy asked several major European states how they managed the security arrangements for their heads of state. Although the information they sent was limited, it would seem that prior to 1900 most of the Great Powers had provided substantially larger and more rigorous systems of security for their leaders than Italy had.

A revolution in protection for heads of state?

A comprehensive history has yet to be written of how security arrangements have evolved for the protection of national leaders, but scattered pieces of evidence from the archives and memoirs give some idea of the situation in the Western world. A case can be made for a major change, if not indeed a revolution, in such arrangements around 1900. As a result of the anarchist threat, a number of important countries carried out police reforms that made protection of leaders bureaucratic, systematic, and official, rather than, as in the past, ad hoc and personal. In the past, aristocratic and military values had strongly influenced rulers' attitudes toward their security. God would protect those who held power by divine right and rulers were supposed to be courageous and unafraid of death in the face of potential assassins.[102] For example, in 1881 Tsar Alexander II stopped his sleigh after a bomb had been thrown at him and confronted his assailant. This courageous but incautious act led to his death. While the notion of the divine right of kingship was in decline by the later part of the nineteenth century, "scientific policing" was increasingly the goal toward which police reform was aimed. Now, for the first time in history, one can speak of the protection of high officials as becoming a kind of science.

We can see this sort of development in Germany. Kaiser Wilhelm II's grandfather, Wilhelm I (reigned 1861–1888) had a single permanent bodyguard, a police captain, who accompanied him everywhere. Wilhelm II (reigned 1888–1918) strongly embraced aristocratic and military values and trusted in God for his safety. He loathed the idea of a police escort, but grudgingly accepted one for "reasons of state" and "in view of the abominable attentats of mad individuals."[103] For his protection Wilhelm did not have one designated bodyguard, as with his grandfather.

[102] For a pioneering article on the subject, see Carola Dietze and Frithjof Benjamin Schenk, "Traditionelle Herrscher in moderner Gefahr. Soldatisch-aristokratische Tugendhaftigkeit und das Konzept der Sicherheit im späten 19.Jahrhundert," *Geschichte und Gesellschaft*, 35 (2009): 368–401.

[103] *Berlin Lokal Anzeiger*, September 12, 1900. For Wilhelm's dislike of all special police precautions and "his trust in God" for his safety, see Louis Schneider, *L'Empereur Guillaume*, trans. Charles Rabany, 3 vols. (Paris and Nancy: Berger-Levrault, 1888): 2:4–5, 3:20.

Rather the officers and men of his security service were chosen from the "criminal police...by the political department of the Royal [Prussian] police bureau."[104] Throughout the 1890s, and in apparent contrast with the situation in Italy, Germany increased its protection for the kaiser and the thoroughness of its preventative policing. In 1898 the authorities added eight civilian and uniformed police to guard the kaiser when in Potsdam.[105] In 1899, the police of provincial German towns routinely asked for any information, including photographs, of "politically suspect persons, particularly anarchists" who might be traveling there prior to visits by the kaiser.[106] In May 1900, the newspapers reported that prior to the kaiser's arrival in a town, persons indicated as "dangerous" would be subject to more intense surveillance. Some might be expelled. An "international information service" (*internationaler signalisirungsdienst*) had been set up at home and abroad to report on possible conspiracies.[107] After the assassination of King Umberto, the German police required photographers, who it feared might possess firearms disguised as cameras, to obtain special permission or to remain 150 meters from the kaiser.[108] Foreign guests staying in hotels along the Unter den Linden, Berlin's main thoroughfare leading to the royal palace, had their passports carefully examined.[109] The kaiser had very little involvement with all these security arrangements and complained of heavy-handed measures during his walks, when, for example, the police chased away any other walkers before the emperor arrived. Wilhelm asked that this practice be stopped.[110]

In 1901, after an assault by a mentally disturbed workingman in Bremen, the kaiser's bodyguard was increased to more than sixty for his travels outside Berlin.[111] (The Political Police, the secret service of Germany whose duties included monitoring the activities of

---

[104] *Berlin Lokal Anzeiger*, September 12, 1900.
[105] *Berlin Lokal Anzeiger*, November 29, 1898.
[106] Polizei-Direktor, Metz, to Polizei Präsidium, Berlin, April 27, 1899, and Polizei Präsidium, Kassel, to Polizei Präsidium, Berlin, March 20, 1899, rep. 30, Berlin C, tit. 94, lit. K, 10972, SP.
[107] *Berliner Landenblatt*, May 9, 1900. As further examples of the thoroughness of German security measures, the *New York Times* speaks of the deploying of hundreds of detectives and the carrying out of numberless house searches during visits to various cities in Germany by the Kaiser and other royalty. "Royalty Guarded at Coburg," April 19, 1894, and "Minor Affairs in Germany," November 14, 1897.
[108] German consul, Gothenburg, Sweden, to Commandant Royal Headquarters, General von Plessen, August 7, 1900 and police memo, Kurt Wachtmeister, Berlin, August 28, 1900, SP, rep. 30, Berlin C, tit. 94, lit. K, 10972.
[109] *Berliner Tageblatt*, September 1, 1900.
[110] *Berliner Landenblatt*, May 9, 1900; Royal Adjutant to Police President von Windheim, n.d., but probably *c.* April 10, 1901, SP, rep. 30, Berlin C, tit. 94, lit. K, 10972.
[111] *Deutsche Warte* (Berlin), March 23, 1901.

"subversives" as well as protecting the kaiser when he resided in Berlin, consisted in 1901 of 120 men, not including officers.[112]) While Edward VII "chaffed Kaiser Wilhelm because of the large phalanx of German Secret Police" which accompanied him "wherever he went," this was more against the kaiser's will than because of it.[113] In Berlin he hated having detectives around him and they had to disguise themselves as butchers, bakers, masons, and carpenters. Wilhelm's massive guard represented the increasing bureaucratization, depersonalization, and professionalization of protection for heads of state rather than the whim of the very idiosyncratic German monarch, who would have preferred to travel everywhere with the freedom of an ordinary tourist. As Gustav Steinhauer, who, before becoming a spy, was for fourteen years part of the kaiser's bodyguard, declared: "the safety for the Emperor had to be considered; that lay in the interests of the State, whether the Kaiser and his adjutants wanted it or not."[114]

Austria-Hungary, like Germany, apparently provided, at least by the end of the nineteenth century, much greater police protection for its monarch than had been customary in Italy.[115] Asked by the Italians in January 1901 how they organized the protection of Franz Joseph, the Austrian government replied that it had established no "separate police office" (as the Italians had just created) devoted exclusively to the task of providing for the security of the emperor, of the imperial household, and of visiting foreign sovereigns.[116] That job was in the hands of the regular police and administrative authorities. In Vienna, as in Berlin, the Police Department (*Polizei-Präsidium*) handled these measures with a special brigade of agents under the command of the chief of the Police-Agent-Institute (*Polizei-Agenten-Institut*). Two inspectors of police were permanently stationed at the Hofburg Palace, the official Habsburg residence in Vienna. At the emperor's summer residence just outside Vienna at Schönbrunn a police commissioner delegated by the Vienna police

[112] *Deutsche Warte* (Berlin), March 23, 1901; for a brief history of the political division of the Berlin police, see Hoerder, *Plutocrats and Socialists*, xxvi–xxxv.
[113] Brust, *"I Guarded Kings,"* 33.
[114] Gustav Steinhauer, *Steinhauer, the Kaiser's Master Spy*, ed. S. T. Felstead (New York: Appleton, 1931): 327–328.
[115] Early in his reign, in 1853, Franz Joseph had been assaulted and almost killed while accompanied by a single equerry, who wrestled the assailant to the ground and saved the Emperor's life.
[116] Note verbale, Italian embassy, Vienna, to Austro-Hungarian foreign minister, January 19, 1901; Polizei Präsidium to Informationsbureau, foreign ministry, Vienna, January 30, 1901. The note verbal communicated to the Italian ambassador, and dated March 16, 1901, omitted some information provided by the Vienna police department, such as the detailed discussion of the policing of the Emperor's routine trips. Informationsbureau 1901, c. 427. HHStA.

chief and a "sufficient number of security agents" guarded the monarch and also resided at the chateau.

On trips, the police devoted themselves principally to a rigorous sur-veillance of the roads. For regular, recurring trips the police carried out a minutely detailed plan of surveillance. The special brigade would in these cases be aided by police officials, agents, and uniformed policemen (*Sicherheitswachen*) from the district office (the *Polizei-Commissariat*).[117] The route travelled by the emperor would be divided into small stretches and each stretch would have assigned to it the same police group, who, having been "most thoroughly instructed," would subject it to "constant and precise control." A vehicle with police would not precede or fol-low His Majesty's, however, except in special circumstances, such as the sojourn in Vienna of foreign sovereigns.

A map preserved in the Viennese police archives dated February 1901 shows the positioning of between 114 to 127 police agents, on both horseback and foot, entrusted with guarding the emperor's journey from the Hofburg to Schönbrunn.[118] Although it was about twenty-eight miles between the two palaces, as opposed to the less than three miles between the Monza stadium and the Royal Villa, the precise system of the Austrian police and the much greater number and variety (i.e., some on horseback) of guards devoted to the task suggests that the Austrian approach to protecting the monarch was more scientific, or at least more thought-out, than that employed in Italy.

The Italians also wanted to know if the imperial security force had at its disposition "special agents either domestically or abroad, notably in those places which are considered anarchist hotbeds." The Austrians did not reply specifically to this question, although evidence does exist that they had placed anti-anarchist agents abroad in the 1890s.

A few days before contacting Austria, Italy had sent a similar list of questions to the British government. Interestingly, when communicating with the British, the Royal Commissariat styled itself as "the Criminal Investigation Department attached to the Royal Household," suggest-ing how influential was the British police model. Since Scotland Yard's Special Branch had been founded in 1883, it had, in the words of one of its detectives, "made Great Britain famed as one place where not only its own rulers but those of foreign countries may walk in safety."[119] Germany, the Netherlands, and other countries, as well as Italy, all wanted to know the secret of the Special Branch's success, but they were almost invariably

---

[117] For an explanation of the organization of the Viennese police, see Fosdick, "Bertillon System," 119–124.

[118] 1901. Scha.St/1. Bibliotek und Archiv. Bundespolizeidirektion, Vienna. See Figure 9.

[119] Brust, *"I Guarded Kings,"* 35.

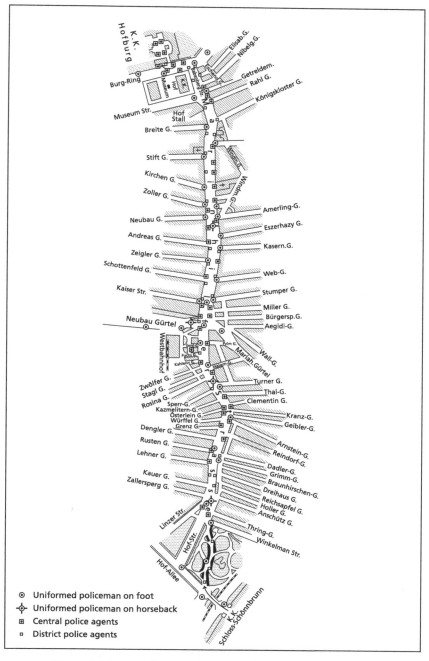

K.K. Hofburg

Burg-Ring
Museum Str.
Hof Museum
K.K.
Hof Stall
Elisab. G.
Nibelg. G.
Getreidem.
Rahl G.
Königskloster G.
Hof Stall
Breite G.
Stift G.
Kirchen G.
Zoller G.
Neubau G.
Andreas G.
Zeigler G.
Schottenfeld G.
Kaiser Str.
Neubau Gürtel
Westbahnhof
Amerling-G.
Eszerhazy G.
Kasern.G.
Web-G.
Stumper G.
Miller G.
Bürgersp.G.
Aegidi-G.
Pzlm G.
Wall-G.
Mariah. Gürtel
Kahlenn.
Halam.
Turner G.
Zwölfer G.
Stagl G.
Rosina G.
Sperr-G.
Kazmelitern-G.
Österlein G.
Würffel G.
Grenz G.
Dengler G.
Rusten G.
Lehner G.
Kauer G.
Zallersperg G.
Thal-G.
Clementin G.
Kranz-G.
Geibler-G.
Arnstein-G.
Reindorf-G.
Dadler-G.
Grimm-G.
Braunhirschen-G.
Dreihaus G.
Reichsapfel G.
Holler G.
Anschütz G.
Thring-G.
Winkelman Str.
Linzer Str.
Hof-Str.
Hof-Allee
K.K. Schloss-Schönbrunn

⊙ Uniformed policeman on foot
⊕ Uniformed policeman on horseback
▣ Central police agents
▫ District police agents

Figure 9 The complex security system for Emperor Franz Joseph during his trips from the Hofburg Palace to Schönbrunn. Based on a Viennese police map, 1901. Scha. St/1. Bibliotek und Archiv. Bundespolizei-direktion, Vienna.

disappointed. Police Commissioner Bradford replied to the Italians in the same way he had replied on August 2, 1900, to a German request for a party of its detectives to study the English police system, including knowledge of police duty in attendance on the royal family.[120]

this duty is necessarily of an extremely delicate nature. Its efficient perform-ance depends not so much on a strict adherence to Police regulations, as on the possession by the Officers engaged of a strong fund of common sense, and of a capacity to deal effectively with emergencies which arise so suddenly as to leave no time for seeking instructions from a Superior officer… to put the German Detectives in touch with the officers actually engaged in such duties would be obviously undesirable.[121]

The Foreign Office told Germany that

the House of Commons and public opinion in this country are excessively sus-picious of cooperation between the English and Continental Police especially in regard to political crimes. On one occasion a Home Secretary was nearly driven out of office on this ground, and it was on another, in 1852, the real cause of the fall of Lord Palmerston's Ministry.[122]

Memoirs left by former Special Branch detectives, supplemented by archival information, provides some insight into why the British were so successful at protecting royalty. The memoirs published by British detectives in 1915 and the mid-1930s (and based on service that began prior to World War I or went back as far as the 1890s), probably reflect practices in place even earlier, but also, no doubt, puff up the abilities of the Special Branch. These memoirs depict a longtime "surveillance duty and guardian service" that was low key, but preventive, rigorous, methodical, and professional to the highest degree. Prior to a royal visit, trains were searched, and crowds thoroughly combed for dan-gerous characters. A pilot train would precede a royal one in order to scout out any danger, which was a practice that went back to the days of the Fenian terror in the early 1880s and further evidence that the Irish dynamiters had partly inoculated Britain against the later threat

120 Rough draft, C. M. [Charles Murdoch] to Italian Vice-Consul, January 1901; Gericke to Lansdowne, London, February 13, 1901. HO144/527/x79683, PRO. The Dutch (Gericke) were interested in studying "public security, the regulation of the surveillance of foreigners and the dispositions decreed in their regard, and the organization of the secret police in order to combat anarchism." It seems odd that the Italians approached the English on such an important and delicate matter through a lowly Vice-Consul. The British were clearly not impressed by this approach, but the fate of the German and Dutch requests suggests that even the Italian ambassador would have met a refusal.

121 Bradford, New Scotland Yard, to undersecretary of state, Home Office, London, August 2, 1900. HO 144/527/x79683, PRO.

122 Copy, T. H. Sanderson, Foreign Office, to Count Hatzfeldt, August 9, 1900. HO527/x79683/2. PRO; Porter, *Vigilant State*, 143.

from the anarchists.[123] Every inch of track would be inspected ahead of time. On the lookout for anarchist assassins renting rooms, the Special Branch acquired an "intimate knowledge" of the "rabbit-warren of tenement houses" that surrounded the big London railway terminals. Moreover:

In key positions, not only around the terminus stations in London but in our ports, our inland cities, and all over the world, are Special Branch men, serving perhaps as barmen in public-houses, stewards on ships, secretaries in working-men's clubs – in fact, in all those places where people talk. Our men listen. Day and night their reports come in to Scotland Yard. Long before any nihilist plot can be successfully hatched, the plotters find themselves confronted by quiet men in soft civilian suits, and learn that they must cease from disturbing the King's peace, or suffer the rigours of the law.[124]

Aliens officers at the ports, assisted by Special Branch agents, would be on the look-out for suspicious characters and false passports, although passports were required for travel to Britain only after 1905. The passenger lists of liners would be meticulously checked. Detective Cheney, alias Brust, speaks of a well-worn "black book" (presumably an updated version of the Anarchists' Register of 1890) at Scotland House, home of the Special Branch and adjacent to Scotland Yard, constantly being consulted and updated, with the names of anarchists, political fanatics, and troublemakers provided by all the police of Europe.[125]

Sir Howard Vincent's semi-official – since no less a person than the chief commissioner of the Metropolitan Police wrote the introduction for several of its editions – *Police Code* devoted several pages under the entry "Anarchism" to a detailed description of how the police should protect heads of state and persons "in authority." These guidelines were tremendously influential since the *Police Code*, both in Britain and throughout the British Empire, possessed a "popularity... [that] seems to be inexhaustible."[126] Vincent, who had founded the CID and been instrumental in the creation of the Special Branch, demanded exceptional rigor of even ordinary constables:

In view of the great facilities given by modern weapons and explosives to the commission of outrages at public processions, etc., the greatest possible vigilance is called for on these occasions. No precautions should ever be neglected, no warning ever be unheeded. It is not the life alone of the Head of a State, or person in authority, which may be endangered. It is that of innocent spectators. In

---

[123] "This had become the general practice by 1883." Porter, *Vigilant State*, 26 and 203n.
[124] Herbert Fitch, *Memoirs of a Royal Detective* (London: Hurst and Blackett, 1936): 22.
[125] Brust, *"I Guarded Kings,"* 184.
[126] *The Dictionary of National Biography*, "Vincent, Sir Charles Edward," by Sir Charles Mathew, describes *The Police Code* as "a standard text book."

addition to securing the control of crowds upon special occasions, the free passage of a procession, the prevention of a rush from adjoining streets, steps should be taken that sufficient police in plain clothes either walk parallel to the carriage conveying the illustrious personages who may be the object of attack, on both sides of the roadway, or are posted thickly along the route.[127]

Queen Victoria had always been followed by seven armed men.[128] By the time Edward VII came to the throne in 1901, the security guard that travelled with the monarch had increased to nine and was headed by a chief inspector. Buckingham Palace, where Victoria had only stayed for short visits, now became the primary residence of the king and was permanently staffed with twenty-eight police. Altogether, sixty-two inspectors, sergeants, and constables were on permanent guard duty either with the monarch or at his four residences (Buckingham Palace, Windsor Castle, Osborne House, and Sandringham).[129]

More important than these numbers, the British police were aided in successfully guarding royalty by the decidedly British knack for doing it without the beneficiaries being made aware. The Special Branch detectives were "trained to be quiet and unostentatious;" to "never intrude," so "that the royal person often does not notice his guardian from one day to another, while still resting assured that he is near, even though invisible."[130] This unobtrusiveness was important if one recalls how much royalty and heads of state in general objected to clumsy police surveillance and therefore often worked to circumvent it.

Empress Elisabeth hated being shadowed by detectives and did everything possible to give them the slip. During a visit to France in 1895, she gave a particularly cold reception to French detective Xavier Paoli, whose duty it was to protect visiting royalty and who was one of those special railway police commissioners that played such an important part during the 1890s in monitoring the activities of France's anarchists. A major-general who was a member of the Empress's entourage explained to the slighted Paoli the reason for his unpleasant reception:

When we go abroad, they [the authorities] generally send us officials who, under the pretense of protecting us, terrorize us. They appear to us like Banquo's ghost,

---

[127] *Police Code*, 15th editon, 10.

[128] Herbert Fitch, *Traitors Within: The Adventures of Detective Inspector Herbert T. Fitch* (London: Hurst and Blackett, 1933): 19.

[129] In 1902, the number of police was increased at Buckingham Palace by as much as eight police and decreased by four at Windsor Castle. Bradford, New Scotland Yard, to Home Office, March 23, 1892; Home Office reply, April 6, 1902; Memorandum, New Scotland Yard, to undersecretary of state, Home Office, March 25, 1902, HO 144/928/A53778, PRO.

[130] Fitch, *Memoirs*, 186–187.

with long faces and rolling eyes; they see assassins on every side; they poison and embitter our holidays. That is why you struck us at first as suspicious.[131]

Given this experience, it is hardly surprising that the Empress refused repeated offers of protection from the Swiss police prior to her fatal trip to Geneva in September 1898.[132]

On this subject, King Umberto shared many of Elisabeth's attitudes and, for example, almost invariably delighted in guessing which route his guards would patrol so that he might drive his carriage along a different road. Moreover, he doubted that any preventive measures could be completely effective.[133] When, after his death, stories spread that Umberto had invited his own assassination by refusing more police protection, Senator Astengo, who in 1897 had carried out an inquest into the king's personal security, denounced this view. He told the Italian parliament: "he [Umberto] wanted [surveillance around his person], but not in a rough [plateale] and ridiculous fashion, as was being done."[134] It has also been implied that the Empress Elisabeth cooperated in her own demise and that she refused to be guarded because she welcomed death as an end to her mental suffering.[135] While the empress was highly neurasthenic and had a fatalistic streak, she did not object to being guarded when it was done cleverly and out of sight. This was what occurred when she traveled in France and came under the protection of Police Detective Paoli and his agents. Paoli earned her and her entourage's trust, and ingratiated himself by serving not only as guardian, but also as tour guide and purveyor of desired newspapers and reviews. So sensitive was he to the empress's every need that, rather than fleeing from him, she came to request his presence on all her trips through France.[136]

Like the exceptionally tactful Paoli, the Special Branch quickly made both the British royal family and visiting foreign monarchs happy to

---

[131] René Lara, "Preface," in Xavier Paoli, *Leurs Majestés*, 13th edition (Paris: Librairie Paul Ollendorff, 1910): ii; Xavier Paoli, *My Royal Clients*, trans. Alexander Teixeira de Mattos (London: Hodder and Stoughton, 1911): 5–6.

[132] Brigitte Hamann, *Elisabeth, Kaiserin Wider Willen* (Vienna: Amalthea, 1982): 598; Liang, *Modern Police*, 159.

[133] Pesci, *Il re martire*, 372–373.

[134] Astengo, *Atti parlamentari*, XXI legislatura, 1st session, Senato, Discussions, November 27, 1900, 242. Grimaldi (*Il re "buono,"* 446) writes that because of Umberto's "fatalism with which he now accepts the risks of his own condition" he did not take special care for his safety on the day of his assassination. Denis Mack Smith, *Italy and its Monarchy* (New Haven and London: Yale University Press, 1989): 139, repeats Grimaldi's misinformation that Umberto had only a single policeman to guard him on July 29, 1900.

[135] Hamann, *Reluctant Empress*, 367.

[136] Paoli, *My Royal Clients*, Chapter 1, especially, 5, 9, 14–16, 28, 30, 33; French President Félix Faure told René Lara, "Preface," viii, that the Empress Elisabeth "unstintingly praises" Paoli's "refinement and tact" ("la distinction et le tact").

concert with it rather than maneuver at cross purposes. The memoirs of the Special Branch detectives make clear that an easy rapport existed between King Edward and his guardians, and that diffident visiting monarchs, such as Tsar Nicholas II of Russia, soon came to appreciate and collaborate in its efforts.[137]

Another reason for the Special Branch's success was that "ordinary detective officers," not to mention the general British citizenry, readily cooperated with it. In the opinion of Detective Fitch, this cooperation stood in distinct contrast with the rivalry that existed between the detectives and the regular police forces in tsarist Russia and in other countries.[138] Detective Piano's fate and the rivalries within and between the Italian police forces, civilian and military, provide further examples in support of Fitch's contention. Another British detective also cited the better pay and education, as well as stricter attention to duty, of the British protective service as reasons for its superiority.[139] While these claims seem likely or at least plausible, British comments about "excitable" and easily distracted detectives from the Latin races being poor guardians seem to be pure Anglo prejudice, especially when measured against the success of the Frenchman Paoli, whom even Detective Fitch admired.[140]

Little is known about how the Italians applied what knowledge they could obtain of British, or of Austrian and German practice, or how exactly the Security Commissariat for the Royal House carried out its work. But due to both luck and design, after 1900, despite several close calls, no other Italian head of state or government was assassinated while in office. By 1908, the Italian police had acquired such a reputation for excellence that the Portuguese government requested their help in securing the safety of the Portuguese king after the assassination of his father and brother in February. According to the report of two Italian police commandants, they devised a detailed plan for crowd management during the funeral service for King Carlos I that was adopted by the government and revolutionized such procedures in Portugal. Among other things, the Italians had the police turn their backs on the funeral procession so as to exercise continual surveillance of the crowds during the passage of the royal cortege, a practice that the Portuguese had never seen before.[141] This was a technique that a British Special Branch

---

[137] For examples, see Fitch, *Memoirs*, 25–27, regarding the tsar, and Fitch, *Traitors*, 260–261, and Brust, *"I Guarded Kings,"* 33, for the easy rapport between the Special Branch and King Edward.

[138] Fitch, *Memoirs*, 188–189.   [139] MacNaghten, *Days of My Years*, 225.

[140] "Excitability is a national trait of the French...effect even upon supposedly case-hardened French detectives." Brust, *"I Guarded Kings,"* 181; Fitch, *Memoirs*, 192–193.

[141] Commissario di p.s. Riccardo Secchi to F. Leonardi, DGPS, Rome, May 19, 1908. DGPS-ufficio riservato, B. 2 (1909), ACS.

detective claimed was crucial to his own country's safeguarding success (and contrasted with the practice of certain continental countries):

I will just say that there have been many occasions when I and my colleagues, on line-of-route duty at a royal function, *never caught a single glimpse of our royal charge, though the carriages rolled along within a few feet distance of us.* We were far too busy in other directions. An old proverb says, "A cat may look at a king"; but a guarding detective's job is to look *not* at a king but at the crowds near that king.[142]

Around this time, Russia also revolutionized its protective service for the tsar, although the pre-eminent danger of assassination came not from the anarchists, but from the Socialist Revolutionaries. When Alexander II was assassinated in 1881, his bodyguard did not lack for resources or numbers, as was the Italian case in 1900, but professional skill and energetic leadership, which Italy also lacked.[143] The four separate guard units designated for the tsar's protection were largely ornamental.[144] In February 1906, in the wake of the outbreak of widespread terrorism during and after the Revolution of 1905, General Trepov, the imperial palace commandant, created a new service for protecting the tsar, a "*corps special d'agents de garde*" or court security force.[145] In the words of Alexander Spiridovitch, the court security force's first commander, the tsar's bodyguard had previously been organized in a "naïve and infantile fashion." It was now to be "firm and rational."[146] Spiridovitch had 275 men at his command; by western European or American standards, this was a gigantic force.[147] Spiridovitch carefully screened applicants for the new corps and instituted a rigorous training and discipline. He created a "museum of terrorism" with photographs, models of bombs, and plans to instruct guards about the most important past political murders and *attentats* and what the police had done wrong and why. He also carried out a systematic registration of the inhabitants at all the imperial residences and insured the careful identification of all new imperial personnel. Those who balked at the strenuous new training were "pitilessly dismissed."[148]

---

[142] Fitch, *Memoirs*, 187.
[143] According to Daly, before Alexander II's assassination "[Interior Minister] Loris-Melikov seemed more concerned with the success of his reforms than with the safety of the emperor." Obvious preventative measures, such as rounding up known members of the People's Will, were neglected. *Autocracy under Siege*, 31.
[144] Daly, *Watchful State*, 18.
[145] Alexander Spiridovitch, *Les deniers années de la cour de Tsarskoïe-Selo*, trans. M. Jeanson. 2 vols (Paris: Payot, 1928): 1:25; Daly, *Watchful State*, 19.
[146] Spiridovitch, *Les deniers années*, 1:26.
[147] Daly, *Watchful State*, 19. Spiridovitch, *Les deniers années*, 25, gives an initial figure of 160 men.
[148] Spiridovitch, *Les deniers années*, 1:135–136. Daly, *Watchful State*, 58.

The itineraries of imperial trips were placed under rigorous surveillance. Bodyguards worked regularly with Russian surveillance police both inside the empire and abroad so as to become familiar with the faces of potential assassins. It is unclear whether Trepov or Spiridovitch patterned their new court security police on European models, although much of what they did reminds one of British practices and continental efforts aimed at more scientific policing. The British were very impressed by Spiridovitch's explanations of his systematic efforts to protect King Edward VII during the latter's visit to Russia in 1908.[149]

The anarchists noticed all the increased security for European monarchs and found in it found some ironic pleasure. "Strange compensation of Fate, that Royalty to-day as it basks on the Riviera [in this case, referring to the German Empress Victoria surrounded by detectives] is forced to share the pangs of the humblest philosophic anarchist 'shadowed' in London!"[150] Once again anarchists and the authorities seemed to be mirroring one another's actions.

Italian policing abroad

Besides working to create a more professional, effective, and "scientific" protective service for the monarch, in August 1900 Italy also began the creation of a far-flung network of police agents to monitor the activities of Italian anarchists residing abroad. As we shall see, this network would expand over the next twelve years as Italian policemen were posted to some eleven cities and towns in the Americas and Europe outside Italy. The impulse for this development grew out of a feeling that one of the major reasons for the assassination was a lack of effective intelligence, especially outside Italy. It also grew out of frustration with the authorities and police in the United States.

The newspapers pointed out that Bresci's name had appeared "on none of the lists of dangerous anarchists" kept by the Italian police; nor had Bresci's name been registered on lists of noted and dangerous anarchists kept by the authorities (presumably a reference to the Secret Service) in the United States.[151] In September 1900 Giovanni Branchi, the Italian consul general in New York and on whose shoulders Rome

---

[149] Spiridovitch, *Les deniers années*, 1:259.
[150] "International Notes," *Freedom* (London), March 1899.
[151] "Negli archivi penali," *La Tribuna* (Rome), July 31, 1900, 3; copy, Consul General G. Branchi, New York, to foreign ministry, Rome, August 31, 1900. I fondi archivistici ... delle rappresentanze diplomatiche italiane negli USA (1848–1901) (hereafter cited as Rap.dip.USA 1848–1901), b. 108, IFM. The Pelloux archive, f. 29, ACS, contains a list, apparently compiled by the DGPS, entitled *"Anarchici italiani all'estero,"* June 4, 1899. There are 408 names and locations given, but no reference to Bresci.

placed the burden for investigating the roots of the alleged conspiracy in Paterson, complained to the ambassador that "the two police [forces of New York and New Jersey] do absolutely nothing for us. The governor of N.Y. [Theodore Roosevelt] has said or communicated nothing."[152] (Governor Voorhees of New Jersey eventually proved more helpful.) Branchi therefore asked the ambassador whether the "Federal Police," i.e., the Secret Service, which at the time was the only national policing organization in America, could be requested to intervene. Ambassador Fava, however, believed that the Secret Service was "incapable of rendering true services because it is employed almost exclusively in the search for counterfeiters and customs defrauders" and recommended that the consul hire private detectives, as even the federal government did on occasion.[153] This Branchi did, but soon asked that the Pinkerton agents be dismissed because their services were excessively expensive and their reports "worthless" (*valgono nulla*).[154] A Newark, New Jersey, lawyer named James M. Trimble also investigated the Paterson and West Hoboken anarchists for the Italian government.[155]

Branchi's temporary resort to the Pinkertons for anarchist surveillance highlights a peculiarity of American law enforcement. Because of its decentralized and ill-coordinated policing system an enormous private detective industry had sprung up. Often police powers were delegated to private detectives who were armed and sometimes deputized temporarily as regular police. On several occasions armed Pinkerton guards engaged in bloody battles with strikers, as at Homestead in 1892. Other Western nations employed private detectives but never on the scale of the United States; moreover, these countries maintained a monopoly of the use of organized force. American detectives frequently had terrible reputations. Often recruited from criminals and ex-convicts, they were decried by a Secret Service agent as "the scum of the earth," or in the words of the reforming detective William Burns, as "one of the most diabolical evils with which we have to contend." While the progressive Burns was influenced by British policing, the Pinkertons had been modeled after the detectives of France's Second Empire, with their penchant for secrecy,

[152] Fava, Washington, DC, to Visconti Venosta, Rome, August 8, 1900, Affari politici, ser. P, b. 49, IFM; Branchi to Baron [Fava], September 10, 1900, Rap.dip.USA 1848–1901, b. 108, IFM.

[153] Fava, Washington, DC, to Visconti Venosta, Rome, July 31, 1900. IFM, Affari politici, ser. "P," b. 49.

[154] Ibid. and Branchi, New York, to Italian foreign ministry, August 6, 1900, and, copy. Branchi, private, to Italian interior ministry, August 28, 1900. IFM, Affari politici, Serie P, politica, b. 49.

[155] David O. Watkins, US District Attorney, Woodbury, New Jersey, to Attorney General Griggs, Washington, DC, February 7, 1901. NA, RG 60, 11717/1900.

lack of regard for civil liberties, and widespread use of informants and *agents provocateurs*.[156]

The local American police proved equally valueless or worse. The police chief of Paterson claimed there were no anarchists in his town and slammed the door in the face of a reporter who had asked too many probing questions. The New York City police proved more accommodating, but detective Captain George W. McClusky's report on the anarchists was full of sensationalistic information "most of which," according to the Secret Service, was "absolutely without foundation."[157] This sensationalistic information included the claim that from London Malatesta had cabled the anarchists in Paterson telling them to carry out the assassination. No such cable has ever been found.

Forced to rely on his own devices, Branchi hired at moderate cost two or three agents from among "a quantity" of local people who, immediately after Umberto's assassination, "wanted to be employed as secret agents." Unfortunately, Branchi thought that their connection to the consulate would soon be discovered and this would render them useless; at least one became so fearful of anarchist reprisals that he had to be dismissed.[158] The anarchist agent whom Branchi had used in past years was also unable to "penetrate very deeply into the counsels of the anarchists" because his dealings with the consulate had become known.[159] Branchi wrote the Italian foreign ministry:

Therefore if one wants to have a serious police service it would be necessary to have here intelligent agents and change them every so often. That would not be possible without sending personnel from Italy. For our purposes, it is not necessary that the selected agents know English. They will have nothing to do with anyone but the Italian element.

But this is not sufficient. This Consulate can direct the service, but it can not maintain it by itself. It is hardly a month that serious and varied research has been undertaken, and we already have such a confused jumble [*farragine*] of names and papers, that finding anything is absolutely impossible without alphabetical indexes, filing cabinets or other things of which this Consulate has neither

---

[156] Ward Churchill, "From the Pinkertons to the PATRIOT Act: The Trajectory of Political Policing in the United States, 1870 to the Present." *CR: The New Centennial Review* 4:1 (2004): 1–72, especially 5–6, 43–44; Robert Hunter, *Violence and the Labor Movement* (New York: Macmillan, 1914): 280–285.

[157] "Searching Among Paterson Anarchists," *New York Times*, August 1, 1900; Copy, McClusky Report, Detective Bureau, New York City, August 1900, appended to letter, Ambassador Fava, Washington, DC, to Acting Secretary Adee, September 19, 1900; John Wilkie to Secretary of the Treasury, November 2, 1900, RG 60, 11717/1900, NA.

[158] Ambassador Mayor, Washington, Foreign Minister Prinetti, Rome, February 17, 1902, PI, b. 35, IFM.

[159] Copy, Branchi, New York City, private, to Italian interior ministry, August 28, 1900, Affari politici, Serie P, politica, b. 49, IFM.

experience nor is able to institute by itself. Therefore, if the Interior Ministry wants to undertake serious investigations and continue them, it is indispensable that an employee experienced in this profession should be sent here immediately to assume the reins of this service. He should know at least a little English. It would be for the best, however, if his ties to the Consulate remained unknown.[160]

In earlier reports to Rome, the Italian ambassador had made the same point: one could not count on the American police and "an efficacious surveillance of the anarchists in the United States" could not be successfully done without "good special, confidential agents of the interested governments."[161]

American efforts to track down the alleged anarchist conspiracy

Because of its decentralized political system, concern to protect civil liberties, and lack of a national police force other than the overworked Secret Service, America's response to anarchist terrorism always disappointed Europe, which wanted more information and faster assistance than the Americans were ever capable of. For example, as the Italian consul general soon discovered, the state of New Jersey had no law against conspiracy so that even if it was proved that Bresci had had accomplices, the police could do nothing against them until the law was changed.[162] Hearing of letters sent from London allegedly with information about an assassination plot against Victor Emmanuel III, the Italian ambassador asked confidentially if these could be sequestered and copied. The postmaster general said the letters could be retained but not opened without a court warrant.[163]

Nonetheless, Washington tried as best it could to meet Rome's requests for help in tracking down the alleged anarchist conspirators against King Umberto. President McKinley and the cabinet indicated their desire to support Italian efforts "within the limits in which their action is circumscribed by the law."[164] Secretary of State Hay authorized direct contacts between Consul General Branchi and the New York and New Jersey authorities, although normally these requests should have been

---

[160] Copy, Branchi, New York City, to [foreign] minister, [Rome], September 10, 1900, Rap. dip. USA 1848–1901, b. 108, IFM.

[161] Fava, Washington, DC, to Visconti Venosta, Rome, August 6, 1900, Affari politici, ser. P, b. 49, IFM. In the margin, the foreign minister specially marked this passage.

[162] Branchi, New York, to foreign ministry, Rome, August 9, 1900, Ser. P, politica, b. 49, IFM.

[163] Fava, Washington, DC, to Visconti Venosta, Rome, February 12, 1901. Ser. P, politica, b. 49, IFM.

[164] Ibid., August 6, 1900. Ser. P, politica, b. 49, IFM.

channeled through the State Department.[165] In early September 1900 Attorney General Griggs informed the Italian ambassador that he had instructed the US attorneys for New York and New Jersey to look into any possible conspiracy, although they had found nothing as of yet.[166] On November 12, 1900, Griggs ordered every US district attorney within whose jurisdiction there resided correspondents of Pedro Esteve (i.e., the subscribers to *La Questione Sociale*) to be investigated.[167] Griggs had somehow acquired a list of more than 500 correspondents, presumably through the Post Office inspector.[168] For want of anything better, the Post Office inspectors now became America's frontline troops in the war on anarchist terrorism, since the various federal attorneys asked them to check up on the activities of these correspondents. Invited to investigate correspondents in New Jersey, one postal inspector complained that this would require far too much work and requested the assistance of a Secret Service agent. He was told none was available.[169]

Other inspectors produced long and interesting reports. Post Office Inspector Frank O'Brien traveled to Yohoghany (Shaner), a small mining town that once existed southeast of Pittsburg, in order to find out about "Joseph Crancibelli" or "Crancabilli" (his name was actually Giuseppe Ciancabilla).[170] According to the report, Ciancabilla, who had arrived in June 1900, began publishing the Italian language *L'Aurora (The Dawn)*, which was sent to every state in the union, and lecturing to Italians on Sundays in an abandoned mine shaft. About twenty-five anarchists lived in Yohoghany that summer. The assistant postmaster of the town told O'Brien that "Crancabilli" "sent out numerous photographs of Bresci." When postmaster Wilson, who also happened to be Ciancabilla's landlord, visited his room, the anarchist "manifested great pride in Bresci's picture and gloried in the act which the latter had committed. The lady who was living with him – presumably his wife[?] – would frequently kiss the picture." In conversation, Ciancabilla often referred to Bresci as a "personal friend." In November, the charismatic anarchist went on to Spring Valley, Illinois. O'Brien's conclusion was: "That the tenets of

---

[165] Ibid., August 22, 1900. IFM, Ser. P, politica, b. 49, IFM.

[166] Copy, Griggs to Italian ambassador, Washington, DC, September 8, 1900, Ser. P, politica, b. 49, IFM. Petacco and Ferraris misspell Griggs as "Briggs."

[167] Blaisdell, "Humbert I," 244; Frank A. O'Brien, Office of Post Office Inspector, Savannah, Georgia, to Daniel Heiner, US District Attorney, Pittsburg [sic], January 17, 1901, RG 60, NA.

[168] Blaisdell's ("Humbert I," 244) figure of 350 is a considerable underestimate.

[169] W. B. Snow, Post office Inspector, Boston, to David Watkins, US Attorney, district of New Jersey, May 18, 1901; Secret Service/Treasury Department to Attorney General, Washington, DC, February 1, 1901, Department of Justice, RG 60, NA.

[170] Until World War I, "Pittsburg" was the correct spelling; later an "h" was added in order to "deGermanize" the city.

anarchism are being propagated in this country I have no doubt, and I am sure the principles advocated by these organizations and papers are against Law, Order and Government." Yet, because these foreign anarchists did "not mingle with the American people," the "ordinary citizen does not give them a thought and they might be hatching all kinds of conspiracies unobserved by any one interested in the welfare of this country."[171] Despite O'Brien's alarming conclusions, in March 1901 the attorney general informed the secretary of state of his conviction, based on the US attorneys' reports, that the subscribers to *La Questione Sociale*, "while they may have indulged occasionally in foolish or violent talk... in no legal sense were co-conspirators."[172]

Italian secret police to New York and Buenos Aires, 1900

Since Italy could not rely on the Americans to provide speedy information about ex-patriot Italians who might become assassins, the government in Rome heeded the advice and repeated requests of Ambassador Fava and Consul General Branchi, and set out to create a professional secret police service in the United States. According to the newspapers, during August 1900 a lively debate had occurred inside the short-lived and little-studied Saracco government (June 1900–February 1901) about the shape of the proposed policing apparatus.[173] Decisive steps were soon taken to expand international policing. In early October 1900 the interior ministry sent Umberto Molossi, a superintendent of police (*delegato di pubblica sicurezza*), from Rome to New York City, where he would remain until 1917, hiring informers and monitoring the activities of Italian subversives throughout the United States.[174] Although his mission was supposed to be secret, the government was embarrassed to see that *La Stampa*, a Turinese newspaper, had published a notice of his departure for America.[175] Another policeman named Aristide Pallini was sent for some months to Paterson, New Jersey, to report on its large resident colony of Italian anarchists.

Rome also assigned a policeman to Buenos Aires, with the initiative again coming from a resident Italian diplomat. The Italian minister to

[171] O'Brien, Savannah, GA, to District Attorney Heiner, Pittsburg, January 1, 1901, Department of Justice, RG 60, NA.

[172] Blaisdell, "Humbert I," 245.   [173] *Berliner Lokal Anzeiger*, August 16, 1900.

[174] Leonardi, DGPS, Rome, to Minister of Foreign Affairs, October 10, 1900, *Affari politici*, ser. P, b. 49, IFM; Molossi's personnel files are in interior ministry, DGPS, versamento 1949, b. 437 and 437bis, ACS.

[175] Ms. Fusinato, foreign ministry, Rome, to interior ministry (PS), October 31, 1900, *Affari politici*, ser. P, b. 49, IFM.

Argentina had noted with alarm the glorification of the murder of King Umberto by a large number of local anarchists, the continual arrival of new Italian emigrants, including many anarchists, and the inadequacy of both Argentine laws and police, and of the Italian Legation to control and monitor all these possibly subversive Italians. According to the Austrian ambassador in Rome, in 1901 the Italian government believed that more than 7,000 anarchists resided in Buenos Aires (population 820,000), and that a thread of anarchist activity ran from that city to Paterson, New Jersey, from there to London, and then on to Switzerland.[176] Given this menace, and on the Legation's recommendation, in October 1900 Rome sent Francesco Parrella, an Italian police officer, to watch over Buenos Aires's large Italian community.[177] An Italian police commissioner would remain in Argentina until at least World War I.

In a report unknown to the Italians, but which arrived at many of the same conclusions, Francisco Beazley, the head of Argentine police of Buenos Aires, warned about the anarchist danger and the need for more police detectives. Beazley wrote the Argentine interior minister that of the approximately 5,000 anarchists in Argentina, which was likely a considerable underestimate, only 1,200 were known to the police. To watch over and investigate all of the anarchists in the capital, where most of the anarchists resided, the police had only four men, who made up the "*brigada de policía secreta*" of the "*Comisaría de Investigacions.*" Beazley asked for an increase in personnel, which was urgently needed given the approaching visit of the president of Brazil and the danger of an *attentat.* On October 18, 1900, the government granted Beazley's request, but it is unclear how many police were added.[178]

In that same crucial month of October 1900, the Italian foreign minister also sent a circular to all Italian diplomats requesting that, in order to assure "quickness and speed" and "unity of direction," they send information on international police work directly to the interior minister, bypassing the foreign ministry. The provincial prefects were also ordered to work through the interior ministry, rather than, for example, making requests directly to diplomats abroad for the arrests of suspected criminals.[179] This

[176] Pasetti, Rome, to Goluchowski, Vienna, secret, April 25, 1901, IB 1901, GZ. 36, HHStA.

[177] Copy of Minister Obizzo Marquis Malaspina, Buenos Aires, to Prime Minister Saracco, Rome, *riservato*, August 22, 1900; Leonardi, DGPS, interior ministry, *reservato*, to Minister of Foreign Affairs, October 19, 1900, Rome, PI, b. 28, IFM.

[178] Francesco Beazley to Felipe Yofre, interior minister, Buenos Aires, September 1, 1900, Ministero del Interior, file 16, n. 3080; decree signed by president and government ministers, Buenos Aires, October 18, 1900. Archivo General de la Nacion (Buenos Aires).

[179] Circular, Rome, October [23,] 1900, to all royal diplomatic and consular agents. In cases of great urgency, the prefects could still make direct contacts. On July 23, 1906,

directive, however, had to be modified in certain cases. The Italian consul general in Geneva, whose office had been monitoring subversives without interruption since 1875, feared that a known anarchist sympathizer in the local Post Office might soon grow suspicious of – and presumably might open – envelopes if he saw them being regularly sent off to the interior ministry.[180] The consul general was therefore given permission to put a second envelope addressed to the interior ministry inside the usual envelope sent to the Foreign Office.

Italian anti-anarchist legislation?

While the Saracco's ministry's creation of a police network overseas to gather intelligence on the anarchists and of a new security guard for the king had lasting influence in Italy and significance for the rest of Europe and the world, its proposals for new anti-anarchist legislation failed. Avoiding the sensitive issue of reintroducing the death penalty, as conservatives had requested immediately after the assassination, on February 2, 1901, Saracco presented a bill to parliament punishing groups that sought the violent overthrow of society, and persons who, either in public or privately, supported violent anarchist crimes or incited others to commit such acts. People guilty of these offences could be deported or placed under strict police surveillance. The law also prohibited the publication of biographies and portraits of anarchist defendants and of the minutes of their trials. Besides these measures, all of which had been suggested at the Rome conference, Saracco's law called for making anarchists liable to prosecution even if they had committed crimes outside Italy and for prohibiting public subscriptions on behalf of anarchist defendants.[181] Three days after the bill's introduction, however, the government was forced to resign and the new, more liberal Zanardelli-Giolitti administration dropped the legislation. The demise of the newly proposed anti-anarchist law proved characteristic, since most of the anti-anarchist legislation of the early twentieth century, whether proposed or enacted, failed or proved to be largely ineffectual. During the next decade, anarchist terrorism would diminish for a variety of reasons, including better intelligence and policing, but not due to frontal assaults on the civil rights of anarchists and other citizens.

the government reiterated the necessity to send all communications "directly" to the interior ministry (DGPS), which suggests that this regulation was not always being obeyed. Affari politici P, b. 47, IFM.

[180] Bassa, Geneva, to foreign minister, Rome, November 6, 1900, Affari politici P, b. 47, IFM.

[181] Italy, *atti parlamentari*, Senato, *legislatura* XXI: 1ª *sessione, documenti*, n. 93.

The attempt on the Persian shah; Turkey and Spain appeal for more anti-anarchist cooperation, August 1900

The assassination of Umberto spurred on the European powers not only to renovate their protective services for heads of state and improve anarchist intelligence-gathering by posting police and secret agents abroad, but it also sparked renewed interest in stronger international anti-anarchist cooperation. While the Rome conference had promoted international police cooperation and other measures, it had obviously failed to prevent many new assassination attempts.

On August 2, almost immediately after the murder of Umberto, a French anarchist named François Salson made an attempt on the life of Muzaffar al-Din, the shah of Persia, while he was visiting Paris. The Italian *Corriere della Sera*, the French police official Paoli, and the London *Times* (not to mention the sensationalist *New York Herald*) linked the new attentat to Bresci's lethal deed.[182] *The Times* opined that "the proverbial force of example on deranged or criminal minds has been once more demonstrated," and Paoli declared that "the recent assassination of King Humbert [Umberto] had suggested [to Salson] this fantastic plan of making away with the unoffending Muzaffr-ed-Din [sic]."[183] Salson refused to disclose his motives (he seemed to have had nothing personally or politically against the shah, other than his status as a monarch) or whether he had been put up to the deed by others. He did say that, if he had succeeded, he would have gone on to attempt the life of the tsar.[184] His Parisian landlady disclosed that the few times she had entered his room it had "always" been "full of newspapers," which might lend credence to the view that Salson's was a copycat crime.[185] After the police arrested and searched him they found in his pocket a page from a newspaper outlining the shah's itinerary; they also discovered that his rented room was filled with anarchist journals.[186]

In another twist to the story, in late August, the French press reported that Salson was a police agent whose assassination attempt had been manipulated by Puibaraud and the Parisian political police. "As a matter

---

[182] "Il regicidio e la scienza," *Corriere della Sera*, August 7–8, 1900, 2, claims that Salson's deed was "without doubt inspired by the atrocious crime of Monza"; *New York Herald*, August, 1900.

[183] *The Times*, August 3, 1900, 3; Paoli, *My Royal Clients*, 86.

[184] *The Times*, August 4, 1900; *Corriere della Sera*, August 4–5, 1900.

[185] *Corriere della Sera*, August 4–5, 1900.

[186] *Corriere della Sera*, August 3–4 and 4–5, 1900.

of fact, the hammer [of Salson's revolver] had been filed just enough to prevent its striking the cartridge at all." According to the *Petite République*, Salson "was suspected [of being a spy] by the Anarchists with whom he has been fraternizing; and that they, to test his loyalty, selected him to make the attempt on the Shah's life." A police officer then fixed the revolver and instructed him to carry out the sham *attentat*. Although the regular, non-political police of Paris attested to the veracity of this account, their reliability may have been skewed by animosities toward Puibaraud's political police fueled by the Dreyfus case.[187] Puibaraud's reputation for using *agents provocateurs*, however, makes the former's claim at least plausible.

The *New York Herald*'s sensationalistic announcement on August 3, supposedly based on information from Italian secret agents and others, of a "Worldwide Anarchistic Plot to Murder Monarchs," a plot hatched in the Jersey mill towns and perfected in Paris, reflected continuing and widespread fears, even if the existence of such a plot was never verified and seems unlikely.[188] For example, the British minister reported in a confidential dispatch that, based on statements from a royal aide-de-camp and the Italian minister, the king of Romania had absented himself from a requiem mass for the late king of Italy because of "the alarm felt lest an attack should be made on his Majesty by Anarchists in Bucharest."

It appears that numerous arrests of Italians and Bulgarians have recently been made in Bucharest, and that proofs have been obtained from correspondence seized, mainly at the house of an Italian, that the international anarchist conspiracy against Crowned Heads and persons of high position extends to Roumania.

The King has also lately received many threatening letters, as my Italian colleague told me, from Bucharest.[189]

The Home Office took this report seriously enough to pass it on to Robert Anderson, the head of Scotland Yard's Criminal Investigation Department.

In Constantinople, the Ottoman sultan was concerned that in July a so-called "Committee" had chosen four anarchists to assassinate, first the king of Italy, and then him. Special precautions were taken at the weekly

---

[187] Both *The Times* (London), August 6, 1900, 4, and the *New York Times*, August 20, 1900, 20, cited reports in the French press. The *New York Times* garbles Puibaraud's name and confuses a few other details, such as the fact that Puibaraud's police brigades were attached to the Paris prefecture and not to the *Sûreté*'s detectives, which were under the interior ministry.

[188] *New York Herald*, August 3, 1900, 3.

[189] Copy, marked "secret," of J. G. Kennedy, Bucharest, to Salisbury, London, August 29, 1900, HO144/545/A55176/34, PRO.

Selamlik, a ceremony held in the palace's public apartments prior to the sultan's departure for his Friday prayers at the mosque and "almost the only occasion on which the Sultan leaves his Palace," to exclude strangers. In the future any foreigner desiring to attend the Selamlik ceremony would be required to obtain a special admission card signed by the diplomatic representative of the country to which he belonged. The Turkish foreign minister: "dwelt on the danger to which all the Sovereigns of Europe were exposed at the hands of the Anarchists and on the advisability of holding a European Conference to consider what measures should be taken by the several Governments against them."[190]

Spain shared Turkey's desires for increased international cooperation against the anarchists. On August 15, 1900 Foreign Minister Ventura García Sancho, Marquis de Aguilar de Campoó, a member of conservative Prime Minister Francisco Silvela's cabinet, composed a confidential circular to all Spanish diplomatic representatives residing in Europe, including the Vatican, and in Washington, DC.[191] He noted how the "execrable crime committed in Monza," as well as the assassination attempts against the prince of Wales and the shah, had "renewed the anxieties" of the public and, "especially" of the "governments of civilized peoples," after the "limited results" of the Rome conference had temporarily numbed (*adormeciendo*) them. The responsibility for these evil deeds, according to García Sancho, rested with anti-religious anarchists opposed to the principle of authority, either acting in conspiracies or alone:

It is an opinion very widely held that all the crimes with which I am concerned are the work of sinister conspiracies... yet it enters the realm of possibility that in the future it may happen, and naturally it has happened in the past, that the assassin may be alone and that only the lack of religious feeling, an excess of sufferings, exaltation produced by books or perverse speeches poorly digested, the desire for notoriety and heroic monomania impel the criminal's hand.

Without specifically mentioning Italy, the Spanish foreign minister pointed out that criminals (i.e., assassins) who had recently acquired a sad fame had belonged to "a certain nationality," which had been disturbed by continual discussions about the "vices of theocracy and the vices of the [pope's] temporal power," discussions that undermined faith and authority to such an extent that now simple country people in their songs exalted and sanctified Caserio, the assassin of President Carnot.

Spain would benevolently examine any proposal for a new anti-anarchist congress, but believed that "prompt and efficacious police

---

[190] Copy, Ambassador N. R. O'Conor, Therapia, to Salisbury, London, August 8, 1900. HO 144/608/B32482/8, PRO.
[191] Circular number 13, OP, L. 2751, expediente 35, SFM.

measures" were needed immediately. The foreign minister called for "the continual exchange of information regarding the meetings, purposes and accords of the anarchist and related associations" between the police of Spain and other countries on a bilateral basis. Spain wanted to rapidly establish close relationships between its police and the police of foreign countries so that they might provide mutual assistance "without losing their autonomy, or altering their laws and customs." As a basis for these negotiations, the Marquess of Aguilar y Campoó sent out copies of the conclusions reached at the Rome conference in 1898.

Spain wanted in particular to improve cooperation with Britain since the latter had not officially adhered to the Rome conference's proposals. Furthermore, in July 1897 and again in April 1900 disputes over the unannounced expulsion of Spanish anarchists to Britain had strained relations between the two countries. In both cases, the Spanish foreign ministry in Madrid, embarrassed by the unauthorized actions of officials in Catalonia, had promised to stop the mass expulsions, and after 1900 they finally ceased. Given this troubled history, the Spanish were pleased when on July 31, 1900, after King Umberto's assassination, Lord Salisbury stated in the House of Lords that society had been too lenient in its treatment of the anarchists. Using language that had now become standard in describing anarchist assassinations, Salisbury asserted that "the secret societies selected and the ruthless executioner [Bresci] struck at [Umberto] in obedience to their decree" even though the Italian king was no tyrant but rather a benefactor of his people. Salisbury believed that this and similar "awful crimes" were due to "that morbid thirst for notoriety which is the bane and curse of our modern civilization ... and which threatens the very existence of society if it cannot be arrested."[192]

This bold statement, highlighting the anarchist danger and implicitly blaming the media for causing it, encouraged the Spanish to think that London might be willing to change its policy and engage in more vigorous efforts against anarchism.[193] Indeed, the duke of Mandas, the Spanish ambassador in London, remarked that, "by its scope [*por su alcance*]" Salisbury's statement had caught "the attention of Europe."[194] When the former spoke with Salisbury after his return from the continent in September 1900, the British prime minister said it would give him great pleasure if Britain could provide information that might help

---

[192] *The Times* (London), August 1, 1900, 10.
[193] Circular number 13, and duke of Mandas, London, to foreign minister, Madrid, September 19, 1900, OP, L. 2751, expediente 35, SFM.
[194] Duke of Mandas, London, to foreign minister, Madrid, October 2, 1900, SFM, L. 2751, expediente 35, SFM.

avoid *attentats* in Spain and suggested that Mandas speak with the home minister.[195]

The Spanish foreign minister indicated in a handwritten phrase inserted between the lines of his dispatch to his ambassador in London that he wished to obtain from Britain the establishment of "a more perfect and effective meshing [*engrane*] between police agents and diplomatic and consular agents."[196] The Spanish marquis hoped it might be possible to institute "between the intermittent action of the police and the continual [efforts] of the diplomatic and consular agents an action more permanent and efficacious."[197] When in November Mandas met the new home secretary, C. F. Ritchie, the latter went a good way toward meeting the Spanish desires. Ritchie promised "to watch in a special manner" anarchist activities that concerned Spain, and to speak with William Melville, the head of the Special Branch, about whether it was better to communicate directly with the Spanish embassy or "for greater rapidity with the Spanish police proper."[198]

Recognizing that the English police had reached "the highest point" of development, a success due, in the opinion of the Spanish foreign minister, perhaps to "greater resources, perhaps because of better organization" than the Spanish police, after 1900 Spain increasingly turned to the British for help.[199] So low was the confidence of Madrid in its own security forces (one recalls how in 1898 the foreign minister had bemoaned Spain's "scant police resources") that it sought on every important occasion, as if clutching at a talisman, to obtain British officers to guard Spain's royal family. In 1902, when the sixteen-year-old king reached his maturity and was to be crowned, the Spanish authorities requested the assistance in Madrid of two British police agents familiar with the anarchists and who possibly spoke Spanish, French, or Italian; the Spanish also requested assistance from the Parisian police.[200] Curiously, and almost comically, adverse to seeing his force considered as a model for the rest of Europe, the chief of the Metropolitan Police wished to decline the Spanish proposal since "we have no police officers who would be of

---

[195] Ibid., September 19, 1900. L. 2751, expediente 35, SFM.
[196] Aguilar y Campoó's note is referred to in Mandas to foreign minister, October 2, 1900, l. 2751, expediente 35, SFM.
[197] Foreign minister, Madrid, to ambassador, London, October 9, 1900, l. 2751, expediente 35, SFM.
[198] Mandas to foreign minister, Madrid, November 16, 1900, in ibid.
[199] Aguilar de Campoó, Madrid, to ambassador, London, September 25 and October 9, 1900, in ibid.
[200] Almodovar, Madrid, to ambassadors, London and Paris, May 5, 1902, in ibid. Ambassador Leon y Castillo reported to the foreign minister that the French were sending two "of their best agents from the anarchist police squad," May 6, 1902.

the slightest use and I can only suggest that a reply should go saying so in courteous terms. It would scarcely do to admit that we have no Spanish speaking officer in the Force!" Spanish-speaking or not, such concerns were, presumably, overruled in the interests of diplomatic politeness, Chief Inspector Quinn and Sergeant McBrien were selected to travel to Madrid, There they were handsomely rewarded for their three days of work, receiving money for expenses as well as a £40 gratuity.[201]

While British police and diplomatic cooperation with Spain, at least of a limited sort, improved after 1900, that between the United States and Spain remained glaringly deficient. Carrying out Madrid's instructions of August 15, 1900, finally in October, the duke of Arcos, the Spanish minister in Washington, DC, obtained a long interview with Secretary of State Hay.[202] While Hay "saw and appreciated the danger" represented by the "anarchist colonies" in Paterson, New York, and other places, he noted that the American government "had its hands tied by federal laws and by the particulars of each state." The American government could not enter into an agreement for information exchange with Spain or any other country since it maintained neither personal nor judicial files on the anarchists, and could therefore not promise reciprocity. Hay volunteered that if the police discovered anything of interest to Spain, the Spanish government would be immediately informed. Moreover, Hay continued, he had no objection to direct correspondence between the Spanish and American police. The Spanish minister believed, however, that these offers amounted to empty promises since the local state police forces – there being no national American police at this time except for the Secret Service – were completely uninterested in the question of the anarchist threat to Europe. The duke of Arcos concluded in his report to Madrid that the only way to acquire solid information was through acquiring a police force of one's own, although "even in that case, it would be very difficult to discover something of true importance." Since the assassination of Umberto, the duke noted, Italy had established its own police force in America, operating out of the Italian consulate in New York, and the Italian consul general "offered to communicate to me anything which he might know that would be of interest to us."

Particularly interesting about Arcos's report, besides its revelation of the ineffectiveness of the American police, was Hay's extraordinary

---

[201] Bradford to K. E. Digby, undersecretary of state, Home Office, May 9, 1902; E. R. Henry to Digby, HO45/10269/86397/7, PRO.

[202] Duke of Arcos, Washington, DC, to foreign minister, Madrid, n. 155, October 19, 1900, l. 2751, expediente 35, SFM. The text is printed in Jensen, "The United States, International Policing and the War against Anarchist Terrorism, 1900–1914," *Terrorism and Political Violence*, 13:1 (2001): 27–28.

encouragement of direct communications, unregulated by any diplomatic accord, between the Spanish and American police forces, a measure that many other countries, such as Britain and Switzerland, saw – at least before 1900 – as infringements on their national sovereignty. The governments of the latter usually insisted on such communication proceeding through normal diplomatic channels. The United States also tacitly allowed the operation of foreign police agents on its soil despite the fact that many other nations forbade this practice since it was likely to lead to the police becoming or hiring *agents provocateurs* who might instigate the very deeds of violence they were supposed to prevent.[203]

Most of the responses to Spain's circular of August 1900 expressed a willingness to increase direct police to police cooperation, but opposed new legislation or a new anti-anarchist conference, since the earlier meeting had led to such paltry results.[204] The Italian ambassador to Berlin told his Spanish colleague that governments rejected "more energetic remedial measures, [because] they were fearful in that way to especially attract the anger of the anarchists." Ambassador Lanza noted that he had just passed on to the German government two anonymous messages from Italy threatening the kaiser with death.[205] Only Turkey and Sweden-Norway, whose King Oscar II had been "deeply stirred" by the recent violent assaults on three monarchs, seemed interested in a new international conference. Oscar and his government believed that, except for the pernicious opposition of Britain, the 1898 conference would have produced the desired results.[206] Both Sweden and the Netherlands pointed out that, since the Rome conference, their police forces had begun to provide information – in the case of the Dutch, monthly reports – on the anarchists to other European police authorities. They would be happy to do the same with Spain, although no new formal understanding on the subject was necessary.[207] Denmark,

---

[203] Porter, *Vigilant State*, 122–123, 225n54 and Liang, *Modern Police*, 139–140, 160–161.

[204] E.g., Foreign Minister Bülow left the Spanish ambassador with the sense that Germany would take "no initiative whatever" in calling an "anti-anarchist congress or Conference." Angel Ruota, Berlin, to foreign minister, Madrid, August 24, 1900; Belgium was very willing to put its police headquarters in direct communication with the Spanish interior ministry, dispatches of August 30 and September 5, 1900; Russia was also in favor of direct police to police communications, duke of Vistahermosa, St. Petersburg, to foreign minister, Madrid, August 29, 1900, l. 2751, expediente 35, SFM.

[205] Angel Ruota, Berlin, to foreign minister, Madrid, August 24, 1900, l. 2751, expediente 35, SFM.

[206] Spanish Minister, Stockholm, to foreign minister, Madrid, August 27, 1900, l. 2751, expediente 35, SFM.

[207] Arturo de Baguer, [The Hague], September 15, 1900, no. 82, to foreign minister, Madrid. SFM. l. 2751, expediente 35; attachment, October 5, 1900, to dispatch, Spanish minister, Stockholm, to foreign minister, Madrid, October 6, 1900, l. 2750 n. 26, SFM.

on the other hand, was happy to exchange official notes with Spain providing for the reciprocal exchange of information regarding particular anarchists residing in Denmark and those recently expelled.[208] Much more vital to Spain than greater cooperation with Scandinavia and the Low Countries would have been better police coordination with France. Although the French police, and especially the French commissioner posted to monitor the anarchists in Barcelona, were often secretly willing to provide Madrid with intelligence regarding dangerous Spanish anarchists, more formal and regularized cooperation remained elusive and a high level political accord impossible.[209]

The Russo-German anti-anarchist proposals of September 1900

Paralleling, and in part replicating, the Spanish diplomatic efforts were calls by imperial Russia, supported by Germany, for stepped up measures against the anarchists. The tsar's government jettisoned the religious sentiments found in the Spanish program, and emphasized the need for new legislation to suppress anarchist propaganda. Given St. Petersburg's greater power, and strong support from the even more powerful government in Berlin, its initiative proved of more significance than Madrid's, and indeed provided the kernel that sprouted within four years to become the anti-anarchist protocol signed at St. Petersburg.

At the end of August 1900 Tsar Nicholas approved Russian Foreign Minister Lamzdorf's proposal for a circular to the Great Powers on the anarchist danger. Before officially circulating the message to the liberal governments of France and Britain, Russia wanted "the conservative Monarchies" to "achieve an agreement" and approached Germany and Austria-Hungary for their reactions, thus reviving the *de facto* Three Emperor's League that had worked together at the Rome conference for tougher anti-anarchist measures.[210] Both Berlin and Vienna welcomed Russia's efforts and its desire to exchange ideas about measures against both propaganda by the deed and propaganda by the word. They agreed with it that the "general mood of public opinion" in Switzerland, Britain, and France, which had been disturbed by the assassination attempts

---

[208] A copy of this agreement, dated September 25, 1900, Copenhagen, is attached to dispatch September 27, 1900, Spanish Legation, Stockholm, to foreign minister, Madrid, L. 2751, expediente 35, SFM.

[209] For the *Sûreté's* and the French commissioner's cooperation with the Spanish, González Calleja, *La razón de la fuerza*, 284–85, 294 (regarding Angiolillo), 356n, 366–368 (Morral), 372.

[210] Aehrenthal, St. Petersburg, to Goluchowski, Vienna, August 20 and September 7, 1900, confidential, Administrative Registratur (hereafter cited as Adm Reg) F52/10, HHStA.

against the prince of Wales and the Persian shah, as well as by the murder of Umberto, was "far better" than in 1898 for the success of a proposed anti-anarchist agreement.[211]

On September 6, 1900 Russia submitted a confidential *Pro memoria* first to the German Foreign Office, and later to other European states and to the United States.[212] The Russians declared that the death of Umberto and the attempts on the two other royal persons proved that "anarchist propaganda instead of diminishing had acquired, in recent times, a new strength." In fact, it represented "the greatest danger menacing contemporary society." Moreover, the "experience of many years had proved that isolated efforts by governments would not suffice to extirpate this evil; common efforts, based on international conventions, would be necessary for that purpose." While "the results obtained by Italy" in calling the 1898 Rome conference were "very important," they remained largely in the "form of desiderata and general principles," unrealized and unenforced. Only one measure had been

in practice applied up until the present, and not yet conspicuously: that is the exchange of information coming from the surveillance exercised on the most well-known anarchists and their movements in the great urban centers.

The direct relations established by this means between the principle police organs of the different countries clearly facilitate the surveillance of dangerous elements, but they do not suffice, as has been proved, in preventing new *attentats*.

Russia believed that the time was right to apply the other desiderata of the 1898 conference "and principally those which, in order to combat the evil in its root, deal with measures of a political and legislative character." Russia sought new laws against propaganda by the word since it believed that it inevitably led to propaganda by the deed.

the greatest danger menacing contemporary society is precisely Anarchist propaganda that penetrates into the popular masses by means of public meetings and by propagation among the working populace of Anarchist journals and tracts exalting the "famous" followers of Anarchism and calling the indigent classes to an armed rising against the well-to-do.

The best means to address this issue was not a new conference but:

a confidential discussion between Cabinets in order to establish to what extent the States who adhered to the [Final] Acte of the Rome Conference, would find

---

[211] Prussian interior minister, Prussian State ministries meeting, Berlin, September 6, 1900, GCSAM, film 1215/56; Aehrenthal, St. Petersburg, to Goluchowski, Vienna, September 7, 1900, Adm Reg F52/10, HHStA.

[212] Copy, originally dated September 4, 1900, GFO, 43 Anarchismus (geheim); a printed copy is in Baron Eckardstein to British Foreign Office, October 9, 1900, FO 881/7711, PRO.

it timely to employ the means recommended by that international meeting for the struggle against Anarchism.

By focusing on new legislation and by seeming to lump together anarchism with any group "advocating violence and the dividing up of property" St. Petersburg guaranteed that its *Pro memoria* would be controversial, as it itself acknowledged in the final paragraph of the diplomatic message.

The German government, while it fully supported the Russian memorandum, hesitated once again to take a leading role. The kaiser and some ministers supported extreme measures, but Chancellor Bernard von Bülow and the majority of ministers in the German government doubted that anything but improved administrative and police cooperation could be obtained. As might be expected, Kaiser Wilhelm's reaction to St. Petersburg's proposal, revealed in his marginalia, was extravagant:

Agreed! [i.e., that anarchism did not deserve the protection afforded other political doctrines] The anarchist must be treated simply as standing *extra leges* [outside the laws], and if possible dealt with only by court martial and immediate execution.[213]

German government policy, as hammered out in meetings of the Prussian state ministry, or cabinet, on September 6 and November 3, 1900, was more cautious. The first ministerial meeting attended by Imperial Chancellor Bülow and presided over by Finance Secretary (State Ministry Vice-President) Johann von Miquel, noted that when the Russian proposal arrived, Bülow had already been planning to propose a new international anti-anarchist agreement. Now that St. Petersburg had acted, Germany would warmly support its efforts, rather than the similar proposal coming out of Madrid. Prussian Interior Minister Georg von Rheinbaben thought America's participation in the agreement "imperative," as did other ministers. Rheinbaben also suggested that anti-anarchist legislation – he came armed with a draft proposal – should be submitted both to the Reichstag and presented to the foreign powers as a possible model for their action. Rheinbaben's proposal called for increased penalties for anarchist crimes, including supporting and glorifying such crimes in public meetings and through the press, and spreading anarchist propaganda in the army and navy. Punishments might comprise, depending on the crime, the revocation of civil rights, mandatory police supervision, deportation to overseas colonies – possibly for life – and prison time. Miquel suggested going even further and

---

[213] Marginalia on Russian *Pro Memoria* forwarded by Richthofen, German foreign ministry, Berlin, to Reich Interior Secretary Posodowsky, September 12, 1900. Reich interior ministry, vol. 7, n. 13688, GCSAM.

introducing corporal punishment for anarchists, but the justice minister thought such a punishment would be ineffective as a "deterrent" in the face of the anarchists' "vanity."[214]

The issue of anti-anarchist legislation surfaced once again at the November 3, 1900, Prussian cabinet meeting attended by both Prussian and Reich ministers, and including Imperial Chancellor Bülow.[215] The imperial secretary of the interior, Arthur Count von Posadowsky, described by one historian as "a stiff, pedantic bureaucrat, fanatical agrarian, and political conservative,"[216] in this case proved to be shrewder and more flexible than both his Prussian counterpart and the ambitious and right-leaning former National Liberal, Miquel. Posadowsky doubted whether the proposed anti-anarchist law would have any chance of being approved by the Reichstag since it would be mistaken for an anti-socialist measure, as had happened with the "anti-revolution" bill of 1894–1895. More helpful in protecting the safety of the kaiser than new laws would be "skillful police measures."

On the other hand, Rheinbaben argued that German leadership, accompanied by tough anti-anarchist measures, might serve to convince hesitant countries, such as Italy, the United States, Switzerland, and Belgium, to adhere to the Russian proposals. Moreover, tough measures might soon be needed inside Germany itself. The *attentat* at the Niederwald monument, the murder of Frankfurt Police Chief Rumpff in 1885, and the dynamite assault against Berlin Police Colonel Krause on June 29/30, 1895, showed what "fertile ground" Germany provided for anarchist teachings. Just recently the anarchist newspaper *Neues Leben* (*New Life*) had been founded. Moreover, "not only in Berlin but also in other large German cities, such as Magdeburg, Elberfeld-Barmen and others, anarchist organizations were surviving." Miquel warned that the "dangerousness" of the anarchists "for all Civilized states [*Kulturstaaten*] was emerging more and more."

In the end, the ministers decided that a cautious anti-anarchist policy was preferable to tough new domestic measures and a prominent international role. The Prussian justice minister argued that too forward a position by Germany could provoke "a very considerable worsening of the anarchist danger...the rage of anarchist fanatics from abroad, where they could make their preparations, would be directed above all against Germany." In his concluding statement Bülow, Wilhelm's ambitious, sycophantic, and

[214] Reichskanzlei, "Bekämpfung der Umsturzbestrebungen," 755/4, GCSAM, Minutes of Prussian Ministry of State, September 6, 1900.

[215] Ibid., Minutes of the Royal [Prussian] Ministry of State, November 3, 1900.

[216] Lamar Cecil, *Wilhelm II: Prince and Emperor*, 2 vols. (Chapel Hill: University of North Carolina Press, 1989 and 1996), 1:253.

manipulative chancellor (nicknamed "the eel" by diplomats in token of his slippery qualities) agreed with this view.[217] He pointed out that other countries were more duty-bound and responsible than Germany, such as Italy, and more capable of taking the lead, such as Russia. After all, "Italian soil," not German, "gave birth to and nurtured ... anarchism," and tsarist Russia lay unhampered by the legal and constitutional restrictions that the German government faced. "The most important means of protection against [the anarchists]," stressed Bülow, was the "surveillance of anarchists abroad, finding information about where they stayed, their communications, their travels etc. General international measures in the police sphere, therefore, would be of special worth."

The assembled Prussian and imperial ministers followed Bülow's line of reasoning and determined that the Reich chancellor should undertake to

ascertain via international soundings out and negotiations to what extent, in connection with the Russian proposal, the *Kulturstaaten* may be united for a partly police, partly legislative action against anarchism and at the same time give cognizance of Germany's willingness [to adopt] suitable measures.[218]

Supporting St. Petersburg, but hoping to remain off center stage and unnoticed, Berlin became the chief proponent of Russia's proposals. Germany, not the tsar's empire, submitted the Russian anti-anarchist program to Britain on October 9, 1900. In his message to the British Foreign Office, the German ambassador, Baron Ekardstein, noted that "the German Government ... were disposed to agree to the proposal but did not think that a fresh Conference on the subject was desirable."[219] Lord Salisbury's reaction was that:

As far as I understand the Russian government would make it penal to advocate anarchist doctrines even where no crime is directly recommended. This would be quite impossible in England.[220]

The Home Office agreed that the suggested joint legislation by all governments against anarchist propaganda was "impossible in this country."[221]

The Germans had no more luck with the United States, although here the chief difficulty was the lack of the technical means to cooperate, as the Spanish had already found out. On October 5, 1900, the

---

[217] Cecil, *Wilhelm II*, 1:258; Katharine Anne Lerman, *The Chancellor as Courtier: Bernhard von Bülow and the Governance of Germany 1900–1909.* (cambridge university press, 1990): 94.

[218] Reichskanzlei, "Bekämpfung der Umsturzbestrebungen," 755/4, Minutes of Royal Ministry of State, November 3, 1900, GCSAM.

[219] Eckardstein to Sanderson, Foreign Office, confidential, London, October 9, 1900, PRO. FO 881/7711; copy of Salisbury to Lascelles, Berlin, October 17, 1900. PRO. HO45/10254/x36450/116.

[220] "S[alisbury]," mss. memo on Eckardstein, October 9, 1900. PRO. FO 83/1970.

[221] Digby, Home office, to FO, Whitehall, October 29, 1900, PRO. FO. 881/7711.

German chargé d'affaires in Washington, DC, submitted a memorandum calling for the reciprocal furnishing of information regarding anarchist movements:

In 1897 the United States Ambassador in Berlin expressed the desire to be kept informed of the departure of Anarchists leaving Germany for the United States. At the time the German government was thoroughly disposed to take up this suggestion on condition of reciprocity in action. At that period the establishment of a central office – in Berlin – was underway which should devote its attention to the whereabouts of Anarchists. This central office has now been definitely established, and it has also met with the approval of the Roman Conference of 1898.

The latest deed committed by the Anarchists has brought the Anarchist question to the front and it would be of greatest value if a record kept in the United States could keep the central office informed of all movements of Anarchists from there to Germany.

The State Department replied on October 13, 1900:

There is no Federal machinery in the United States by which Anarchists may be found out and their movements followed. Neither State nor Federal legislation provides for civil registry or other means of following up the life of individuals within our territory.

The arrangement suggested in 1897, that the United States Ambassador in Berlin should be advised of the departure of Anarchists from Germany to the United States, was with a view to enabling the Secretary of the Treasury to apply those provisions of our immigration statutes which related to the sending back of certain prescribed classes of immigrants.

Whilst this government would welcome all information of the proposed character which might aid toward the application of our immigration statues, and would endeavor to procure reports through state or Federal agencies of the movements of any suspicious characters who might be indicated to it, – yet the absence of Federal laws or means for adequately detecting and watching suspicious individuals throughout the great expanse of the national territory and among some seventy millions of inhabitants, would make it impracticable for the Government of the United States to assume a reciprocal obligation the value of which would lie mainly in its effective execution.

The Russian Promemoria to which the German Memorandum refers, was made recently the occasion of an oral inquiry by the Russian Chargé, which was in like manner orally answered.[222]

Belgium also refused to commit itself to the Russian proposals, citing constitutional constraints and the belief that existing legislation was enough to oppose "anarchist excesses."[223] Approached by both Germany and Russia, the kingdom of Greece made the surprising declaration that

[222] Copies of memoranda, forwarded by Secretary of State Hay to the Attorney General, October 13, 1900, RG 60, file no. 11717/1900, NA.
[223] Koziebrodzki, Brussels to Goluchowski, Vienna, November 6, 1900, Adm.Reg. F52/10, HHStA.

it had not believed it necessary to institute a [central anti-anarchist] office because, from the investigations carried out by various Royal authorities, it had resulted that persons who professed anarchist opinions and had interactions with adherents of that sect did not exist in Greece.

The Italian foreign minister indicated his well-founded doubts about the truth of this assertion by placing next to it in the margin a big question mark.[224] Greece was not the only country that lived in the false belief that it had no anarchists and faced no danger from anarchist terrorism. Given this complacency and the reluctance or opposition of other European states and America to champion new repressive laws and police practices, the Russo-German initiative of 1900 failed.

Conclusion

In the liberal states, be they constitutional monarchies or republics, the three assassination attempts of 1900 failed to move public opinion sufficiently to cause their governments to abandon scruples regarding civil liberties and to join the conservative monarchies in repressing propaganda by the word as well as by the deed. The failure to revive the program of the Rome conference, whose largely unfulfilled mandates continued to provide the model for international anti-anarchists efforts throughout the pre-World War One era, left it up to individual states unilaterally to expand their policing efforts abroad. Italy, above all, but also Germany created new networks of police in the Americas and in Spain, since the assassination of King Umberto pointed out the potential danger from discontented individuals in emigrant communities largely unmonitored by local police in New York, Buenos Aires, and Barcelona. European states realized that they knew little about what anarchist and other activities might be transpiring in these groups of migrants and needed better intelligence than the indigenous police were able, or willing, to provide.

Besides the development of new police apparatuses abroad, 1900 also marked an important change, or even revolution, in the way some countries protected their heads of state. Personal security systems for top political leaders became bureaucratic, systematic, and official, rather than, as before, ad hoc and personal. In both the business of protecting heads of state and of gathering anti-anarchist intelligence the British provided a model esteemed by the rest of Europe. The success of British methods, as careful and unostentatious as they were, was no doubt somewhat

---

[224] Italian Minister Avarna, Athens, to Italian foreign minister, Rome, November 25, 1900, PI, b. 32, IFM.

exaggerated by foreign observers. In 1900, at least, Britain did not need to contend with discontented groups of British subjects overseas.

The print media played a complex part in stoking the fires of terrorism. Its understanding of anarchist terrorism was often shallow and it remained obsessed with a phantom threat from international conspiracies. The media largely created the image of a looming specter of anarchism, a powerful specter that terrified both ordinary people and governments (one thinks of the timidity of the German authorities about provoking anarchist anger), and inspired potential assassins. The press erroneously linked Sipido, Salson, and Bresci's deeds with Lucheni's although they had little in common. While the latter may have had, to cite Lord Salisbury, a "morbid thirst for notoriety," this does not appear to have been a prominent factor with the three other assassins. On the other hand, a virulent Anglophobic press played a role in precipitating the attempt of the callow, teenaged Sipido; Salson's deed may have been a copycat crime based on much reading about Umberto's assassination. (Or it may have been the act of a police spy and an example of how the police itself contributed to creating the phenomenon of anarchist terrorism.) The Italian king's murder, however, was a conscious political act by the thirty-year-old Bresci, who was familiar with the classics of anarchist thought, as well as with the writings of journalists. If the media often misunderstood the anarchists, so did governments, whose ignorance of the anarchist movement and faulty intelligence often mistook a peaceful libertarian for a homicidal conspirator. The next great anarchist assassination would lead to more misleading press coverage but also to more successful efforts at forging international police cooperation.

7

The murder of President McKinley, 1901

The Buffalo, New York, Pan-American Exposition's spectacular, pompous Temple of Music, looking much like a set from a D. W. Griffith epic film, provided the locale for the most stunning of all anarchist assassinations, the murder of President McKinley in early September 1901. McKinley, both head of government and head of state, was the most powerful leader that the anarchists ever managed to kill. Even more than the murder of Umberto, the assault on the US president signaled that anarchist terrorism had spread in dramatic fashion from Europe to the Western Hemisphere. After 1901, it soon became a global phenomenon, since not only North America, but also South America, particularly Argentina, North Africa, and finally Asia provided sites for anarchist, or allegedly anarchist, outrages. Australia worried about anarchists immigrating to its shores and new terrorist attacks after a single act of propaganda by the deed in 1893.[1] While during the late 1880s and early 1890s dynamite blasts had been the signature "deeds" of the anarchist terrorists, beginning in 1894 assassinations of heads of state and government had become their most characteristic – and publicized – acts, culminating in the twin murders of Umberto and McKinley in 1900–1901. McKinley's assassination also triggered unprecedented efforts at anti-terrorist cooperation. It led directly, albeit only after some years of negotiation, to the signing of the most concrete international anti-anarchist accord ever formulated. McKinley's assassination also highlighted once again the glaring inadequacies of measures for safeguarding heads of state.

Leon Czolgosz, the handsome, introverted twenty-eight-year-old American of Polish-German descent who shot McKinley, is probably the most controversial of all the anarchist assassins.[2] Why did he kill McKinley? Was he in fact an anarchist? Was he sane? More than

---

[1] For Australian worries after 1900 about new acts of terrorism, see Gianfranco Cresciani, *The Italians in Australia* (Cambridge University Press, 2003): 48.
[2] Detective Sergeant Vallely asked Czolgosz "Where were your parents born?" and he said: "I am a Polish German." Supreme Court, Erie County. The People of the State of New York, against Leon F. Czolgosz, 103 (hereafter, cited as trial transcript).

a century after the event, the answers to these questions still remain controversial.

Even if some questions regarding the McKinley assassination remain open to dispute, its basic facts are fairly clear. McKinley arrived in Buffalo on September 5, 1901, planning to see the sights of the Pan-American exhibition and deliver a major address promoting trade agreements within the Western Hemisphere. In his speech, McKinley claimed that:

trade statistics indicate that this country is in a state of unexampled prosperity. The figures are almost appalling. They show that we are utilizing our fields and forests and mines and that we are furnishing profitable employment to the millions of workingmen throughout the United States, bringing comfort and happiness to their homes and making it possible to lay by savings for old age and disability. That all the people are participating in this great prosperity is seen in every American community.[3]

Czolgosz was in the crowd listening to McKinley. When asked later why he had shot the president, Czolgosz replied, "McKinley was going around the country shouting about prosperity when there was no prosperity for the poor man."[4] Scholarly estimates of poverty in the United States around 1900, based on contemporary, rather than today's, judgments, range from one-third to half or more of the population.[5] Many children were unable to attend school due to lack of shoes or an overcoat, and good medical care was usually unavailable for the poor and disabled, as Czolgosz experienced after falling ill in 1897.[6]

The day after McKinley's speech, September 6, 1901, Czolgosz waited, apparently for hours, in the humid heat in order to be one of the first to enter the highly ornate, gilt-domed Hall of Music for a brief – ten minute – public reception for the president that Czolgosz had read about in the newspapers. After entering the building, Czolgosz took his right hand, wrapped round with a handkerchief, out of his jacket pocket

---

[3] Charles Olcott, *The Life of William McKinley* (Boston: Houghton Mifflin, 1916), 2:381.

[4] Carlos MacDonald, a doctor at Bellevue, interviewed Czolgosz on September 20, 1901. MacDonald, "The Trial, Execution, Autopsy and Mental Status of Leon F. Czolgosz, Alias Fred Nieman, the Assassin of President McKinley," *American Journal of Insanity*, 58:3 (1902): 384.

[5] Robert Plotnick, Eugene Smolensky, Eirik Evenhouse, and Siobhan Reilly, "The Twentieth Century Record of Inequality and Poverty in the United States," Institute for Research on Poverty. Discussion Paper no. 1166–98, July 1998, 23–25; www.ssc.wisc.edu/irp (accessed August 25, 2013); Robert J. Goldstein, *Political Repression in Modern America: From 1870 to 1976* (Urbana: University of Illinois Press, 2001): 66.

[6] Plotnick et al, "Twentieth Century Record," 25; L. Vernon Briggs, *The Manner of Man That Kills* (Boston: Richard G. Badger, 1921): 30.

and held it close to the front of his body. In the palm of his hand was a short-barreled revolver with Czolgosz's forefinger upon the trigger. He passed by exposition guards and ten Marines in dress uniform, who were there for crowd control and untrained in preventing assassination. The three Secret Service agents near the president were distracted by the onrush of people, "pressed to each other's backs," and being quickly, but erratically, hurried past to shake McKinley's hand.[7] Others in line looked more suspicious than the short (five foot seven-and-a-half inch), narrow-shouldered Czolgosz, who was nicely dressed in a dark striped suit, collar, and necktie. Czolgosz hardly looked menacing with his light blue eyes, mop of light brown wavy hair, and pleasant, freshly shaved face that years later one eyewitness remembered as "kind and intelligent." Reaching the president, Czolgosz, a practiced shot who often hunted squirrels and rabbits, used both hands to hold his revolver steady as he pumped two bullets into McKinley's corpulent body. The firing weapon set Czolgosz's handkerchief ablaze. One bullet somehow (by hitting a button?) bounced off, merely grazing McKinley's sternum, but the other pierced both walls of his stomach, and lodged somewhere deep inside his body. Deathly pale, the president staggered from beside one of the potted trees on stage to another one, where he braced himself and was then helped to a seat. Putting his hand under his vest, he located the wound, which was oozing blood. An ambulance took McKinley to the exposition first aid station where a gynecologist, the only doctor who could be located immediately, assisted by two other surgeons, performed an operation. They were unable to locate the bullet. For some days the president seemed to be recuperating, but a week later, on September 14, due to shock, loss of fluids, and ultimately, heart failure, McKinley died. While many criticized the doctors for botching McKinley's operation, today medical opinion holds that, given the state of knowledge at the time, nothing could have been done to save the president's life.[8]

[7] Trial testimony of Secret Service Agent George Foster, trial transcript, 78. The published trial record, which is a condensation, omits this quotation.

[8] This description of Czolgosz and the assassination is based primarily on the testimony of Louis Babcock, marshal of the Pan American Exhibition, Harry Henshaw, superintendent of music, Albert Gallaher, Secret Service Agent, John Branch, in charge of toilet rooms, and of Secret Service Agent Samuel Ireland. All of these men were eyewitnesses. Louis Babcock, "The Assassination of President McKinley," *Niagara Frontier Miscellany* 34 (1947): 27; Gallaher, Henshaw, and Branch, trial record, 70, 95, 100–101, and Ireland's Daily Report, September 6, 1901, written some time later at Rochester. RG 87, US Secret Service, box 144, file 161, NA. Several authors refer to Czolgosz's large hands (all the better with which to conceal a revolver), but the autopsy concluded that "his hands were not in any way notable." Edward A. Spitzka, "The Post-Mortem Examination of Leon F. Czolgosz," appended to MacDonald, "Trial, Execution, Autopsy," 398. See also

Czolgosz's motivations

Why did Czolgosz fire on President McKinley? Like Bresci, Czolgosz wished to protest against an unjust political and economic system as well as against his personal sufferings. He also shared personal similarities with the Italian since both were handsome, older men: Czolgosz twenty-eight and Bresci thirty. In contrast, Lucheni had been twenty-five and Caserio twenty at the time they carried out their famous assassinations. Czolgosz's sensitivity, intelligence, and idealism led him to react strongly against the harsh labor conditions of late nineteenth-century America. With five and a half years of school, including six months of evening classes, Leon was the best-educated member of his family. He read "all the time" and became especially fascinated with Edward Bellamy's *Looking Backward*.[9] This bestselling book envisioned a utopian United States where vicious conflicts between capital and labor had been replaced by a benevolent society in which a big government-owned trust worked for the common interest of every American.

Certainly the brutal labor struggles of these years marked Czolgosz. He worked at a bottle-producing plant and then, for seven years, at a wire factory. His foreman later told an investigator that "Leon had been a steady worker; he never gave any trouble, never quarreled nor got into any disputes with other workmen ... [He] was as good a boy as we had ever had."[10] Twice he was injured on the job; on one occasion a piece of wire scarred his face.[11] The turning point in his life, both as a worker and a person, came during the panic and depression of 1893. When the wire mill in Cleveland where Czolgosz worked cut wages, Czolgosz, his brother Waldeck, and the other workers went out on strike. During this crisis Czolgosz and his brother "prayed very hard," since, as faithful Catholics, they "always believed what the priest taught them – that if they were in need or trouble and prayed their prayers would be answered."[12] But their prayers were not answered and both were fired and blacklisted

Jack Fisher, *Stolen Glory: The McKinley Assassination* (La Jolla: Alamar Books, 2001): 152–157, and Eric Rauchway, *Murdering McKinley: The Making of Theodore Roosevelt's America* (New York: Hill and Wang, 2003): 3–11. Fisher is a physician.

[9] Testimony of Joseph and Waldeck Czolgosz. Waldeck, Leon's closest sibling, said that "Leon had studied [*Looking Backward*] for seven or eight years." Vernon Briggs interviewed Waldeck and other members of Leon's family, as well as other acquaintances. Briggs later published this information in a work of fundamental importance for our understanding of Czolgosz (*The Manner of Man That Kills*, 305, 312), even if one disagrees with Briggs's diagnosis of the assassin as insane.

[10] Briggs, *The Manner of Man That Kills*, 314.

[11] Briggs, *The Manner of Man That Kills*, 242.

[12] Briggs, *The Manner of Man That Kills*, 304; Rauchway, *Murdering McKinley*, 166. Rauchway's book is especially valuable because he has consulted the unpublished

from further employment. Czolgosz was only able to resume work, at lower pay, by changing his name to "Nieman," (or Nimen), which, as he explained, meant "nobody" in German. Waldeck Czolgosz later told an interviewer that his brother now "got quiet and not so happy."[13] It was at this time that Czolgosz started to read *Looking Backward*, joined the Socialist Club, and abandoned his Catholic faith. He began to read radical, including anarchist, pamphlets and journals. Like Lucheni, who had begun as a monarchist and faithful servant of an aristocrat but then had become disillusioned, Czolgosz drifted into anarchist circles and thinking in an attempt to find meaning for an increasingly embittered life.

He also sought in anarchism a way to protest against injustice, whose increasing occurrence troubled him. A few months before he shot McKinley, Czolgosz told a Cleveland anarchist that "things were getting worse and worse – more strikes and they were getting more brutal against the strikers, and that something must be done."[14] Like Sipido, Czolgosz was also upset by the brutality of Western imperialism. He told Abraham Isaak, a Chicago anarchist and editor of *Free Society*, that the "outrages committed by the American government in the Philippine islands [against a native uprising in favor of independence] ... [did] not harmonize with the teachings in the public schools about our flag."[15] After all, the United States had pledged to liberate the Filipinos from Spanish rule but then ended up imposing American control and occupying their country for almost fifty years. McKinley was directly responsible for American actions in the Philippines and could be blamed for the sufferings of American workers due to his cozy relationship with the leaders of big business. For years Hearst's vastly influential *New York Journal* had hammered away at McKinley both in print and in brilliant cartoons that depicted him as the child and puppet of the great business trusts and wealthy financiers. Despite allegations to the contrary, Czolgosz certainly read English and may have been affected by the anti-McKinley attitudes of the *Journal* and other newspapers, although no evidence links his actions directly with, for example, an editorial and a poem approving assassination (indeed the assassination of McKinley!) that appeared in the pages of the *Journal* in 1901.[16]

---

papers of Briggs and Walter Channing, the most important contemporary investigators of Czolgosz and his family.

[13] Briggs, *The Manner of Man That Kills*, 303.

[14] Briggs, *The Manner of Man That Kills*, 321.

[15] Rauchway, *Murdering McKinley*, 102.

[16] Czolgosz spoke and read English fluently, as well as Polish. Briggs, *The Manner of Man That Kills*, 306, 314, 317; David Nasaw, *The Chief: The Life of William Randolph Hearst* (Boston and New York: Houghton Mifflin, 2001): 154–158. Brian Thornton, "When a Newspaper was Accused of Killing a President," *Journalism History* 25:3 (2000): 108–116.

Controversy has raged over whether Czolgosz was in fact an anarchist or, in the words of *Free Society*, acted out "of purely personal idiosyncrasy and not of any doctrine or propaganda."[17] While *Free Society*'s objectivity was no doubt clouded by its anxiety to deflect anger from itself and from the anarchist movement in the United States, whose adherents had suffered a series of violent reprisals after the assassination, it is uncertain how many anarchist meetings Czolgosz attended and how much anarchist literature he read. At his trial, one witness said Czolgosz told him he had been studying the "doctrines of Anarchy" for "several years" and another said "seven" (which would be around 1893–1894, when Czolgosz underwent his unemployment and personal crisis).[18]

Most witnesses agree that he idolized the famous anarchist orator, Emma Goldman, whom he had met briefly on May 5 and then again on July 12, 1901.[19] Police Superintendent Bull thought Czolgosz was in love with her.[20] Czolgosz also made a deep impression on Goldman, who years later vividly remembered his "large dreamy eyes" and "a most sensitive face … a handsome face made doubly so by his curly golden hair."[21] On the other hand, Czolgosz's extravagant "confession" implicating Goldman in McKinley's assassination is almost certainly a fake. The *New York Times* and many other newspapers, and later on many periodicals and books down to the present day, reported that Czolgosz made a statement to the police asserting that a lecture by Goldman "started the craze to kill … Her doctrine that all rulers should be exterminated was what set me to thinking so that my head nearly split with the pain."[22] Erie County District Attorney Thomas Penney, the alleged source, denied the confession the next day. Nor does any such allegation appear in the trial record or in eyewitness reports.[23]

Czolgosz's own testimony about his involvement with the anarchists is confusing and contradictory. Several doctors, headed by Dr. Joseph Fowler, a police surgeon, were entrusted with examining him for signs of insanity, but also asked him about his political beliefs. They claimed in a report dated September 28, 1901 that he belonged to a "nameless"

[17] Cited by Briggs, *The Manner of Man That Kills*, 322.
[18] James Quackenbush, an attorney who accompanied Czolgosz to jail after the assassination, gives "several" and Buffalo Police Superintendent Bull says "seven," trial transcript, 59, 106
[19] Goldman, *Living My Life*, 289–290; Paul Avrich and Karen Avrich, *Sasha and Emma*, (Cambridge, MA: Harvard University Press, 2012): 152–154, 156–158.
[20] Briggs, *The Manner of Man That Kills*, 267; Rauchway, *Murdering McKinley*, 89.
[21] Emma Goldman, "The Psychology of Political Violence," in *Anarchism and Other Essays* (New York: Dover, 1970): 90; Goldman, *Living My Life*, 290.
[22] "The Assassin Makes A Full Confession," *New York Times*, September 8, 1901, 1.
[23] "'Czolgosz's Confessions' Manufactured," *Buffalo Evening News*, September 9, 1901.

circle of people who "called themselves Anarchists." The doctors quoted Czolgosz as saying, "At this circle we discussed Presidents and that they were no good."[24] It seems likely, though, that this circle was the Sila Club that he mentioned in 1901 to the anarchist Emil Schilling.[25] The Sila Club was ostensibly socialist, but fell apart in 1900 due to factionalism. Subsequently most of the members joined either the radical Social Labor Party or Eugene Debs's more moderate Socialist Party. Disgusted by the quarrelling, Czolgosz abandoned the club. Since at the grassroots level, the affiliates and ideas of anarchism and Marxist socialism often intermingled, it is possible or even likely that Czolgosz first began to pick up some anarchist ideas in the Sila Club.

In the same year that the Sila Club broke up, Gaetano Bresci shot down King Umberto. According to his parents, as reported by Dr. Channing, Czolgosz was fascinated by the assassination. He "spent a great deal of time reading the account of the murder of King Humbert [Umberto]...The paper was very precious to him as he took it to bed every night."[26] He kept the paper for more than half a year and would allow his brothers or sisters to read it if they liked.[27] Czolgosz was obsessed with reading newspapers and would walk a half mile every afternoon to get them, reading everything he could find in English or Polish.[28] In May 1901, he sought out the treasurer of an anarchist association in Cleveland, saying "I hear the Anarchists are plotting something like Breschi [sic]; the man was selected by the comrades to do the deed that was done." When the anarchist treasurer denied these stories, Czolgosz confessed that he had not read of them in any anarchist publication but "in some capitalist paper."[29] (Indeed the American mass circulation dailies gave enormous coverage to Umberto's murder, e.g., on July 30, the *New York World* devoted its entire front page to the assassination, including large photos.) In July Czolgosz went to Chicago to hear Emma Goldman and to find

---

[24] Report by Fowler, Floyd Crego, and James Putnam, reprinted in Briggs, *The Manner of Man That Kills*, 244.

[25] Schilling's testimony is recorded in Briggs, *The Manner of Man That Kills*, 316.

[26] Walter Channing, "The Mental Status of Czolgosz, the Assassin of President McKinley," *The American Journal of Insanity* 59:2 (1902): 263.

[27] February 16, 1902, copy of interview with Czolgosz family for Dr. Walter Channing, from A. B. Spurney, Butler Hospital, Providence, RI, to H. C. Eyman, Massillon State Hospital, Massillon, Ohio. Papers of Walter Channing, Channing Family Papers. Massachusetts Historical Society, Boston. I am grateful to Eric Rauchway for supplying me with this information. I can find no primary evidence for published reports that Czolgosz kept a newspaper clipping of Umberto's assassination in his pocket and read it constantly or slept with it under his pillow.

[28] According to his brother Waldeck as reported by Briggs, *The Manner of Man That Kills*, 306.

[29] Briggs, *The Manner of Man That Kills*, 317.

out if he could attend the "secret meetings" of the local anarchists, but the latter denied holding any such gatherings.[30]

All of this shows how strong Czolgosz's desire to become an anarchist was, even if his interactions with anarchists and knowledge of their literature was limited. Later he said that all he knew of anarchism came from the speeches of Goldman and reading *Free Society*, a Chicago anarchist journal edited by Abraham Isaac. But Czolgosz, secretive and in the habit of denying even evident truths – at one point he denied he had shot McKinley! – may not have been entirely candid on this question. After the assassination, the police declared that they had found anarchist literature on his person and anarchist books in his room.[31] At his initial interrogation and his trial, he repeatedly asserted that he was an anarchist.[32]

Like almost all the famous anarchist assassins about whom we have much information, Czolgosz was caught up in the anarchist mystique, that powerful image of the dangerous, powerful anarchist, either demonic or justifiably vengeful, constructed by the mass media, fearful authorities, the public, and the anarchists themselves. Czolgosz said that the idea of murdering McKinley had been suggested by something he read in *Free Society*. While *Free Society* did contain some articles criticizing assassination attempts, such as a reprint of Leo Tolstoy's reaction to the shooting of Umberto, it contained many others honoring the sacrifices of anarchist martyrs. A piece published on May 12, 1901, noted that "most Anarchists regard with unqualified approval acts like Bresci's," but that:

Bresci did not represent an organization when he assassinated Italy's king. It was the act of an individual. Bresci, who was a kind hearted and humane man (not a "wretch"), was deeply touched by the great suffering and misery caused by the oppressive measures of the Italian government, and so resolved to utter his protest by killing the king, the official symbol of all this tyranny.[33]

If one replaced Bresci's name with "Czolgosz," Italian with "American," and king with "president," these sentences could easily describe the motives and deeds of the loner Polish-American assassin convinced that McKinley was the pawn of Hanna and other great monopoly capitalists exploiting the common man.[34] An essay in *Free Society* by Goldman, published on June 2, 1901, made the same points as the anonymous contributor, although Goldman was careful to write that anarchism, "the philosophy of liberty and human independence … can have nothing to

[30] Goldman, *Living My Life*, 290–291; Rauchway, *Murdering McKinley*, 101.
[31] Channing, "Mental Status of Czolgosz," 268.
[32] Trial transcipt, 60–61, 103, 105; Rauchway, *Murdering McKinley*, 17.
[33] "Should Bresci's Torture Be Avenged?", *Free Society*, May 12, 1901, 1.
[34] Briggs, *The Manner of Man That Kills*, 320; Rauchway, *Murdering McKinley*, 206.

do with violence, nor have the representatives of this idea ever advocated it." At the same time she praised Bresci, noting that he "loved" his "kind,...felt the existing wrongs in the world, and...dared to strike a blow at organized authority."[35]

An issue of *Free Society*, published a week before Czolgosz's attack and commemorating the assassination of the Italian king, lauded the figure of a quasi-mythic "monster-slayer," associating Jack the giant-killer, Hercules, and Perseus, and other heroes with Bresci, Lucheni, and Angiolillo. "A true monster slayer," according to C.[harles] L. James, an anarchist writer from Eau Claire, Wisconsin, was "born for a holy purpose," after which he would die. The article concludes that "it is an infallible preservative to read in our daily papers that monster-slayers walk the earth once more."[36] Czolgosz may have read this article (Goldman later thought he must have seen that issue), but even if he did not, it replicates the attitude and vision that inspired him. A day after the assassination Leon told his interviewer that "I planned killing the President three or four days ago, after I came to Buffalo. Something I read in the *Free Society* suggested the idea...I realized that I was sacrificing my life. I am willing to take the consequences."[37]

Czolgosz, the monster-slayer, told his interrogators the evening of the shooting, and later his brother Waldeck, that:

I killed President McKinley because I done my duty. I didn't believe one man should have so much service and another man should have none.[38]

That same evening he also said, using words similar to those of Alexander Berkman's "that he didn't believe in rulers; he thought that all rulers were tyrants and should be removed."[39]

---

[35] Reprinted in Emma Goldman, *Emma Goldman: A Documentary History of the American Years*, ed. Candace Falk, 2 vols. (Berkeley: University of California Press, 2003): 1:455–456.

[36] Monster-slayers also used "enchanted weapons," like "a dynamite bomb." "The Monster-Slayer," *Free Society*, September, 1 1901, 1–2. The Cleveland anarchist, Emil Schilling, told Briggs that this issue of *Free Society* was published "a week before McKinley was shot." It was the same issue in which Isaac denounced Czolgosz as a possible spy, a charge that Emma Goldman was sure Leon had read before he assaulted the President. Goldman, *Living My Life*, 309.

[37] Report by Fowler, Putnam and Crego, in Briggs, *The Manner of Man That Kills*, 243. James Quackenbush reported that Czolgosz said the following during his interrogation on September 6: "he had been thinking about killing the President for three or four days prior to the time of the shooting, that he fully determined that he would kill the President the day before the shooting. He also made another statement that he had determined it at an earlier period." Trial transcript, 60.

[38] Quackenbush, trial transcript, 64. Waldeck quotes Czolgosz's words in Briggs, *The Manner of Man That Kills*, 309.

[39] Quackenbush, trial transcript, 69. For Berkman's statement, see Chapter 1.

Numerous commentators claimed that Czolgosz's actions were the product of insanity, the same accusation leveled erroneously against Bresci and many other anarchist assassins.[40] He was secretive, moody, obsessively fastidious, and in his later years showed intermittent signs of depression, such as wanting to sleep all the time. He may have suffered a nervous breakdown in 1897, and the doctors whom he then consulted told him to stop working, although he continued to work at odd jobs with considerable skill. But the physicians who examined the assassin at the time of his arrest and in prison and the historian Eric Rauchway all conclude that Czolgosz was not insane. Czolgosz's father spoke of a "crazy aunt" back in Prussia, but it was never definitely proven that any of his family or ancestors had suffered from insanity.[41] Leon was a brooding, alienated loner, not crazy or even "half-mad."

Besides his alienation from American society, whose injustices he felt intensely, and his identification with the anarchist "monster-slayer," one other important factor may have influenced Czolgosz's fatal decision to murder McKinley. Unlike previous anarchist assassins, Czolgosz thought that he would soon die of natural causes. This was because Czolgosz seems to have believed that he had advanced syphilis, although his autopsy, while revealing genital scars, showed no signs of that disease. Nonetheless, Czolgosz took medication to treat syphilis, and in July of 1901, told his brother that he was not going to live long. Since he was going to die soon anyway, why not strike a blow against a system that he found so unjust?[42]

Voltairine de Cleyre, an anarchist intellectual from Philadelphia, wrote of "a Saint Bartholomew of the Anarchists," a "stamping-out craze" that swept the country after the murder of McKinley.[43] This popular backlash against the anarchists did more than any acts of repression by the federal government to discourage copycat crimes and prevent a new cycle of anarchist violence. In various parts of the United States, from the Northwest to the Southwest, from the Midwest to the East, individuals

[40] Both doctors, Channing and Briggs, concluded that Czolgosz was "insane," although neither had ever met the young man. Briggs, following a Dr. William A. White, suggests that he suffered from "the paranoid forms of dementia precox", *The Manner of Man That Kills*, 332. Briggs's conclusions on this point are not persuasive. According to Emma Goldman, Clarence Darrow thought Czolgosz insane, although he had never met him (Goldman, *Living My Life*, 303). Theodore Roosevelt was of the same opinion. Sidney Fine also accepts this conclusion, "Anarchism and the Assassination of McKinley," 780.

[41] Briggs, *The Manner of Man That Kills*, 244–249, 289; Rauchway, *Murdering McKinley*, 39–43, especially 114–116, 204–206.

[42] Briggs, *The Manner of Man That Kills*, 308; Rauchway, *Murdering McKinley*, 177–182, for the best discussion of Czolgosz and syphilis.

[43] Avrich, *An American Anarchist*, 133–134.

and bands of armed men forced anarchist-identified families from their homes and harassed anarchists in various other ways. Anarchists lost their jobs and had their possessions confiscated; on occasion they were beat up. Anarchists were arrested simply because they were anarchists. In Rochester a grand jury was asked to indict the city's 100 anarchists on the charge of conspiracy to overthrow the government, although eventually it refused to do so for lack of evidence. Giuseppe Ciancabilla, the anarchist leader and editor who had known Bresci, was run out of Spring Valley, Illinois, and forced to suspend publication of the journal he edited. The office of the New York City Yiddish-language anarchist paper, *Freie Arbeiter Stimme* was attacked and wrecked, and its editor later beaten up.[44] New York's City's police commissioner ordered a census of all anarchists residing in the city to "make conditions disagreeable for those named."[45]

More than fifty suspected anarchists, including Emma Goldman, were arrested in Chicago and held without bail for seventeen days on suspicion of involvement with the assassination. After Goldman protested against this injustice, an officer slugged her, knocking out a tooth and covering her face in blood. After her release for lack of evidence, Goldman had to adopt a pseudonym since, when she used her own name, she could find neither work nor an apartment. On October 3, Goldman was prevented from giving a lecture on anarchism. In Newark, New Jersey, bars and other establishments serving liquor were threatened with revocation of their licenses if they allowed anarchists to meet on their premises.[46] While all this persecution of the anarchists was rarely legal and occasionally brutal, its sporadic and relatively short-lived quality produced no inspiring martyrs. Unlike Spain, no systematic torture or killing of anarchists, aside from Czolgosz, took place in the United States.

As for the most hated anarchist of them all, Czolgosz was soon rushed to trial. It lasted less than three days (although this was better than Bresci's single day in court) and was characterized by many irregularities. Czolgosz was probably tortured during his incarceration, perhaps by using a light to burn his eyes.[47] But at least the formalities of justice were better followed than in some European countries and whatever torture Czolgosz received was minor compared to what the Spanish anarchists had suffered. Moreover, unlike the latter, evidence of the torture was never widely publicized or even clearly established, and this left little incentive for anarchist acts of revenge.

[44] Fine, "Anarchism," 786–787.
[45] Candace Falk, "Forging Her Place: An Introduction," in Goldman, *A Documentary History*, 1:80.
[46] Goldstein, *Political Repression*, 67.   [47] Rauchway, *Murdering McKinley*, 216–217.

American newspapers and journals were full of condemnations of the anarchists, with editorials most frequently demanding the exclusion of anarchist immigrants from entering the United States. Some editors and authors asked for very extreme measures. Even the staid *American Law Review* demanded that not only anarchist assassins but also those who attempted assassinations be subjected to "death in some disgraceful form."[48] In the media and even in Congress calls went out for subjecting anarchists to "police control," declaring, by international agreement, that anarchism was the equivalent of piracy, and deporting all anarchists to an island.[49]

Lack of presidential security

The assassination of President McKinley, as with the murder of King Umberto, revealed the glaring inadequacy of the measures taken for the security of the head of state. America had a long tradition of providing scant security for its leaders. Had they been given even a minimal amount of protection, both Lincoln and Garfield would almost certainly have been saved from assassination. Garfield had no guard at the time of his murder and Lincoln's had wandered off. The response to McKinley's death marked a significant step toward professionalizing and institutionalizing executive protection in the United States, although this change had its roots in the mid-1890s and was not fully consummated until 1906. This development paralleled similar changes going on in Italy and other European countries.

In 1901, however, the forces that protected the president were cobbled together in an ad hoc fashion without effectiveness or, in the case of the Secret Service, full legal authorization. They lacked central direction and coordination, as well as training in crowd control and protective procedures. On the other hand, the number of police and military agents available in Buffalo to protect McKinley was probably sufficient. At the Temple of Music reception, the three Secret Service operatives were joined by two Buffalo city detectives and their chief, the head of the exposition detectives, a squad of about fifteen to eighteen exposition police guards (plus their colonel), and ten coastal artillerymen and their corporal: about thirty-five men altogether.[50] More guards waited outside the hall. Overall coordination of the security arrangements was in the hands of George Cortelyou, the president's very able personal secretary, but Louis Babcock,

---

[48] "Notes," *American Law Review* (September–October 1901), 744.
[49] Fine, "Anarchism," 786–788; Jensen, "The United States."
[50] Babcock, "Assassination," 19; Trial transcript, 91.

the grand marshal of the exhibition, also took a leading role. At the last minute Babcock brought in the artillerymen, who could help with crowd control, but were not instructed to look for suspicious characters.[51] Their presence may even have been detrimental since by lining and narrowing the passage along the aisle, they obstructed the Secret Service agents' view of the oncoming line.[52] The president added to the muddle, by asking that the reception line be speeded up so that he could shake as many hands as possible, which made it more difficult to maintain an orderly procession as the crowd pressed into the Temple of Music.

Instead of taking a leading role in protecting the president, the three Secret Service agents acted passively, letting Cortelyou allocate their positions.[53] They simply stood around as guards, occupied with watching out for the president and managing the crowd. One agent stood ten feet away from McKinley directing people toward the exit and was thus of little use in preventing an assassination.[54] The principle Secret Service agent, George Foster, was a stout, "solid tub of a man," a former door-keeper of the Ohio House of Representatives, and an acquaintance of McKinley's.[55] Normally he stood to the president's left in order to observe everyone who approached him, but on this occasion John Milburn, the president of the exposition, occupied that position. Instead, Foster stood six to eight feet across the aisle from McKinley and Milburn, facing them. Foster never noticed Czolgosz's handkerchief-covered right hand, and seems to have focused as much, or more, on observing people's faces as their hands.[56] Even those who did see Czolgosz's handkerchief were not alarmed given the prevalence of white handkerchiefs, and one bandaged hand, in the lineup of people.[57] Earlier in the day thousands of people had used their handkerchiefs to wave at McKinley in a sign of welcome, as well as to wipe their faces in the late summer heat.[58] Thus,

---

[51] Testimony of artillerymen Francis O'Brien and Louis Neff, trial transcript, 84, 89.
[52] Margaret Leech, *In the Days of McKinley* (New York: Harper, 1959): 591.
[53] Ireland's Daily Report, September 6, 1901, RG 87, US Secret Service, box 144, file 161, NA.
[54] Frederick Kaiser, "Origins of Secret Service Protection of the President: Personal, Interagency, and Institutional Conflict," *Presidential Studies Quarterly* Winter 1988: 112 and notes.
[55] Leech, *Days of McKinley*, 561.
[56] Trial transcript, 78–79. Robert A. Pinkerton criticized the failure of the Secret Service agents to focus on the crowd's hands. "Detective Surveillance of Anarchists," 39–40.
[57] Samuel Ireland, Daily Report, September 6, 1901, RG 87, US Secret Service, box 144, file 161, NA, and trial testimony of Harry Henshaw, superintendent of music, Pan American Exposition, trial transcript, 95, 97. Admittedly Henshaw was not there to guard McKinley.
[58] A. Wesley Johns, *The Man Who Shot McKinley* (South Brunswick and New York: A. S. Barnes, 1970): 90.

even if Foster, whose trial testimony does leaves the impression that he was not a man of particularly acute intelligence, had stood next to the president, this might have made no difference in preventing the assassination. Given the somewhat chaotic way in which people were herded on through and McKinley's commendably democratic desire to greet "50-a-minute," Foster might easily have let pass the innocent looking Czolgosz until it was too late.[59] Secret Service Chief Wilkie later claimed that "the admission [into the Music Hall] of a miscellaneous crowd carrying cameras, lunch boxes, souvenirs and bundles of every description" meant that "no human being could have forseen [sic] or averted the catastrophe that followed."[60] This was a highly self-serving conclusion, however, since it was certainly a major lapse that no detectives or Secret Service men stood along the right side of the aisle and to the left of McKinley and Milburn.

After the assassination, the actions of Foster and the other Secret Service men also appear unprofessional. All three, together with "six or more" others jumped on Czolgosz, leaving the president essentially unguarded and open to attack in the case of a second assassin. In 1881 Tsar Alexander II had escaped the assault of his first assailant only to succumb to the bomb of a second nihilist. In McKinley's case, Agent Ireland soon turned back to look at the president, observing that he was being led away by Cortelyou and Milburn, but did nothing himself to shield or assist him. Agent Foster, after helping to wrestle away the assassin's weapon, "hit him [Czolgosz] between the eyes when he stood up," knocking him down.[61] This purely emotional and unnecessary action, since Czolgosz had already been disarmed and was not resisting arrest, hardly seems consistent with a high standard of conduct.

Shortly after McKinley's assassination, presidential protection became regular, permanent, and better coordinated, rather than ad hoc and temporary. The precedent for Secret Service protection of the president and his family went back to 1894 although protection had only been intermittent and unauthorized by Congress. President Cleveland and his wife had requested more security due to a fear of anarchists, Colorado gamblers, cranks, and sympathizers of Coxey's Commonweal army of the unemployed who marched on Washington, DC, in May of that year. The crucial step took place in early October 1901 due to Cortelyou, who had continued in

---

[59] Trial transcript, 75–80; Fisher, *Stolen Glory*, 58.

[60] John E. Wilkie, memorandum on protection of the president, March 1910, in Charles Norton file, box 27, Franklin MacVeagh Papers, Manuscript Division, Library of Congress (hereafter cited as LC).

[61] Foster, trial transcript, 76; Ireland, Daily Report, September 6, 1901, RG 87, US Secret Service, box 144, file 161, NA.

his position as personal secretary to the president. Despite the assassination of three presidents in the previous thirty-seven years, Roosevelt had initially resisted increased protection. He was "fearless," impulsive, and had a "lifelong habit of moving about freely."[62] On the morning of October 4, however, the new president finally acknowledged the wisdom of his personal secretary's arguments about taking precautions and told him that he should go ahead and do whatever he thought best.[63]

On the evening of the very day that Roosevelt gave his consent, Cortelyou convened a meeting at the White House on presidential security. He invited the Secret Service, Richard Sylvester, the head of the Washington, DC, police, and the Post Office's chief inspector, and sought closer coordination between these three "protective bureaus" and the White House in order to safeguard the president's life. At the meeting, W. H. Moran, chief clerk of the Secret Service, complained that his agency had been "badly hampered...for years since its business [had] been of large volume, by the failure of Congress to provide sufficient men and means for their expenses."[64] As a result of the gathering, besides asking for larger Congressional appropriations for both the Secret Service and the Washington police, it was decided that two Secret Service agents should be on duty at all times at the president's office (previously he had had only one), and more would be available when the president went on trips. Sylvester would continue to provide police guards for the White House grounds and entrances and mounted guards to accompany Roosevelt everywhere he went in the capital. Postal inspectors were to work with the Secret Service to develop plans for presidential visits outside of Washington. The post office would also provide information regarding threatening letters sent to the White House for investigation by the Secret Service and the DC police. This meeting also revealed that the Washington police and the Secret Service had alphabetical lists of many anarchists and criminals throughout the country, located by city. The State Department was also involved in these security efforts and promised to help in locating "anarchists and people of similar classes."[65]

While no legislation allowed for the Secret Service to investigate suspected anarchists or other persons and to compile records on them, it did so anyway. Lists and booklets containing the names of hundreds of

---

[62] Don Wilkie and Mark Lee Luther, *American Secret Service Agent* (New York; Frederick A. Stokes, 1934): 143.

[63] Cortelyou and B. F. Barnes, memorandum on presidential security, October 4, 1901, 6, 11–12, reel 453, Theodore Roosevelt Papers, LC.

[64] Ibid.

[65] Fisher, *Stolen Glory*, 142–43; Richard B. Sherman, "Presidential Protection during the Progressive Era: The Aftermath of the McKinley Assassination," *The Historian*, 46:1 (1983): 3, 13–14; Kaiser, "Origins of Secret Service Protection," 113.

suspected anarchists can be found in the archives of the Secret Service, apparently from 1901–1902, but they are very primitive records, especially when compared to those compiled by the Europeans. They merely give the name of the anarchist and the town where he lived; the addresses are mostly perfunctory. Sometimes there is a comment next to a name such as "very dangerous." But there is no biographical information or exact physical descriptions, let alone Bertillonage measurements or fingerprints. A few names of anarchist groups are also provided, e.g., "Debatter [sic] Club, Social Science, Liberator." An "Italian French" group is spoken of, although what exactly this refers to is unclear (most of the names listed are Italian). A few foreign cities are mentioned, but under Paris, for example, no anarchist is named.[66]

In the memorandum about presidential security drawn up at the October meeting, mention was also made that "the national police system of cooperation between cities which is coming into vogue greatly increases the possibility of a full and efficient record of these people [i.e., 'the criminal and anarchist classes']."[67] This was undoubtedly a reference to the International Association of Chiefs of Police (IACP), which, despite its name, was made up predominantly of American municipal police forces. The IACP had established a National Bureau of Identification to keep tabs primarily on common criminals, but also on anarchists. For many years the driving force behind both these organizations was Washington, DC, Police Chief Sylvester. Despite Sylvester's desire to make the IACP a great international organization, it never achieved that status, in part because few European police forces joined it, and even more importantly, the rival New York City police force refused to join. The National Bureau of Identification (NBI) acquired "many thousands of photographs and Bertillon measurements of criminals, anarchists and suspects," but its effectiveness was hamstrung by a lack of funding. The federal government refused to give the NBI more than an occasional subsidy. It could therefore only afford to pay a superintendent and a secretary to carry out its myriad tasks. European governments were usually frustrated when inquiring about the whereabouts of suspected anarchists who had emigrated to or lived in the United States.[68]

While intelligence-gathering regarding dangerous anarchists improved somewhat in the United States after 1901 (although it continued to

---

[66] RG 87 5/46/35/5, NA.

[67] Cortelyou and Barnes, memorandum on presidential security, October 4, 1901, 11, Theodore Roosevelt Papers, LC.

[68] Sylvester to Francis B. Loomis, assistant secretary, Department of State, Washington, DC, April 26, 1903, cited in Jensen, "The United States," 29–30.

be of little use internationally until after the founding of the Bureau of Investigation in 1908), an important shift occurred regarding the professionalization of executive protection. It became a necessity of government rather than a personal choice – or whim – of the head of state. McKinley's bodyguard and security arrangements were very much the product of his personal desires. His chief bodyguard was an acquaintance from Ohio, not a long time Secret Service professional. Three times McKinley overruled Cortelyou and others when they advised him to cancel what they feared might be a dangerous public reception in Buffalo.[69] In regard to Roosevelt, Secret Service Chief Wilkie seconded Cortelyou's position. He pointed out to the peripatetic Roosevelt that he "owed it to the nation to cooperate with the Secret Service in its efforts to protect him."[70] Or, as he later put it, "perhaps when one becomes President he forfeits the right to expose himself to danger of any sort."[71] This was all in the context of Wilkie's efforts to depoliticize the Secret Service and raise its standards to the highest professional level. His son's biography of his father captures this new spirit. When Wilkie took office in 1898, "he found the service crippled by politics" since "members of Congress had packed it with their henchmen." Wilkie proceed to cleanse the organization, ousting "every man on whom rested the slightest suspicion of political affiliations." He then rebuilt it by choosing agents with "specific abilities" trained as "shadow men, linguists, banker types, business types ... Detective methods were installed and detective brains were secured."[72] This was the American version of "scientific policing" championed by the criminologists of Europe.

The belief of some congressmen that the Secret Service was too political, that it had failed to protect the president at Buffalo, or that strengthening it might somehow undermine state or local rights led to legislative proposals stipulating that the guardians of the president be appointed from the army. This in turn provoked fears of creating a "praetorian guard" more suitable for the monarchs of Europe than the leaders of a republic. In the end, Congress acquiesced in the Secret Service's assumption of executive protective duties because no other solution seemed preferable. It was only in 1906, however, that it became entirely legal, since only then the Congress officially authorized and funded the

[69] Leech, *Days of McKinley*, 584.
[70] Wilkie and Luther, *American Secret Service*, 143.
[71] Wilkie memorandum for Taft's personal secretary Charles Norton, January 1911, cited in Sherman, "Presidential Protection," 14.
[72] Wilkie and Luther, *American Secret Service*, 7. Despite the fact that the Secret Service became part of the Civil Service in 1894, which should have made it immune from political influence and appointees, complaints about this continued through 1901. Pinkerton, "Detective Surveillance," 609, 610.

Secret Service to protect the president in addition to its duties apprehending counterfeiters.[73]

Stimulated by its new duties, the size of the Secret Service greatly expanded (although the exact figures were kept a secret – and remain so until the present day – as was almost everything else that had to do with presidential protection). On May 1, 1893, twenty-five agents were employed for both presidential protection and anti-counterfeiting services but by 1909 the number had expanded to fifty-six agents in thirty-one offices.[74] It may have been even larger than this if one includes part-time employees (and contemporary newspaper articles suggest that it was larger).[75] The police detail of the District of Columbia metropolitan police force assigned to protecting the White House increased from three in 1895 to more than fifty by around 1905.[76] In 1910, the Justice Department (and therefore the newly formed Bureau of Investigation) was also authorized to protect the president.[77]

The changes that had taken place in the Secret Service in reaction to the murder of McKinley became very evident early in 1902, when the service had to protect Prince Henry, the kaiser's brother, during his extensive tour of the United States. According to the Italian ambassador, the American government held "lively apprehensions … about possible attentats [against the prince], especially in Chicago and New York."[78] Admiral Robley Dunglison Evans, who was involved in security arrangements, relates the following details about providing protection for the prince:

Chief Wilkie worked with energy and perfect system, and before many days had passed every anarchist of much importance was under observation. Each one

---

[73] President's Commission on the Assassination of President Kennedy, *Hearings*, vol. 25 (Washington, DC: US Government Printing office, 1964), exhibit no. 2550; Kaiser, "Origins of Secret Service Protection," 112–114; Sherman, "Presidential Protection," 6–13.

[74] The 1893 source is from an unidentified comment in Secret Service Chief William Hazen's file and the 1909 figure is from U.S. House of Representatives, Extracts from Hearings Before the Subcommittee of the House of Representatives' Committee on Appropriations, Relative to the Secret Service. I owe this information to a June 27, 2003, communication from Mike Sampson at the U.S. Secret Service archives. Sherman, "Presidential Protection," 15, speaks of fifty to sixty agents around the year 1908.

[75] "How The 'Secret Service' Does Its Work," *New York Times*, 27 December 1908, pt. 5, p. 6, estimated that each of the thirty-eight offices of the Secret Service, if one includes its Washington, D.C., headquarters, had four to five agents, which would lead to an exaggerated figure of 152 to 190 agents for the entire country.

[76] Sherman, "Presidential Protection," 13.

[77] Sherman, "Presidential Protection," 18; Kaiser, "Origins of Secret Service Protection," 118.

[78] Draft, Italian embassy, Washington, DC, to Prinetti, Rome, March 18, 1902. Draft, Mayor des Planches to Prinetti, Washington, DC, February 5, 1902. Rap.dip.USA 1848–1901, b. 205, IFO.

had a friend who observed him carefully; in some special cases these friends even went so far as to dine with the objectionable people and then accompany them to the theatre or some other place of amusement. In this way we very soon knew what the most prominent anarchists were doing, saying, and thinking. So complete was the system by which all this was done that Wilkie felt confident that he would know in advance if any mischief was contemplated [...]

The only case that really threatened to give serious trouble was that of a doctor in New York who had prepared and printed a most villainous attack on the Prince. The pamphlet containing this attack was a very innocent-looking document with a flattering notice of the Prince on the cover [...] Wilkie secured one of the advance copies, and the entire edition of 25,000 copies was burned before the ink was dry [...] Many of the more violent among the anarchists were locked up, and found habeas corpus proceedings so slow that they only regained their liberty when it was too late for them to do any harm [...] Chief Wilkie and his able assistants ... were constantly with [Prince Henry and his party].[79]

None of these precautions, some of which seem scarcely legal, had been undertaken before McKinley's fatal visit to Buffalo. If these measures, together with other procedures that soon became standard, such as not publishing the precise route of the president before his visits, carefully examining all persons meeting the president, and maintaining a wider clear space in front of the president, had been implemented when McKinley visited Buffalo, he would not have been assassinated.[80]

American anti-anarchist legislation

As was the case in Italy, the shock of the murder of the head of state caused the proposal of much anti-anarchist legislation, but resulted in the approval of few laws. Those that were passed accomplished relatively little, leading only to the expulsion of a handful of anarchists and the harassment of others. Laws debated during 1902–1903 to provide for the death penalty for persons who killed the president, those in line of succession to the presidency, ambassadors of foreign countries, and the sovereigns of foreign nations all failed to pass Congress.[81] The states of New York, New Jersey, and Wisconsin enacted anti-anarchist laws. In January 1903, the Italian Consul General in New York City described these state laws as "draconian," but dead letters. He pointed out several specific instances in which they could have been enforced, but were not. Since "these laws do not accord with the notion of unlimited liberty [*l'opinione di sconfinata libertà*] that prevails here among the masses, they were

---

[79] Robley Dunglison Evans, *An Admiral's Log* (New York and London: Appleton, 1910): 27–29. Don Wilkie verifies Evans's account. *American Secret Service*, 150.
[80] Fisher, *Stolen Glory*, 163–168; Robert Donovan, *The Assassins*, 116–121.
[81] Fine, "Anarchism," 790–793.

destined to remain a dead letter and such they have in fact remained."[82] The consul general somewhat underestimated their impact since they did lead to the harassment of prominent anarchists such as Emma Goldman. In New York the new legislation was used to put pressure on landlords to deny her permission to rent halls for public speeches and, in January 1907, to arrest her and Alexander Berkman; they were soon released, however, and all charges dropped. In general these state laws exercised relatively little impact until after World War I.[83]

The only anti-anarchist measure that Congress ended up passing, at the request of Theodore Roosevelt, the new president, was in March 1903 when it amended the immigration law in order to exclude anarchists from entering the United States. This law would have done nothing to prevent McKinley's assassination since Czolgosz had been born in Detroit and his parents were not anarchists.[84] It was based on the widespread assumption that most anarchists were foreigners. The US legislation banned "anarchists, or persons who believe in or advocate the overthrow by force or violence of all governments, or of all forms of law, or the assassination of public officials."[85] Section 38 of the law clarified that assassins of foreign officials, as well as American, would be excluded from entering the country. By in this way defining anarchists in very broad terms, rather than, as with the 1892 definition of the Institute of International Law, more narrowly, since according to the latter anarchists only included those culpable of "criminal" attack against "the bases of *all social* organization," or, as in the definition adopted by the Rome conference of 1898, of those aiming at the "violent" destruction of "*all social* organization," the American definition opened the way for punishing non-anarchists. This indeed turned out to be a result of the law, since in 1919 it was used to expel a left-wing member of the socialist party.

Another result of the new immigration law was the exclusion from the United States of prominent European anarchists such as Kropotkin

[82] Copy Consul General Branchi, New York City, to interior minister, Rome, January 7, 1903; Branchi to Italian ambassador, Washington, DC, March 2, 1903. Rap.dip.USA 1901–1909, b. 119, IFM.

[83] Fine, "Anarchism," 793–794. Falk, in Goldman, *A Documentary History*, 2:16. "New York's law lay essentially dormant until it was used against the Communist Party in 1919." Robert J. Goldstein, "The Anarchist Scare of 1908: A Sign of Tensions in the Progressive Era," *American Studies* 15 (1974): 68.

[84] Not Alpena (cf. Jensen, "The United States," 17), relying on James Clarke, *American Assassins* (Princeton University Press, 1982): 42, where the family moved later and which is 200 miles north of Detroit. Czolgosz's sister Victoria told L. Vernon Briggs that Czolgosz was born in Detroit and Briggs visited his birthplace there at 141 Benton Street. Briggs, *The Manner of Man That Kills*, 280–281, 286.

[85] *United States Statutes at Large*, December 1901 to March 1903, vol. 32, (sec. 2) 1214, (sec. 38) 1221.

and Malatesta (and public lectures by famous, eloquent speakers was an important means of spreading anarchist thought). In 1904, due to this law and after a long court battle that went all the way to the Supreme Court, where Clarence Darrow acted for the defense, the well-known British anarchist John Turner was expelled.[86] Since Turner did not advocate violence, his case earned the anarchists much sympathy from Americans who believed in the right of free speech. Goldman and others believed that both the Turner case and the authorities' efforts to harass her ultimately redounded to the benefit of the anarchist cause by providing much, and often favorable, publicity.[87] Until the Red Scare of 1919, however, the law led to the exclusion or expulsion of only about fifty people.[88] Preston, Sherman, and other scholars have pointed out that in 1903 "congress wrote into American immigration law the first test of political opinion" ever enacted in American history.[89] It reflected the same kind of thinking as that of the more conservative European powers at the Rome conference, i.e., that anarchism was non-political.

Conclusion

One historian has cited the "immense significance" of the American federal and state anti-anarchist laws of 1902–1903, since they opened the way for unprecedented government, particularly federal government, involvement in political repression (unprecedented at least since the infamous Alien and Sedition Act of 1798).[90] But their impact on anarchist terrorism – if any – was short-lived, since it flared up in 1908 and again between 1914 and 1920. The laws probably backfired by disproportionately affecting moderate anarchists, such as Goldman, and excluding people like Turner, who advocated participation in labor-organizing, not violence. In France and Italy, such participation would prove to be the single more important outlet for anarchist energies after 1900, energies that otherwise might have been channeled into terrorism and less peaceful means of trying to change society.

As had also been the case with the Rome accords of 1898, new police measures proved more effective than legislative ones. American policies to provide for the safety of the president succeeded in expanding, institutionalizing, and professionalizing this protective service. Although

---

[86] Fine, "Anarchism," 796–798.
[87] Falk, "Raising Her Voices," in Goldman, *A Documentary History*, 2:9, 10, 18–19, 23.
[88] Fine, "Anarchism," 793. For the statistics of exclusion and expulsion, William Preston, *Aliens and Dissenters: Federal Suppression of Radicals, 1903–1933* (Cambridge, MA: Harvard University Press): 33.
[89] Sherman, "Presidential Protection," 12; Preston, 32.
[90] Goldstein, "Anarchist Scare," 68.

less extensive, they were comparable to those already in use in Europe and served to safeguard him for more than sixty years. While on occasion Wilkie's preventive tactics used to protect high-ranking dignitaries bent the law and can be cited as another example of the way in which terrorism causes governments to act illegally, there is no evidence that the Secret Service resorted to *agents provocateurs* as a means of fighting anarchist assassins and bomb-throwers.

8 The St. Petersburg Protocol, 1901–1904

In the same speech to Congress of December 3, 1901, in which Roosevelt had called for imposing restrictions on the immigration of anarchists, he had also called for international cooperation against them. Although this was sweet music to the ears of several of the more conservative European governments, who now thought that at last there was an opportunity to enact wide-ranging anti-anarchist measures on a global scale, both legislatively and in terms of police cooperation, Roosevelt's rhetoric proved much bolder than his actions. Why the United States refused to join a new international anti-anarchist league deserves analysis. Even more important is understanding how such a league came into being in 1904, encompassing about two-thirds of the European states, although, significantly, without the participation of the three Great Powers of Western Europe (Britain, France, and Italy). Germany now emerged from its position behind the scenes and took a leading public role in this attempt to create an international anti-anarchist league.

On December 3, 1901, in his first message to Congress as president, Roosevelt had violently condemned the anarchists as "depraved" and as "not merely the enemy of system and of progress, but the deadly foe of liberty. If ever anarchy is triumphant, its triumph will last but one red moment, to be succeeded for ages by the gloomy night of despotism." Given this catastrophic possibility, Roosevelt called for an international anti-anarchist agreement:

Anarchy is a crime against the whole human race; and all mankind should band against the anarchist. His crime should be made an offense against the law of nations, like piracy and that form of manstealing known as the slave trade; for it is of far blacker infamy than either. It should be so declared by treaties among all civilized powers. Such treaties would give to the Federal Government the power of dealing with the crime.[1]

---

[1] Congress, Senate, President Roosevelt's Message to the Senate and House of Representatives, 57th Congr., 1st sess., Congressional Record (December 3, 1901), vol. XXXV, 82.

Russia and Germany responded eagerly to Roosevelt's clarion call for "all mankind" to "band against the anarchist" since this fit in perfectly with the diplomatic efforts they had been making since the assassination of Umberto to revive and expand the resolutions of the 1898 Rome conference.

Germany now assumed the leading role, while working closely with the Russian government. German leadership in the anti-anarchist crusade may seem quixotic, since few native anarchists remained in Germany.[2] In 1900 one German newspaper even claimed there were none.[3] While this was inaccurate, a 1905 police report gave relatively low figures: a mere 170 anarchists residing in Berlin and 1,500 throughout Germany.[4] Moreover, during the kaiser's reign no clearly identifiable anarchist attempt took place against his life, although a few *may* have been nipped in the bud or barely avoided, such as the murky plot foiled in August 1895 when he visited Lowther Castle in England.[5] Claims by a popular biographer that Hungarian gypsies had twice predicted Wilhelm's death by the hand of an assassin and that "a subject of daily thought and preoccupation" was "the bullet from the anarchist's revolver that may put an end to his existence" appear to be unsubstantiated sensationalism.[6] Moreover, no anarchist bombs exploded in Germany after 1895, unless a handful of mysterious explosions were due to the anarchists. In 1913 a single, presumably anarchist *attentat* occurred in Munich killing two people.[7]

One can explain Germany's anti-anarchist lead, first of all, by noting the kaiser's and his government's genuine fears for his life, even if most later proved to be unfounded. In March 1901 Dietrich Weiland, a workman, threw a piece of iron at the kaiser, causing a deep wound under the right eye, but Weiland was deranged and not an anarchist. This attack, as well as an earlier one by a crazy, ax-wielding woman, frayed Wilhelm's nerves and led to doubts about the German population's sense of respect for authority.[8] The German media further stoked the fears of Wilhelm and his government with warnings such as that of the *Die Post* in 1902

---

[2] If discovered, foreign anarchists were immediately expelled.

[3] *Deutsche Tagezeitung*, August 30, 1900.

[4] Berlin Police President Borries to interior minister, Berlin, May 20, 1905. CA. 1282.05. Reichskanzlei, 755/4. GCSAP.

[5] Röhl, *Wilhelm II: The Kaiser's Personal Monarchy*, 501, 776.

[6] Anonymous [Margaret Cunliffe-Owen], *The Private Life of Two Emperors. William II. of Germany and Francis-Joseph of Austria* (London: Eveleigh Nash, 1904): 6–7.

[7] See the list of German bombings and assassinations compiled in Wagner, *Politischer Terrorismus*, 14–16. On May 13, 1913, Johannes Strasser, allegedly an anarchist, shot Major von Lewinski, the Prussian military attaché, and a policeman. *The Times* (London), May 15, 1913. Wagner's dating of this event is incorrect.

[8] John C. G. Röhl, *Wilhelm II. Der Weg in den Abgrund 1900–1941* (Munich: C. H. Beck, 2009): 167–173.

of "the anarchist danger, which is becoming more and more noticeably threatening."[9] Wilhelm took these warnings to heart since he was an avid newspaper reader, even of obscure newspapers, and had developed a fanatical hatred of the anarchists.[10] Finally, Germany desired to exploit anti-anarchism to forge a link with Russia that would weaken the latter's alliance with France.[11]

On the topic of combating and preventing assassination attempts and violent revolutionary activity, the tsar was happy to cooperate with his German neighbor since these issues were of even more vital concern to the Russian Empire. The Russian police had been able to destroy the People's Will within a few years after the assassination of Alexander II in 1881. For almost twenty years most terrorist activity had ceased in Russia. At the end of the 1890s, however, a new era of social upheaval began with labor unrest, strike activity, and student disorders; soon after came the founding of the Socialist Revolutionary Party. Following in the footsteps of the populists, the Socialist Revolutionaries promoted the use of political terrorism. Beginning in February 1901 terrorism once again became a prominent feature of Russian life with the assassination of Education Minister N. P. Bogolepov by a disgruntled student who later became a Socialist Revolutionary terrorist. Assassinations of other high-ranking tsarist officials ensued, almost all engineered by members of the SR party. Yet the tsarist government frequently failed to make a distinction between the Socialist Revolutionaries and the anarchists. In August 1902 the tsar told the German ambassador that: "There is no doubt, that an anarchist crime is present" in the case of the *attentat* on Prince Obolenski, Governor of Kharkov, on July 29.[12] Later it turned out that Grigori Gershuni, the head of the SR Combat Organization, had personally coached a woodworker in carrying out the attempted assassination; any anarchist involvement was completely chimerical.[13] Of course, it was exactly because of this failure to distinguish between revolutionary socialists and anarchists that the British and others hesitated to join in an anti-anarchist crusade.

---

[9] *Die Post*, April 24, 1902. After Umberto and McKinley's assassinations, the newspapers repeatedly asked "who will be next?"

[10] For example, Wilhelm's concern about an inaccurate article on the "Anarchist Movement" in the *Wedekindschen Korrespondenz*, May 16, 1905. Verbal note, Reich Chancellor to Interior minister, May 18, 1905. Reichskanzlei, 755/4. GCSAP.

[11] Lerman, *Chancellor as Courtier*, 84, speaks of Wilhelm's "anxiety about anarchists and assassins," which, "throughout 1904...intensified his nervousness about Social Democracy."

[12] Alvensleben, St. Petersburg, to Foreign Office, Berlin, August 13, 1902. Eur. Gen. 91, GFO.

[13] Geifman, *Thou Shalt Kill*, 50.

Czolgosz's assault on President McKinley profoundly shocked both the tsar and the German kaiser. The kaiser ordered that reports of McKinley's condition be wired to him hourly.[14] After the president's death, Wilhelm personally ordered not only that the flags of his fleet be lowered to half-mast, but also that the American colors be flown.[15] When he heard the painful news, Tsar Nicholas II, on his way to make important diplomatic visits to both Germany and France, was still in Denmark, visiting his grandparents, the Danish king and queen.[16] Edward VII and Alexandra, Edward's Danish-born queen, soon joined the other monarchs; King George of Greece, himself of Danish descent, was also in Denmark. Count Lamzdorf (or Lamsdorff), the Russian foreign minister, later informed the Germans that Queen Alexandra had said to him in Copenhagen: "it is time to act energetically against the anarchists."[17]

When on September 12, Nicholas, together with his foreign minister, arrived on his yacht *Standart* off the coast of Danzig and met the kaiser and Chancellor Bülow, they apparently spoke of the recent startling assassination attempt, although the precise content of their discussions has never been revealed. Before the Russian tsar left Danzig on September 13, after reviewing the German fleet, news that, following a few days of apparent recovery, McKinley's health was worsening would have reached Europe and formed a topic for imperial conversation. The newspapers reported that Wilhelm met for "a considerable time" with Count Lamzdorf, the phenomenally hard-working, intelligent, but reclusive and insecure Russian foreign minister. Lamzdorf's friend, Count Sergei Witte, described him as "too sensitive," effeminate in appearance, yet "very firm at critical moments and in difficult times."[18] The next day, the kaiser told the burgomaster of Danzig that he had "just come from a highly important meeting with my friend the Emperor of Russia. Our meeting has passed off to the complete satisfaction both of his Majesty and of myself." According to the London *Times*: "In well-informed quarters here [in Berlin] great pleasure is expressed at the manner in which the visit has passed off."[19] It seems highly likely that among the causes of the kaiser's satisfaction was an informal anti-anarchist agreement

[14] *New York Times*, September 9, 1901, 2.
[15] Olcott, *William McKinley*, 2:331; *The Times* (London), September 16, 1901.
[16] *New York Times*, September 7, 1901.
[17] Tel. Pückler, St. Petersburg, September 28, 1901 to chargé des affaires, Berlin. Eur. Gen. 91, reel 109, GFO.
[18] Dominic Lieven, *Russia's Rulers Under The Old Regime* (New Haven: Yale University Press, 1989): 166–167. In Bülow, *Correspondance secrete*, 54.
[19] Bülow, *Memoirs*, 1:622–623; 666; *The Times* (London), September 14 and 16, 1901.

reached with the tsar.[20] The Russian foreign minister alluded to this in August 1902 when he told Bülow at a meeting in Reval, Estonia, that:

The continuation of the campaign against anarchism agreed to in Danzig a year ago on the basis of the order of the two emperors was urgently needed.[21]

Whatever the two emperors and their advisers spoke about, Wilhelm's reaction to reports of McKinley's impending death was immediate and dramatic. By 6 p.m. eastern standard time on Friday, September 13, bulletins had gone out announcing that McKinley was dying (he passed away in the early hours of September 14).[22] Already at 4:20 a.m. on September 14, following the kaiser's orders after a "discussion [*Entrevue*]" in Danzig, Chancellor Bülow was telegraphing the German Foreign Office that:

His Majesty orders that the Russian government be asked if it is willing together with us to submit proposals to the Powers regarding joint, swift and effective measures against the anarchist danger, which has just again shown itself in such a frightening manner. His Majesty doubts whether all the Continental Powers will respond, but he hopes for America's agreement and he would if need be proceed even without England. I ask that you please draft for me this evening a pertinent telegram for St. Petersburg.[23]

By this time the tsar and his foreign minister had proceeded to Compiègne for an important meeting with Russia's French ally, but Prince Obolenski, Lamzdorf's representative at the Russian Foreign Office in St. Petersburg, responded enthusiastically. He told the Germans that he would "promptly submit" their proposal to the tsar, and that "this proposal agrees with the ideas of the Russian government all the more as last year's Russian memorandum [following the murder of King Umberto] forms a suitable basis for further agreements." Moreover it seemed to him "advisable…to make use of the present attitude in the United States, where a strong popular indignation prevails about the monstrous crime."[24] On

[20] Röhl notes the sudden improvement in German-Russian relations after the Danzig meeting, but he does not explain why this occurred. The improvement was all the more surprising since at the time the Kaiser managed to insult the Russian foreign minister. Röhl, *Wilhelm II. Der Weg in den Abgrund*, 104.

[21] Copy, Bülow to German diplomats and the Kaiser, completely secret, Reval, August 8, 1902. "In connection with the Danzig discussion [*An die Danziger Entrevue anknüpfend*], we suggested to the Russian government that they try, by means of joint German-Russian measures, to get the Powers to agree to a more effective international fight against anarchism." "Note regarding the Fight against Anarchism," probably by Bülow, dated Berlin, October 27, 1901, Eur. Gen. 91, GFO.

[22] Leech, *Days of McKinley*, 600.

[23] Tel., Bülow to Foreign Office, Kreuz, September 14, 1901. Eur. Gen. 91, GFO.

[24] Pückler, St. Petersburg, to Foreign Office, Berlin, September 16, 1901. Eur. Gen. 91, reel 109, GFO.

September 21, even before he had journeyed back to Russia, Nicholas let the Germans know that he "fully agree[d]" with their "proposals for joint steps for the suppression of anarchism."[25] On his return to St. Petersburg, Lamzdorf assured the German representative that, in regard to supporting the anti-anarchist proposals, "the Russian government will go through thick and thin '*nous ne nous arrêterons pas à mi-chemin* [we will not stop halfway].'" The Russian foreign minister feared, however, that "owing to the opposition of the ultra-constitutional states," the "summoning of a Conference" would lead to "nothing." What was needed was "not to pass resolutions, but to take and carry out practical measures." Pückler, the German chargé d'affaires, assured him that this was also the view of his government. "Regarding America," Lamzdorf thought, one must strike while "the fire is hot" (*das Eisen schmieden, solange es warm*). He also believed that, due to the anarchist *attentat* against Edward in Brussels in 1900, the British monarch probably shared the view recently expressed by Queen Alexandra that energetic measures should be taken against the anarchists.[26]

With Russian agreement secured, Bülow acted promptly to draw up a memorandum to be sent to all the German and Russian diplomatic representatives to the major European states and the US. Both Russia and Germany agreed that an exchange of views between governments, rather than the convening of a new conference, was preferable, since the Rome conference had passed impressive resolutions, but had carried out only a few of them. Since November 1900 Bülow had argued that administrative and police measures should take center stage in the "battle" (*Bekämpfung*) against anarchism. Therefore after noting that the rate of anarchist assassinations of heads of state was increasing at an alarming rate and that only a uniform and strict enforcement of measures carried out internationally could guarantee success against them and the anarchist movement, he put these administrative proposals at the forefront of his draft memorandum.[27] This was unlike the Russian memorandum of 1900, which had emphasized legislative proposals. Bülow's draft also called, "where possible," for each nation to strengthen anti-anarchist measures in its legal code. But at this point Bülow did not want to become bogged down in too much detail since that would only lead

[25] Pückler, St. Petersburg, to German Foreign Office, September 21, 1901, and Bülow, Klein Flottbek, to Kaiser, Rominten, September 23, 1901. Eur. Gen. 91, reel 109, GFO.
[26] Pückler, St. Petersburg, to German Foreign Office, 28 Sept. 1901, Eur. Gen. 91, reel 109, GFO.
[27] Copy, "*Angesichts der in immer kürzeren Fristen sich wiederholenden anarchistischen Verbrechen und Anschläge gegen die Staatsoberhäupter*," Bülow to Pückler, St. Petersburg, secret, October 1, 1901, Eur. Gen. 91, reel 109, GFO.

to "fruitless" and "wearisome discussions." "The main thing" was to use the present favorable atmosphere to obtain "the quickest possible agreement" for the "high points and essential features" of the memorandum, even from governments that might wish only "to participate in part."[28] Toward the end of October 1901 the tsar's government readily agreed to the German draft circular, asking only that two sentences be changed so as to request specifically that countries introduce into their legal codes a precise definition of an anarchist crime and measures against anarchist publications. Bülow quickly included these additions, although he thought his initial draft already implied them.[29]

The German-Russian anti-anarchist proposal was conveyed to the major European states at the end of November 1901 and eventually to all those countries that had participated in the Rome conference plus the United States.[30] On November 27 the Russian diplomatic representative Baron Grævenitz called on Foreign Secretary Lansdowne in London and read him the anti-anarchist memorandum. That same day German Ambassador Count Metternich visited Lansdowne, stating

that the Russian and German Governments intended to approach his Majesty's Government informally with a view to ascertaining whether we were prepared to join with them in a discussion of the measures which might be taken to counteract the designs of the Anarchist Societies which now infested so many communities.[31]

In early December the smaller European states were approached as well and on December 12 the German and Russian ambassadors handed the anti-anarchist memorandum to John Hay, the American secretary of state.

Bülow's desire to gain widespread agreement for anti-anarchist action before proceeding to the discussion of detailed measures was largely achieved, although Britain, Switzerland, and the United States were more reserved or non-committal. Furthermore most countries held considerable reservations about implementing new anti-anarchist laws and expulsion regulations. Every state, however, was at least willing to discuss the idea of improving purely police measures against the anarchists.

---

[28] Ibid., and "Note regarding Combatting Anarchism," Berlin, October 27, 1901, Eur. Gen. 91, bd. 2, reel 109, GFO.
[29] "Note regarding Combatting Anarchism," Berlin, October 27, 1901, Eur. Gen. 91, bd. 2, reel 109, GFO.
[30] A December 31, 1901 memo from the German Foreign Office to the interior undersecretary and the Reich justice ministry makes an explicit connection with the 1898 Conference. Interior ministry, bd. 7. 33/13688, GCSAP.
[31] Landsdowne to C. Hardinge, and Lansdowne to Buchanan, FO, November 27, 1901, FO 881/7711, PRO.

The Russo-German proposal would probably have received a more enthusiastic response from every country if it had closely followed upon the death of McKinley. Although on September 23 the tsar had fully approved Germany's suggested diplomatic initiative, it took more than two months for the two countries to draw up and deliver to the Great Powers a simple, one-page memorandum. The shock and outrage over McKinley's assassination had subsided considerably by the end of November following the trial and execution of the assassin and the determination that Czolgosz's act had not been part of a larger conspiracy. Russia seems to have been dragging its feet. Since neither the shy and uncertain tsar nor his reclusive foreign minister were forceful leaders, Russian foreign policy lacked strong and purposeful direction. In a marginal note on a January 30, 1902, message from the German ambassador in St. Petersburg regarding Nicholas's recent expression of enthusiasm for the anti-anarchist agreement, a German official, presumably the kaiser or Chancellor Bülow, complained that "in October" the tsar "expounded to me with verve and energy, [but] since that time I have heard nothing more about it [i.e., the joint anti-anarchist action]."[32] Working against the success of the agreement was also the fact that outside Russia, and with the one exception of the failed assault on King Leopold II in December 1902, no *attentats* or terrorist bombings, anarchist or otherwise – at least that received much publicity – occurred between the end of 1901 and 1903 in Europe or the Americas (or perhaps in the entire world).

Germany's participation was also somewhat uncertain, since in public it often seemed to want to let Russia take the lead, e.g., it was the Russian, not the German, ambassador who delivered the initial anti-anarchist note to many of the Great Powers, although Germany immediately backed up Russian efforts. The Italian ambassador to Berlin even received the false impression that Russia was the driving force behind this initiative, with Germany simply "associating itself with it" and was not "nurtur[ing] ... great faith in reaching an effective result."[33]

The ever-manic kaiser, fierce in his enthusiasms, was certainly avid to crush the anarchist viper. Mild comments about Czolgosz and McKinley printed in *Neues Leben* (Berlin), the only anarchist journal still published in Germany, led to the confiscation of all its copies and the arrest and four month imprisonment of its editor, "Herr Maurer."[34] The German

[32] Alvensleben, St. Petersburg, to Bülow, Berlin, January 30, 1902. The Kaiser's marginal note on Pückler's October 21, 1901 dispatch from St. Petersburg also indicates imperial impatience with Russian slowness: "how far along are they with the completed proposals?!", he asks. Eur. Gen. 91, reel 109, GFO.

[33] Lanza, Berlin, to Prinetti, Rome, December 8, 1901, *DDI*, ser. 3, vol. 5, 628.

[34] *The Times* (London), September 24, 1901, 3; *New York Times*, October 18, 1901, 9.

interior minister tried to ban all public anarchist meetings, but the courts blocked this.[35]

While these steps were an overreaction, evidence exists of anarchist assassination plots against Wilhelm that may have posed concrete threats. While the kaiser was relatively safe inside Germany, he was a compulsive traveler and his frequent trips outside the country greatly increased the danger of assassination. If the memoirs of one of his principal bodyguards is to be believed, Russian anarchists were barely prevented from attempting Wilhelm's life during Queen Victoria's funeral procession in February 1901; in April reports surfaced of another, apparently serious, anarchist plot against the kaiser originating in Buenos Aires, with the alleged collaboration of the "nest of conspirators in Paterson, N.J.").[36] A few years later in 1904, when the emperor had wanted to land at Bari, in southern Italy, in order to visit the ruins of churches from the Hohenstaufen period, his venture had to be cancelled because of a feared assassination attempt. The Italian authorities subsequently arrested a "band" of fourteen Italian, French, and Greek anarchists.[37] A Russian historian reports that "a number of Russian anarchist units and isolated anarchists abroad" contemplated the assassination of the kaiser in 1903, 1906, and 1907.[38] When Wilhelm made his famous landing at Tangier in March 1905, the Germans felt compelled to pay the numerous Spanish anarchists residing there substantial sums to guard the kaiser so as to prevent them from assassinating him.[39] This unorthodox approach toward preventing anarchist violence appears to have been unique (although more recently General Petraeus implemented a comparable counterterrorist strategy in Iraq).

Germany also had an interest in pursuing an international anti-anarchist policy as a means of fostering its relationship with Russia. In a secret dispatch of October 1901, the German chargè d'affaires in St. Petersburg wrote that:

In the interest of German-Russian relations it may have been an auspicious [günstige] stroke that just in those days, during which the Tsar's trip invited so many comparisons between Danzig and Compiègne, the attention of the [Russian] regime was directed again to the anarchist danger. The battle against the powers

[35] Interior Minister Bethmann Hollweg to Reichschancellor,
[36] Steinhauer, *Steinhauer*, 310–319; "German Police Fear Plot to Kill Kaiser," *New York Times*, April 23, 1901.
[37] Lascelles, Berlin, to Lansdowne, London, May 18, 1904. *British Documents on Foreign Affairs*, series F, vol. 19, 175.
[38] Geifman, *Thou Shalt Kill*, 36.
[39] Röhl, *Wilhelm II: Der Weg in den Abgrund 1900–1941*, 381. Richard von Külmann, *Erinnerungen* (Heidelberg: Lambert Schneider, 1948), 226–227. Several European countries feared that, because of Morocco's weak central authority, Tangier was becoming a refuge for anarchists and "a center of international anarchist propaganda." Aide-memoire, German ambassador, to Italian foreign ministry, Rome, October 1900. PI, b. 34, IFM.

of revolution is surely the sphere in which the Russian regime again finds it easiest to connect to the Central powers and in the first rank to Germany.[40]

Britain and the Russo-German proposals

Britain's response to the Russo-German *démarche* was of great importance not only because of the large number of foreign anarchists in London, but also because other countries once again looked to Britain for guidance and leadership. Prior to giving their own responses, Switzerland, Greece, and Italy all asked Britain how it would reply to the Russo-German proposal.[41] Lord Lansdowne, who in October 1900 had succeeded the aging Lord Salisbury as foreign secretary, told the Austrian ambassador that the "the question is very ticklish, since England at present had little to complain of the anarchist movement." The many anarchists residing in Britain had behaved "very quietly" until now and did not wish to forfeit their place of asylum. Count Deym reproached the foreign secretary for taking such an "egotistical" viewpoint, since these same anarchists who found refuge in Britain went to other countries to carry out criminal *attentats*. Lansdowne recognized the justice in the ambassador's remarks, and held that it was desirable to take action against those who instigated others to carry out crimes, either by words or deeds. On the other hand English public opinion was against expelling all anarchists given the difficulty of specifying exactly who should be viewed as an anarchist.[42]

After Lansdowne heard from the Home Office and the head of the Criminal Investigation Department, he responded formally to the Russians and the Germans in a "very confidential" dispatch dated February 4, 1902.[43] The British position remained essentially the same as in 1898 at the time of the Rome conference, despite the numerous assassinations and attempted assassinations that had taken place since then. Lansdowne, renowned for his aristocratic good manners, "possibly the greatest gentleman of his day," clothed his reply in the friendliest language.[44] He stressed that Britain was "sincerely desirous of cooperating

---

[40] Pückler, St. Petersburg, to Bülow, October 21, 1901. Eur. Gen. 91, GFO.

[41] Foreign Office memo, November 26, 1901; Sanderson, memorandum, February 12, 1902. FO83/1970, PRO.

[42] Deym, London, to Goluchowski, Vienna, secret, December 20, 1901. Adm. Reg. F52/9, HHStA.

[43] Lansdowne, London, to Sir C. Scott, St. Petersburg, February 4, 1902. FO412/68, PRO. The same dispatch, but addressed to the British ambassador in Berlin, can be found in *BDIL*, 6:72–75.

[44] The description of Lansdowne is that of his brother-in-law, Lord Ernest Hamilton. Barbara Tuchman, *The Proud Tower: A Portrait of the World Before the War: 1890–1914* (New York City: Bantam Books, 1972): 43.

with other Powers...for the purpose of preventing such acts [anarchist crimes], and checking the propagation of incitements to these atrocities." But, just as the British representatives had previously explained at the Rome conference, British law and practice limited what could be done. No law allowed for the expulsion of persons back to their homes or to any other country, nor could amendments be made, with any chance of parliamentary success, to the press laws regarding advocating and inciting to crime.[45] In his dispatch, Lansdowne asserted that British measures for anarchist surveillance "work well," but in a note meant only for the Foreign Office, Undersecretary of State Sanderson pointed out that "There is no legal provision for surveillance."[46] CID Chief E. R. Henry, asked to comment on the Russo-German proposal, advocated "more co-operation, within well-defined limits, between the police forces of the several [European] States." But Henry also pointed out that, although the "sustained observation" of a "number of suspects" was absolutely necessary, it was "not sanctioned by express provision of the laws but by usage only, and by the general acquiescence in it of the community."[47] American Secret Service Chief Wilkie would have understood Henry's position entirely, given that neither Secret Service protection for the president nor anarchist surveillance were sanctioned by US law, although both were carried out in practice.

In 1902, as it had in 1898, Britain also promised to amend its 1883 law on the criminal possession of explosives, including making crimes committed with explosives grounds for extradition, and "to define 'political' offences in such a manner as to prevent assassination or attempts or conspiracies to assassinate being...regarded as a political offence." But Britain could give no assurance that these laws could be passed "in the near future." Privately Lansdowne seemed embarrassed by this failure to keep the earlier promise.[48]

According to Lansdowne, Britain could be more helpful in the surveillance of anarchists if the police forces of the continent provided more and speedier information, especially since, according to the police's anarchist register, 97 percent of the anarchists in Britain came from

---

[45] Not that Britain was totally disarmed in this regard. Laws passed in 1860–1861 penalized those who conspired or encouraged other people to murder a person, whether "within the Queen's Dominions or not." This legislation, together with the common law on libel regarding the justification of assassination, was used successfully to convict and imprison Johann Most and others associated with publishing articles in *Freiheit* applauding the assassination of Alexander II and British officials in Ireland. Porter, *"Freiheit."*

[46] T. H. Sanderson, memorandum, December 6, 1901, FO83/1970, PRO.

[47] E. R. Henry, memorandum, January 7, 1902, inclosure 2 in no. 2, FO412/68, PRO.

[48] Lansdowne's handwritten note in red ink appended to Sanderson's memo, December 6, 1901, FO83/1970, PRO.

abroad. If the continental states only lived up to the Rome conference's injunction "invariably" to deport anarchists back to their countries of origin, Britain's anarchist problems would largely be resolved. Lansdowne, relying on the report of CID Chief Henry, complained that Britain never received notices of the impending arrivals of anarchists expelled from other countries. Furthermore, the British police "more than once had to complain of wholesale deportation of foreign anarchists to British ports."[49] Lists of expellees were sent by certain countries (but not by Germany, Spain, Russia, and Italy[?]), but irregularly and after the fact.[50] If information and photos regarding dangerous expelled persons with "revolutionary or violent opinions" were supplied, London would be prepared to pass on this information to countries where the expelled person subsequently traveled. In any case, "in the event of credible information being obtained of a plot" or some other anarchist crime to be committed abroad "immediate information" would be "forwarded to the police of that country." For "obvious and practical reasons" this information sharing "should be made as confidentially and with as little outward appearance of combination as possible."

In short, Britain wanted a few of the Rome conference's resolutions enforced, but not the majority. Moreover, it was able, or at least willing, to do relatively little in return and, for the most part, that had to be carried out in the greatest secrecy. It may be asked whether Britain could not have done more at this time and, for example, have passed legislation authorizing expulsion. But in the opinion of the country's rulers this measure was politically impossible, since they still held fast to many of Britain's bedrock mid-Victorian liberal values, including the right of unrestricted asylum for refugees.[51]

France, Italy, and the United States

France, like Britain, wanted to avoid participation in an international police system and felt disinclined to pass new anti-anarchist laws.[52] This was not because of its liberalism, but because its anti-anarchist legislation was already "in advance of various other states," as was its "application of police measures."[53] Indeed the French legislation of 1893 and 1894 had

---

[49] E. R. Henry, Memorandum, January 7, 1902, inclosure 2 in no. 2, FO412/68, PRO.

[50] Police Commissioner Bradford later added Italy to the list of those countries, along with France and Belgium, that provided the names of expelled anarchists, although only after the fact. Bradford memo, April 29, 1902, inclosure in no. 10, FO412/68, PRO.

[51] Porter, *Vigilant State*, 112, 115.

[52] Copy, Austrian Ambassador Wolkenstein, Paris, to Austrian foreign ministry, Vienna, November 29, 1901. IB 1901/GZ36, K.431, HHStA.

[53] Tornielli, Paris, to Prinetti, Rome, December 12, 1901, Ser. P, b. 47, IFM.

served as a *"fil conducteur"* at the Rome conference, as the formal French
reply to Germany at the end of December 1901 explained. Moreover, "foreign [police] administrations, in conformity with the resolutions adopted
at Rome, are regularly informed of all they are interested in knowing on
the subject of the anarchist movement." Although France was already coping well with the anarchists, it was still willing to authorize the director
of the *Sûreté General* to negotiate with other police authorities regarding
useful administrative changes to facilitate everyday practice.[54] These gestures and promises aside, in its response to the Russo-German proposals,
France once again seemed to be following its traditional police strategy of
"défense du territoire," eschewing international entanglements and focusing
on the policing of its own territory in a self-centered and opportunistic
fashion.[55] A few months later, Paris reiterated its general agreement with
the proposed administrative propositions, but refused any idea of expelling
anarchists back to their homelands, unless this was expressly provided for
in extradition treaties.[56]

Initially Italy was more favorable to the proposal of its ally in the Triple
Alliance. Foreign Minister Prinetti informed the German ambassador
that, "appreciating the high value of the considerations that inspire the
initiative of the cabinets of Berlin and St. Petersburg," Italy was ready
"in principle, to take part with all the interested powers in an *entente*
aimed at a better social defense against anarchist crime." Rome was
particularly in agreement with the call for "the creation of bureaus in
each country for centralizing information [on the anarchists]."[57] But,
in the words of the Italian ambassador in Berlin a few days later, Italy
also doubted that it would be possible "to modify the dispositions of our
penal code."[58]

Both Portugal and Spain willingly accepted the anti-anarchist initiative. Portugal, poverty-stricken and ruled by an authoritarian, monarchical government and a factious, but largely submissive, parliament, already
possessed extremely harsh anti-anarchist legislation passed in 1896.
These were employed against not only anarchists, but also socialists.[59] In
a report to Berlin, German Minister Tattenbach pointed out that this law

---

[54] Copy, French reply, December 20, 1901, forwarded by Radolin, Paris, to Bülow, Berlin,
December 27, 1901. Pol.An. Gesandtschaft Bern, Anarchistisches, bd. 3, GFM.
[55] Liang, *Modern Police*, 46.
[56] C. Radolin, Paris, to Bülow, Berlin, June 20, 1902. Pol.An, Gesandtschaft Bern,
Anarchistisches, bd. 4, GFM.
[57] Prinetti, Rome, to German ambassador, confidential, December 2, 1901. IFM, Ser. P,
b. 47.
[58] Lanza, Berlin, to Foreign Minister Prinetti, Rome, December 6, 1901. Prinetti, Rome,
to Lanza, Berlin, December 7, 1901. DDI, ser. 3:5, 624–625.
[59] Merten, *Anarchismus*, 50.

made it "easy" to sentence "persons who admit to spreading anarchist teachings, and the sentence is always deportation" to Portuguese colonies in "Africa or on the island of Timor." Foreign anarchists were also treated harshly. They were held "in prison with little food and even less light." At the least hint from their native countries, the Portuguese government was ready to deport these anarchists back to their homelands. As for anarchist surveillance, the German minister noted that between Spain and Portugal a certain surveillance procedure had developed in which the Spanish government sent descriptions and photographs of anarchists to the Spanish consul in Lisbon, who gave the local Portuguese police any information it desired. Given this background, Tattenbach thought Portugal agreeable to any German-Russian anti-anarchist proposal.[60]

Portugal's ruthless anti-anarchist policies hardly served it in the long run, since they fueled political opposition that called for more liberty and greater social justice, and increasingly looked to violent stratagems for political solutions. On February 1, 1908, King Carlos I and the Prince Royal Luís Filipe were brutally assassinated in Lisbon. While the identity of those behind this deed remains unknown, it seems that, despite the allegations of some contemporary writers and authorities, the culprits were revolutionary republicans, rather than anarchists. Radical republicans finally overthrew the monarchy and seized control of the country in 1910.[61]

Like Portugal, the Balkan countries were very willing to join the anti-anarchist fight. The Serbian interior minister told the German chargé d'affaires, however, that it would be inopportune to take any legislative measures, since they would be incomprehensible to the populace, given that there were "no anarchists in our country." Belgrade, however, would assist in all measures for the surveillance of anarchists and the expulsion or extradition of foreign anarchists who came into Serbia. It would join

[60] Copy, Tattenbach, Lisbon, to Bülow, December 17, 1901. Pol.An. Gesandtschaft Bern, Anarchistisches, vol. 3, GFO. Close Portuguese-Spanish anti-anarchist cooperation went back to the early 1890s. The Portuguese monarchs visited Spain in the fall 1892 to concert Iberian anti-anarchist policy. González Calleja, *La razón de la fuerza*, 270n. In 1907, the Spanish minister noted the continuing severity of Portuguese policies. The "political criminals," who were not anarchists, but had planted a bomb intended for the king and which exploded in Lisbon on November 18, 1907, were to be shipped to Timor without any judicial procedure whatsoever. Spanish Legation, Lisbon, to foreign minister, Madrid, November 19, 1907. Allendesalazar archive, B-16, SFM.

[61] Stanley Payne, *A History of Spain and Portugal* (Madison: University of Wisconsin Press, 1973), 2:552–560. German Ambassador Radolin, Paris, wrote Chancellor Bülow that the assassination had been supported by "international anarchists" and the free masons. Copy, July 15, 1908, Rep. 30 Berlin, tit. 94, 12247, lit A, nr. 468, SP. Relying on little documentation, Jùlio Carrapato insists that the assassins were anarchists. *The Almost Perfect Crime: The Misrepresentation of Portuguese Anarchism* (Sacramento, CA: Black Powder Press, 2005): 2.

with other states in all these measures so that anarchism would never take root in Serbia.[62] Romania explained that "a part of the administrative provisions of the Rome Conference of 1898" had "already been put into application" and the royal government was ready to study and propose new anti-anarchist legislation once agreement had been established between the Great Powers.[63] Incidentally, despite Romania's apparent willingness to cooperate against the anarchists, the Austrians were soon complaining that Bucharest was "failing...to strictly implement the decisions of the international Anti-Anarchist Conference," particularly regarding the expulsion of anarchists.[64]

Berlin and St. Petersburg nurtured great hopes that the United States would join their efforts due to the outburst of popular rage that followed the murder of McKinley. On December 12 the Russian and German ambassadors delivered their diplomatic note inviting the United States to join in international anti-anarchist measures, and confidently expected a favorable answer. They were not disappointed on December 16 when John Hay presented them with a memorandum presenting the views of President Roosevelt. The secretary of state informed the ambassadors that: "I am directed by the President to express his cordial sympathy with the views and the purposes...set forth [in the Russo-German memorandum]." Hay then referred them to the various recommendations made in the president's December 3 address to Congress in which he had called for the exclusion and prompt deportation to their home countries of those "hostile to all government and justifying the murder of those placed in authority." "The Federal courts should be given jurisdiction over any man who kills or attempts to kill the President" and "anarchy should be declared an offense against the law of nations through treaties among all civilized powers." The president's memorandum concluded by stating his:

earnest desire to adopt every practicable means to eradicate this deadly growth from our body politic. The President will be glad to adopt such administrative measures as are within his constitutional power to cooperate with other governments to this end.

Legislative matters were in the hands of Congress, but Roosevelt promised to urge "the adoption of such measures for the suppression of anarchy as may be found acceptable to the national Legislature and which

---

[62] Chargè d'Affaires Wuitch, Belgrade, to German Foreign Office, January 13, 1902, Pol. An. Gesandtschaft Bern, Anarchistisches, GFO.
[63] Foreign Minister Sturdza to Chargé d'Affaires Count de Linden, Bucharest, December 2/15, 1901. Pol.An. Gesandtschaft Bern. Anarchistisches, vol. 3, GFO.
[64] See Austrian foreign ministry dispatch, Vienna, to Austrian Ambassador Pallavicini, Bucharest, February 21, 1903. Adm. Reg. F52/9, HHStA.

may enable the Executive to act in the matter with greater effectiveness in concert with other powers."[65] Writing to Vienna ten days later, the Austro-Hungarian ambassador pointed out a difference between the attitudes of the young Roosevelt and the sixty-three-year-old Hay. "The honesty and seriousness of Mr. Roosevelt's wishes to fight anarchism and the anarchists are beyond any doubt." On the other hand Hay "speaks with great reservations about the practical arrangement [*Gestaltung*] of the matter and its implementation."[66]

In the end, the caution and reservations of Hay won out over the enthusiasm of Roosevelt. While eventually the United States proved unwilling to sign an anti-anarchist accord with Europe, it was happier to reach a more limited agreement if confined to the Western Hemisphere. On January 28, 1902, the United States, together with sixteen Latin American countries attending the Second Pan-American Conference in Mexico City, signed a "Treaty for the Extradition of Criminals and for Protection against Anarchism." This treaty provided for the extradition of assassins (Art. 1st. III.1), thus removing anarchist assassins from the protection of the political exemption clause found in most extradition treaties. The Rome anti-anarchist conference had also recommended this measure, i.e., the so-called Belgian clause. Art. 13 provided that: "The extradition of any individual guilty of acts of anarchism can be demanded when ever the legislation of the demanding State and of that on which the demand is made has established penalties for such acts."[67]

Having received a favorable response to at least part of their initial inquiry, Germany and Russia sent a detailed outline of their proposal to the major European states on April 9, 1902, and to the United States on May 1. Since only the United States seemed on the verge of passing new anti-anarchist legislation and the European states were unwilling to amend their penal codes, Russia and Germany dropped their call for a legal definition of anarchism and for measures to restrict anarchist publications. What remained was a detailed set of measures regarding the expulsion of anarchists and the creation and interaction of central anarchist surveillance centers in each country. But the devil proved to be in the details, because despite having jettisoned the most controversial

---

[65] Department of State, *Papers Relating to the Foreign Relations of the United States* (1901), 2:196–197; John Bassett Moore, ed., *A Digest of International Law* 8 vols. (Washington, DC: Government Printing Office, 1906), 2, 432–435.

[66] Hengelmüller, Washington, DC, to Goluchowski, Vienna, December 26, 1901, secret. Adm Reg. F52/19, HHStA.

[67] International American Conference (2nd: 1901–1902, Mexico), *Actas y documentos. Minutes and documents* (Mexico City, 1902): 749–755. While Brazil attended the conference, it did not sign the draft treaty.

parts of the proposed anti-anarchist accord, it still took almost two more years to negotiate a binding agreement.

The rupture of diplomatic relations between Switzerland and Italy

For a time the breakdown of relations between Switzerland and Italy in April 1902 over the question of extremist anarchist publications in the former seemed to favor the creation of the new anti-anarchist league. The incendiary articles published in the anarchist press and other anarchist activities, particularly in the Ticino, that wedge of Italian-speaking Swiss territory sticking like a fat dagger into the back of northern Italy, and the half-hearted, merely sporadic efforts by the Swiss authorities to clamp down on the extremists proved to be a continual source of irritation for the Italian government.

On the other hand, on issues of extradition and expulsion, Switzerland increasingly tried to cooperate with the Italian authorities. In March 1898, for example, Berne let Rome know that it would indicate the border to which it was expelling Italian anarchists, although it would not provide the same information about Italian socialists.[68] This was despite the rule "always followed in Switzerland" of refusing to communicate such information ahead of time. In April 1901, the Swiss courts extradited Vittorio Jaffei, an alleged accomplice of Bresci, to Italy rejecting the argument that anarchism was a legitimate political doctrine and denying that Jaffei deserved the right to political asylum. This was a rather momentous and controversial decision. The *attentat* against King Umberto, said the Swiss court, was essentially the same as that against the Empress Elisabeth: common murder, not political crime.[69] This ruling harked back to earlier Swiss treaties and the extradition law of January 1892, which established the so-called "Swiss clause" or "proportionality theory" that extradition must be conceded in cases where, even if a political motive was alleged, the act under review constituted principally a common crime.[70]

---

[68] Italian Legation, Berne, to foreign ministry, Rome, March 2, 1899, b. 35, PI, IFM.

[69] Swiss Federal Tribunal decision, March 30, 1901. Francoise Grivaz, "L'extradition en matière de crimes politiques et sociaux: Affaire Jaffei," *Revue générale de droit international public* 9 (1902): 701–718; Maurice Travers, *Le Droit Pénal International*, 5 vols. (Paris: Recueil Sirey, 1921): 4:531–532. Like many other international law experts, both Grivaz and Travers were critical of the Swiss tribunal's ruling.

[70] *Nuovo digesto italiano*, "Estradizione," by Ugo Aloisi, 696; *Enciclopedia giuridica italiana*, "Estradizione," by Pietro Lanza, 456; Wijngaert, *Political Offence*, 126–132; Roger Corbaz, *Le Crime Politique et la Jurisprudence du Tribunal Fédéral Suisse en matière d'extradition* (Lausanne: G. Vaney-Burnier, 1927): 136–139.

Some contemporaries and subsequent legal scholars have thought this decision peculiar and suggested that it may have been due to Switzerland's adherence to the 1898 Rome protocol.[71] But in fact Switzerland had refused to agree to that portion of the Rome accord, and its action in the Jaffei case should rather be seen as a more general response to enormous domestic and international pressure to suppress the anarchists following the deaths of the Austrian empress and the Italian king.[72] Ironically, Jaffei turned out to be a loudmouth with no connection to the assassination of Umberto. He had merely written an ill-advised letter to Bresci supporting his deed and had to be released by the Italian authorities after a year in prison. Sent back to Switzerland, he was expelled, ending up in Antwerp, where the Belgian authorities expelled him to Dover, much to the chagrin of the British authorities, who only received news of the arrival of this unwelcome visitor after the fact.[73] Notorious now as a dangerous anarchist, in London Jaffei seems for a short time to have been taken into the employ of the Italian secret police.[74] The Jaffei case was emblematic of the continuing chaos of European expulsion policies as well as of the mystique of the Rome conference.

The immediate background to the diplomatic rupture regarded apparent Swiss tolerance for extremist publications advocating or approving of violence inside Italy. At the end of 1899 the anarchist Carlo Frigerio published a *Socialist-Anarchist Almanac* for the year 1900 calling for violent action against the Italian monarchy. Brought to trial for violating the Swiss law of April 1894 regarding "crimes tending to spread terror or to disturb the general security," the court acquitted Frigerio and his associates, Luigi Bertoni and Emile Held.[75] In July 1900, Bertoni, a Swiss citizen and a printer by trade, founded in Geneva the anarchist journal *Il Risveglio socialista anarchico* (*The Socialist Anarchist Awakening*), with a French supplement, *Le Réveil*.[76] It claimed to publish, on an average,

---

[71] "A propos d'un fait," *Le Réveil* (Geneva), April 27, 1901; Vincenzo Manzini, *Trattato di Diritto penale italiano*, 11 vols. (Turin: UTET, 1961): 1:487n35; Clunet's editorial note also suggests as much, see Ernest Lehr, "Quelques mots sur un cas d'extradition recent," *Journal de droit international privé* 29 (1902): 78–79n1.

[72] The Swiss accepted the 1898 accord's recommendations regarding expulsion, e.g., sending expellees back to their home countries, but declined to go further than current Swiss extradition treaties and the law of January 22, 1892. Swiss Legation, Rome, to Italian foreign ministry, May 16, 1899, PI, b. 32, IFM.

[73] Correspondence, HO, October–November 1901, HO144/668/x84164/2, PRO.

[74] A. Calvo, March 12, 1902, letter forwarded by Italian embassy, London, to interior ministry, Rome, DGPS 1908, b. 5, ACS.

[75] Reichesberg, "Anarchisme," 316; Grivaz, "L'extradition en matière," 704–705; Johann Langhard, *Die anarchistische Bewegung*, 379–388.

[76] Leonardo Bettini, *Bibliografia dell'anarchismo 1: Periodici e numeri unici anarchici in langua italiana pubblicati all'estero (1872–1971)*, (Florence: CP, 1972), 243. Gianpiero Bottinelli,

2,000 copies a day.[77] In January 1902, *Il Risveglio* published an article glorifying the assassination of King Umberto.

This was the straw that broke the camel's back of Italian patience. Italy dispensed with diplomatic niceties and demanded that the Swiss government take action. Contributing to the brusque Italian response was the personality of the recently appointed (September 10, 1901) Italian minister to Berne, Giulio Silvestrelli. In the words of a Belgian minister who knew him, Silvestrelli was "imperious" and "abrupt" in his manner; an Italian diplomat commented on his "inflexibility."[78] The Swiss government replied that it could do nothing under Swiss law unless Italy made a formal request and guaranteed reciprocal treatment for Switzerland should it make a similar application. Silvestrelli, supported by Foreign Minister Prinetti, refused to do either of these things and instead called on the Swiss government to undertake "the observance of its international duties." Italy seemed to be expanding its complaint regarding a single article or newspaper into a wholesale protest "against the impunity accorded in Switzerland to similar [i.e., extremist and subversive anti-Italian] publications."[79] The Swiss government found the imperious Italian note "wounding" (*blessante*) in both "form" and "content."[80] On April 10 Berne broke off relations with Silvestrelli; Rome took similar action with the resident Swiss minister.[81] After the diplomatic rupture between the two countries, some Swiss officials thought it wise to prepare for war, but the Italian government never intended to go that far.[82]

Indeed only a few months later, on July 30, Italo-Swiss relations were restored through the mediation of the three eastern and central European empires, and particularly through the efforts of Germany. Although nothing was made public, the Swiss president gave a spoken promise to the Italians that Switzerland would intervene should a subversive journal once again preach regicide.[83]

"Bertoni" in *Dizionario biografico degli anarchici italiani*, ed. Maurizio Antonioli et al (Pisa: BFS, 2003): 159–164.

[77] Prinetti, April 26, 1902, *Atti parlamentari*, Chamber of Deputies, *discussioni*, 943, cited in Mario Ferrigni, *Les Souverains Ètrangers et le Droit Italien: Notes* (Florence: Bernard Seeber, 1903). The British ambassador thought the influence of *Il Risveglio* much less, i.e., that it "was not known but to a 100 people in Switzerland." April 20, 1902, DDS, 4:868.

[78] Swiss Minister, Bourcart, London, to Swiss President J. Zemp, April 14, 1902. DDS, 4: 867.

[79] Swiss Federal Council to the Italian chargé d'affaires, Berne, February 25, 1902; Silvestrelli, to Zemp, Berne, March 8, 1902. DDS, 4:840.

[80] Zemp, Berne, to Carlin, Rome, March 12, 1902. DDS, 4:839.

[81] Zempt to Silvestrelli, Berne, March 12, 1902. DDS, 4:841.

[82] Lardy, Paris, to Zemp, April 11, 1902. DDS, 4:863.

[83] Verbal note, Italian foreign ministry to German embassy, Rome, July 23, 1902, DDI 3:7, 25. This note gives the German government entire credit for the mediation.

The three empires, spearheaded by Russia, also put pressure on Switzerland to take action against anarchist publications. Russia informed Berne that it was too indulgent toward the anarchist press, a fact with international implications since the vast majority of the anarchists in Switzerland were foreigners and their efforts were directed against foreign states, especially monarchies. "The cabinet of Berne ought to take into account its international duties and its moral responsibility vis-à-vis the governments of the European states which, since 1815, safeguard the neutrality of the Republic." The Silvestrelli case was therefore of "general," and not just Italian, "interest" and "represented a political incident of very great importance."[84] Secret Swiss assurances that both administrative and legal measures against the anarchists were in the works headed off a larger diplomatic confrontation or the harsher measures desired by St. Petersburg. Germany was willing to settle for Switzerland's voluntary compliance with some of the desires of the imperial powers so as to avoid pushing it further into the orbit of France.[85] The following December the Swiss government introduced a law, which had been in consideration since the permissive ruling on the *Socialist-Anarchist Almanac*, that penalized the public incitement to crime. On March 30, 1906, the Swiss parliament finally enacted an amended version that specifically punished those who extolled or called on others to commit an "anarchist crime."[86] The Swiss justified their tardiness in filling this lacuna in their legislation by contending that, prior to Bertoni, no anarchists with Swiss citizenship had existed. Even without press restrictions, foreign anarchists could always be expelled from the country if they produced outrageous publications.[87]

The rupture in Italo-Swiss relations over an anarchist publication and the involvement of the three empires was significant since it led to, or at least speeded up, steps to curtail the widespread freedom of the anarchists in Switzerland, a process that would continue almost until the outbreak of the First World War. It also reinforced the close relationship and leadership of Berlin and St. Petersburg in the drive for a pan-European anti-anarchist agreement, although in the end it failed to persuade Italy to participate in that agreement.

---

[84] Copy, *Traduction d'un projet d'instruction au Ministre de Russie à Berne.* [May 1902] Adm. Reg. F52/9, fol. 450r-454v, HHStA.
[85] Dannecker, *Schweiz und Österreich-Ungarn*, 170; Chancellor Bülow, Berlin, to kaiser, June 15, 1902, secret. Eur. Gen. 91, GFO.
[86] Dannecker, *Schweiz und Österreich-Ungarn*, 166; Reichesberg, "Anarchisme," 317.
[87] "L'article de la 'Nuova Antologia,'" *Gazette de Lausanne*, May 9, 1902.

The St. Petersburg Protocol of 1904

Throughout 1902, both before and after the Italo-Swiss crisis and its resolution, Germany and Russia continued to work to secure a Europe-wide
anti-anarchist accord. A long report by German Undersecretary of State
Otto von Mühlberg, explained that Great Britain refused any formal participation in the agreement, but would "in the meantime secretly [*unter den
hand*] comply as much as possible." The United States "apparently wants
to go its own way and confront anarchism legislatively."[88] Switzerland
was in basic agreement but wanted amendments. The draft protocol
called for empowering border authorities, without having to resort to
diplomatic procedures at the national level, to hand over or receive anarchists. This could be done when the anarchist's nationality was "clearly
established" by his identification papers or "other evidence," and also
"when the only ground for expulsion [was] that the expelled party [was]
known as an anarchist to the police of both countries or [had] committed acts that prove[d] him to be an anarchist." Switzerland wanted the
arrangement to remain as the Rome conference had established it and
as the Swiss government had decreed on March 21, 1899, i.e., declining
to authorize the border police to act independently. Germany hoped the
Swiss would change their minds and opt for the simpler border exchange
procedure, but, remaining obstinate, they refused.

Furthermore, Berne asked that the questions which all the central
police authorities were required by the protocol to answer be limited
specifically to matters regarding the *anarchist* movement. The Swiss also
suggested that countries exchange the names of the frontier authorities
whom they should notify of the imminent arrival of anarchists being
expelled or voluntarily leaving their territories.[89] Eventually Berlin and
St. Petersburg accepted all of the Swiss-recommended changes. Given
the willingness of Germany and Russia to adopt its proposed amendments, Berne felt unable to back out once the protocol was ratified in
St. Petersburg on March 1, 1904.[90] The Austro-Hungarian ambassador
thought an important factor, the reason the Swiss had engaged in these
negotiations in the first place, was "the hope to redeem themselves from
the stain of the bloody deed in Geneva [i.e., the assassination of the
Empress Elisabeth]." The Swiss finally adhered to the protocol despite
the fact that they felt very uneasy about committing to a secret accord

---

[88] Von Mülhberg, Berlin, to Alvensleben, St. Petersburg, January 12, 1903, Anarchismus
(Geheim) 43, GFO.
[89] *Reservations du Conseil federal suisses*, Berne, May 23, 1902, Pol.An., Gesandtschaft Bern.
Anarchistisches, bd.4, GFO.
[90] March 14, according to the Russian calendar.

with such Balkan states as Turkey, Serbia, and Bulgaria when the "liberal" powers Britain, France, America, and even Italy refused to go along.[91]

Given that the western European Great Powers failed to join, it is somewhat surprising that the Scandinavian states adhered to the St. Petersburg Protocol. Denmark and the dual (but soon to be separated) country of Sweden-Norway, saw the St. Petersburg accord as basically a continuation of the Rome conference, whose resolutions they had for the most part already implemented, at least regarding administrative measures. The protocol's simplified expulsion procedure, which many western European countries objected to, had already been enacted in a Danish-German extradition treaty.[92] The Scandinavians merely asked that the police of their capitals be allowed to assume the functions of central anti-anarchist offices, as the protocol stipulated, rather than being forced to create new ones. The Danes said that a new office was unnecessary, given the "little importance of the anarchist movement" in their country.[93]

From a broader perspective, the reasons for the Scandinavians' concurrence with the protocol was that neither Denmark nor Sweden wished to antagonize their powerful neighbors, Germany and Russia. Sweden's authoritarian King Oscar II was sympathetic to Germany, which he looked upon as a model state. At least since the time of the Rome conference, Sweden had worried about becoming an asylum for anarchists, a development that the St. Petersburg Protocol might conceivably help prevent.[94] The Swedish government's concern about a developing revolutionary workers' movement, which included anarchists and was stronger in Sweden than in the rest of Scandinavia, may also have affected policy.[95] As for Denmark, besides a desire for keeping up good relations with bordering Germany, a factor may have been that the Russian tsar was the grandson of the reigning King Christian IX. Since the Danish king was "father-in-law" of Europe with so many of his children and relations married into European royal houses, there were anxieties over possible anarchist *attentats* during these relatives' frequent visits. In 1902, concern

---

[91] Heidler, Berne, to Goluchowski, Vienna, January 8, 1907, cited by Liang, *Modern Poilce*, 173–174.

[92] Aide-mèmoire, German embassy, [to Italian Foreign Office], Rome, July 28, 1902, secret. IFO, Series P, busta 47.

[93] See former Norwegian Prime Minister Blehr's newspaper article reported by the *Frankfurter Zeitung*, November 27, 1904; copy, von Schoen, German Legation, Copenhagen, to Chancellor Bülow, Berlin, May 26, 1902. Pol.An., Gesandtschaft Bern. Anarchistisches, bd.4, GFO.

[94] Austro-Hungarian Ambassador Wodzicki, Stockholm, to Goluchowski, Vienna, November 26, 1898. IB 1898. K.390, HHStA.

[95] See the English summary in Jonas Bals's Norwegian-language thesis, "Holy Alliances and Dangerous Classes: Anarchism and Anti-Anarchism, 1885–1914" (University of Copenhagen, 2008): 102–104.

that the Russian dowager empress might be assassinated during a visit to Copenhagen led the Danish minister in Paris to be swindled by a conniving informer's tale of an anarchist plot.[96]

While Germany and Russia were able to coax the Scandinavians and the Swiss into agreeing to the St. Petersburg Protocol, Italy refused, despite the fact that it had been in the vanguard confronting anarchism ever since the Rome conference and most recently with the Silvestrelli affair. Italy's apparent change of policy is doubly significant because after 1900 anarchist violence, which had been such a disturbing issue in the 1890s, greatly diminished in importance. In February 1901 the coming to power of Giuseppe Zanardelli, Giovanni Giolitti, and the progressive liberals marked an important change in Italian politics. The rigidly repressive social and political policies of the 1890s were abandoned and an era inaugurated of what might be termed "New Liberalism" and an opening to the left.

Zanardelli was the titular prime minister between 1901 and 1903, but, old and ailing, he was overshadowed by Giolitti, his minister of the interior. In 1903 Giolitti became prime minister and continued to dominate Italian politics, whether in office or out, until 1914. People who knew Giolitti well, both friends and critics, described him as a man with a "genius" for administration, who could make the bureaucratic machinery of the Italian state work "to perfection."[97] This ability was based on twenty years of service in the government, particularly in the finance ministry, before entering political life. Sparing of words and gestures, hating highflown rhetoric, his personality seemed more that of a northern European than a stereotypical Italian. Born near the Alps in Piedmont, all his life he retained a love of hiking in the countryside. After he embarked on his political career, he would walk in Rome's great Villa Borghese park for an hour before entering the lion's den of Montecitorio, the seat of parliament. On his long, solitary walks in northern Italy, Giolitti enjoyed talking to and occasionally helping local country people, whom he admired. The closeness that he felt to ordinary, hardworking people was presumably one reason for his devotion to the principle of social justice and his willingness to tackle the "Social Question" without fear.[98] After graduating from university, Giolitti served briefly in the office of the *avvocatura de'poveri*, the lawyers for the poor, as his father had done for many

---

[96] Italian Legation, Copenhagen, to foreign ministry, Rome, October 9, 1902, Ser. P, b. 47, IFM.

[97] Natale, *Giolitti e gli italiani*, 45; General Arturo Cittadini to General Angelo Gatti, 20 March 1922, in Aldo A. Mola, *Giolitti. Lo statista della nuova Italia* (Milan: Mondadori, 2003): 454.

[98] Natale, *Giolitti e gli italiani*, 8, 10.

Figure 10 Italian Prime Minister Giovanni Giolitti, 1892–1893, 1903–1905, 1906–1909, 1911–1914, and 1920–1921. Building on the groundbreaking efforts of his predecessor, he was initiator of continental Europe's most successful policies to counter anarchist terrorism.
Source: Fondo Giolitti Chiaraviglio-Revelli, Centro europeo "Giovanni Giolitti" per lo studio dello stato, Dronero.

years.[99] Physically large and with a commanding personality, Giolitti was often capable of bold and unexpected initiatives. One keen observer of his later career compared his tactics to that of the chessman's knight, able unexpectedly to leap over and confound his opponents.[100] There was something of this "knight's move" in his reaction to massive strikes, which in 1901 broke out throughout Italy and that Giolitti refused to repress despite the fears of conservatives that this was the beginning of a revolution. There was also something of the knight's move in his response to the problem of anarchist terrorism, when he abandoned his policy of 1892–1893 and supported a far-reaching, and expensive, intelligence network of policemen and informers posted abroad.

Giolitti's answer in 1902 to Germany and Russia's call for an anti-anarchist league is therefore of importance and deserves to be quoted at length. It shows his concern for the anarchist danger, his practical approach to dealing with it, and his larger commitment to careful law enforcement, basic liberties, and to upholding the principle of liberty itself. In many ways this new Italian approach paralleled that of Britain, a country that Italy tried to remain in close touch with regarding its anti-anarchist views.[101] After Foreign Minister Prinetti asked for Giolitti's response to the Russo-German anti-anarchist proposal, on May 12, 1902, Giolitti sent him a memo marked "private" and "confidential." He wrote that:

Worried as I am about the danger that anarchy presents and convinced of the necessity to devise opportune means to secure to the social order a greater and more effective defense against that persistent menace, I do not hesitate to declare myself in general favorable to an international understanding, regarding measures to take administratively, in order to prevent anarchist crime.

Giolitti restricted himself to discussing "preventative measures," leaving questions of repression and changes to the penal law to the justice ministry.

I'm not going to stop to discuss the principle, if anarchism in itself, in the theoretical sense of the word, even if it doesn't express itself in those acts that the law foresees and punishes, should be considered as a criminal organism; but it is certainly difficult to establish who is an anarchist and, even when one succeeds in this, it is also certain that Italian law does not punish this qualification as a crime...

---

[99] Alexander De Grand, *The Hunchback's Tailor. Giovanni Giolitti and Liberal Italy from the Challenge of Mass Politics to the Rise of Fascism, 1882–1922* (Westport, CT: Praeger, 2001): 13.

[100] Cittadini in Mola, *Giolitti*, 455.

[101] At his request and "confidentially," the Foreign Office gave the Italian ambassador copies of the British responses in 1902 to the Russo-German proposals. T. H. Sanderson,

In the first section of those [Russo-German] proposals it speaks of the obligation to consign an expelled anarchist to the authorities of the country to which the anarchist belongs by birth.

Giolitti remarks that although Italy had "no interest in having back on its own territory Italian anarchists," foreign states were certainly free to expel them. At the same time Italy was concerned that the Russo-German proposals amounted to disguised extradition.

Therefore, in my view, the first point of the proposals should be modified in the sense that, while leaving every country free, as is now the case, to expel an anarchist, or not, however many times an expulsion may have been decided, the expulsion itself should be preceded by notifying the authorities of the state to which the expellee belongs and those of the state that the expellee has to cross to reach his own country; but all of this [should be done] without the express obligation to deliver, *a delivery that should be carried out only in the case that the expellee himself would consent to it of his own free will.* And such norms, it seems to me, must be imposed on the conduct of the Italian government, in homage to the principle of liberty, which informs all our legislation ....

For that which regards the other particulars of those proposals I note that for the most part they are already enforced in Italy.

Already for very many years a special office has existed at the Directorate General of Public Security that has the task of gathering all the information that comes from the other domestic and foreign offices regarding anarchists and of following the anarchist movement in Italy and abroad. And the Directorate General of Public Security, even before the international anti-anarchist conference gathered in Rome, had begun direct relations with many of the central [police] authorities of foreign states for communications and information relative to the anarchists, and after the conference, these relations were extended to other authorities with which they had not existed previously; whence one can say that on that point there may be nothing to add from our point of view, except rendering more frequent the communications exchanged between the General Directorate of Public Security and the central [police] offices of the other states, in order to facilitate surveillance of the anarchists and to closely follow their movement.[102]

Foreign Minister Prinetti's formal reply to Germany and Russia followed Giolitti's recommendations exactly, without additions from the Italian justice minister or anyone else.[103] On the morning of June 6, the German and Russian ambassadors met with Giolitti and Prinetti to see if they could iron out their differences over the proposed anti-anarchist measures. Giolitti provided further practical reasons why he objected

memorandum, February 12, 1902; note from C. A. H. to Sanderson, June 9, 1902. FO83/1970, PRO.

[102] Giolitti to Prinetti, Rome, May 12, 1902, Ser P, b. 47, IFM.

[103] Prinetti, Rome, to the ambassadors of Germany and Russia, May 28, 1902, N. 140 (CXVIII), *Documenti diplomatici a stampa*, IFO.

to a simplified procedure for anarchist expulsion that amounted to "administrative extradition." He claimed that presently no *foreign* anarchists, or at least dangerous ones, sojourned in Italy. Moreover, according to his reports, no dangerous Italian anarchists resided in Germany or Russia. According to Giolitti, the "breeding places of anarchism" were in Britain, Switzerland, the United States, Brazil, Argentina, and Egypt (all important sites of Italian immigration, although Giolitti does not mention this), but it would be difficult to change the situation in those locations. Under present conditions, it would not be in the interests of Italy to ask for the deportation of Italian anarchists. In any case, as an earlier Italian message had indicated, it was hard to define anarchism and many nondangerous people said they were anarchists only out of braggadocio. Italy could not change its expulsion policy without obtaining parliamentary approval. In his dispatch to Berlin, the German ambassador added that Giolitti wanted to avoid creating the public appearance of being repressive and provoking ill will among his socialist friends in parliament. Moreover the German ambassador had received the impression from Giolitti's remarks that he did not want to ease the return of Italian anarchists to the peninsula, since they were a "sect" that "thrives in [Italian] soil." Since the US Congress had just given the government power to expel all foreign anarchists, Giolitti expected a "shipment of this species" back to Italy.[104]

Three weeks later the Germans tried again, arguing first of all that the simplified expulsion procedure would have the advantage, even from a liberal point of view, of ending the "always more or less long" detention time that suspected anarchists endured at the borders. Moreover, Germany, Russia, and Denmark had already successfully enacted this measure between themselves. Finally, only the "unanimous concurrence" of the "great powers … could curb the harmful [*nèfaste*] activity of the anarchists."[105] But Italy refused to budge, with Giolitti emphasizing even more strongly than before that the protocol was "contrary to every principle of liberty and for this primary reason" it was impossible for Italy to adhere. Despite several new requests (twice in 1904, once by Germany and once by Spain; by Germany again in 1908), Italy never did sign the St. Petersburg Protocol.[106]

[104] Copy, Wedel, Rome, to Bülow, June 6, 1902. Pol.An., Gesandtschaft Bern, Anarchistisches, bd.4, GFO.

[105] Aide-mèmoire, German embassy, Rome, [to Italian Foreign Office], July 28, 1902, secret. Series P, b. 47, IFO.

[106] Pro-memoria, Italian foreign ministry to German embassy, August 1, 1902; German embassy, Rome, to Tittoni, Italian foreign ministry, May 3, 1904; November 1904 Spanish request (Italian foreign ministry to interior ministry, December 5, 1904, and Giolitti, interior ministry, to foreign ministry, December 8, 1904); Giolitti, interior ministry, to foreign minister, Rome, August 30, 1908, Ser. P, b. 47, IFO.

Instead of adhering to this international agreement, Giolitti chose to act unilaterally and, building on the work of his predecessor, to create the largest anti-anarchist police and informer network in the world. The focus of his policy therefore switched from what it had been in 1892–1893 – essentially "repression, not prevention" – to an enlightened version of "prevention, not repression" aimed at intelligence-gathering. The only comparable system was that of Russia and this was mostly restricted to Europe and focused on Russian socialists and Socialist Revolutionaries, not anarchists. Giolitti followed in Saracco's groundbreaking footsteps, expanding the system that the latter had begun in New York City and Buenos Aires and posting Italian policemen to other major centers of Italian immigration. Giolitti came to preside over a network of police stationed permanently in at least eleven cities on three continents and temporarily in other urban areas. In June 1901 he sent a policeman to Brazil, and in July 1901 to London. By May 1904, after long and frequent trips to New England, Pennsylvania, Ohio, Illinois, New Orleans, and Florida, Police Superintendent Molossi had set up an extensive spy network made up of twenty-one informers, about half drawn from local policemen.[107] In 1905 a police officer was posted to Marseilles and in 1906 to Berne. In 1907 police commissioners were dispatched to Lyon, France, in order to monitor Italian anarchists in nearby Switzerland, and to Montpellier, Vermont, in order to keep track of the militant anarchist editor Luigi Galleani and the Italian anarchist stonecutters working in the quarries of Barre. In September 1908, Giolitti decided to reestablish the police office in Paris that had been left vacant since the first months of 1894.[108] In August 1911, an Italian police commissioner went very briefly to Constantinople and returned there in November 1912 following the Turkish-Italian war over Libya. There was also an Italian policeman in Nice and Italian informers in several Egyptian cities, Luxembourg, Barcelona, and the Ticino, Switzerland.[109]

This huge and expensive system provided increasingly good intelligence about the anarchists. Initially one major scandal took place. In 1902 Gennaro Rubino (or Rubini), an Italian informant in London who had been exposed by the local anarchists and who wished to regain his subversive credentials, tried to assassinate the king of Belgium.[110] This misstep was due in part to the faulty actions of Ettore Prina, Rubino's

[107] Canali, *Le spie del regime*, 31; Consul Fara Forni to consulate general, New York, December 10, 1904, PI, b.35, IFM.
[108] Giolitti, interior ministry, to Ambassador Gallina, Paris, August 31, 1908; Gallina, Paris to DGPS, Rome, September 5, 1908, DGPS (1909), b. 2, ACS.
[109] Canali, *Le spie del regime*, 18-32. Tugini, Cairo, to Prinetti, Rome, July 2, 1901, PI, b. 28, IFM. Jensen, "National, Bilateral, and Regional Anti-Anarchist Policing, 1900-1914," *Terrorism and Political Violence*, forthcoming.
[110] Di Paola, "Spies," 201–204; Porter, *Vigilant State*, 126.

Italian police handler, who was soon replaced. Subsequently Giolitti was careful to avoid similar episodes and there were no more scandals with poorly handled informers. His director general of public security reined in confidents who threatened to become *agents provocateurs*.[111]

Forewarned by confidential informers both at home and abroad, the Italian police seem to have prevented a number of assassination attempts. In early June 1906 the police discovered several bombs (and a considerable quantity of explosives) at the shop of an anarchist barber in Ancona, and two weeks later, they discovered three bombs secreted near the railway track over which the king was scheduled to journey for his visit to the Adriatic port, one of Italy's greatest anarchist centers.[112] In 1911, with the assistance of the Italian consuls in Geneva and New York City (and doubtless with the help of the Italian police official and informants), three anarchists were arrested at Genoa and Turin. Apparently they were intending to strike at the king and Giolitti as they visited the International Exposition being held in Turin to celebrate the fiftieth anniversary of Italian unification. Giuseppe Notario and Pietro Costelli, the anarchists arriving in Genoa from New York, were in the possession of arms, explosives, and publications glorifying the assassin Bresci.[113]

Britain, like Italy and for some of the same or similar reasons, refused to accept the Russo-German anti-anarchist proposals, although eventually it agreed to abide by some of the administrative measures unilaterally and secretly. Britain also, like Italy, determined to protect itself from possible anarchist *attentats* by relying on the information provided by its confidential agents. Responding to the proposals on June 16, 1902, Lord Lansdowne followed closely the reasoning of London's Metropolitan Police, and repeated many of the same arguments that he had made in February.[114] According to the Italian ambassador, London was loath to join an "international police organization.[115] It feared it might be required to create an "institution...separate from Scotland Yard – with secret agents and political police."[116] The pragmatic British, however, were happy to cooperate on a case-by-case basis. Moreover,

---

[111] Di Paola, "Spies," 204; Vigliani, DGPS, Rome, to Italian Minister, Berne, October 9, 1911. PS 1911, b. 43, ACS.

[112] *Corriere della Sera*, June 25–26, 28, 1906, 3–7. The bombs found around June 23, 1906, were in a castle wall at Castelferretti, near Falconara. For Giolitti's close attention to these matters and concern that "nothing ought to be neglected in order to guard the life of His Majesty," see, Giolitti to foreign minister, Rome, June 16, 1906. DGPS, B. 5, ACS.

[113] Fiorentino, *Ordine pubblico*, 81–82; DGPS, 1911, b. 43, ACS.

[114] Lansdowne's message is printed in BDIL, 6: 75–77; Bradford's memo, April 29, 1902, is an inclosure in no. 10, Kenelm Digby, HO, to FO, May 13, 1902, FO412/68 PRO.

[115] Pansa, London, to Prinetti, Rome, December 20, 1901. Ser. P, b. 47, IFM.

[116] Bradford's comments in Sanderson, May 13, 1902, FO 83/1970, PRO.

both the British Home Office and the foreign secretary liked the Swiss approach to the protocol, since their adherence was unilateral, voluntary, and *de facto*, rather than contractual and *de jure*. London informed St. Petersburg that they had designated "the Commissioner of Metropolitan Police ... [as] the official with whom foreign police authorities should communicate when necessary on this subject ... [A]ll possible assistance and information" would be given by him "to foreign police authorities." Like the Swiss, the British wished to "reserv[e] to themselves full liberty to modify their own arrangements for the repression of anarchical crime as occasion may arise."[117] Lansdowne emphasized once again that all this must remain "as secret as possible."[118] An unmentioned concern was that cooperation with reactionary continental governments might come before parliament or get into the newspapers. In some cases, we know that the responsible British minister preferred not to be informed of contacts reached with foreign security forces because this made it easier in the House of Commons.[119] The British were apparently also invited to join the St. Petersburg Protocol *"par acte separate,"* like the Swiss or Luxembourg, but in the end refused to advance to that level of adhesion.[120]

The most interesting points made in Police Commissioner Bradford's April 1902 memorandum forwarded to Lansdowne were only hinted at in the latter's communication to the Germans and Russians.[121] These points regarded the nature of Britain's successful strategy for monitoring the anarchists and preventing their crimes and why this disfavored systematic international communications. Since information coming from the continental police was sparse or out of date, the British had to rely on informants ("private agency") to monitor anarchists arriving in the country and living there. In Bradford's words:

they [the police] have to rely upon private agency for much of their information, as the difference in habits and language makes it difficult for any but a few specially

[117] Lansdowne to Benckendorff, London, June 17, 1904. The confidential HO memorandum on the subject makes it even clearer than the diplomatic note that the British desired to adhere *informally* to much of the St. Petersburg Protocol, while at the same time retaining their freedom of action. M. D. Chalmer, HO, to FO, May 30, 1904, which restates much of E. R. Henry's confidential letter, New Scotland Yard, to the undersecretary of state, May 18, 1904. FO. 881/928/x and HO144/757/118516 PRO.

[118] Lansdowne memorandum, June 16, 1902, in BDIL, 6:77.

[119] Jeyes and How, *Howard Vincent*, 70; Porter, *Vigilant State*, 69, 142–44; Di Paola, "Spies," 197.

[120] In a private letter of June 8, 1904 French Ambassador Cambon inquired of the British Foreign Office if "le Gouvernement Britannique a-t-il accueilli favorablement la suggestion, qui a du lui être faite par l'Allemagne et la Russie d'adherer, par acte separate (come l'a fait récemment le Gouvernement Suisse), aux dispositions du Protocol signe a Petersbourg le 1/14 Mars ...." FO83/1970, PRO.

[121] These closely followed the recommendations of CID Assistant Commissioner Henry.

qualified officers to continue mixing with these aliens without being detected. It is quite certain that if intelligence acquired through this private agency were communicated to the police of other countries, the identity of informants must sooner or later become known and then this important source of information would become closed.

Moreover, much of the information thus obtained is not susceptible of verification and may or may not prove trustworthy. The London police are careful not to act on it to the prejudice of the persons affected until they have tested it, and are not prepared to communicate to others information the credibility of which they cannot vouch for. One of the obligations of Contracting Parties is clearly stated in the [Russo-German] Memorandum to be that of answering all the questions of other Central Bureaux and is an obligation which, if enforced would speedily operate to create scares and prevent effective inquiries being made anywhere.

The experience of the London police is that communications from a private agency cannot be too cautiously dealt with, and should be tested in every way possible before action is taken.

Reliable intelligence derived from evaluating secret information (itself dependent on the great tact and secrecy with which the police handled informants) was at the heart of British success in dealing with the anarchists. British fears about poorly used or managed intelligence and spies were well taken as the experience of the Spanish, Italians, and Russians with informants and *agents provocateurs* demonstrated. The danger of the anarchist threat was doubtless exaggerated by the unverified reports of continental spies being circulated among the police departments and foreign ministries of Europe. Moreover Bradford worried that too much contact with foreign police methods might corrupt the British police and lower their high standards. Therefore the commissioner of police had objected to the sending of "two detectives to Madrid [as] asked for by the Spanish. Emb[assy] ... [because] they would be indoctrinated into the foreign methods of political espionage."[122]

On March 1, 1904, nine countries signed a secret anti-anarchist protocol in the Russian capital.[123] The signatories, represented by their ambassadors in St. Petersburg as plenipotentiaries, were Germany, Austria-Hungary, Denmark, Romania, Russia, Serbia, Sweden-Norway, Turkey, and Bulgaria. Belgium, France, Greece, Britain, Italy, Spain, and the United States received copies of the document in case they might be

---

[122] T. H. Sanderson reports Bradford's comments in a minute to Lansdowne, May 13, 1902, FO 83/1970, PRO.

[123] For the original French text of the protocol, see appendix, and Anarchismus (Geheim) 43, Abschrift zu III a. 3382, GFO. Leo Stern has published a German translation of the protocol, found in the archives of Saxony, that differs slightly from the version in De Martens. *Die Auswirkungen der ersten russischen Revolution von 1905–1907 auf Deuschland*, 2 vols. (Berlin 1955): 1:19–21.

disposed to join the agreement at a later date. The signatories declared themselves

convinced of the necessity to oppose an energetic resistance to the development of the anarchist movement, recognizing that the best way to attain that end ... is to maintain before everything the understanding [*entente*] so successfully established between themselves on that subject and to assert together their common interest ... in the repression of anarchist crimes and *attentats*.

The 1904 protocol made no attempt to define an anarchist act or to suggest possible improvements in legislation and extradition procedures affecting anarchists. This was no doubt a weakness in the protocol, although all the 1904 signatories had earlier subscribed to the somewhat fuzzy definition provided by the Rome conference's Final Act. What the St. Petersburg Protocol concentrated on was expanding and spelling out in practical detail what had been the administrative section of the Rome proposals dealing with expulsion and police organization and communication. In neither the 1898 nor 1904 agreements was there a proviso that the signatories *must* expel *all* foreign anarchists (despite the fact that conservative monarchies, especially Russia, might have desired such a clause). The St. Petersburg covenant also made no specific mention of *portrait parlé*. This may be because it was now somewhat out of vogue given the emergence of fingerprinting as the most accurate method of criminal identification, or it could be that its universal adoption after the Rome conference rendered superfluous any further injunction. Instead, each central police agency was asked to provide the affected country with the description, background data, and if possible, the photograph of any anarchist being expelled there.

While the Rome conference had suggested in general fashion that the contracting states exchange "all useful pieces of information," the 1904 accord was more specific. Now the central authorities were charged with immediately informing every other police bureau if perchance an anarchist should clandestinely quit the territory of one country and his whereabouts were unknown. The central bureau entrusted with watching anarchists in each country was asked to inform the others without delay of any anarchist conspiracy it had learned about; in addition, the Central Bureau, should, at least every six months, inform all the other bureaus of every important development within the anarchist movement in its territory. The rest of the protocol dealt with the setting up of agencies to watch the anarchists and procedures to be followed in their expulsion.

Of the signatories to this agreement, only Romania and the Ottoman Empire wished to append substantive reservations. Romania withheld to itself the right to determine at all times for the purposes of the treaty whether a person was indeed an anarchist. In its reservation, Turkey referred back to its declaration of September 6, 1899, made in response to the Rome conference, in which it had maintained its "right to not admit [the return of] its anarchist subjects expelled from other countries if the right to judge them for their past crimes was refused." The Ottoman government also stated that the 1904 protocol would not affect the existent accords between the Sublime Porte and St. Petersburg on the subject of certain categories of Armenians (who the Ottomans and the press often times labeled "anarchists") residing in Russia.[124] Despite its limited scope, the St. Petersburg accord was the single most "practical" result of the Rome conference, whose resolutions had been only advisory.

Between late March and June 1904 Switzerland, Luxembourg, Spain, and Portugal associated themselves with the protocol. On March 31, 1904, the Swiss declared that: "we [will] adopt all the administrative measures referred to [in the St. Petersburg Protocol] and that we will give the necessary orders to ensure their execution." On the other hand Berne rejected any contractual obligation and retained full liberty to modify its adherence when "circumstance or a change in legislation" made this "opportune."[125] On May 8, Luxembourg, in a trilateral convention concluded only with Germany and Russia, agreed to the terms of the St. Petersburg accord except for the first section of the protocol calling for the expulsion of anarchists back to their homelands after prior notification.[126] Spain and Portugal adhered to the protocol on June 15 and 25, respectively, with some minor reservations. Spain designated the ports of Barcelona and Vigo for the expulsion of foreign anarchists and Cádiz and Santander for the reception of expelled Spanish anarchists until such time as France and Portugal adhered to the protocol. Like Switzerland, Spain joined unilaterally, reserving for itself the "freedom to modify or revoke [the protocol] when by reason of circumstances or of any change in legislation it would be considered opportune."[127] The Netherlands, which, like Luxembourg, had reservations about the protocol's provisions on expulsion procedures, said it would join at a later date but never did.[128] Nor did Greece and Belgium, although as late as January 1905 Germany hoped these countries might adhere via a "special agreement"

---

[124] Annex A and C to the St. Petersburg Protocol.
[125] Swiss Federal Council to Russian minister at Berne, inclosure 2, in Bernstorff, London, to Lansdowne, April 28, 1904. FO 881/928/x, PRO.
[126] Russian embassy, Vienna, to Goluchowski, June 6, 1904. Adm, Reg F52/9, HHStA.
[127] Copy, Spanish foreign ministry to German ambassador, very confidential, Madrid, June 15, 1904. OP, l. 2753, SFM.
[128] For Dutch assurances, see excerpt, report, March 16, 1904, St. Petersburg. Adm, Reg F52/9, HHStA.

(*Sonderabkommen*) similar to that signed by Luxembourg.[129] In the end, almost two-thirds, thirteen out of twenty, of the European states, excluding such microstates as Monaco, San Marino and Andorra, adhered to the St. Petersburg Protocol.

Why did the United States, the assassination of whose president had served as the catalyst triggering negotiations that led to the St. Petersburg accord, refuse to participate?[130] Political prejudices and practical concerns both played a part. Traditionally the US had avoided European entanglements. Moreover John Hay, the American secretary of state, was a staunch Anglophile, along with many other high officials in the Roosevelt cabinet, and a decided Germanophobe. He had little eagerness to sign, with Britain's main rival, an international treaty that Britain itself opposed. Roosevelt himself had some liking for Germany, but harbored very mixed feelings about the kaiser, and disliked the Russian ambassador and his despotic government. Just at the time that the anti-anarchist negotiations were underway, the economic and political rivalry between the United States and Germany in Latin America and Asia reached a critical point. Both the American public and government were angered by Germany's heavy-handed actions in 1902–1903 when the kaiser sent gunboats to the Venezuelan coast in order to force the corrupt Castro government to pay up its debts.

It would also have been difficult for the United States to sign a secret anti-anarchist treaty since the constitution required the Senate to approve all treaties and this would have inevitably led to the revelation of the protocol's provisions. Washington could perhaps have gotten around this barrier by taking the Swiss route and agreeing to a *de facto* adherence. Indeed Switzerland, with its long traditions of neutrality, political liberty, and federalism, resembled the United States politically more than any other country in Europe. But the US still faced the insuperable hurdle posed by its lack of a centralized police force and criminal record-keeping agency that could have routinely exchanged information with the European police forces. In 1901–1902, the Secret Service had begun to compile a register of anarchists, but the surviving records suggest that this was cursory and incomplete, lacking standardized identification terminology and photographs.[131] Moreover the Secret Service, while willing to respond to urgent requests for information about men suspected of being dangerous anarchists, lacked the manpower and had too many other tasks to provide the information that the Europeans desired. It

---

[129] Franzius, Royal Prussian foreign ministry, to interior minister, Berlin, January 14, 1905. bd. 7, n. 8, GCSAM.

[130] For a more detailed analysis, Jensen, "The United States," 15–46.

[131] See Chapter 7 and Jensen, "The United States," 20.

was not until July 1908 that Roosevelt ordered the attorney general to create the embryonic investigative service that would eventually grow into the Federal Bureau of Investigation (FBI). Initially this service had only ten men; it was not until 1910 and the passage of the Mann Act against white slavery that the "Bureau of Investigation" would begin its phenomenal expansion. On the eve of American entrance into the First World War, there were 300 Bureau of Investigation agents, enough to fight both white slavery and the anarchists, but by this time any interest in joining the Russo-German- led anti-anarchist league had evaporated. Moreover it was not until 1924 that Congress funded the creation of America's first national bureau of criminal identification in the form of the Identification and Information Division of the Justice Department's Bureau of Investigation. This division merged the files on suspects and criminals maintained by the federal prison system in Leavenworth with the files of the National Bureau of Criminal Identification, a service created and maintained by the International Association of Chiefs of Police, a private association of mostly American and Canadian police heads.

Conclusion

On May 20, 1904, in a front page article, the Parisian newspaper *Le Matin* leaked word of the signing of the St. Petersburg Protocol, denouncing the agreement as seeming "to date to the time of the Holy Alliance." *Le Matin* believed that France and Britain had refused to sign because the accord would abolish all the rules regulating extradition between the two states and "would repudiate the right of exile accorded until now to political refugees."[132] *Le Matin*'s claims were exaggerated and alarmist since no provision of the protocol required a country to expel those anarchists to whom it wished to grant asylum. On the other hand, the protocol certainly made anarchists more vulnerable to police harassment and political repression. Subsequently one historian has asserted that the anti-anarchist protocol was designed to create "a league that would, if necessary align the conservative powers against the Western democracies."[133] This is also a considerable exaggeration since from the beginning Germany and Russia had intended to enroll as much of Europe as possible, as well as the United States. If the design was to create a league of conservative powers, why were repeated efforts made to induce Britain, Italy, and the United States to reconsider and adhere to the protocol? As the German ambassador in Rome had told the Italians in 1902, only the "unanimous concurrence" of the "great powers... could curb the harmful activity

[132] *Le Matin* (Paris), May 20, 1904.   [133] Liang, *Modern Police*, 169; 171.

of the anarchists." Nor was the agreement "directed above all against liberal Switzerland."[134] While it is true that, during the Silvestrelli affair, Germany and Russia had pressured Switzerland to clamp down on anarchist propaganda, in the negotiations leading up to the St. Petersburg Accord, the Eastern empires had sought Switzerland's cooperation, not its subjugation. In order to entice Switzerland to join, they had offered it substantial concessions, thereby weakening the final agreement.

The St. Petersburg Protocol was significant as an important part of a continuing and overlapping series of anti-anarchist initiatives, unilateral, bilateral, and multilateral, and as a key benchmark in pre-war efforts to prevent and contain anarchist terrorism. Its failure to distinguish decisively between peaceful and violent actors and activities, a failure made all the more ominous by the fact that, during the 1890s and later, many countries had lumped together in the same category terrorists with peaceful anarchists and socialists, limited the number of its adherents. Its potential and actual effectiveness was further undermined by different national traditions of policing and by many states' lack of effective public security organizations and identification bureaus that could effectively cooperate with one another.

---

[134] Linse, *Organisierter*, 26.

The negotiation of the St. Petersburg Protocol represented the high point of international anti-anarchist collaboration, but in many countries it was accompanied or followed by a new series of terrorist attacks. After a pause around the turn of the century, in 1903 anarchist assassinations and bombings resumed in Spain, reaching a grisly climax in May 1906 with a bloody assault on the Spanish king, his bride, and innocent onlookers. Even after that date, explosions continued for years in Barcelona, bestowing on it the grim title: "City of Bombs." The outbreak of the 1905 Revolution in Russia inspired many revolutionaries and some terrorists throughout the world, inaugurating a new, and more genuinely global, wave of terrorism than had ever occurred before. Anarchism and anarchist terrorism had previously been insignificant in Russia but now suddenly assumed great importance. Immigrating Russian anarchists and violent revolutionaries, fleeing the ruthless tsarist repression that followed the end of the 1905 Revolution, brought terrorist attacks to continental Europe, Britain, and North and South America. In 1907–1909 terrorist incidents took place for the first time in Sweden. The United States experienced both an anarchist resurgence and, in 1908, a terrorist scare; a new series of anarchist bombings began in 1914 and continued into the 1920s. Between 1905 and 1910 Argentina suffered a series of anarchist assassination attempts and explosions, culminating in fall 1909–summer 1910. Beginning in 1908 Indian "anarchists" (labeled as such by the newspapers and British government authorities, but actually nationalists) assassinated and bombed in India and London. Real or alleged anarchist incidents also occurred in Austria-Hungary, Italy, Belgium, Germany, Denmark, the Ottoman Empire, and Japan. In France, while *attentats* against political leaders and purely symbolic bourgeois targets ceased after the turn of the century, in the early 1900s and in 1911–1912 criminal anarchist bands stole cars, robbed banks, and killed people for short, but highly publicized, periods. In China, where "assassinationism" – associated with both anarchist and nihilist influence – was in vogue between 1905 and 1912, anarchists and nationalists plotted to murder the imperial regent. In Guangzhou an anarchist attack in October 1911 led to the death of twenty people.[1]

As will be discussed in both this chapter and the next, nations responded to the new wave of anarchist *attentats* in several different ways. In terms of multilateral action, new calls went out for an international accord to prevent and repress anarchist crimes, but these proved fruitless. Repeated efforts were undertaken to render the recently signed St. Petersburg Protocol a functioning and more effective agreement, although attempts to increase its membership failed. Continued international pressure on Switzerland led it to pass new anti-anarchist legislation, sign extradition treaties aimed at the anarchists, and expel more anarchists in close, if sometimes highly secret, cooperation with its neighbors. Britain and other countries made efforts to reduce bureaucratic delays and improve communications regarding anarchist information exchange. Provoked by massive strikes instigated by anarchist-dominated unions, several South American countries signed a multilateral treaty to improve antisubversive police cooperation.[2] Continuing problems remained regarding the expulsion of anarchists, especially between Spain and France, Belgium and Britain, and Switzerland and its neighbors. Moreover, by 1913–1914, the St. Petersburg accord gave signs of coming unraveled.

The implementation of the St. Petersburg accord

The new anti-anarchist league created in 1904 and championed by Germany and Russia proved to be a continual work in progress. Most of the signatory countries to the accord designated an office in their interior ministries or the police of their capitals as the center for exchanging anti-anarchist information. Switzerland designated its Federal

---

[1] In April 1910 a bomb was discovered along the route the Regent Prince Chun (or Zaifeng) traveled. Robert A. Scalapino and George T. Yu, *The Chinese Anarchist Movement* (Westport, CT: Greenwood Press, 1980); Dirlik, *Anarchism in the Chinese Revolution*, 71–72; Edward J. M. Rhoads, *Manchus and Han: Ethnic Relations and Political Power in Late Qing and Early Republican China, 1861–1928* (Seattle: University of Washington Press, 2000), 154–155. For the Guanzhou bombing, Edward Krebs, *Shifu, Soul of Chinese Anarchism* (New York: Rowman and Littlefield, 1998), 69. Daniel Tretiak provides a list of bombings and assassination attempts during the final years (1905–1912) of the Ch'ing, "Political Assassinations in China, 1600–1968," in James F. Kirkam, Sheldon G. Levy, and William J. Crotty (eds.), *Assassination and Political Violence: Report to the National Comission on the Causes and Prevention of Violence* (Washington, DC: US Government Printing Office, 1969): 644.
[2] Convention signed in Buenos Aires on October 20, 1905, by the police forces of the capital cities of Argentina, Brazil, Chile, and Uruguay. Adolpho Rodriquez, *Historia de la Policia Federal Argentina vol. 6* (Buenos Aires, 1975): 6:523–535.

Prosecutor's Office. Germany set up a special bureau inside the Berlin police presidency's seventh department (VII. *Abteilung*), the political police section. This office was abbreviated as the CA or the CfA, signifying the *Centralstelle für die Überwachung der anarchistischen Bewegung.* The CA was in fact not an entirely new creation, but an expansion of the office set up in 1898 to collect information on anarchists throughout the German Empire. The *Dirigent*, or director of the political police, was also the head of the anti-anarchist office. To handle the expected increase in international correspondence, two additional clerks were hired, making a total of five employees under the *Dirigent*'s overall control.[3] Besides additional employees and new furniture, including cabinets with pigeonholes, the new office ordered copies of Neumann's *Geographisches Lexikon des Deutschen Reichs*, railway maps of Europe, and English–German and French–German dictionaries. It also acquired standardized forms to expedite the communication of information about and photos of anarchists to be found in the anarchist list and the *Anarchisten Album.* There were also forms for recording information about subscribers to anarchist newspapers.[4] In 1908, citing the need to communicate with various foreign and domestic authorities, the office requested an atlas, von Ritter's *Geographisch-statistischen Lexikon,* and an Italian–German dictionary (indicating the extent to which the anti-anarchist office interacted with Italy, even if the latter was not formally a part of the anti-anarchist league).[5]

At least through early 1905, Germany hoped, although in vain, that ongoing negotiations with Greece, the Netherlands, and perhaps Belgium, might lead to their joining the St. Petersburg Protocol, or at a minimum, to their concluding separate anti-anarchist agreements similar to that which Luxembourg had signed with Russia and the German Reich. Eventually Berlin wanted to extend the truncated Luxembourg agreement, which was restricted to the exchange of information about anarchists, to all the member states of the St. Petersburg Protocol, as well as to all those countries that had not joined, as long as the latter were committed to reciprocity. The German Foreign Office believed that such an exchange was in the "common interest of all civilized states [*Kulturstaaten*] in stemming and combating Anarchism."[6]

---

[3] Police president Borries to interior minister, Berlin, March 24, 1904. GCSAM, vol 7, no. 8, tit. 2512.

[4] Mss. Memos. Berlin April 21, 1904, and August 7, 1906. Polizei Präsidium. SP, PR.BR. Rep.30. Berlin. C tit.95.15701.

[5] Abteilung VIII/C.A. to Abt. I, Berlin police, February 5, 1908. SP. PR.BR.Rep.30. Berlin. C tit.95.15701.

[6] Frantzius, Foreign Office, to interior ministry, Berlin, January 14, 1905, GCSAM, vol. 7 no. 8, tit. 2512.

The revival of anarchist terrorism, the May 1906 Madrid bombing, and new calls for international cooperation

For several years around the turn of the century anarchist terrorism largely vanished, perhaps due in part – if only temporarily – to police repression and popular revulsion against anarchist *attentats*, but also to the greater prosperity that enveloped much of the world in the early years of the twentieth century and the emergence of more progressive governments in France, Italy, and the United States.[7] In the latter three countries, the public backlash against the murder of their heads of state chastened the anarchists. In the wake of McKinley's assassination, many anarchists, including Emma Goldman and Alexander Berkman (who, in prison, rejected the "social necessity" of Czolgosz's act), abandoned their support for propaganda by the deed – at least in the United States.

About the time of Russia's 1905 Revolution, however, terrorism, although often not directly linked to anarchism, revived in much of the world.[8] Writing decades after this period, Special Branch Detective Herbert Fitch claimed: "In the years 1906 and 1907 London seems to have been the world's storm-centre of anarchism."[9] Although Fitch repeatedly confuses every sort of left-wing extremist with an anarchist, during this period (1905–1906) the letter registers of the Home Office also show a "significant increase" in the amount of correspondence on anarchism.[10] In several countries, e.g., the United States and Italy, economic crises and high unemployment during 1907–1909 added fuel to the flames of working-class discontent and strengthened the appeal of anarchism. Another sign of increasing radicalism was that the number of Italian anarchist groups in Switzerland grew from about ten in 1902 to around thirty in 1915.[11] In 1906, the Parisian newspaper *Le Gaulois* calculated that anarchist journalism, which had hardly existed a decade before, was now of "a certain importance," with an impressive 250

---

[7] Peter Latouche, *Anarchy! An Authentic Exposition of the Methods of Anarchists and the Aims of Anarchism* (London: Everett, 1908): 147, makes the questionable claim that this lull was due to "the Boer War and the Russian and Japanese Conflict," which "caused the comrades to indulge in speculations concerning the results of these events, rather than indulge in 'removals' and other outrages."

[8] For a detailed discussion of this new wave of anarchist terrorism, Jensen, "The First Global Wave of Terrorism and International Counter-terrorism, 1905–14," in Jussi Hanhimäki and Bernhard Blumenau (eds.), *An International History of Terrorism: Western and Non-Western Experience* (London and New York: Routledge, 2013): 16–33.

[9] Fitch, *Traitors*, 33.   [10] Porter, *Vigilant State*, 155.

[11] In 1907 there were also ten French-speaking Swiss anarchist groups. "Bertoni," in *Dizionario biografico degli anarchici italiani*, 1:160.

anarchist periodicals serving a relatively small number (40,000) of anarchists throughout the world.[12]

As already mentioned, in Spain, terrorism re-emerged even before the 1905 Russian Revolution.[13] Once again a cycle uncoiled of socioeconomic protest, police brutality, and anarchist revenge. The chain of events began with an August 1903 strike at Alcalà del Valle in southern Spain, followed by heavy-handed repression and reports of the police use of torture that led to the deaths of two workers.[14] The Spanish historian Núñez Florencio emphasizes that the "reports of tortures" exercised "a decisive influence in the perpetuation of new attentats." Within a year a revenge-seeking anarchist attempted the life of Antonio Maura, the conservative prime minister, wounding him very slightly with a kitchen knife.[15] More serious was an attempt on King Alfonso XIII's life in May 1905 during an official visit to Paris when, together with the French president, he was riding in a carriage along the Rue Rohan. Two pineapple-shaped bombs were thrown, injuring eleven people, but leaving the two heads of state unhurt. While Spanish and English anarchists were suspected of engineering this *attentat*, due to insufficient proof and the dramatic testimonials of such prominent Spanish and French political figures as Alejandro Lerroux and Jean Jaurés, all the defendants were exonerated. Lerroux argued, and Jaurés believed, that the *attentat* had been concocted by the Spanish police, a claim that did not seem entirely absurd given the lingering memory of police misbehavior at the time of the Montjuich tortures.[16]

A terrible explosion and assassination attempt at the end of May 1906, exactly one year after the Parisian *attentat* and the bloodiest act of anarchist terrorism up until this point in terms of the total number of casualties, spurred on new efforts to expand international policing.[17] On May 31, 1906, shortly after his wedding, Alfonso and his new bride were riding in their horse-drawn carriage down the Calle Mayor in Madrid past crowds of people lining the street. A powerful bomb concealed in a bouquet of flowers was thrown at the royal procession just as it had reached a point opposite the residence of the captain-general of Madrid. The explosion resulted in the deaths of between 23 and 33 soldiers and bystanders,

[12] "*Bloc-Notes Parisien: La presse anarchiste*," *Le Gaulois*, June 6, 1906, 1; *The Times* (London), June 7, 1906, 2.
[13] Romero Maura, "Terrorism," 132; Núñez Florencio, *Terrorismo*, 59.
[14] Kaplan, *Anarchists*, 203.
[15] Núñez Florencio, *Terrorismo*, 61–62, 69–70, 72, 102–103.
[16] Avilés Farré, "Contra Alfonso XIII", 142–148.
[17] In 1858, the bombs of the nationalist Orsini probably caused the most bloodshed of any terrorist act of the nineteenth–early twentieth centuries: 150 casualties, including eight deaths and 142 injured people.

THE FAMOUS PHOTOGRAPH OF THE MADRID OUTRAGE TAKEN AT THE MOMENT OF THE EXPLOSION.

Figure 11 Attempted assassination of Alfonso XIII, May 30, 1906. Probably the first photograph of a terrorist incident in progress. *The Illustrated London News*, June 9, 1906, 850–851.

with more than 100 people wounded.[18] Once again the Spanish king, as well as his consort, escaped unharmed – this was Alfonso's third escape from assassination during his reign. This time the culprit was discovered: it was Mateo Morral Roca, a former colleague of Francisco Ferrer, the well-known anarchist educator.

Morral, the son of a wealthy Catalonian industrialist, differed from most anarchist terrorists of the period with their artisan and working-class backgrounds. Morral, deeply serious with a long, thin face, narrow moustache, and blue eyes, was well travelled and very well educated. In Germany he had studied, among other subjects, Nietzsche and chemistry; later on this training in chemistry apparently proved useful to him in constructing bombs. Like Bresci, he was a fine and fastidious dresser. Puritanical regarding women, socially he embraced advanced ideas, and even instructed the workers at his father's factory on how to go out on strike! Although he had become interested in anarchism earlier, in 1905, after a decisive break with his family, he became a full-time militant. Ferrer hired him as a librarian and publishing assistant at the Modern School in Barcelona. Morral probably participated in some fashion (helping mail bomb components to Paris?) in the assassination attempt on Alfonso in May 1905. While older Spanish historiography has denied that Morral threw the 1905 bomb, Avilés Farré's recent biography of Ferrer, based on extensive archival research, forcefully argues that he did.[19]

Since Morral subsequently committed suicide, we do not know his motivation for trying to kill the king while risking the lives of dozens

[18] For a detailed narrative of the assault, see Albert J. Calvert, *The Spanish Royal Wedding: An Account of the Marriage of HM Alfonso XIII of Spain and HRH Pincess Victoria Eugénie of Battenberg* (Taunton: Phoenix Press, 1906). Similar casualty figures are cited by Romero Maura, "Terrorism," 146 (23 dead and 108 wounded), and Joan Connelly Ullman, *The Tragic Week: A Study of Anticlericalism in Spain, 1875–1912* (Cambridge, MA: Harvard University Press, 1968), 45 (24 dead and 107 wounded). In 1909, the Spanish prosecutor charged Ferrer with responsibility for "2 frustrated regicides, 24 murders, and 107 woundings and maimings." William Archer, *The Life, Trial, and Death of Francisco Ferrer* (London: Chapman and Hall, 1911): 79. According to María Teresa Puga, *Alfonso XIII* (Barcelona: Planeta, 1997): 107, citing Count Romanones, the interior minister, there were "twenty-five deaths and more than 100 wounded." Italian Ambassador Silvestrelli, an eyewitness to the bombing who had obtained photos of the event from another Italian, claimed that "*una trentina*," around 30, had been killed. "But now one realizes [that the number of dead is] superior to the figure indicated by me above." Silvestrelli believed that the Spanish authorities wished to downplay the number of fatalities. Silvestrelli, Madrid, to Foreign Minister Tittoni, Rome, June 5 and 7, 1906. PI, b. 35, IFM. In his well-documented text, González Calleja, *La razón de la fuerza*, 374, apparently supports Silvestrelli's estimates, giving a figure of 33 (or is this a typographical error?) killed and 108 gravely wounded.

[19] Núñez Florencio, *Terrorismo*, 147, and Pére Solá, "Morral y Ferrer vistos por Alban Rosell," *Tiempo de Historia* 43 (1978): 45, deny that Morral was the 1905 bomb-thrower. Avilés Farré, *Francisco Ferrer*, 193.

of innocent bystanders. Although in the past this has often been cited as a crucial factor, it was probably not because of any desire to impress Soledad Villafranca, Ferrer's girlfriend with whom Morral was allegedly, but apparently falsely, in love.[20] Presumably, he carried out his deed for the same reason that motivated so many anarchist assassins, the hope that the death of the head of state might lead to a social revolution. Despite what some historians have implied, the demise of the childless Alfonso would not have left the Spanish throne vacant, since the king's four-and-a-half-year-old cousin, the Infante Alfonso, duke of Calabria, had been designated heir presumptive. Nonetheless, with all the enemies confronting the restoration regime – Carlists, Catalonians, syndicalists, and radical republicans, as well as anarchists – the prospect of a revolution was more likely in Spain than elsewhere.

The allegation, made both at the time of the events and subsequently, that Ferrer was the mastermind behind the 1905 and 1906 *attentats* on King Alfonso's life has often been denied. The historians Pére Solá and Núñez Florencio in their carefully reasoned analyses conclude that Ferrer may have had prior knowledge of the 1905 *attentat*, but that it is "highly improbable," although still possible, that he was implicated in the 1906 bombing. In 1906 Ferrer was fully engaged in his experiment in rationalistic education, rather than in plotting violent deeds.[21] More recently, Juan Avilés Farré and others have revived the charges against the anarchist leader.[22] While impressively argued and documented, Avilés's claim perhaps relies too heavily on the testimony of informants such as "Sannois," Aristide Jalaber de Fontenay, the main Spanish secret agent in Paris, given the general unreliability of such agents and Sannois's mistakes on other occasions.[23]

Even if one accepts Avilés's argument, Ferrer and Lerroux's (Lerroux was the charismatic leader of the radical Republicans, who at this time

---

[20] Núñez Florencio, *Terrorismo*, 147; Solá, "Morral y Ferrer," 41.

[21] Solá, "Morral y Ferrer," 45. Núñez Florencio concludes that "Morral, Ferrer, Vallina and their French collaborators – probably had [*tuvieron*] some participation in the attentats [of 1905 and 1906]" but to make this into a "plot" is too much of a "stretch." (*Terrorismo*, 72–73, 151).

[22] Avilés Farré, *Francisco Ferrer*, 193. Romero Maura ("Terrorism," 145–146), also argues for Ferrer's culpability.

[23] For example, in 1905, Sannois reported that the Spanish anarchist Charles Malato had been involved in the assassination of King Umberto. This is typical of the era's pervasive fear of anarchist conspiracies, but no concrete proof has ever been produced for this allegation. Sannois also alleged that the famous anarchist editor Joan (or Juan) Montseny, aka Federico Urales, was a one-time government spy. This seems highly unlikely, unless Montseny was playing the game of double agent. González Calleja, *La razón de la fuerza*, 380n. Relying on an unnamed informant in Paris, the Spanish authorities also took very seriously news in 1906 of a great international conspiracy against several heads of state, this time originating in London. After investigating, the British police denied the allegation as groundless. Bunsen, Madrid to Foreign Office, June 19, 1906; Home Office reply, June 25, 1906. PRO, FO 371/136.

often collaborated with the anarchists) level of participation in Morral's plot appears to have been minimal. Sitting together in a café in Barcelona on May 31 for news of – presumably – the assassination, Ferrer and Lerroux appear as distant onlookers, ready to take advantage of the situation but uninvolved in the details and mechanics of the assassination attempt. If they had really been determined to kill the king, why had they not involved more people in the actual attempt? Why was not a second or third bomb prepared for tossing at the royal carriage? Since bombing as a means of assassination was notoriously unreliable, such "back up" bombs were clearly needed. As Ferrer and Lerroux would have been well aware, the bombs thrown at Alfonso in Paris in 1905 and at Captain General Martínez Campos in 1893 had injured and killed bystanders but had failed to do away with their intended targets. After failing in many prior attempts, in March 1881 the Russian nihilists had finally required two bombers and two bombs in order to murder Tsar Alexander. Of the seven monarchs and heads of government and state assassinated by the anarchists between 1894 and 1921, none died due to a bomb.

For many Spaniards, the Calle Mayor explosion was the most stunning act of terrorism in their history. Bernaldo de Quirós y Pérez, the well-known criminal anthropologist, declared that "the *attentat* of Mateo Morral against Alfonso XIII and Queen Victoria [Alfonso's bride, Victoria Eugenia of Battenberg] ... represents the summit, the apex [*vértice*] of anarchist criminality." Not only was it an assassination attempt on the young king and queen that very nearly succeeded, but also a murderous assault on scores of innocent bystanders in a city that for almost thirty years had been immune to *attentats*. For Spain such a combination of regicide and bloodbath was unprecedented. The idea of the lovely Victoria Eugenia – considered the most beautiful Spanish queen in 400 years – as a radiant bride one moment and the next emerging from a wrecked carriage in her blood-spattered white wedding dress while streams of blood flowed along the cracks of the pavement caught the public imagination and added to the horror of the scene, which in any case much of the Spanish and world press exaggerated.[24] One British publication

[24] Constancio Bernaldo de Quirós y Pérez, *Derecho penal adaptado al programma de judicatura* (Madrid: Reus, 1926): 242. *L'Osservatore romano* (Rome), June 2, 1906, 1, the semi-official spokesman of the Vatican, qualified it as: "this horrible *attentat*, more hateful still, if that is possible, and more infamous than the others." Professor Enrique de Benito y Llaves cited this "*attentat* that absorbed the attention of all Spaniards, and that produced an indescribable emotion in the entire world" (*La Anarquía y el Derecho Penal: discurso leído en la solemne aperture del curso academic de 1906 a 1907* [Oviedo: Adolfo Brid, 1906]: 9). The *Daily Telegraph* described it as "an outrage of unutterable horror, which ... stands unmatched for murderous impulse, devilish calculation, and heartrending results in the history of political crime." Cited by Calvert, *Spanish Royal Wedding*,

went so far as to suggest that if the newly married monarchs had been killed, Spain might have been plunged into civil war.[25] In Barcelona, radical republicans and the anarchists, massively armed with revolvers and knives, were planning to storm the Montjuich fortress on news of Alfonso's death.[26] Lerroux had also contacted sympathizers inside the military and in various other provinces to be prepared.[27]

The attempt on Alfonso was also noteworthy because of the wide publication and groundbreaking status of the photographs of the bomb blast, perhaps the world's first photographs to register an image of a terrorist act just at the moment of its occurrence.[28] Aware of the significance, picture postcards of the explosion were printed, with careening horses and carriage.[29] *The Illustrated London News* offered for sale enormous copies, as large as small posters, of the "famous photograph" either by themselves or framed in stained oak.[30] Besides such media stunts, alarm was increased by incoming reports of suspected anarchist conspiracies against other European monarchs and by the notice a few days later of the discovery of anarchist bombs in Ancona apparently prepared for use against the Italian king during his forthcoming visit to the city.[31] Madrid's *El Liberal*, the leading liberal newspaper with one of the largest circulations in the country, declared that: "one [anarchist] crime after another appears, and the contagion spreads amongst all countries. One can't deny that a truly universal plot endures [*subsiste*] in a latent state. It is not possible to avoid *attentats*."[32] This feeling of helplessness

302. See the description of the *attentat* in the *New York Times*, June 2, 1906, 4, and in Bunsen, Madrid, to Grey, London, June 1, 1906, in BDFA. Series F, vol. 27: 148–150, and in *Illustrierte Zeitung* (Leipzig), June 14, 1906, 950. According to María Teresa Puga, *Alfonso XIII* (Barcelona: Planeta, 1994): 105, all the commentators of the time considered Victoria Eugenia the most beautiful Spanish Queen since Isabella, wife of Charles V, the Holy Roman Emperor.

[25] "Festivity and Outrage," *The Illustrated London News*, June 9, 1906, 829.

[26] González Calleja, *La razón de la fuerza*, 373–74; José Alvarez-Junco, *The Emergence of Mass Politics in Spain* (Brighton and Portland: Sussex Academic Press, 2002): 115.

[27] Avilés Farré, *Francisco Ferrer*, 192.

[28] See pictorial section 1 of the *New York Times*, June 17, 1906, and the even more dramatic photographs reproduced by *The Illustrated London News*, June 9, 1906, 850–851, courtesy of the Spanish journals *Blanco y Negro* and *ABC*.

[29] A picture of such a postcard is reproduced following page 288 in José Alvarez-Junco, *El Emperador del Paralelo: Lerroux y la demagogia populista* (Madrid: Alianza Editorial, 1990).

[30] Two sizes were possible: 18 by 13 inches or, upon card mount, 24 by 20. *The Illustrated London News*, June 16, 1906, 879.

[31] "Dispatches" coming out of New York spoke of a plot against President Roosevelt, King Edward II, Kaiser Wilhelm II, and the tsar. "Bloc-Notes Parisien," *Le Gaulois*, June 6, 1906; *The Times* (London), June 4, 1906, 3; *The Times* (London), June 6, 1906, 5; "Plot Not Hatched in London," *New York Times*, June 4, 1906, 1; *L'Illustrazione italiana*, June 10, 1906.

[32] *El Liberal*, June 4, 1906.

in the face of *attentats*, that protective measures could never be extensive enough to prevent the determined lone anarchist assassin or bomber from getting through, affected not only Spain, but also Germany, Italy and other countries. It helped to account for the pervasive fear of anarchist terrorism.

Spain's reaction was to call for an "international accord for the repression and prevention of anarchist crimes."[33] The Spanish interior minister emphasized that "in order to be effective, the surveillance of the anarchists must be worldwide, because it is a universal social evil."[34] Besides the demands of the European and American press,[35] several notables urged Madrid to take action. In Stockholm King Oscar visited the Spanish minister to Sweden at his home to encourage Spain "to take the initiative" in proposing "energetic measures against anarchism." The anarchists, according to the king, deserved to be "exiled from society" and "imprisoned like ferocious beasts." Only the British might object to this and even they might accept it after the "treacherous attack" on the Spanish sovereigns.[36] In Paris, Sir Howard Vincent, who had represented Britain at the Rome conference, gave a widely publicized interview calling for "European nations and the United States of America to take vigorous and concerted action against anarchic crime."[37] Encountering the Spanish chargé d'affaires at a social event on June 5, Vincent reiterated his proposal for an anti-anarchist campaign and assured the skeptical diplomat that in recent years British opinion regarding international anti-anarchist action "had changed much." He pledged to do what he could to make such action possible.[38] The prince of Wales, who had attended the wedding in Madrid, may also have joined in pressuring the British government. After the explosion on Calle Mayor, the Spanish prime

---

[33] This phrase referring to the foreign minister's instructions in his telegram of June 14 can be found in: Duke of Arcos, Rome, to foreign minister, Madrid, June 19, 1906. OP. L. 2751/336. SFM.

[34] Count de Romanones, interview in the French newspaper, *Le Journal*, June 6, 1906, cited by González Calleja, *La razón de la fuerza*, 376.

[35] Editorial, *Le Temps* (Paris), June 2, 1906. London's *Daily Express* called for an international conference to study measures of repression; The *Daily Chronicle* wanted more police surveillance; the *Standard* asked for more restrictions on the sale and manufacture of explosives and a crackdown on anarchist meetings, public and private (see the review of the English press published in *Corriere della Sera*, June 2, 1906, 1). "Hostes Humani Generis", *New York Times*, June 5, 1906, 6, called for international action, perhaps at the next [peace] conference of The Hague, aimed at "the summary suppression of avowed 'enemies of the human race.'"

[36] Count de Chacon, Spanish Legation, Stockholm, to foreign minister, Madrid, June 2, 1906. L. 2751/336. SFM.

[37] *The Times* (London), June 5, 1906, 3. The *New York Times* reprinted Vincent's interview on June 17, 1906, 3:6.

[38] Riaño, Paris, to foreign minister, Madrid, June 7, 1906. L.2751/336, SFM.

minister "urgently requested" that he use his influence for "the severest measures against the anarchists in England since ... against their criminal solidarity one must have defensive solidarity; in this endeavor the missing link is England." Reportedly the prince concurred and offered to act accordingly.[39]

The Ottoman Empire was eager for new international anti-anarchist measures since for years the sultan had tended to label all his political enemies as "anarchists." Basing its views on newspaper reports, Constantinople believed wrongly that Italy was about to take the initiative (a misconception repeated by later historians).[40] In 1901 Sultan Abdul Hamid II, dubbed the "Great Assassin" for massacring so many of his subjects, particularly Armenians, sought to have the Great Powers deport as an anarchist, according to the terms of the Rome conference's Final Protocol, his own brother-in-law.[41] Damad Mahmud Celâleddin was a Young Turk, and although neither he, nor the Armenians, who looked to the Russian nihilists for inspiration, were anarchists, the sultan frequently condemned them as such.[42] Abdul Hamid's anarchist fears, which must have been at least partly feigned for political reasons, were not totally chimerical. On July 21, 1905, as the sultan was leaving Friday prayers at the mosque near his enormous palace complex at Yildiz, outside of Constantinople, a melinite bomb packed inside a carriage exploded. The sultan remained unscathed, but twenty-six people were killed and fifty-seven injured. Afterwards, bombs were discovered in various buildings in the Ottoman capital.

While most of the dozens of conspirators behind this plot were Armenian nationalists, the Belgian anarchist Eduard Joris (or Carolus Eduard Joris)

---

[39] Tel. Radowitz, Madrid, to Foreign Office, Berlin, June 4, 1906. Eur. Gen. 91, bd. 4, GFO.

[40] G. de Martino, Therapia, to Tittoni, Rome, June 20, 1906. Ser.P, b. 47, IFM. No evidence exists in the Italian archives of an Italian initiative to convoke a new anti-anarchist meeting. This rumor was simply based on the fact that it had called for a conference in 1898. Many of the same reasons that Giolitti and the Italian government gave for not adhering to the St. Petersburg Protocol explain their lack of interest in any new conferences. González Calleja's analysis (*La razón de la fuerza*, 376, 377n) is mistaken.

[41] Copy, Turkish circular telegram to the European powers, December 24, 1901, included with Sanderson, FO, to undersecretary, HO, January 2, 1902, reporting conversation with the Turkish ambassador. PRO. HO144/608/B32482/14. The Sultan also wanted the deportation of a "Hodja Kadri."

[42] For the Sultan's efforts to brand the young Turks as anarchists, see François Georgeon, *Abdülhamid II. Le sultan calife (1876–1909)* (Paris: Fayard, 2003): 380–383. "Turkey ... considers the Armenian refugees in Bulgaria as anarchists without exception." Memo on a report of the Austrian minister to Bulgaria, November 3, 1898. IB 1898, k. 390, HHStA. "Both the Hunchakian and Dashnaktsutiun [two Armenian revolutionary groups] were very strongly influenced by the Russian Narodniks." Manoug Joseph Somakian, *Empires in Conflict: Armenia and the Great Powers, 1895–1920* (London and New York: Tauris Academic Studies, 1995): 16.

played an important role. Joris, who was living in Constantinople, was motivated by his deep interest in the Armenian problem. The plotters generally met in Joris's apartment where he stored explosives that he had imported from abroad labeled as "white soap." Joris also lent his passport and hat to the Armenians so that they might travel in disguise in order to test the explosives. Joris wanted to participate in the actual assassination attempt, but the Armenian terrorists refused to allow him because he was a foreigner. After Joris had been arrested, tried, and sentenced to death, the sultan released him under pressure from the Belgian government, which was itself responding to pro-Joris demonstrations inside Belgium. According to some sources, the sultan subsequently paid Joris to spy on the Armenian revolutionaries, but Belgian historians have now rejected this view.[43]

As for Spain, on June 9, in the royal response to the address of the president of the chamber of deputies congratulating him on his escape from harm, King Alfonso alluded to an anti-anarchist accord. The foreign minister, the duke of Almodóvar del Río, sent out a formal proposal on June 14.[44] Educated in England, more businessman than aristocrat since he had acquired his title through marriage, Almodóvar was universally admired for, according to British Ambassador Bunsen, his "agreeable and conciliatory manners," as well as his "tact and firmness" when chairing the great international conference at Algeciras during the early months of 1906.[45] Russian Ambassador Cassini praised his "exquisite urbanity," and declared that he was "one of the most likeable [*sympathique*] diplomats" that he had encountered in his long career.[46] In 1898 Almodóvar had also been foreign minister during the meeting of the Rome conference. This experience together with the duke's impressive diplomatic skills might possibly have led to some progress on an accord. Ill and overworked, however, he died on June 23 at the age of fifty-five. With him died the possibility of an extensive, new international agreement, as remote as that might have been, although as late as December 1906 Spain was still thinking of appealing to the Great Powers for an "international agreement" to establish "general measures" against the anarchists.[47]

[43] Georgeon, *Abdülhamid II*, 390–391; *The Times* (London), July 24, 1905, 5, and January 25, 1906, 4, and January 26, 1906; Walter Resseler and Benoit Suykerbuyk, *Dynamiet voor de Sultan: Carolus Eduard Joris in Konstantinopel* (Antwerp: B+B, 1997).
[44] Duke of Arcos, Rome, to foreign minister, Madrid, June 19, 1906. OP. L. 2751. SFM.
[45] Bunsen, Madrid, June 25, 1906. FO371/136. PRO.
[46] L. 225/no. 12454, "Almodóvar del Río," SFM.
[47] Conversation between the German ambassador and Spanish Prime Minister Vega Armijo. Copy, German ambassador, Madrid, to Chancellor Bülow, December 30, 1906. Rep. 30, 8756, GSAP.

Even before Almodóvar's death, Prime Minister Moret indicated that Spain would be satisfied with an international police accord alone. Interviewed on a June 11 by a reporter from the Parisian daily, *Le Temps*, the Spanish prime minister said that:

the most useful [measure] would be the organization of an *entente* between the police of all civilized states. The anarchist is in essence a nomad and a cosmopolitan. It is his perpetual migrations that make him at once difficult to monitor and dangerous...The police of the different States should...keep the other [police] *au courant* of the [anarchists'] movements and communicate reciprocally lists and personal descriptions of those of their nationals noted for their suspect doctrines. Previously, such an *entente* existed between the Italian, English and French police, and rendered the greatest services. Little by little, that organization was allowed to decline [*péricliter*]. I consider that one ought to re-establish it and extend it to the entire civilized world. We are now witnessing a fresh outbreak of anarchist activity; in consequence one ought to take measures. [48]

It is unclear what Moret meant by the *entente* of the Italian, English, and French police. The agreements of the mid-1890s regarding closer anti-anarchist police cooperation between Italy and France had not included the English.

The Italian response to Almodóvar's dispatch indicated both European willingness to meet some of the Spanish desires and the limitations of their commitment. When the Spanish ambassador met with the Italian foreign minister on June 19, Tittoni mentioned that he had recently had a conversation with Prime Minister Giolitti, regarding the measures they might adopt against anarchist attacks. "Both were convinced that it was urgent that they concern themselves very seriously with this question and find the means to defend against such barbarous *attentats.*" At the same time they thought that no legislative measures were "necessary or even useful." Nor was an international conference advisable, since with all its publicity, it would be impossible to keep measures secret. Instead agreements ought to be adopted:

to organize the reciprocal intelligence [*mútual inteligencia*] of the different police forces, in a way that each one of them would be constantly informed of the movements of the anarchists and, as far as possible, of their plans [*projectos*].

Each government should privately come to an agreement with the others. In Tittoni's judgment, to make this intelligence service effective, governments would have to "spend considerable sums." The Spanish ambassador commented to Madrid that:

I know that the secret expenditures of the Italian government are very great. Both in Italy and in other countries, there is no anarchist center where there are

---

[48] Pierre Mille, "Une conversation avec M. Moret," *Le Temps*, June 13, 1906, 1.

not numerous spies. Some of these services are very complete particularly in the United States and in England.[49]

The viewpoint of Giolitti and Tittoni was also that of most of western Europe. As in 1893, 1898, and 1901, it proved impossible to achieve consensus on measures for repressing and preventing anarchist crimes, except in the area of more effective police action and greater police cooperation. In late June, when the Spanish ambassador spoke to King Edward about the need for action in the common defense against the anarchist danger, the king reacted heatedly that anarchist surveillance in Britain was better organized than anywhere else, and that a good police force was the best protection.[50] Even restricting itself to police measures alone, Spain was unable to achieve its goals of an *international* police accord, but succeeded in establishing better bilateral police communications with Britain, Italy, and some other countries that had not signed the St. Petersburg Protocol. On June 20, Spain sent the United States a despatch conveying its desire:

to keep the several Governments and police of the Great Powers as much in touch as possible with regard to the movements and schemes of anarchists … and with the hope that reciprocal warnings and information may be communicated by and exchanged between all the governments interested in thwarting the criminal designs of the anarchists.[51]

Washington made no promises but passed this request onto the Secret Service.[52]

Spain also took up the Italians on their willingness for an accord to facilitate intelligence-gathering. An exchange of diplomatic notes on July 4 and August 17 established an agreement between the two countries to provide "personal data" regarding each other's anarchists.[53]

Spain and Anglo-French police cooperation

In July 1906, at the behest of the Spanish prime minister, a former minister of finance, Guillermo J. de Osma y Scull, made a secret visit to London, and in August to Paris, seeking "to work out confidentially the

---

[49] Duke of Arcos, Rome, to foreign minister, Madrid, June 19, 1906. OP. l. 2751. SFM.
[50] Report of the German ambassador after a conversation with Polo de Bernabé, the Spanish ambassador. Metternich, London, to Bülow, June 28, 1906. Eur. Gen. 91. Bd. 4. GFO.
[51] William Miller Collier, American Legation, Madrid, to Elihu Root, Washington, DC, June 20, 1906. M31, roll 134, NA.
[52] RG 87. E14, box 5 (70333–71083), NA.
[53] Minute, undersecretary, foreign ministry, Madrid, to Spanish ambassador, Italy, July 4, 1906. Ambassador, Rome to foreign minister, Madrid, August 17, 1906. L.2751/336. SFM.

means by which in some manner the surveillance services of the anarchists could be coordinated in several countries."[54] Osma spoke with the permanent undersecretary at the Home Office and then three times with Sir Edward Henry, head of the Metropolitan Police. Henry answered all his questions and put at his disposal confidential Home Office reports from recent years. Osma became convinced, without "the least doubt" of Henry's "absolute sincerity," "although [Henry's view that the English were doing their anti-anarchist duty] contradicts the universal belief that attributes to the English police a policy which one could define as the intentional appeasement [*contemporización*] of the anarchists who respect the public peace of England."[55]

Osma suggested, more as a general topic of discussion than as a concrete proposal, creating an "International Branch" (*Sección internacional*) under Sir Henry's "orders, selected by and dependent on him," made up of "one or two Inspectors" and of:

whatever the desired number of Spanish, and above all of Catalan agents; while in the same fashion we would have English Inspectors and Agents in Madrid and Barcelona selected and paid for by us, although proposed by him; [also] having to organize, in each case, analogous Branches with personnel, namely, French and Italians in London and Madrid, and with Italian, Catalan, etc. personnel in Paris, Rome, etc.: in sum, where one desires in one's own interest, and not for philosophic or philanthropic considerations, the heads of police, whether they be called Commissioner of Police, Director of the *Sûreté*, or as each calls itself, want to work together for the more efficacious monitoring of anarchism, so far as preventative ends might be achieved.

Neither Sir Henry, although he discussed the measure thoroughly with Osma, nor the director of the French *Sûreté* thought this form of international policing a viable option (although, as we shall see, a version of it was adopted by Barcelona). Nonetheless, in retrospect, the Spanish proposal appears to be rather remarkable and groundbreaking, as well as an indication of the tremendously high esteem in which the Spanish held the British police. One reason for the tepid British response to this proposal for international policing was the fear that it would needlessly

---

54 Osma is presumably the author of an unsigned typed memorandum, *"Tanteo confidencial sobre concertar la repression internacional del anarquismo de accion* [written in blue pencil], *Entente cordiale,"* dated July 1906 and deposited in the Archivo Maura (Madrid), Arm. Inf.N.3/G.2. Hereafter cited as *Tanteo confidencial.* The reference to M. Huart's departure from the directorship of the French *Sûreté* shows that this document was written after January 1907. A British Home Office docket sheet minute by E. G. B. and dated August 27, 1906 mentions that: "I believe Señor Osma, late Spanish minister of finance called on Comr. [Metropolitan Police Commissioner] & had some conversation with him." Osma was Spanish minister of finance [Hacienda] December 1903–December 1904.
55 Literally: "the anarchism that respects."

spread "unproven suspicions and confidences" and thus "maintain the alarm, that spreads more after each *attentat*." The Italian police service set up in London, according to Henry, had only produced criticisms of the British police, without unearthing a single plot: "not one single time has it been known that an offense was plotted in England that the English police might have been able to observe in order to give a preventative warning about it" (although Rubino's *attentat*, and perhaps Angiolillo's, would seem to contradict this assertion).

The chief commissioner also pointed out all of the limitations on British police powers. While it was true that, with the passage of the Aliens Act of 1905, the authorities for the first time obtained the right to expel foreigners, they were still unable "to expel anyone for mere suspicion without a previous conviction." Despite these limitations, Henry expressed the belief, which impressed Osma, that, during his long experience in office, even if he had possessed greater powers, he did not remember "a single occasion" on which he might have used such powers to "detain, expel or hand over an anarchist" meriting serious suspicion of having been involved in an *attentat*.[56]

Some of Police Commissioner's Henry's most interesting comments to Osma were his explanation of the various safety valves in English society that rendered the anarchist threat harmless.

The Commissioner of Police believes that in fact it is not in England where *attentats* are hatched: he believes that the atmosphere of English society is a sedative [*un sedante*]; that in any case one does not encounter in this atmosphere passions, on the contrary they evaporate in the clubs and in the special press in which advanced ideas are ventilated; and yet he cites the fact that no anarchist periodical manages to prosper in England, nor even to survive moderately well. The police tries, by means of its confidants, to stay in contact with these people, and it seems that it even follows a policy of finding them work; and he [i.e., Commissioner Henry] believes to have observed that by this procedure, which might seem to be like the cultivation of microbes, the anarchist virus in individuals loses much of its intensity... regarding the most sensational [anarchist] newspaper articles, they deserve, according to the Commissioner, to be viewed as of a complete and even ridiculous insignificance, treating of trashy papers [*papeluchos*] without circulation and without any more notoriety than that which they momentarily achieve due to parliamentary questions formulated about what they have said.[57]

---

[56] *Tanteo confidencial*, 3–5.
[57] *Tanteo confidencial*, 5–6. Henry is presumably referring to Sir William Evans-Gordon's query in parliament on June 14, 1906, regarding articles in the London anarchist press that approved of Morral's *attentat*. The commissioner of police provided the Home Office with the following information about the anarchist press (22 June 1906, 144/834/144519/2, PRO): "In London there are issued 6 papers which may be considered as giving a measure of support to doctrines that may be construed as Anarchistic. One of these papers is in English and issues monthly; 5 are in Yiddish – one being issued

This remarkable statement by Henry reaffirmed the English view that freedom of the press was a better guarantee against anarchist extremism, and by implication anarchist terrorism, than police repression or censorship, which only threatened to provide the anarchists the oxygen on which extremism and terrorism thrive: publicity. Even more remarkable was the police commissioner's willingness, if necessary, to find anarchists jobs, thus potentially integrating them into society and rendering them innocuous.

Osma seems not to have been particularly persuaded that British policy was effective and enlightened. Rather, he noted disappointedly that, given the lack of anarchist "terror" in Britain and the British public's "worship ... of individual liberty," the police would do nothing that might cause controversy by involving "some expansion of its powers" or taking some "novel action." The only thing that could be hoped for ("and it would be a start") was to establish "a relationship of reciprocal correspondence," that might be "official or confidential," between interior ministries and central police departments that might communicate "by mail, by telegraph, in cipher etc., but without the necessity of having recourse to embassies or other centers." Each country would be free to communicate what it wished.

If what I just mentioned were possible, if the [police] centers were in constant communication, and even if it became clear through this daily or possibly weekly communication that they had nothing to say to each other, a special warning would become unnecessary, and there would be no need to feel directly or seemingly responsible for it. In fact, should this concept be adopted, it could very well become a habit, just as having a phone available creates the habit of using it more frequently. I cannot even say for sure whether the Commissioner of Police in London would be favorable to such a practice but my feeling is that he would be and – this is not only my opinion but that of a much more authoritative [or authorized] person – that it would not be an insignificant thing if this relationship of habitual correspondence came to be, even though its scope will not be defined by any text.[58]

After Osma journeyed to Paris he received a similar message, i.e., that such constant, habitual, and direct communication, established by verbal understanding rather than by written accord, was the most that could be hoped for from the French *Sûreté*. This French reluctance was not due to a desire to maintain traditional "constitutional guarantees" and civil rights,

at irregular intervals, 1 monthly, 2 fortnightly and one being issued at irregular intervals, 1 monthly, 2 fortnightly and 1 weekly. Their influence & circulation will be increased if they get the advantage of being advertised through the medium of questions in the House."

[58] *Tanteo confidencial*, 9–10.

as in Britain, but to the dominance of purely political concerns. French governments were afraid of the press, and above all, of the power exercised in parliament by "the most advanced elements, who did not blindly sympathize with any attentat, but sympathize with those who profess ideas that lead to those" ideas that "bring forth attentats." Osma is presumably referring to some of the radicals and socialists who were increasingly influential both in parliament and on the government. According to a story that Osma heard from the French police and in reference to the bombing attack on President Loubet and King Alfonso in May 1905, these advanced elements included even the president of France. "One could not be more papal than the Pope and if the Presidents of the Republic were glad that the [assassins] were throwing bombs at them, there was not much the Justice [ministry] and the *Sûreté* could object to."[59]

As startling as this observation was Osma's conclusion that, regarding anti-anarchist police cooperation, "at present the [police] of London and Paris in fact volunteer nothing reciprocally." While the *Entente Cordiale*, the informal diplomatic alliance between France and Britain, functioned at many levels, including police cooperation, it did not include the surveillance of anarchists.

I [i.e., Osma] have to say that one of the things that most caught my attention in the conversations with Sir Edward Henry was the observation that regarding the aims we're discussing, i.e. cooperation between police forces, at present in fact [the police] of London and Paris volunteer nothing reciprocally, to the point that, [while] an Entente cordiale exists politically, administratively, socially and for all police functions except for this, as regards monitoring anarchist elements and preventively communicating news depending on the case, not only do you have nothing organized, but nothing is being done: except perhaps criticizing each other. I'll not enter into the very graphic details of the extremes to which a lack of confidence has arrived: the fact that[,] even to obtain a photograph of some individual abroad that it is interested in possessing, the English police prefers to send out one of its agents from London to photograph him, instead of applying to the police of that country (and I am not alluding to France).[60]

Furthermore, according to Osma, the British police had taken no interest in the French judicial proceedings regarding the 1905 bomb attack in Paris against the French president and the Spanish king.

Why this lack of British interest and an unwillingness to exchange information on the anarchists with France? Presumably it was because of France's alliance with Russia and the presence of a large Russian secret police agency in Paris with which the French authorities, especially the *Sûreté*, fully cooperated. One historian has qualified the *Sûreté*–Russian Foreign Agency relationship as "symbiotic": the *Sûreté* provided

---

[59] *Tanteo confidencial*, 12.   [60] *Tanteo confidencial*, 10.

information and other forms of assistance to the Russians and the Russians in turn provided employment for retired French detectives and surveillance over the activities of the Russian revolutionaries, thus reducing the *Sûreté*'s workload.[61] Therefore any information that the British supplied to Paris might easily make its way into the hands of the Russian police. When William Melville was head of the Special Branch (1893–1903), this might have mattered less, since Melville was happy to work closely with the Russian police in Paris and elsewhere and had to be restrained by his superiors from cooperating even more. But in March 1903, the fifty-one-year-old master detective abruptly resigned under somewhat mysterious circumstances. E. Thomas Wood speculates that Edward Henry, the new chief commissioner of the Metropolitan Police (1903–1918), engineered a quiet purge of the Special Branch to get rid of Melville and some other long-serving CID officers. Besides collaborating with Russia, Melville had been notorious for bending the rules in combating the anarchists and suspected of employing *agents provocateurs*.[62] Since many British officials, not to mention the general public, were uncomfortable with these tactics as well as deeply distrustful of the tsarist police, Henry may have wished to make a clean break with the past by forcing Melville out of office.

A second question raised by Osma's report is the extent to which Britain was responsible for "nurturing the microbes" of the anarchist virus, leading to *attentats* abroad. This belief was widely held on the continent. In 1906, the *Journal du droit internationale privé* (Clunet), a distinguished French international law publication, opined that the attacks of May 31, 1905, in Paris and 1906 in Madrid were both "very likely" (*trés vraisemblablement*) plotted in London.[63] Of the more than 200 anarchist "incidents" (assassinations, bombings, discovery of bombs presumably planted by anarchists or alleged anarchists) that occurred between 1880 and 1914 throughout the world, outside of Russia and of Britain itself, only two can be directly linked to the latter, i.e., Angiolillo's assassination of Cánovas in 1897, after seeing victims of Spanish torture who had arrived in London, and Rubino's assault on King Leopold in 1902.[64] While it is true that Émile Henry took refuge in London at various times before returning to Paris to resume his bombings, he had already begun

[61] Ben Fischer, *Okhrana: The Paris Operations of the Russian Imperial Police* (Washington DC: History Staff, Center for the Study of Intelligence, CIA, 1997); Zuckerman, *Abroad*, 175; Andrew and Gordievsky, *KGB*, 23–24.

[62] Porter, *Vigilant State*, 143–144; 149; Wood, *Wars on Terror*, Chapters 2 and 5.

[63] The *Journal du droit internationale privé* (Clunet) 33 (1906): 769.

[64] Hermia Oliver, *The International Anarchist Movement*, 115–116, has cast doubt on the report that Angiolillo saw Spanish torture victims in London. However, she has not consulted Rudolf Rocker, *En la borrasca* (Buenos Aires: Americalee, 1949), 63. Rocker was an eyewitness to Angiolillo's meeting with such a victim.

his terrorist career under the nose of the French police who had been unable to locate him. There is no evidence that he received much support or direction while in the British capital.[65] No proof has ever been produced demonstrating that the 1905 and 1906 *attentats* against Alfonso were planned in London. Indirectly, perhaps, a case could be made for a greater degree of British responsibility for anarchist terrorism, since so many prominent anarchist leaders lived for long periods in the British metropolis. Only one of these, Johann Most, was a vigorous advocate of violent anarchist tactics during his stay there in 1878–1882. In the early 1890s Kropotkin (in London 1886–1917) and Malatesta (1881–1882, 1889–1897, 1900–1913, 1914–1919) had abandoned their advocacy of propaganda by the deed, although they remained sympathetic to anarchist assassins. During Kropotkin and Malatesta's London sojourns, evidence is lacking that would connect them to terrorist acts, although suspicions linger about Malatesta's possible involvement with planning, or at least suggesting to Bresci, the assassination of King Umberto. On the other hand, the Italian nationalist Orsini had not only plotted his famous attack against Napoleon III in England but had also procured and tested his bombs there. This deed may well have colored subsequent views about Britain's responsibility for anarchist terrorism.

If the view of London as the world's prime incubator of anarchist plots was largely a myth, Paris had more claim to that title, at least as regarded Spain. Much evidence suggests that the revolutionary republicans and anarchists in the French capital played a key role in the assassination attempts of 1905 and 1906 and they were often protected by highly placed figures in French politics.

Returning to a discussion of Anglo-Spanish relations, in reaction to Osma's efforts, the shock of the attack on Alfonso and his British bride, and against the background of increasingly cordial diplomatic and dynastic relations between the two countries, London agreed to an unprecedented degree of police cooperation with Madrid. This was despite the fact that the British did not particularly trust the Spanish police – one official in the Home Office expressed the fear that the Spanish police itself might contain anarchists![66] In the fall of 1905, Scotland Yard sent over two officers to help in providing security during the state visit of French President Loubet to Madrid. In May 1906 two British policemen were again sent to the Spanish capital to assist in security matters,

[65] According to a French police report, an anarchist grocer in London gave Henry 300 francs in appreciation and "eagerness that he would continue his work," but Émile was "indignant that the sum was so small." Merriman, *The Dynamite Club*, 128.

[66] Docket sheet minute, M. D. Chalmers, undersecretary HO, August 30, 1906, HO144/757/118516/36, PRO.

all expenses defrayed by the Spanish government. In an unprecedented move, a police sergeant from the Special Branch accompanied Princess Victoria Eugenia to the Spanish border; previously only the king and queen and the prince and princess of Wales had received publicly funded police protection when traveling outside the metropolis.[67]

Then on July 17, 1906 the British ambassador informed the Spanish foreign minister of a significant step forward in Anglo-Spanish anti-anarchist police cooperation.

In my note of the 3rd instant I had the honor to communicate to the Department of State for the information of the Spanish Government information received from the London police authorities as to the anarchist movement. I am now directed to inform Your Excellent that any further information on this subject that might be of interest to the Spanish police will be communicated direct to them by the London police. This course has, I believe, been followed occasionally in the past and is in the opinion of the competent authorities the most effective.[68]

The Spanish were delighted by this "formal pledge" (*promesa formalizada*) that Foreign Minister Gullón thought had "never been ... as expedient and opportune as in the present circumstances" due to "a certain activity among the anarchists" and tentative plans for the Spanish sovereigns to travel outside of Spain and inside the Peninsula. He also asked that when the British police obtained information of "urgent interest," it should in addition be sent to the Spanish ambassador.[69] On August 15, 1906, the British Foreign Office agreed to this request.[70] A month later, and despite some Home Office reservations about targeting "ordinary political discontents," Secretary Gladstone promised "that anything which comes to the knowledge of the police in this country as to the relations suspected to exist between anarchists and the extremists of Spanish political parties shall be promptly and confidentially communicated to the Spanish Government."[71] This was in reaction to Spanish concerns about evidence that Carlists, Catalans, and republicans, as well as anarchists, were involved in plotting the assassination of the king.

On the other hand, the Metropolitan Police balked at too close a degree of cooperation. Speaking with the British ambassador in early August

---

[67] Minutes on docket sheet, Edward Henry and HO Officials, New Scotland Yard, to undersecretary of state, FO, May 22, 1906, HO45/10332/136042, PRO.

[68] Bunsen, to Pio Gullón, San Sebastian, July 17, 1906. OP, l. 2751, SFM.

[69] Minute, Pio Gullón, to British ambassador, San Sebastian, July 18, 1906. OP. l. 2751, SFM.

[70] Eric Barrington (for Edward Grey), FO, to Ambassador Luis Polo de Bernabé, London, August 5, 1906. OP, l. 2751, SFM; Troup, HO to undersecretary of state, FO, July 10, 1906, and Bunsen, San Sebastian, to Grey, London, July 31, 1906. FO371/136, PRO.

[71] Undersecretary Chalmers minute, August 30, 1906 HO144/757/118516/36; Gladstone to Grey, September 17, 1906. FO371/136, PRO.

1906, Spanish Queen Dowager Maria Christina expressed her admiration for Scotland Yard and said that on "one occasion the information supplied [by them] had enabled the Spanish police to arrest an anarchist who had come to Spain to take her life." She continued that "she would be glad if a small number of intelligent Spanish police officers could be sent to England to study the latter's methods."[72] While the queen dowager's wish never became a formal Spanish request, the Metropolitan Police made clear that they would oppose such contact for the same reasons they had opposed Italian and German requests to work directly with the police inside Britain. First, because the Criminal Investigation Department's methods were "in accordance with local conditions. The methods employed in London would not be the same as those appropriate to Madrid or Barcelona." Moreover "the Commissioner of police is further of the opinion that the proposed visit would make his own task more difficult, as the arrival of the Spanish officers would at once become known, and would stir up excitement in quarters where it is better that excitement should not exist."[73]

The deficiencies of the Spanish police

The repeated, poignant attempts by the Spanish to obtain foreign police help in combating the anarchists highlighted an uncomfortable truth: the Spanish public security forces were woefully inadequate and ineffective. The Spanish police lacked technical expertise and were undermanned, underfunded, and often made up of the dregs of society due to the pitiful wages and low social status of this career. In his memoirs, Juan de La Cierva, a famous minister of the interior and police reformer under Antonio Maura, described the situation in these terms:

The police of that time was a dangerous and infected conglomeration of agents appointed and discharged at the caprice of the [provincial] governor and the minister [in Madrid] ...With salaries of 1,250, 1,500 or 2,000 pesetas [in 1914 a family with two children needed a minimum of 2,000 pesetas per year to survive], one can imagine how those functionaries would act, in contact with every office and every corruption.[74]

In March 1908, Angel Ossorio, the captain general of Barcelona, where most of the terrorism in Spain occurred, even referred to the police of his city as, until recently, "a true manure heap" (*verdadero estercolero*).[75] In a

---

[72] Bunsen, San Sebastian, to Grey, August 4, 1906. FO371/136, PRO.
[73] Private letter, Gladstone, Home Office, to Grey, September 17, 1906. FO371/136. PRO.
[74] *Notas de mi vida* (Madrid: Reus, 1955), 57–58, cited by Antonio Viqueira Hinojosa, *Historia y Anecdotario de la policía española 1833–1931* (Madrid: San Martin, 1989): 106.
[75] Cited in González Calleja, *La razón de la fuerza*, 414.

book published in 1913, a Spanish journalist reported that, except for a few rare exceptions, there were no "expert detectives" (*detectives especialistas*) in the Spanish police. Funding went to top bureaucrats, not skilled detectives.[76]

Another source of Spanish ineffectiveness was the division of the Spanish police into competing and ill-coordinated organizations. More than a half dozen separate police forces existed in nineteenth-century Spain. While to some degree these divisions also existed in Italy and France, the situation was much worse in Spain. As previously mentioned, in September 1896 the government created, on the French model, a special body of judicial, or investigative, police to enforce the provisions of the severe anti-anarchists laws passed in 1894 and 1896.[77] This police was divided into two sections, one for Madrid made up of thirteen men, and one for Barcelona, a center of much greater anarchist activity, with twenty-five. The army appointed military officers to be the heads of both sections, but the courts, on the recommendation of the military commander and civil governor of each province, nominated the rest of the agents. The anti-anarchist police depended on the ministry of justice rather than forming an integral part of the police system under the interior ministry. Nicknamed the "social brigade" (*brigada social*), it soon came into bad repute, accused of torturing people, faking evidence, and planting bombs or other incriminating material upon innocent people. Both the corrupt, semi-illiterate Tressols and the infamous torturer Portas of Montjuich fame were members of the *brigada social*. Sometimes paid informers recruited by the squad planted bombs in order to be rewarded for subsequently finding them.[78]

The largest of the Spanish police bodies was the heavily militarized *Guardia Civil* with its distinctive shiny, tricorn hats. Unlike some of the others, the *Guardia Civil* was incorruptible and better paid, but its rigid military discipline did not encourage personal initiative and imagination. Always armed and never alone, civil guards became known everywhere in Spain as *la Pareja*, "the Pair." Parading around in twos in semi-military

---

[76] Juan José López-Serrano, *Descubriendo los misterios ó un detective á la fuerza (informaciones de un periodista). Sensacionales relatos de los complots y atentados anarchistas, realizados en España en los últimos años*. (Madrid: Artistica Española, 1913): 78.

[77] The anti-anarchist law passed on July 10, 1894, punished the criminal use of explosives, conspiracy, and instigation to commit such crimes either by word of mouth or by other means of publicity. The law also banned associations aimed at executing such crimes. In 1896 the penalties of the earlier law were exacerbated, and the more serious crimes handed over to military tribunals for adjudication.

[78] The decree establishing the *brigada social* is reprinted in Ferdinando Cadalso, *El anarquismo y los medios de repression* (Madrid: Romero, 1896): 129–134. Brenan, *Spanish Labyrinth*, 30–33.

formation, however, was often unhelpful when investigating and solving crimes – and finding terrorists. Aloof from the population, a trait that helped keep it incorruptible, the *Guardia Civil* was generally hated.[79]

Effective government coordination of and control over the *Guardia Civil* and the other police forces was also thwarted by the chronic instability of Spanish political life. Between 1901 and 1914 twenty-three cabinets and twenty-nine interior ministers, who in theory coordinated the actions of the police, succeeded each other in office at a dizzying pace. Because of this and other reasons, the *Guardia Civil* was largely autonomous (at least during peacetime) from both the interior and war ministries.[80] Another source of administrative fecklessness was the fact that, as previously mentioned, the governor and military command in Barcelona often resisted or failed to follow the policies laid down by the central government in Madrid.

Given all these problems, it is not too surprising that Spanish security arrangements broke down at the time of the king's wedding with the influx of between 100,000 and 200,000 people into Madrid to witness the grand festivities. The king himself had made it more difficult for the police by choosing for his wedding a church right in the middle of Madrid and planning a mile-and-a-half processional route that provided maximum exposure to the public.[81] This presented a splendid opportunity to popularize the monarchy; it also provided a splendid opportunity for terrorists to murder the king.

The government, in particular Count Romanones who was interior minister, hoped to make up for the deficiencies of the Spanish police by importing foreign detectives, all expenses paid, to watch out for potential assassins. British, French, German, and Italian policemen soon traveled to Madrid. According to Romanones's memoirs, police attention was focused on safeguarding the church of St. Jeronimo and preventing the entrance of any assassin.[82] Given the recent attack on the king in the streets of Paris, however, it should have been very obvious that the processional route was an even more dangerous locale. Italian Ambassador Silvestrelli, the same man who, as minister to Berne, upbraided the Swiss for deficiencies in anti-anarchist action and provoked a rupture of diplomatic relations in 1902, witnessed the bombing from the Italian embassy.

[79] Brenan, *Spanish Labyrinth*, 157.
[80] Manuel Ballbé, *Orden público y militarismo en la España constitucional (1812–1983)* 2nd edition (Madrid: Alianza, 1983): 147.
[81] "The Spanish Wedding," *The Times* (London), June 1, 1906; *New York Times*, June 1, 1906, 1.
[82] Alvaro Figueroa y Torres, *Notas de Una Vida*, 2 vols. (Madrid: Renacimiento, 1928): 2:158–160.

The embassy was virtually next door to the site of the *attentat*, separated from 88 Calle Mayor by only a narrow street.[83] The ambassador
criticized the Spanish police for failing to carry out "effective preventative surveillance." The police did not take such minimal precautions as
checking the names of the lodgers in the hotels along the route of the
wedding procession. It was in just such a place, a *huespedes* or third-class
hotel, that Morral took up residence several days prior to the wedding,
fabricated a bomb in his room, and threw it from his fifth-storey balcony.
Despite the presence of numerous police and soldiers, after the explosion no attempt was made to seal off the building at 88 Calle Mayor,
an oversight that allowed Morral to escape. Nor had the police realized that Morral was in town although, according to Silvestrelli, he was
relatively well-known as an anarchist associated with Ferrer, who was
a suspect in the 1905 attempt on Alfonso's life. In other words Morral
should have been on a list of anarchists to be watched, although he was
not. Romanones's defense was that the police were blindsided because
they lacked his photograph.[84] In contrast to these Spanish deficiencies,
Silvestrelli asserted that he had undertaken "draconian measures of precaution" to secure the Italian embassy, preventing any strangers from
entering the rooms (some of which were living quarters for the servants)
that faced Calle Mayor.[85]

The British ambassador's dispatches show him in essential agreement
with Silvestrelli's criticisms:

it is feared that the adoption of severe measures against anarchism [by the Spanish
government] may again entail retaliation against their author, as happened in the
case of Señor Canovas nine years ago.

What is most needed is an efficient police organization, to enforce existing laws
and keep an eye on suspicious persons, as is done in England, but no one expects
that this desirable end will be attained.[86]

So convinced were the British of the "hopeless" state of the Spanish police
and the danger of anarchist attack that, despite Alfonso's repeated invitations, for years they refused to allow King Edward to step on Spanish

[83] The Italian embassy was located in the former Palace of the Dukes of Abrantes where
today the Italian cultural institute has its offices. Although Karl Baedeker, *Spain and
Portugal*, 3rd edition (Leipzig: Baedeker, 1908): 103, writes that the bomb was thrown
from the fourth floor of 88 Calle Mayor, in American usage, this would be the fifth floor
since Americans normally refer to the ground floor as the first floor.

[84] Figueroa y Torres, *Notas de Una Vida*, 2:164.

[85] Silvestrelli, Madrid, to Foreign Minister Tittoni, Rome, June 1 and 4, 1906. PI, b.
35, IFM.

[86] See Silvestrelli to Tittoni, June 5, 1906, PI, b. 35, IFM, and Bunsen to Grey, June 7,
1906, in BDFA. Par I, Series F, vol. 27, p. 152.

soil. The most he would do was meet the Spanish monarch onboard ship off the coast of Cartagena.[87]

Arrow's police in Barcelona

Since the Spanish were frustrated in their desire to observe and import British police tactics (although eventually they did send a civilian observer to London), they did the next best thing.[88] They imported a British police officer. Actually, it was not the Spanish government that did this, although it gave its authorization, but Catalan politicians and the municipal authorities of Barcelona angry at the failures of the national police.

In Barcelona, anonymous explosions in obscure corners of the city had begun in 1903 and went on for years and years, bestowing on the capital of Catalonia the grim title of "city of bombs."[89] According to one historian, between 1903 and 1909 (when the bombings stopped, except for one explosion in 1910), more than eighty bombs exploded in Barcelona, as many as six a week, killing at least eleven people and wounding seventy.[90] Other sources give somewhat lower figures, but whatever the exact statistics, these bombings and the continual discovery of unexploded bombs and petards caused a "psychosis of panic in the population."[91] According to the British ambassador: "the series of outrages...have made Barcelona a byword for lawlessness and anarchy throughout the world."[92] In early 1907 "a positive reign of terror set in" as explosion followed explosion, leading to "a considerable exodus of well-to-do people."[93] "In recent years...many thousands of people" left Barcelona, the previously flourishing tourist trade came to an end, and

---

[87] Hardinge's comment on the Spanish police in Lee, *King Edward VII*, 2:535. Gordon Brook-Shepherd, *Uncle of Europe. The Social and Diplomatic Life of Edward VII* (New York and London: Harcourt Brace Jovanovich, 1975): 279–280.

[88] The Metropolitan Commissioner of Police agreed to see a representative of the Barcelona municipality who wished to study British detective methods. Apparently a civilian observer presented fewer problems for the British than a Spanish policeman. Redford Roberts, Consul General Barcelona, to Grey, January 28, 1907, and W. P. Byrne, HO, to undersecretary of state, FO, February 26, 1907, FO371/335, PRO.

[89] Núñez Florencio, *Terrorismo*, 75.   [90] Romero Maura, "Terrorism," 149–150.

[91] Núñez Florencio, *Terrorismo*, 194–197, gives a detailed chronology of terrorist *attentats* between 1888 and 1909. For the period 1903–1909, this yields figures of 49 explosions, and more than 48 injured and four killed in Barcelona. One incident in 1905 lists the number of dead and injured as "some." For the sense of panic, see Núñez Florencio, *Terrorismo*, 75.

[92] Bunsen, San Ildefonso, to Grey, August 2, 1907. FO371/336. PRO.

[93] Bunsen, *General Report on Spain, 1906*, to Grey, April 27, 1907, FO371/336, PRO, as well as the British ambassador's 1907 *Annual Report*, February 14, 1908, FO371/525, p. 13, PRO. 92

prosperity declined. This led some of those who remained to declare at a protest meeting that "Barcelona was being killed" by terrorist attempts and the authorities' mishandling of the situation.[94] In the words of the Catalan nationalist leader Enric Prat de la Riba, the Spanish police was "impotent":

> It is an apparatus of a primitive type, an unusable fossil. To treat the modern illness that afflicts Catalonia (that is to say, anarchism) with these [police] organizations is like using flint spears and stone hatches to fight against multitudes armed with Mausers and Krups.[95]

Osma's proposal for the Metropolitan Police to create an "international branch," i.e., to appoint an British officer to coordinate anti-anarchist efforts in Spain, seemed to be coming true in the summer of 1907, although not in the way that Madrid would have liked since it was outside of its immediate supervision. In July, after negotiations involving the British consulate in Barcelona, the Spanish ambassador in London, and with the permission of the Metropolitan commissioner, the city of Barcelona hired a twenty-six year veteran, newly retired, of Scotland Yard, a detective named Charles Arrow. This was despite the fact that he did not speak Spanish, let alone Catalan. Arrow set up a British-style Office of Criminal Investigation in order to find the authors of the Barcelona bombings. In early 1908 a police force of thirty Catalans was finally put at his disposal.[96] By August he had "compiled registers of some 400 suspected anarchists, who are watched and their movements noted on the Scotland Yard system."[97] Arrow discovered that the Barcelona anarchists were "in communication with other Anarchist centers such as Switzerland and Paris and their bombs [were] chiefly manufactured in the Pyrenees and in the mountainous regions of Catalonia."[98] Arrow tried valiantly and soon learned Spanish, but he could do relatively little, caught up as he was in a maelstrom of warring Castilian and Catalan politicians and policemen.[99]

---

[94] Consul General Roberts, Barcelona, to Grey, January 28, 29, and 31, 1907, FO.371/335, PRO. Partially due to the persistence of terrorist violence, the Vega Armijo government fell in January 1907. González Calleja, *La razón de la fuerza*, 392.

[95] Author's translation, "Les bombes," *La Veu de Catalunya*, July 27, 1906, cited by González Calleja, *La razón de la fuerza*, 391.

[96] Bunsen, San Sebastian, to Grey, August 13, 1908. FO371/526/29643, PRO.

[97] Bunsen, San Sebastian, to Grey, August 13, 1908. FO371/526/29643, PRO.

[98] Memorandum in E. Grant Duff, November 22, 1907, FO371/336, PRO.

[99] Charles Arrow, *Rogues and Others* (London: Duckworth, 1926): Chapter 23; Ullman, *Tragic Week*, 104–106; British Consul George R. Smithers, confidential memo, inclosed in n. 116, Ambassador Bunsen to Foreign Secretary Grey, August 2, 1907; and confidential memo in E. Grant Duff, Madrid, to FO, n. 175, November 22, 1907. FO 371/336, PRO; Bunsen's annual report to Grey, February 14, 1908, FO 371/525, PRO; Romero Maura, "Terrorism," 163–164.

While several Spanish politicians and later historians judged Arrow's police as "of no use whatsoever," some contemporary domestic and foreign observers were more impressed.[100] A well-known Barcelona resident told the British vice-consul that Arrow "earned his salary before he arrived" in Barcelona since the Madrid government, seeing in the British policeman a rival to its authority, tried harder than ever before to round up terrorists.[101] The fall of 1907, until December 23, was free of terrorist bombings, and this may have been due to Arrow's vigilance (or to chance).[102] The British Foreign Office, with which Arrow stayed in very close contact, thought he deserved credit for the successful, incident-free visits of the Spanish king and queen to Barcelona during 1908.[103] Previously royalty had usually avoided that city as too dangerous. Arrow also made a very favorable impression on the military attaché attached to the German embassy in Madrid. In January 1908 Von Bronsart lauded him as "a smart and thoughtful man who is at the same time energetic and goal-oriented. He has a firm grip on the Spanish situation and in all human probability, despite all the difficulties, he will be able to fulfill his task." During their discussions the optimistic Arrow expressed the hope that if his "anarchist surveillance service" worked satisfactorily in Barcelona, it could be extended "to other large European cities." The kaiser's marginal comment was: "for Berlin very necessary" and that "Mr. Arrow must come to Berlin sometime."[104]

Arrow came to believe, and his views were largely seconded by the British ambassador, that "the outrages are not all caused by Anarchists; but some of them by interested persons in Madrid who desire to discredit Barcelona and the Catalan movement." Surprisingly, on Arrow's list of persons suspected of involvement in the bombings were the distinguished liberal statesmen Segismundo Moret and the Count de Romanones.[105] Other observers agreed with Arrow that the liberals might be complicit in terrorism, and still others in Spain blamed the Catalan regionalists, the Radical Party, the Catholic religious orders, and clerical politicians![106] Perhaps even more

---

[100] Romero Maura, "Terrorism," 163, provides the harshest critique; Núñez Florencio, *Terrorismo*, 101–102, agrees with his evaluation.

[101] Cited in González Calleja, *La razón de la fuerza*, 403n285.

[102] González Calleja, *La razón de la fuerza*, 407.

[103] See docket sheet comments by G. W. and W. L., Bunsen to Grey, November 28, 1908, n.168, FO371/526/42033, PRO, and Bunsen's *Annual Report on Spain for 1908*, February 5, 1909, BDFA, Part 1, Series F, vol. 28, p. 24.

[104] Copy, Von Bronsart, Madrid, to Royal War Ministry, Berlin, January 31, 1908, in Radowitz, Madrid, to Bülow, Berlin, February 4, 1908, Eur. Gen. 91, bd. 4, GFM.

[105] Memorandum in E. Grant Duff, no. 175, November 22, 1907, FO371/336, PRO; Maurice de Bunsen, *Annual Report on Spain for the year 1908*, BDFA, Part 1, Ser. F, 28:24.

[106] Ullman, *Tragic Week*, 105–106.

surprisingly, Arrow told the German military attaché in Spain that many believed a Genoese group was behind the bombings, since the Italian port city wished to damage the trade of its great commercial rival.[107] The chief conclusion that should be drawn from all this is that once again "anarchist terrorism" proved to be more the product of local political and socioeconomic conditions than of anarchist ideology. Many of the terrorists may not have been anarchists at all, despite the charges of the press, the police, and various politicians.

Another, more general point to be made about Spain, Britain, and anti-anarchist policing has been overlooked by the diplomatic historians, i.e., that Spanish desires for foreign help against terrorism was an important factor moving Spain toward closer dynastic and diplomatic connections with Britain (and France). British assistance in stopping anarchist assassination attempts and bombings, along with admiration for the British fleet and need for Anglo-French assistance in Morocco, helped push Spain into formally aligning itself with the *Entente cordiale* in April 1907. While the marriage between Alfonso and Victoria Eugenia proved to be a true love match, it was clear from the beginning that the Spanish king, as well as the Spanish government, was prejudiced in favor of an English bride. Before Alfonso's engagement to Victoria, Kaiser Wilhelm had dangled beautiful German duchesses before his eyes, but the reputation of the Berlin police presidency in controlling anarchists could not compete with Scotland Yard's (which was also located in that world center of the anarchist community-in-exile that *seemed* to be giving Spain so many difficulties).

Germany and Russia after 1906

The bloody Madrid bombing deeply concerned Germany and Russia, as well as Britain and Italy. Berlin thought that now might be the time to achieve closer anti-anarchist cooperation with London, if possible getting it to adhere to the St. Petersburg Protocol or at least a modified version of it. On June 7, 1906, a week after the assassination attempt on Alfonso and his bride, the German chargé d'affaires in London asked the British foreign secretary "whether the British government would change its attitude with regard to measures for dealing with anarchists." Presumably because the negotiations had been secret, Sir Edward Grey, a Liberal, replied that in this matter he could "not remember what the attitude of the previous

---

[107] Copy, Von Bronsart, Madrid, to Royal War Ministry, Berlin, January 31, 1908, in Radowitz, Madrid, to Bülow, Berlin, February 4, 1908. Eur. Gen.91, Bd. 4, GFM.

[Conservative] Government had been."[108] Before replying to the German inquiry, the foreign secretary consulted his colleagues, particularly the Home Office and the chief commissioner of the Metropolitan Police. Even before hearing their views, an internal Foreign Office memo of June 8 reiterated the continuing British objections to signing the accord (but pointing out, significantly, Britain's *de facto* adherence to much of it):

We have always held out against having our hands tied by the stipulation of a convention. And practically we carry out most of the provisions of the general protocol signed by the 9 powers on March 1, 1904. Switzerland takes up the same attitude as Great Britain; or, to be more correct, we adopted her attitude as our model.[109]

In July, the Home Office chimed in that E. R. Henry's objections to "any formal adherence" remained the same as in 1904. As in the past, of key importance was the desire not to undermine England's delicate intelligence-gathering system based on "*the private informer.*" It would also have difficulty applying the St. Petersburg Protocol's provisions regarding the expulsion of foreign anarchists since despite the Aliens Act of 1905 there was "still no power to expel anarchists as such."[110]

A few months later, the British rebuked Russian feelers for closer cooperation. London refused St. Petersburg's request on November 21, 1906, for direct inter-police communications regarding the anarchists. The excuse offered was that: "as the use of a cipher would be necessary, there could be but little saving of time, and there would, he [Home Office Secretary Gladstone] considers, be an increased risk of serious results arising from the possible misspelling of different Russian and Polish names."[111] In early 1909, after émigré Latvians, allegedly anarchists but actually members of the Latvian (or Lettish) Social Democratic Party, robbed the Schnurmann Rubber Factory in Tottenham, killing a policeman and a child and injuring more than twenty others, the Russian government planned once again to urge Britain to adhere to the St. Petersburg Protocol. The tsarist government eventually demurred from taking this step, however, realizing that the increasingly strained relations between London and Berlin made the former loath to become involved in any

---

[108] Copy, extract from dispatch, FO to Lascelles, Berlin, n. 149, June 7, 1906, in HO144/757/118516/15, PRO; Stumm, German embassy, London, to Bülow, Reich chancellor, Berlin, June, 8 1908. Eur. Gen.91, Bd. 4, GFO.

[109] W. E. Davidson, June 8, 1908, FO371/78, PRO.

[110] A. H. D[ixon], "Memorandum as to the Protocol of 1904 respecting Anarchist Crimes," July 13, 1906. HO144/757/118516, PRO

[111] The Russian note, November 21, 1906. Copy of this and Secretary Gladstone's reply in HO144/757/118516/47 and /51, PRO; Porter, *Vigilant State*, 159.

international agreement signed by the Germans.[112] It may well be true, as Bernard Porter claims, that, although they would provide information on a case-by-case basis if this assistance remained secret, "all in all the British police appear to have given less help than most other European police forces to the Okhrana in these years [i.e., 1905 and after]."[113]

The British reticence proved deeply disappointing to the German government, whose concern for the safety of the kaiser had been greatly heightened by the bloody anarchist attack in Madrid. The Madrid massacre also raised the possibility of passing new anti-anarchist legislation in Germany. After the attack, the spies and police of various European states passed on stories of possible assassination attempts against the lives of the German kaiser, the Spanish king, and the Russian tsar. This included an unverified French government report of anarchists bent on regicide who "would hide the explosive devices in their luggage among their laundry and, especially, their shoes."[114] Chancellor Bülow telegraphed the German Foreign Office regarding his (perhaps insincere and certainly sycophantic) worries about Wilhelm, who was scheduled to visit Austria in a couple of days. "There is only one real danger in Vienna, namely that there could be an assassination attempt against His Majesty. This is the only question in the world that makes me nervous."[115] Wilhelm read the telegram and responded in characteristically extravagant fashion:

The best way to prevent assassinations is simply to seize and imprison known anarchists, as well as those that are suspects. This was done by the Sultan during our visit there [in October 1898], and it proved successful. I recommend that you advise this to Vienna. By the way, I find it amazing that there is no suggestion by anyone, and that no government is taking steps against these creatures. If, in response to an assassination, all countries would arrest and just behead known anarchists, this mess would soon end. But no government, including ours, has that kind of nerve.[116]

---

[112] Russian diplomatic notes of January 30 and April 17, 1909, cited in Johnson, *Okhrana Abroad*, 65–66, and Zuckerman, *Abroad*, 65. Johnson and Zuckerman mistakenly translate Schnurmann as "Sherman." For the "Tottenham Outrage" and the secret Latvian revolutionary groups in England, see F. B. Clarke, *Will-o'-the wisp: Peter the Painter and the Anti-tsarist Terrorists in Britain and Australia* (Melbourne: Oxford University Press, 1983): 33–37. The English press frequently identified the two Tottenham robbers as "foreign anarchists;" they were also repudiated by the Social Democratic Party. Donald Rumbelow, *The Houndsditch Murders and the Siege of Sidney Street* (London: W. H. Allen, 1988): 32, 43, 45.

[113] Porter, *Vigilant State*, 157–158.

[114] Flotow, Paris, to Foreign Office, Berlin, June 8, 1906. Eur. Gen. 91, Bd. 4. GFO. "Virgilio," the Italian spy in London, reported on a new attempt against King Alfonso, August 4, 1906. DGPS. Div. AAGGR. b. 6, ACS.

[115] Bülow, Norderney, to Foreign Office, Berlin, June 4, 1906, Eur. Gen. 91, Bd.4, GFO.

[116] Reported in Bülow, Norderney, to Foreign Office, Berlin, June 5, 1906, Eur. Gen. 91. Bd.4, GFO.

To Tsar Nicholas (who had expressed his concern about the attack in Madrid), Wilhelm complained in his stilted English that:

the arrangements [presumably the St. Petersburg Protocol] made by our two Governments for the control of these fellows [the anarchists], have completely miscarried. Because they can live with absolute impunity in London, there [they] mature their murderous designs. The right place for these fiends is the scaffold, sometimes the imprisonment for life in a lunatic asylum. All Continental Powers should send London a joint invitation to ask the English Government to join them by an International agreement to fight these beasts. I should think that it would be possible, by a common consent, in the defense of life & culture, to legally place the fabrication of chemicals for the filling & use of bombs under capital punishment.[117]

It was statements like these that led many to wonder whether Wilhelm was in his right mind.[118]

Yet other statesmen of the time championed measures almost as extreme. In a speech on August 12, 1906, Charles Bonaparte, the American secretary of the navy, advocated that the death penalty be "unequivocally imposed" whenever the anarchist sought "directly or indirectly" to take life, even if unsuccessful. Flogging should be used for lesser anarchist crimes.[119]

In late August 1906 Chancellor Bülow met with the Prussian cabinet to discuss the anarchist threat.[120] Bülow conveyed the kaiser's message suggesting that, in light of the recent bloody assassination attempt in Madrid, new anti-anarchist measures should be taken. The chancellor also presented a progress report on the status of international anti-anarchist efforts. He noted that the countries at the Rome conference had "agreed to mutually monitor any dangerous socialist and anarchist elements" and "established... an international intelligence service." Since in fact the Rome conference had *not* aimed at monitoring socialists, this comment is either a revealing memory lapse or else indicative of the reactionary spin German conservatives wanted to place on its deliberations.

Since 1898, the chancellor continued, the Swiss and Americans had taken some positive steps, but Britain still proved to be the major stumbling

---

[117] Neues Palais [Potsdam], June 14, 1906. The text of this letter (in slightly different English versions) can be found in *Briefe Wilhelms II. an den Zaren: 1894–1914* (Berlin: Ullstein, 1920) 389–392, and in *The Kaiser's Letters to the Tsar*, edited and with an introduction by N. F. Grant. London: Hodder and Stoughton, 1920), 228–233.

[118] See the assessment of Wilhelm's mental condition in chapter one of John C. G. Röhl, *The Kaiser and his Court: Wilhelm II and the Government of Germany* (Cambridge University Press, 1994) and in Röhl, *Wilhelm II: The Kaiser's Personal Monarchy,* 1056–1067.

[119] *New York Times*, August 13, 1906, 1. An editorial on August 15, 1906, 5, opposed Bonaparte's proposals.

[120] Minutes, *Staatsministerium*, Berlin, August 31, 1906, MI, bd. 7, nr. 13689. GCSAP.

block to international anti-anarchist action. Swiss federal authorities had acted more strictly against anarchist activities in Switzerland, and newly passed legislation had made it possible to intervene against bomb-makers (undoubtedly a reference to the anti-anarchist law of March 1906).[121] There was also, according to the chancellor, more willingness on the part of the United States to consider preventive measures (and here the reference was presumably to new legislation in the works, ultimately enacted in February 1907, to deport immigrant anarchists). On the other hand:

> The greatest difficulty is in England which cannot decide to break with her tradition of political asylum. King Edward is also of the opinion that anarchy can be fought with police measures in his own country and that international agreements would not be successful. As long as England insists on this viewpoint, no international organization could successfully fight the dangers of anarchy.

As for monitoring the "terrorist movement...most closely," as His Majesty desired, Bülow declared that the interior minister and the Berlin police department were already doing that, as well as dealing "with the question of how to combat social democratic and revolutionary aspirations, and prevent their penetration into the army." Nonetheless, Bülow added, "the subject of preventing assassination is especially urgent since His Majesty will travel to Silesia," a hotbed of violent socialist activity.

Interior Minister von Bethmann-Hollweg commented that precautionary measures had already been taken but "there is no real protection against assassination attempts." Ultimately, as Bethmann-Hollweg had already told the kaiser, "his life was in God's hands." As for "additional anti-anarchist legislation," it would require changes in the criminal code and approval by the Reichstag, which was "highly doubtful." Both the interior and agriculture ministers noted the threat posed by dangerous elements, including anarchists and other revolutionaries, among Russian students and other Russian immigrants in Germany. Recently a Russian bomb factory had been discovered in Hamburg.

The minister of finance, Georg von Rheinbaben, worried that more needed to be done for the security of the kaiser. "Although the speed of automobile travel ensures greater safety than before, His Majesty is dangerously vulnerable on other occasions [...] especially his return from parades at the head of the color guard column...presents an opportune moment for an assassination attempt." Should the kaiser, who loved military pomp and circumstance, be warned of this danger? The chancellor thought not, since it would only undermine his self-confidence. Besides, the kaiser's fatalism, his belief that his personal safety was in the hands

---

[121] *Journal du droit international privé*, **33** (1906): 955.

of God, "would make it difficult [for him] to agree to restrict his movements." "Fortunately," according to Bülow:

There is no German parallel to the situation in Russia and preventive measures – not always successful – that have been put into place in Russia would never be understood by the population here. There is no guarantee against assassination bombs, as was again demonstrated by the sad event in Madrid.[122]

The Prussian cabinet therefore concluded to do nothing more than to study the question of further legislation and to maintain the vigilance of the security forces. The kaiser's sound and fury vented against the anarchists had once again resulted in nothing (as it would again in 1908 when he became alarmed by the discovery in Berlin of a Russian revolutionary cache of weapons and revolutionary leaflets). Despite their protestations about the emperor's fatalism, more fatalistic was the attitude of Bülow and his ministers, who were content to leave Wilhelm's security in God's hands. This is all the more surprising given that for years the government had provided abundantly for the emperor's personal security. It reflects traditional views about divine right monarchy, as outdated as they were, as well as the continuing power of the anarchist mystique, i.e., that no system of protection could prevent an unknown anarchist bomber or assassin from getting through to his victim. Of course, relying on God to protect the kaiser was also a convenient excuse not to push for the unreasonable measures of harsh police prevention and repression that Wilhelm desired but that neither the German parliament nor the public would have stood for.[123]

The St. Petersburg Protocol, 1906–1918

The failure to secure new international measures involving Britain, Italy, and other states in the aftermath of the Madrid bloodbath was perhaps the last chance for such an accord or for an enlargement of the anti-anarchist league. Nonetheless, the system set up by the St. Petersburg Protocol continued to be fine-tuned, refined, and in some cases strengthened.

In February 1907, Switzerland agreed to improve the procedures calling for prior notification before anarchists were expelled across the Austro-Hungarian border. These procedures were spelled out in writing, but this did not mean that Switzerland formally signed onto the St.

---

[122] Minutes, *Staatsministerium*, Berlin, August 31, 1906, MI, bd. 7, nr. 13689. GCSAP.
[123] In 1908 Bülow emphasized once again that the best response "against the anarchist movement" was not new repressive legislation, but "thorough and skillful police surveillance of anarchist groups." Bülow to interior minister, January 3, 1908, Reichskanzlei, 755/4, GCSAP.

Petersburg Protocol, as has been alleged.[124] The negotiations leading up to this agreement provide a window into the fragile and secretive nature of Swiss adherence to the anti-anarchist accord. In August 1905 Switzerland expelled the anarchists Siegfried Nacht (aka Arnold Roller) and Josef Urban, but despite Swiss efforts to forewarn the Austrians, they managed to evade the Austrian authorities and enter Tyrol, where the Emperor Franz Joseph was observing army maneuvers. Taken aback by this possible exposure of the Austrian emperor to an attack by supposedly dangerous anarchists, the Swiss made a detailed verbal promise to improve communications regarding expulsions. The Austrians worried that this verbal promise made by Ernst Brenner, the head of the justice and police department, would be forgotten after he vacated his post. Further compounding the difficulties of enforcement was that neither the Swiss parliament nor the cantonal authorities knew that Switzerland had adhered to the St. Petersburg Protocol, if only unilaterally and without a formal signature. Nor did the government want parliament and the cantons to know about this accord since the Radicals, who formed part of the majority in the national and most of the cantonal assemblies, would strongly object.

To facilitate anarchist expulsions in the future, the Austro-Hungarian ambassador and a reluctant Brenner agreed on a draft proposal whereby a Swiss justice department employee would verbally inform an official of the Austrian embassy about any impending expulsion. Moreover the justice ministry would prescribe to the cantonal authorities the exact day of the expulsion. In the future, photographs and detailed descriptions of the deportees were also to be provided. The Austrian ambassador noted that the federal attorney general (*Bundesanwaltschaft*) had an extensive and updated collection of anarchist photographs and that anarchists to be expelled were photographed and measured anthropometrically (i.e., utilizing Bertillonage). Interestingly, the ambassador commented that "although descriptions [of anarchists] have improved since the introduction of anthropometry, these measurements are not reliable enough for identification." To mask what was essentially an act of administrative extradition, the anarchists would be escorted to the border by detectives in civilian clothes, rather than by police and officials in uniform as was done with other expelled or extradited persons.[125] On June 15, 1907, Switzerland followed up its accord with Austria with an agreement with Germany designating border places for the exchange of expelled anarchists.[126]

---

[124] Liang, *Modern Police*, 174. The first provision of the St. Petersburg Protocol had called for such prior notification.

[125] Heidler, Bern, to Aehrenthal, Vienna, February 7, 1907, Adm. Reg. F52/9, HHStA.

[126] Schmidt-Dargitz, foreign ministry, to interior ministry, Berlin, January 8, 1914. Interior ministry, 13689. F. 449, GSAP.

Switzerland also moved in other ways toward a severer approach to the anarchists and violent revolutionaries. For years Switzerland had been willing, even eager, to cooperate in secret with the Russian, German, and Austrian police in monitoring anarchists and other subversives. The Russian Foreign Agency in Paris maintained extremely good relations with the Geneva police. In 1903, the chief of the department of police and justice in Geneva wrote that it was "useful" to maintain a good rapport with the Russian government regarding expulsions, i.e., by providing it with prior warning.[127] Due to this excellent relationship, Geneva became one of the two most important centers outside of Russia for the secret opening of the correspondence of Russian émigrés.[128] After 1905 Switzerland adopted harsher public policies of expulsion, extradition, and repression. In 1906 two Italians were expelled as anarchists spreading anti-militarist propaganda.[129] In November, a Swiss court applied the recently passed law penalizing support for anarchist crimes and sent the publicist Luigi Bertoni to jail for a month for commemorating the actions of the assassin Bresci.[130] In August 1912, under pressure from the Italians and perhaps the Germans as well, Bertoni was once again arrested, although soon released, for glorifying regicide.[131] Also in 1906, to avoid punishment for a similar deed in Italy, Armando Borghi, editor of the weekly anarchist publication *Aurora*, fled to Switzerland. He was stopped at the border "as a dangerous anarchist, due to an international convention against the anarchists of which I don't know the year" (presumably the 1898 Rome accord). The Swiss informed the Italian police, who arrested Borghi. The irrepressible anarchist returned to Switzerland in 1912 on a propaganda speaking tour but was arrested and spent a few weeks in prison before being expelled.[132]

In June 1906, May 1907, June 1908, and September 1909 the Swiss judiciary ordered the extradition back to their homeland of four Russian revolutionaries. These were Alexander Belenzow, George Kilatschitsky and, curiously, two Victor Wassilieffs, although with different patronymics.[133] Of these four, the first and last were extradited for robbing banks,

[127] Marc Vuilleumier, "La police politique," 59–60.
[128] Marc Vuilleumier, "La police politique," 60, who cites Michael Confino, "Pierre Kropotkine et les agents de l'Okhrana. Étude suivie de treize letters de Kropotkine à M. Goldsmith et à un groupe anarchiste russe," *Cahiers du monde russe et soviétique* 24:1–2 (1983): 98.
[129] Saint-Aubin, *L'extradition*, 1:440.
[130] According to Casagrande, "Mises en fiche," 76, this was both the first and the last conviction under the so-called Silvestrelli anti-anarchist law.
[131] Casagrande, "Mises en fiche," 78–79.
[132] Armando Borghi, *Mezzo Secolo di Anarchia (1898–1945)* (Naples: Edizioni scientifiche italiane, 1954), 97, 129–130.
[133] Victor Platonovitch and Victor Gavrilov Wassilieff (also spelled Vassilief or Vasiliev).

the second for murdering a Russian railroad manager, and the third for killing a police chief.[134] In each case the Swiss federal tribunal refused to accept the argument that these were political crimes. Swiss public opinion was not entirely pleased with these rulings and in particular the 1908 decision regarding Victor Platonovitch Wassilieff (actually an alias for a man named Bromar) caused a great deal of controversy.[135] According to one historian, Bromar's extradition had been arranged by the head of the Russian police abroad, i.e., the Foreign Agency, who traveled to Geneva to arrange for "Wassilieff's" return to Russia.[136] On February 22 and March 18, 1908, Bern also made agreements with, respectively, Russia and Italy that provided for the extradition of persons who used explosives abusively.[137] While Switzerland had not completely caved in to foreign pressure, since it still frequently provided refuge for political immigrants, it was no longer an automatic place of asylum for anarchists – or terrorists – as seemingly it once had been. This change in Swiss practice deeply impressed international opinion.[138]

Besides integrating the Swiss more closely into their anti-anarchist pact, Germany and Russia worked to make the provisions of the St. Petersburg Protocol operational. This took a surprisingly long time. Ten years after the signing of the agreement, some of the signatories had still not designated either the border points or the authorities who were to receive expelled anarchists or both. By October 1913 Germany had the names of Russia's and by January 1914 Austria's border *authorities* but

---

[134] All claimed to be Socialist Revolutionaries, although Victor Gavrilov Wassilieff was involved with a gang of "anarchist communists." Corbaz, *Le Crime Politique*, 113.

[135] Saint-Aubin, *L'extradition*, 1:430–433; *Dictionnaire historique & biographique de la Suisse*, "Wassilieff," 5:179; Corbaz, *Le Crime Politique*, 102–107, 112–114, 116–125. Johnson, *Okhrana Abroad*, 88, 111, identifies Victor Platonovitch as Bromar.

[136] Johnson, *Okhrana Abroad*, 111–112. The Swiss extradited Bromar before Harting arrived.

[137] *Repertoire de droit international privè et de droit penal international* (1929), "Anarchiste," 1:429; [Polizeidirektion, Vienna], *Die socialdemokratische und anarchistische Bewegung im Jahre 1908* (Vienna: Druck der kaiserlich-königlichen Hof- und Staatsdruckerei, 1909), 69, Amtsbibliothek der Polizeidirektion Wien; Charles Lardy, "Notes Historiques Sur L'extradition en Suisse," *Zeitschrift Für Schweizerisches Recht* 38 (1918): 322.

[138] Writing *c.* 1910 in the authoritative *Enciclopedia giuridica italiana*, "Estradizione," 548n, Pietro Lanza observed that: "recently Switzerland has conceded to Russia extradition for common crimes connected to political ones which, until some years ago, it would not have dreamed of conceding." The equally authoritative *Journal de doit international privé* [*Clunet*] 33 (1906): 767–768, noted that recent expulsions placed Switzerland in the first rank of those democratic republics, like the United States, which rejected bomb-throwers. "England alone remains a land of exile for these public enemies." See also Saint-Aubin, *L'extradition*, 1:440, 442. In a February 19, 1909, letter to Foreign Minister Izvolskii, Russian Prime Minister Stolypin noted that, in terms of handling Russian revolutionary émigrés, Switzerland, as well as Germany and Austria, were "becoming more helpful while France, *an ally*, is less so." Johnson, *Okhrana Abroad*, 59.

not their border transit *points*.[139] Only in January 1914 did Denmark and Norway, and only in June 1914 did Austria communicate to Germany the names of the requisite border posts; in January of the same year Denmark finally informed Germany of its designated border authorities.[140] Also in January 1914, Berlin noted that the German federal states were frequently observing neither the St. Petersburg Protocol nor the regulations governing the internal German anti-anarchist system as promulgated in the circulars of November 28, 1898, and May 23, 1908. Updated lists of border points and police authorities needed to be sent in and some states, e.g., the Grand Duchy of Hesse, were receiving neither Berlin's annual overview of the anarchist movement nor anarchist photos.[141]

Why these delays and omissions? It is not in fact entirely clear why simple administrative decisions should have taken such a long time to implement and communicate, but one can offer a variety of explanations. Perhaps the overarching reason was that the European countries and the constituent members of the German Empire which failed for many years to comply with the requirements of the St. Petersburg accord were not important centers of anarchist activity. Nor were they, with the possible exception of Berlin, centers of large scale Russian emigration with active revolutionary subcultures. Moreover the outbreak of the Russo–Japanese War in February 1904 and the subsequent 1905 Revolution diverted the attention of the Russian government from the anarchist threat abroad. Finally, the friendly relations between Germany and Russia that had been crucial to the creation of the St. Petersburg accord became increasingly strained after Russia's conclusion of an entente with Britain in August 1907.

Various efforts, both political and geographical, were made to broaden the scope of the Petersburg agreement. In August 1907, A. I. Trusevich, the head of the Russian police, met with German officials in Berlin for exploratory talks to see if the 1904 accord could be informally expanded to: "include all persons involved in revolutionary movements" who resorted to "terrorists acts like murder, armed robbery, etc., to achieve this goal [i.e., the overthrow of the government]." In Russia this would include socialist revolutionaries, social democrats, and the "small number

---

[139] Mss. German Foreign Office, Berlin, to von Lucius, St. Petersburg, October 11, 1913; mss. German Foreign Office to von Tschirschky, Vienna, January 8, 1914; Russia provided its *points-frontière* on December 13, 1913, copy, Sazonov, St. Petersburg to German foreign ministry, no. 130, bd. 35, no. 72, 35972, GCSAP.

[140] German ministry, Denmark, to Bethmann Hollweg, January 8, 1914; Tschirschky, Vienna, to Bethmann Hollweg, Berlin, June 8, 1914, bd. 35, no. 72, 35972, GCSAP.

[141] Copy, Schmidt-Dargitz, foreign ministry, to interior ministry, Berlin, January 8, 1914, interior ministry 13689, CGSAP. For the May 23, 1908 circular, see interior ministry to German federal states, 13689, GCSAP.

of genuine anarchists." Regarding anarchists and violent revolutionaries, Russia also wanted to authorize the police of the two countries to communicate directly with regional police offices, including on the Russian side the Foreign Agency in Paris, as well as with each country's central police office, which the St. Petersburg Protocol already provided for. Trusevich raised the possibility of sending Russian agents to watch over revolutionaries in Berlin and he also wanted the Germans to forewarn the police in St. Petersburg about any of their actions, including expulsion, taken against these revolutionaries. The Germans objected to all these proposals, except for unilaterally providing information to Russian regional police offices in Warsaw, etc. (but not to the Paris office). Presumably the Germans wanted to avoid information getting into the hands of the French given the close, symbiotic relationship between the Russian and French police that existed in the French capital. The Germans also did not want communications between their regional police offices and the Russians.[142] In this case, then, and rather surprisingly, a common police culture did not suffice to bridge the widening political gap between Germany and Russia, each ever more tightly enmeshed in their respective rival alliances.

In 1912–1913 Germany and Spain proposed additional measures to strengthen the anti-anarchist dragnet. On April 19, 1912, Germany suggested that all signatories to the St. Petersburg Protocol agree to a convention providing for direct negotiations between central police bureaus regarding the expulsion and transfer of anarchists, including the hour and place of delivery. This was designed to execute what was already prescribed by numeral IV paragraphs 1 and 2 of the protocol.[143] While eight years seems an amazingly long time to wait to implement one of the central provisions of the St. Petersburg accord, the fact that Germany was already communicating with "some" other countries in this fashion perhaps rendered it something of an afterthought.[144] Several countries' objections to the convention led Berlin to drop the whole matter.[145] In May and December 1912, Berlin suggested to Constantinople that the judiciaries of each country be authorized to bypass diplomatic channels

---

[142] Zuckerman, *Abroad*, 65–67, gives a very dramatic reading of this encounter, which he cites as occurring in July 1907. The German documents date the meeting as August 11, 1907. See memorandum dated August 11, 1907, Berlin, Eur. Gen. 91, GFO. This memo indicates that two representatives of the German Foreign Office as well as Police Director Eckhardt and Trusevich (or Trussewitsch) were present.

[143] Ratibor, German embassy, Madrid, to Marquis d'Alhucemas, foreign minister, April 19, 1912. OP, l. 2753, SFM.

[144] Spain's central police bureau was already communicating directly with Berlin.

[145] German embassy in Spain, to Lopez Muñoz, foreign minister, Madrid, October 14, 1913. OP, l. 2753, SFM.

and communicate directly regarding anarchist extraditions and expulsions. Waiting a year to reply, Turkey refused to agree to this amendment to the secret protocol (although the Turks were happy to facilitate direct police-to-police communications).[146] In July 1913, Spain requested that Germany provide the date, as well as the site, or port of arrival, of anarchist expulsions, which for some reason had not been done in the past.[147] The Berlin police soon agreed to proceed according to Spanish wishes.[148]

Several attempts were made to expand the number of nations adhering to the St. Petersburg accord. Besides putting a feeler out to Britain in June 1906, Germany invited Italy to join two years later after several acts of anarchist violence in the United States and the assassination of the king and prince royal of Portugal. Despite these alarming incidents and Berlin's suggestion that Rome could adhere to the accord on the same abridged terms as Switzerland or Luxembourg, Prime Minister Giolitti turned down the informal German offer of June 1908 for the same reasons that he had given in 1904.[149] Nonetheless, Italy assured Germany that it would continue to carry out surveillance and provide information on the anarchists directly to the Berlin police as provided for "exclusively" in the 1898 Rome conference accord and as it had done frequently in the past.[150]

Another failed initiative involved Japan. In 1908 Japan had approached Austria-Hungary, wanting information about domestic laws and regulations used to monitor the "activity of the anarchists and other persons belonging to radical socialist parties that foment ideas judged dangerous to the state." Vienna replied that Austria and Hungary exercised surveillance over the anarchists in conformity with the St. Petersburg Protocol.[151] In February 1909 Tokyo contacted Berlin regarding possible adherence to the protocol, expressing concern about anarchists arriving

---

[146] German *Notes Verbales*, May 10 and December 20, 1912. Copy, Minister of Foreign Affairs, Sublime Porte, to German ambassador, December 4, 1913. *Auswärtiges Amt*, 35972, GCSAP.

[147] Copy, José de Landecho, Spanish embassy, to Jagow, foreign secretary, Berlin, July 31, 1913. OP, l. 2753, SFM.

[148] Berlin police memorandum to German foreign ministry, August 23, 1913, Auswärtiges Amt, 35515, GCSAP.

[149] Wedel, German embassy, Rome, to secretary general, Italian foreign ministry, June 20, 1908; Giolitti, interior ministry, DGPS, to foreign minister, Rome, August 30, 1908, Ser. P. b. 47, IFO.

[150] Leonardi, DGPS, Rome, to minister of foreign affairs, Rome, July 12, 1908, Ser. P, b. 47, IFM.

[151] Japanese embassy, Vienna, to Aehrenthal, June 18, 1908, and copy, Austrian foreign ministry to Japanese ambassador, Vienna, October 8, 1908. Adm. Reg F52/9, HHStA.

in Japan from the American Northwest (referring, perhaps, to the establishment in 1906 by Kotoku Shusui, the leading Japanese anarchist, of a Social Revolutionary Party among Japanese Americans in San Francisco and Oakland).[152] Tokyo first heard about the secret St. Petersburg agreement from information leaked to *Le Matin* in May 1904. Japan had reason to be concerned and not only about anarchists arriving from abroad. During the year or so before their arrest in May 1910, Japanese anarchists had apparently been plotting to murder the emperor and talked about assassinating government figures, blowing up buildings, and consummating a "revolution of terror."[153] The Japanese anarchists turned to terror after the government responded to strikes, demonstrations, and other peaceful means of protest with brutal repression.[154]

In 1909 Germany responded to the Japanese request by first sounding out Russia, which raised no objections to Tokyo's adherence, and then consulting the other members of the anti-anarchist pact.[155] Some eight months later, after examining the protocol, Japan informed Germany that regretfully, as things stood in Japan, it was "not in a position" to join the agreement. Why Japan declined is unclear. At the time of the "Great Treason Incident" of 1911 involving anarchist plotters, the Italian ambassador observed that the Japanese government was uncertain which course to follow "in the struggle against the currents destructive [*correnti demolitrici*] of the social order." In combating this new phenomenon Japan was prone to look abroad for solutions, but here, according to the Italian diplomat, Europe was no help: "the long experience of the European governments provides little instruction, [since] among them the system of severity, like that of moderation, has so far not given very satisfying results."[156] This brush with anarchist terrorism, while nipped early in the bud, left a permanent mark on Japan. It marked "the end of the Meiji socialist movement" and in 1911 led to the "establishment of the first Tokkô [political policing] section" in Japan, within the Tokyo Metropolitan Police.[157] The lack of such a section in 1909 may explain why the Japanese government felt unable to adhere to the St. Petersburg Protocol with its requirement for systematic reporting on and information exchange about the anarchists.

---

[152] Ira Plotkin, *Anarchism in Japan: A Study of the Great Treason Affair 1910–1911* (Lewiston, NY: Edwin Mellen, 1990): 26–27.

[153] Plotkin, *Anarchism in Japan*, 104–115.

[154] Plotkin, *Anarchism in Japan*, 13–14, 24–25, 108.

[155] Von Schoen, Berlin, February 7, 1909, to German Legation Bern, Pol.An. Anarchistisches, Gesandtschaft Bern, bd. 7, GFO.

[156] Guiccioli, Tokyo, to Di San Giuliano, Rome, January 20 and especially 22, 1911. Ser. Z, B. 47, IFO.

[157] Elise Tipton, "The Tokkô and Political Police in Japan, 1911–1945," in Mark Mazower (ed.), *The Policing of Politics in the Twentieth Century* (Oxford: Berghahn, 1997): 217, 219;

In late November 1913 Spain wished to return to the question of enlarging the anti-anarchist league and making it more effective. The assassination of Prime Minister Canalejas a year earlier had led to a reorganization and centralization of the Spanish police under a *Direccion General de Seguridad* (DGS). This culminated a whole series of police reforms since 1908 that in effect led to the foundation of the modern Spanish police.[158] It exemplifies how powerful terrorism has been historically in the modernization of public security forces. At the request of the DGS, Madrid suggested to Germany, as initiator of the St. Petersburg pact, that Italy and the United States, as well as the Latin American countries of Argentina, Brazil, Cuba, and Panama, be invited to adhere because they were "very important centers [*focos importantisimos*] of the universal anarchist movement."[159] Spain also asked for more effective and continuous exchange of information about the anarchists (including their organization of revolutionary strikes), the use of a single language in communication, and the establishment of the requirement that, at the request of consular officials, captains keep track of the anarchists on board their vessels. Little seems to have come of the Spanish proposals, and none of the states listed by Spain subsequently adhered to the protocol. Berlin informed Madrid that, given their earlier flat refusals, it was pointless to ask once again for the United States and Italy to join the accord. Furthermore, single-language countries might object to being forced to renounce using their own tongue when communicating with their officials internally.[160]

Decline of the St. Petersburg "system"

Before World War I, some signs appeared that anti-anarchist cooperation between the European states was diminishing. Besides its growing entente with Britain, several other developments undermined Russia's reliability and capability as a partner, at least as far as Germany and Austria were concerned, in carrying out anti-anarchist actions abroad. Contributing to the decline were the devastating actions of Vladimir Burtsev, the self-declared revolutionary "policeman," who exposed a large number of Russian government agents operating inside

Elise Tipton, *The Japanese Police State: the Tokkô in Interwar Japan* (Honolulu: University of Hawaii, 1990).
[158] Antonio Viqueira Hinojosa, *Policía española*, 110; Turrado Vidal, *Estudios*, 37–38.
[159] Director general, DGS, to undersecretary, Spanish foreign ministry, August 12, 1913; Marques de Lema (Madrid) to Spanish ambassador (Berlin), November 22, 1913. OP, l. 2753, SFM.
[160] Confidential German memorandum forwarded by Spanish embassy, Berlin, to Spanish foreign minister, n. 329, December 24, 1913, OP, l. 2753, SFM.

revolutionary organizations (the most famous of whom was E. F. Azef). Astonishingly, and this was almost without parallel in any other country, Burtsev was assisted by a number of turncoat policemen, some of whom had formerly served in the highest ranks of the Russian police. This was detrimental to police morale, and if Zuckerman is correct, undercover agents began to refuse to inform because they were terrified that they might be found out by Burtsev's "police" with its moles inside the Foreign Agency itself.[161] In 1908, Burtsev exposed the energetic and able head of the Russian Foreign Agency in Paris, A. M. Garting (or Harting), as a former *agent provocateur*, forcing his resignation and the evacuation of his organization from the Russian embassy to a secret Parisian apartment. Garting's successor was inexperienced. In 1913 the Foreign Agency was officially dissolved and ostensibly replaced by a detective agency headed by two French citizens. Although this was a façade to allow Russian political policing in the French capital to continue (and secretly approved of by the French authorities), the effectiveness of this policing was compromised.[162]

At the end of September 1913 Switzerland refused to transfer Italian anarchists being expelled from Germany directly into the hands of the Italian police, as they had done in the past; henceforth the Swiss insisted that, as was the practice before the signing of the St. Petersburg Protocol, diplomatic channels be used. The Germans thought that this change of policy was due to internal Swiss politics and concern for the viewpoint of the Socialist Party.[163] At the beginning of the next year, Sweden, Norway (which had now broken away from Sweden to become a fully independent state), and Portugal (which had overthrown its monarchy in 1910 and become a republic) informed Berlin that, despite the provisions of the St. Petersburg Protocol, they would no longer permit direct police to police communications regarding the expulsions of anarchists. Instead, such communications would have to go through diplomatic channels.[164]

---

[161] Zuckerman, *Abroad*, 202, 205–208, writes that Burtsev unmasked one-third of the undercover agents working abroad, including the most important ones. Daly, *Watchful State*, 104, 109, 111, points out that besides damaging the Russian police, and government, the exposures hurt the revolutionary parties, which seemed to be honeycombed with spies and *agents provocateurs*.

[162] Daly, *Watchful State*, 134–135, notes discussions in 1912 about "the necessity to reorganize the security bureau in Paris" but the "failure to do so."

[163] Note, Department IIIb. Foreign ministry, Berlin, November 13, 1913, *Auswärtiges Amt*, bd. 3, n. 19, 35515, GCSAP.

[164] Mss. Foreign Office, Berlin, to Staatsministerium, Munich, January 8, 1914, bd. 35, 72/35972, GFO.

Conclusion

The violence unleashed by the Russian Revolution of 1905 and the diaspora that it spawned contributed to a number of anarchist *attentats* and re-energized the anarchist mystique. In an era of unprecedented international migration, the specter of the anarchist migrant – against whose attempts at assassination no foolproof protection was believed possible – stoked officialdom's exaggerated fears. This helps explain continuing efforts to expand multilateral anti-anarchist cooperation.

How should one assess the overall impact of the St. Petersburg Protocol before World War I? Historians of the Russian secret police *abroad* do not see it as having played an important role in the tsar's efforts to thwart anarchists and violent revolutionaries. Diplomatic and bilateral police ties appear to have been the normal channels for interaction between the Paris-based Russian police organization and foreign authorities.[165] This made all the more sense because the Russian political police abroad was centered in a country that had not signed the protocol. Spain clearly appreciated it (as well as the help and information provided by foreign governments through other channels), only wanting to expand the protocol's sphere and effectiveness.

The best way to assess the protocol, as well as the Final Act of the Rome conference, is to look at them in a larger context. Both diplomatic agreements resulted in more effective and wider police cooperation and information exchange, and they operated in conjunction with a web of bilateral accords that had been signed in the mid-1890s among a number of European states who never adhered to the protocol. Among the latter was France, which was tied into intra-European anti-anarchist policing not only by these agreements, but also by its alliance with Russia and the close cooperation between the Russian and French police. Britain was also informally tied into this anti-anarchist system through its conscious mimicking of Switzerland's unilateral adherence to the protocol. London was more deeply involved in anti-anarchist actions than would appear from the Anglophobic statements in the continental press and among continental leaders. The strongly anti-anarchist attitudes of policemen throughout Europe, including Britain, helped create another dimension of cooperation outside of the formal agreements. While those agreements certainly affected scores of individual anarchists, who were arrested and deported according to the rules laid down in the 1898 and 1904 agreements, did they actually prevent violent deeds? The state

[165] Johnson, *Okhrana Abroad*, 62.

of research does not allow one to point to specific cases where they stopped terrorists, but the anti-anarchist accords were part of general trends toward better European intelligence, which in the Italian case and perhaps others, can plausibly be shown to have prevented some acts of terrorism.

10   The decline of anarchist terrorism, 1900–1930s

One can point to the various examples showing that better police cooperation and intelligence forestalled assassinations and bombings, but still conclude that the decline of the incidence and importance of anarchist terrorism that became noticeable in many countries during the first decade and a half of the twentieth century was due primarily to other developments.[1] Heavy-handed repression during the 1890s had frequently led to anarchist acts of revenge, setting off chain reactions of violence that had often seemed impervious to police repression. Since the mystique of the powerful anarchist terrorist, viewed by some as a martyr ready to give up his life for humanity, held such a strong grip on the imagination of the age, the allure of propaganda by the deed was most effectively countered by undermining and devaluing this image and by opening up alternate outlets for the energies of discontented proletarians and middle-class idealists, a few of whom might otherwise become terrorists and assassins. These developments – some at the initiative of governments, some due to the anarchists, and others to broad socio-economic changes – took place most strikingly in France and Italy, but, disastrously, not in Spain (or for that matter in Argentina and Russia). Because the subject is a vast one, this chapter will merely attempt to present a brief sketch.

---

[1] Writing *c.* 1906, Pietro Lanza noted that "to tell the truth for some years we have had a little truce from anarchist attentats." *Enciclopedia giuridica italiana,* "*Estradizione,*" vol. 5, 547n5. In an interview with the former anarchist Francesco Saverio Merlino published in the Turinese newspaper *La Stampa* (June 18, 1907), the interviewer noted "the evident and comforting diminution of anarchist attentats," an opinion with which Merlino agreed (cited in Aldo De Jaco, ed., *Gli anarchici: Cronaca inedita dell'Unità d'Italia* (Rome: Editori Riuniti, 1971): 699. For additional comments on the decline of anarchist attentats after 1900 see Vizetelly, *The Anarchists,* 293; Maitron, *Histoire,* 244–246; Joll, *The Anarchists,* 126–129; Masini, *Storia degli anarchici italiani:* 2:184; G. D. H. Cole, *A History of Socialist Thought. Vol. 2: Marxism and Anarchism* (London: Macmillan, 1954): 335. It needs emphasizing, however, that alarming anarchist *attentats* continued to occur after 1900 in Argentina, Spain, Russia, the United States, and several other countries and that after World War I they revived dramatically.

Italy

Italy merits special attention, since after 1900, terrorism diminished dramatically as a political and social problem. During the 1890s clumsy and excessive Italian policies of repression had politicized anarchist violence, creating martyrs and a thirst for revenge that in 1900 culminated, after a whole series of assassinations by Italian anarchists, in the murder of King Umberto. After the beginning of the new century, however, the policies of the Italian government worked in a significant fashion to diminish, downplay, and redefine the role of anarchist terrorism. While isolated terrorist incidents still occurred, the Italian government was able to break the chain reaction of violence, repression, and revenge that had characterized the relationship between the anarchists and the authorities during the 1890s. Due to the progressive social policies of Giolitti, the dominant political figure first as interior minister and then as premier, a number of crucial developments took place. May Day processions and labor union and strike activity (outside the public sector) were no longer prohibited or harassed and became available as a safety valve for proletarian action.[2] The growing socialist party, together with mushrooming labor organizations – including syndicalist groups – and widespread strike activity, all served to absorb and domesticate anarchist and proletarian energies, diverting them away from individualistic acts of propaganda by the deed and toward more organized and non-violent efforts to alter society.[3]

Since the age of anarchist terrorism coincided with the development of New Journalism and the birth of the era of mass media, it is noteworthy that Prime Minister Giolitti worked consistently and, since the public proved receptive to his messages and policies, relatively effectively to shape public perceptions of anarchist violence by limiting, reconfiguring, or denying it publicity. This was crucial since, as many scholars have observed, publicity and media coverage are a key factor in nurturing and sustaining terrorism.[4]

One way Giolitti downplayed anarchist violence was to refuse it special treatment outside of established law. In a remarkable speech made in March 1897, Giolitti explained why he had voted against the

---

[2] Masini, *Storia ... Bakunin a Malatesta*, 2:177.

[3] For Malatesta's comments on how Giolitti integrated the Italian working class into society and the economy, see Levy, "Malatesta in Exile," particularly 278. For the reactions of and adjustments needed by the anarchists to the freer atmosphere of Giolittian Italy, see the memoirs of the anarchist Armando Borghi, *Mezzo Secolo di Anarchia,* 47–50, and the historian Gino Cerrito, *Dall'insurrezionalismo alla settimana rossa: per una storia dell'anarchismo in Italia (1881–1914)* (Florence: Crescita politica editrice, 1977): 51–53, 79–116.

[4] Laqueur, *Age of Terrorism*, 121–127; Bruce Hoffman, *Inside Terrorism* (New York: Columbia University Press, 1999): 176–178.

anti-anarchist laws passed by the Italian parliament in 1894 (and why in the future he would prove to be both a brilliant administrator and psychologist of the body politic). He believed that exceptional laws were "inefficacious and therefore in themselves harmful."

Exceptional measures render popular whoever is affected [*colpito*] by them; they create martyrs and converts; they are a cause of discredit to the country that resorts to them; putting in doubt the solidity of the social order, they increase the audacity of the extremist parties, and, making go away the outward appearance [*l'apparenza*] of danger, they distance [*allontanano*] the government from truly serious measures ... [T]hen, being by their very nature temporary, they leave the situation worse when their action is terminated.

The ordinary laws, if constantly and severely applied[,] are more than sufficient for the guardianship of society; nevertheless, I admit that, if there should be some lacunae in those laws, they may be filled in, but as a normal and enduring regulation [*ordinamento*], not as a tumultuous measure that takes on the appearance of violence and of vendetta, and that therefore cannot have an enduring efficacy.[5]

After he returned to power in 1901, Giolitti pursued "micro" policing policies of prevention through careful intelligence-gathering together with "macro" preventive strategies designed to respond to and alleviate the great social problems of the day. While opposed to special anti-anarchist measures, Giolitti proved a tough-minded upholder of law and order and no friend of anarchists.[6] As he telegraphed the prefect of Livorno (Leghorn) in 1902: "A liberal government has the duty to guard order with greater energy than any other since liberty is irreconcilable with disorder."[7] Yet he also refused to pass new anti-anarchist laws or to employ that dubious practice of preventive policing, the administrative detention (*domicilio coatto*) of anarchists shipped en masse to remote islands, as had been done in the 1890s.[8] The use of *domicilio coatto* was restricted to habitual criminals; political suspects were no longer affected. Again in stark contrast with the 1890s, Giolitti carefully limited the army's role and virtually ended martial law as a tool in the maintenance of public order or the struggle against terrorism.[9] While troops continued to be

---

[5] Giovanni Giolitti, *Discorsi extraparlamentari*, intro. Nino Valeri (Torino: Einaudi, 1952): 187. Francesco Tamburini's article, "L'attentato anarchico di fine secolo e l'evoluzione della legislazione penale italiana contro il 'Delitto sociale'," in Aldo A. Mola (ed.), *La svolta di Giolitti. Dalla reazione di fine Ottocento al culmine dell'età liberale*, ed. (Foggia: Bastogi, 2000): 52, brought this passage to my attention.

[6] Levy, "Italian Anarchism."

[7] Telegram, February 3, 1902, cited by Natale, *Giolitti e gli italiani*, 498.

[8] Jensen, "Italy's Peculiar Institution."

[9] When railway workers threatened a strike in February 1902, Giolitti called up the army reservists among them, since he saw the railways as an essential public service, i.e., necessary for provisioning the cities with food, in which strikes could not be permitted. He soon settled the dispute by granting some of the railwaymen's demands. This militarization of the railways was not repeated. Natale, *Giolitti e gli italiani*, 494–496; Seton-Watson, *Italy*, 239.

used in emergencies, they were almost always employed under the close supervision of the civilian authorities. In the years after 1900 and until the outbreak of the First World War, Rome declared martial law only once, and then not in connection with any terrorist incident or social protest, but following a powerful earthquake that leveled the city of Messina.

Nor did Giolitti give special attention to anarchism by signing on to new anti-anarchist diplomatic accords (although he adhered to those already agreed to, such as the bilateral treaties between Italy and neighboring states signed during the 1890s and the administrative provisions of the Rome Final Act of 1898). Giolitti was always willing to improve international police cooperation, as with Spain in 1906, if it was done confidentially and as an administrative measure. As we have seen, after 1901 Giolitti proved to be a great supporter of enlightened preventative policing by creating an unprecedented global network of police and informers to secretly gather intelligence about the anarchists.

In other ways as well, Giolitti's policies succeeded in directly or indirectly shaping the message that the media presented of anarchist terrorism and in reducing its importance. On the one hand he refused to follow the recommendations of the Rome conference of 1898 and enact new press restrictions or to adopt the Spanish practice of officially limiting or banning altogether the publication of news about violent anarchist deeds. The press was a necessary safety valve for discontent and enjoyed unprecedented freedom under Giolitti. Even if anarchist journals were on occasion (and sometimes frequently) censored and individual issues confiscated, a vigorous anarchist press developed in the peninsula.[10]

Where possible, the prime minister downplayed anarchist plots and deeds of violence or kept them secret. In his memoirs, Giolitti omits any mention of anarchism when discussing Bresci's assassination of King Umberto, instead describing this deed as the act of a "deranged mind" (*cervello squilibrato*).[11] In public little was made of a series of violent incidents, any of which might have been used as an excuse to pass new anti-anarchist laws or stage massive crackdowns against the anarchists. These include the October 26, 1902, bombing of the bishop's palace in Livorno, which killed a child and injured two others (the most lethal deed of terrorism during the Giolittian era, yet soon forgotten),[12] the

---

[10] Masini, *Storia … Bakunin a Malatesta*, 2:201, 226. Cerrito, *Dall'insurrezionalismo*, 52–53, 59, refers to the "anarchist press of the period" as becoming "always more numerous and interesting."

[11] Giovanni Giolitti, *Memorie della mia vita* (Milan: Treves, 1922): 162–163.

[12] *Corriere della Sera*, November 1–2, 1902; *L'Osservatore romano*, November 4, 1902; Giovanni Giolitti, *Quarant'anni di politica italiana*, 3 vols., ed. Piero d'Angiolini et al. (Milan Feltriuelli, 1962): 2:275–276. Natale, a close associate of Giolitti's, mentions

January 17, 1904, attack on an army officer in Milan, the June 1906 discovery of bombs outside Ancona apparently intended for use against the king, the November 17, 1906, anarchist murder of Professor Rossi in Naples,[13] and an explosion the next day in Rome inside St. Peter's Basilica while mass was being celebrated.[14] The prime minister made no public statements regarding these events. If possible, Giolitti kept an anarchist deed secret, as with the discovery, and arrest, of a would-be anarchist assassin in the Swiss exhibit at the 1906 Milan exposition.[15] In March 1912 Giolitti declined to mention the word "anarchist" in connection with the attempted regicide and self-declared anarchist, Antonio D'Alba. Speaking to parliament, Giolitti dismissed D'Alba as a man with a record of robberies and manhandling his parents. The authorities refused to release D'Alba's photograph to the newspapers.[16] All of these efforts were doubtless aimed at preventing the glorification of anarchist *attentats* and a surge of copycat crimes, but by means of low-key administrative and police measures rather than by highly publicized crackdowns or new legislation.

Through these and other measures, Giolitti built upon and encouraged certain attitudes already present in Italian society. He helped shift the frame of reference for understanding and dealing with anarchist acts of violence from that of deeds of political and social protest to crimes committed by juvenile delinquents and psychopaths. These were best dealt with by the courts and the psychiatrists, rather than by the government and the legislature.[17]

Of help in nurturing a mindset congenial to Giolitti's new approach to anarchist violence was the increasing permeation throughout Italian society of the ideas of Cesare Lombroso and other criminal anthropologists. In 1894 Lombroso had argued in a famous and controversial book that anarchists, and in particular anarchist assassins and bomb-throwers, were epileptic, insane, the victims of congenital disease of various sort, degenerate, hysterical, and often suicidal. While later on Lombroso's

---

this incident (which Giolitti took very seriously), although his dating is incorrect. Natale, *Giolitti e gli italiani*, 475.

[13] "L'anarchico Laganà arrestato," *Corriere della Sera*, November 20, 1906.

[14] The congregation panicked and fled after the bomb exploded, but no one was injured. This event followed the discovery in Rome of a bomb on the threshold of the Café Aragno, an event that the press linked to the St. Peter's explosion. *Corriere della Sera*, November 19, 1906.

[15] The plot was kept in "the most profound secrecy," in the words of the Spanish ambassador who was one of the few who eventually found out about it. Duke de Arcos, Rome, to foreign minister, Madrid, June 6, 1906. OP, l. 2751, SFM.

[16] Jensen, "Criminal Anthropology and Anarchist Terrorism in Spain and Italy," *Mediterranean Historical Review* 16:2 (2001), 31–44.

[17] Jensen, "Criminal Anthropology."

ideas became increasingly discredited, at the time Italians accepted them as for the most part legitimate.[18]

The best example of a successful application of Lombrosianism to defuse an act of terrorism was that of Augusto Masetti.[19] In October 1911, Masetti, newly inducted into the army and awaiting shipment to fight in a colonial war in Libya, shot his commanding colonel and let out a shout of "Long live anarchy!" Prior to this incident Masetti had never specifically identified himself as an anarchist, nor did the authorities believe that he was one (although the anarchists soon celebrated him as a hero and one of their own).[20] Anarchist or not, according to the military code of justice, Masetti should have been brought before a court martial and shot. Instead, a commission of inquest appointed by the military court placed him in an asylum for the criminally insane, where he was initially diagnosed as suffering from "morbid furor" and later from "psychic degeneration with a disposition to fall into psychopathic states."[21] To contemporaries the message was clear. As the anarchist Armando Borghi wrote in his well-known memoirs: "Giolitti was not a man of extreme measures. In order to avoid a trial, that is a death sentence, he thought of... Cesare Lombroso, and had Masetti interned."[22] This "Lombrosian" solution got Masetti out of the way without creating an anti-war martyr in the midst of Italy's invasion of Libya, a controversial colonial war vehemently opposed by the Italian left. Borghi's statement suggests that Giolitti resorted to such a solution from purely Machiavellian considerations. No evidence exists, however, that he disagreed with the various doctors' diagnoses of Masetti, as strange as their conclusions may seem to us today.[23] While the authorities' decision led to a long drawn-out campaign by the extreme left to free Masetti, it certainly had far fewer detrimental consequences than dragging Masetti before a firing squad. The pro-Masetti agitation never became violent and Masetti's incarceration

---

[18] Jensen, "Criminal Anthropology" and Mary Gibson, *Born to Crime: Cesare Lombroso and the Origins of Biological Criminology* (New York: Praeger, 2002). Even anarchists such as Pietro Gori were influenced by and "gladly publicized" Lombroso's ideas. Levy, "Italian Anarchism," 37.

[19] The most thorough study of the Masetti case is Laura De Marco, *Il soldato che disse no alla guerra. Storia dell'anarchico Augusto Masetti (1888–1966)* (Santa Maria Capua Vetere: Edizioni Spartaco, 2003).

[20] Delegato P. S. Brandi, Persiceto, to Police Chief, Bologna, December 7, 1911. Masetti file, n. 3125, CPC, ACS.

[21] Masetti file, no. 3125, CPC, ACS.

[22] Borghi, *Mezzo Secolo*, 118.

[23] A note dated November 21, 1913, unsigned but in Giolitti's handwriting on the prime minister's stationary, orders: "publish the medical examination [*la perizia medica*] which demonstrated [Masetti's] madness thus one should be able to cut short [*troncherebbe*] the [pro-Masetti] campaign of the extremist parties." Masetti file, n.3125, CPC, ACS; De Marco, *Il soldato*, 119n.

in an asylum never led to violent acts of revenge. In early January 1914, the authorities transferred Masetti from a criminal to a civilian asylum, which virtually ended the pro-Masetti campaign in Italy (although not the anti-militarist movement).[24] In 1919 Masetti was finally released.

While the spread of Lombrosian ideas helped the Italian government to finesse its way out of the Masetti incident in a relatively humane way that did not provoke a terrorist response, it hardly needs mentioning that Lombrosianism had retrogressive as well as potentially progressive aspects. While Giolitti embraced its reformist and seemingly more "scientific" side (which fit in with his plans to modernize the Italian police), other countries chose different approaches. For the most part, the French and Spanish governments ignored Lombroso, although in Spain he had many followers, including Rafael Salillas, dubbed Spain's "little Lombroso," who held several important government positions and edited a journal of criminal anthropology.[25] On the other hand, the oligarchy that dominated Argentina's politics until 1916 fervently embraced criminal anthropology, specifically ideas of "social defense," to justify draconian legislation hastily enacted in 1902 and 1910 that led to thousands of arbitrary arrests, imprisonments, torture, and expulsions, as well as to the suppression of anarchist publications and associations.[26] Between 1906 and 1910, it also helped provoke a whole series of assassination attempts and other terrorist acts carried out by the anarchists in revenge.

Britain and Germany

As should be clear from previous chapters, Britain pioneered much of the approach that Italy followed after 1900, and became famous internationally for its domestic success in dealing with the anarchists and avoiding terrorism. Britain's first class police force and intelligence-gathering system was the iron fist behind the country's "velvet" façade, i.e., a normally laissez-faire attitude toward the anarchists living in its midst. Generally speaking, British informants provided information that was considerably more reliable and less alarmist than that provided by their continental counterparts. This was in large part because, as was pointed out earlier,

---

[24] Luigi Lotti, *La settimana rossa* (Florence: Felice Le Monnier, 1972), 56–59.

[25] Jensen, "Criminal Anthropology," 36–37.

[26] Julia Rodriguez, *Civilizing Argentina: Science, Medicine, and the Modern State* (Chapel Hill: University of North Carolina Press, 2006), 247–257, provides a devastating critique of the Argentine state and elite's exploitation of science, including criminology and medicine, in the name of promoting civilization and repressing crime, but actually for the "marginalization of the masses and control and repression of their opponents."

Special Branch officers cooperated better with each other and with other police detectives, and were more careful in sifting through and evaluating the often-unreliable information provided by spies. Too often continental authorities passed on unverified information that needlessly exaggerated the anarchist threat and led to rumors about plots to assassinate all the crowned heads of Europe. The British were also better at keeping the identity of their informants secret, a secrecy that they have maintained up until the present day despite the complaints of historians.[27] The divisions and rivalries on the continent between spies, and their handlers, operating either out of embassies or out of interior ministries, between military and civilian police forces, between *Sûreté* and Parisian detectives – little or none of this existed in the Metropolitan Police. Moreover the British police could more often count on information being provided by the general public than was the case on the continent.

Usually very well informed about what was going on in anarchist circles, the authorities, if necessary, could locate and come down hard on potential bomb-throwers or assassins, as they did with Farnara and Polti in the 1890s. They might also prosecute the occasional anarchist publication that went too far (as with the Italians Adolfo Antonelli and Francesco Barberi who were tried and imprisoned in Britain in 1909).[28]

But in general the British believed that, as Metropolitan Police Supervisor Henry suggested in his conversations with the Spanish politician Osma, an open society exercised the firmest grip of all on the phenomenon of anarchist terrorism. Allowing the anarchists in London to expend their passions in loquacious meetings and in alarming, but little read, publications dissipated energy that might otherwise have gone into *attentats*. The "sedative" of an open British society rendered anarchism innocuous. The British police increased the potency of the sedative by, on occasion, finding jobs for the anarchists, and, above all, by not annoying them with useless, minor vexations. If measures needed to be taken against an anarchist, they were done discretely or even secretly, so as to avoid adverse publicity. These various actions taken in the context of a free society, rather than cultivating the anarchist "microbe," as Osma feared, rendered it harmless. The British, like the Italian, authorities did not conflate anarchism with socialism or trade unionism (which would only have exponentially multiplied its threat). Neither they nor the Italians under Giolitti tried to exploit the terrorist menace for ulterior political goals. The British anti-anarchist "system" (although a better term might be "approach," given its ad hoc and pragmatic nature), for thirty years the wonder of the world, only began to show its defects

---

[27] Butterworth, *World That Never Was*, xxxi.   [28] Porter, *Vigilant State*, 160.

in 1909–1911 when violent revolutionists escaping a despotic Russia proved impervious to the British sedative and carried out several bloody acts culminating in the Sidney Street Siege. Since, like the Bonnot gang in France (see below), the Baltic terrorists were essentially criminals who were burdened with little, if any, ideological baggage – and were seen as such even by left-wing public opinion – and since their deaths inspired no revenge-seekers, the significance of these violent deeds can to a degree be discounted.

Despite the brutal impulses of their often overexcited kaiser, the German government and police understood and acted in accordance with some of the same crucial lessons about anti-anarchist policing that the British and Italians had learned. In 1898 the Prussian interior minister wrote Wilhelm, who was worried about a report of a recent anarchist meeting, that too much heavy-handed prevention tended to be counterproductive. First of all this was because suppressing anarchist meetings gave them a significance they did not merit – and for this reason the anarchists themselves would find such police action "very agreeable" (*sehr genehm*). Moreover, on practical grounds, the wholesale suppression of anarchist meetings and organizations would make surveillance more difficult. In limited numbers, these groups could be carefully monitored, with the views and tendencies of each person noted and the entrance of new elements into the movement discovered. Breaking up these groups would lead to the formation of "a multitude of smaller groups, whose surveillance could not be managed with the same reliability. As experience taught, it was precisely in these small groups that criminal plans were fabricated and ripened" (*die verbrecherischen Pläne geschmiedet und zur Reife gebracht*). The police also cited the legal and political difficulties of banning anarchist meetings when nothing illegal had transpired.[29]

France

In France, policies and socio-economic developments comparable to those in Italy (although, as previously mentioned, the French rejected Lombrosianism early on) also defused the anarchist menace. In the late 1890s the French anarchists were drawn more and more into both the political mainstream and the organized labor movement. One of the precipitating factors in this development was the Dreyfus affair, the political battle over the guilt or innocence of Captain Alfred Dreyfus, a French Jew wrongly imprisoned as a German spy. Although initially the anarchists

---

[29] Von der Recke to Kaiser, Berlin, October 26, 1898, Prussian Royal Secret Cabinet, Rep. 89H, Abt. 23, n. 18, vol. 2, GCSAM.

were indifferent to the plight of Dreyfus, by the end of 1898 most of them had plunged into the battle for his vindication. The common struggle to free Dreyfus promoted contacts and solid friendships between French anarchists and Dreyfusard liberals, many of whom started to work for the release of anarchists earlier imprisoned for crimes of opinion.[30]

After the mid-1890s a change also occurred in the workings of French justice since anarchists began to receive fairer trials and more moderate sentencing. During the *attentat* era, French courts and juries had acted harshly, consigning anarchist journalists to long terms in jail or on Devil's Island and guillotining Vaillant for a largely symbolic act that caused almost no serious injuries. (It should also be pointed out that, notwithstanding France's draconian anti-anarchist laws, jurisdiction over anarchist crimes remained in civilian hands and was never turned over to military courts.) In August 1894 the tide turned against a policy of blind repression when, in the "Trial of the Thirty," a jury acquitted a group of well-known anarchist journalists and writers who had been arrested en masse after the assassination of President Carnot. After 1894, the French government and courts refused to create new anarchist martyrs. In an 1898 case the government commuted the defendants' sentence from death to life imprisonment. In 1905 a Parisian jury acquitted all four of those accused of conspiring in an assassination plot against the visiting king of Spain, a plot whose bombs also endangered the French president.[31] Despite having had his life put in jeopardy, President Loubet was content with this politically convenient outcome.[32]

The development of anarcho-, or revolutionary, syndicalism, which began after the anarchist Fernand Pelloutier became secretary general and driving force behind the *Fédération des Bourses du Travail* in 1895, increasingly brought the anarchists into the labor movement, both in France, and later, in Italy. During the mid-1890s, the example of militant British unionism had deeply impressed the French anarchists who had taken exile in London and proved very influential for the development of anarcho-syndicalism on the continent. The anarchists were impressed by "the mass strikes and the great wave of unionization that followed."[33] One could argue therefore that Britain exercised a double influence on anarchist terrorism, both from the top and the bottom, by inspiring (and diverting) anarchist participation into the labor movement and by providing a government model for effective anti-anarchist policing. While, at least outside Russia, the syndicalists were militant and could be disruptive, they did not engage in terrorism.

[30] Maitron, *Histoire*, 311–322.   [31] Ibid, 241–242; 386–388.
[32] See Chapter 9.   [33] Bantman, "Internationalism," 975.

After 1900 several incidents of anarchist "expropriationism" or "individual recovery" took place in France, harking back to the Parmeggiani and Pini robber band of the 1890s, and the anarchist robberies and murders in Vienna during the 1880s. The fact that after 1900 no expropriationism took place in Italy (nor did Italians imitate Parmeggiani and Pini elsewhere in Europe) may provide further evidence of the effectiveness of Giolitti's policies in diverting anarchist energies. These anarchist misdeeds in France, however, failed to lead either to government overreaction and the creation of martyrs or to new cycles of violence, repression, and revenge. Before being apprehended in 1903, the Frenchman Marius Jacob and his band of *illégalistes* claimed to have instigated more than 100 robberies in France, Belgium, and Italy. Jacob proposed that gang members donate 10 percent of their loot to the cause of anarchist propaganda, but some refused. The 1911–1912 rampages of the Bonnot gang, the "Tragic Bandits," were even more spectacular and bloody. Most of the bandits were French, but a few were Belgian. Many of the gang's members, although not Jules Bonnot himself, had originally been associated with *L'Anarchie*, founded in 1905 as the premier anarchist journal advocating individualist anarchism and "individual restitution," i.e., robbery. In December 1911 the Tragic Bandits began to steal cars, rob banks, and kill people. They were the first individuals to use automobiles for terrorist or criminal purposes. (Incidentally, fearing that the anarchists might move on from fast automobiles to airplanes for their nefarious deeds, in February 1912 French authorities required flight schools throughout the country to report on all students taking flying lessons.)[34] Prominent anarchists in both Britain and France denounced the Bonnot gang for being out for individual, bourgeois gain rather than for the collective good. Even a former editor of *L'Anarchie* rejected illegalism as a dead end. After the surviving gang members were apprehended and tried, they abandoned their anarchist faith and, unlike the anarchists of the 1890s, failed to make any stirring anarchist declarations prior to being guillotined.[35] Before World War I, the *Bande à Bonnot* had no imitators and only one afterwards.

Spain

The situation in Spain differed from that in France and Italy, since in the Iberian Peninsula anarchist violence remained an important phenomenon after the turn of the century. As we have seen, anarchists

---

[34] Sonn, *Sex, Violence*, 172
[35] Laqueur, *Age of Terrorism*, 106, 130. Maitron, *Histoire*, part 3, chapter 5: "L'illégalisme." Sonn *Sex, Violence*, 188–89.

made serious attempts on Alfonso XIII's life in 1905, 1906, and 1913, missing the king but resulting in the death of many,[36] and assassinated Prime Minister Canalejas in 1912 after he had quashed much of the anarchist press and labor movement. Spain's worst outbreak of violence before World War I occurred during Barcelona's "Tragic Week" of 1909. Madrid's inept response to this event stands in marked comparison with Giolitti's shrewd handling of the Masetti case. Both situations ultimately focused on an anarchist during a contentious colonial war. In July 1909 Prime Minister Maura called up army reservists to fight in Morocco, leading to protests in Barcelona. A precipitous decision to declare a state of siege and turn over pacification of Barcelona to the military proved provocative without being effective. Anarchists, republicans, Catalan nationalists and others rampaged through the city, burning or damaging scores of convents and churches. After a week, the Spanish army crushed the revolt, shooting and executing more than 100 people. Ferrer was falsely charged with leading the rebellion and tried by a court martial. His execution by firing squad, however, far from dealing a deathblow to the movement he symbolized, only created a martyr and sympathy for the anarchists.[37] This judicial murder provoked massive, violent rioting in many of the major cities of Europe and of North and South America; attacks – including a bombing – against Spanish consulates and embassies; bombings in Barcelona that resulted in at least one death, and possibly as many as five; scores of injured persons, and the death of a French policeman.[38] Moreover, the desire to avenge Ferrer's death was very likely a factor in the assassination of Canalejas and certainly one in Sancho Alegre's assault on Alfonso XIII in April 1913.[39]

[36] According to the press, in addition to the three major assaults, five other attempts were made on Alfonso's life between 1903 and 1913, although they resulted in no casualties or injuries and were due to "lunatics" as well as anarchists. "Anarchist Shot at King Alfonso," *New York Times*, April 14, 1913, 1 and 3.
[37] On some occasions, Spanish liberals, such as the Count de Romanones, claimed that "the best arm against the anarchists, is still liberty," but given their sporadic control of power, they were unable to enforce this policy, particularly in Barcelona. Romanones interview, *Le Journal*, June 6, 1906, cited by González Calleja, *La razón de la fuerza*, 376.
[38] One report stated that five died and twenty-one had been injured in the last four days. "Bombs Fatal in Barcelona," *New York Times*, October 18, 1909; *The Times* (London), October 16 and 18, 1909, reported the death of a "señor Bonaventure" due to a bomb that exploded near the cathedral on October 15. *Le Gaulois* (Paris), October 16, 1909, 2, reported six bombs, one death, and eight wounded. See also, "Six nouvelles bombes a Barcelona" and "Violents incidents au conseil municipal," *Le Gaulois*, October 17, 1909, 2. The Spanish consulate in Rosario Argentina was damaged by an anarchist bomb on October 14, 1909. "La ejecucion de Ferrer: Manifestaciones de protesta," *La Nación* (Buenos Aires), October 15, 1901, 9. Avilés Farré, *Francisco Ferrer*, 247–258, neglects to mention the bombings inside Spain.
[39] Since Pardiñas committed suicide, we have no way of knowing his precise motivation in murdering Canalejas. The Spanish historian Susana Sueiro Seoane, "El asesinato

In Spain, the passage of special anti-anarchist laws, the creation of anti-anarchist police squads, and the frequent suspension of constitutional liberties and imposition of martial law exacerbated rather than ameliorated the problem of anarchist violence. This was because these measures were frequently followed by cases of police and military cruelty and arbitrariness, and by examples of judicial injustice. The failure of even the Spanish liberals to fully understand this was exemplified in a 1906 speech given in the Cortes by Count de Romanones, a prominent liberal statesman. He praised the effectiveness of the Italian system of police-mandated internal exile, *domicilio coatto*, viewing it as having been crucial to Rome's successful prevention of anarchist crimes.[40] Yet *domicilio coatto* was an extremely arbitrary and illiberal form of preventive social control that even a conservative Italian prime minister referred to as a "verminous plague" and "a real legal crime."[41] It corrupted and radicalized those whom it afflicted. As mentioned, after 1900 Giolitti abandoned *domicilio coatto* as a weapon against the anarchists.

Madrid's constant suspensions of constitutional rights and declarations of martial law in response to strikes and demonstrations of political and social protest also undermined the prestige of the civil authorities and increasingly discredited Spanish justice. Between 1890 and 1914 martial law was declared once for Spain as a whole and more than forty-five times for various Spanish provinces. Between December 1900 and July 1909 the government suspended constitutional guarantees of civil liberties in Barcelona four times for periods ranging from three-and-a-half months to almost twelve months.[42] As Giolitti had predicted in 1897, resort to extraordinary and temporary legal measures, including "special" treatment for the anarchists, undermined the rule of law and fanned the flames of extremism. The frequent resort to military courts

de Canalejas y los anarquistas españoles en Estados unidos," in Juan Avilés and Ángel Herrerín (eds.), *El nacimiento del terrorismo en occidente* (Madrid: Siglo XXI, 2008): 159–188, documents the international anarchist community's calls during 1909–1912 for violent revenge against the Spanish authorities for the execution of Ferrer and argues that these might very possibly have influenced Pardiñas. According to two problematic sources, shortly before the assassination Pardiñas attended a meeting regarding Ferrer. López-Serrano, *Descubriendo los misterios*, and Cristóbal Buñuel Zaera et al, *El asesinato de D. José Canalejas* (Madrid: Juan Perez Torres, 1912): 20; "Anarchist Shot at King Alfonso," *New York Times*, April 14, 1913, 1, 3.

[40] Romanones. *Cortes españoles. Congreso de los diputados. Diario de las Sesiones*, December 29 and 30, 1906, 5052 and 5065–66. Commissions composed of government bureaucrats and police officials consigned the accused to *domicilio coatto*. Those affected had no recourse to the judicial system.

[41] Prime Minister Antonio di Rudinì in an 1896 letter. Jensen, "Italy's Peculiar Institution."

[42] González Calleja, *La razón de la fuerza*, 411.

and military rule increased the sense that in Spain anarchists and others received irregular justice at the hands of a new Spanish Inquisition.

The instability and divided authority of Spanish government also undercut efforts to forge an effective anti-anarchist policy (and this stood in dramatic contrast with Italy, whose government during this period was even more stable than that of France). In Spain, civilian governments shared – and sometimes disputed – control over policing with the military; the ministry of the interior, or *Gobernación*, changed hands an incredible twenty-nine times between 1901 and 1914. Moreover, the interior minister often lacked full control over Barcelona, after 1900 the major center of terrorist activity, either because the army had assumed authority under martial law or because its governor, as during Maura's 1907–1909 ministry, enjoyed a semi-autonomous position.[43]

This compares with Italy, where Giolitti proved to be the most effective administrator in Italian history. He ran the interior ministry and police with an iron hand. Between 1901 and 1914, as both the dominant political figure – whether in office or not – and for ten years minister of the interior, Giolitti brought a centralized control, consistency, and dynamism to Italian public security policy impossible in Spain or even in France. Moreover, Italy's directors general of public security, the powerful interior ministry officials responsible for day-to-day issues of public order, reinforced the continuity of policy. Only two directors served between 1898 and 1917, and one held office continuously for twelve-and-a-half years, surviving cabinet change after cabinet change, and finally dying at his post.[44] The unification of all public security forces under the directing mind of Giolitti bears comparison with the similar coordination achieved by the Metropolitan Police. While the Italian public never came to the aid of the police in the way that the British did, Giolitti was able to lessen the alienation between the policing forces and those policed to an unprecedented, if still inadequate, degree. One prominent socialist even claimed that he and his friends were "acting as cops for free," although this was not in the context of preventing terrorism but resolving potentially explosive labor disputes.[45]

Madrid signed the Rome and St. Petersburg accords in the hope of benefiting from international police cooperation and intelligence

---

[43] Governor Ossorio reported directly to Maura, rather than to Interior Minister Cierva. Ullman, *Tragic Week*, 103–104. For Cierva's complaints about Ossorio, see Juan de la Cierva y Peñafiel, *Notas de mi Vida* (Madrid: Reus, 1955): 101, 136–137.

[44] Francesco Leonardi, August 1, 1898–February 24, 1911, and Giacomo Vigliani, February 26, 1911–August 29, 1917.

[45] Filippo Turati, June 3, 1902, Chamber of deputies. Jensen, "Police Reform and Social Reform: Italy from the Crisis of the 1890s to the Giolittian Era," *Criminal Justice History: An International Annual*, 10 (1989): 194.

exchange in the fight against anarchist terrorism. But the results of its participation in these agreements proved to be mixed. Since no Spanish police official had attended the 1898 conference, Spain had failed to take part in secret, informal talks that had improved anti-anarchist police cooperation. Possible benefits from the 1904 agreement were diminished by the refusal of neighboring France and nearby Italy to participate. On several occasions France refused to extradite, or transport across its territory from other European states, anarchists wanted in Spain.[46] Spain was also hampered by the lack of money and trained personnel needed to set up an anti-anarchist police network abroad on the scale of the Italians.

Spain's labor movement also served it badly, since it failed to function, or functioned only sporadically, as a safety valve for worker and anarchist discontent. Before World War I, the Spanish proletariat remained poorly organized and prone to bursts of intense, but short-lived, activity rather than to sustained efforts. The Spanish Socialist Party and its affiliated labor union grew very slowly, and continuous, large-scale anarchist involvement with the organized labor movement did not commence until 1910–1911, with the founding of the *Confederacion Nacional del Trabajo* (CNT). For the first few years, however, the CNT was weak, its membership only 15,000–30,000. In 1912 Prime Minister Canalejas banned the CNT, causing its temporary collapse and forcing it to operate clandestinely. Not until 1917–1918, when it reorganized along strictly syndicalist lines, did it begin to become a really effective organization representing hundreds of thousands of workers.[47] Intransigent employers and hostile government policies also hindered the evolution of the Spanish labor movement.

Spain's slow rate of economic and social development, which was much behind that of France and Italy, combined with the Spanish government's policy of brutally and arbitrarily repressing dissent and strike activity and its failure to develop an effective policing apparatus, explain the continued incidence in the Iberian peninsula of extreme forms of political violence. The Spanish government's inability to remold the public image of the anarchist, which remained more that of a persecuted martyr than of a common criminal, exacerbated the problem of anarchist violence in Spanish society.

---

[46] Saint-Aubin, *L'extradition*, 1:422–429.

[47] In September 1911 the CNT had 7,776 members in Barcelona. Angel Smith, "From Subordination to Contestation: The Rise of Labour in Barcelona, 1898–1918," in Angel Smith (ed.), *Red Barcelona: Social Protest and Labour Mobilization in the Twentieth Century* (London and New York: Routledge, 2002): 31–32. There were 30,000 throughout Spain, but government repression caused the membership to go into steep decline. Angel Smith, *Anarchism, Revolution and Reaction: Catalan Labour and the Crisis of the Spanish State, 1898–1923* (New York: Berghahn Books, 2007): 195–200, 211, 218, 234–235, Bookchin, *Spanish Anarchists*, 144, 147–48, 160, 164, 169–171.

Argentina

Similar to the situation in Spain, Argentina's labor movement failed to act as an anodyne for violent extremism. Indeed the history of terrorism in Argentina presents a reverse mirror image of Italy's. During the 1890s, despite a growing anarchist movement and press that glorified dynamite, the South American country remained free of terrorism. Unlike Italy, the early twentieth-century integration of Argentina's anarchists into the labor movement did not serve as a safety valve for extremist discontent since the government reacted to this development with crude attempts at repression and brutal police crackdowns. The anarchists responded with assassination attempts and bombings.

A combination of economic, social, and political factors, together with a systematic government effort to redefine and downplay the nature and importance of anarchist terrorism provides the best explanation for why this form of violence declined in certain countries but not in others before World War I. Careful police intelligence work and international police cooperation, together with a more rigorously professional system of protection for monarchs and heads of state, could and did aid in reducing the problem of anarchist terrorism, but heavy-handed prevention and repression only worsened it.

Epilogue: anti-anarchist policing and anarchist terrorism after 1914

Eventually political and ideological divisions between rival governments, culminating in World War I, undermined and destroyed the St. Petersburg Protocol's attempt to create a formal anti-anarchist alliance. A rump alliance, however, operated among the central powers and neutral states to the end of the war.[48] For example, in August 1914, the German government wished to deport three Spanish anarchists back to Spain (it is amusing to note that the Spanish government sought to prevent this by attesting to the anarchists' good character; no doubt Madrid, like Rome, preferred keeping its anarchists abroad). Wartime conditions, however, made deportation impossible from the usual exit port of Hamburg and the land route too difficult and expensive.[49] Berlin and Vienna continued to send out their

---

[48] For example, on June 4, 1917 the Ottoman embassy in Berlin informed the German foreign ministry that the Directorate General of Police was no longer occupied with "the international measures adopted regarding the anarchists by the powers signatory to the [St. Petersburg] Convention" and that in future information should be sent to the Judicial Proceedings Section of the Directorate of General Security "in conformity with articles 2 and 6 of the secret Protocol." Note Verbale. CGSAP, Auswärtiges Amt, bd. 36, 72/35973.

[49] Police Chief Dusseldorf to police presidency, Berlin, August 25, 1914; Note Verbale, Spanish embassy, Berlin, September 23, 1914. GCSAP, 35972.

secret annual reports on the anarchist and social democratic movement. In February 1917 the Viennese police's *Die socialdemokratische und anarchistische Bewegung im Jahre 1915* went out to Berlin and the German states, Sweden, Norway, Denmark, and Switzerland but not, for some reason, to the Ottoman Empire. The Netherlands also received a copy although it was unaffiliated with the St. Petersburg Protocol. The Austrian foreign ministry memo forwarding this material noted that, due to the present "difficulties," no information had been reported from the Austrian representatives in the United States, South America, and Spain.[50]

During the war the Rome Anti-Anarchist Final Act also remained in force, at least for some countries. After an "educated anarchist," who may have had some mental problems, assassinated King George I of Greece in March 1913,[51] the Greek government instituted a special public security service to protect sovereigns and other noted personages. In April 1914 Athens asked that this organization receive "all notices regarding the movement of anarchists and other dangerous persons."[52] In October it also asked various European states to send "a list as complete as possible of the names of all anarchist militants who are considered dangerous for the public order or the security of prominent persons."[53] Italy's response was to refuse to send a complete list of militant Italian anarchists, while pledging to make available to Athens news of the "departure for Greece of dangerous anarchists and of all other relevant information as stipulated for in letter C paragraph II of the propositions determined on December 21, 1898 by the international conference for the defense of society against the anarchists."[54] While Italy had cause to worry that with a list of militants in hand, Greece might quickly make Italian anarchist emigrants into unwelcome home comers, Germany and Austria had no such concerns. They readily turned over names, descriptions, and photographs of the "militant anarchists" residing in their countries.[55]

The phenomenon of anarchist terrorism after 1914 has been much less studied than the pre-war variety. Although the single most lethal act

---

[50] Austrian foreign ministry to Austrian diplomatic representatives Berlin etc., confidential, Vienna, February 23, 1917. HHStA, PA I, 706.

[51] "King's Murderer is Educated Anarchist," and "The Assassin Lived Here," *New York Times*, March 20, 1913, 3.

[52] The new service was instituted by decree on January 3, 1914. Italian foreign ministry, April 27, 1914, Div. AA.GG.RR. Massime, b. 3/A3, ACS.

[53] Note Verbale, Greek Legation, to Italian foreign ministry, Rome, October 23, 1914, Z contenzioso b. 49, IFM.

[54] Vigliani, DGPS, Rome, November 5, 1914, to foreign ministry, Rome. Z contenzioso, b.49, IFM.

[55] Mss. German foreign ministry to Greek Legation, Berlin, February 22, 1915, CGSAP, 341/35972; Note Verbale, Greek Legation, Vienna, to Austro-Hungarian foreign ministry February 3/16, 1916. Adm. Reg. F52/9, HHStA.

of anarchist terrorism in its entire history took place during this period, i.e., the Wall Street bombing of September 1920, on the whole anarchist terrorism was a much less salient feature of international life. In effect anarchism lost its publicity, or at least much of it, displaced in the newspapers and in popular imagination by the notoriety, above all, of the Bolshevik Revolution, but also by other events, such as the Irish struggle for independence, which unleashed its own formidable terrorist campaign. As David Rapoport has described it, after World War I a new, anti-imperialist and anti-colonialist era in the history of terrorism developed and increasingly displaced anarchist terrorism.

Based on a cursory analysis of newspaper accounts and on various other sources, one can conclude that at least ten countries in the Americas and Europe witnessed acts of anarchist violence after 1914. These were, by degree of importance, Spain, the United States, Russia, Italy, Argentina, France, Uruguay, Brazil, Portugal, and Bulgaria. Anarchist terrorism in these countries led to the death, excluding those killed in Spain during 1919–1921 and the 1930s and in Russia during its Revolution and civil war, of at least ninety-seven people and to the injury of at least 376.

Following a wartime pause, the Russian Revolution of 1917, much like the Russian Revolution of 1905 but to an even greater degree, re-energized the far left, destabilized a number of countries, and opened the way for the final phase of anarchist terrorism. Compounding its impact was the severe social and economic dislocation that followed the war and demobilization. After initially welcoming the Bolshevik Revolution, Russian anarchists soon came to see Lenin's government as the worst tyranny in history. Anarchist terrorist groups arose, especially in the south of Russia, where they carried out bombings and "expropriations." Anarchists broke into city jails and freed the prisoners and called on the people to revolt. The most spectacular example of anarchist terrorism took place in Moscow on September 25, 1919. Seeking revenge for the arrests of their comrades, members of the group Underground Anarchists and left SRs blew up the headquarters of the Moscow Committee of the Communist Party while a meeting was in session. Twelve members of the committee were killed and fifty-five wounded, including Nikolai Bukharin. While the anarchists hoped that this would be the beginning of a new "era of dynamite" that would destroy Bolshevik despotism, it instead provoked a massive series of arrests and the destruction of the Underground Anarchists.[56]

For this period Spain must be examined separately because of the extraordinary conditions of quasi-civil war that prevailed there, or to be

---

[56] Paul Avrich, *The Russian Anarchists*, (New York: W. W. Norton, 1978): 185–190.

more precise, in Catalonia in the years 1919–1921. In Barcelona virtual civil war raged between the labor movement and intransigent employers supported by the Spanish authorities, particularly by the army. Rival groups of gunmen, *pistoleros*, some affiliated with the government and the employer associations and others with the anarchists and the CNT, carried out tit-for-tat assassinations and bombings. According to one source, between January 1919 and December 1923, more than 700 people were murdered by the rival gangs and, presumably, roughly half of these victims were due to the anarchists.[57] At the conflict's height in Barcelona an average of sixteen people were being assassinated weekly. The government and employer-affiliated forces threw bombs into a workman's music hall and murdered dozens of syndicalist leaders, including many moderates who opposed violence. In revenge anarchist "action groups" assassinated employers; the editor of a newspaper; Count Salvatierra, the former civil governor of Barcelona; Prime Minister Eduardo Dato (March 8, 1921); and the Cardinal Archbishop of Saragossa, Juan Soldevila Romero (April 4, 1923). Dato proved to be history's last head of government or state murdered by the anarchists.[58]

After Spain, the United States experienced the bloodiest wave of anarchist terrorism post-1914. In a cycle of accelerating violence comparable to what Europe experienced during the 1890s, government repression was met by anarchist revenge. Between July 1914 and September 1920, spurred on by police persecution, anti-war sentiment, and anger over the Sacco and Vanzetti case, anarchists set off explosions that killed fifty-seven to sixty-seven people in the United States, including eight anarchists whose bombs blew up prematurely.[59] Among the more famous events of the post-war "Red Scare," at the end of April 1919, was the mailing of thirty bombs to various high ranking officials, from the Attorney General and a Supreme Court justice to mayors, congressmen, and a Bureau of Investigation agent. On June 2, 1919, explosions at the homes of various officials took place almost simultaneously in seven American cities. These two series of bombings were the most widespread coordinated attacks in anarchist history. The wave of anarchist violence

---

[57] Gerald Brennan, *The Spanish Labyrinth* (Cambridge University Press, 1971): 73–74n.

[58] Robert Kern, *Red Years/Black Years: A Political History of Spanish Anarchism, 1911–1937* (Philadelphia: Institute for the Study of Human Issues, 1978): 53–63; Woodcock, *Anarchism*, 379. A few symbolic anarchist attacks also occurred during the Primo de Rivera dictatorship, i.e., the November 6–7, 1924, attacks on the Atarazanas prison in Barcelona and the Vera de Bidasoa frontier station. Kern, *Red Years/Black Years*, 66; Bookchin, *Spanish Anachists*, 191.

[59] Paul Avrich, *Sacco and Vanzetti: The Anarchist Background* (Princeton University Press, 1991): 99–103, 137–162.

finally climaxed in the Wall Street explosion of September 16, 1920, the most lethal act of terrorism in American history prior to the Oklahoma City bombing of April 1995 and the single deadliest anarchist *attentat* in world history in terms of the total number killed. The large dynamite bomb, hauled to the site opposite the Morgan Bank by a horse-drawn wagon, was filled with heavy cast-iron slugs, apparently window weights. The explosion killed 38 people and injured over 143.[60] Several historians argue convincingly that the bomber was Mario Buda, an anarchist follower of Galleani and a close friend of Sacco and Vanzetti.[61] At the time, however, many, including the famous William J. Burns, head of the Bureau of Investigation, and J. Edgar Hoover, believed the bomb was due to a Soviet or American communist plot. This is one of many examples demonstrating how the Bolshevik revolution tended to overshadow anarchist terrorism.[62] The persecution and martyrdom of Sacco and Vanzetti was not only a probable contributing cause of the Wall Street bloodbath, but also led to a series of later bombings and violent demonstrations in the United States and around the globe. At least three people died in these incidents and hundreds were injured.[63] It was the Francesco Ferrer case all over again.

After Spain and the United States, and almost on a par with Russia, Italy experienced the worst terrorist incidents following World War I. Bombings, apparently by anarchists, killed a few people in Milan (Hotel Cavour, October 14, 1920) and Turin (May 11, 1921). Then on March 23, 1923, an anarchist bomb exploded at the Diana Theatre in Milan, killing 21 and injuring more than 70 people, the deadliest terror attack in Italian history until August 1980. While Italians had earlier acquired the reputation of being the foremost assassins in Europe, this bloodbath slaughtering of a large number of people uninvolved in politics was unprecedented in Italy. In fact the anarchists intended the bomb for the *Hotel* Diana, where they believed the police chief of Milan was staying, and only by mistake killed the theatergoers in the building next

[60] Beverly Gage's excellent *The Day Wall Street Exploded* (Oxford University Press, 2009) places this event in the context of decades of violent class conflict in the United States. The final count of victims appears on page 161. Charles H. McCormick, *Hopeless Cases: The Hunt for the Red Scare Terrorist Bombers* (Lanham: University Press of America, 2005): 157n8, citing the *New York Times*, gives a figure of forty victims by mid-November.

[61] Gage, *Wall Street*, 325–326, accepts Avrich's hypothesis in *Sacco and Vanzetti*, 205–205, as does Pernicone, "Luigi Galleani," 469.

[62] For Burns's attempt to pin the blame on the Soviets, see Gage, *Wall Street*, 261–308. After the multi-city anarchist bombing attacks of June 1919, the *New York Times* editorialized that "these crimes are plainly of Bolshevist or I.W.W. origin." June 4, 1919, 14.

[63] Avrich, *Sacco and Vanzetti*, 205–207, 212–213. Moshik Temkin, *The Sacco-Vanzetti Affair: America on Trial* (New Haven: Yale University Press, 2009): 40–41, 50–53, 57, 129.

door.[64] In the mid-1920s to early 1930s, Italian anarchists made one or two (depending on how the youthful Anteo Zamboni's beliefs should be characterized) *attentats* on the life of Mussolini and were involved in various conspiracies against *il Duce*.[65]

In France anarchists shot Prime Minister Clemenceau in the shoulder on February 19, 1919, and on July 14, 1922, mistakenly fired shots at the Paris police prefect while intending to slay President Millerand (or perhaps Raymond Poincaré).[66] On July 25, 1921, the anarchist Jacques Mécislas Charrier, together with two criminals he had met in prison, robbed first class passengers on a Paris-Marseilles train, resulting in the death of one man. André Salmon (who knew Charrier's father) claims that Charrier, previously convicted for blackmail, wanted to imitate the Tragic Bandits of 1912. Charrier justified his actions as revenge for his sufferings and his disgust at social inequality. He was the last French "illegalist" and the last French anarchist to be guillotined for his crimes.[67] In May 1923 a Russian Jewish anarchist assassinated Simon Vasilievich Petliura, former leader of the Ukraine, while he was dining in a Parisian restaurant. This act was in revenge for Petliura's perpetration of pogroms during the Russian Civil War.[68]

On January 22, 1923, the individualist anarchist Germaine Berton (or Berthon) became one of the few – perhaps the only – female anarchist assassins when she murdered Marius Plateau, an editor at the right-wing *Action Française* newspaper and chief of the "Camelots du Roi" propaganda organization. The newspapers cited police evidence that she was also involved in a plot to kill the American ambassador, Myron Herrick, on October 19, 1921. The ambassador's valet was injured when a hand grenade blew up inside a perfume box that had been mailed to Herrick.[69] Once again, the deed was initially attributed to the communists rather than the anarchists.[70] If the anarchist May Picqueray's

---

[64] Vincenzo Mantovani, *Mazurka blu: la strage del Diana* (Milan: Rusconi, 1979).

[65] Riccardo Lucetti, *Gino Lucetti, l'attentato contro il Duce, 11 settembre 1926* (Carrara: Cooperativa Tipolitografica, 2000); Brunella Dalla Casa, *Attentato al Duce. Le molte storie del caso Zamboni* (Bologna: Mulino, 2000); Lorenzo Del Bocca, *Il ditto dell'anarchico. Storia dell'uomo che sognava di uccidere Mussolini* (Casale Monferrato: Piemme, 2000).

[66] *New York Times*, January 9, 1923.

[67] André Salmon, *El terror negro. Crónica de la acción anarquista* (Mexico City: Editorial extemporaneos, 1975 [translation of *La terreur noire*, Paris: Pauvert, 1959]): 431–436. "Charrier, Jacques, Mecislas," *Dictionnaire international des militants*. http://militants-anarchistes.info (accessed July 8, 2013).

[68] Sonn, *Sex, Violence*, 140–143.

[69] *New York Times*, October 20, 1921, 1, and January 25, 1923, 1; T. Bentley Mott, *Myron Herrick, Friend of France: An Autobiographical Biography* (Garden City, NY: Doubleday, Doran, 1929): Chapter 35.

[70] *New York Times*, October 20, 1921, 1. Berton flitted between various anarchist and syndicalist groups and had at one point been close to the communist party. "Berton Germaine, Jeanne, Yvonne." *Dictionnaire international des militants*. http://militants-anarchistes.info.

memoirs are to be believed, however, it was she, not Berton, who was the actual attempted assassin of the ambassador.[71] A bomb explosion on November 8, 1921, that damaged the American consulate at Marseilles was also probably due to anarchist anger over the treatment of Sacco and Vanzetti, as was the bombing of the US consulate in Sofia, Bulgaria, in August 1927.[72]

In South America, anarchist bomb explosions and fear of revolutionary Bolshevism led to the signature of the last specifically anti-anarchist agreement.[73] A Brazilian diplomat expressed fear of the "contagion of Russian anarchism" and that Uruguay might turn into a "center for anarchist propaganda."[74] On February 29, 1920, Argentina, Bolivia, Brazil, Chile, Paraguay, Peru, and Uruguay signed a police convention "for the purpose of... social defense" and providing for the exchange of information about "anarchical or similar acts," anarchist propaganda, and conspiracies (Art. 1).[75] Among the targets of anarchist bombing in this period were the Palace of Justice in Buenos Aires (August 15, 1920) and the Stock Exchange and foreign minister buildings in Rio De Janeiro (February 9, 1921).[76] In 1923, Argentine Colonel Varela was assassinated in Buenos Aires for ruthlessly repressing striking ranch laborers in Patagonia.[77] In March 1927 two American-identified banks in Buenos Aires were bombed, killing two people, in apparent protest against the approaching execution of Sacco and Vanzetti. The same protest was also behind two more bombs that went off in the Argentinean capital in July 1927 and in Rosario in August.[78] Giovanni di Severino, a refugee from fascist Italy, and his gang carried out numerous bombings between 1926 and 1930, including the US embassy in Buenos Aires (May 1926). The latter was in protest against the death sentence pronounced on Sacco and Vanzetti. Di Giovanni's most spectacular deed was in May 1928 when he bombed the Italian consulate in Buenos Aires, killing nine and injuring thirty-four. Between 1926 and 1928, Miguel Arcangel Roscigna, leader of the Argentinean "anarchist expropriators," who on one occasion collaborated in crime with Buenaventura Durutti, the famous Spanish anarchist,

[71] Picqueray, *May La Refractaire*, 60–61. See Chapter 2.
[72] Sonn, *Sex, Violence*, 178; Temkin, *Sacco-Vanzetti*, 40.
[73] "Bomb Outrages Stir Buenos Aires," *New York Times*, June 21, 1917, 7.
[74] Eugenio V. Garcia, "Antirevolutionary Diplomacy in Oligarchic Brazil, 1919–30, *Journal of Latin American Studies* 36 (2004) 771–796, especially 777–778.
[75] Rodriquez, *Historia de la Policia Federal Argentina*: 523–525; *Control of Terrorism: International Documents*, ed. Yonah Alexander et al. (New York: Crane Russak, 1979) 11–16; "South Americans Uniting to Keep Track of Anarchists," *New York Times*, April 19, 1920, 17.
[76] *New York Times*, August 15, 1920, 2:1, and February 10, 1921.
[77] *New York Times*, 26 January 1923, 19.   [78] Temkin, *Sacco-Vanzetti*, 40.

robbed several banks, leading to the death of a policeman.[79] Having fled to Uruguay, the expropriators were captured and tortured by Luis Pardeiro, the police chief of Montevideo. In February 1932, revenge-seeking anarchists gunned down Pardeiro and his chauffeur.[80]

The post-World War I resurgence of anarchist violence petered out in most of the world between the mid-1920s and early 1930s as prosperity (at least during the twenties) and political stability, sometimes under dictatorial regimes, returned to Europe and the world. International migration, which before 1914 had done so much to spread anarchism and which was a distinguishing feature of the first era of globalization, declined markedly as some countries enacted severe restrictions. Moreover, powerful dictatorships and totalitarian regimes led by more or less charismatic leaders ruthlessly repressed the anarchists in Russia, after the Bolshevik revolution of 1917, in Italy, after the 1922 fascist takeover, and in Spain, following military coups by General Primo De Rivera, 1923–30, and General Franco, 1939–75. These were three countries that had earlier been key centers of anarchism and anarchist terrorism. Anarchists found in these dictatorships an enemy more to be reviled than the former targets of their wrath; but yet, the anarchists were often impotent to strike with terrorist acts against such powerful police states. While before 1914 brutal acts of prevention and repression had more often exacerbated than diminished anarchist terrorism, the new style postwar dictatorships with their political parties that mobilized the masses and with their mastery of the media – and public opinion – through propaganda and censorship proved capable of stifling the anarchist threat.

In countries outside the dictatorships, anarchists were more factionalized and marginalized than ever before. Beginning in 1914, bitter divisions over whether anarchists should have supported the Allies (as Kropotkin and several prominent French anarchists did) or not, continued to impact the post-war anarchist movement and helped lead to a general decline.[81] Anarchist violence only revived briefly in Republican Spain in the mid-thirties and at the onset of the Spanish Civil War. The

---

[79] Osvaldo Bayer, *Los anarquistas expropriadores, Simon Radowitzky y otros ensayos* (Buenos Aires: Planeta, 2003): 11–88.

[80] Osvaldo Bayer, "L'influenza dell'immigrazione italiana nel movimento anarchico argentino," in Bruno Bezza (ed.), *Gli italiani fuori d'Italia* (Milan: Franco Angeli, 1983): 531–548, especially 546–547.

[81] In 1928, Sebastien Faure, a prominent anarchist leader, cited as factors in the decline of French anarchism, besides the defection of Kropotkin and others over the war issue, the fact that the unions had rejected anarchism, becoming either reformist or communist. In 1932 an anarchist journal also blamed the individualist anarchists for discrediting the movement by focusing too much on issues of sexuality. Sonn, *Sex, Violence,* especially 2–3.

Bolsheviks were now in the limelight as the greatest threat to Western, capitalist civilization, not the anarchists. Some anarchists had initially tried to co-opt the attractive power of the Bolshevik image by styling themselves "Anarcho-Bolsheviks," as in Spain, but soon came to realize that Soviet Communism championed a ruthless dictatorial state that was the opposite of what they desired.[82]

In the postwar United States use of terrorism as a weapon of class warfare went into decline after the early 1920s.[83] The most dedicated anarchists, like Emma Goldman and the terrorism-advocates Alexander Berkman and Luigi Galleani, were deported, and in 1924 new laws heavily restricted the Italian and Eastern European Jewish immigration that had previously brought so many anarchists into the country. The annual number of immigrants declined over 50 percent from what it had been in the prewar years. Having lost many of their leading figures, the anarchists became increasingly ineffective, fragmented "by incessant rivalries and disputes."[84] Despite this – or perhaps because of it – sporadic bombings associated with the Sacco and Vanzetti case continued until September 1932 when they ended after an explosion had destroyed the home of Judge Thayer, the man who had presided at the infamous trial. Reform also played a role in the decrease of terrorism in the United States. In the mid-1930s Franklin Delano Roosevelt, whose New Deal makes one recall Giolitti's pro-labor policies of the early 1900s, enacted the federal protections that the American labor movement had been demanding since the 1870s.[85]

Symbolic of the end of the age of anarchist terrorism were changes in international legal thinking that in turn reflected a fundamental shift in the climate of opinion. Ever since a resolution passed in 1892 by the Institute of International Law, anarchist, or "social," crimes had been defined as "criminal acts directed against the bases of the entire social order, and not against only a certain State or a certain form of government."[86] In 1934 the International Conference for the Unification of Penal Law, held in Madrid, replicated this definition almost exactly when it wished to devise a legal formulation punishing terrorism:

---

[82] For the anarcho-bolsheviks, see Kern, *Red Years/Black Years*, 54, 56. "In the first few years of the Bolshevik regime many anarchists and syndicalists saw 'sovietism' as a kind of Russian internationalist direct action" and Malatesta wanted to include the Bolsheviks with the anarchists in a new international organization, *La Mondiale*. Levy, "Anarchism, Internationalism," 341.

[83] Gage, *Wall Street*, 310–311.

[84] Avrich, *Sacco and Vanzetti*, 211.   [85] Gage, *Wall Street*, 311.

[86] *Annuaire de l'Institut de Droit International* 12 (1892–1894): 167.

He, who with the aim of destroying every social organization [or the entire social order, *toute organization sociale*] employs any means whatsoever to terrorize the population, will be punished.[87]

After three Croatian nationalists, with Mussolini's support, assassinated Yugoslav King Alexander and French Foreign Minister Barthou while they were being driven through the streets of Marseille in April 1934, it was no longer possible to view terrorist deeds as primarily the acts of anarchists. In the uproar over the assassinations, the League of Nations convened an international conference to draw up a convention for the prevention and punishment of terrorism. Completed in November 1937, although never fully ratified, this accord made no mention of anarchist or social crimes.[88] Subsequently, the menacing advances of Nazi Germany, the Soviet purges, and even more, the horrors of World War II and the Holocaust, made most people forget that anarchist violence had once been considered the greatest single threat to civilization.

In the final accounting, the international campaign against anarchist terrorism between the end of the 1870s and the 1930s deserves a much larger place in the history books than it has so far received. It exercised an important impact on a largely secret diplomacy, influencing the actions and attitudes of the European (and to a lesser extent, the American and Asian) states in ways that have seldom been assessed. Efforts to fight the perceived threat of anarchist terrorism influenced extradition law and practice, stimulated the spread of new methods of criminal identification, promoted police expansion, modernization, and centralization, and led to the development of more professional forms of guardianship for both democratically elected and dynastic rulers. They also led to Italy's creation of the most extensive global policing network in history up until that point, although quite modest by later standards. In terms of combating terrorism, however, the results of this campaign were mixed. At best they proved complimentary to and supportive of the more important social, political, and economic policies and reforms designed to extricate nations from the impasses that had caused anarchist violence to erupt in the first place. At worst they exacerbated the very problems they were designed to alleviate. At best the violent *danse macabre* of anarchists, the media, the authorities, and the public went into an extended intermission; at worst its bloody gyrations continued on and on.

---

[87] Bogdan Zlataric, "History of International Terrorism and its Legal Control," in M. Cherif Bassiouni (ed.), *International Terrorism and Political Crimes* (Springfield, IL: Charles C. Thomas, 1975): 480, omits "*toute*" in his translation of "*toute organization sociale*." Cf. *Ve Conference Internationale pour l'unification du droit penal* (Madrid, October 14–20, 1933). *Actes de la conférence* (Paris: A. Pedone 1935): 335.

[88] Zlataric, "History," 483.

Appendix A

The Final Act of the Anti-Anarchist Conference of Rome, 1898[1]

PROPOSALS adopted by the International Conference in Rome under the auspices of the Italian Government for the purpose of examining and establishing the most effective [*efficacies*] means of combatting anarchist propaganda, submitted for approval to the governments represented there.

I. The Conference believes that there is no commonality between anarchism and politics, and that anarchism may in no way be considered as a political doctrine.

II. From the point of view of its resolutions, the Conference finds that any act whose objective is the destruction of all social organization [*toute organization sociale*] by violent means is an anarchist act.[2]

Anyone who commits an anarchist act as defined above is considered to be an anarchist.

III. From an administrative point of view.

The Conference sets forth [*emet*] the following proposals [*vœux*]:

A) Each State should carefully observe the anarchists within its territory.

B) Each State should appoint a central authority to perform this surveillance.

C) The central authorities of the various nations should be directly interconnected and share all useful information.

---

[1] CIR, 61–65. French text published in *Early Writings on Terrorism*, edited by Ruth Kinna, 4 vols. (London and New York: Athena Press, 2006): 3:326–329. The translation is by the author and Ken Berri.

[2] "The term 'anarchical act,' to give it its real meaning, is one which is directed towards destroying by violent measures *all* social organization." Salisbury to Currie, London, December 2, 1898. FO 881/7179, PRO.

D) Insofar as the legislation of the country that orders extradition does not disagree, any foreigner extradited as an anarchist should be conducted to the border of his country of origin, and if the expelled party is not a citizen of a border country, the intermediary countries should provide at their own expense for his transit to the border of his country, unless they see fit to allow him to remain within their territory. Police authorities should advise each other in a timely manner [*en temps utile*] of all extraditions of anarchists.

E) Should the foreigner to be extradited be accountable in a court of law in his own country or a transit country for infractions preceding his extradition, the interested States may reach an agreement as to the appropriate actions to take concerning [*sur les suites á donner*] the expulsion, according to their laws and extradition treaties.

F) In conformity with the proposal made by the chiefs of security and the police of the various States represented at the Conference, all Governments should adopt "*portrait parlé*" as the only [personal] description [*signalement*] used to ensure that wrongdoers in general and anarchists in particular are properly identified.

IV. Concerning extradition, the Conference sets forth the following proposals:

A) It declares that any anarchist act that constitutes a crime or offense according to the laws of the soliciting country and the solicited country should be liable to extradition.

B) Under the same conditions, the regime of extradition should be extended to include the deeds specified in the following resolutions formulated in regard to legislative measures (Art. V – § 1, 2, 4).

C) Anarchist acts should not be considered as political offenses from the standpoint of extradition.

D) An attempt on the life or liberty of a Sovereign or Head of State, as well as an attempt on the life or liberty of the members of their family should, in all cases, be included in the list of acts providing grounds for extradition.

V. From the legislative standpoint.

The Conference sets forth the following proposals:

A) In addition to suppressing the violent act having an anarchist nature, all countries should repress the following deeds [*faits*] with criminal penalties [*par des dispositions pénales*]:

    1 The direct preparation of this act: in particular, the construction or possession of lethal or incendiary devices, of any type of explosives, or of substances intended to be part of their composition, with the intention of committing said action or with knowledge that they would assist in committing it.

    2 Any association formed or agreement established with the intent of perpetrating or preparing this very act, regardless of the number of associates or members, membership in an association, or agreement established for this purpose.

    3 Any assistance willingly or knowingly offered to anarchists by persons who either participate in the associations or agreements described in the preceding paragraph or act individually, by providing them with instruments of crime, means of correspondence, lodging, or meeting places.

    4 The public or non-public provocation to commit an act of an anarchistic nature, the same [*même*] for the defense of such acts.

    5 The manufacture and possession, without legitimate reason, of any explosive and any substance intended as a component of an explosive.

    6 The propagandizing of anarchist doctrine in the army as well as the instigation of soldiers to indiscipline with an anarchist objective.

B) That the various sets of legislation should recognize the necessity of condemning complicity in anarchist acts.

C) That the various sets of legislation should forbid by penal sanction:

    1 The distribution, sale, exhibition, and transportation of all writings, works, newspapers and other printed matter, all portraits, images, figures, and emblems constituting the provocation to commit a violent act of an anarchist nature.

    2 The publication or reproduction of proceedings and debates concerning an anarchist act, in particular the publication of the testimony of the accused; minimally, presiding judges should be allowed to block this publication by legal sanction when they deem it a danger to public order.

D) Governments should examine the appropriateness of restricting to a certain extent reports on anarchist acts published by the press.

E) All countries should provide for and agree to:

    1 The preventive seizure of all writings, printed matter, and other objects whose distribution, sale, or exhibition would otherwise be forbidden.

    2 A system of solitary confinement in the case of a guilty verdict regarding an act of anarchy that provides for such punishment.

    3 Judges' authority to attach to the punishment for any anarchist crime or offense the prohibition of any change of address without notifying the administrative authority, or residence in certain pre-determined places.

F) That the anarchist attempt to take the life of a Sovereign or Chief of State or the lives of their family members should be punishable by the death penalty in all countries where this attempt constitutes the crime of assassination.

G) That the execution of those condemned to capital punishment for anarchist crimes should not be in public.

H) That anarchist crimes be considered and addressed as such, independently of the motives for which they were committed.

The above provisions [*propositions*] were adopted by a majority after the declarations and with the reservations appended to this protocol. (See *appendix*.)[3]

It is agreed that the Governments may communicate, within three months' time, their intentions as to the sequel [*sur la suite*] to be given to the present provisions, especially those concerning the agreement to be established regarding provisions of an administrative order.

The Conference considers that it is desirable that the minutes of its deliberations, as well as the provisions of an administrative order, should remain secret.

Furthermore, it considers it desirable that the provisions found in the documents emanating from its deliberations should not be made public except as necessary.

Signed in Rome, December 21, 1898.

---

[3] CIR, 67–76. The *Annexe* includes England's lengthy declarations and reservations, and also those by Sweden and Norway, Denmark, Greece, Romania, France, Switzerland, Belgium, Netherlands, Portugal, Turkey, and Italy. These regarded primarily reservations concerning proposed expulsion and extradition measures, the death penalty, and about various proposals in conflict to a greater or lesser degree with national legislation. Many countries had voted "yes" on various proposals with the reservation that a word or phrase in the motion be suppressed.

For Germany:

A. SAURMA

E. DE PHILIPSBORN
F. VON MARTITZ

For Austro-Hungary:

M. PASETTI

Deputy delegates for Austria:
Dr SCHROTT
Dr HOEGEL
K. BRZESOWSKY
Deputy delegates for Hungary:
Dr SÉLLEY
Dr E. DE BALOGH

For Belgium:

VAN LOO

DE LATOUR

For Bulgaria:

Dr SIRMAGIEFF

For Denmark:

REVENTLOW

For Spain:

CIPRIANO DEL MAZO

FELIX DE ARAMBURU

For France:

CAMILLE BARRÈRE

VIGUÉ
G. BOUTET

For Greece:

D. COUNDOURIOTIS

G. STREIT

For Italy:

N. CANEVARO

TANCREDI CANONICO
L. SORMANI-MORETTI
F. FASSATI DI BALZOLA

For the Principality of Monaco:

MAC CARTHY

BARON DE ROLLAND

For Monténégro:

NÉLIDOW

For the Netherlands:

WESTENBERG KIST

For Portugal:

M. DE GARVALHO E VASCONCELLOS QUEIROZ RIBEIRO

For Romania:

ALEXANDRE EM. LAHOVARY AL. GIANNI

For Russia:

NÉLIDOW SLOUTCHEVSKY

S. ZWOLIANSKY

For Serbia:

ALEX. Z. YOVITCHITCH Dr V. VELJKOVITCH

For Sweden and Norway:

BILDT

For Sweden:

SEMMY RUBENSON

For Norway:

HARALD SMEDAL

For Switzerland:

CARLIN SCHERB

J. ISELIN

For Turkey:

M. RÉCHID NOURY

I. HAKKI

Appendix B

St. Petersburg Protocol, 1/14 March 1904[1]

Germany, Austria-Hungary, Denmark, Romania, Russia, Serbia, Sweden and Norway, Turkey [sic] and Bulgaria, convinced of the necessity to oppose an energetic resistance to the development of the anarchist movement, recognize that the best way to attain the end they have proposed is first of all to maintain the agreement [*entente*] so successfully established between themselves on that subject and to assert together their common interest that they are taking in the repression of anarchist crimes and *attentats*.

The undersigned, duly authorized thereto by their governments, are accordingly agreed to the following provisions:

I. Every anarchist expelled from one of the contracting States shall be taken back, by the shortest route, to the State under whose authority they were at the time of the expulsion.

If the country of origin of the expelled party should not be coterminous with the expelling State, the expelled party shall be accompanied to the frontier of the bordering country that is on the most direct route between the expelling country and the country of origin of the expelled party.

The transfer of an expelled anarchist to the frontier of his country of origin should be preceded by a notice sent in good time [*en temps utile*] to the authorities of the police of the last country.

If the country of origin of the expelled party should not be coterminous with the expelling State, the expelled party shall be transported through the territory of the interjacent state or states and in the charge of the authorities of such states, unless the Government of one of them should prefer to hold the expelled party within its

---

[1] Anarchismus (Geheim) 43, GFO. Author's translation with assistance from Christine Ferrell.

territory. If the transfer of an anarchist to the frontier of his country of origin necessitates transport through the territory of one or more intermediary countries, the authorities of the bordering country shall be advised in good time of the arrival of the transfer; the authorities of the country of origin shall be equally advised in good time of the expulsion and of the direction in which the transfer is routed.

The general designation of the authorities that should be advised of the expulsion and transport of anarchists, as well as the places on the border for the reception of expelled anarchists remains to be determined in an agreement among the contracting countries.

The cost of transportation, unless otherwise provide for, shall be borne by each State to the extent of the expenditure occasioned by the transportation of the expelled through its territory.

II. There shall be established in each State a Central Bureau of Police whose duties will be to gather information concerning anarchists and their doings [agissements].

III. It shall be for the central authority of each State to determine the manner in which it will supply its Central Bureau with the necessary information concerning anarchists within its territory, and their machinations.

IV. Each Central Bureau shall inform the bureaus of the contracting countries:

1. a. of the expulsion;
    b. of the spontaneous departure of an anarchist from its territory.

2. This warning [avis] shall be accompanied by a description, by an account [notice] of the past record [antecedents], and when practicable, by a photograph of the anarchist in question. It is desirable that the warning should mention the time and place of the anarchist's passage into the neighboring state and be communicated with the greatest possible expedition, so that immediate surveillance may be facilitated.

3. If an anarchist should clandestinely leave the province of a Central Bureau and his whereabouts be unknown, all the other bureaus should be simultaneously advised so as to facilitate investigations.

4. If the place at which the anarchist is to cross the boundary in the event of expulsion or spontaneous departure be known in advance, it would be advisable to inform [of this fact] not only the Central Bureau but also the authorities on the border of the State. The Central Bureau of each country shall communicate to all the other bureaus a list of the authorities on the border appointed for this purpose.

V. Each Central Bureau shall communicate without delay to the Bureaus of the contracting countries all information on criminal plots of an anarchist character about which it has knowledge.

VI. Each Central Bureau is obliged to communicate to the other Bureaus, within six months, all the information concerning important events connected with the anarchist movement that may have taken place within its jurisdiction [*rayon*].

The Bureaus must, in addition, reply to all the inquiries referring to the anarchist movement that they may receive from the other Bureaus.

The stated measures will be put into execution starting from the day of the signature of the present protocol.

The signatory powers commit to place themselves, without delay, in connection with each of the other signatory powers in accordance with the provisions of this Protocol. The countries which have not signed this Protocol may adhere to its provisions by a separate act.

The adherence of each Power is made known [*notifiée*], through diplomatic channels, to the Russian Government, and by the latter to all the signatory states or adherents.

It involves the full acceptance of all the above stated obligations.

Attesting that this Protocol is and will remain strictly secret, it has been signed and sealed by the Plenipotentiaries of the said powers.

Done at St. Petersburg, 1/14 March 1904, in a single copy that will remain deposited in the archives of the Russian Ministry of Foreign Affairs, and from which certified copies will be sent by the diplomatic channel to the signatory and adhering states.

For Germany: Alvensleben,	(L.S.)[2]
For Austria and Hungary: Ambassador L. Aehrenthal	(L.S.)
For Denmark: P. Lövenörn	(L.S.)
For Romania: G. Rosetti-Solesco	(L.S.)
For Russia: [Foreign Minister] Count Lamsdorff	(L.S.)
For Serbia, Stojan Novakovi	(L.S.)
For Sweden and Norway: Aug. F. Gyldenstolpe	(L.S.)
For Turkey [sic]: Husny	(L.S.)
For Bulgaria: Staneioff	(L.S.)
By certified copy: Director of the Second Department of the Ministry of Foreign Affairs: Malewsky	(L.S.)

Appendix to the 1/14 March 1904 Protocol.

At the time of signing the protocol on the subject of international measures against the anarchists the Ambassador of Turkey and the Ministers:

---

[2] *Locus sigilli*, i.e., the place of the seal.

of Denmark, Romania and of Sweden and Norway have tendered [*remis*] the following communications (*note verbales*):

A. His Excellency the Marshal Husny Pasha

The undersigned, Ambassador Extraordinaire and Plenipotentiary of His Majesty the Emperor of the Ottomans, in signing the protocol on this day on the subject of international measures against the anarchists, refers to the declaration of the Imperial Ottoman Government communicated to the cabinet of Rome, 6 September 1899 and makes the reservations that the clauses of the aforementioned protocol do not affect at all the agreements between the Sublime Porte and the Russian Government in that which concerns the return of certain categories of Armenian emigrants present in Russia.

St. Petersburg, 1/14 March 1904
(signed) Husny.

B. Monsieur P. de Lövenörn

The undersigned, Envoy Extraordinaire and Minister Plenipotentiary of His Majesty the King of Denmark, in signing the protocol on this day on the subject of international measures against the anarchists, declares, in the name of his Government, that the functions attributed by articles II to VI of the aforementioned protocol to the central bureau will be exercised by the police of the city of Copenhagen.

St. Petersburg, 1/14 March 1904
(signed) P. Lövenörn

C. Monsieur G. Rosetti-Solesco.

The undersigned, Envoy Extraordinaire and Minister Plenipotentiary of His Majesty the King of Romania, in signing the protocol on this day on the subject of international measures against the anarchists, declares that the Romanian Government maintains its exclusive right to identify the anarchist character of any individual against whom it is called to apply the measures provided, and that in general, each time that a difference of opinion arises on this point between the State on whose territory one finds the individual and that of which he is the subject, it belongs to the first to identify his anarchist character.

St. Petersburg, 1/14 March 1904
(L. S.) (signed) G. Rosetti-Solesco.

D. Monsieur Count Gyldenstolpe.

The undersigned, Envoy Extraordinaire and Minister Plenipotentiary of His Majesty the King of Sweden and Norway, in signing the protocol on this day on the subject of international measures against the anarchists, declares, in the name of his Government, that the functions attributed by articles II to VI of the aforementioned protocol to the central bureau will be exercised in Sweden by the chief of police of Stockholm and in Norway by the bureau of police of Christiania.

St. Petersburg, 1/14 March 1904
(signed) Aug. F. Gyldenstolpe.

Select bibliography

ARCHIVAL SOURCES

Archive of Antonio Maura, Madrid, Spain
Archivo Centrale dello Stato, Rome, Italy
Archivo General de la Nación, Ministero del Interior, Buenos Aires, Argentina
Brandenburgischen Landeshauptarchive, Orangerie, Potsdam, Germany
Haus- Hof- and Staatarchiv, Vienna, Austria
Bundespolizeiarchiv, Vienna
Foreign Office papers, the National Archives (formerly Public Record Office),
 London, United Kingdom
German Central State Archive, Potsdam, Germany
Deutsches Zentrales Staatsarchiv, formerly in Merseburg, now in Berlin-Dahlem,
 Germany
German Foreign Office (records filmed at Whaddon Hall, Bucks,
 December 1958
Home Office papers, The National Archives (formerly Public Record Office),
 London
Italian foreign ministry archive, Rome
Library of Congress, Manuscript Division, Washington, DC, United States
 John Hay Papers
 Franklin MacVeagh Papers
 Cortelyou Papers
 Theodore Roosevelt Papers
National Archives, College Park, Maryland, United States
Spanish foreign ministry, Archivo Histórico, Madrid
Manuel Allende-Salazar papers
Spanish National Archives, Madrid
Trial transcript, Supreme Court, Erie County, People of the State of New York
 against Leon F. Czolgosz, September 23, 1901. Buffalo and Erie County
 Historical Society library.

PRIMARY PRINTED SOURCES

American Historical Association, Committee for the Study of War Documents.
 *A Catalogue of Files and Microfilms of the German Foreign Ministry Archives
 1867–1920.* Whaddon Hall, 1959.

Anderson, Robert. *The Lighter Side of My Official Life*. London: Hodder and Stoughton, 1910.

Andrieux, Louis. *Souvenirs d'un Prefect de Police*. Montréal: Memoire Du Livre, 2002 [1885].

Anselmo, Lorenzo. *El proletariado militante. Memorias de un internacional.* 2 vols. Toulouse: Editorial del Movimiento libertario español CNT en Francia, 1946.

Araquistain, Luis. "Contra el anarchismo: un remedio," *El Liberal*. April 21, 1913.

Arrow, Charles. *Rogues and Others*. London: Duckworth, 1926.

Barrère, Camille. "Lettres à Delcassé." *Revue de Paris* 44 (April 15, 1937), 721–763.

Berkman, Alexander. *Prison Memoirs of an Anarchist*. New York: Schocken, [1912] 1970.

Borghi, Armando. *Mezzo Secolo di Anarchia*. Naples: Edizioni scientifiche italiane, 1954.

Brandes, Georg. *Correspondance*, ed. P. Krügre. 3 vols. Copenhagen, Rosenkilde og Bagger, 1952–66.

British Documents on Foreign Affairs-Reports and Papers from the Foreign Office Confidential Print. Part I, *from the Mid-Nineteenth Century to the First World War.* Series F, Europe, 1848–1914. General editors, Kenneth Bourne and D. Cameron Watt; editor, David Stevenson. 35 volumes. University Publications of America, 1987–1991.

Brust, Harold [Peter Cheyney]. *"I Guarded Kings." The Memoirs of a Political Police Officer*. London: Stanley Paul, 1935.

Bülow Bernard von. *Correspondance secrete de Bülow et de Guillaume II*, trans. Gilbert Lenoir. Paris: Bernard Grasset, 1931.

Cierva y Peñafiel, Juan de la. *Notas de mi Vida*. Madrid: Reus, 1955.

Conferencia Internacional Sudamericana de Policia: Convenio y Actas. Buenos Aires: De José Tragan, 1920.

Congrès international d'anthropologie criminelle. Compte rendu de travaux de la quatrième session. Geneva. August 24–29, 1896.

Documents diplomatiques suisses. Vols. 4 and 5. Bern: Benteli, 1983 and 1994.

Dugdale, Edgar T. S. *Maurice de Bunsen: Diplomat and Friend*. London: John Murray, 1934.

Early Writings on Terrorism, ed. Ruth Kinna. 4 vols. London and New York: Athena Press, 2006.

Evans, Robley Dunglison. *An Admiral's Log*. New York and London: Appleton, 1910.

Ferri, Enrico. "In difesa di Antonio D'Alba," *L'Eloquenza* fasc. 9–10 (1912): 301–321.

Figueroa y Torres, Alvaro. *Notas de Una Vida*. 2 vols. Madrid: Renacimiento, 1928.

Fitch, Herbert T. *Memoirs of a Royal Detective*. London: Hurst and Blackett, 1936.

Traitors Within: The Adventures of Detective Inspector Herbert T. Fitch. London: Hurst and Blackett, 1933.

France, Jean. *Souvenirs de la sureté générale: autour de l'affaire Dreyfus.* Paris: Rieder, 1936.

Trente ans a la rue des Saussaies: Ligues et complots. Paris: Gallimard, 1931.

German Foreign Office. Records filmed at Whaddon Hall, Bucks, December 1958.

Germany. Auswärtiges Amt. *Dokumente aus den russischen Geheimarchiven: soweit sie bis zum 1. Juli 1918 eingegangen sind.* Berlin: Reichsdruckerei [1918?].

Giolitti, Giovanni, *Discorsi extraparlamentari,* intro. Nino Valeri. Torino: Einaudi, 1952.

Memorie della mia vita. Milan: Treves, 1922.

Quarant'anni di politica italiana. 3 vols., ed. Piero d'Angiolini, Claudio Pavone and Giampiero Carocci. Milan: Feltrinelli, 1962.

Gladstone, William Ewart. *The Gladstone Diaries,* vol. 13. Oxford: Clarendon Press. 1994.

Goldman, Emma. *Anarchism and Other Essays.* New York: Dover, 1911.

Emma Goldman: A Documentary History of the American Years, ed. Candace Falk, 2 vols. Berkeley: University of California Press, 2003–2005.

Goron, Marie François. *Les Mémoires de M. Goron. Volume one: De L'invasion à L'anarchie,* Paris: E. Flammanion, 1980.

Holstein, Friedrich von. *The Holstein Papers,* ed. Norman Rich and M. H. Fisher, 5 vols. Cambridge University Press, 1955.

International American Conference (2nd: 1901–1902, Mexico). *Actas y documentos: Minutes and documents.* Mexico: Tip. De la Oficina Impresora de Estampillas, 1902.

Italy. Ministero degli Affari Esteri. *I Documenti diplomatici italiani.* Series 3, vols. 4–7. Rome: Istituto poligrafico dello stato, 1962–2000.

León y Castillo, F. de. *Mis Tiempos.* 2 vols. Madrid: Sucessores de Hernando, 1921.

Malatesta, Errico. *Rivoluzione e lotta quotidiana,* ed. Gino Cerito. Milan: Edizioni Antistato, 1982.

Picqueray, May. *May La Refractaire.* Paris: Marcel Jullian, 1979.

Polizeidirektion [Vienna]. *Die socialdemokratische und anarchistische Bewegung im Jahre 1908.* Vienna: Druck der kaiserlich-königlichen Hof- und Staatsdruckerei, 1909.

Ponsonby, Henry. *Queen Victoria's Private Secretary: His Life from his Letters.* New York: Macmillan, 1944.

Raynaud, Ernest. *Souvenirs de Police au temps du Ravachol.* With preface by M. Louis Barthou. Paris: Payot, 1923.

La vie intime des commissariats. Paris: Payot, 1926.

Rocker, Rudolf. *En la Borrasca: Memorias.* Puebla, Mexico: Ediciones Cajica, 1962.

Rodd, James Rennell. *Social and Diplomatic Memoires (Second Series) 1894–1901: Egypt and Abyssinia.* London: E. Arnold, 1923.

Roosevelt, Theodore. *An Autobiography.* New York: Macmillan. 1913.

Schoen, Wilhem Edward von. *The Memoirs of an Ambassador.* London: George Allen and Unwin, 1922.

Spiridovitch, Alexander. *Les deniers années de la cour de Tsarskoïe-Selo,* trans. M. Jeanson. 2 vols. Paris: Payot, 1928.

Spring Rice, Cecil. *The Letters and Friendships of Sir Cecil Spring Rice: A Record*, ed. Stephen Gwynn. 2 vols. London: Constable, 1929.
Steinhauer, Gustav. *Steinhauer, the Kaiser's Master Spy*, ed. S. T. Felstead. New York: Appleton, 1931.
Stern, Leo, ed. *Die Auswirkungen der esten russischen revolution von 1905–1907 auf Deutschland*. 2 vols. Berlin: Hütten and Loening, 1955.
Tarrida del Marmol, F. *Les Inquisiteurs d'Espagne. Montjuich–Cuba–Philippines*. 3rd edition. Paris: P.–V. Stock, 1897.
Torrigiani Malaspina, Cristina. *Dal mio diario di mezzo secolo*. Preface by Paulo Boselli, Florence: Le Monnier, 1928.
Victoria, Queen. *The Letters of Queen Victoria: 1896–1901*. Vol. 3, 3rd Series. New York: Longmans, Green, 1932.
Wensley, Frederick Porter. *Detective Days. The Record of Forty-Two Years' Service in the Criminal Investigation Department*. London: Cassell, 1931.
White, Andrew Dickson. *Autobiography*. 2 vols. New York: Century, 1907.
William II. *Briefe Wilhelms II. an den Zaren 1894–1914*. Berlin: Ullstein, 1920.
The Kaiser's Letters to the Tsar, ed. and intro. N. F. Grant. London: Hodder and Stoughton, 1920.
William II and Nicholas II. *The Willy-Nicky Correspondence: Being the Secret and Intimate Telegrams Exchanged between the Kaisser and the Tsar*, ed. Herman Bernstein. New York: Knopf, 1918.
Wyndham, George. *Life and Letters of George Wyndham*. 2 vols. London: Hutchinson & co., 1925.
Zedlitz-Trüzschler, Robert. *Zwölf Jahre am deustchen Kaiserhof*. Berlin: Deutsche Verlags-Anstalt, 1924.

SECONDARY SOURCES: SELECTED ARTICLES, BOOKS, AND PAMPHLETS

Acevedo Agosti, Valentin. *Anarquismo y Derecho penal*. Oviedo: de Flórez, Gusano, 1911.
Alvarez-Junco, José. *Anarchism Today*, ed. David E. Apter and James Joll. Garden City, NY: Doubleday, 1971.
El Emperador del Paralelo: Lerroux y la demagogia populista. Madrid: Alianza Editorial, 1990.
The Emergence of Mass Politics in Spain. Brighton and Portland: Sussex Academic Press, 2002.
El Anarquismo en América Latina, ed. Carlos M. Rama and Angel J. Cappalletti, prologue and chronology, Angel J. Cappelletti. Caracas, Venezuela: Biblioteca Ayacucho, 1990.
Andreucci, Franco and Tommaso Detti. *Il Movimento operaio italiano: dizionario biografico, 1853–1943*. Rome: Riuniti, 1975–1979.
Andrew, Christopher. *For the President's Eyes Only: Secret Intelligence and the American Presidency from Washington to Bush*. New York: HarperCollins, 1996.
Her Majesty's Secret Service: The Making of the British Intelligence Community. New York: Viking, 1986.
Andrew, Christopher and Oleg Gordievsky. *KGB: The Inside Story of Its Foreign Operations from Lenin to Gorbachev*. New York: HarperCollins, 1990.

Anon [Margaret Cunliffe-Owen], *The Private Life of Two Emperors. William II. of Germany and Francis-Joseph of Austria*. London: Eveleigh Nash, 1904.

Antonioli, Maurizio. "Colombo, Carlo." In *Dizionario biografico degli anarchici italiani*. Pisa: BFS, 2003–2004.

Antonioli, Maurizio and Giampietro Berti, "Bresci, Gaetano," In *Dizionario biografico degli anarchici italiani*. Pisa: BFS, 2003–2004.

Apter, David E. and James Joll. *Anarchism Today*. Garden City, NY: Doubleday, 1972.

Araquistain, Luis. "Contra el anarchismo: un remedio," *El Liberal*. April 21, 1913.

Archer, William. *The Life, Trial, and Death of Francisco Ferrer*. London: Chapman and Hall, 1911.

Arcos, Duke of. "International Control of Anarchists," *North American Review* 173 (1901): 758–767.

Avilés Farré, Juan. "Contra Alfonso XIII: Atentados frustrados y conspiración revolucionaria," in Juan Avilés Farré (ed.), *El nacimiento del terrorismo en occidente*. Madrid: Siglo XXI de España, 2008, 141–158.

Francisco Ferrer y Guardia: pedagogo, anarquista y mártir. Madrid: Marcial Pons Ediciones de Historia, 2006.

Avilés Farré, Juan and Angel Herrerin, eds. *El nacimiento del terrorismo en occidente, Anarquia, Nihilismo, y Violencia revolucionaria*. Madrid: Siglo XII, 2008.

Avrich, Paul. *An American Anarchist: The Life of Voltairine de Cleyre*. Princeton University Press, 1978.

The Haymarket Tragedy. Princeton University Press, 1984.

The Russian Anarchists. New York: W. W. Norton, 1978.

Sacco and Vanzetti: The Anarchist Background. Princeton University Press, 1991.

Avrich, Paul and Karen Avrich. *Sasha and Emma*, Cambridge, MA: Harvard University Press, 2012.

Babcock, Louis. "The Assassination of President McKinley," *Niagara Frontier Miscellany* 34 (1947): 11–30.

Badrawi, M. *Political Violence in Egypt 1910–1924: Secret Societies, Plots and Assassinations*. Richmond, Surrey: Curzon Press, 2000.

Baedeker, Karl. *Spain and Portugal*, 3rd edition. Leipzig: Baedeker, 1908.

Baily, Samuel L. *Immigration in the Lands of Promise: Italians in Buenos Aires and New York City 1870–1914*. Ithaca and London: Cornell University Press, 1999.

Bakunin, Mikhail. *The Political Philosophy of Bakunin: Scientific Anarchism*, ed. G. P. Maximoff, intro. Rudolf Rocher. Glencoe, IL: The Free Press, 1953.

Balestra, Demetrio. 'Il diritto d'estradizione nei rapporti italo-svizzeri.' Dissertation, University of Zurich, 1927.

Ballbé, Manuel. *Orden público y militarismo en la España constitucional (1812–1983)*, 2nd edition. Madrid: Alianza, 1983.

Bassiouni, M. Cherif. *International Terrorism and Political Crimes*. Springfield, IL: Charles C. Thomas, 1975.

Bayer, Osvaldo. *Los anarquistas expropiadores, Simon Radowitzky y otros ensayos*. Buenos Aires: Editorial Galerna, 1975.

Beauchet, Ludovic. *Traité de l'extradition*. Paris: A. Chevalier-Marescq, 1899.

Beaudéant, Jean. *L'Attentat contre les chefs d'Etat.* Toulouse: Divion, 1911.

Beck, James M. "The Suppression of Anarchy," *American Law Review* 36 (1902): 190–203.

Bekzadian, Alexander. *Der Agent-Provocateur (Lockspitzel) mit besonderer Berücksichtigung der politischen Provokation in Russland. Ein Beitrag zum Strafrecht und zur Kriminalpolitik.* Zurich: Leemann, 1913.

Beltrani Scalia, Marino. "La Conferenza internazionale contro l'anarchia ed il riordinamento della P.S. in Italia," *Rivista di discipline carcerarie* 23 (November 1898): 501–510.

Benito y Llaves, Enrique de. *La Anarquia y el Derecho Penal: Discurso leido en la solemne apertura del curso academico de 1906 a 1907.* Ovideo: Adolfo Brid, 1906.

Berlière, Jean-Marc. *Le Monde des polices en France XIXe-XXe siècles.* Paris: Le Monde, 1996.

"A Republican Political Police? Political Policing in France under the Third Republic, 1875–1940," in Mark Mazower (ed.), *The Policing of Politics in the Twentieth Century.* Providence and Oxford: Berghahn Books, 1997, 27–55.

Bernecker, Walther L. "The Strategies of 'Direct Action' and Violence in Spanish Anarchism," in Wolfgang Mommsen and Gerhard Hirschfeld (eds.), *Social Protest, Violence and Terror in Nineteenth- and Twentieth- Century Europe.* New York: St. Martin's Press, 1981, 88–111.

Berti, Giampietro. *Errico Malatesta e il movimento anarchico italiano e internazionale, 1872–1932.* Milan: FrancoAngeli, 2003.

Bertillon, Alphonse. *Identification Anthropométrique. Instructions Signalétiques.* 2 vols. Melun: Imprimerie administrative, 1893.

"Résultats obtenus par l'Antropométrie au point de vue de la criminalité. Quelles sont les lacunes à combler?" *Compte Rendu: Congrés International d'Antropologies Criminelle.* 24–29 August, 1896. 63–66.

Bertoni, Luigi. *Gli anarchici ed il regicidio di Monza: autodifesa. Con prefazione di Pietro Gori.* Roma: Mentella, 1907.

Bettini, Leonardo. *Bibliografia dell'anarchismo 1: Periodici e numeri unici anarchici in lingua italiana pubblicati all'estero (1872–1971).* Florence: CP, 1972.

Bézos, Paul. *L'extradition en Italie.* PhD dissertation, University of Paris, 1908.

Bianco, Gino. "Rivoluzionarismo anarchico in Lunigiana nel 1894," *Il Movimento operaio e socialista in Liguria* 6 (1961): 335–352.

Billot, Albert. *La France et L'italie: histoire des années troubles: 1881–1899.* Paris: Librairie Plon, 1905.

Biron, Chartes and Kenneth Chalmers. *The Law and Practice of Extradition.* London: Stevens and Sons, 1903.

Bishop, Joseph Bucklin. "Theodore Roosevelt and His Time," *Scribner's* 66 (September; October; November; December 1919): 257–275; 385–408; 515–533; 650–662.

Blaisdell, Lowell. "The Assassination of Humbert I," *Quarterly of the National Archives* 27:3 (1995): 241–247.

Bloxham, Donald. "Terrorism and Imperial Decline: The Ottoman-Armenian Case," *European Review of History* 14 (2007): 301–324.

Bonfils, Henry. *Manuel de droit international public,* ed. Paul Fauchille, 7th edition. Paris: Rousseau, 1914.

Bookchin, Murray. *The Spanish Anarchists: The Heroic Years: 1868–1936*. New York: Free Life Editions, 1977.

Borghi, Armando. *Errico Malatesta*, 2nd edition. Milan: Istituto editoriale italiano, 1947.

Botz, Gerhard, Gerfried Brandstetter and Michael Pollak. *Im Schatten der Arbeiterbewegung: Zur Geschichte des Anarchismus in Österreich und Deutschland*. Vienna, 1977.

Bourquin, Maurice. "Crimes et délits contre la Sûreté des états etrangers," *Recueil des Cours* 16 (1927): 119–246.

Brandenburg, Broughton. "Menace of Anarchism," *Hampton Magazine*. 20 June 1908, 265–274.

Brandl, Franz. *Kaiser, Politiker und Menschen. Erinnerungen eines Wiener Polizeipräsidenten*. Leipzig and Vienna: Johannes Günter, 1936.

Brennan, Gerald. *The Spanish Labyrinth*. Cambridge University Press, 1971.

Briggs, L. Vernon. *The Manner of Man That Kills*. Boston: Richard G. Badger, 1921.

British Digest of International Law, ed. Clive Parry. Part 6: *The Individual in International Law*. London, 1965.

Brook-Shepherd, Gordon. *Uncle of Europe: The Social and Diplomatic Life of Edward VII*. New York and London: Harcourt Brace Jovanovich, 1975.

Burgmann, Verity. *Revolutionary Industrial Unionism: The Industrial Workers of the World in Australia*. Cambridge University Press, 1995.

Butterworth, Alex. *The World That Never Was: A True Story of Dreamers, Schemers, Anarchists and Secret Agents*. New York: Pantheon, 2010.

Cahm, Caroline. *Kropotkin and the Rise of Revolutionary Anarchism, 1872–1886*. Cambridge University Press, 1989.

Calhoun, A. Fryar. *The Politics of Internal Order: French Government and Revolutionary Labor, 1898–1914*. PhD Dissertation, Princeton University, 1973.

Calón, Eugenio C. "La delincuencia anarquista," *La Lectura* (July 1908): 265–277, and (August 1908): 436–446.

Calvert, Albert J. *The Spanish Royal Wedding: An Account of the Marriage of HM Alfonso XIII of Spain and HRH Princess Victoria Eugénie of Battenberg*. Taunton: Phoenix Press, 1906.

Canali, Mauro. *Le spie del regime*. Bologna: Mulino, 2004.

Cappon, Santo. "L'histoire de l'assassin d'Élisabeth, dite Sissi, impératrice d'Autriche et reine de Hongrie," in Luigi Lucheni, *Mémoires de l'assassin de Sissi*. Paris: Le cherche midi, 1998.

Carabelli, Giovanni. *Il Delitto anarchico: Studio di diritto penale*. Dissertation, University of Turin, 1910.

Carey, George W. "*La Questione Sociale*, an Anarchist Newspaper in Paterson, NJ (1895–1908)," in Lydio F. Tomasi (ed.), *Italian Americans. New Perspectives in Italian Immigration and Ethnicity*. New York: Center for Migration Studies, 1985, 289–297.

Carfora, Francesco, "Delitto politico," in *Il Digesto Italiano: Enciclopedia metodica e alfabetica di Legislazione, Dottrina e Giurisprudenza*, vol. 9, Part I. Turin: UTET, 1926, 832.

Carlson, Andrew R. "Anarchism and Individual Terror in the German Empire, 1870–90," in Wolfgang J. Mommsen and Gerhard Hirschfeld (eds.), *Social*

Protest, Violence and Terror in Nineteenth and Twentieth-Century Europe. New York: St. Martin's Press, 1982, 175–200.

Anarchism in Germany. Vol. 1: The Early Movement. Metuchen, NJ: Scarecrow Press, 1972.

Carr, Raymond. *Spain 1808–1975,* 2nd edition. Oxford: Clarendon Press, 1982.

Casagrande, Giovanni. "Mises en fiche du début du siecle: le cas Luigi Bertoni," in *Cent ans de police politique en Suisse (1889–1989).* Lausanne: Editions d'enbas, 1992, 63–80.

Castro y Casaleiz, Antonio de. "La extradición." In *La Extradición y el procedimiento judicial internacional en España,* ed. Manuel Walls y Merino. Madrid: Victoriano Suárez, 1905, 13–84.

Cecil, Lamar. *Wilhelm II: Prince and Emperor.* 2 vols. Chapel Hill: University of North Carolina Press, 1989 and 1996.

Cerrito, Gino. *Cent ans de police politique en Suisse.* Lausanne: Association pour l'etude de l'histoire du mouvement ouvrier and Editions D'en Bas, 1992

Dall'insurrezionalismo alla settimana rossa: per una storia dell'anarchismo in Italia (1881–1914). Florence: Crescita politica editrice, 1977.

L'antimilitarismo anarchico in Italia nel primo ventennio del secolo. Pistoia: Edizioni RL, 1968.

Chapel, Edward Charles. *Finger Printing: A Manual of Identification.* New York: Coward McCann, 1941.

Charlot, Claude. "Brigades." In *Histoire et Dictionnaire de la Police,* ed. Michel Aubouin, Arnaud Teyssier and Jean Tulard. Paris: Robert Laffont, 2005.

Churchill, Ward. "From the Pinkertons to the PATRIOT Act: The Trajectory of Political Policing in the United States, 1870 to the Present," *CR: The New Centennial Review* 4:1 (2004): 1–72.

Cini, Bettino. *Il Reato politico e particolarmente l'attentato alla vita del capo dello Stato in rapporto alla estradizione.* Montevarchi: Tipografia varchi, 1900.

Civolani, Eva. *L'Anarchismo dopo la comune: I casi italiano e spagnolo.* Milan: Franco Angeli, 1981

Clarke, Francis Gordon. *Will-o'-the-wisp: Peter the Painter and the Anti-tsarist Terrorists in Britain and Australia.* Melbourne: Oxford University Press, 1983.

Colao, Florian. *Il delitto politico tra ottocento e novecento. Da "delitto fittizio" a "nemico dello Stato."* Milan: Giuffrè, 1986.

Cole, G. D. H. *A History of Socialist Thought. Vol. 2: Marxism and Anarchism.* London: Macmillan, 1954.

Cole, Simon. *Suspect Identities: A History of Fingerprinting and Criminal Identification.* Cambridge, MA: Harvard University Press, 2001.

Collyer, Michael. "Secret Agents: Anarchists, Islamists and Responses to Politically Active Refugees in London," *Ethnic and Racial Studies* 28:2 (2005): 278–303.

Confino, Michael. "Pierre Kropotkine et les agents de l'Okhrana. Étude suivie de treize letters de Kropotkine à M. Goldsmith et à un groupe anarchiste russe," *Cahiers du monde russe et soviétique* 24:1–2 (1983): 83–149.

Control of Terrorism: International Documents, ed. Yonah Alexander, M. A. Browne and A. S. Wanes. New York: Crane Russak, 1979.

Comin Colomer, Eduardo. *Historia del anarquismo español*, 3 vols, 2nd edition. Barcelona: Editorial AHR, 1956.

Un siglo de atentados politicos en España. Madrid, 1951.

Corbaz, Roger. *Le Crime Politique et la Jurisprudence du Tribunal Fédéral Suisse en matière d'extradition*. Lausanne: G.Vaney-Burnier, 1927.

Corti, Egon. *Elizabeth, Empress of Austria*, trans. Catherine Alison Phillips. New Haven:Yale University Press, 1936.

Crewe, Robert. *Lord Rosebery*. NewYork and London: Harper, 1931.

Crispi, Francesco. *Discorsi parlamentari*. 3 volumes. Rome: Tipografia della Camera dei deputati, 1915.

Culla i Clarà, Joan B. *El Republicanisme Lerrouxista a Catalunya (1901–1923)*. Barcelona: Curial, 1986.

Dalla Casa, Brunella, Fiorenza Tarozzi and Angelo Varni. *Disciplina militare e territorio: il tribunale militare territoriale di Bologna: prime riflessioni su una ricerca in corso*. Perugia: atti del Convegno di studi, 1989.

Daly, Jonathan. *Autocracy under Siege: Security Police and Opposition in Russia, 1866–1905*. DeKalb: Northern Illinois University Press, 1998.

"Security Services in Imperial and Soviet Russia," *Kritika* 4:4 (2003): 955–973.

The Watchful State: Security Police and Opposition in Russia 1906–1917. DeKalb: Northern Illinois University Press, 2004.

Dannecker, Rudolf. *Die Schweiz und Österreich-Ungarn: Diplomatische und militärische Beziehungen von 1866 bis zum ersten Weltkrieg*. Basel and Stuttgart: von Helbing and Lichtenhahn, 1966.

Dedijer,Vladimir. *The Road to Sarajevo*. NewYork: Simon and Schuster, 1966.

Deflem, Mathieu. "International Policing in 19th-Century Europe: The Police Union of German States, 1851–1866," *International Criminal Justice Review* 6 (1996): 36–57.

Policing World Society: Historical Foundations of International Police Cooperation. Oxford University Press, 2002.

De Jaco, Aldo, ed. *Gli anarchici: Cronaca inedita dell'Unità d'Italia*. Rome: Editori Riuniti, 1971.

De Marco, Laura. *Il soldato che disse no alla guerra. Storia dell'anarchico Augusto Masetti (1888–1966)*. Santa Maria Capua Vetere: Edizioni Spartaco, 2003.

Derechef, Ralph. "Anarchism in England." In Felix Dubois, *The Anarchist Peril*, trans. and ed. Ralph Derechef. London:T. Fisher Union, 1904, 262–284.

Deriabin, Peter. *Watchdogs of Terror: Russian Bodyguards from the Tsars to the Commissars*. New Rochelle: Arlington House, 1972.

Deubert, Ernst. *Der Agent Provocateur und Seine Beurteilung nach dem Reichsstrafgesetzbuche*. Neunkirchen: C. A. Ohle, 1910.

Dhavernas, Marie-Josèphe. "La surveillance des anarchistes individualistes (1894–1914)," in Philippe Vigier (ed.), *Maintien de l'ordre et polices en France et en Europe au XIXe siècle*. Paris: Créaphis, 1987, 347–360.

Dictionnaire biographique du movement ouvrier française, ed. Jean Maitron, Jean Dautry, Roger Dufraisse, Georges Duveau, Rémi Gossez and Jean Vidalenc. Paris: Editions ouvrières, 1976–1977.

Diemoz, Erika. *A morte il tiranno. Anarchia e violenza da Crispi a Mussolini*. Turin: Giulio Einaudi, 2011.

Diena, Giulio. "I provvedimenti contro gli anarchici e la prossima conferenza internazionale," *Rivista di diritto internazionale e di legislazione comparata* 1:6 (1898): 241–262.

"Les délits anarchistes et l'extradition," *Revue générale de droit international public* 2 (1895): 303–336.

Principi di diritto internazionale. I: Diritto internazionale pubblico. Naples: Luigi Pierro, 1914.

Di Paola, Pietro. "The Spies Who Came in from the Heat: The International Surveillance of the Anarchists in London," *European History Quarterly* 37:2 (2007): 189–215.

Dirlik, Arif. *Anarchism in the Chinese Revolution.* Berkeley: University of California Press, 1991.

Documenting Individual Identity: The Development of State Practices in the Modern World, ed. Jane Caplan and John Torpey. Princeton University Press, 2001.

Dizionario biografico degli anarchici italiani, ed. Maurizio Antonioli, G. Berti, S. Fedele and P. Iuso. Pisa: BFS, 2003.

Donnedieu de Vabres, H. *Les principes modernes du droit pénal international.* Paris: Sirey, 1928.

ed. *Traité de Droit Criminel et de Législation pénale comparée.* Paris: Librairie du Recueil Sirey, 1947.

Donovan, Robert. *The Assassins.* New York: Harper, 1955.

Dupuy, Micheline. *Le Petit Parisien.* Paris: Plon, 1989.

Echegaray, José. "Los Explosivos," *La Lectura* 61 (1894): 54–61, and 62 (1894): 59–65.

Ehrenberg, John. *Proudhon and his Age.* Atlantic Highlands, NJ: Humanities Press, 1996.

Ely, Richard T. "Anarchy," *Harper's Weekly* 37 (December 23, 1893): 126.

Emerson, Donald. *Metternich and the Political Police: Security and Subversion in the Hapsburg Monarchy (1815–1830).* The Hague: Martinus Nijhoff, 1968.

Emsley, Clive. "Introduction: Political Police and the European Nation-State in the Nineteenth Century," in Mark Mazower (ed.), *The Policing of Politics in the Twentieth Century.* Providence and Oxford: Berghahn Books, 1997, 1–25.

Esenwein, George Richard. *Anarchist Ideology and the Working-Class Movement in Spain, 1868–1898.* Berkeley: University of California Press, 1989.

Españoles y franceses en la primera mitad del siglo XX. Madrid: Centro de Estudios Históricos, Departamento de Historia Contemporánea, 1986.

Etienne, Genovefa and Claude Moniquet. *Histoire de l'espionnage mondial. Les services secrets, de Ramsès II à nos jours.* Paris: Luc Pire and du Fèlin, 1997.

"Extradition et terrorisme," *Revue de Droit penal et de criminologie* 1–2 (1980).

Fabbri, Luigi. *Malatesta, L'uomo e il pensiero.* Napoli: Edizioni RL, 1951.

Malatesta: Su Vida y su Pensamiento, trans. Diego A. de Santillan. Buenos Aires: Editorial Americalee, 1945.

Farré, José Maria. *Los atentados sociales en España: Las teorías Los Hechos; Estadistica,* preface by Quintiliano Saldaña, Madrid: Casa Fauvre, 1922.

Felici, Alfredo. "Le Associazioni anarchiche e la legge penale," *Studi e giudicati illustrativi del codice penale italiano* 6 (1897): 178–185.

Felisatti, Massimo. *Un delitto della polizia? "Oggi, 2 maggio 1897, Romeo Frezzi si è suicidato nel carcere di San Michele."* Milan: Bompiani, 1975.

Feraud, H. and E. Schlanitz. "La coopération policière international," Division des Etudes du Secretariat General de l'OIPC – Interpol. 475–497.

Fernandez Almagro, Melchor. *Cánovas. Su vida y su politica.* Madrid: Ambos Mundos, 1951.

Fernandez Cadenas, Maria. *La vida intima de Canalejas.* Madrid: Afrodisio Aguado, 1959.

Ferracuti, Franco "Ideology and Repentance: Terrorism in Italy," in *Origins of Terrorism*, ed. Walter Reich. Cambridge and New York: Woodrow Wilson International Center for Scholars and Cambridge University Press, 1990, 59–64.

Ferraris, L. V. "L'assassinio di Umberto I e gli anarchici di Paterson," *Rassegna storica del Risorgimento* 60 (1968): 47–64.

Ferri, Enrico. "Difesa sociale e difesa di classe nella giustizia penale," *Scuola Positiva* 10 (1899): 577–591.

Ferrigni, Mario C. *Les Souverains Étrangers et le Droit Italien: Notes.* Florence: Bernard Seeber, 1903.

Fetscher, Iring. *Terrorismus und Reaktion mit einem Anhang, August Bebel, Attentate und Sozialdemokratie.* Cologne: Europäische Verlagsanstalt, 1978

Feuilloley, G. "Moyen pratiques d'assurer la répression des crimes et delits internationaux," *Journal du droit international privé* 32 (1905): 785–796.

Fiamingo, G. M. "Italian Anarchism," *The Contemporary Review* 78 (1900): 339–243.

Fiestas Loza, Alicia. "Los Delitos Politicos (1808–1936)". Thesis, Faculty of Law, University of Salamanca, 1977.

Figueroa Torres, Alvaro and Conde de Romanones. *Moret y su Actuación en la Politica exterior de España.* Madrid: Gráfica Ambosmundos, 1921.

Fine, Sidney. "Anarchism and the Assassination of McKinley," *American Historical Review* 60 (1955): 777–799.

Fiorentino, Fiorenza. *Ordine pubblico nell'Italia giolittiana.* Rome: Carecas, 1978.

Fischer, Ben. *Okhrana: The Paris Operations of the Russian Imperial Police.* Washington DC: History Staff, Center for the Study of Intelligence, CIA, 1997.

Fischer, Henry. *Private Lives of Kaiser William II and his Consort.* New York: W. C. Adams, 1909.

Fisher, Jack. *Stolen Glory: The McKinley Assassination.* La Jolla: Alamar Books, 2001.

Fleming, Marie. "Propaganda by the Deed: Terrorism and Anarchist Theory in Late Nineteenth-Century Europe," *Terrorism* 4 (1980): 1–23.

Florian, Eugenio. *Parte Generale del Diritto Penale.* 2 vols., 3rd edition. Milan: Vallardi, 1926.

Trattato di Diritto Penale. 2: Introduzione ai delitti in ispecie delitti contro la sicurezza dello Stato, 2nd edition. Milan: Vallardi, 1915.

Ford, Auguste. "Luccheni," *Archivio di psichiatria, antropologia criminale e scienze penale.* 20 (1899): 11–25.

Ford, Franklin L. *Political Murder: From Tyrannicide to Terrorism.* Cambridge University Press, 1985.

Fosdick, Raymond. "The Passing of the Bertillon System of Identification," *Journal of Criminal Law and Criminology* 6 (1915): 363–369.

Francos Rodríguez, José. *La vida de Canalejas*. Madrid: Revista de arqueología, bibliografia, y museos, 1918.

Frantel, Max. *Caserio*. Paris: Emile-Paul Freres, 1934.

Frassati, Alfredo. "I dinamitardi e il codice penale," *Rivista Penal di dottrina, legislazione e giurisprudenza* 35 (1892): 565–577.

Gabaccia, Donna R. and Franca Iacovetta, eds. *Women, Gender, and Transnational Lives: Italian Workers of the World*. University of Toronto Press, 2002.

Gabriel, Elun. *Anarchism, Social Democracy and the Political Culture of Imperial Germany*. DeKalb: Northern Illinois University Press, 2014.

Gage, Beverly. *The Day Wall Street Exploded*. Oxford University Press, 2009.

Galzerano, Giuseppe. *Gaetano Bresci*. Casalvelino Scalo: Galzerano, 2001.

Garcia, Eugenio V. "Antirevolutionary Diplomacy in Oligarchic Brazil, 1919–30," *Journal of Latin American Studies* 36 (2004): 771–796.

Gauthier, Alfred. "Le procès Lucheni," *Revue Pènale Suisse* (1898): 334–354.

Geifman, Anna. *Thou Shalt Kill: Revolutionary Terrorism in Russia, 1894–1917*. Princeton University Press, 1995.

Geill, Christian. "Les services actuels d'identification dans les pays scandinaves," *Archives d'anthropologie criminale* 22 (1907): 57–60.

Gelvin, James L. "Al-Qaeda and Anarchism: A Historian's Reply to Terrorology," *Terrorism and Political Violence* 20:4 (2008): 563–581

Gli Italiani fuori d'Italia: gli emigrati italiani nei movimenti operai dei paesi d'adozione, 1880–1940, ed Bruno Bezza. Milan: Franco Angeli, 1983.

"Gli italiani nella statistica del regicidio: Fatti e note," *Civiltà Cattolica* 9 (January 27, 1903): 257–270.

Goldman, Emma. "The Assassination of McKinley," *American Mercury* 24 (1931), 53–67.

Goldstein, Robert J. "The Anarchist Scare of 1908: A Sign of Tensions in the Progressive Era," *American Studies* 15 (1974): 50–75.

Political Repression in Modern America: From 1870 to 1976. Urbana: University of Illinois Press, 2001.

Goll, August. "Signalement," in *Salmonsens Konversations leksikon*, Vol. 22, 26 vols, 2nd edition. Copenhagen: J. H. Schultz, 1926, 377.

González Calleja, Eduardo. *La razón de la fuerza: orden publico, subversión y violencia política en la España de la Restauración (1875–1917)*. Madrid: Consejo superior de investigaciones científicas, 1998.

Goyens, Tom. *Beer and Revolution: The German Anarchist Movement in New York City, 1880–1914*. Urbana and Chicago: University of Illinois Press, 2007.

Green, James. *Death in the Haymarket: A Story of Chicago, the First Labor Movement, and the Bombing that Divided Gilded Age America*. New York: Anchor Books, 2006.

Greenway, Judy. "Anarchists, Aliens, and Detectives," *History Today* 55:12 (2005): 4–6.

Gregory, Charles Noble. "The Expulsion of Aliens," in *Proceedings of the American Society of International Law at its Fifth Annual Meeting held on April 27–29, 1911*. New York: Kraus Reprint Corporation, 1960, 119–139.

Grimaldi, Ugoberto Alfassio. *Il re "buono,"* 5th edition. Milan: Feltrinelli, 1973.

Grivaz, Francoise. "L'extradition en matière de crimes politiques et sociaux: Affaire Jaffei," *Revue générale de droit international public* 9 (1902): 701–718.

Gross, Feliks. "Political violence and terror in Nineteenth and Twentieth Century Russia and Eastern Europe," in James Kirkham, Sheldon Levy, and William Crotty (eds.), *Assassination and Political Violence: A Report to the National Commission on the Causes and Prevention of Violence*, vol. 8. Washington, DC: US Government Printing Office, 1969, 448–451.

Violence in Politics: Terror and Political Assassination in Eastern Europe and Russia. The Hague and Paris: Mouton, 1972.

Gundle, Stephen and Lucia Rinaldi, eds. *Assassinations and Murder in Modern Italy: Transformations in Society and Culture.* Italian and Italian American Studies Series. New York: Palgrave Macmillan, 2007.

Hackworth, Green H. *Digest of International Law*, 8 vols. Washington, DC: US Government Printing Office, 1940–1944.

Hall, William E. *A Treatise on International Law*, 7th edition. Oxford: Clarendon Press, 1917.

Halstead, Murat. *The Illustrious Life of William McKinley.* Chicago: Printed by the author, 1901.

Hamann, Brigitte. *Elisabeth, Kaiserin Wider Willen.* Vienna: Amalthea, 1982.

The Reluctant Empress. New York: Knopf, 1986.

Hanioğlu, M Şükrü. *The Young Turks in Opposition.* New York: Oxford University Press, 1995.

Hart, John M. *Anarchism and the Mexican Working Class, 1860–1931.* Austin: University of Texas Press, 1987.

Harvard Law School. *Research in International Law: Supplement to the American Journal of Law*, 2 vols. Washington, DC: American Society of International Law, 1935.

Havens, Murray Clark, Carl Leiden, and Karl Michael Schmitt. *The Politics of Assassination.* Englewood Cliffs, NJ: Prentice-Hall, 1970.

Heehs, Peter. *The Bomb in Bengal: The Rise of Revolutionary Terrorism in India, 1900–1910.* Oxford University Press, 1993.

"Foreign Influences on Bengali Revolutionary Terrorism 1902–1908," *Modern Asian Studies* 28:3 (1994): 533–556.

Hingley, Ronald. *The Russian Secret Police: Muscovite, Imperial Russian and Soviet Political Security Operations, 1565–1970.* London: Hutchinson, 1970.

Histoire générale de la presse française, ed. Claude Bellanger, Jacques Godechot, Pierre Guiral and Fernand Terrou. Paris: Presses universitaires de France, 1969–1976.

Hoerder, Dirk. *Plutocrats and Socialists: Reports by German Diplomats and Agents on the American Labor Movement, 1878–1917.* Munich: K. G. Saur, 1981.

Holoff, Gustov, ed. *Schulthess' Europaischer Geschichtskalender: 1898.* Munich: C. H. Beck, 1899.

Hopff, U.-A. "De la lutte contre le criminalisme international," *Journal du droit international privé* 34 (1907): 631–639.

Hough, Richard. *Edward and Alexandra: Their Private and Public Lives.* New York: St. Martin's Press, 1992.

Howerth, Ira W. "The Social Question of Today," *The American Journal of Sociology* 12:2 (1906): 254–268.

Hunter, Robert. *Violence and the Labor Movement*. New York: Macmillan, 1914.

Ingraham, Barton. *Political Crime in Europe: A Comparative Study of France, Germany, and England*. Berkeley: University of California Press, 1979.

Iviansky, Ze'ev. "Individual Terror: Concept and Typology," *Journal of Contemporary History* 12 (1977): 43–63.

Jacker, Corinne. *The Black Flag of Anarchy: Anti Statism in the United States*. New York: Scribner's, 1968.

James, Bob. "Introduction," in *A Reader of Australian Anarchism, 1886–1896*. Canberra Publishing, 1979.

Jaquet, Cocinne. *La Secrète à 100 ans: histoire de la police de sûreté Genevoise*. Geneva: Nemo, 1993.

Jardí, Enric. *La Ciutat de les Bombes (El terrorisme anarquista a Barcelona)*. Barcelona: Rafael Dalmau, 1964.

Jensen, Richard Bach. "Daggers, Rifles and Dynamite: Anarchist Terrorism in Nineteenth Century Europe," *Terrorism and Political Violence* 16:1 (2004): 116–153.

"The Evolution of Anarchist Terrorism in Europe and the United States from the Nineteenth Century to World War I," in Brett Bowden and Michael Davis (eds), *Terror from Tyrannicide to Terrorism*. St. Lucia: University of Queensland Press, 2008, 134–160.

"The International Anti-Anarchist Conference of 1898 and the Origins of Interpol," *Journal of Contemporary History* 16 (1981): 323–347.

"Italy's Peculiar Institution: Internal Police Exile, 1861–1914," in June K. Burton (ed.), *Essays in European History*. Lanham: University Press of America, 1989. 99–114.

Liberty and Order: The Theory and Practice of Italian Public Security Policy, 1848 to the Crisis of the 1890s. New York: Garland, 1991.

Nineteenth Century Anarchist Terrorism: How Comparable to the Terrorism of al-Qaeda?" *Terrorism and Political Violence* 20:4 (2008): 589–596.

"The United States, International Policing, and the War against Anarchist Terrorism, 1900–1914," *Terrorism and Political Violence* 13:1 (2001): 15–46.

Jeyes, S. H. and F. D. How. *The Life of Sir Howard Vincent*. London: George Allen, 1912.

Johns, A. Wesley. *The Man Who Shot McKinley*. South Brunswick and New York: A. S. Barnes, 1970.

Johnson, Richard J. "The Okhrana Abroad, 1885–1917: A Study in International Police Cooperation." PhD Dissertation, Columbia University, 1971.

"*Zagranichnaia Agentura*: The Tsarist Political Police in Europe," in George Mosse (ed.), *Police Forces in History*. London: Sage Publications, 1975, 17–38.

Joll, James. *The Anarchists*. 2nd edition. Cambridge, MA: Harvard University Press, 1980.

Jouffray, Theodore L. "Warnings and Teachings of the Church on Anarchism," *The Catholic World* 74 (1901): 202–209.

Junco, José Alvarez. *El Emperador del Paralelo: Lerroux y la demagogia populista*. Madrid: Alianza Editorial, 1990.

Kahn, Ely Jacques. *Fraud: The US Postal Inspection Service*. New York: Harper and Row, 1973.

Kaiser, Frederick. "Origins of Secret Service Protection of the President: Personal, Interagency, and Institutional Conflict," *Presidential Studies Quarterly* Winter 1988: 101–127.

Kaplan, Temma. *Anarchists of Andalusia, 1868–1903*. Princeton University Press, 1977.

Kennedy, A. L. *Old Diplomacy and New, 1876–1922: From Salisbury to Lloyd-George*. London: John Murray, 1922.

Salisbury, 1830–1903: Portrait of a Statesman. London: John Murray, 1953.

Kennedy, Paul. *The Realities Behind Diplomacy: Background Influences on British External Policy, 1895–1980*. London: George Allen and Unwin, 1981.

Kern, Robert W. *Red Years/Black Years: A History of Spanish Anarchism, 1911–1937*. Philadelphia: Institute for the Study of Human Issues, 1978.

Kirchner, Francis J. *Index to the Police Forces of the British Empire, the United States of America, and Foreign Countries, to which Has Been Added a Treatise on Fugitive Offenders and Extradition and a Motor Index*. London: John Kempster, 1908.

Kirkam, James F., Sheldon G. Levy, and William J. Crotty. *Assassination and Political Violence: Report to the National Commission on the Causes and Prevention of Violence*. Washington, DC: US Government Printing Office, 1969.

Knott, Stephen F. *Secret and Sanctioned: Covert Operations and the American Presidency*. Oxford University Press, 1996.

Kohut, Thomas A. *Wilhelm II and the Germans: A Study in Leadership*. Oxford University Press, 1991.

Krebs, Edward S. *Shifu, Soul of Chinese Anarchism*. New York: Rowman and Littlefield, 1998.

Kropotkin, Peter. *The Essential Kropotkin*, ed. Emile Capoya and Keitha Tompkins. New York: Liveright, 1975.

Lacher, Adolf. *Die Schweiz und Frankreich vor dem Ersten Weltkrieg. Diplomatische und politische Beziehungen im Zeichen des deutsch-franzosischen Gegensatzes 1883–1914*. Basil: Helbing and Lichtenhahn, 1967.

La Iglesia y Garcia, Gustavo. *Caracteres del Anarquismo en la actualidad*. Madrid: Asilo de Huérfanos del S.C. del Jesús, 1905.

Land, Isaac, ed. *Enemies of Humanity: The Nineteenth-Century War on Terrorism*. New York: Palgrave Macmillan, 2008.

Langhard, Johann. *Die anarchistische Bewegung in der Schweiz von ihren Anfängen bis zur Gegenwart und die internationalen Führer*. Berlin: O. Häring, 1903.

Die politische Polizei der schweizerischen Eidgenossenschaft. Bern: Stämpfli, 1909.

Langum, David J. *Crossing Over the Line: Legislating Morality and the Mann Act*. University of Chicago Press, 1994.

Lanza, Pietro. "Estradizione," in *Enciclopedia giuridica italiana. Vol. 5*. Milan: L. Vallardi, 1910, 456ff.

Lapradelle, Albert Geouffre de. *Répertoire de droit International: Condition des étrangers.—Conflit des lois.—Respect des droits acquis.—Lois pénales.—Nationalité.—Jugements.—Procédure, etc.* Paris: Librairie du Recueil Sirey, 1929–1931.

Laqueur, Walter. *The Age of Terrorism*. Boston: Little, Brown, 1987.

Lara, René, Preface to *Leurs Majestés*, Xavier Paoli. 13th edition. Paris: Librairie Paul Ollendorff, 1910.

Latouche, Peter. *Anarchy! An Authentic Exposition of the Methods of Anarchists and the Aims of Anarchism*. London: Everett, 1908.

Laurens, Jean-Paul. *De l'extradition en matière politique*. Toulouse: Bonnet 1921.

Le Clère, Marcel. *Histoire de la police*. Paris: Presses universitaires de France, 1947.

Lee, Sidney. *King Edward VII*, 2 vols. New York: Macmillan, 1925–1927.

Lee, W. L. Melville. *A History of Police in England*. London: Methuen, 1901.

Lehr, Ernest. "Quelques mots sur un cas d'extradition recent," *Journal de droit international privé* 29 (1902): 74–78.

Lerman, Katharine Anne. *The Chancellor as Courtier: Bernhard von Bülow and the Governance of Germany, 1900–1909*. Cambridge University Press, 1990.

"Les 50 ans du bureau central Suisse de police 1904–1955," *Revue internationale de criminologie et de police technique* (1955): 311–318.

Leroy, Constant [Miguel Villalobos Moreno]. *Los secretos del anarquismo (sensacionales revelaciones de un decepcionado). Asesinato de Canalejas y el caso Ferrer*. Mexico City: Librería Renacimiento, 1913.

Levy, Carl. "Anarchism, Internationalism and Nationalism in Europe, 1860–1939," *Australian Journal of Politics and History* 50:3 (2004): 330–342.

"The Anarchist Assassin and Italian History, 1870s to 1930s," in Stephen Gundle and Lucia Rinaldi (eds.), *Assassinations and Murder in Modern Italy: Transformations in Society and Culture*. New York: Palgrave Macmillan, 2007, 207–222.

"Italian Anarchism, 1870–1926," in David Goodway (ed.), *For Anarchism: History, Theory, and Practice*. London: Routledge, 1989, 25–78.

"Malatesta in Exile," *Annali della Fondazione Luigi Einaudi* 15 (1981): 245–280.

"Malatesta in London: The Era of Dynamite," in L. Sponza and A. Tosi (eds.), *A Century of Italian Immigration to London 1880s-1980s. Five Essays*. Supplement to *The Italianist* 13 (1993): 25–42.

Liang, Hsi-Huey. "International Cooperation of Political Police in Europe, 1815–1914," *Mitteilungen des Österreicheschen Staatsarchivs* 33 (1980): 193–217.

The Rise of Modern Police and the European State System from Metternich to the First World War. Cambridge University Press, 1992.

Linse, Ulrich. "Der deutsche Anarchismus 1870–1918: Eine politische Bewegung zwischen utopie und wirklichkeit," *Geschichte in Wessenschaft und Unterricht* 20 (1969): 513–519.

Organisierter Anarchismus im Deutschen Kaiserreich von 1871. Berlin: Dunker and Humbolt, 1969.

"'Propaganda by Deed' and 'Direct Action': Two Concepts of Anarchist Violence," in Wolfgang Mommsen and Gerhard Hirschfeld (eds.), *Social Protest, Violence and Terror in Nineteenth- and Twentieth-century Europe*. New York: St. Martin's Press, 1982, 201–229.

Lindholm, Frederick. *El anarquismo según las fuentes suecas y extranjeras*, trans. Emilio Miñana y Villagrasa. Madrid: De Góngora, 1906.

Lithner, Klas. "Assassination in Sweden," in James F. Kirkham, Sheldon G. Levy, and William J. Crotty (eds.), *Assassination and Political Violence: Report to the National Commission on the Causes and Prevention of Violence*, vol. 8. Washington, DC: US Government Printing Office, 1969. 578–580.

Livi, Rodolfo. *Antropometria*. Milan: Hoepli, 1900.

Locard, Edmond. "Les Services actuels d'identification et la fiche international," *Archives d'anthropologie criminelle et de criminologie* 21 (1906): 145–206.

Traité de criminalistique, 7 vols. Lyon: J. Desvigne, 1931–1940.

Lombroso, Cesare. "Anarchico-monarchico con doppia personalità," *Archivio di psichiatria, scienze penali ed antropologia criminale* 20 (1899): 26–29.

Crime: Its Causes and Remedies. Montclair, NJ: Patterson Smith Publishing Corporation, 1968.

"G. Bresci giudicato da Cesare Lombroso," *L'Adriatico (Venice)*, September 23 1900, 1–2.

Gli anarchici. Turin: Bocca, 1894.

"Luccheni e l'antropologia criminale," *Archivio di psichiatria scienze penali ed antropologia criminale* 20 (1899): 1–10.

Lombroso, Cesare and Rodolfo Laschi. *Il delitto politico e le rivoluzioni.* Turin: Bocca, 1890.

Longo, Michele. "Anarchismo e delinquenza," *Cassazione Unica* 11:44 (1899–1900): 1378–1380.

Longoni, Joseph Claude. *Four Patients of Dr. Deibler: A Study in Anarchy.* London: Lawrence and Wishart, 1970.

Longuet, Jean and Georges Silber. *Terroristes et policiers.* Paris: F. Juven, 1909.

López-Serrano, Juan José. *Descubriendo los misterios ó un detective á la fuerza (informaciones de un periodista): Sensacionales relatos de los complots y atentados anarchistas, realizados en España en los últimos años.* Madrid: Artistica Española, 1913.

Lorenzo, César. *Les Anarchistes espagnol et la pourvoir 1868–1969.* Paris: Éditions du Seuil, 1969.

Lösche, Peter. "Terrorismus und Anarchismus – Internationale und historische Aspecte," *Gewerkschaftliche Monastschefte* 2 (1978): 106–116.

Lotti, Luigi. *La settimana rossa.* Florence: Felice Le Monnier, 1972.

Loubat, William. *Code de la legislation contre les anarchistes.* Paris: Chevalier-Marescq etc., 1895.

"De la legislation contre les anarchistes au point de vue international," *Journal du Droit international privé* 22 (1895): 1–22; 23 (1896): 294–320.

Lozzi, Carlo. *L'ambiente anarchico dell'odierna società.* Turin: UTET, 1899.

McCormick, Charles H. *Hopeless Cases: The Hunt for the Red Scare Terrorist Bombers.* Lanham: University Press of America, 2005.

Maitron, Jean. *Histoire du Mouvement Anarchiste en France (1880–1914)*, 2nd edition. Paris: Société universitaire d'éditions et de librairie, 1955.

Le mouvement anarchiste en France. Paris: Maspero, 1983.

Manduca, Filippo. "Il delitto anarchico e il diritto penale italiano," *Giustizia Penale* 5 (1899): 225–232.

Manopulo, Aristide. "Polizia internazionale," *Novissimo digesto italiano* 13 (1966): 215–216.

Mantovani, Vincenzo. *Mazurka blu: la strage del Diana.* Milan: Rusconi, 1979.

Manzini, Vincenzo. *Trattato di Diritto penale italiano*, 11 vols. Turin: UTET, 1961.

Marabuto, Paul. *La collaboration policière internationale en vue de la prévention et de la répression de la criminalité; les institutions internationales de la police.* Nice: École professionnelle Don-Bosco, 1935.

Marinoni, Aldo. *Il Delitto Anarchico*. Bergamo: Stabilimento Tipo-Litografico Mariani, 1906.

Marks, Steven G. *How Russia Shaped the Modern World: from Art to Anti-semitism, Ballet to Bolshevism*. Princeton University Press, 2003.

Marucco, Dora. "Processi anarchici a Torino tra il 1892 e il 1894." In *Anarchici e anarchia nel mondo contemporaneo*. Turin: Einaudi, 1971.

Masini, Pier Carlo. *Storia degli anarchici italiani da Bakunin a Malatesta (1862–1892)*. Milan: Rizzoli, 1969, 217–241.

Storia degli anarchici italiani nell'epoca degli attentati. Milan: Rizzoli, 1981.

Matray, Maria and Answald Krüger. *Das Attentat: Der Tod der Kaiserin Elisabeth in Genf*. Vienna: Langen Müller, 1980.

May, Arthur. *The Hapsburg Monarchy, 1867–1914*. Cambridge, MA: Harvard University Press, 1951.

Melanson, Philip H. *The Politics of Protection: The US Secret Service in the Terrorist Age*. New York: Praeger, 1984.

Mena, Antonio Maria de. *Del Anarquismo y su represión*. Madrid: Imp. "Revista de Archivos", 1906.

Mérignhac, Alexandre. *Traité de Droit Public International*, 2 vols. Paris: Librairie générale de droit e de jurisprudence, 1905–1912.

Merlino, Francesco. "The End of Anarchism," interviewed by *La Stampa* (June 18, 1907). Reprinted in Aldo de Jaco (ed.), *Gli anarchici: Cronaca inedita dell'unità d'Italia*. Rome: Riuniti, 1971.

Merriman, John. *The Dynamite Club: How a Bombing in Fin-de-Siécle Paris Ignited the Age of Modern Terror*. Boston: Houghton Mifflin Harcourt, 2009.

Merten, Peter. *Anarchismus und Arbeiterkampf in Portugal*. Hamburg: Libertäre Association, 1981.

Miller, Martin A. "The Intellectual Origins of Modern Terrorism in Europe," in Martha Crenshaw (ed.), *Terrorism in Context*. University Park, Pennsylvania: State University Press, 1995. 27–62.

Ordinary Terrorism in Historical Perspective," *Journal for the Study of Radicalism* 2:1 (2008): 125–154.

Miller, Scott. *The President and the Assassin: McKinley, Terror, and Empire at the Dawn of the American Century*. New York: Random House, 2011.

Milza, Pierre. *Français et Italiens à la fin du XIX e Siècle, aux origines du rapprochement franco-italien de 1900–1902*. 2 vols. Rome: École Française de Roma, 1981.

Mola, Aldo A., ed. *Istituzioni e metodi politici dell'età giolittiana*. Turin: Centro Studi Piemontesi, 1979.

Mommsen, Wolfgang J. and Gerhard Hirschfeld, eds. *Social Protest, Violence and Terror in Nineteenth and Twentieth-Century Europe*. New York: St. Martin's Press, 1982.

Moore, John Bassett, ed. *A Digest of International Law*. 8 vols. Washington, DC: Government Printing Office, 1906.

Morel, Jean-Paul. "Préface," in Louis Andrieux, *Souvenirs d'un préfet de police*. Paris: Mémoire du Livre, 2002.

Morel, Pierre. *La police á Paris*. Paris: Sociéte d'édition e de publications, 1907.

Moscatelli, Alfredo. "I delitti politici e gli attentati anarchici in materia di estradizione," *Rivista Penale* 49 (1899): 356–366.

Moulaert, Jan. *Le mouvement anarchiste en Belgique*, trans. Sophie Haupert. Ottignies, Belgium: Quorum, 1996.

Moya, Jose. *Cousins and Strangers: Spanish Immigrants in Buenos Aires, 1850–1930*. Berkeley: University of California Press, 1998.

"Italians in Buenos Aires's Anarchist Movement: Gender Ideology and Women's Participation, 1890–1910," in Donna Gabaccia and Franca Iacovetta (eds.), *Women, Gender, and Transnational Lives: Italian Workers of the World*. Toronto University Press, 2002, 189–216.

The Positive Side of Stereotypes: Jewish Anarchists in Early-Twentieth-Century Buenos Aires," *Jewish History* 18:1 (2004): 19–48.

Munck, Ronaldo. "Cycles of Class Struggle and the Making of the Working Class in Argentina, 1890–1920," *Journal of Latin American Studies* 19:1 (1987): 19–39.

Murphy, J. Palmer and Margaret Murphy. *Paterson & Passaic County: An Illustrated History*. Northridge, CA: Windsor Publications, 1987.

Natale, Gaetano. *Giolitti e gli italiani*. Milan: Garzanti, 1949.

Nelson, Bruce C. *Beyond the Martyrs: A Social History of Chicago's Anarchists, 1870–1900*. New Brunswick: Rutgers University Press, 1988.

Nettlau, Max. *Geschichte der Anarchie*. 7 vols. Vaduz: Topos Verlag, 1981–.

A Short History of Anarchism, ed. Heiner M. Becker, trans. Ida Pilat Isca. London: Freedom Press, 1996.

Newsinger, John. *Fenianism in Mid-Victorian Britain*. London: Pluto Press, 1994.

Nichols, Francis H. "The Anarchists in America," *The Outlook in America* 68 (1901): 859–863.

Nichols, J. Alden. *Germany after Bismarck: The Caprivi Era, 1890–1894*. Cambridge, MA: Harvard University Press, 1958.

Nitti, Francesco. "Italian Anarchists," *The North American Review* 167 (1898): 598–608.

Noel, John Vavasour. *History of the Second Pan-American Congress*. Baltimore: Guggenheimer, Weil, 1902.

Noël, Léon. *Camille Barrère, Ambassadeur de France*. Paris: Tardy, 1948.

Novak, D. "Anarchism and Individual Terrorism," *The Canadian Journal of Economics and Political Science* 20:2 (1954): 176–184.

Núñez Florencio, Rafael. *El Terrorismo Anarquista (1888–1909)*. Madrid: Siglo veintiuno, 1983.

Olcott, Charles. *The Life of William McKinley*. Boston: Houghton Mifflin, 1916.

Oliver, Hermia. *The International Anarchist Movement in Late Victorian London*. London: Croom Helm, 1983.

Ortolani, Giovanni. "L'associazione anarchica e il Codice Penale," *Manuale del Funzionario di Sicurezza Pubblica e di Polizia Giudiziaria* 39:15 (1901): 228–232; 39:16 (1901): 241–243, 258–261.

O'Squar, Flor. *Les Coulisses de Anarchie*. Paris: Les nuit rouges, 2000.

Ostuni, Maria Rosaria. "Inmigración política italiana y movimiento obrero argentino," in F. Devoto and G. Rosoli (eds.), *La Inmigración Italiana en la Argentina*. Buenos Aires: Biblos, 1985. 105–126.

Ottolenghi, Salvatore. "L'estensione del Bertillonage e la lotta contro gli anarchici," *Rivista d'Italia*, fasc. 6, 1901.

Oved, Iaacov. *El anarquismo y el movimiento obrero en argentina*. Mexico City: Siglo XXI, 1978.

Packe, Michael St. John. *The Bombs of Orsini*. London: Secker and Warburg, 1957.

Paoli, Xavier. *Leurs Majestés*. 13th edition. Paris: Librairie Paul Ollendorff, 1910.

My Royal Clients, trans. Alexander Teixeira de Mattos. London: Hodder and Stoughton, 1911.

Parker, Leroy. "International Agreement for the Treatment of Anarchy," in *Report of the 21st Conference of the International Law Association, at Antwerp*. London: Newman, 1904. 405–417.

Parry, Richard. *Bonnot Gang: Story of the French Illegalists* London: Rebel Press, 1987.

Pella, Vespasian. "La repression des crimes contre la personalité de l'état," *Recueil des Cours: Académie de Droit International* 3 (1930): 673–837.

Pelloux, Luigi. *Quelques souvenirs de ma vie*. Ed. and intro. Gastone Manacorda. Rome: Insituto per la storia del risorgimento italiano, 1967.

Pennetti, Vincenzo. "Anarchismo socialismo e diritto internazionale," *Progresso giuridico* 1:10 (1896): 1–20.

Pérez Guerero, José. *Regicidios y crímenes politicos*. Madrid: Los Sucesos, Libertad, 1908–1909.

Pérez y Gómez, Antonio. *Don Juan de la Cierva. Ministro de Alfonso XIII (1864–1938)*. Murcia: Academia de Alfonso X el sabio, 1965.

Pernicone, Nunzio. *Carlo Tresca: Portrait of a Rebel*. New York: Palgrave Mamillan, 2005.

Italian Anarchism, 1864–1892. Princeton University Press, 1993.

"Luigi Galleani and Italian Terrorism in the United States," *Studi emigrazione/Etudes migrations* 30:11 (1993): 469–488.

Perrie, Maureen. "Political and Economic Terror in the Tactics of the Russian Socialist Revolutionary Party before 1914," in Wolfgang Mommsen and Gerhard Hirschfeld (eds.), *Social Protest, Violence and Terror in Nineteenth-and Twentieth-Century Europe*. New York: St. Martin's Press, 1982. 63–79.

Pesci, Ugo. *Il re martire: la vita e il regno di Umberto I: date, aneddoti, ricordi, 1844–1900*. Bologna: Ditta Nicola Zanichelli, 1901.

Petacco, Arrigo. *L'anarchico che venne dall'America*. Milan: Mondadori, 1974.

Pichon, Paul. *Histoire et organisation des services de police en France*. Issoudun: Laboureur, 1949.

Pick, Daniel. "The Faces of Anarchy: Lombroso and the Politics of Criminal Science in Post-Unification Italy," *History Workshop: A Journal of Socialist Historians* 21:1 (1986): 60–81.

Piggott, Francis. *Extradition: A Treatise on the Law Relating to Fugitive Offenders*. London: Butterworth, 1910.

Pinkerton, Robert A. "Detective Surveillance of Anarchists," *The North American Review* 173 (1901): 609–617.

Plotkin, Ira L. *Anarchism in Japan: A Study of the Great Treason Affair 1910–1911*. Lewiston, NY: Edwin Mellen, 1990.

Popplewell, Richard. *Intelligence and Imperial Defence. British Intelligence and the Defence of the Indian Empire, 1904–1924*. London: Frank Cass, 1995.

"The Surveillance of Indian Revolutionaries in Great Britain and on the Continent, 1905–1914," *Intelligence and National Security* 3:1 (1988): 57–76.

Porch, Douglas. *The French Secret Services from the Dreyfus Affair to the Gulf War.* New York: Farrar, Straus and Giroux, 1995.

Porter, Bernard. "The British Government and Political Refugees, c. 1880–1914," *Immigrants and Minorities* 2:3 (1983): 23–48.

The Origins of the Vigilant State: The London Metropolitan Police Special Branch Before the First World War. London: Weidenfeld and Nicolson, 1987.

Preston, William. *Aliens and Dissenters: Federal Suppression of Radicals, 1903–1933.* Cambridge, MA: Harvard University Press, 1963.

Prothero, Margaret. *The History of the Criminal Investigation Department.* London: Herbert Jenkins, 1931.

Pugliese, G. A. "Anarchia ed anarchici," *Rivista di giurisprudenza* 22 (1899): 5–26.

Quail, John. *The Slow Burning Fuse.* London: Paladin, 1978.

Quintavalle, Ferruccio. *Storia della unità italiana (1814–1924).* Milan: Hoepli, 1926.

Rapoport, David C. *Assassination and Terrorism.* Toronto: Canadian Broadcasting Corporation, 1971.

"The Four Waves of Modern Terrorism," in Audrey Kurth Cronin and James M. Ludes (eds.), *Attacking Terrorism: Elements of a Grand Strategy.* Washington, DC: Georgetown University Press, 2004, 43–76.

Inside Terrorist Organizations. New York: Columbia University Press, 1988.

Rauchway, Eric. *Murdering McKinley: The Making of Theodore Roosevelt's America.* New York: Hill and Wang, 2003.

Read, Philip M. *Paterson.* Charleston, SC: Arcadia, 2003.

Redlich, Joseph. *Emperor Francis Joseph of Austria.* Hamden, CT: Archon Books, [1929] 1965.

Reichesberg, Naum. "Anarchisme," in *Dictionnaire Historique et Biographique de la Suisse*, 316.

Reid, Whitelow. "Some International Questions," in *American and English Studies.* 2 vols. Reprint, Yale University Press: 1968. 75–106.

Reis, R. A. *Manuel du Portrait parlé (Signalment).* Paris: G. Roustan; Lausanne: Th. Sack, 1914.

Relyea, Harold C. *Evolution and Organization of Intelligence Activities in the US.* Laguna Hills, CA: Aegean Park Press, 1992.

Resseler, Walter and Benoit Suykerbuyk. *Dynamiet voor de Sultan: Carolus Eduard Joris in Konstantinopel.* Antwerp: B+B, 1997.

Rhodes, Henry T. F. *Alphonse Bertillon: Father of Scientific Detection.* New York: Abelard-Schuman, 1956.

Rhodes, James Ford. *The McKinley and Roosevelt Administrations, 1897–1909.* Port Washington, NY: Kennikat Press, 1965.

Roberts, Andrew. *Salisbury: Victorian Titan.* London: Phoenix, 1999.

Rock, David. *Argentina 1516–1982.* Berkeley: University of California Press, 1985.

Rodriquez, Adolfo Enrique. *Historia de la Policía Federal Argentina. Vol. 6. 1880–1916.* Buenos Aires: Policía Federal Argentina, 1975.

Rodriguez, Julia. *Civilizing Argentina: Science, Medicine, and the Modern State.* Chapel Hill: University of North Carolina Press, 2006.

Rogers, Colin. *The Battle of Stepney, The Sidney Street Siege: Its Causes and Consequences.* London: Robert Hale, 1981.

Röhl, John C. G. *Germany without Bismarck: The Crisis of Government in the Second Reich, 1890–1900.* Berkeley: University of California Press, 1967

Wilhelm II. Der Weg in den Abgrund 1900–1941. Munich: C. H. Beck, 2009.

Wilhelm II: The Kaiser's Personal Monarchy, 1888–1900, trans. Sheila de Bellaigue. New York: Cambridge University Press, 2004.

Rolin, Albéric. "Quelques questions relatives a l'extradition," *Recueil des Cours: Académie de Droit International* 1 (1923): 177–226.

"Rapport Supplémentare et Propositions avec motifs à l'appui," *Annuaire de l'Instituto de Droit International* 12 (1892–1894): 156–168.

Rollin, Henri. *L'Apocalypse de notre temps. Les dessous de la propaganda allemande d'apeès des documents inédits.* Paris: Allia, 1991 [1939].

Romero Maura, Joaquín. *"La rosa de fuego," Republicanos y anarchists: la politica de los obrerors barceloneses entre el desastre colonial y la semana trágica, 1899–1909.* Barcelona: Grijalbo, 1975.

"Terrorism in Barcelona and its Impact on Spanish Politics, 1904–1909," *Past and Present* 41 (1968): 130–183.

Rotelli, Ettore. "Governo e amministrazione nell'età giolittiana," in Aldo Mola (ed.), *Istituzioni e metodi politici dell'eta giolittiana.* Turin: Centro Studi Piemontesi, 1979, 63–75.

Ruggeri, Stefania. "Il fondo 'Polizia Internazionale'," in F. Grassi and G. C. Donno (eds.), *Il movimento socialista e popolare in Puglia dalle origini alla Costituzione (1874–1946).* Bari: Laterza, 1986, 153–157.

Rumbold, Horace. *Francis Joseph and His Times.* New York: D. Appleton, 1909.

Saint-Aubin, Francois Joseph. *L'extradition et le droit extraditionnal: Théorique et Appliqué.* 2 vols. Paris: A. Pedone, 1913.

Saldaña, Quintiliano. *La Défense Sociale Universelle.* Coueslant: CAHORS, 1924.

Salillas, Rafael. "La celda de Ferrer," *Revista Penitenciaria* 4:6 (1907): 321–347.

Salmon, André. *El terror negro. Crónica de la acción anarquista.* Mexico City: Editorial extemporaneos, 1975.

Saltman, Richard B. *The Social and Political Thought of Michael Bakunin.* Westport, CT: Greenwood Press, 1983.

Samaritani, Fausta. "Il pasticciaccio di Monza," *Il Carabiniere* April 1992: 88–93.

Sandonnini, Giuseppe. *Dei reati politici in materia d'estradizione.* Modena: Società tipografica, 1901.

Saracini, Emilio. *I crepuscoli della polizia: Compendio storico della genesi e delle vicende dell' amministrazione di pubblica sicurezza.* Naples: SIEM, 1922.

Schmitt, Kar. "Assassination in Latin America," in James F. Kirkham, Sheldon G. Levy, and William J. Crotty (eds.), *Assassination and Political Violence; Report to the National Commission on the Causes and Prevention of Violence.* Washington, DC: US Government Printing Office, 1969. 537–543.

Schulthess' Europaischer Geschichtskalender: 1898, ed. Gustav Holoff. Munich: C. H. Beck. 1899.

Schultz, Hans. *Das schweizerische Auslieferungsrecht.* Babel: Verlag für recht und Gesellschaft, 1953.

Scott, James Brown, "Editorial Comment: 'Political Offence' in extradition treaties," *American Journal of International Law* 3 (1909): 459–461.

Senn, Alfred Eric. *The Russian Revolution in Switzerland 1914–1917.* Madison: University of Wisconsin Press, 1971.

Sernicoli, Ettore. *Gli attentati contro sovrani, principi, presidenti e primi ministri.* Milan: Fratelli Treves, 1894.

I delinquenti dell'anarchia: Nuovo studio storico e politica. Rome: E. Voghera, 1899.

L'anarchia e gli anarchici. Studio storico e politico. 2 vols. 2nd edition. Milan: Treves, 1894.

Seuffert, Hermann. *Anarchismus und Strafrecht.* Berlin: Otto Liebmann, 1899.

Sevilla Andrés, Diego. *Canalejas,* intro. Jesús Pabón. Barcelona: AEDOS, 1956.

Shearer, Ivan Anthony. *Extradition in International Law.* Manchester University Press, 1971.

Short, Kenneth. *The Dynamite War: Irish-American Bombers in Victorian Britain.* Dublin: Gill and Macmillan, 1979.

Sibley, N. W. and Alfred Elias. *The Aliens Act and the Right of Asylum.* London: William Clowes and Sons, 1906.

Silió, César. "El anarquismo y la defensa social," *España Moderna* 61 (1894): 141–148.

Simarro, Luis. *El proceso Ferrer y la opinión Europea.* Madrid: Eduardo Arias, 1910.

Smith, Angel. *Anarchism, Revolution and Reaction: Catalan Labour and the Crisis of the Spanish State, 1898–1923.* New York: Berghahn Books, 2007.

Smith, Phillip Thurmond. *Policing Victorian London: Political Policing, Public Order, and the London Metropolitan Police.* Westport, CT: Greenwood Press, 1985.

Somakian, Manoug Joseph. *Empires in Conflict: Armenia and the Great Powers, 1895–1920.* London: Tauris Academic Studies, 1995.

Söderman, Harry and Ernst Fontell. *Handbok i Kriminalteknik.* Stockholm: Wahlström und Widstrand, 1930.

Sonn, Richard. *Anarchism and Cultural Politics in Fin de Siècle France.* Lincoln, NE, and London: University of Nebraska Press, 1989.

Sex, Violence and the Avant-Garde: Anarchism in Interwar France. University Park: Pennsylvania State University Press, 2010.

Sottile, Antoine. "Le Terrorisme International," *Academie de Droit Internationale: Recueil Cours* 3 (1938): 89–184.

Spira, Leopold, ed. *Attentate, die Österreich erschütterten.* Vienna: Löcker, 1981.

Spiridovitch, Alexander. *Histoire du terrorisme russe, 1886–1917.* Paris: Payot, 1930.

Staudacher, Anna. *Sozialrevolutionäre und Anarchisten: Die Andere Arbeiterbewegung vor Hainfeld: die Radikale Arbeiter-Partei Österreichs (1880–1884).* Vienna: Verlag für Gesellschafts Kritik, 1988.

Stockis, Eugène. *L'identification Judiciaire et le Signalement International.* Bruxelles: Larcier, 1908.

Sueiro Seoane, Susana. "El asesinato de Canalejas y los anarquistas españoles en Estados Unidos." In Juan Avilés and Ángel Herrerín (eds.), *El nacimiento del terrorismo en occidente.* Madrid: Siglo XXI, 2008. 159–188.

Suriano, Juan. *Trabajadores, anarquismo y Estado represor: de la Ley de residencia a la Ley de defensa social (1902–1910)*. Buenos Aires: CEAL, 1988.

Tamburini, Francesco. "L'attentato anarchico di fine secolo e l'evoluzione della legislazione penale italiana contro il 'Delitto sociale'," in Aldo A. Mola (ed.), *La svolta di Giolitti. Dalla reazione di fine Ottocento al culmine dell'età liberale*. Foggia: Bastogi, 2000. 42–54.

"La conferenza internazionale di Roma per la difesa sociale contro gli anarchici (24 Novembere-21–21 Dicembre 1898)," *Clio* 32:2 (1997): 227–265.

"Michele Angiolillo e l'assassinio di Cánovas del Castillo," *Spagna contemporanea* 4:9 (1996): 101–130.

Tarizzo, Domenico. *L'anarchia: Storia dei movimenti libertari nel mondo*. Milan: A. Mondadori, 1976.

Tarrida del Mármol, Fernando. *Les Inquisiteurs d'Espagne*. Paris: Stock, 1897.

Tays, Dwight L. "Presidential Reaction to Security: A Longitudinal Study," *Presidential Studies Quarterly* 10 (1980): 600–609.

Temkin, Moshik. *The Sacco-Vanzetti Affair: America on Trial*. New Haven: Yale University Press, 2009.

Tipton, Elise. "The Tokkô and Political Police in Japan, 1911–1945," In Mark Mazower (ed.), *The Policing of Politics in the Twentieth Century*. Oxford: Berghahn, 1997, 213–240.

Tomasi, Lydio. *Italian Americans: New Perspectives in Italian Immigration and Ethnicity*, ed. Lydio F. Tomasi. New York: Center for Migration Studies, 1985.

Tosatti, Giovanna. "L'anagrafe dei sovversivi italiani: origini e storia del Casellario politico central," *Le Carte e la Storia* 2 (1997): 133–150.

"Il Ministero degli interni: le origini del Casellario politico central," in *Le reforme crispine: Amministrazione statale*. Milan: Giuffrè, 1990, 447–485.

"La repressione del dissenso politico tra l'età liberale e il fascismo. L'organizzazione della polizia," *Studi storici* 38 (1997): 217–255.

Tosti, Gustavo. "Anarchistic Crimes," *Political Science Quarterly* 14 (1899): 404–417.

Trautmann, Frederic. *The Voice of Terror: A Biography of Johann Most*. Westport, CT: Greenwood Press, 1980.

Travers, Maurice. *Le Droit Pénal International*. 5 vols. Paris: Recueil Sirey, 1921.

Truche, Pierre. *L'anarchiste et son juge: à propos de l'assassinat de Sadi Carnot*. Paris: Fayard, 1994.

Tuchman, Barbara. *The Proud Tower: A Portrait of the World Before the War: 1890–1914*. New York City: Bantam Books, 1972.

Turone, Giuliano. "Il proceso per il regicidio di Umberto I," *Risorgimento* 34 (1982): 36–47.

Turrado Vidal, Martin. *Estudios sobre historia de la policia*. Madrid: Ministerio del interior: Secretaria General Tecnica, 1986.

Tussel, Javier. "Las relaciones Hispano-Francesas en el Gobierno Largo de Maura: El Archivo de D. Manuel Allendesalazar come Fuente (1907–1909)." *Espanoles y franceses en la primera mitad del siglo XX*. Madrid: Centro de Estudios Historicos, Departamento de Historia Contemporánea, 1986, 51–64.

Ullman, Joan Connelly. *The Tragic Week: A Study of Anticlericalism in Spain, 1875–1912*. Cambridge, MA: Harvard University Press, 1968.

United States Warren Commission. *Report of the President's Commission on the Assassination of President John F. Kennedy.* Washington, DC: US Government Printing Office, 1964.

Vandereychken, Walter and Ron VanDeth. "The Anorectic Empress: Elisabeth of Austria," *History Today* 46:4 (1996): 12–19.

Varennes, Henri [Henri Vonoven]. *De Ravachol à Caserio: (notes d'audience).* Paris: Garnier Frères, 1895.

Van Hamel, Gerard-Anton. "La lotta contro l'anarchismo," *Scuola positiva* 6 (1897): 535–545.

Vené, Gian Franco. "Il braccio della legge contro gli anarchici," *Storia illustrata.* October 1973: 147–154.

Vigier, Philippe, ed. *Maintien de l'ordre et polices en France et en Europe au XIXe siècle.* Paris: Créaphis, 1987.

Vigo, Pietro. *Annali d'Italia. Storia degli ultimi trent'anni del secolo XIX,* 7 vols. Milan: Treves, 1908–1915.

Vincent, Charles Edward Howard. *The Police Code and General Manual of the Criminal Law.* 15th and 17th editions. London: Butterworth, 1912 and 1931.

Viqueira Hinojosa, Antonio. *Historia y anecdotario de la policía española, 1833–1931,* vol. 1. Madrid: San Martin, 1989.

Vizetelly, Ernest Alfred. *The Anarchists.* London: John Land, 1911.

Vuilleumier, Marc. "L'emigrazione italiana in Svizzera e gli avvenimenti del 1898," in *Anna Kuliscioff e l'età del riformismo. Atti del convegno di Milano. December 1976.* Milan: Mondo Operaio, 1978, 85–103.

Immigrés et réfugiés en Suisse. Aperçu historique. 2nd edition. Zurich: Pro Helvetia, 1989.

"La police politique en Suisse, 1889–1914. Aperçu historique," in *Cent ans de police politique en Suisse.* Lausanne: Association pour l'etude de l'histoire du mouvement ouvrier and Editions D'en Bas, 1992, 31–62.

Wagner, Joachim. *Politscher Terrorismus und Strafrecht im Deutschen Kaiserreich von 1871.* Heidelberg and Hamburg: R.v. Decker's Verlag, G. Schenk, 1981.

Wilkie, Don and Mark Lee Luther. *American Secret Service Agent.* New York: Frederick A. Stokes, 1934.

Wood, E. Thomas. *Wars on Terror: French and British Responses to the Anarchist Violence of the 1890s.* M. Phil, University of Cambridge, 2002.

Woodcock, George. *Anarchism: A History of Libertarian Ideas and Movements.* New York: World Publishing Co., 1962.

Woodward, P. H. *The Secret Service of the Post-Office Department.* Hartford, CT: Winter, 1886.

Zlataric, Bogdan. "History of International Terrorism and its Legal Control," in M. Cherif Bassiouni (ed.), *International Terrorism and Political Crimes.* Springfield, IL: Charles C. Thomas, 1975, 474–484.

Zuckerman, Frederic Scott. "Political Police and Revolution: The Impact of the 1905 Revolution on the Tsarist Secret Police," *Journal of Contemporary History* 27 (1992): 279–300.

The Tsarist Secret Police Abroad: Policing Europe in a Modernising World. Hampshire: Palgrave Macmillan, 2003.

Index

Lightning Source UK Ltd.
Milton Keynes UK
UKOW06f0948120816

280544UK00008B/302/P